SCHAUM'S OUTLINE OF

THEORY AND PROBLEMS

OF

PROGRAMMING WITH ASSEMBLY LANGUAGE

•

DAVID E. GOLDBERG, Ph.D.
Professor of Chemistry
Brooklyn College

JACQUELINE A. JONES, Ph.D.
Assistant Professor of Computer and Information Science
Brooklyn College

PAT H. STERBENZ, Ph.D.
Professor of Computer and Information Science
Brooklyn College

•

SCHAUM'S OUTLINE SERIES
McGRAW-HILL BOOK COMPANY

New York   St. Louis   San Francisco   Auckland   Bogotá   Hamburg   London
Madrid   Mexico   Milan   Montreal   New Delhi   Panama   Paris
São Paulo   Singapore   Sydney   Tokyo   Toronto

DAVID E. GOLDBERG received his Ph.D. in chemistry from Pennsylvania State University and joined the faculty at Brooklyn College in 1959. His primary interests are chemical and computer science education. He is the author or coauthor of six books, over 30 journal articles, and numerous booklets for student use.

JACQUELINE A. JONES received her Ph.D. from the Unviersity of Pennsylvania in 1974. She is currently an Assistant Professor of Computer and Information Science at Brooklyn College. Her interests are artificial intelligence and computer science education. She is the coauthor of *Problem Solving Using Turbo Pascal* and *Problem Solving Using IBM PC Pascal*.

PAT H. STERBENZ received his Ph.D. in mathematics from the Ohio State University and worked for IBM for many years. He has been Professor of Computer and Information Science at Brooklyn College since 1974. His primary interest is the design and use of computers for scientific computation. He is the author of *Floating-Point Computation*.

Schaum's Outline of Theory and Problems of
PROGRAMMING WITH ASSEMBLY LANGUAGE

Copyright © 1988 by McGraw-Hill, Inc. All rights reserved. Printed in the United States of America. Except as permitted under the Copyright Act of 1976, no part of this publication may be reproduced or distributed in any form or by any means, or stored in a data base or retrieval system, without the prior written permission of the publisher.

1 2 3 4 5 6 7 8 9 10 11 12 13 14 15 16 17 18 19 20 SHP SHP 8 9 2 1 0 9 8 7

ISBN 0-07-033011-5

Sponsoring Editors, John Aliano and Jeffrey McCartney
Production Supervisor, Denise Puryear
Editing Supervisor, Marthe Grice

Library of Congress Cataloging-in-Publication Data

Goldberg, David E. (David Elliott)
   Schaum's outline of theory and problems of
assembly language.

  (Schaum's outline series)
  1. Assembler language (Computer program language)
I. Jones, Jacqueline A. II. Sterbenz, Pat H.,
       . III. Title.
QA76.73.A8G65 1987   005.13'3   87-3239
ISBN 0-07-033011-5

Preface

This book is an introduction to assembly language programming on the IBM 360/370 series of machines. Although it is primarily intended as a supplement to existing textbooks, many instructors may want to use it as the primary textbook in an introductory assembly language course. We have class-tested the book as a textbook at Brooklyn College with a great deal of success.

We have attempted to make the book as useful as possible, no matter what approach a teacher might wish to use. Therefore, we have arranged the material so that, after Chapters 1 through 6, the remaining chapters are largely independent of one another and may be covered in any order. While some of the problems in the later chapters may assume knowledge of material in other chapters, the examples and the bulk of the problems depend only on the material in the introductory chapters and the current chapter. You may use the index to find the material which you need.

The great majority of students studying assembly language programming already know how to program in at least one high-level language. Since they thus know the elements of good style and how to plan a program we have concentrated on the details of assembly language programming without spending a great deal of time on overall program design. If you are having trouble in writing programs despite a good knowledge of the details of the instructions, your background in computer science may be weak.

Assembly language programming is extremely detailed. Even more than most computer languages, it requires extensive practice. It is impossible to memorize all the details, so you must try to understand what you are doing, and you need repeated practice to reinforce the concepts.

In using this book, you should read the text before attempting the problems, as the problems may assume that you know a technique introduced in the text. Answers are provided for many of the problems; however, you should not look at the answer before you have tried to work out the problem yourself. There is a tremendous difference between being able to produce the answer yourself and merely reading an answer that someone else has produced, even if you can readily understand the answer when you read it. Many of the problems, expecially in the early chapters, have multiple parts. Try every other or every third part at first. If you get those correct, you probably do not need to do the others. However, if you do not get nearly all of them correct, you should do the remaining parts.

There are many correct answers to some problems. Just because your answer differs from the answer provided does not necessarily mean that your answer is wrong. If it is a programming problem, run your solution on the computer to see that you get the correct answer with all types of data. If your answer is wrong, try to figure out where and why. If your answer works, try to analyze how it differs from the answer provided. Are the algorithms different? Are you using more (or unnecessary) instructions? Use the printed answer to help improve your answer, if yours was different.

There are a number of people who have provided invaluable assistance to us as we have written this book. We would first like to thank those who taught us what we know of assembly language. Second, we would like to thank all the

PREFACE

students, too numerous to mention individually, who have tested every problem and every example to help eliminate errors. Third, we would like to thank those at Schaum's who have helped in the production of the book: Jeff McCartney, John Aliano, Meg Tobin, and Marthe Grice. We also would like to thank Professor Lawrence Newcomer for his outstanding job of reviewing the manuscript. Without these people, this book would not exist.

DAVID E. GOLDBERG
JACQUELINE A. JONES
PAT H. STERBENZ

Contents

Chapter 1 NUMBER SYSTEMS 1

    1.1 Introduction 1
    1.2 Positional Number Systems 2
    1.3 Binary to Decimal Conversion 3
    1.4 Hexadecimal to Decimal Conversion 3
    1.5 Decimal to Binary and Decimal to Hexadecimal Conversions 3
    1.6 Another Method for Conversion from Decimal to Binary or to Hexadecimal 5
    1.7 Hexadecimal to Binary and Binary to Hexadecimal Conversions 7
    1.8 Addition of Binary and Hexadecimal Numbers 8
    1.9 Subtraction of Binary and Hexadecimal Numbers 9
    1.10 Bytes, Words, and Halfwords 9
    1.11 Representation of Negative Binary Numbers 10

Chapter 2 ASSEMBLY LANGUAGE FORMAT 22

    2.1 Introduction 22
    2.2 Registers and Memory 22
    2.3 Assembly Language Format 22
    2.4 Defining Storage in Memory 24
    2.5 How the Program Works 25
    2.6 Literals 27

Chapter 3 ARITHMETIC OPERATIONS 38

    3.1 Introduction 38
    3.2 The Multiply (M) Instruction 38
    3.3 The Divide (D) Instruction 39
    3.4 RR Instructions 41
    3.5 LPR, LNR, and LCR Instructions 42
    3.6 Halfword Instructions 43

Chapter 4 ADDRESSING 61

    4.1 Introduction 61
    4.2 Machine Language format for RR and RX Instructions 61
    4.3 Effective Addresses 63
    4.4 The Effects of BALR and USING 66
    4.5 Boundary Requirements 67
    4.6 Explicit Notation 68
    4.7 Further Extensions of Addressing 69
    4.8 Putting an Address into a Memory Location 70
    4.9 Load Address 71
    4.10 Debugging Programs 73
    4.11 Addressing Long Programs 74
    4.12 Equivalence Pseudo-Instruction 76

CONTENTS

Chapter 5 COMPARE AND BRANCH INSTRUCTIONS 85
    5.1 The Condition Code and Branching 85
    5.2 Load and Test Register 89
    5.3 Compare Instructions 90

Chapter 6 ARRAYS AND LOOPING 106
    6.1 Introduction 106
    6.2 The BCT and BCTR Instructions 106
    6.3 Arrays 109
    6.4 Address Modification 111
    6.5 The BXLE and BXH Instructions 118

Chapter 7 CHARACTER STRING MANIPULATION 136
    7.1 Representation of Character Strings 136
    7.2 Declaration of Character Strings 137
    7.3 Move Character (MVC) 139
    7.4 Logical Comparisons 141
    7.5 Immediate Instructions 144
    7.6 Arrays of Character Strings 146
    7.7 Move Character Long and Compare Logical Character Long 150

Chapter 8 PACKED DECIMAL NUMBERS 171
    8.1 Introduction 171
    8.2 Packed Decimal Number Format 171
    8.3 Declaration (Definition) of Packed Decimal Numbers 172
    8.4 Packed Decimal Operations and Formats 173
    8.5 Zero and Add Packed 175
    8.6 Multiplication and Division of Packed Numbers 175
    8.7 Compare Packed 178
    8.8 Arrays of Packed Decimal Numbers 179

Chapter 9 ADVANCED PACKED DECIMAL CONCEPTS 189
    9.1 Introduction 189
    9.2 Fractional Packed Decimal Numbers 189
    9.3 Shift and Round Packed 192
    9.4 Move Zone and Move Numeric 195
    9.5 Move with Offset 197
    9.6 Number Conversions 200
    9.7 Input/Output 203
    9.8 Edit and Edit with Mark 204

Chapter 10 SUBPROGRAMS 230
    10.1 Introduction 230
    10.2 Control Sections 231
    10.3 Branching to and Returning from a Subprogram 232
    10.4 Load Multiple and Store Multiple 234
    10.5 Passing Parameters 235
    10.6 Saving Register Contents 239
    10.7 Establishing Addressability 240

CONTENTS

    10.8 Returning a Value from a Function 242
    10.9 Subprograms Which Call Other Subprograms 243

Chapter 11   **BIT AND BYTE MANIPULATION** **268**

    11.1 Introduction 268
    11.2 Shift Operations 268
    11.3 Logical Operations 272
    11.4 Test under Mask 276
    11.5 Insert Character and Store Character 278
    11.6 The ICM, STCM, and CLM Instructions 278

Chapter 12   **FLOATING-POINT OPERATIONS** **295**

    12.1 Introduction 295
    12.2 Format of Floating-Point Numbers 296
    12.3 Declaration of Floating-Point Numbers 300
    12.4 Floating-Point Registers and Floating-Point Instructions 300
    12.5 Floating-Point Arithmetic 302
    12.6 Instructions Which Yield Unnormalized Answers 306

Chapter 13   **ADVANCED INSTRUCTIONS** **319**

    13.1 Introduction 319
    13.2 Translate 319
    13.3 Translate and Test 322
    13.4 The Execute Instruction 324

Chapter 14   **MACROS AND CONDITIONAL ASSEMBLY** **334**

    14.1 Introduction 334
    14.2 Simple Macros 335
    14.3 Symbolic Parameters 337
    14.4 System Macros and Systems Variables 341
    14.5 Keyword Parameters 342
    14.6 Set Symbols 343
    14.7 Conditional Assembly 346

Appendix 1   **ASSEMBLY AND MACHINE LANGUAGE INSTRUCTIONS AND FORMATS** **359**

Appendix 2   **INPUT/OUTPUT** **364**

Appendix 3   **INTERRUPTS** **369**

ANSWERS TO SELECTED SUPPLEMENTARY PROBLEMS **371**

INDEX **395**

INSTRUCTIONS AND PSEUDO-INSTRUCTIONS INDEX **404**

Chapter 1

Number Systems

1.1 Introduction

We are familiar with numbers in various formats—integers, numbers with a fixed number of decimal places, and floating-point numbers. The first two of these types are called *fixed-point numbers*.

EXAMPLE 1.1

> 90   Fixed-point integer
> 75.3   Fixed-point number with one decimal place
> 2.3×10^3 Floating-point number

We will deal mostly with fixed-point numbers in this book, with the exception of Chap. 12, where floating-point numbers are discussed.

Numbers also come in different *bases*. Numbers can be fixed-point or floating-point in any base system. Our ordinary number system, the decimal system, has 10 different digits (0 through 9), probably because our ancestors had 10 fingers. Thus the decimal system has a base of 10. With digital computers, we use a binary number system, with a base of 2. A binary digit is called a *bit*, and can have values of 0 or 1 only. The choice of the binary system is dictated by the fact that an electric circuit, or a magnetic field, etc., can be either off or on. The binary number system matches that duality because in the binary system there are only two digits. If we start counting at zero in the binary system, we get

Binary	*Decimal Equivalent*
0	0
1	1

and we have run out of digits. When that happens the first time in the decimal system, we put a 1 in the next column and start again with zero in the right-hand column. We do the same thing in binary:

Binary	*Decimal Equivalent*
10	2
11	3

Again we have run out of digits in both columns. We start yet another column:

Binary	*Decimal Equivalent*
100	4
101	5
110	6
111	7

We keep going that way, adding new columns much more frequently than we do in the decimal system.

Because the binary number system needs so many binary digits—bits—to represent reasonably sized numbers, the IBM 370 assembler also uses hexadecimal notation to represent binary numbers. Each hexadecimal digit represents 4 bits. In the hexadecimal system there are 16 digits. Arabic numerals are used for the first 10 of them, and the first six letters of the alphabet are used for the rest. We therefore get the following equivalent representations of the numbers from 0 through 16.

Binary	Decimal	Hexadecimal
0	0	0
1	1	1
10	2	2
11	3	3
100	4	4
101	5	5
110	6	6
111	7	7
1000	8	8
1001	9	9
1010	10	A
1011	11	B
1100	12	C
1101	13	D
1110	14	E
1111	15	F
10000	16	10

It is important to be able to convert numbers from each of these systems to either of the others. There are several methods for each of the conversions. You should learn one method for each conversion well. The conversions needed are decimal to binary, decimal to hexadecimal, binary to decimal, binary to hexadecimal, hexadecimal to decimal, and hexadecimal to binary.

1.2 Positional Number Systems

In order to understand some of the conversions which we must do, it is necessary to understand the positional number system. The decimal number 123 does not mean the same as the decimal number 321. What is the difference? Each place is 10 times as important as the one to its right. Each place represents 10 to a power; the rightmost digit is the number of ones (tens to the zero power). The next digit is the number of tens. The third digit from the right is the number of hundreds (ten squares), etc. Thus the number 123 means

$$
\begin{array}{l}
1\ 2\ 3 \\
\ 3 \text{ ones } (3 \times 10^0) 3 \\
\ 2 \text{ tens } (2 \times 10^1) 20 \\
1 \text{ hundred } (1 \times 10^2) \underline{100} \\
 123
\end{array}
$$

Similarly, the decimal number 753,812 means

$$7 \times 10^5 + 5 \times 10^4 + 3 \times 10^3 + 8 \times 10^2 + 1 \times 10^1 + 2 \times 10^0$$

CHAP. 1] NUMBER SYSTEMS 3

The same positional number system is used for binary and hexadecimal, but in binary the powers are powers of 2, and in hexadecimal the powers are powers of 16. For example, the binary number 1011011 means

$$1 \times 2^6 + 0 \times 2^5 + 1 \times 2^4 + 1 \times 2^3 + 0 \times 2^2 + 1 \times 2^1 + 1 \times 2^0$$

and the hexadecimal number 73A5 means

$$7 \times 16^3 + 3 \times 16^2 + 10 \times 16^1 + 5 \times 16^0$$

1.3 Binary to Decimal Conversion

To convert from binary to decimal, we merely interpret the positional number system. This time, however, we are using base 2. Therefore we have the 1's column, the 2's column, the 4's column, the 8's column, etc.

EXAMPLE 1.2

Convert the binary number 10111 to decimal.

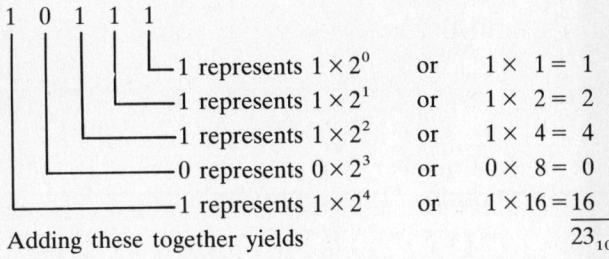

```
1  0  1  1  1
            └─ 1 represents 1 × 2⁰    or    1 ×  1 =  1
         └──── 1 represents 1 × 2¹    or    1 ×  2 =  2
      └─────── 1 represents 1 × 2²    or    1 ×  4 =  4
   └────────── 0 represents 0 × 2³    or    0 ×  8 =  0
└───────────── 1 represents 1 × 2⁴    or    1 × 16 = 16
   Adding these together yields              23₁₀
```

The subscript 10 denotes the base.

1.4 Hexadecimal to Decimal Conversion

In this type of conversion the process is the same, but the base is different. Hexadecimal is base 16, so now each column represents 16 times the value of the same digit in the column to its right. The rightmost column is the 1's (16^0) column; the next column is the 16's (16^1) column; the next one is the 256's (16^2) column; etc.

EXAMPLE 1.3

Convert $2A6_{16}$ to decimal.

```
2  A  6
      └─ 6 × 16⁰ =  6 ×   1 =   6
   └──── A × 16¹ = 10 ×  16 = 160
└─────── 2 × 16² =  2 × 256 = 512
                              ─────
                              678₁₀
```

1.5 Decimal to Binary and Decimal to Hexadecimal Conversions

We will give two methods for converting decimal numbers to binary (or to hexadecimal). The first method for converting a number to binary is to express the number as a sum of powers of 2. To illustrate this approach, we convert the decimal number 212 to binary.

1. Find the largest power of 2 which is less than or equal to the decimal number given.   128 (2^7) is the largest power of 2 less than or equal to 212

2. Subtract that power of 2 from the original number, and write down a 1 representing that power of 2. $212 - 128 = 84$ 1

3. (a) If the next lower power of 2 is smaller than the remainder, subtract that power of 2 and place a 1 to the right of what you have already written down.
   $2^6 = 64$
   $84 - 64 = 20$ 11

   (b) If the next lower power of 2 is larger than the remainder, write a zero to the right of what you have already written (and don't subtract anything).

4. Repeat step 3 until you have tried to subtract $2^0 = 1$.

   $20 < 32$ 110
   $20 - 16 = 4$ 1101
   $4 < 8$ 11010
   $4 - 4 = 0$ 110101
   $0 < 2$ 1101010
   $0 < 1$ 11010100

Thus we have written the original number as a sum of powers of 2, and missing powers of 2 are represented by 0 in the proper position. Thus we have used

$$212 = 1 \times 128 + 1 \times 64 + 0 \times 32 + 1 \times 16 + 0 \times 8 + 1 \times 4 + 0 \times 2 + 0 \times 1$$
$$= 1 \times 2^7 + 1 \times 2^6 + 0 \times 2^5 + 1 \times 2^4 + 0 \times 2^3 + 1 \times 2^2 + 0 \times 2^1 + 0 \times 2^0$$
$$\ 1 \qquad\quad 1 \qquad\quad 0 \qquad\quad 1 \qquad\quad 0 \qquad\quad 1 \qquad\quad 0 \qquad\quad 0$$

The binary number is built up from left to right in this method. The last value is the binary equivalent of the original decimal number.

$$212_{10} = 11010100_2$$

Conversion of a number from decimal to hexadecimal form may be done similarly, except that a multiple of the highest power of 16 is subtracted, and that multiple is written down. The conversion steps are outlined in the following example that converts 2010 to hexadecimal.

1. Find the largest power of 16 which is less than or equal to the decimal number given.   256 (16^2) is the largest power of 16 less than or equal to 2010.

2. Divide the decimal number by this power of 16 to get a quotient and a remainder.

   $$256 \overline{)2010}$$
   $$\underline{1792}$$
   $$218$$

3. Write down the quotient (which is one hexadecimal digit).   7

4. Divide the remainder by the next lower power of 16 to get a new quotient and a new remainder. Write down the new quotient (one hexadecimal digit).

   $$16\overline{)218} \qquad D$$
   $$\underline{16}$$
   $$58$$
   $$\underline{48}$$
   $$10$$

5. Repeat step 4 until you have divided by $16^0 = 1$.

$$\begin{array}{r} 10 \\ 1\overline{)10} \\ \underline{10} \\ 0 \end{array} \quad A$$

6. The number in hexadecimal is obtained by writing the hexadecimal digits in the order in which they were produced.

7DA

Thus, we have found that

$$2010 = 7 \times 256 + 218$$
$$= 7 \times 256 + 13 \times 16 + 10$$

or
$$2010 = 7 \times 16^2 + 13 \times 16^1 + 10 \times 16^0$$
$$= 7 \times 16^2 + D \times 16^1 + A \times 16^0$$

which is written in hexadecimal as 7DA.

1.6 Another Method for Conversion from Decimal to Binary or to Hexadecimal

The methods discussed in Sec. 1.5 for converting from decimal to binary and to hexadecimal are convenient if the number is relatively small. However, if the number is large, they have the disadvantage that a table of powers of 2 or powers of 16 is required. The methods discussed in this section do not have this drawback. To understand the approach discussed in this section, note that if we divide a decimal number by 10, each of the digits in the quotient represents one power of 10 less than it did in the dividend, and the last digit of the dividend becomes the remainder.

EXAMPLE 1.4

Let's divide a decimal number by 10, and repeatedly divide the quotient of each prior division by 10. What does the collection of remainders represent? What possible values does each remainder have? Use the numbers 123,456 and 9,073,050 as examples.

```
                Remainder              Remainder
   10)123456                10)9073050
   10)  12345   6           10)  907305   0
   10)   1234   5           10)   90730   5
   10)    123   4           10)    9073   0
   10)     12   3           10)     907   3
   10)      1   2           10)      90   7
             0   1           10)       9   0
                                       0   9
```

The remainders, from bottom to top, represent the number in decimal. Each remainder could be a digit from 0 through 9.

Since the same positional number system is used for binary and hexadecimal, a similar result would be obtained if a binary number were repeatedly divided by 2 or a hexadecimal number were repeatedly divided by 16.

Thus another way to convert a number from decimal to another base is to repeatedly divide the decimal number, or the quotients obtained, by the base you are converting to until a quotient of zero is reached. The remainders obtained in this way are written from *bottom to top* to obtain the result.

EXAMPLE 1.5

Convert the decimal number 43 to binary.

```
           Remainder
   2)43
     21   1     2 into 43 yields 21, with 1 remainder
   2)21
     10   1     2 into 21 yields 10, with 1 remainder
   2)10
      5   0     2 into 10 yields 5, with 0 remainder
   2) 5
      2   1     2 into 5 yields 2, with 1 remainder
   2) 2
      1   0     2 into 2 yields 1, with 0 remainder
   2) 1
      0   1     2 into 1 yields 0, with 1 remainder
```

Thus our answer is

$$101011$$

Note two important details:

1. Divide until you get to zero.
2. Read the remainders from bottom to top. (The bottom number is the *leftmost digit* in the binary form of the number; the top number is the *rightmost digit*.)

To check, convert the binary number back to decimal:

$$
\begin{array}{l}
1\ 0\ 1\ 0\ 1\ 1 \\
1 \times 2^0 = 1 \\
1 \times 2^1 = 2 \\
0 \times 2^2 = 0 \\
1 \times 2^3 = 8 \\
0 \times 2^4 = 0 \\
1 \times 2^5 = 32 \\
\hline
43
\end{array}
$$

EXAMPLE 1.6

Convert 438_{10} to hexadecimal.

```
   16)438
       27     remainder 6
   16) 27
        1     remainder B (11)
   16)  1
        0     remainder 1
                              1  B  6
```

The answer is $1B6_{16}$.

EXAMPLE 1.7

Convert 212 to binary by successive division. Perform the same operations on the binary equivalent of 212. Show that each successive quotient in the binary format is the equivalent of the corresponding quotient in decimal format. Note that the sequence of remainders is the same in both cases. Note also that $2_{10} = 10_2$.

Decimal	Binary equivalent
2)212	10)11010100
2)106 0	10) 1101010 0
2) 53 0	10) 110101 0
2) 26 1	10) 11010 1
2) 13 0	10) 1101 0
2) 6 1	10) 110 1
2) 3 0	10) 11 0
2) 1 1	10) 1 1
0 1	0 1

1.7 Hexadecimal to Binary and Binary to Hexadecimal Conversions

These conversions are the simplest of all. Their simplicity stems from the fact that $2^4 = 16$. Four binary digits are equivalent to one hexadecimal digit. To convert from binary to hexadecimal, therefore, go through the number from *right to left* and divide it into groups of 4 bits. (If the leftmost group has fewer than 4 bits, pad it with zeros or consider these bits to be blank.) Convert each group of 4 bits to the corresponding hexadecimal digit (see the table on p. 2, if necessary).

EXAMPLE 1.8

Convert 11010010 to hexadecimal.

$$1101 \quad 0010$$
$$D \quad 2$$

The answer is D2.

EXAMPLE 1.9

Convert 1100111100011100101001101 to hexadecimal.

$$11 \quad 0011 \quad 1100 \quad 0111 \quad 0010 \quad 1001 \quad 1101$$
$$3 \quad 3 \quad C \quad 7 \quad 2 \quad 9 \quad D$$

The answer is $33C729D_{16}$.

Hexadecimal to Binary Conversion

For this conversion, simply substitute the 4 equivalent binary bits for each hexadecimal digit. (Be sure to use leading zeros to make a full 4-bit equivalent, except for the leftmost digit.)

EXAMPLE 1.10

Convert 3CF1 to binary.

$$3 \quad C \quad F \quad 1$$
$$0011 \quad 1100 \quad 1111 \quad 0001$$

or

$$11 \quad 1100 \quad 1111 \quad 0001$$

Note that the number in the computer would have no blanks between sets of 4 bits, and would look like this:

$$0011110011110001$$

Note also that the leading zeros of the hexadecimal 1 at the right cannot be omitted, but those of the 3 at the left can be omitted. If the three leading zeros of the rightmost hexadecimal digit were omitted, the resulting binary number would be 111 1001 1111, a completely different number which is equivalent to 7 9 F.

Methods for representing negative fixed binary and hexadecimal numbers on the IBM 370 system will be discussed in Sec. 1.11.

1.8 Addition of Binary and Hexadecimal Numbers

When two binary numbers are added (the computer never adds more than two numbers at a time), it is necessary to "carry" a digit to the next place when the sum exceeds 1. Consider the following decimal example and its binary equivalent, in which only the rightmost digit has been added thus far.

```
        Decimal              Binary
           1                    1
          19                  10011
          17                  10001
           6                      0
           ↑                      ↑
       Put down 6;          Put down 0;
        carry the 1          carry the 1
```

The problem is finished in the same way.

```
          1               1  11
         19              10011
         17              10001
         36             100100
```

As a check, we convert 100100_2 to decimal, as follows:

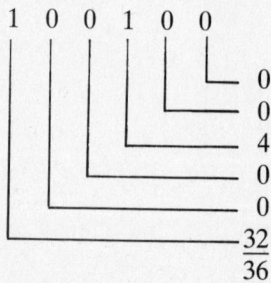

Addition of hexadecimal numbers is similar, except that carrying is required only when the sum exceeds F (15). That is, we write the sum of the digits in hexadecimal, and there is a carry if the sum exceeds F (15). For example, $8 + D = 21_{10} = 15_{16}$, so we would write down the 5 and carry the 1. On the other hand, $8 + 7 = 15_{10} = F_{16}$, so there is no carry.

EXAMPLE 1.11

Perform the following hexadecimal additions:

```
    9      11      17A2     84 2A    F 9 4B
    5      1F      8D5F      DAD    7ABC
```

The solutions are as follows:

```
              1         1 1 1      1  1    1 1 1 1
    9        11        17A2       84 2A    F 9 4B
    5        1F        8D5F        DAD     7ABC
    E        30        A501       91 D7    174 0 7
    ↑         ↑
    No     First column
  carry    sum exceeds
           $15_{10}$; hence
           1 is carried
```

1.9 Subtraction of Binary and Hexadecimal Numbers

When numbers are subtracted, borrowing from the next digit to the left is often required. In decimal,

$$
\begin{array}{r} 113 \\ -\ 44 \\ \end{array} \quad \text{Step 1} \quad \begin{array}{r} 0_1 \\ 1\!\!\!/\,3 \\ -\ 4\ 4 \\ \hline 6\ 9 \end{array}
$$

In binary and hexadecimal arithmetic, borrowing may be done in a similar manner. However, when borrowing is done, 2 in binary or 16 in hexadecimal (not 10, as in decimal) is borrowed.

Binary

$$
\begin{array}{r} 110 \\ -\ 11 \\ \end{array} \quad \text{Step 1} \quad \begin{array}{r} 0_1 \\ 1\!\!\!/\,0 \\ -\ 1\ 1 \\ \end{array} \quad \text{Step 2} \quad \begin{array}{r} 0_1 0_1 \\ \!\!\!/\,\!\!\!/\,0 \\ -\ 1\ 1 \\ \end{array}
$$

Step 1. 1 cannot be subtracted from 0 in column 1, so 1 from the next column is borrowed. This leaves 0 in the second column, and 10 (decimal 2) in the first. When 1 is subtracted from 10, 1 remains.

Step 2. 1 cannot be subtracted from the 0 now in column 2, so 1 is borrowed from column 3. Column 3 is now 0, and column 2 has 10. Subtraction in column 2 leaves 1, and in column 3, 0 from 0 leaves 0.

Hexadecimal

$$
\begin{array}{r} 1A42 \\ -\ B83 \\ \end{array} \quad \text{Step 1} \quad \begin{array}{r} 3_1 \\ 1A\!\!\!/\,2 \\ -\ B8\ 3 \\ \hline F \end{array} \quad \text{Step 2} \quad \begin{array}{r} 9_1 3_1 \\ 1\!\!\!/\!A\!\!\!/\,2 \\ -\ B8\ 3 \\ \hline B\ F \end{array} \quad \text{Step 3} \quad \begin{array}{r} 9_1 3_1 \\ 1\!\!\!/\!A\!\!\!/\,2 \\ -\ B8\ 3 \\ \hline E\ B\ F \end{array}
$$

Step 1. 3 cannot be subtracted from 2 in column 1, so 1 is borrowed from column 2, leaving 3 there and 12 (equivalent to decimal 18) in column 1. 3 from 12 leaves F.

Step 2. 8 cannot be subtracted from the 3 remaining in column 2, so 1 is borrowed from column 3. That leaves 9 in column 3 and 13 in column 2. 8 from 13 is B (remember, it is hexadecimal).

Step 3. The B in column 3 cannot be subtracted from the 9 remaining there, but it can be subtracted from 19, leaving E.

Try this binary subtraction:

$$
\begin{array}{r} 100 \\ -\ 11 \\ \end{array}
$$

In column 1, 1 cannot be subtracted from the 0, so 1 must be borrowed. However, there is a 0 in column 2. Thus 1 must be borrowed from column 3 first, changing column 3 to 0 and making column 2 equivalent to 10. Then 1 is borrowed from column 2, leaving column 2 with 1 and making column 1 equal to 10, from which 1 can be subtracted:

$$
\begin{array}{r} 100 \\ -\ 11 \\ \end{array} \quad \begin{array}{r} 0_1 \\ 1\!\!\!/\,0\ 0 \\ -\ 1\ 1 \\ \end{array} \quad \begin{array}{r} 0\ 1_1 \\ 1\!\!\!/\,\!\!\!/\,0 \\ -\ 1\ 1 \\ \hline 0\ 0\ 1 \end{array}
$$

1.10 Bytes, Words, and Halfwords

The IBM 370 system holds fixed binary numbers in 16 general-purpose registers (used for computation) and in main memory (also called *core* or *internal storage*).

The computer memory contains millions of bits—each one having a value which is either 0 or 1 at any time. In the IBM 370 system, 8 bits constitute 1 *byte*, which is the smallest accessible (*addressable*) unit of memory. Since the byte contains only a small amount of information, we will usually deal with a *word* (or *full word*), which consists of 4 bytes. Most fixed binary arithmetic operations on the IBM 370 are performed on numbers stored in full words. Since each full word is composed of 32 bits (4 bytes × 8 bits per byte), it can thus hold 2^{32} different numbers (from $-2,147,483,648$ to $+2,147,483,647$). Addition, subtraction, and multiplication operations can also be performed on halfwords if the programmer specifies. A halfword consists of 2 bytes, or 16 bits. Double words, 64 bits long, are used with floating-point operations. Thus the value of a fixed binary variable is usually held in a 32-bit (fullword) or 16-bit (halfword) portion of memory.

Fullword	32 bits	4 bytes
Halfword	16 bits	2 bytes
Double word	64 bits	8 bytes

In the computer, each bit has a value of either 0 or 1. There is no bit which contains "nothing"; each bit must have a value of 0 or 1. (The current value may have no meaning to the program which is running, in which case it is often referred to as "garbage." Nonetheless, the value is there.)

Thus a variable X with a value of 3_{10} might be stored in a halfword as

$$0000\ 0000\ 0000\ 0011$$

or as the full word

$$0000\ 0000\ 0000\ 0000\ 0000\ 0000\ 0000\ 0011$$

Although the leading zeros are usually left out when a human writes down the number, in the computer we store the number in a fixed amount of storage, so the leading zeros are present.

1.11 Representation of Negative Binary Numbers

In the IBM 370, we use either a fullword, 32 bits, or a halfword, 16 bits, to hold a binary number. Thus a positive number is written with enough leading zeros to fill either a full word or a halfword allotted to it. Fixed binary negative numbers are represented in a form called *2's complement notation*. In this notation, if a number is negative, the first bit is 1; otherwise, the first bit is 0. The first bit is called the *sign bit*. If we are using n-bit numbers, the 2's complement of a number is obtained by subtracting the number from 1 followed by n zeros. A consequence of this definition is that the complement of a complement is the original number. That is, if x is the complement of y, then y is the complement of x.

Before considering binary numbers, let's consider the more familiar decimal numbers. Using a fixed number of digits for all numbers is familiar to us in the automobile odometer (mileage indicator), which usually has six digits (dials).

$$\boxed{9|9|9|9|9|9}$$

After the odometer reads all 9s, the next number is zero. Thus, 999999 can be used to represent -1 on an odometer because adding 1 to the 999999 produces zero on the instrument, just as adding 1 to -1 produces zero logically. In general, we can use the odometer to represent five-digit signed numbers. Then we represent $-n$ by a number obtained by subtracting n from 1 followed by six 0s. The leading digit specifies the sign, where 0 is positive (or zero) and 9 is negative.

EXAMPLE 1.12

What reading should an odometer be set to in order to get a reading of zero after the car has been driven 4 miles?

$$999996$$

Adding 4 to 999996 gives the result

$$\begin{array}{r} 999996 \\ + 4 \\ \hline 1000000 \end{array}$$

| 9 | 9 | 9 | 9 | 9 | 6 |

1 | 0 | 0 | 0 | 0 | 0 | 0 |
↗
lost

But since the odometer has only six digits, the 1 ("carried" from the addition) is lost, and a zero reading results. The 999996 represents −4, since it represents 4 more miles to a zero reading. This is the 10's complement of 4.

EXAMPLE 1.13

What is the six-digit 10's complement of 432?
To get the complement, subtract the number from 1,000,000 (a 1 followed by six 0s).

$$\begin{array}{r} 1\ 000\ 000 \\ -432 \\ \hline 999\ 568 \end{array}$$

The same type of representation is used for fixed binary numbers in the computer, except, of course, the only digits are 0s and 1s. If the leading digit is 1, the number is negative; 0, positive or zero. We will use halfwords in many of our examples, since they have fewer digits; however, the same things are also true of full-word binary numbers. The following two halfword numbers (the first positive, the second negative) are complements of each other, since they add up to zero:

$$\begin{array}{r} 0000\ 0000\ 1010\ 1110 \\ +\ 1111\ 1111\ 0101\ 0010 \\ \hline 1\ 0000\ 0000\ 0000\ 0000 \end{array} \quad \text{Leftmost bit is lost}$$

(In general, the complement of a complement is the original number.)

In decimal arithmetic, it is easy to subtract one number from another number of equal or greater length whose digits are all 9s. There is never any borrowing. In contrast, subtracting from a number 1 greater than all 9s gives an answer 1 greater, but that subtraction requires a lot of borrowing:

$$\begin{array}{r} 999\ 999 \\ -\ 123\ 478 \\ \hline 876\ 521 \end{array} \qquad \begin{array}{r} 1\ 000\ 000 \\ -\ 123\ 478 \\ \hline 876\ 522 \end{array}$$

To get the complement of a halfword binary number, we could subtract it from a 1 followed by sixteen 0s (thirty-two 0s for a full word). (See Problem 1.24.) However, an easier way to accomplish the same result is to subtract the number from 16 bits of 1, then add 1 to the difference. This method of subtraction has two advantages. (1) there is no borrowing, and (2) each bit of the result is 0 if the corresponding bit of the original number is 1, and vice versa. Thus the first step in getting the complement is accomplished by "switching the bits" (from 1 to 0 and from 0 to 1). Then the final result is obtained by adding 1.

EXAMPLE 1.14

What is the halfword complement of 0000 1001 1100 1011?

$$\begin{array}{rl} 1111\ 1111\ 1111\ 1111 & \text{You really don't need this line} \\ -\ 0000\ 1001\ 1100\ 1011 & \text{Do this subtraction, or just} \\ \hline 1111\ 0110\ 0011\ 0100 & \quad \text{change every 0 to 1, every 1 to 0} \\ +1 & \text{Add 1} \\ \hline 1111\ 0110\ 0011\ 0101 & \text{2's complement} \end{array}$$

The complement of a negative number is, of course, a positive number:

$$\begin{array}{rl} \text{Negative number} & 1011\ 1101\ 1010\ 1001 \\ \text{Switched bits} & 0100\ 0010\ 0101\ 0110 \\ \text{Add 1 to get the positive complement} & 0100\ 0010\ 0101\ 0111 \end{array}$$

The result obtained by subtracting a number from n ones (or switching the bits) is called the 1's complement of the number. The 2's complement is obtained by adding 1 to the 1's complement of the number. (The only negative number whose 2's complement is not positive is 1000 0000 0000 0000. The computer cannot hold the absolute value of this number in a halfword space.)

To get the complement of a binary number in hexadecimal format, merely subtract the number from all F's and add 1. (A hexadecimal number consisting of all F's has a binary equivalent which consists solely of 1s. For example, $FFFF_{16} = 1111\ 1111\ 1111\ 1111_2$.)

EXAMPLE 1.15

Find the fullword complement of 12AB34CD.

$$\begin{array}{r} FFFF\ FFFF \\ -12AB\ 34CD \\ \hline ED54\ CB32 \\ +\qquad\qquad 1 \\ \hline ED54\ CB33 \end{array}$$

To prove that they are complements, add them:

$$\begin{array}{r} 12AB\ 34CD \\ +\ ED54\ CB33 \\ \hline 1\ 0000\ 0000 \end{array} \quad \text{The leftmost digit is lost}$$

EXAMPLE 1.16

Explain how you can tell whether or not an eight-digit hexadecimal number (in 2's complement notation) is negative.

The number is negative if the leftmost bit of the binary number is 1. This will be true if the leftmost hexadecimal digit is one of the digits 8 through F.

The magnitude of a negative number in complement form may be estimated by the position of its first zero. Just as leading 0s may be ignored for positive numbers, leading 1s in a negative number are merely copies of the sign bit, and do not represent significant digits. For example, 1111 1111 1111 1111 represents decimal -1. All the leading 1s are replications of the sign bit. In contrast,

$$1011\ 1101\ 1111\ 1111$$

represents a negative number (because its first bit is 1) with a large magnitude (its next bit is 0, not merely a copy of the sign bit).

EXAMPLE 1.17

Determine the decimal values of the halfwords

$$1011\ 1101\ 1111\ 1111 \quad \text{and} \quad 1111\ 1101\ 1111\ 1111$$

Switched bits	0100 0010 0000 0000	0000 0010 0000 0000
Add 1	0100 0010 0000 0001	0000 0010 0000 0001
Decimal value	$-16{,}897$	-513

Note that the number with its first 0 farthest left (the first number) has a greater magnitude. In general, the farther left the first 0 in a negative number, the farther left the first 1 in its complement and the greater the magnitude of the number.

Solved Problems

1.1 Convert the following unsigned binary (base 2) numbers to decimal (base 10).

(a)	1101	(e)	1111000	(i)	11110011101
(b)	1001010001	(f)	1000001010	(j)	1001111001
(c)	111110	(g)	1010	(k)	1000111
(d)	1011100011	(h)	101011111	(l)	110000001

(a) $1101_2 = 13_{10}$ (g) $1010_2 = 10_{10}$
(b) $1001010001_2 = 593_{10}$ (h) $101011111_2 = 351_{10}$
(c) $111110_2 = 62_{10}$ (i) $11110011101_2 = 1949_{10}$
(d) $1011100011_2 = 739_{10}$ (j) $1001111001_2 = 633_{10}$
(e) $1111000_2 = 120_{10}$ (k) $1000111_2 = 71_{10}$
(f) $1000001010_2 = 522_{10}$ (l) $110000001_2 = 385_{10}$

1.2 Convert the following hexadecimal (base 16) numbers to decimal (base 10).

(a)	C	(e)	6AB	(i)	AA
(b)	10A	(f)	9908	(j)	549
(c)	45	(g)	FACE	(k)	2ABC
(d)	69	(h)	80953	(l)	BAD

(a) $C_{16} = 12_{10}$ (g) $FACE_{16} = 64206_{10}$
(b) $10A_{16} = 266_{10}$ (h) $80953_{16} = 526675_{10}$
(c) $45_{16} = 69_{10}$ (i) $AA_{16} = 170_{10}$
(d) $69_{16} = 105_{10}$ (j) $549_{16} = 1353_{10}$
(e) $6AB_{16} = 1707_{10}$ (k) $2ABC_{16} = 10940_{10}$
(f) $9908_{16} = 39176_{10}$ (l) $BAD_{16} = 2989_{10}$

1.3 Convert the following decimal (base 10) numbers to binary (base 2).

(a)	32	(e)	47	(i)	10,973
(b)	198	(f)	765	(j)	95
(c)	14	(g)	1102	(k)	250
(d)	12,457	(h)	301	(l)	25,121

(a) $32_{10} = 100000_2$ (g) $1102_{10} = 10001001110_2$
(b) $198_{10} = 11000110_2$ (h) $301_{10} = 100101101_2$
(c) $14_{10} = 1110_2$ (i) $10{,}973_{10} = 10101011011101_2$
(d) $12{,}457_{10} = 11000010101001_2$ (j) $95_{10} = 1011111_2$
(e) $47_{10} = 101111_2$ (k) $250_{10} = 11111010_2$
(f) $765_{10} = 1011111101_2$ (l) $25{,}121_{10} = 110001000100001_2$

1.4 Convert $41{,}152_{10}$ to hexadecimal using the algorithm presented in Sec. 1.5.

The largest power of 16 in 41,152 is $16^3 = 4096$.

$$
\begin{array}{r}
10 \quad \text{A}\\
4096\overline{)41152}\\
4096\\
\hline
192\\
0\\
\hline
192
\end{array}
$$

$$
\begin{array}{r}
0 \quad 0\\
256\overline{)192}\\
0\\
\hline
192
\end{array}
$$

$$
\begin{array}{r}
12 \quad \text{C}\\
16\overline{)192}\\
16\\
\hline
32\\
32\\
\hline
0
\end{array}
$$

$$
\begin{array}{r}
0 \quad 0\\
1\overline{)0}\\
0\\
\hline
0
\end{array}
$$

The hexadecimal equivalent of decimal 41,152 is A0C0.

1.5 Convert the following decimal (base 10) numbers to hexadecimal (base 16).

(a) 13   (e) 50   (i) 8888
(b) 99   (f) 987   (j) 777
(c) 244   (g) 22,412   (k) 69
(d) 5549   (h) 645   (l) 462

(a) $13_{10} = D_{16}$ (g) $22{,}412_{10} = 578C_{16}$
(b) $99_{10} = 63_{16}$ (h) $645_{10} = 285_{16}$
(c) $244_{10} = F4_{16}$ (i) $8888_{10} = 22B8_{16}$
(d) $5549_{10} = 15AD_{16}$ (j) $777_{10} = 309_{16}$
(e) $50_{10} = 32_{16}$ (k) $69_{10} = 45_{16}$
(f) $987_{10} = 3DB_{16}$ (l) $462_{10} = 1CE_{16}$

1.6 Convert the following hexadecimal (base 16) numbers to binary (base 2).

(a) B   (e) 48   (i) AC4
(b) 145   (f) 457A   (j) 144E
(c) AF   (g) BA   (k) 1984
(d) 9B9   (h) 9771   (l) 2001

(a) $B_{16} = 1011_2$ (g) $BA_{16} = 10111010_2$
(b) $145_{16} = 101000101_2$ (h) $9771_{16} = 1001011101110001_2$
(c) $AF_{16} = 10101111_2$ (i) $AC4_{16} = 101011000100_2$
(d) $9B9_{16} = 100110111001_2$ (j) $144E_{16} = 1010001001110_2$
(e) $48_{16} = 1001000_2$ (k) $1984_{16} = 1100110000100_2$
(f) $457A_{16} = 100010101111010_2$ (l) $2001_{16} = 10000000000001_2$

CHAP. 1] NUMBER SYSTEMS 15

1.7 Perform the following additions in hexadecimal.

(a) 9
    +4

(e) DB
    +CA

(i) F1 3 5
    +ABCD

(b) FACE
    + BAD

(f) 515
    +1984

(j) 1000
    +5461

(c) 9 9
    +7A

(g) ACE1
    +EA52

(k) 23458
    +99FA3

(d) 5 7776
    +ABFEE

(h) 45
    +69

(l) BB4
    +ACE

(a) D   (e) 1A5   (i) 19D02
(b) 1067B   (f) 1E99   (j) 6461
(c) 113   (g) 19733 (k) BD3FB
(d) 103764   (h) AE   (l) 1682

1.8 Perform the following additions in binary.

(a) 111
    + 10

(e) 1011
    +1111

(i) 10110
    +10100

(b) 1101
    + 10

(f) 101011
    +111111

(j) 110111011011
    + 11100011111

(c) 1011101
    + 111001

(g) 100011
    +111000

(k) 1010
    + 110

(d) 100011111
    +101101110

(h) 111001001110
    +100111100111

(l) 11011
    +100001

(a) 1001   (g) 1011011
(b) 1111   (h) 1100000110101
(c) 10010110   (i) 101010
(d) 1010001101   (j) 1010011111010
(e) 11010   (k) 10000
(f) 1101010   (l) 111100

1.9 Perform the following subtractions in hexadecimal.

(a) 69
    −45

(e) EC
    −24

(i) F2
    −C5

(b) 987
    −3A3

(f) 124C
    −10CB

(j) 1F92
    −1BC3

(c) 598ED
    − 79AF

(g) 777E
    −4EEE

(k) FACE
    − BAD

(d) 499F
    −1DAC

(h) DAC
    −ACE

(l) 94497
    − 8AAB

(a) 24   (e) C8   (i) 2D
(b) 5E4   (f) 181   (j) 3CF
(c) 51F3E   (g) 2890   (k) EF21
(d) 2BF3   (h) 2DE   (l) 8B9EC

1.10 Perform the following subtractions in binary.

(a) 1110
− 111

(b) 110110
− 10111

(c) 111
− 110

(d) 1111110
− 1100111

(e) 10011011
− 1110001

(f) 10001110
− 1011110

(g) 101110110
− 100011110

(h) 10011011011
− 1000010111

(i) 1110001100010
− 1000111101110

(j) 11111
− 10110

(k) 11100011
− 1111111

(l) 1110110
− 1000111

(a) 111 (e) 101010 (i) 101001110100
(b) 11111 (f) 110000 (j) 1001
(c) 1 (g) 1011000 (k) 1100100
(d) 10111 (h) 1011000100 (l) 101111

1.11 Using 16-bit binary numbers, compute the 1's and 2's complements of the following decimal numbers.

(a) 77 (e) 20,202 (i) 700
(b) 938 (f) 3499 (j) 515
(c) 2001 (g) 5198 (k) 818
(d) 1984 (h) 27 (l) 2474

(a) 0000 0000 0100 1101 = 77
1111 1111 1011 0010 = 1's comp.
1111 1111 1011 0011 = 2's comp.

(b) 0000 0011 1010 1010 = 938
1111 1100 0101 0101 = 1's comp.
1111 1100 0101 0110 = 2's comp.

(c) 0000 0111 1101 0001 = 2001
1111 1000 0010 1110 = 1's comp.
1111 1000 0010 1111 = 2's comp.

(d) 0000 0111 1100 0000 = 1984
1111 1000 0011 1111 = 1's comp.
1111 1000 0100 0000 = 2's comp.

(e) 0100 1110 1110 1010 = 20,202
1011 0001 0001 0101 = 1's comp.
1011 0001 0001 0110 = 2's comp.

(f) 0000 1101 1010 1011 = 3499
1111 0010 0101 0100 = 1's comp.
1111 0010 0101 0101 = 2's comp.

(g) 0001 0100 0100 1110 = 5198
1110 1011 1011 0001 = 1's comp.
1110 1011 1011 0010 = 2's comp.

(h) 0000 0000 0001 1011 = 27
1111 1111 1110 0100 = 1's comp.
1111 1111 1110 0101 = 2's comp.

(i) 0000 0010 1011 1100 = 700
1111 1101 0100 0011 = 1's comp.
1111 1101 0100 0100 = 2's comp.

(j) 0000 0010 0000 0011 = 515
1111 1101 1111 1100 = 1's comp.
1111 1101 1111 1101 = 2's comp.

(k) 0000 0011 0011 0010 = 818
1111 1100 1100 1101 = 1's comp.
1111 1100 1100 1110 = 2's comp.

(l) 0000 1001 1010 1010 = 2474
1111 0110 0101 0101 = 1's comp.
1111 0110 0101 0110 = 2's comp.

1.12 Using eight hexadecimal digits, convert the following decimal (base 10) numbers to hexadecimal (base 16).

(a) −7 (e) −44 (i) −103
(b) −713 (f) −9999 (j) −6543
(c) −547 (g) −200 (k) −55
(d) −2 (h) −29 (l) −501

CHAP. 1] NUMBER SYSTEMS 17

(a) FFFFFFF9   (e) FFFFFFD4   (i) FFFFFF99
(b) FFFFFD37   (f) FFFFD8F1   (j) FFFFE671
(c) FFFFFDDD   (g) FFFFFF38   (k) FFFFFFC9
(d) FFFFFFFE   (h) FFFFFFE3   (l) FFFFFE0B

1.13 Suppose we are using halfword (16-bit) numbers. Then the following numbers are all negative. Convert them to decimal.

(a) 1111111111110010   (g) 1111111101100110
(b) 1111111101101110   (h) 1111111100111111
(c) 1111111111100011   (i) 1111111111011101
(d) 1111111101111111   (j) 1111101011001111
(e) 1111111111110011   (k) 1111111101101000
(f) 1111000000001110   (l) 1111111111100111

(a) −14   (e) −13   (i) −35
(b) −146   (f) −4082   (j) −1329
(c) −29   (g) −154   (k) −152
(d) −129   (h) −193   (l) −25

1.14 Using 16-bit binary numbers, convert the following decimal (base 10) numbers to binary (base 2).

(a) −4   (e) −8812   (i) −66
(b) −88   (f) −3456   (j) −8
(c) −301   (g) −745   (k) −92
(d) −517   (h) −205   (l) −105

(a) 0000 0000 0000 0100 = 4
    1111 1111 1111 1011 = 1's comp.
    1111 1111 1111 1100 = 2's comp.
(b) 0000 0000 0101 1000 = 88
    1111 1111 1010 0111 = 1's comp.
    1111 1111 1010 1000 = 2's comp.
(c) 0000 0001 0010 1101 = 301
    1111 1110 1101 0010 = 1's comp.
    1111 1110 1101 0011 = 2's comp.
(d) 0000 0010 0000 0101 = 517
    1111 1101 1111 1010 = 1's comp.
    1111 1101 1111 1011 = 2's comp.
(e) 0010 0010 0110 1100 = 8812
    1101 1101 1001 0011 = 1's comp.
    1101 1101 1001 0100 = 2's comp.
(f) 0000 1101 1000 0000 = 3456
    1111 0010 0111 1111 = 1's comp.
    1111 0010 1000 0000 = 2's comp.
(g) 0000 0010 1110 1001 = 745
    1111 1101 0001 0110 = 1's comp.
    1111 1101 0001 0111 = 2's comp.
(h) 0000 0000 1100 1101 = 205
    1111 1111 0011 0010 = 1's comp.
    1111 1111 0011 0011 = 2's comp.
(i) 0000 0000 0100 0010 = 66
    1111 1111 1011 1101 = 1's comp.
    1111 1111 1011 1110 = 2's comp.
(j) 0000 0000 0000 1000 = 8
    1111 1111 1111 0111 = 1's comp.
    1111 1111 1111 1000 = 2's comp.
(k) 0000 0000 0101 1100 = 92
    1111 1111 1010 0011 = 1's comp.
    1111 1111 1010 0100 = 2's comp.
(l) 0000 0000 0110 1001 = 105
    1111 1111 1001 0110 = 1's comp.
    1111 1111 1001 0111 = 2's comp.

1.15 Using eight-digit hexadecimal numbers, find the complements of the following hexadecimal numbers.

(a) 000001AC (f) E12B319C
(b) 025A81FE (g) 32FF415B
(c) 1A325AB0 (h) FFFFFFFF
(d) 718D183B (i) F2A3E5AB
(e) FFF1A28B (j) 80001234

(a) FFFFFE54 (f) 1ED4CE64
(b) FDA57E02 (g) CD00BEA5
(c) E5CDA550 (h) 00000001
(d) 8E72E7C5 (i) 0D5C1A55
(e) 000E5D75 (j) 7FFFEDCC

1.16 What is the complement of 0000 0000 0000 0000? Answer two ways—by logic and by following the technique outlined above.

    Switching the bits 1111 1111 1111 1111
    Adding 1   0000 0000 0000 0000 (carried 1 is lost)

Logically, $-0 = 0$.

1.17 What is the value of $1F0402_{16}$ after 60_{10} has been added to it?

          1F043E

1.18 Determine the sum of the two numbers in each part (expressed in different bases). Express the answers in hexadecimal.

	Hexadecimal Value	Decimal Value
(a)	1AB342	102
(b)	1A0342	66
(c)	1F0502	26
(d)	0F134A	98
(e)	F0F142	258

(a) 1AB3A8 (b) 1A0384 (c) 1F051C (d) 0F13AC (e) F0F244

1.19 What is the difference in decimal between the following pairs of hexadecimal numbers?

(a) 10F3A4 − 10F11C (c) 1AB202 − 1AAAAA
(b) AB1818 − AB0FF4 (d) 0975CC − 083DF0

(a) 648 (b) 2084 (c) 1880 (d) 79,836

1.20 How can you tell immediately if a binary number is even or odd? Does your method work for negative numbers in 2's complement notation? How can you tell if a binary number is evenly divisible by 4? by 8? by 16?

 If its last bit is 0, the number is even; if its last bit is 1, the number is odd. This method works for negative numbers in complement notation as well as for positive numbers and 0. If a binary number is divisible by 4, its last 2 bits are 0. If a binary number is divisible by 8, its last 3 bits are 0. If a binary number is divisible by 16, its last 4 bits are 0.

1.21 What is the decimal value of the negative number with the greatest magnitude which can be represented in 16 bits?

$-2^{15} = -32,768$

1.22 What hexadecimal digits represent 4-bit strings in which the last 2 bits are 0?

0	0000
4	0100
8	1000
C	1100

1.23 Prove that a hexadecimal number which ends in 0, 4, 8, or C, no matter what the values of its other digits, must be evenly divisible by 4.

Since it ends in 0, 4, 8, or C, its last 2 bits must be 0. Dividing it by 100_2 causes these 2 bits to be lost, with no remainder. That is, the number is evenly divisible by 4.

1.24 (a) Explain why the results of the following two binary subtractions differ by 1.

```
  100000        11111
-  10101      - 10101
  ------       ------
  01011        01010
```

(b) Explain why the results of the following two hexadecimal subtractions differ by 1.

```
  1 0 0 0        F F F
-   A 1 3      - A 1 3
  -------       -------
    5 E D        5 E C
```

(c) Which subtraction is easier to do in each case? Devise a method to subtract a number from another number which consists of a 1 followed by any number of zeros [like the numbers in the first part of each of (a) and (b)]

In (a) and (b) the answers differ by 1 because the same value is being subtracted from two numbers which differ by 1. In (c) the point is that it is easy to subtract from the smaller number in each case, so that if we have to subtract from the larger, we can subtract from the smaller and add 1 to the result to get the final answer.

Supplementary Problems

1.25 Convert the following unsigned binary numbers to decimal.

(a) 11110010 (g) 111101100110
(b) 111101101110 (h) 111100111111
(c) 111111100011 (i) 111111011101
(d) 111101111111 (j) 1111101011001111
(e) 11110011 (k) 111101101000
(f) 1111000000001110 (l) 111111100111

1.26 Convert the following hexadecimal numbers to binary and also to decimal. Check your work by converting the binary number to decimal.

(a) ABC   (c) F1   (e) BF   (g) DAD
(b) FFF   (d) BAD   (f) 1000   (h) 111

1.27 Convert the following positive binary numbers to decimal and also to hexadecimal. Check your work by converting the decimal number to hexadecimal.

(a) 1110111111101111   (e) 11111111
(b) 10000000   (f) 10101010
(c) 00011100   (g) 00000001
(d) 11100   (h) 1100101010

1.28 If the dividend of Example 1.4 (123456) had been divided by 2 instead of 10 in each case, (a) what possible values would each remainder have? (b) What result would the successive divisions have?

1.29 If the dividend of Example 1.4 (123456) had been divided by 16 instead of 10 in each case, (a) what possible values would each remainder have? (b) What result would the successive divisions have?

1.30 Repeat Example 1.7, using decimal 109 instead of 212.

1.31 Repeat Problem 1.30, using the algorithm for converting decimal notation to binary presented in Sec. 1.5.

1.32 Convert the following decimal numbers to binary and also to hexadecimal. Check your work by converting the binary number to hexadecimal.

(a) 123   (e) 98   (i) −132
(b) 777   (f) 200   (j) −333
(c) 512   (g) 256   (k) −1048
(d) 77   (h) 900   (l) −1001

1.33 Consider the following numbers in 2's complement notation. Are the 32-bit number and 64-bit number equal in magnitude?

11101110101010100111011111110001
0000000000000000000000000000000011101110101010100111011111110001

1.34 Which of the following hexadecimal numbers (in complement notation) are negative?

(a) 1FA02003   (e) 8FA02003
(b) FFFFF000   (f) ABCDEF12
(c) 7FFFFFFF   (g) 80000000
(d) 00000000   (h) C03D8F2B

1.35 Which of the signed numbers below is largest? smallest? Would your answer differ if the numbers were unsigned hexadecimal numbers?

(a) 1FA02003   (e) 8FA02003
(b) FFFFF000   (f) ABCDEF12
(c) 7FFFFFFF   (g) 80000000
(d) 00000000   (h) C03D8F2B

CHAP. 1] NUMBER SYSTEMS 21

1.36 Write the 16-bit equivalent of each of the following 32-bit numbers which are in 2's complement notation.

   (*a*) 1111 1111 1111 1111 1010 1010 1010 1010
   (*b*) 0000 0000 0000 0000 0000 0000 0000 0000
   (*c*) 1111 1111 1111 1111 1111 1011 1111 1111
   (*d*) 0000 0000 0000 0000 0001 0000 0000 0000

1.37 Explain why it is impossible to write 16-bit equivalents of the following 32-bit numbers written in 2's complement notation.

   (*a*) 1110 1111 0101 0001 0101 0101 0000 1111
   (*b*) 1111 1111 1111 1111 0101 0101 0101 0101
   (*c*) 0000 0000 0000 0000 1000 0000 0000 0000

1.38 Expand each of the following halfword numbers to full-word numbers, maintaining the 2's complement notation.

   (*a*) ABCD   (*e*) 1234
   (*b*) 8010   (*f*) C104
   (*c*) CCCD   (*g*) 7F5F
   (*d*) 80AC   (*h*) 9031

1.39 Show how the algorithm in Sec. 1.7 for converting from binary to hexadecimal is related to the algorithm of Example 1.4 for converting decimal to decimal.

1.40 The number of grains of rice in a 1-gallon jar of rice can be represented by a decimal number, a hexadecimal number, or a binary number. If we divide the grains of rice into groups of 16, and there are 14 grains left over, what is the last digit in the hexadecimal representation of the number of grains? Does it matter if the original number was counted in hexadecimal, in decimal, or in binary?

1.41 Convert 20,000 seconds to hours, minutes, and seconds, using the two different algorithms (methods) presented in this chapter. The number in hours, minutes, and seconds can be regarded as being in base 60 as long as the time is less than 60 hours. You can invent 60 symbols to represent the digits (10 decimal digits, 25 capital letters, and 25 lowercase letters, for example) or merely separate the hours, minutes, and seconds with slashes (as in 1/20/30, meaning 1 hour, 20 minutes, and 30 seconds).

1.42 Divide the hexadecimal number 7A32 by hexadecimal A, and the quotient by A, repeating until the final quotient is zero. What value will the collection of remainders represent? If the value were divided by 2, what would the remainders represent?

Chapter 2

Assembly Language Format

2.1 Introduction

High-level languages use compilers to generate machine language instructions from the source program. Assembly language programs use an assembler to generate machine language object code. The major difference is that a typical statement in a higher-level language produces many machine language instructions, but there is a one-to-one correspondence between assembly language instructions and machine language instructions. Writing assembly language programs helps immeasurably in understanding how the computer actually works. This chapter introduces the assembly language program, using only a few instructions; the main emphasis is on the format of assembly language itself.

2.2 Registers and Memory

There are three areas of the computer where the programmer can store information:

16 general-purpose registers (GPRs)

Main memory (also called core or internal storage)

4 floating-point registers (FPRs)

The 16 general-purpose registers, often simply referred to as *registers*, are numbered from 0 through 15. Registers 2 through 12 are used for regular work. (By convention, registers 0, 1, 13, 14, and 15 are used for communication with subprograms, and the low-numbered registers are also used by the computer to return answers when some advanced instructions are executed.) Each GPR holds 32 bits of information. Thus a register can hold 2^{32} different combinations—for example, 2^{32} different numbers. Since the machine uses the 2's complement representation for negative numbers, a register can hold any integer from -2^{31} to $+(2^{31} - 1)$. (2^{31} is a little over 2 billion; hence a register can hold any 9-digit decimal number and even some 10-digit decimal numbers.)

Main memory sizes are described in bytes. Each byte consists of 8 bits. The byte is the smallest addressable portion of memory (see Chap. 4), but we rarely store information in only 1 byte. For example, fixed-point binary numbers are held in either full words or halfwords. A full word consists of 4 consecutive bytes, while a halfword consists of 2 consecutive bytes. At times we shall also be interested in a double word, which consists of 8 consecutive bytes.

The four floating-point registers will be discussed in Chap. 12.

2.3 Assembly Language Format

There are essentially two kinds of statements in assembly language: (1) instructions which are translated into machine language instructions, and (2) data definitions, which define the type and amount of storage for variables. (Some statements are a combination of these types; see Sec. 2.6.)

We will also encounter several assembly language instructions, called *pseudo-instructions*, which are not translated into machine language at all. These are instructions to the assembler, telling it how to proceed to assemble the program. START, CSECT, USING, and END are four frequently encountered pseudo-instructions.

We shall describe the format of assembly language statements by considering the program shown in Fig. 2-1. Note that assembly language programs are written in uppercase (capital) letters.

There are four fields in an assembly language statement—the Name field, the Operation field, the Operand field, and the Comment field. If there is a Name field, it must start in column 1. (If column 1 is blank, it means that there is no Name field, and the statement begins with the Operation

```
Col.1      Col.10 Col.16         Col.30
  ↓          ↓      ↓              ↓
PROGRAM1   START  0               START-UP INSTRUCTIONS
           BALR   12,0               TO BE DISCUSSED
           USING  *,12               IN LATER CHAPTERS
*
           L      2,X             LOADS THE VALUE FROM MEMORY POSITION X INTO
*                                    REGISTER 2
           A      2,Y             ADDS THE VALUE FROM Y TO THAT IN
*                                    REGISTER 2
           S      2,Z             SUBTRACTS THE VALUE OF Z FROM THE REGISTER
           ST     2,W             COPIES THE VALUE FROM THE REGISTER TO
*                                    MEMORY LOCATION W
*
           BR     14              THIS INSTRUCTION STOPS EXECUTION
*                                    OF THE PROGRAM
*
X          DC     F'7'
Y          DC     F'-3'
Z          DC     F'17'
W          DS     F
           END
Name       Oper-  Operand         Comment    (These comments would be very
field      ation  field           field       poor for any later program,
           field                              after you know what the
                                              operation symbols mean.)
```

Fig. 2-1 A simple assembly language program to calculate $W = X + Y - Z$.

field.) One or more blanks separate the fields, so there cannot be any blanks within any of the first three fields (except in character strings enclosed in quotation marks). Good style requires that the Operation field, the Operand field, and the Comment field each start in a given column; columns 10, 16, and 30 are most often used.

Only columns 1 through 71 can hold information to be used by the assembler. If more information is required for an instruction, any nonblank symbol can be entered in column 72, which signifies that the next line will be a continuation. Continuation lines begin in column 16. No more than two continuation lines can be used for a single instruction (for a total of three lines).

Names are used in the Name field and the Operand field. They can be up to a maximum of eight characters in length and must start with a letter or a national character ($, #, or @); however, the national characters are conventionally used for special purposes. The characters (if any) after the first character must be letters or digits (or national characters). No blanks, hyphens, or underbar symbols may be used within a name. Names should be meaningful for best style.

EXAMPLE 2.1

The accompanying table lists incorrect and correct names, respectively.

Incorrect Name	Correct Name	Reason Incorrect
a	A	Lowercase
A 1	A1	Embedded blank
A_ONE	AONE	Underscore
VAR-NAME	VAR	Hyphen
NAME2LONG	LONGNAME	Too long
12	ONE2	Does not start with letter

In the Operation field, each operation is denoted by a mnemonic operation code—a string of from one to five letters—which specifies which operation is to be performed. For example, A is used for add, S for subtract, M for multiply, and D for divide. L is used for load, which means to copy a value from a memory location into a register. This instruction erases whatever was previously stored in the register. ST is used for store, which means to copy a value from a register into a memory location (erasing what was previously there). Each of the other operation codes also uses a letter or combination of letters to help the programmer remember what operation is to be performed. Note that it is also permissible to use these same letters or sequences of letters for names of variables.

The Operand field usually contains one to three operands. With the instructions L, A, S, and ST, there are two operands; the first of these is a register and the second a memory location.

The Comment field is printed by the assembler, but is otherwise ignored. An asterisk (∗) in column 1 means that the whole line is a comment. The assembler will print the line, but otherwise ignore it. As many full comment lines as are desired can be used consecutively. No entirely blank line can be included, so a line with an asterisk in column 1 is a good way to separate major portions of a program.

Each program contains only one START and one END statement. The END statement ends assembly of the program.

2.4 Defining Storage in Memory

At the end of the sample program in Fig. 2-1, there are statements with DC or DS in the Operation field. DC (short for Define Constant) reserves memory space and, in addition, places an initial value in that memory location. Despite the word "constant," it is quite possible to change the value in that memory location during execution of the program. Each DC instruction has its initial value indicated within single quotation marks. *Values written in an assembly language program are always in decimal notation*, unless the programmer explicitly states otherwise. The use of decimal values is not limited to defining constants but extends throughout the entire assembly language program. The decimal values are translated into binary (represented as hexadecimal) by the assembler as it assembles the machine language form of the program.

EXAMPLE 2.2

```
X         DC      F'17'           INITIAL VALUE IS THE BINARY EQUIVALENT OF
*                                 DECIMAL 17
Y         DC      F'-3'           THE MINUS SIGN IS PERMITTED
Z         DC      F'17110'        NOTE THAT NO COMMAS ARE PERMITTED
```

DS (short for Define Storage) merely reserves space in memory but does not place a value into memory. If the programmer writes DS and also indicates a value in the instruction, the assembler does *not* enter an initial value. Thus the two following statements both have the same effect:

```
NAME      DS      F'10'
NAME      DS      F
```

The programmer may allocate portions of memory with various sizes, as needed. The designations for the most common sizes are given in Table 2-1.

The programmer designates the type of storage required in a DS or DC instruction. A full word can hold a value up to $(2^{31} - 1)$—a little over 2 billion. A halfword can hold a value up to $(2^{15} - 1)$—about 32,000. Values in storage locations defined as full word and halfword are stored as binary integers. The use of double words will be discussed later.

Table 2-1 Declarations of Memory Space

Designation	Meaning	Length
F	Full word	32 bits (4 bytes)
H	Halfword	16 bits (2 bytes)
D	Double word	64 bits (8 bytes)

EXAMPLE 2.3

```
VARIABLE  DS   F
HALFWD    DS   H
DBLWD     DS   D
HALF      DC   H'-19'
```

The first three declarations allocate a full word of memory for the variable VARIABLE, a halfword of memory for the variable HALFWD, and a double word of memory for the variable DBLWD, respectively. The last declaration allocates a halfword of memory for HALF as well as giving HALF an initial value of −19.

Numbers may be included in a program in scientific notation. In normal scientific notation, 2000 may be represented as 2×10^3. In the assembly language program, such a number is represented as follows:

$$2 \times 10^3 \quad \text{is represented} \quad 2E3$$

Here, 2 is the coefficient (or mantissa) of the number. The exponent (to the base 10) is 3, which is preceded by E for exponent. Here are two more examples:

$$7 \times 10^{-3} \quad \text{is represented} \quad 7E-3$$
$$-6 \times 10^{-4} \quad \text{is represented} \quad -6E-4$$

Fullword and halfword numbers are integers. If a decimal fraction is used in a DC statement with an F or H format, the value is rounded to the nearest whole number. Thus,

```
NUM1   DC   F'7.4'     YIELDS 7 IN NUM1
NUM2   DC   F'7.5'     YIELDS 8 IN NUM2
```

2.5 How the Program Works

The program shown in Fig. 2-1 works in the following way. [Note: The first three instructions set up the program, but they will not be discussed until later. The last statement (END) indicates the end of the program to be assembled.] Instructions are executed sequentially unless a branch is encountered (see Chap. 5).

Load

The Load (L) operation copies a value from a full-word memory location (designated second in the Operand field) to a register (designated first in the Operand field). The previous value in the register is erased, and the register is filled with the new value. The value in memory is left unchanged. Thus L 2,X copies into register 2 the value 7 from the memory location denoted by X, replacing the "garbage" which was previously in register 2. The value in memory location X is still the binary equivalent of decimal 7. (Of course, the contents of the register are also in binary form.) Thus, as in *most* operations, the first operand is changed and the second one is not.

Add and Subtract

The Add (A) and Subtract (S) operations also change the value of the first operand (the register) and leave the second operand (the memory location) unchanged. The operation A 2,Y causes the value in the full-word memory location Y (the binary equivalent of decimal −3) to be added to the contents of register 2. After execution of the add instruction, register 2 will contain the binary equivalent of 7 + (−3) = +4. Memory location Y still contains −3.

The subtract operation S 2,Z causes the value at memory location Z (which is 17) to be subtracted from the present contents of register 2 (which is +4), yielding a result in register 2 of the binary equivalent of decimal −13. The value at Z is still the binary equivalent of decimal 17.

Store

The Store (ST) operation moves information in the opposite direction from the load, add, and subtract operations. The store operation copies the value from the register (first operand) to the full-word memory location (second operand), erasing whatever was at that memory location previously. Thus the execution of ST 2,W causes the binary equivalent of −13 to be copied to memory location W. This same value still exists in register 2.

If the value in a register is no longer needed, the register may be used for some other purpose. The programmer can load a new value into the register and replace whatever was there. Using a register for any other operation, such as add or subtract, will require another step first to clear the register.

Halting Execution

The BR 14 instruction is a special instruction which halts execution of the program (if the contents of register 14 have not been changed by the programmer during the course of the program). Certain installations may halt execution in alternative ways.

The whole program has the effect of executing the following high-level language assignment statement:

$$W = X + Y - Z$$

We note that we will not see any results from the execution of this program, since we have not asked for anything to be printed.

EXAMPLE 2.4

A portion of an assembly language program is shown which will compute and store the value of ANS = A + B, where A has the initial value 15 and B has the initial value 25.

```
          L     2,A           LOADS A INTO REGISTER 2
          A     2,B           ADDS THE VALUE IN B TO THE VALUE IN REGISTER 2
          ST    2,ANS         STORES THE SUM FROM REGISTER 2 AT MEMORY
*                             LOCATION ANS
           ...
* THE A IN THE OPERATION FIELD IS NOT RELATED TO THE A IN THE
* NAME FIELD
A         DC    F'15'
B         DC    F'25'
ANS       DS    F
```

The result of this program is to store 40, the sum of A + B, at ANS. Note that the letter A was used both as the name of a variable in the first instruction and as the operation code in the second instruction.

EXAMPLE 2.5

How can we write a portion of an assembly language program which will compute and store the value of ANS, as indicated below?

$$W = M + N$$
$$ANS = P + Q - W$$

Assume that M has the initial value 20, N has the initial value 30, P has the initial value 40, and Q has the initial value -50.

We can write the code in the following way:

```
        L     2,M
        A     2,N           M + N
        ST    2,W           W = M + N STORED
        L     2,P           SAME REGISTER CAN BE USED AGAIN
        A     2,Q           P + Q
        S     2,W           P + Q - W
        ST    2,ANS
        ...
M       DC    F'20'
N       DC    F'30'
P       DC    F'40'
Q       DC    F'-50'
W       DS    F
ANS     DS    F
```

This portion of program works as follows: First, the value of M is loaded into register 2. The value of N is added to the value in that register. Then the sum in the register is copied into memory location W by the ST operation. We reuse register 2 to load the value of P. (That operation erases the value previously in register 2, but since we have the value of W stored in memory, we don't need it in the register.) We then add the value of Q and finally subtract the value of W. The answer, in register 2, is copied into memory location ANS by the store operation. (You will be able to write a more efficient program to perform this task after a few more instructions are introduced in Chap. 3.)

2.6 Literals

How would you write instructions to add a constant value, say 9, to a memory location (for example, $X = X + 9$)? First you load X into a register, after which you want to add 9 to it. One way to do this is to define a constant, say NINE, and add its value into the register, as shown in Example 2.6.

EXAMPLE 2.6

```
        L     2,X
        A     2,NINE
        ST    2,X
        ...
X       DC    F'101'
NINE    DC    F'9'
```

The first instruction loads the value of X into register 2. The second instruction adds the value of NINE to that value. The value of NINE is defined to be 9 in the last statement. The third instruction stores the sum as the new value of X.

A second way to perform this task is to include the constant in the instruction—to use a *literal*. A literal is expressed as an unnamed constant, with an equal sign in front of it.

EXAMPLE 2.7

```
        L    2,X
        A    2,=F'9'
        ST   2,X
        ...
X       DC   F'101'
```

This will be assembled in exactly the same way as the instructions used in the preceding example. However, this time we did not set up the memory location NINE. Instead, the assembler will define a memory location, called a literal, initialize it to 9, and give it a special name. Then it will add the value at that location to the value in register 2. The F'9' has the same meaning that it has in DC statements (which define constants). The equal sign tells the assembler that this is a literal. If =F'9' is used again in the program, the original memory location will be reused. The assembler places the declaration of the literal after the END statement, providing a special name, such as

```
.LIT0001 DC    F'9'
```

Literals have the advantage over programmer-defined constant locations that their values are less likely to be changed by mistake. Literals also have some disadvantages. If the same literal (e.g., =F'9') is used in many places throughout a program, and the programmer later wants to change the constant to 10, many modifications must be made. If a constant were defined and used, only the value of that constant would have to be changed. The user-declared variable makes the program more flexible.

Solved Problems

2.1 (a) What are the numbers of the general-purpose registers in hexadecimal notation?

(b) Explain why the registers are numbered from 0 through 15, as they are.

(c) Are hexadecimal or decimal numbers used to represent registers in the assembly language program?

(d) Are hexadecimal or decimal numbers used to represent registers in the machine language program?

(a) 0 through F (0 through 9 and A through F)
(b) Each register can be represented in machine language by one hexadecimal digit.
(c) Decimal
(d) Hexadecimal

2.2 Can a register hold more positive numbers than negative numbers or vice versa? If so, how many more? Explain.

A register can hold one more negative number. The number of negative numbers equals the number of positive numbers plus one 0 number. Half the numbers start with a 1 bit and are negative. The other half, starting with a 0 bit, include zero and the positive numbers.

2.3 Which registers are most available for ordinary work?

2 through 12

2.4 What, if anything, is wrong with each of the following names for variables?

(a)	END	(d)	FIRST_ONE	(g)	N123	(j)	$10
(b)	START	(e)	FIRSTTHREE	(h)	two	(k)	#MEN
(c)	USING	(f)	123	(i)	TWO FOUR	(l)	STOCK@

(a) through (c), (g), and (j) through (l) are legal. (There are no reserved words in assembly language.)

(d) The underbar symbol is not allowed, and the name is too long.
(e) The name is too long.
(f) A name cannot start with a digit.
(h) Lowercase letters are not allowed in assembly language.
(i) An embedded blank is not permitted.

2.5 Which of the following operations moves information from the first operand to the second? What happens to the original value that was stored in the first operand?

   A   S   ST   L

ST; with ST, the first operand is not changed.

2.6 A student states that a certain register which has not yet been initialized contains nothing. What is wrong with this statement?

Registers contain 32 bits of 0 or 1. Before the register is initialized, the information is usually meaningless, but it is there.

2.7 The machine language instructions assembled from a program with single blanks between the fields would be identical to instructions assembled from a program in the format suggested in the text. In light of this fact, suggest reasons for use of the format suggested in the text.

This format is easier for humans to understand, which aids program construction and modification.

2.8 What is wrong with the format of each of the following statements? State whether there is a syntax error, poor style, or nothing wrong.

	Col. 1 ↓	Col. 10 ↓	Col. 16 ↓	Col. 30 ↓
(a)	L	2,A		
(b)		VAR	DC	F'4'
(c)	X		DC	H'2'
(d)		VAR	DS	F'4'
(e)	X		DS	H'2'

(a) The operands are in the Operation field (and presumably the operation is in the Name field). Syntax error.
(b) The name is in the Operation field, the operation is in the Operand field, and the operands are in the Comment field. Syntax error.
(c) The format is poor, but the assembler will have no trouble with the instruction. Poor style.
(d) In addition to the problems in (b), which are syntax errors, the statement is a DS with a value given, which is at best confusing, but not an error.
(e) The operation is in the Operand field, and a DS statement is given with a value. Poor style.

2.9 What value, if any, will be stored in memory by each of the following statements? How many bytes of memory are reserved in each case?

(a) A DC F'1234'
(b) B DC H'1234'
(c) C DS F'1234'
(d) D DS D'1234'

(a) 1234, 4 bytes
(b) 1234, 2 bytes
(c) No value is stored because this is a DS statement; 4 bytes are reserved
(d) No value is stored; 8 bytes are reserved

2.10 Show how to set up storage for the following values.

(a) 164 expressed as a full word called NUM
(b) −11 expressed as a halfword called HW
(c) a full word called VAR, with no initial value
(d) a halfword called HALF, with no initial value

(a) NUM   DC F'164'
(b) HW   DC H'−11'
(c) VAR   DS F
(d) HALF DS H

2.11 Explain what, if anything, is wrong with each of the following statements.

(a) VAR   DC F'1A'
(b)   A   VAR1,VAR2
(c)   S   F,VAR
(d) VAR   DC F12
(e) VAR   DC F '12'
(f) VAR   DC F 12
(g) VAR1   DC F'VAR2 − 1'
(h)   A   2, VAL
(i) VARI   DC F'1,000,000'
(j) HALFW DC H'1000000'
(k) VAR   DC F'− 10'
(l) *VAR   DS F
(m) VAR   DS F'123'

(a) Hexadecimal values are not used in the F format in the assembly language program.
(b) The first operand must be a register for an add instruction.
(c) A hexadecimal value (or variable name) is not permitted for the value of a register.
(d) The value after the F must be enclosed in single quotes.
(e) No blanks are permitted in the Operand field.
(f) See (d) and (e).
(g) Expressions are not permitted in DC statements with F formats.

(h) See (e).
(i) No commas are permitted in the number.
(j) The number is too big for a halfword value.
(k) See (e).
(l) Nothing is wrong if this line is intended to be a comment, which is the effect of the asterisk in column 1. The * cannot be part of a name.
(m) A value is given in a DS statement, which is legal but confusing since the value will not be stored.

2.12 Write a portion of assembly language code to do each of the following.

(a) ANS = A + B + C
(b) ANS = −A + B − C
(c) ANS = A + 1
(d) ANS = 2 ∗ A   (using addition)
(e) ANS = 0
(f) ANS = ANS + 1
(g) ANS = −A − B

```
(a)  L    2,A        (d)  L    10,A       (g)  L    5,=F'0'
     A    2,B             A    10,A            S    5,A
     A    2,C             ST   10,ANS          S    5,B
     ST   2,ANS                                ST   5,ANS
(b)  L    9,B        (e)  L    7,=F'0'
     S    9,A             ST   7,ANS
     S    9,C
     ST   9,ANS
(c)  L    8,A        (f)  L    6,ANS
     A    8,=F'1'         A    6,=F'1'
     ST   8,ANS           ST   6,ANS
```

2.13 Explain what will be accomplished by each of the following sequences of instructions (or write a high-level language equivalent).

```
(a)  L    2,A        (b)  L    2,A        (c)  L    2,=F'1'
     A    2,B             A    2,=F'1'         A    2,A
     ST   2,TEMP          ST   2,A             ST   2,A
     L    3,C
     S    3,D
     S    3,TEMP
     ST   3,ANS
```

(a) TEMP = A + B   (b) A = A + 1   (c) A = 1 + A
ANS = C − D − TEMP

2.14 How could the following sets of instructions be simplified?

```
(a)  L    2,A        (c)  L    2,X        (e)  L    2,N
     S    2,A             A    2,=F'0'         ST   2,N
(b)  L    6,=F'0'    (d)  L    2,=F'0'
     L    6,A             A    2,A
```

In each case, there are redundant operations.

(a) L   2,=F'0'   (c) L   2,X   (e) L   2,N
(b) L   6,A   (d) L   2,A

2.15 Write two sections of assembly language code for the following sequence of statements. First, write code using one register for the entire sequence of statements. Then, write code using a different register for each equation.

$$ANS1 = A + B$$
$$ANS2 = C + 1$$
$$ANS3 = D - ANS2$$

L	2,A		L	2,A
A	2,B		A	2,B
ST	2,ANS1		ST	2,ANS1
L	2,C		L	3,C
A	2,=F'1'		A	3,=F'1'
ST	2,ANS2		ST	3,ANS2
L	2,D		L	4,D
S	2,ANS2		S	4,ANS2
ST	2,ANS3		ST	4,ANS3

2.16 The following portions of a high-level program produce the same value for ANS.

(a) How many ST instructions (minimum) would an assembly language translation need for each?

(b) How many L instructions (minimum) would an assembly language translation need for each?

(c) Under what circumstances might you prefer the first approach?

(d) Under what circumstances might you prefer the second approach?

(i) ANS1 = A + B
    ANS2 = C + D
    ANS3 = E + F
    ANS = ANS1 + ANS2 + ANS3

(ii) ANS = A + B + C + D + E + F

(a) 4 stores for (i), 1 store for (ii).

(b) 3 loads for (i), 1 load for (ii).

(c) If the intermediate values are needed, ANS1, ANS2, and ANS3 should be stored.

(d) If the intermediate answers are not needed, the second method uses fewer instructions and less storage.

2.17 Assume that, before each instruction below is executed, the contents of memory locations X and Y and registers 2 and 3 are as follows.

	Hexadecimal	Decimal
Register 2	00000000	0
Register 3	00000100	256
X	00000064	100
Y	FFFFFFFF	−1

For each instruction, specify which register or memory location is changed, and give its new value in both hexadecimal and decimal.

CHAP. 2] ASSEMBLY LANGUAGE FORMAT

			Item Changed	Hexadecimal	Decimal
(a)	L	2,X			
(b)	L	3,X			
(c)	A	2,X			
(d)	A	3,X			
(e)	ST	2,X			
(f)	ST	3,X			
(g)	ST	3,Y			
(h)	A	3,Y			
(i)	S	3,Y			
(j)	S	2,Y			

			Item Changed	Hexadecimal	Decimal
(a)	L	2,X	Register 2	00000064	100
(b)	L	3,X	Register 3	00000064	100
(c)	A	2,X	Register 2	00000064	100
(d)	A	3,X	Register 3	00000164	356
(e)	ST	2,X	Location X	00000000	0
(f)	ST	3,X	Location X	00000100	256
(g)	ST	3,Y	Location Y	00000100	256
(h)	A	3,Y	Register 3	000000FF	255
(i)	S	3,Y	Register 3	00000101	257
(j)	S	2,Y	Register 2	00000001	1

2.18 Complete the table showing the contents of the memory location(s) or the register(s) changed after execution of each set of instructions. Give your answers in both decimal and hexadecimal. For each part, the initial values are as follows.

	Hexadecimal	Decimal
Register 2	00000000	0
Register 3	00000100	256
X	00000064	100
Y	FFFFFFFF	−1

			Item Changed	Hexadecimal	Decimal
(a)	L	2,X			
	A	2,Y			
(b)	L	2,=F'0'			
	S	2,X			
(c)	L	2,Y			
	L	2,X			
	S	2,=F'7'			
(d)	L	2,X			
	S	2,=F'64'			
(e)	L	2,Y			
	A	2,X			
	S	2,=F'64'			
(f)	L	2,X			
	ST	2,Y			

			Item Changed	Hexadecimal	Decimal
(g)	L	2,Y			
	L	3,X			
	S	2,=F'7'	_____	_____	_____
			_____	_____	_____
(h)	L	2,Y			
	ST	2,X			
	S	2,=F'7'			
	ST	2,Y	_____	_____	_____
			_____	_____	_____
			_____	_____	_____
(i)	L	2,X			
	ST	2,Y			
	S	2,=F'64'	_____	_____	_____
			_____	_____	_____

			Item Changed	Hexadecimal	Decimal
(a)	L	2,X			
	A	2,Y	Register 2	00000063	99
(b)	L	2,=F'0'			
	S	2,X	Register 2	FFFFFF9C	−100
(c)	L	2,Y			
	L	2,X			
	S	2,=F'7'	Register 2	0000005D	93
(d)	L	2,X			
	S	2,=F'64'	Register 2	00000024	36
(e)	L	2,Y			
	A	2,X			
	S	2,=F'64'	Register 2	00000023	35
(f)	L	2,X			
	ST	2,Y	Register 2	00000064	100
			Location Y	00000064	100
(g)	L	2,Y			
	L	3,X			
	S	2,=F'7'	Register 2	FFFFFFF8	−8
			Register 3	00000064	100
(h)	L	2,Y			
	ST	2,X			
	S	2,=F'7'			
	ST	2,Y	Register 2	FFFFFFF8	−8
			Location X	FFFFFFFF	−1
			Location Y	FFFFFFF8	−8
(i)	L	2,X			
	ST	2,Y			
	S	2,=F'64'	Register 2	00000024	36
			Location Y	00000064	100

2.19 What is wrong with each of the following assembly language segments?

(a) L   2,A   (b) L   2,A   (c) L   2,−A
     blank line   A   2,B
     A   2,B   L   2,C
     ST   2,C   ST   2,E

(a) No blank lines are allowed.

(b) The first two instructions are wasted, since the contents of register 2 are erased by the third instruction.

(c) Wrong format. The value at memory location A can be loaded, but there is no memory location −A.

2.20 A programmer was using V2 for a "second variable" and C2 for the constant 2. The programmer accidentally used the instruction

        ST   7,C2   instead of   ST   7,V2

Would an error message be produced? Describe the effect this error could have on the rest of the program. Could such an error be made if the programmer used a literal (=F'2') for the constants?

    No error message would be produced, but the value in the "constant" memory location will not be what the programmer had intended, yielding a logical error. This means that the value in register 7 would be used when the program expected to use the value 2. Using a literal reduces the chances for this type of error.

2.21 Does the following pair of statements make sense?

        L   2,=F'0'
        ST   2,=F'9'

The assembler does not allow one of these instructions. Which one?

    The assembler will not allow use of a literal with the ST instruction.

2.22 Show how to subtract 19 from a variable in memory (a) by adding a literal and (b) by subtracting a defined variable.

```
(a)   L    2,X          (b)        L    2,X
      A    2,=F'-19'                S    2,NINETEEN
      ST   2,X                      ST   2,X
                                    ...
                         NINETEEN DC   F'19'
```

2.23 A student sought to subtract 19 from a variable X in memory. Criticize the code:

        L   2,X
        S   2,=F'−19'
        ST   2,X

Subtraction of −19 causes an increase of 19 in the value of the number.

Supplementary Problems

2.24 Simplify the following sequences of instructions.

(a)   L   3,=F'13'   (c)   ST   3,N
       A   3,N   A   3,=F'6'
       S   3,=F'20'   L   3,N

(b)   ST   3,N   (d)   L   3,N
       L   3,N   S   3,=F'0'

2.25 Which of the following sets of instructions yield the same results?

(a)   ST   3,N   (b)   ST   3,N   (c)   L   3,=F'0'
       S   3,N   L   3,=F'0'   ST   3,N

2.26 Which of the following names for variables are incorrect?

(a)   BR14   (c)   BR 14   (e) $1
(b)   BALR   (d)   SMALLLOOP   (f)   %1

2.27 What value, if any, is in register 10 after execution of the following sequence of instructions?

           L   10,=F'9'
           A   10,=F'17'
           ST   10,ANSWER

2.28 Write assembly language instructions corresponding to the following high-level language statements. Do each two ways: (1) by simplifying the algebraic expression, and also (2) by using a temporary memory location called TEMP.

(a)   ANS = (A − B) − (C − D)
(b)   ANS = A − (B − C) − D
(c)   ANS = A − (B − (C − D))

2.29 Explain why L   2,X and A   2,X yield the same answer in Problem 2.17.

2.30 Repeat Problem 2.17, assuming that the instructions are a complete sequence of instructions. What final values would there be in registers 2 and 3 and in memory locations X and Y?

2.31 Write high-level language statements for the following sequence of assembly language instructions.

           L   2,A
           A   2,B
           S   2,=F'44'
           ST   2,TEMP
           L   4,TEMP
           ST   4,F

2.32 Show the binary or hexadecimal representation of the contents of register 2 as the program in Fig. 2-1 is executing.

2.33 Write a portion of an assembly language program which will compute and store the value of ANSWER, as indicated below. Copy the first three instructions from the example in Fig. 2-1, except possibly for the name of the program.

$$\text{ANSWER} = X - Y - Z$$

Assume that X has an initial value of −2, Y has a initial value of 23, and Z has an initial value of 17.

2.34 Explain precisely the difference between

$$\text{BR} \quad 14 \quad \text{and} \quad \text{END}$$

2.35 Simplify:

$$\begin{array}{ll} \text{ST} & 5,\text{A} \\ \text{L} & 5,\text{E} \\ \text{A} & 5,\text{A} \end{array}$$

2.36 Compare the size of number which a register can hold to that which can be stored in a full word.

2.37 What is the value (in decimal format) stored in memory by the following DC statements?

(a) FRACT1   DC   F'1.5'   (e) POWER3   DC   F'.5E7'
(b) FRACT2   DC   F'1.4'   (f) POWER4   DC   F'−0.5E7'
(c) POWER1   DC   F'1.0E7'   (g) POWER5   DC   F'0.5E−7'
(d) POWER2   DC   F'1.5E7'

Chapter 3

Arithmetic Operations

3.1 Introduction

In this chapter, the following kinds of instructions are presented:

1. Multiplication and division instructions (there is no exponentiation operation in assembly language)
2. Instructions, called RR instructions, in which both operands are registers
3. Instructions involving halfwords in memory, which require less memory space
4. Instructions which control the sign of the value in a register

All these operations involve fixed binary integer arithmetic with 2's complement notation for negative numbers (see Chap. 1). Also, they all involve general-purpose registers.

3.2 The Multiply (M) Instruction

When two integers with m and n digits, respectively, are multiplied together, the product may contain as many as $m + n$ digits. This statement is true for decimal multiplication, binary multiplication, and hexadecimal multiplication. For example,

	Decimal	Binary	Hexadecimal
Three digits	900	110	B52
Two digits	× 90	× 11	× A7
	000	110	4F3E
	8100	110	7134
Five digits	81000	10010	7627E

If two 32-bit numbers are multiplied, as many as 64 bits may be produced in the product. For this reason, the designers of the IBM 370 system have put the product of a fullword multiplication in a double register. The multiplication operation uses an *even-odd pair* of registers to hold the answer. An even-odd pair of registers is an even-numbered register and the next higher odd-numbered register. The even-odd pair is specified by the number of only the even register. One of the integers to be multiplied is placed in the *odd* register of the pair. The original contents of the even register are immaterial. The number in the odd register is multiplied by a full word in memory, and the answer is placed in the even-odd pair of registers. If the answer is less than about 2 billion, it will be contained in the odd register; the even register will contain only copies of the sign bit. The mnemonic operation code for multiply is M.

EXAMPLE 3.1

To multiply A by B:

```
        L    3,A       One number is placed in the odd register.
        M    2,B       The EVEN register number is used in the M operation.
        ST   3,PROD    Store the answer (assuming it fits in one register).
```

EXAMPLE 3.2

If A has the value 7 and B has the value 2, what happens is shown step by step (in memory and the registers) as these two numbers are multiplied and the product is stored in PROD.

		Register 4	Register 5	PROD
L	5,A	Garbage	00000007	Garbage
M	4,B	00000000	0000000E	Garbage
ST	5,PROD	00000000	0000000E	0000000E

EXAMPLE 3.3

Example 3.2 is redone with A having the value 7 and B the value −3.

		Register 4	Register 5	PROD
L	5,A	Garbage	00000007	Garbage
M	4,B	FFFFFFFF	FFFFFFEB	Garbage
ST	5,PROD	FFFFFFFF	FFFFFFEB	FFFFFFEB

If two very large numbers are multiplied together, the answer cannot be stored from the odd register of the even-odd pair. If the product exceeds 2^{31}, the answer will occupy the first bit of the odd register and perhaps some or all of the even register. Storing the odd register would assume that the first bit holds the sign bit, which is not true. Moreover, part of the number might be in the even register.

3.3 The Divide (D) Instruction

The mnemonic operation code for divide is D. The Divide operation uses an even-odd pair of registers for the dividend and a fullword memory location for the divisor. As in the multiply instruction, the first operand is the number of the *even* register. After execution of the divide operation, the quotient winds up in the odd register, and the remainder is found in the even register. Any nonzero remainder has the same sign as the dividend. Specifically, if we divide A by B, producing the quotient Q and the remainder R, then

$$A = B * Q + R$$

where R has the same sign as A (unless $R = 0$), and R has a smaller absolute value than divisor B does ($|R| < |B|$).

The dividend is loaded into the odd register. But since the computer acts as if the dividend occupies the even-odd register pair, both registers of the pair must be initialized before the divide instruction is executed. If the dividend fits into the odd register, then the even register must be filled with sign bits before execution of the instruction. (One way to get more than 31 significant bits into the even-odd register pair for use as a dividend is as the result of a multiplication operation.)

Thus we load the dividend into the odd register, initialize the even register, and then divide. Afterward, we may print or store the quotient from the odd register and, if needed, the remainder from the even register. But how do we know how to initialize the even register? If the dividend is positive or 0, we want all 0s in the even register (L 2,=F'0'). However, if the dividend is negative, we want all 1s in the even register (L 2,=F'−1'). To do either one of these, we must know the sign of the dividend. But better than testing the sign of the dividend, we can merely multiply the dividend by 1. Multiplying a number by 1 does not change its value, but it spreads the value throughout the even-odd pair of registers, just as is required for the division. That is, it extends the sign bit of the dividend through the 32 bits of the even register.

The instructions for assembly language implementation of

$$X = A/B$$

would be

```
        L       3,A
        M       2,=F'1'         SPREADS SIGN BIT THROUGH EVEN REGISTER
        D       2,B
        ST      3,X             STORE QUOTIENT
        ST      2,REM           STORE REMAINDER, IF NEEDED
```

If A = 17 and B = 5, the registers would change as follows (using hexadecimal notation) during these instructions:

		Register 2	Register 3
Beforehand		Garbage	Garbage
L	3,A	Garbage	00000011
M	2,=F'1'	00000000	00000011
D	2,B	00000002 (remainder)	00000003 (quotient)

EXAMPLE 3.4

Show the register contents (in hexadecimal) before and after each of the preceding instructions, using the values A = −17, B = 5.

		Register 2	Register 3
Beforehand		Garbage	Garbage
L	3,A	Garbage	FFFFFFEF
M	2,=F'1'	FFFFFFFF	FFFFFFEF
D	2,B	FFFFFFFE (remainder)	FFFFFFFD (quotient)

EXAMPLE 3.5

Code the following in assembly language, where A, B, and C are large numbers (>1 million but <2 billion).

$$X = (A * B)/C$$

```
        L       5,A
        M       4,B             A * B IS IN THE EVEN-ODD PAIR
        D       4,C             X IS IN REGISTER 5, REMAINDER IN 4
```

Here we wish to do two operations—multiply and then divide. Before we divide, we need not multiply by 1 in addition to multiplying by B; the multiplication by B will extend the sign bits. If $A * B$ is less than 2^{31}, the M 2,=F'1' is merely a waste of time. However, if the product $A * B$ exceeds 2^{31}, multiplication by 1 will cause an error because multiplication by 1 after multiplication by B will use the value in the odd register only. Here is an example.

EXAMPLE 3.6

Consider what happens to the values in registers 4 and 5 as the following program segment is executed.

```
        L       5,A
        M       4,B             A * B IS IN THE EVEN-ODD PAIR
        M       4,=F'1'
        D       4,C             INCORRECT (WHY?)
        ...
A       DC      F'4000000'
B       DC      F'20000'
C       DC      F'100000'
X       DS      F
```

ARITHMETIC OPERATIONS

		Register 4	Register 5
Beforehand		Garbage	Garbage
L	5,A	Garbage	003D0900
M	4,B	00000012	A05F2000
M	4,=F'1'	FFFFFFFF	A05F2000
D	4,C	Incorrect	Incorrect

The product A * B occupies part of the even register. The second multiplication operation (M 4,=F'1') completely ignores the portion of the A * B product which is in register 4, and it treats the first bit in register 5 as the sign bit. Thus an incorrect answer (but no error message) will be produced.

3.4 RR Instructions

The instructions that have been used so far—L, A, S, ST, M, D—have operands which include a register and a memory location. They are termed *RX instructions*; the R stands for register and the X for indexed memory location. In RX-type instructions, the second operand is a memory location whose value is used (with L, A, S, M, D) or overwritten (with ST). In a second similar set of instructions, both operands are registers, and there is no memory location involved. These are called RR instructions. All RR instructions have the letter R as the last letter in their mnemonic operation code. The second operand is never changed in an RR instruction.

Operation	RX Type	RR Type
Load	L	LR
Add	A	AR
Subtract	S	SR
Multiply	M	MR
Divide	D	DR
Store	ST	....

In each of these RR instructions, the first operand is changed, using the information in the second operand—a register. There is no store register instruction, which by analogy would copy information from one register to another, because the LR instruction does precisely that.

EXAMPLE 3.7

LR	2,3	Copies the value from register 3 into register 2
AR	6,4	Adds the value in register 4 to that in register 6
SR	3,3	Subtracts the value in register 3 from itself, leaving zero in register 3
MR	2,5	Multiplies the value in register 3 by that in register 5, leaving the answer in the 2-3 register pair
DR	6,2	Divides the value in the 6-7 register pair by the value in register 2, leaving the quotient in register 7 and the remainder in register 6

RR instructions are slightly more efficient than the corresponding RX instructions; moreover, they often allow a saving of one or more instructions and/or memory locations.

EXAMPLE 3.8

Explain in words what each of the following instructions does:

(a) AR 4,4   (b) SR 2,2   (c) MR 4,5

(a) The value in register 4 is doubled (added to itself).

(b) Zero is placed in register 2 (whatever was there was subtracted from itself).

(c) The value in register 5 is squared. [The value in register 5 (the odd register of the even-odd pair) is multiplied by the value in register 5.]

EXAMPLE 3.9

How can we code the following in two ways: (a) without any RR instructions? (b) with at least one RR instruction?

$$X = (A + B)/(C + D)$$

	(a) Without		(b) With
L	3,A	L	3,A
A	3,B	A	3,B
L	4,C	L	4,C
A	4,D	A	4,D
ST	4,DENOM	M	2,=F'1'
M	2,=F'1'	DR	2,4
D	2,DENOM	ST	3,X
ST	3,X		

DR is slightly faster than D, and the ST 4,DENOM instruction has been eliminated entirely using the RR instruction (DR). Moreover, the memory location DENOM is not needed.

3.5 LPR, LNR, and LCR Instructions

Three sign control instructions are related to the LR instruction. LPR, LNR, and LCR all move values the way that LR does, but, in addition, they may affect the sign of the number put into the first register in the following ways:

LPR (Load Positive Register) loads the absolute value

LNR (Load Negative Register) loads the negative of the absolute value

LCR (Load Complement Register) changes the sign of the value

If the second register contains x, the results of these operations, placed in the first register, are

LPR	$|x|$
LNR	$-|x|$
LCR	$-x$

EXAMPLE 3.10

For a second operand of -1 or $+1$, what result would be obtained by each instruction?

		Result in Register 2	Using Value in Register 3	First Operand Changed to
LPR	2,3	+1	−1 ⎫	Positive, no matter what the value in the second register
LPR	2,3	+1	+1 ⎭	
LNR	2,3	−1	−1 ⎫	Negative, no matter what the value in the second register
LNR	2,3	−1	+1 ⎭	
LCR	2,3	+1	−1 ⎫	Oppposite sign to that in second register
LCR	2,3	−1	+1 ⎭	

These instructions often use the same register for both operands. For example, to get the absolute value of the number in register 2, we can code

                              LPR   2,2

To change the sign of the value we can code

                              LCR   2,2

Note that it would be pointless to use the same registers for an LR instruction, because LR would merely load the value of the register into itself. But the job of the LPR, LNR, or LCR instruction is to change the sign of the value in the register, if necessary.

EXAMPLE 3.11

Write code to place a value for A − |B| in register 2.
Either of the following solutions will do this:

```
    L    2,A        or better    L    2,B
    L    3,B                     LNR  2,2
    LPR  3,3                     A    2,A
    SR   2,3
```

3.6 Halfword Instructions

The set of halfword instructions is very similar to the full-word set of RX instructions. These are also RX instructions.

Operation	Full Word	Halfword
Load	L	LH
Add	A	AH
Subtract	S	SH
Multiply	M	MH
Divide	D	...
Store	ST	STH

Each halfword instruction uses a 2-byte integer from memory as its second operand. Since the registers are still 32 bits, the machine pads the halfwords with sign bits to 32-bit lengths before the LH, AH, or SH operations are carried out. It does this without changing the number in memory, however. STH causes the rightmost 16 bits of the register to be stored. Here is an example using LH.

```
Before LH:  Memory                                   1111 1111 1010 1010
            Extended to 32 bits    1111 1111 1111 1111 1111 1111 1010 1010
After LH:   Register               1111 1111 1111 1111 1111 1111 1010 1010
```

EXAMPLE 3.12

For a Subtract Halfword operation, the order of adding the sign bits and the subtraction are critical.

```
Before SH:  Register               1111 1111 1111 1111 1111 1111 1111 1110
            Memory                                     1111 1110 1110 1110
            Extended to 32 bits    1111 1111 1111 1111 1111 1110 1110 1110
After SH:   Register               0000 0000 0000 0000 0000 0001 0001 0000
```

EXAMPLE 3.13

What value is stored after the SH operation of Example 3.12 by the operation STH?

$$0000\ 0001\ 0001\ 0000$$

The rightmost 16 bits are stored in the designated memory location.

MH uses only a single register, either odd or even. The contents of the register (32 bits) are multiplied by the halfword (16 bits), and an answer (as much as 48 bits) is obtained. *Only the rightmost 32 bits are retained in the register*!

There is no Divide Halfword (DH) instruction.

Halfwords are defined in memory just like full words, except that H is used in place of F.

HW	DC	H'4'
HWD	DS	H
HALF	DC	H'−3200'

The values of halfword variables can range from -2^{15} to $+(2^{15}-1)$ (2^{15} is a little over 32,000).

Please note that a memory location which is declared with one format, F for example, can be used with values in other formats, H for example. It is up to the programmer to understand how the memory locations are used, no matter how they are declared initially. Later in this book, we will intentionally declare a memory location with one attribute and use it for another. Right now, you must be aware that such a possibility exists but you should avoid doing such a thing. The assembler will not create an error message but will assume that you have done what you intended to do. Moreover, a value actually stored as a result of a DC instruction depends on the format declared.

Solved Problems

3.1 What values will remain in registers 2 and 3 after execution of the following sets of instructions? Simplify each set.

	(a)	L	2,=F'4'	(b)	L	2,=F'−4'
		L	3,=F'3'		L	3,=F'−3'
		M	2,=F'2'		M	2,=F'2'

	Register 2	Register 3
(a)	00000000	00000006
(b)	FFFFFFFF	FFFFFFFA

Loading a value into register 2 in each sequence is a waste of time, since the value originally in the even register is ignored and then overwritten by the multiply operation.

3.2 Explain why register 4 in Example 3.6 is filled with F's by execution of M 4,=F'1'.

The hexadecimal A in register 5 represents binary 1010. Since the first bit is 1 and the computer treats the first bit as a sign bit, it copies that bit through register 4.

3.3 What values in hexadecimal will be placed in registers 2 and 3 by each of the following pairs of instructions?

    (a) L   3,=F'20'
           M   2,=F'5'

    (b) L   3,=F'−20'
           M   2,=F'5'

    (c) L   3,=F'1118481'   EQUAL TO 111111_{16}
           M   2,=F'131072'   EQUAL TO 20000_{16}

	Register 2	Register 3
(a)	00000000	00000064
(b)	FFFFFFFF	FFFFFF9C
(c)	00000022	22220000

3.4 Fill in the register numbers to calculate X = (A + B) * C.

    L   __,A
    A   __,B
    M   __,C
    ST __,X

One possible set is 3, 3, 2, 3.

3.5 Write portions of assembly language programs which will calculate and store the following quantities. Assume that the partial and final results each fit into one register and that integer arithmetic is used.

(a) $x = a + b$
    $y = x + c$

(b) $x = a - b - c$
    $y = x - 23$

(c) $x = a + b$
    $y = 2x + c$

(d) $x = a - 23$
    $y = x^2 + 1$

(e) $x = a - 23$
    $x = x^2 + 1$

(a) L   2,A
      A   2,B
      ST 2,X
      A   2,C
      ST 2,Y

(b) L   2,A
      S   2,B
      S   2,C
      ST 2,X
      S   2,=F'23'
      ST 2,Y

(c) L   7,A
      A   7,B
      ST 7,X
      AR 7,7
      A   7,C
      ST 7,Y

(d) L   3,A
      S   3,=F'23'
      ST 3,X
      MR 2,3
      A   3,=F'1'
      ST 3,Y

(e) L   3,A
      S   3,=F'23'
      MR 2,3
      A   3,=F'1'
      ST 3,X

There is no need to store an intermediate value (x) which will be erased before it is used.

3.6 A factorial, such as n!, is defined as

$$n! = n \times (n-1) \times \cdots \times 2 \times 1$$

Use a hand calculator to determine the largest n value such that $n!$ will fit into a single general-purpose register and be stored correctly.

    12! (12! = 479,001,600, equivalent to hexadecimal 1C8CFC00; 13! = 6,227,020,800, equivalent to hexadecimal 17328CC00, which is too long for one register.)

3.7 State one way a large number (>3 billion) can be placed in an even-odd register pair.

That large a value can be placed in the register pair by multiplication of two smaller numbers in a preceding instruction.

3.8 Write a portion of an assembly language program which will store the quotient of *x/y* in QUOT and the remainder of *x/y* in REM.

```
        L     5,X
        M     4,=F'1'
        D     4,Y
        ST    5,QUOT
        ST    4,REM
```

3.9 Why does L 2,=F'−1' place sign bits into register 2 for later division of a negative number in register 3? (*Hint*: Write the hexadecimal notation for the 32-bit 2's complement of decimal 1.)

The 2's complement of −1 is FFFFFFFF (all bits are 1). This is exactly what is needed if the sign bit in register 3 is 1.

3.10 What is the difference in value between the following?

(*a*)   00000000 00001234   and   00001234

(*b*)   FFFFFFFF FFFF1234   and   FFFF1234

(*a*) No difference.

(*b*) No difference, assuming 2's complement notation.

3.11 Correct each set of code so that it performs the same calculation as the indicated high-level statement.

(*a*) X = (A + B)/C
```
        L     3,A
        A     3,B
        D     3,C
        ST    3,X
```

(*b*) X = (A + B)/C
```
        L     3,A
        A     3,B
        D     2,C
        ST    3,X
```

(*c*) X = (A * B)/C
```
        L     3,A
        M     2,B
        M     2,=F'1'
        D     2,C
        ST    3,X
```

(*d*) X = A + B/C
```
        L     2,A
        L     3,B
        M     2,=F'1'
        D     2,C
        AR    3,2
        ST    3,X
```

(*a*) Add, after the A instruction,

$$M \quad 2,=F'1'$$

Change the register number in the divide instruction to 2.

(*b*) Add, after the A instruction,

$$M \quad 2,=F'1'$$

(c) Delete the M   2,=F'1' instruction.

(d) A in register 2 is erased by the multiply instruction. Use

$$L \quad 7,A$$
$$\ldots$$
$$AR \quad 3,7$$

3.12 In multiplication, what is the number with the most bits called? Does it exist before or after execution of the operation? In division, what is the number with the most bits called? Does it exist before or after execution of the operation?

Product, after; dividend, before.

3.13 Show step by step what values are in each register as the instructions of Example 3.5 are executed with A = 3,145,728 (300000_{16}), B = 1,048,576 (100000_{16}), and C = 2,097,152 (200000_{16}).

		Register 4	Register 5
Beforehand		Garbage	Garbage
L	5,A	Garbage	00300000
M	4,B	00000300	00000000
D	4,C	00000000 (remainder)	00180000 (quotient)

3.14 Repeat Example 3.4, using A = −17 and B = −5.

		Register 2	Register 3
Beforehand		Garbage	Garbage
L	3,A	Garbage	FFFFFFEF
M	2,=F'1'	FFFFFFFF	FFFFFFEF
D	2,B	FFFFFFFE (remainder)	00000003 (quotient)

3.15 Explain why the even register has to be "initialized" for the divide operation but not for the multiply operation.

The multiply operation ignores the contents of the even register; the divided operation uses both registers.

3.16 If the instructions of Example 3.5 are executed with the values of Example 3.6, should we have coded the assembly language program to divide first and then multiply, so that we would not have such large numbers to calculate in hexadecimal?

No. Division first would cause a fractional answer, which would give a truncation error. Try it with the values (in decimal) in Problem 3.13.

3.17 What would happen in Problem 3.13 if C were 2 instead of more than 2 million?

When we divide such a large number by 2, the answer won't fit into a single register, and a division exception (error) will occur.

3.18 Write assembly language instructions for the calculations described by the following sequence of equations. Be sure to follow the precedence rules. Assume that the partial and final results each fit into one register. *Note*: ** means exponentiation.

(a) X = 7 + A + B   (d) VAR = A ** 2 + 4 * C
(b) Y = A/B − C   (e) M = (Y ** 2 * 3) + 10
(c) Z = A + Q − X

(a) L   9,=F'7'   (d) L   3,A
     A   9,A   MR 2,3   A ** 2 IN 3
     A   9,B   L   7,C
     ST 9,X   M   6,=F'4'
                                    AR 3,7
                                    ST 3,VAR

(b) L   5,A   (e) MR 4,5   FROM PART (B)
     M   4,=F'1'   M   4,=F'3'
     D   4,B   A   5,=F'10'
     S   5,C   ST 5,M
     ST 5,Y

(c) L   10,A
     A   10,Q
     SR 10,9   FROM PART (A)
     ST 10,Z

3.19 What is the value of the remainder (r) in terms of the dividend (d), divisor (s), and quotient (q)?

$$r = d - q * s$$

3.20 Write portions of assembly language programs which will calculate and store the following quantities. Integer arithmetic is assumed. Be sure to follow the precedence rules. Assume that the partial and final results each fit into one register.

(a) $x = ab$ (d) $x = a + \dfrac{b}{c+d}$
     $y = (x+1)(x-1)$

(b) $x = \dfrac{a}{b}$ (calculates the quotient)   (e) $x = a + \dfrac{b}{c} + d$
     $y = a - xb$ (calculates the remainder)

(c) $x = \dfrac{(a+b)}{(c+d)}$ (f) $x = \dfrac{ab}{cd}$

(a) L   3,A   (c) L   3,A   (e) L   3,B
     M   2,B   A   3,B   M   2,=F'1'
     ST 3,X   L   4,C   D   2,C
     LR 5,3   A   4,D   A   3,A
     A   3,=F'1'   M   2,=F'1'   A   3,D
     S   5,=F'1'   DR 2,4   ST 3,X
     MR 2,5   ST 3,X
     ST 3,Y

(b) L   3,A   (d) L   3,B   (f) L   3,A
     M   2,=F'1'   L   4,C   M   2,B
     D   2,B   A   4,D   D   2,C
     ST 2,Y   M   2,=F'1'   M   2,=F'1'
     ST 3,X   DR 2,4   D   2,D
                           A   3,A   ST 3,X
                           ST 3,X

CHAP. 3] ARITHMETIC OPERATIONS 49

3.21 Write assembly language instructions corresponding to the following algebraic equations. Assume that the partial and final results each fit into one register.

(a) $y = b^3$ (b) $y = b^4$ (c) $y = (a+b)^3$ (d) $y = (a+b)^4$

(a) L   5,B
    MR 4,5
    M   4,B
    ST 5,Y

(c) L   5,A
    A   5,B   A + B
    LR 6,5   COPY OF A + B
    MR 4,5   (A + B) ** 2
    MR 4,6   (A + B) ** 3
    ST 5,Y

(b) L   5,B
    MR 4,5   SQUARE
    MR 4,5   FOURTH
    ST 5,Y

(d) L   5,A
    A   5,B
    MR 4,5   SQUARE
    MR 4,5   FOURTH
    ST 5,Y

3.22 Write assembly language instructions corresponding to the following algebraic equation. Assume that the partial and final results each fit into one register.

$$y = (a+b) + (a+b)^2 + (a+b)^3$$

L   3,A
A   3,B   (A + B)
LR 5,3
MR 4,3   (A + B) SQUARED IN 5
LR 7,5
MR 6,3   (A + B) CUBED IN 7
AR 7,5
AR 7,3
ST 7,Y

3.23 State at least two ways that you could initialize register 2 to zero for later accumulation of SUM.

(a) L   2,=F'0'
(b) LH   2,=H'0'
(c) MH   2,=H'0'
(d) SR   2,2   (Best choice, since it doesn't require memory)
(e) M   2,=F'0'   (But this also affects register 3)

3.24 What is the effect of each of the following sequences of instructions?

(a) L   2,X
    L   3,Y
    MR 2,3

(b) L   2,X
    L   3,Y
    MR 2,2

Assume that the products are less than 2 billion. (a) The square of Y is placed in register 3. The instruction L 2,X is a wasted instruction. (b) The product X * Y is placed in register 3. (Register 2 contents are destroyed.)

3.25 Write a high-level language statement corresponding to each of the following sequences of assembly language code.

(a) L   2,A
     A   2,B
     L   5,C
     S   5,D
     M   4,=F'1'
     DR   4,2
     ST   5,ANS

(b) L   2,A
     A   2,B
     L   5,C
     S   5,D
     MR   4,2
     ST   5,ANS

(c) L   3,A
     A   3,B
     M   2,=F'1'
     D   2,C
     S   3,D
     ST   3,ANS

(d) L   3,A
     M   2,A
     S   3,A
     S   3,=F'1'
     ST   3,ANS

(e) L   3,A
     M   2,=F'1'
     D   2,B
     ST   2,R

(a) ANS = (C − D)/(A + B)
(b) ANS = (A + B) ∗ (C − D)
(c) ANS = ((A + B)/C) − D
(d) ANS = A ∗ A − A − 1
(e) R = MOD(A,B)   That is, R = remainder of A/B.

3.26 Explain precisely why there is no STR (Store Register) instruction.

By analogy with ST, STR would copy the contents of the first operand into the second—in this case, one register into another. But LR copies one register into another, so STR is unnecessary.

3.27 In a DR operation, can the first operand be odd? Can the second operand be odd?

The first operand must be even (representing an even-odd pair), but the second may be any register.

3.28 Redo Example 2.5 and Problems 2.12(g), 2.13(a), 2.14(a), and 2.15, using the more advanced operations, such as LCR and SR, that you learned in this chapter.

Example 2.5	Problem 2.12(g)	Problem 2.13(a)	Problem 2.14(a)
L 2,M	L 2,A	L 2,A	SR 2,2
A 2,N	A 2,B	A 2,B	
ST 2,W	LCR 2,2	L 3,C	
L 3,P	ST 2,ANS	S 3,D	
A 3,Q		SR 3,2	
SR 3,2		ST 3,ANS	
ST 3,ANS			

Problem 2.15	
Using Two Registers	Using One Register
L 2,A	L 2,A
A 2,B	A 2,B
ST 2,ANS1	ST 2,ANS1
L 2,C	L 2,C
A 2,=F'1'	A 2,=F'1'
ST 2,ANS2	ST 2,ANS2
L 3,D	S 2,D
SR 3,2	LCR 2,2
ST 3,ANS3	ST 2,ANS3

3.29 Write code to switch the values of three numbers—A, B, and C. Move A to C, C to B, B to A (a) using three registers, (b) using two registers.

(a)	L	2,A	(b)	L	2,A	
	L	3,B		L	3,C	
	L	4,C		ST	2,C	OLD VALUE IN 3, SAFE TO OVERWRITE
	ST	2,C		L	2,B	C NOW STORED, SAFE TO OVERWRITE
	ST	3,A		ST	3,B	OLD B IN 2, SAFE TO OVERWRITE
	ST	4,B		ST	2,A	OLD A LOADED PREVIOUSLY

3.30 Write a program segment to compute the following:

$$ANS = 4 * F/Q + 4 * F/S + 4 * F/R$$

Remember, multiplication and division are done before addition and subtraction.

```
L    3,F
M    2,=F'4'
LR   5,3
M    4,=F'1'
D    4,Q
LR   7,3
M    6,=F'1'
D    6,S
AR   5,7
LR   7,3
M    6,=F'1'
D    6,R
AR   5,7
ST   5,ANS
```

3.31 If A has the value 17 and B has the value 200, show what happens step by step (in memory and the registers) as these two numbers are multiplied and the product is stored in PROD.

			Register 4	Register 5	PROD
	L	5,A	Garbage	00000011	Garbage
	M	4,B	00000000	00000D48	Garbage
	ST	5,PROD	00000000	00000D48	00000D48

3.32 Simplify: LR   2,2

    Delete the entire instruction. This operation copies the value from register 2 into register 2, which is essentially no operation.

3.33 Which of the following, if any, are incorrect?

(a) MR   3,3   to square the number in register 3
(b) MR   2,2   to square the number in register 2
(c) MR   2,3   to square the number in register 3
(d) MR   2,7   to get a product in register 3

(a) MR   2,3   First operand must be even.
(b) This operation multiplies the contents of register 3 by those of register 2; it is not a squaring operation (unless the two numbers happen to be the same).
(c) and (d) are correct.

3.34 Simplify:

(a) SR   2,2
     L   2,DATUM

(b) L   2,X   LOAD X INTO REGISTER 2

(c) SR   2,2
     A   2,X

(a) L 2,DATUM (There is no need to zero the register before a load.)
(b) L 2,X   (Omit the comment, which is totally uninformative.)
(c) L 2,X   (Loading X is faster than adding X to zero and has the same effect.)

3.35 Write three equivalent ways of doubling the value in register 3.

(a) M 2,=F'2'   (b) AR 3,3   (c) MH 3,=H'2'

3.36 Write two ways of squaring a number. Store the result in SQUARE.

(a) L   3,X   (b) L   3,X
    M   2,X   MR 2,3
    ST 3,SQUARE   ST 3,SQUARE

3.37 Write two ways to initialize register 2 before doing division on a negative number in register 3.

(a) L 2,=F'−1'   (b) M 2,=F'1'

3.38 (a) Suppose we wish to load a number into a register to become the dividend in a divide instruction. Its sign must be extended into all bit positions of the even-numbered register of the register pair. If the sign is unknown, what is one way to extend it?

(b) Using the method described in (a), divide a variable B by C and store the answer in Q and the remainder in R.

(a) Multiply by 1.   (b) L   3,B
                         M   2,=F'1'
                         D   2,C
                         ST 3,Q
                         ST 2,R

3.39 What is the effect of LCR, LPR, and LNR on a register with a value of zero if the first and second operands are both that same register, e.g., LPR 2,2?

No effect.

3.40 Simplify.

(a) L 2,X   (c) L 3,X   (e) L   4,B
    A 2,X   M 2,Y   L   5,C
    A 2,X   M 2,=F'1'   M   4,D
    A 2,X   D 2,Z
(b) L 3,X   (d) L   2,X   (f) LCR 9,8
    M 2,X   LCR 2,2   AR   9,8
    M 2,X   A   2,X   ST   9,RESULT
    M 2,X

(a) L   2,X   (c) L   3,X   (e) L   5,C
     AR   2,2   M   2,Y   M   4,D   (Loading 4 first is wasted.)
     AR   2,2   D   2,Z
(b) L   3,X   (d) SR   2,2   (f) SR   9,9
     MR   2,3   ST   9,RESULT
     MR   2,3

3.41 Write code to place a value in register 2 corresponding to each of the following.

(a) $|A| - |C - D|$ (b) $|A| - (|C - D|)^2$ (c) $|A - C - D|$

(a) L   2,A   (b) L   2,A   (c) L   2,A
     LPR 2,2 |A| LPR 2,2 |A| S   2,C
     L   3,C   L   5,C   S   2,D
     S   3,D   S   5,D   LPR 2,2
     LPR 3,3 |C − D| MR   4,5   (C − D) ** 2
     SR   2,3 |A| − |C − D| SR   2,5
                                       (No need to change sign;
                                       square must be positive.)

3.42 Write portions of assembly language programs which will calculate and store the following quantities. Integer arithmetic is assumed.

(a) $x = |a - b| - |c - d|$ (c) $x = -|a - b|$
(b) $x = |a + |b||$ (d) $x = -x$

(a) L   2,A   (c) L   2,A
     S   2,B   S   2,B
     LPR 2,2   LNR 2,2
     L   3,C   ST   2,X
     S   3,D
     LNR 3,3
     AR   2,3
     ST   2,X

(b) L   2,B   (d) L   2,X
     LPR 2,2 |B| LCR 2,2
     A   2,A   A + |B| ST   2,X
     LPR 2,2 |A + |B||
     ST   2,X

3.43 Describe the result which gets stored in RESULT after the following sets of instructions are executed.

(a) L   3,A   (d) L   6,MEAN   (g) L   9,A
     LNR 2,3   LR   7,6   M   8,A
     ST   2,RESULT   LCR 6,6   ST   9,RESULT
                              AR   6,7
                              ST   6,RESULT

(b) L   5,B   (e) L   8,POS
     A   5,=F'4'   LNR 9,8
     ST   5,RESULT   AR   9,8
                              ST   9,RESULT

(c) L   4,C   (f) L   4,VAR
     ST   4,RESULT   A   4,D
                              ST   4,RESULT

(a) $-|A|$ is placed in RESULT.
(b) $B + 4$ is placed in RESULT.
(c) C is placed in RESULT.
(d) 0 is placed in RESULT.
(e) $POS - |POS|$ is placed in RESULT (0 if POS is positive; 2 times POS if POS is negative).
(f) $VAR + D$ is placed in RESULT.
(g) A^2 is placed in RESULT.

3.44 Write a portion of an assembly language program to calculate each of the following expressions. Declare each variable as a halfword.

(a) $A = B/C$
(b) $QUOT = (A + B)/(C + D)$
(c) $REM = MOD(B,C)$ (remainder when B is divided by C)

(a)	LH	3,B	(b)	LH	3,A	(c)	LH	3,B
	M	2,=F'1'		AH	3,B		M	2,=F'1'
	LH	4,C		M	2,=F'1'		LH	4,C
	DR	2,4		LH	4,C		DR	2,4
	STH	3,A		AH	4,D		STH	2,REM
				DR	2,4			
				STH	3,QUOT			

3.45 Using the following register and memory location contents (in decimal), state what values (in decimal) will be calculated and the locations at which they will be placed by each of the following instructions. This is not a sequence; each part should deal with the original values.

Register	Contents		Declarations	
2	0	A	DC	F'2000'
3	7	B	DC	F'0'
4	−1	C	DC	F'−15'
5	−10	D	DC	F'20'
6	1000000	E	DC	F'1'
7	2000001	F	DC	F'200'
8	0	G	DC	H'0'
9	2000001	H	DC	H'75'
		I	DC	H'−10'
		J	DC	H'−25'

(a)	D	4,E	(j)	LCR	4,6	(r)	MR	6,7
(b)	D	2,C	(k)	DR	8,6	(s)	MR	6,6
(c)	M	2,D	(l)	AR	7,4	(t)	LH	6,G
(d)	MR	2,3	(m)	SR	7,4	(u)	LNR	6,6
(e)	MR	2,6	(n)	SH	5,J	(v)	SR	2,5
(f)	DR	4,3	(o)	MH	5,J	(w)	SR	7,7
(g)	LH	7,J	(p)	LNR	7,4	(x)	AR	6,6
(h)	STH	5,H	(q)	STH	5,G	(y)	M	6,=F'7'
(i)	LPR	4,4						

	Value	Location	Value	Location
(a)	0	Register 4	−10	Register 5
(b)	7	Register 2	0	Register 3
(c)	0	Register 2	140	Register 3
(d)	0	Register 2	49	Register 3
(e)	0	Register 2	7000000	Register 3
(f)	−3	Register 4	−1	Register 5
(g)	−25	Register 7		
(h)	−10	Location H		
(i)	1	Register 4		
(j)	−1000000	Register 4		
(k)	1	Register 8	2	Register 9
(l)	2000000	Register 7		
(m)	2000002	Register 7		
(n)	15	Register 5		
(o)	250	Register 5		
(p)	−1	Register 7		
(q)	−10	Location G		
(r)	$(2000001)^2$	Registers 6 and 7		
(s)	2000001000000	Registers 6 and 7		
(t)	0	Register 6		
(u)	−1000000	Register 6		
(v)	10	Register 2		
(w)	0	Register 7		
(x)	2000000	Register 6		
(y)	0	Register 6	14000007	Register 7

3.46 Repeat Problem 3.45, with these more involved instructions. Explain in words why each of these instructions is more involved.

(a) DR 4,5 (c) DR 2,2   (e) D 2,B
(b) LCR 2,2 (d) D 4,=F'1' (f) LR 3,3

	Value	Location	Comment
(a)	0	Register 4	Assuming only sign bits in register 4, the remainder is 0
	1	Register 5	The quotient is 1 when a number is divided by itself
(b)	0	Register 2	−0 = 0
(c)	Interruption		The machine cannot divide by 0; therefore, the instruction is not executed, and some diagnostic information is printed
(d)	0	Register 4	Remainder is 0 when a number is divided by 1
	−10	Register 5	Quotient is equal to dividend when the divisor is 1
(e)	Interruption		Cannot divide by 0
(f)	7	Register 3	No change is made by this operation

3.47 Suppose that these are the initial contents in decimal in certain registers and storage locations:

> Register 2: 0
> Register 3: 48 Location U: 16
> Register 4: −1 Location Y: −5
> Register 5: −80 Location HW: 16
> Register 7: 12
> Register 9: −30

What are the results of the following instructions, assuming the above are the contents before each of these instructions. Where are the answers located?

(a) MR 8,9   (e) DR 2,7
(b) MR 6,9   (f) DR 4,7
(c) M 8,U   (g) DR 4,9
(d) MH 7,HW   (h) D 2,Y

(a) 900: register 9; 0: register 8   (e) 4: register 3;   0: register 2
(b) −360: register 7; −1: register 6   (f) −6: register 5; −8: register 4
(c) −480: register 9; −1: register 8   (g) 2: register 5; −20: register 4
(d) 192: register 7   (h) −9: register 3;   3: register 2

3.48 (a) Name at least two possible advantages to halfword instructions. (b) Name at least one possible disadvantage.

(a) They save space in memory, and they do not need register pairs for multiplication.

(b) They do not hold values as large as may be necessary, and they do not permit division.

3.49 How many bytes does the L operation load (a) when its second operand is defined as a fullword location? (b) when its second operand is defined as a halfword location?

(a) 4   (b) 4 (L always loads 4 bytes)

3.50 Tabulate all load, store, and arithmetic operations that you have learned so far, under the headings RR type, RX full word type, and RX halfword type.

RR Type	RX Fullword Type	RX Halfword Type
LR	L	LH
....	ST	STH
AR	A	AH
SR	S	SH
MR	M	MH
DR	D	....
LPR		
LNR		
LCR		

3.51 Is it possible that register 3 will not hold the correct value for the product of X and Y after the following pair of instructions is executed?

$$\text{LH} \quad 3,X$$
$$\text{MH} \quad 3,Y$$

Since X and Y are halfwords, they are limited to 16 bits each. Their product cannot exceed 32 bits, so the register will always hold the correct product.

3.52 How many halfwords would fit into 16 bytes?

    Eight. Each halfword memory location is 2 bytes long.

3.53 Since there is no DH operation, how would you divide one halfword by another?

LH	3,DIVIDEND
LH	4,DIVISOR
M	2,=F'1'
DR	2,4
STH	2,REM
STH	3,QUOT

3.54 Convert the numbers from Example 3.12 to decimal. What answer would you expect to get by subtracting the number in memory from the number in the register? What value did result? What value would have resulted if the sign bit had not been extended before the subtraction?

```
Before SH:  Register   -2     1111 1111 1111 1111 1111 1111 1111 1110
            Memory     -274                       1111 1110 1110 1110
            Extended   -274   1111 1111 1111 1111 1111 1110 1110 1110
After SH:   Register   +272   0000 0000 0000 0000 0000 0001 0001 0000
```

The +272 is expected and obtained. If the sign bit were not extended, we would have gotten

```
After SH:   Register          1111 1111 1111 1111 0000 0001 0001 0000
```

equivalent to −65,264.

3.55 What is wrong with each of the following instructions?

(a) M 3,A   (b) DH 2,HW   (c) DR 3,6   (d) MR 4,PROD

(a) An even register must be specified.
(b) There is no DH instruction.
(c) An even register must be specified as the first operand.
(d) RR instructions take two registers, not a register and a memory location.

3.56 Write a portion of an assembly language program to calculate each of the following expressions. Declare each variable as a halfword. Assume that the result in each case fits into a halfword. *Note*: ** means exponentiation.

(a) E = A + B + 15   (c) G = A ** 2 + B ** 2   (e) A = A + D
(b) F = (A + B) * (A − B)   (d) H = E * F * A * C   (f) B = B − C

```
(a) LH   2,A        (c) LH   2,A        (e) LH   2,A
    AH   2,B            MH   2,A            AH   2,D
    AH   2,=H'15'       LH   3,B            STH  2,A
    STH  2,E            MH   3,B
                        AR   2,3
                        STH  2,G

(b) LH   3,A        (d) LH   2,E        (f) LH   7,B
    LR   5,3            MH   2,F            SH   7,C
    AH   3,B            MH   2,A            STH  7,B
    SH   5,B            MH   2,C
    MR   2,5            STH  2,H
    STH  3,F
```

3.57 Suppose that the initial contents of registers and storage locations are as follows:

            Register 5   0000 002E
            Register 6   4567 89AB
            Register 7   0000 001D
            Location K   FFFF
            Location P   8765
            Location Q   8765 4321
            Location R   FEDC

Assuming that these are the contents before each of the instructions, show the result of each instruction.

(a) AH 6,P   (f) ST 5,Q
(b) LPR 9,5   (g) L 8,Q
(c) STH 6,K   (h) LNR 10,7
(d) S 5,Q   (i) SR 6,5
(e) LH 6,R   (j) LCR 5,6

	Value	Stored in
(a)	4567 1110	Register 6
(b)	0000 002E	Register 9
(c)	89AB	Location K
(d)	789A BD0D	Register 5
(e)	FFFF FEDC	Register 6
(f)	0000 002E	Location Q
(g)	8765 4321	Register 8
(h)	FFFF FFE3	Register 10
(i)	4567 897D	Register 6
(j)	BA98 7655	Register 5

3.58 An instructor wants to multiply the class average, in register 3, by 25, but all the other registers are being used. Show two ways that the instructor can accomplish the multiplication.

(a) MH   3,=H'25'   (b) ST   2,SAVE
                                  M   2,=F'25'
                                  L   2,SAVE

3.59 An instructor wants to multiply the class average, in register 3, by the value in halfword NUMINCLS. Show how the instructor can accomplish the multiplication.

                          MH   3,NUMINCLS

3.60 In a large program, an instructor wants to multiply the class average, in register 3, by the value in full word NUMINCLS, but all the other registers are being used. Show two ways that the instructor can accomplish the multiplication.

(a)   ST   2,SAVE   (b)   STH   3,SAVE
           M   2,NUMINCLS   L   3,NUMINCLS
           L   2,SAVE   MH   3,SAVE
           ST   3,ANSWER   ST   3,ANSWER
           ...   ...
SAVE DS   F   SAVE DS   H

Supplementary Problems

3.61 (a) Write the hexadecimal value for the decimal value 3,000,000,000. (*Hint*: 1 billion in decimal is 3B9ACA00 in hexadecimal; 2 billion is 77359400.)

(b) How many bits does this value occupy, excluding leading zeros?

(c) If this were a product calculated by a multiply instruction, would you get a correct answer by storing only the odd register? Explain.

3.62 In the sequence of instructions below, state the effect of the store and load instructions involving BEGIN and END.

```
        L     3,A
        M     2,B
        ST    2,BEGIN
        ST    3,END
        ...
        L     2,BEGIN
        L     3,END
        D     2,X
        ST    3,ANS
```

Use the following declarations:

```
A       DC    F'200000'
B       DC    F'400000'
BEGIN   DS    F
END     DS    F
X       DC    F'1000'
```

3.63 What happens if an instruction requires division by a variable whose value happens to be zero?

3.64 (a) What is the decimal value of the "garbage" produced by M 2,=F'1' in Example 3.6?

(b) What is the sign of that value?

(c) What are the "quotient" and the "remainder," in hexadecimal, produced by the divide instruction?

3.65 Explain precisely what happens if a halfword instruction is used with a full-word memory location.

3.66 What is the effect of dividing by a halfword in this example?

```
        D     2,HW
        ...
HW      DC    H'2'
HW2     DC    H'3'
```

3.67 Write assembly language code to swap the values in two variables A and B.

3.68 Judy wants to go on a diet. She counts her calories daily so she can figure out how many pounds she can lose in a week. To lose a pound you must eat 3500 fewer calories. If in 1 week she eats 31,500 calories, how many calories does she consume a day (on the average)? How many calories may she consume a day in order to lose 3 pounds in 1 week? What is the number of calories by which she should cut down each day? Write a program that does these calculations.

3.69 (a) Shelley's Discount Store had the following items in stock at the beginning of the month:

    1000 pairs of gloves
    500 hats
    350 pairs of socks
    350 pairs of sunglasses
    100 leg warmers

Write a program to figure out how many of each item were sold by the end of the month if the following were left:

    350 pairs of gloves
    90 hats
    53 pairs of socks
    62 pairs of sunglasses
    67 leg warmers

(b) Write a program to calculate Shelley's gross sales if the prices of the items are as follows:

    Pair of gloves $15
    Hat $20
    Pair of socks $2
    Pair of sunglasses $12
    Pair of leg warmers $4

3.70 A room measures 240 by 150 feet. Write a program which calculates how much it costs to put a carpet in this room if 1 square yard of carpet costs $13.

3.71 Four students coded the following high-level statement as shown, where x, a, b, and c are integer variables. Which give(s) correct results?

$$x = a/(b * c)$$

(a)		(b)		(c)		(d)	
L	3,A	L	3,A	L	3,B	L	3,B
M	2,=F'1'	M	2,=F'1'	M	2,C	M	2,C
D	2,B	D	2,C	L	5,A	D	2,A
M	2,=F'1'	M	2,=F'1'	M	4,=F'1'	L	5,=F'1'
D	2,C	D	2,B	DR	4,3	M	4,=F'1'
ST	3,X	ST	3,X	ST	5,X	DR	4,3
						ST	5,X

3.72 What will be stored in memory by the following DC statements?

    A   DC   F'1.4'
    B   DC   F'1.5'

3.73 Write assembly language instructions corresponding to the following algebraic equations.

(a) $y = |(a-b)^2|$ (b) $y = -|(a-b)^2|$

3.74 Suppose that x and y have m and n digits, respectively, in base B. (In each case, the first digit is nonzero.) Prove that xy has either $(m+n)$ or $(m+n-1)$ digits in base B.

3.75 Suppose that we divide A and B and get a quotient Q and a remainder R. For the following (decimal) values of A and B, give the corresponding values of Q and R (in decimal).

(a) A = 17, B = 5   (d) A = −153, B = 10   (g) A = 28, B = −5
(b) A = 198, B = 30   (e) A = −21, B = 8   (h) A = −172, B = −20
(c) A = 8, B = 10   (f) A = 51, B = −7   (i) A = −59, B = −17

Chapter 4

Addressing

4.1 Introduction

Instructions, constants, and variables used in an assembly language program are stored in memory at specific locations which do not change during execution of the program. To specify places in memory, each byte is given an *address*. Addresses on the IBM 370 system are 24 bits long, so the machine can address a maximum of 2^{24} bytes, which is more than 16 million bytes. (Most IBM 370 installations have less memory than this.) If a machine has N bytes of memory, these bytes will have addresses 0 through $N-1$. An instruction, or an operand which requires more than 1 byte of storage, say a full word or a halfword, must be located in consecutive bytes of memory, and its address is taken to be the address of the first byte. Thus the full word whose address is 1AB370 is stored in bytes 1AB370, 1AB371, 1AB372, and 1AB373.

For example, suppose the contents of part of memory is shown in Fig. 4-1. The contents of the full word whose address is 1AB370 is 5C7269B4, that of the halfword whose address is 1AB374 is CA28, and that of the byte whose address is 1AB377 is C1. The contents of the halfword at 1AB370 is 5C72.

Address	Contents (*hexadecimal*)
1AB370	5C
1AB371	72
1AB372	69
1AB373	B4
1AB374	CA
1AB375	28
1AB376	47
1AB377	C1
1AB378	00

Fig. 4-1 A portion of memory.

When the machine language program is executed, it places the address of a point near the beginning of the program into a register which is called the *base register* for the program. This address is called the *base address*, and it is specified by the USING statement (see Sec. 4.4). Every address used in the program is specified by its *displacement*, which is the number of bytes from the base address. The instructions and data are stored sequentially in memory in the order that they were written in the source program. An instruction requires 2, 4, or 6 bytes of storage, depending on what type of instruction it is. As the program is assembled, the assembler keeps track of how many bytes have been used, so it can determine the displacement of each instruction or location in the program. Similarly, when the assembler encounters a variable, it determines its displacement from the base address. Thus, one important part of the job of the assembler is to determine the displacement of every name appearing in the Name field.

4.2 Machine Language Format for RR and RX Instructions

Machine language is expressed in the hexadecimal equivalent of the binary numbers used by the computer. Although the format of the instruction depends on what type of instruction it is, for all instructions considered in this book the first byte is the *operation code* (*op code*). The assembler replaces the mnemonic operation code used in the source program by the 8-bit machine language operation code shown in Appendix 1.

RR-Type Instructions

The simplest instructions are the RR instructions, in which both operands are registers. These instructions require only 2 bytes, one to specify the operation code and the other to specify the two registers, designated R1 and R2. Thus

$$\text{BALR} \quad 12,0 \quad \text{is translated to} \quad 05C0$$

where the op code is 05 (see Appendix 1), R1 is C (the hexadecimal represention for decimal 12), and R2 is 0. We customarily show the form of the RR instructions schematically as

op	R1 R2

EXAMPLE 4.1

The machine language instruction corresponding to the assembly language instruction AR 2,11 is

$$\begin{array}{ccc} \underline{1A} & 2 & B \\ \downarrow & \downarrow & \downarrow \\ \text{op} & \text{R1} & \text{R2} \end{array}$$

The op code for AR is 1A. This is followed by the hexadecimal digits for registers 2 and 11 (which in one case happens to be the same as the decimal digit).

RX-Type Instructions

For a typical RX instruction (such as A 2,X) there are two operands, one in a register and the other in memory. The object code for this instruction must specify which register to use (register 2) and where to find the second operand (X) in memory. The register is denoted R1 and is specified just as in RR instructions. The memory location is identified by specifying an index register (X2), a base register (B2), and a displacement (D2). The 2 in each means second operand. RX instructions have the following format:

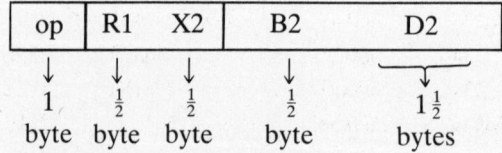

Thus if the variable A were 294 bytes (126 hexadecimal) from the base address in register 12, the instruction L 2,A would have this machine language code:

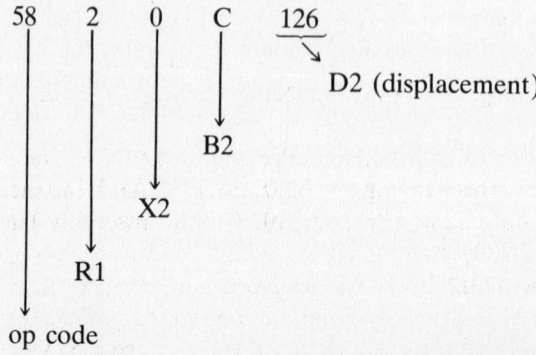

The meaning of base register, index register, and displacement will be introduced in the following sections.

Appendix 1 gives the instructions, together with their operation codes and instruction formats. This information can be used to determine the number of bytes a given instruction occupies.

EXAMPLE 4.2

The Add (A) instruction occupies 4 bytes. A is an RX instruction, which specifies the op code (1 byte), a register (half byte), and a memory location ($2\frac{1}{2}$ bytes).

EXAMPLE 4.3

The MH instruction also occupies 4 bytes of memory. Since MH is an RX instruction, it must specify the op code (1 byte), a register (half byte), and a memory location ($2\frac{1}{2}$ bytes). We say that MH is a halfword instruction because it operates on a halfword in memory. However, the amount of storage required for the instruction itself is 4 bytes because it is an RX instruction.

4.3 Effective Addresses

As noted previously, the address of a memory location is the address of its first byte. That is, if a full word named A is stored in the 4 bytes starting at 1AB164, its address is 1AB164. The operation

L   2,A

is a fullword operation, and it loads the 4 bytes starting at the address of A, which is 1AB164. In contrast, LH is a halfword operation, which loads only 2 bytes. The instruction

LH   2,A

would load the 2 bytes starting at 1AB164.

For RX operations, the type of operation determines the number of bytes to be acted on. The name of the variable determines the address of the first byte.

The program shown in Fig. 4-2 performs the equivalent of the high-level language instruction C = A + B. We assume that the program begins in memory at the address 1AB340.

Address	Location		Source Statement	
1AB340	000000	PGM	START	0
1AB340	000000		BALR	12,0
1AB342	000002		USING	*,12
1AB342	000002		L	2,A
1AB346	000006		A	2,B
1AB34A	00000A		ST	2,C
1AB34E	00000E		BR	14
1AB350	000010	A	DC	F'9'
1AB354	000014	B	DC	F'−3'
1AB358	000018	C	DS	F
			END	

Fig. 4-2 Sample assembly language program.

Let's examine the program to understand addressing more fully. The assembler assigns a location of 0 to the first instruction, corresponding to the 0 in the START instruction. The operating system assigns an address to that statement, say 1AB340. Certain assembly language statements, such as START and USING, serve only to direct the assembler and do not get translated into machine language. Since START and USING do not get stored in memory, they occupy 0 bytes each. As a result, BALR starts at 1AB340. It is an RR instruction, which takes 2 bytes (1AB340 and 1AB341). The next instruction, USING, therefore starts at 1AB342. Since USING takes 0 bytes, the L (load) instruction also starts at 1AB342. Load and add are RX instructions, requiring 4 bytes each. The A (add) instruction thus starts at 1AB346. Similarly, the ST (store) instruction starts at 1AB34A. (See Fig. 4-3.) The rest of the instructions have addresses which are calculated similarly, until the DC and DS statements are reached.

		Address	Location
BALR	05	1AB340	000000
	C0	1AB341	000001
LOAD	58	1AB342	000002
	20	1AB343	000003
	C0	1AB344	000004
	0E	1AB345	000005
ADD	5A	1AB346	000006
	20	1AB347	000007
	C0	1AB348	000008
	12	1AB349	000009
STORE	50	1AB34A	00000A
	20	1AB34B	00000B
	C0	1AB34C	00000C
	16	1AB34D	00000D
	⋮	1AB34E	00000E

Fig. 4-3

Before execution, the entire program will appear in memory as shown in Fig. 4-4, starting at address 1AB340 (each box is a byte). We have added the mnemonic labels to identify the statements. During execution, the last 4 bytes will be changed to 00 00 00 06 by the store (ST) instruction.

BALR		LOAD				ADD				STORE			
05	C0	58	20	C0	0E	5A	20	C0	12	50	20	C0	16
07	FE	00	00	00	09	FF	FF	FF	FD	\multicolumn{4}{c}{4 bytes of garbage}

BR   A   B   C

Fig. 4-4

In the preceding example, since the operand of START is zero, the "Location" column begins with location 0. The actual addresses will depend on where the operating system places the program, so the column headed "Address" is merely an example which assumes that the program is loaded into memory beginning at address 1AB340.

When the machine executes the program, it must be able to find the operands in memory. It does this by computing the address of the operand and then going to that spot in memory to find the value of the operand. The machine language instruction specifies the address of the operand by selecting a base address near the beginning of the program and adding a displacement to this address. For example, if the base address is 1AB342, the operand whose actual address is 1AB368 has a displacement of 26 (hexadecimal). In general, the displacement is obtained by subtracting the base address from the actual address. The actual address used by the instruction is called the *effective address*.

An RX instruction specifies for every memory location a displacement and two registers, the base register and the index register. The displacement is an unsigned 12-bit integer (three hexadecimal digits), so it can be any integer from 0 to 4095 (FFF_{16}). The effective address of the memory location is defined to be the contents of the base register plus the contents of the index register plus the displacement. If this procedure produces a result which requires more than 24 bits (six hexadecimal digits), only the rightmost 24 bits are retained. Another wrinkle is that if 0 is used for either the base register or the index register, the number 0 is used instead of the contents of register 0. (Consequently, register 0 can never be used as either a base register or an index register.) Since we will not have any reason to use an index register until Chap. 6, we shall use 0 for the index register here.

The addresses of DS and DC statements are vitally important, because they are the addresses of the corresponding variables. When an assembly language instruction refers to a variable name, the corresponding machine language instruction must be able to calculate the address of that variable. The displacement of the address from the base address is stored in the machine language instruction. RX instructions use the base address and the displacement, as well as the contents of the index register, to calculate the effective address of the variable in memory. Other instructions (see Chap. 6 and following) use the base register and displacement, but do not use an index register. Displacements of labeled instructions are calculated in the same way that all other displacements are calculated.

The displacement of A in the sample program in Fig. 4-2 is the difference between its address and the contents of the base register (established by the BALR and USING instructions):

```
    Address of A            1AB350
  − address in reg 12      − 1AB342      (placed there by BALR)
    displacement              00E
```

This calculation is done during assembly.

The effective address of variable A in the program in Fig. 4-2 is calculated during execution as the sum of the displacement, the contents of the base register, and the contents of the index register. For example,

```
    Base register contents     1AB342
  + index register contents         0
  + displacement             +    00E
    effective address          1AB350
```

Note that if the base register number and/or the index register number is zero, then 0 is added, not the contents of register zero.

Only three hexadecimal digits can fit into the displacement (D2) part of the RX instruction, so the maximum displacement is FFF, corresponding to 4095 (decimal) bytes. This means that our programs cannot be too long unless we take some appropriate steps (see Sec. 4.11).

EXAMPLE 4.4

Calculate the effective address of a variable with displacement 0FE (hexadecimal) from the base register contents 001AB142 and index register value of 0. (Register 0 holds 000000AC.)

The address is calculated as follows:

Base register contents	1AB142
index register value	0
displacement	0FE
effective address	1AB240

Remember, the specification of the index register as 0 means that we use 0, not the contents of register 0.

EXAMPLE 4.5

How is the effective address of the variable in the following machine language instruction calculated?

$$5C20C046$$

The register contents to calculate the answer are as follows:

Register	Contents
0	000000AC
2	00000020
12	001AB042

The op code (5C) identifies the instruction (M, multiply) as an RX instruction, so the instruction has the following meaning:

```
5C   2   0   C   046
 ↓   ↓       ↓   ↓
op   X2          D2
     ↓       ↓
     R1      B2
```

The base register is 12 (C); its contents are	1AB042
The index register is not used; the value used is	0
The displacement in hexadecimal is	046
The effective address is	1AB088

The contents of registers 0 and 2 are not used in calculating the address.

4.4 The Effects of BALR and USING

In Sec. 4.3, we discussed how to calculate effective addresses using the base address. How does the assembler know which register to use as the base register and what value to put into it? There are two aspects to be considered. First, we must tell the assembler which register to use and what address it will contain, and second, we must arrange to put the proper address into the register. The USING *,12 statement handles the first problem. USING is a pseudo-instruction, which is an instruction that gives information to the assembler but is not translated into machine code. The asterisk (*) in the Operand field means "the current address," that is, the address that appears in the Address field of the instruction in which the asterisk is used. This is the address at which the instruction is stored. (Since USING is not stored in memory, the current address is also the address of the next instruction following USING, for example, 1AB342 in Fig. 4-2.) The USING *,12 instruction tells the assembler that, at execution time, register 12 will contain the current address. Thus the assembler will use register 12 as the base register and compute displacements from the address current at the USING statement. The USING *,12 statement is a promise to the assembler that, at execution time, register 12 will contain the current address, in this case 1AB342. Execution of BALR 12,0 during program execution is the fulfillment of that promise, and thus solves the second problem. The instruction BALR 12,0, during execution, loads into register 12 the address of the executable instruction which follows it. Thus, for the example in Fig. 4-2, the BALR 12,0 instruction places the address 1AB342 into register 12.

In summary, the BALR instruction puts an address into the base register, and the USING instruction tells the assembler to use that register as the base register and that address as the base address. This pair of instructions is used to establish addressability.

4.5 Boundary Requirements

Variables are stored in memory in the order in which they are defined. Assume that a program has the following definitions:

```
A    DS    F
B    DS    F
C    DS    F
```

A will be stored at a certain location. B will be stored starting 4 bytes later, and C will be stored 4 bytes after that. Occasionally, some bytes of memory are left unused. The IBM 370 system works most efficiently when the first byte of every full word in memory has an address which is divisible by 4. This is called a *fullword boundary*. Thus a fullword boundary has an address whose last hexadecimal digit must be 0, 4, 8, or C.

EXAMPLE 4.6

(*a*) We can determine whether a decimal number is divisible by 5 by merely seeing whether the last digit is 0 or 5. That is, we merely check whether the last digit is divisible by 5. This works because 5 is a divisor of 10 and the number is written in decimal. We cannot use this approach in the decimal system to determine whether a number is divisible by some other number, such as 3.

(*b*) Since 4 is a divisor of 16, we can check whether a hexadecimal number is divisible by 4 by seeing whether the last digit is divisible by 4. That is, we merely check whether the last digit is one of the digits 0, 4, 8, or C. (See Problem 1.20.)

The assembler automatically starts a full word at an address which is divisible by 4, even if it means that 1 to 3 bytes of memory are unused.

EXAMPLE 4.7

```
1A8340          BR    14
1A8344    A     DS    F
```

The BR instruction occupies 2 bytes—1A8340 and 1A8341. The storage location A does not start at 1A8342, however, since that is not a fullword boundary. The assembler "wastes" 2 bytes, and starts A at 1A8344.

Similarly, halfwords and double words should be stored at addresses divisible by 2 and 8, respectively. These are called *halfword* and *double-word boundaries*.

	Length	Permitted Last Digit of Address
Full word	4 bytes	0, 4, 8, C
Halfword	2 bytes	0, 2, 4, 6, 8, A, C, E
Double word	8 bytes	0, 8

Fullword operations operate on 4 bytes in memory, preferably on memory locations starting on fullword boundaries. For example, once the program has been assembled, the L (load) instruction will operate on 4 bytes starting at the given address regardless of the declaration(s) for those bytes. (It would even load part or all of an instruction.)

EXAMPLE 4.8

```
            L      2,FW       Loads FW
            L      2,HW1      Loads both HW1 and HW2 (4 bytes)
*                             Result will be 000D0002 (decimal 851,970)
            . . .
FW          DC     F'7'       Must be on fullword boundary
HW1         DC     H'13'      Is on fullword boundary (4 bytes past FW)
HW2         DC     H'2'       Is on halfword boundary
```

The LH instruction will work with either halfword, naturally.

```
            LH     2,HW1
            LH     2,HW2
```

A halfword instruction will use only the first 2 bytes of a full word:

```
            LH     2,FW       Loads zero (the first 16 bits of FW)
            . . .
FW          DC     F'100'     00000064 (base 16)
```

Instructions have the same boundary requirements as halfwords, regardless of whether they are 2, 4, or 6 bytes long and regardless of the length of the data they control. Thus, they must start at even addresses. For example, the instruction L   2,A may start at any even address, despite the fact that it is 4 bytes long and its data is a full word which should start at an address evenly divisible by 4.

4.6 Explicit Notation

So far, we have always used variable names in our assembly language programs to refer to locations in memory. It is sometimes necessary to refer to the memory location explicitly, using the format D2(X2,B2) for RX instructions. Here the D2 stands for the displacement of operand 2, X2 stands for the index register for operand 2, and B2 refers to the base register for operand 2. If there is no index or base register, a zero is used in its place. For example, if VAR has displacement of 100 bytes (decimal) from the address in register 12 (the base register) with no index register being used, then the following two instructions will have the same effect:

```
            L      3,VAR
            L      3,100(0,12)
```

Either instruction assembles to the same machine language instruction, which contains an effective address for the second operand. This address is computed as follows:

Contents of register 12	base address
contents of index register (none)	0
displacement (in decimal)	100
effective address	base address + 100

The displacement is given in decimal form in assembly language programs (and is converted to hexadecimal, i.e., binary, by the assembler).

Displacements can be between 0 and 4095 (FFF), and no negative displacements are allowed.

In order to use explicit notation, the programmer must calculate the displacement. Any later change in the program might necessitate recalculation. Obviously, it is both easier and less error-prone to use the symbolic format, using the name of the variable. However, there are certain situations (see Chaps. 5, 7, 8, and 10) where explicit notation is needed. These situations will be discussed in detail in later chapters. Here we can simply say, in summary, that explicit notation is essential to know, but the student may not find situations in which it is useful until later.

CHAP. 4] ADDRESSING 69

EXAMPLE 4.9

The following portion of an assembly language program is rewritten using explicit notation only:

```
1AB340              BALR    12,0
1AB342              USING   *,12
       ...
1AB350              L       2,A
1AB354              A       2,B
1AB358              S       2,C
       ...
1AB480     THERE    LH      7,H
1AB484              S       7,A
       ...
1AB500     A        DC      F'6'
1AB504     B        DC      F'9'
1AB508     C        DC      F'-88'
1AB50C     H        DC      H'55'
```

The explicit program is as follows:

```
1AB340              BALR    12,0
1AB342              USING   *,12          THIS INSTRUCTION IS NOT NECESSARY IN
         *                                THIS FORM OF THE PROGRAM
              ...
1AB350              L       2,446(0,12)
1AB354              A       2,450(0,12)
1AB358              S       2,454(0,12)
              ...
1AB480     THERE    LH      7,458(0,12)
1AB484              S       7,446(0,12)   NOTE THE SAME DISPLACEMENT
         *                                IN THIS INSTRUCTION AS IN
         *                                THE L INSTRUCTION ABOVE
              ...
1AB500     A        DC      F'6'
1AB504     B        DC      F'9'
1AB508     C        DC      F'-88'
1AB50C     H        DC      H'55'
```

Note: The labels in the first program column are not used in this form of the program and may be omitted.

There are shorthand methods of writing explicit notation when either the base register or the index register is not to be used. We can use any of the following formats instead of supplying a zero for the index register and/or the base register:

$D2(X2)$ is the same as $D2(X2,0)$
$D2(,B2)$ is the same as $D2(0,B2)$ (note the required comma)
$D2$ is the same as $D2(0,0)$

4.7 Further Extension of Addressing

It is possible to address a memory location using certain simple expressions instead of a variable name.

EXAMPLE 4.10

It is possible to address a memory location 4 bytes past location VAR by use of the following notation:

```
        L     2,VAR+4
        ...
VAR     DC    F'4'
VAR2    DC    F'9'
```

Execution of this load instruction loads the value of VAR2 into register 2.

EXAMPLE 4.11

The address 4 bytes before VAR is accessed by the following instruction:

```
        L     2,VAR-4
        ...
A       DC    F'6'
VAR     DC    F'11'
```

Execution of this instruction loads the contents of A into register 2. Since VAR has a certain displacement, VAR−4 has a displacement 4 bytes smaller. As long as the constant (4) is not greater than the displacement of VAR, this type of reference is legal.

EXAMPLE 4.12

The following instruction is illegal:

$$L \quad 4,VAR-4096$$

The displacement of VAR has a maximum value of 4095 (FFF). Thus the displacement of VAR−4096 must be negative, which is not permitted. [VAR is at most 4095 bytes beyond the base address. Thus, although the address calculated here is not negative, the displacement is negative. The address is smaller than the base address of the program (unless multiple base registers are used). See Sec. 4.11.]

Each of the names we have been using is said to be *relocatable*, because the address each refers to is the sum of the base address and the displacement. Constants, which do not depend on the base address, are said to be *absolute*. A constant may be added to a relocatable symbol, as in A+4, but another relocatable value cannot be added. Thus the following instruction is not legal:

$$L \quad 4,A+B \quad \text{(not legal)}$$

Two relocatable values may be subtracted from each other, and an absolute answer (not a relocatable answer) is obtained. Such an expression can be used in an assembly program.

EXAMPLE 4.13

```
        LR    3,B-A
        ...
A       DC    F'7'
B       DC    F'28'
```

The Load Register (LR) operation has the same effect as LR 3,4 since B−A is 4 regardless of the base address. (Such an instruction might be used to make a program more flexible. If the number of bytes between B and A might be used in a number of places in a program, and that number might change each time the program is run, this type of notation saves the trouble of changing the constant everywhere it is used each time.)

4.8 Putting an Address into a Memory Location

We can put the address of a variable into a memory location with a DC instruction, similar to the way we initialize a fullword constant. Instead of F, we use A to identify the constant type. Parentheses instead of single quotation marks are used with the A specification. Thus the first of the following definitions places the address of the variable VAR in the memory location corresponding to ADDVAR:

```
ADDVAR   DC    A(VAR)
VAR      DC    F'8'
```

The specification A reserves 4 bytes of memory on a fullword boundary, just as F does. Since the address uses only 3 bytes (24 bits), the first byte is filled with zeros.

EXAMPLE 4.14

The address of the variable VAR will be in register 2 after execution of the following instruction:

```
         L     2,ADDVAR
         ...
VAR      DC    F'8'
ADDVAR   DC    A(VAR)
```

The instruction loads the contents of the memory location ADDVAR, which happens to be the address of the variable VAR. Thus the address of VAR is in register 2. (Register 2 could now be used as a base register in some explicit instruction, if desired.) For example,

```
         L     5,0(0,2)
```

would load the full word at the memory location whose address is in register 2, and therefore has the same effect as

```
         L     5,VAR
```

We can also set up an address literal and load its value into register 2, with the same result as in Example 4.14.

```
         L     2,=A(VAR)
```

These examples show two ways to get the address of a variable (rather than its value) into a register. Another method is shown in the following section.

4.9 Load Address

The Load Address (LA) instruction computes an effective address in the usual way and loads that address into the rightmost 24 bits of a register, with 8 leading bits of zero. Thus the following instruction

```
         LA    2,VAR
```

loads the address of VAR into register 2. The contents of VAR are irrelevant; it is the address of VAR which is loaded into the register. The LA instruction may be used to put an address into a register for future use as a base register or an index register. (Note that until addressability has been established, LA cannot be used with the name of a variable. This is why BALR must be used to establish addressability.)

Explicit addressing can be used with the LA instruction. Thus

```
         LA    2,20(3,12)
```

calculates an address by adding the value in register 12 plus the value in register 3 plus 20. It then loads that address into register 2. Note that LA loads into register 2 the calculated address, not the contents of the memory location at that address. As usual, if zero is used in place of the index register and/or the base register, the value zero is used, not the contents of register 0.

EXAMPLE 4.15

The difference between the LA instruction and other operations is shown in the accompanying table.

Operation	Action	
	First	Then
LA 2,X	Finds effective address	Loads that address
L 2,X	Finds effective address	Loads contents at that address
A 2,X	Finds effective address	Adds contents at that address
LA 2,4(3,7)	Finds effective address	Loads that address
L 2,4(3,7)	Finds effective address	Loads contents at that address
A 2,4(3,7)	Finds effective address	Adds contents at that address

The LA instruction can also be used for special purposes, such as initializing a register. For example, the following instruction loads the value 4 into register 2:

$$LA \quad 2,4(0,0)$$

The effective address is found by

$$\begin{aligned} \text{Base register} &\quad 0 \\ \text{Index register} &\quad 0 \\ \text{Displacement} &\quad \underline{4} \\ \text{Total} = \text{effective address} &= 4 \end{aligned}$$

This allows us to place any permitted displacement value (that is, any value from 0 through 4095) into a register without use of a literal. As shown earlier, we can use the short form of the explicit notation:

$$LA \quad 2,4$$

This is the same as

$$LA \quad 2,4(0,0)$$

EXAMPLE 4.16

Consider the following possible instructions, intended to initialize a register:

```
LA    2,5280
LA    2,-2(0,0)
LA    2,5000(0,0)
LA    2,400(0,0)
LA    2,400
```

Only the last two instructions are permitted. Displacements cannot be negative, nor can they exceed 4095 (FFF); therefore, the first three instructions are illegal. The fourth instruction loads 400 into register 2. The fifth instruction does exactly the same thing as the fourth instruction; the default values for the index and base registers are zero.

EXAMPLE 4.17

Often, load address can also be used to increment the contents of a register:

$$LA \quad 2,4(0,2)$$

The address is calculated by adding the contents of register 2 plus a displacement of 4. The LA instruction causes the address calculated to be loaded into register 2. The net effect of the instruction is that the contents of register 2 have been incremented by 4. Note that the value 4(0,2) is evaluated before the contents of register 2 are amended. There are two restrictions on this use of the LA instruction to increment a register:

1. The displacement must be between 0 and 4095.
2. The result must fit into 24 bits in the register; LA changes the first 8 bits to zeros. Thus the original contents of the register plus the increment should be positive or zero. If it were negative, the leading sign bits would be lost.

Explicit addressing allows access to memory locations which do not have names, as well as to those which do. For example,

$$L \quad 2,202(0,12)$$

will load the contents of the word whose address is 202 bytes more than the address in register 12, whether or not the word has a name in the Name field. Thus either of the following constant declarations, provided that it is 202 bytes past the address in register 12, could be accessed by this load instruction:

$$VAR \quad DC \quad F'4' \quad \text{or} \quad DC \quad F'4'$$

The use of an expression as the second operand in an instruction also allows access to memory locations which might not happen to be named. For example,

$$L \quad 2,A+4$$

accesses the full word 4 bytes after A, whether that memory location has a name in the first field or not:

```
A       DC      F'4'
        DC      F'8'

A       DC      F'4'
B       DC      F'8'
```

The instruction loads the value 8 into register 2, no matter which pair of definitions is used. The name B is irrelevant in this case.

We can also use LA to load the address of a literal into a register.

EXAMPLE 4.18

The address of the literal =F'2' is loaded into register 2 by execution of the following instruction:

$$LA \quad 2,=F'2'$$

This instruction causes the assembler to create a memory location and initialize its value to 2. The literal has an address greater than that of the last DS or DC statement written by the programmer, because the literal is added by the assembler after the END statement. But the literal is a memory location, and it is the address of that memory location which is loaded by the LA instruction.

4.10 Debugging Programs

Knowledge of addressing is useful in program debugging. When the program is being executed, there are various errors that can arise that will cause execution of the program to be interrupted and an error message printed. (Examples are division by zero, illegal operation code, illegal address.) When such a program interruption occurs, the operating system usually prints the value of the Program Status Word (PSW). The PSW is a collection of 64 bits which describe the current state of the machine. The last six hexadecimal digits of the PSW are the address of the instruction immediately following the one which caused the difficulty. The knowledge of which instruction caused the problem is a big step in determining how to correct it. (You might have to add a value given somewhere in your printout to the LOC value printed beside the instructions in your source program to determine the address of the instruction.)

A memory dump can also be useful in debugging a program. Knowing what values are stored in each memory location might help you to find an error. The values in the memory dump must be located by means of their addresses—otherwise the memory dump is merely a collection of alphanumeric nonsense. Remember, the memory dump is given in hexadecimal. Some assemblers give a memory dump each time the program ends execution while others do not. To get the computer to execute a memory dump when you need one, follow the instructions for the SNAP macro in Appendix 2.

4.11 Addressing Long Programs

Suppose a program, including declarations of storage, is more than 4095 bytes long. (An array of 1000 full words will occupy 4000 bytes by itself.) How can larger displacements be handled? One approach is to use more than one base register, because no displacement can exceed 4095 (FFF) bytes. For example, a 12,000-byte program might be addressed with the following set of instructions:

```
        BALR    10,0
        USING   *,10,11,12
        ...
```

Three registers are reserved as base registers, and the current address is placed in the first of these. The second and third (11 and 12) must have values placed in them by the programmer, perhaps as follows:

```
        LA      12,2048(0,0)        Loads 2048 (half of 4096) into 12
        LA      11,2048(12,10)      Loads the address in 10 plus 2048 from 12 plus
                                    2048 displacement into 11 (4096 bytes after
                                    the address in 10)
        LA      12,2048(12,11)      Loads the address in 11 plus 2048 from 12 plus
                                    2048 displacement into 12
```

Registers 11 and 12, respectively, now contain addresses 4096 and 8192 bytes past the address in register 10. These addresses are exactly what must be in registers 11 and 12 to use them as base registers.

EXAMPLE 4.19

The effects of the above instructions on the contents of registers 11 and 12 are shown step by step, assuming that the value in register 10 is 1FA342.

```
        LA      12,2048(0,0)        Loads hexadecimal 800 (decimal 2048) into register 12
        LA      11,2048(12,10)      Loads   1FA342   from 10
                                    plus       800   from 12
                                    plus       800   displacement
                                    Equals  1FB342   into 11
        LA      12,2048(12,11)      Loads   1FB342   from 11
                                    plus       800   from 12
                                    plus       800   displacement
                                    Equals  1FC342   into 12
```

When the assembler encounters an address greater than 4095 bytes past the address in register 10, it automatically uses register 11 or 12, whichever is appropriate, for the base register. Thus the addresses in the accompanying table would be assigned base registers and displacements as follows (assuming that the original base address is 1FA342 and that the pseudo-instruction USING *,10,11,12 has been used).

Address	Base	Displacement	Bytes from Register 10 Address	
			Hexadecimal	Decimal
1FA400	10	0BE	0BE	190
1FB400	11	0BE	10BE	4286
1FC400	12	0BE	20BE	8382

LTORG

Occasionally, a program plus its data area will be longer than 4095 bytes, yet the programmer will not have to set up more than one base register. The additional registers may not be necessary if the last part of storage is a large array, for example. An array is addressed by its first byte (Chap. 6), so that if that byte is within 4095 bytes of the base address and no other memory locations follow the array, then one base register will do. However, literals are normally placed by the assembler at the end of a program, after the large array in our example. To overcome this difficulty, it is useful to use the LTORG (Literal Organization) pseudo-instruction. Placing this instruction in the Operation field at any point in the program will cause the assembler to assign memory space at that point (on a double-word boundary) to the literals used since the last LTORG instruction (or since the beginning of the program), rather than assigning their memory space at the end of the program. Note that the use of LTORG may mean that there will be duplicate copies of commonly used literals like =F'1' or =F'4'.

EXAMPLE 4.20

LTORG may be used as follows:

```
1BC400   LONGPGM   START   0
1BC400             BALR    12,0
1BC402             USING   *,12
                   ...
1BC444             A       4,=F'4'
                   ...
                   LTORG
1BD300             DC      F'4'       (THIS LINE IS INSERTED BY THE ASSEMBLER.
                                       IT MIGHT HAVE A NAME SUCH AS .LIT0001
                                       IN THE NAME FIELD.)
1BD304   A         DC      F'17'
                   ...
1BD360   ARRAY     DS      1000F
                   END
```

In this program, the literal will be assembled before the memory location for A, within addressability limits. If the LTORG pseudo-instruction had not been included, the literal would have been assembled after the array, beyond 4095 bytes from the base address.

4.12 Equivalence Pseudo-Instruction

One name can be set equivalent to another, or a name can be set equivalent to a number, using the EQU pseudo-instruction.

Name Field	Operation Field	Operand Field	Comment Field
A	EQU	B	SETS A EQUIVALENT TO B
REG	EQU	9	SETS REG EQUIVALENT TO 9

This allows us to substitute the name on the left for the name or number on the right. (Note that as the value of B changes during execution of the program, the value of A also changes.) Thus after these instructions, the following instruction loads the value of B into register 9.

    L   REG,A

If a sum is being accumulated in register 10, the following equivalence instruction might make the program more readable:

```
SUM        EQU    10
           ...
           A      SUM,NUM
```

If a program uses a given constant many times, but the constant might be changed for future runs, an equivalence instruction such as the following might be useful:

    COUNT   EQU   100

Each time the program is run, the constant may be amended by changing only the one EQU statement, instead of changing the many occurrences of the constant throughout the program. The program is more flexible than one with the constant explicitly stated throughout.

Solved Problems

4.1 Consider the following portion of an assembly language program. If the starting address is 0FA340, (a) write the address of every byte to the right of each instruction, and (b) write the starting address of every instruction to the left of each instruction.

```
0FA340     PGM         START  0
                       BALR   12,0
                       USING  *,12
                       L      10,A
                       LR     3,10
                       M      2,B


0FA340     PGM         START  0
0FA340                 BALR   12,0           0FA340 0FA341
0FA342                 USING  *,12
0FA342                 L      10,A           0FA342 0FA343 0FA344 0FA345
0FA346                 LR     3,10           0FA346 0FA347
0FA348                 M      2,B            0FA348 0FA349 0FA34A 0FA34B
```

4.2 What is the effective address (in hexadecimal) of the memory location in each of the following machine language instructions? The register contents in hexadecimal are

0	00000010	3	00000030
2	00000020	12	001FA342

(a) 41300004   (e) 4A20C044   (i) 41200004
(b) 58A3C056   (f) 5823C102   (j) 5030C042
(c) 5A20C05A   (g) 582C0506
(d) 5020C012   (h) 5C70C30A

(a) 000004   (e) 1FA386   (i) 000004
(b) 1FA3C8   (f) 1FA474   (j) 1FA384
(c) 1FA39C   (g) 1FA848
(d) 1FA354   (h) 1FA64C

4.3 Of the variables A, B, and C in Fig. 4-2, which would have their displacements altered if the instruction A 2,=F'1' were added (a) after the instruction A 2,B? (b) before the instruction A 2,B?

(a) All.
(b) All.

The displacements depend on the base address and the address where the variables are declared, not where they are used. The displacements are changed in all the cases because the extra instruction takes memory space, and the declarations are farther from the base address.

4.4 Calculate the address of each statement in the following portion of a program in which locations are given. The starting address is found (elsewhere in the program listing) to be 0FA500.

```
              000000    PGM    START  0
              000000           BALR   12,0
              000002           USING  *,12
              000002           L      2,X
              000006           A      2,Y
              00000A           LR     7,2
              00000C           A      2,Z
              000010           MR     6,2
              000012           ST     7,ANS

0FA500        000000    PGM    START  0
0FA500        000000           BALR   12,0
0FA502        000002           USING  *,12
0FA502        000002           L      2,X
0FA506        000006           A      2,Y
0FA50A        00000A           LR     7,2
0FA50C        00000C           A      2,Z
0FA510        000010           MR     6,2
0FA512        000012           ST     7,ANS
```

4.5 What is the effective address of the variable in each of the following machine language instructions? Use these register contents:

78   ADDRESSING   [CHAP. 4

	Register	Contents
	0	00000010
	2	00000020
	11	001AB34A
	12	001AB042

(a) 5A22B054   (b) 5D20C072

(a) 1AB3BE   (b) 1AB0B4

4.6 How many displacements would have to be recalculated in the program in Fig. 4-2 if A were declared A   DC   H'1'? Explain fully.

None. The boundary requirement for full word B would keep the subsequent addresses from being changed.

4.7 Explain why every fullword boundary is a halfword boundary, but not every halfword boundary is a fullword boundary.

Every address divisible by 4 is also divisible by 2, but not every address divisible by 2 is divisible by 4.

4.8 Write machine language instructions corresponding to the second, third, and fourth instructions in each part.

```
(a) 1AB342           USING  *,12      (b) 1AB342           USING  *,12
                     L      5,A                            LH     5,HA
                     A      5,B                            AH     5,HB
                     ST     5,SUM                          STH    5,HSUM
                     ...                                   ...
    1AB740   A       DC     F'7'          1AB740   HA      DC     H'7'
             B       DC     F'-3'                  HB      DC     H'-3'
             SUM     DS     F                      HSUM    DS     H

(a) 5850C3FE  L   5,A       (b) 4850C3FE  LH   5,HA
    5A50C402  A   5,B           4A50C400  AH   5,HB
    5050C406  ST  5,SUM         4050C402  STH  5,HSUM
```

4.9 Prove that an eight-digit hexadecimal number ending in 4 is divisible by 4. (*Note*: An eight-digit hexadecimal number ending in 6 is not necessarily divisible by 6.)

The first seven digits represent some integer times a power of 16, which is divisible by 4. The last digit is also divisible by 4, so the sum of these two—the number itself—is divisible by 4.

4.10 What is the maximum number of bytes of memory which might be "wasted" by the double-word boundary requirement?

Seven. A double word is 8 bytes. If the last variable ended with its last byte on an address divisible by 8, the assembler would have to skip 7 bytes to the next such address.

4.11 Which of the following instructions presents a boundary alignment problem? Explain why. Assume that the contents of register 12 are 1AB032.

```
        L    2,100(0,12)
        LA   2,100(0,12)
```

The effective address is not a fullword boundary. The load instruction fetches information from that address, which presents the boundary alignment problem. The load address instruction merely calculates the effective address and places that address in the register, but does not reference that memory location. Therefore, there is no boundary alignment problem with this instruction.

4.12 Translate each of the following portions of a program from machine language into explicit assembly language.

(a) 05C05820C0425830C0461B231B235020C04A
(b) 05C05870C1025A70C10613775070C052
(c) 05B04130000458A3B0565AA0B05A112A5B20B1025023B106
(d) 05C04820C0404A20C0445020C102
(e) 05C05830C102417000011C275D20C106

(a)	BALR	12,0	(c)	BALR	11,0	(e)	BALR	12,0
	L	2,66(0,12)		LA	3,4(0,0)		L	3,258(0,12)
	L	3,70(0,12)		L	10,86(3,11)		LA	7,1(0,0)
	SR	2,3		A	10,90(0,11)		MR	2,7
	SR	2,3		LNR	2,10		D	2,262(0,12)
	ST	2,74(0,12)		S	2,258(0,11)			
				ST	2,262(3,11)			
(b)	BALR	12,0	(d)	BALR	12,0			
	L	7,258(0,12)		LH	2,64(0,12)			
	A	7,262(0,12)		AH	2,68(0,12)			
	LCR	7,7		ST	2,258(0,12)			
	ST	7,82(0,12)						

4.13 (a) Write the explicit assembly language instruction for

    AH   2,HW

where HW is 100 bytes past the base address, which is stored in register 12.

(b) Write the machine language code for this instruction.
(c) How many bytes of memory does the instruction occupy?
(d) How many bytes does the memory location referenced by the second operand occupy?

(a) AH 2,100(0,12)   (b) 4A20C064   (c) 4   (d) 2

4.14 For which of the following assembly language instructions can you write machine language instructions with no additional information? Which instructions don't need BALR or USING? Which do not need an entry in the Name field?

(a) L   2,A   (c) L   2,0(2,7)   (e) L   8,=F'4'
(b) LR   2,4   (d) L   4,104(0,12)

(a) L   2,A   Needs additional information, BALR and USING, and a name in a declaration Name field
(b) LR   2,4   No additional information, no BALR or USING, no entry in the Name field
(c) L   2,0(2,7)   No additional information, no BALR or USING, no entry in the Name field

(d) L   4,104(0,12)   No additional information; this explicit use of register 12 does not require BALR and USING

(e) L   8,=F'4'   Needs additional information, BALR and USING, but provides its own name in a literal Name field

4.15 Write a machine language instruction for each of the following.

(a)	LA	2,0(0,4)	(d)	S	7,0(7)	(g)	BALR	12,0
(b)	LA	2,4	(e)	MR	6,7	(h)	LPR	4,4
(c)	LR	9,2	(f)	A	5,0(2,12)	(i)	D	2,10(,10)

(a)	41204000	(d)	5B770000	(g)	05C0	
(b)	41200004	(e)	1C67	(h)	1044	
(c)	1892	(f)	5A52C000	(i)	5D20A00A	

4.16 Write assembly language instructions corresponding to each of the following machine language instructions.

(a)	05C0	(d)	4826B004	(g)	5C47B000	
(b)	1A27	(e)	05EF	(h)	4CB0C000	
(c)	1166	(f)	5A20C042			

(a)	BALR	12,0	(d)	LH	2,4(6,11)	(g)	M	4,0(7,11)
(b)	AR	2,7	(e)	BALR	14,15	(h)	MH	11,0(0,12)
(c)	LNR	6,6	(f)	A	2,66(0,12)			

4.17 What is the difference between

          A   2,A−4   and   S   2,A+4

The first adds the value at a memory location 4 bytes before A; the second subtracts the value at a memory location 4 bytes after A (8 bytes after the first).

4.18 How are the contents of register 2 affected by each of the following instructions, assuming the following values are stored prior to execution of each instruction?

        A   DC   F'14'
        B   DC   F'15'
        C   DC   F'16'

(a) A   2,B−4   (d) L   2,C−8
(b) A   2,B+4   (e) L   2,A+8
(c) S   2,B−4

(a) A   2,B−4   14 is added to the prior contents of register 2
(b) A   2,B+4   16 is added
(c) S   2,B−4   14 is subtracted
(d) L   2,C−8   14 is loaded
(e) L   2,A+8   16 is loaded

4.19 Calculate the effective address (in hexadecimal) of the second operand in each of the following instructions. Use register 12 containing 0FA342 (hexadecimal), register 2 containing 00000100 (hexadecimal), and register 0 containing 00000020 (hexadecimal).

(a)	A	2,2(2,12)	(e)	A	2,14(,12)	(i)	LA	2,2(0,0)
(b)	A	2,6(0,12)	(f)	A	2,26(12)	(j)	LA	2,0(0,2)
(c)	A	2,10(2,12)	(g)	LA	2,4(,12)	(k)	LA	2,2(2,12)
(d)	A	2,6(12,2)	(h)	LA	2,100	(l)	LA	2,0(0,0)

(a)	0FA444	(e)	0FA350	(i)	000002
(b)	0FA348	(f)	0FA35C	(j)	000100
(c)	0FA44C	(g)	0FA346	(k)	0FA444
(d)	0FA448	(h)	000064	(l)	000000

[Some assemblers give a warning with the format of part (f).]

4.20 Consider these memory locations:

    1AB400   ADDX   DC   A(X)
    1AB404   X   DC   F'4'

What will be loaded into register 2 by each of the following instructions?

(a) LA   2,ADDX   (d) L   2,X
(b) LA   2,X   (e) L   2,=A(X)
(c) L   2,ADDX   (f) L   2,=A(ADDX)

(a) 001AB400   (d) 00000004
(b) 001AB404   (e) 001AB404
(c) 001AB404   (f) 001AB400

4.21 Simplify the following, if possible.

(a) LA   2,A   (b) LA   7,0(0,3)
    A   2,=F'4'

(a) LA   2,A+4   (*Note*: LA loads the address of A, so adding 4 to it gives the address of A+4.)
(b) LR   7,3   (*Note*: These instructions are equivalent only if the first byte of register 3 is zero, since the LA instruction zeros out the first byte of register 7.)

4.22 Which of the following initialize a register, and which increment it?

(a) LA   2,10(0,2)   (d) LA   2,10(2,0)
(b) LA   2,10   (e) LA   2,10(0,3)
(c) LA   2,10(0,0)

(a) and (d) increment the register; (b), (c), and (e) initialize it.

4.23 What is the effect of each of the following instructions? Assume that the first byte in register 2 is zero.

(a) LA   2,0(2,2)   (b) LA   2,0(0,2)

(a) The value in the register is doubled (provided that the value of the result is less than 2^{24}). (b) There is no change.

82   ADDRESSING   [CHAP. 4

4.24 Why can't the following instruction be used to prepare register 11 as another base register in a long program? (See Sec. 4.10.)

$$\text{LA} \quad 11,4096(0,10)$$

The displacement is too large.

4.25 (a) What would the following section of code accomplish in a long program?
(b) What limitations are there on the location of the DC statement?

```
          BALR   10,0
          USING  *,10,11,12
          ...
          L      3,FOUR096
          LA     11,0(3,10)
          LA     12,0(3,11)
          ...
FOUR096   DC     F'4096'
```

(a) The code loads registers 11 and 12 with the proper addresses to allow their use as base registers.
(b) The DC statement must be written within 4095 bytes of the base address (in register 10).

4.26 What is accomplished by the LA instruction in the following sequence?

```
          A    EQU   4
          LA   A,A(A,A)
```

It loads into register 4 a value which is 4 more than twice the value originally in register 4, assuming that the final contents would have a zero first byte. The second instruction is the same as

$$\text{LA} \quad 4,4(4,4)$$

4.27 Explain why register 0 cannot be used as a base register or an index register, while any other register can theoretically be used for either of these purposes.

When 0 appears in an instruction, the value 0 is used rather than the contents of register 0. Thus the contents of register 0 are inaccessible for use as a base register or an index register.

4.28 Repeat Problem 3.45, with these more involved instructions. Explain in words why each of these instructions is more involved.

(a) LH   2,C   (d) ST   6,H
(b) L   7,G   (e) STH   3,D
(c) ST   2,I   (f) MH   4,=F'9'

	Value	Location	Comment
(a)	-1	Register 2	C is full word: first 2 bytes FFFF
(b)	75	Register 7	4 bytes (two halfwords) are loaded, starting at G
(c)	0 0	Location I Location J	4 bytes (two halfwords) are stored, starting at I
(d)	1,000,000	Locations H, I	$000F_{16}$ in H; 4240_{16} in I
(e)	70014_{16} $(=458,772_{10})$	Location D	Only the first 2 bytes of D are changed
(f)	0	Register 4	Fullword literal is 00000009; only the first 2 bytes are used by MH

CHAP. 4]   ADDRESSING   83

4.29 How many MH instructions would fit in 16 bytes?

Four. Each instruction is 4 bytes long, because each is an RX instruction.

Supplementary Problems

4.30 What occupies the first byte of every machine language instruction?

4.31 When the machine language version of a program is executing, how does the computer tell from the current address and the machine language instruction what the address of the next instruction is?

4.32 Which register cannot be used as a base register? Why not?

4.33 From your background in computer science, state one example of referencing a memory location which did not have a specific name.

4.34 How would the execution of an RX instruction be affected if a student mixed up the base register and the index register in an explicit instruction? Explain. Do you suppose that your answer holds for all types of instructions?

4.35 How many bytes of a machine language instruction does R1 occupy? Explain why there are not more than 16 general-purpose registers.

4.36 Is the base register for the whole program necessarily the base register for every instruction in it? Explain.

4.37 What is the difference in the order of D2, X2, and B2 in assembly language format and machine language format? Which two are in the same order in both formats?

4.38 If a zero is omitted from an assembly language explicit instruction, such as LA 2,4(2) for LA 2,4(2,0), is the zero also omitted from the machine language instruction? (*Hint*: If it were, how long would the machine language instruction be?)

4.39 Calculate the effective addresses for the instructions in Figs. 2-1, 4-2, and 4-3. Assume a starting address of 0FA340 in each case.

4.40 Calculate the address of each of the memory locations B through G:

1AA358	A	DS	F
	B	DS	H
	C	DS	H
	D	DS	F
	E	DS	H
	F	DS	F
	G	DS	D

4.41 Explain how memory space could have been saved by reordering the declarations of Problem 4.40.

4.42 Explain why the computer cannot execute DS and DC statements. What happens if it tries to do so?

4.43 How does the computer know whether it should look for R2 or X2, B2, and D2 (or other things) in an instruction?

4.44 Rewrite the program in Fig. 4-2, defining at least one equivalence name and using the defined name at least twice.

4.45 Use halfword instructions to do the following computation involving fullword memory locations. Assume that each value will fit in 2 bytes.

$$X = A * B$$

4.46 What are the contents of ANS after execution of the following instructions?

	LH	2,C
	AH	2,A+2
	MH	2,B
	ST	2,ANS
	BR	14
A	DC	F'12'
B	DC	F'−32'
C	DC	H'9'
ANS	DS	F

4.47 Is it legal to have an instruction which refers to a DS or DC statement and which follows that statement? If not, why not?

4.48 Redo Problem 3.60 more efficiently with the additional power of the instructions learned in this chapter.

4.49 Describe in words what gets stored in RESULT after the following sets of instructions are executed.

    (a) LA   5,B   (b) LA   4,VAR
         A   5,=F'5'   LR   3,4
         ST   5,RESULT   A   3,D
                                    ST   3,RESULT

4.50 Assume that the one literal shown in Example 4.20 is the only literal in the program, and that the address of A is given correctly.

(a) At what address will the literal be assembled?

(b) If the LTORG instruction were not present, what would be the address of A?

(c) If the LTORG instruction were not present, what would the address of the literal have been? Show that this address is not addressable with only one base register.

Chapter 5

Compare and Branch Instructions

Instructions in assembly language are normally performed sequentially. That is, the next line in the program listing will be the next instruction executed. In order to perform more complicated tasks, it is necessary to be able to branch, which enables us to execute one sequence of instructions under one set of conditions and another sequence under another.

In a high-level language, branching is usually performed by a GOTO statement (GOTO 70, or GOTO L1) or by something like an IF-THEN statement:

> IF A > B
> THEN B = B + 1;

In assembly language, there are two types of branch instructions. Corresponding to the GOTO is the *unconditional branch* instruction, which causes a branch every time it is executed. Comparable to the IF-THEN statement is the *conditional branch* instruction, which causes a branch only if a certain condition is true. In order to translate the PL/1 IF-THEN statement above into assembly language, we would have to break it up into two statements—in particular, a comparison statement and a branch statement. Here is a revision which approximates what happens in assembly language:

> IF A $\Leftarrow$ B
> THEN GOTO L1;
> B = B + 1;
> L1: next statement

The comparison in assembly language can be done by a compare instruction; it establishes the conditions under which we branch. Several other instructions can also set up the conditions under which to branch. These instructions, marked with an asterisk (*) in Appendix 1, are those which set the condition code.

5.1 The Condition Code and Branching

An unconditional branch instruction causes a branch every time it is executed. Also available is the conditional branch, which causes a branch only if a certain condition is true. Whether or not to branch is determined by the status of a 2-bit *condition code* (*cc*). This condition code is set as part of the operation of certain instructions, discussed below. With 2 bits, we can represent four values: 00, 01, 10, 11, and these are the four settings of the condition code; in decimal, these are 0, 1, 2, and 3. Each of these settings has a specific meaning depending upon the type of instruction which has set the code.

Arithmetic Instructions and the Condition Code

Since several instructions which we have already discussed set the condition code, it will be useful to examine them before looking at the compare instructions. When performing arithmetic, it is often useful to know the result of the latest operation—for example, to prevent using zero as a divisor or to determine whether the result fits into one register. To take action in any of these circumstances requires being able to branch to a section of code which makes the appropriate adjustments. For this reason, certain arithmetic instructions set the condition code as shown in Table 5-1. The instructions we have already covered which set the condition code are A, AH, AR, S, SH, and SR, the special load instructions (LPR, LCR, LNR), as well as a new instruction, LTR.

Table 5-1 Meaning of the Condition Code Settings

CC Setting	Meaning
0	Result of the operation is zero
1	Result of the operation is negative
2	Result of the operation is positive
3	Result of the operation is an overflow

An *overflow* occurs when the result of an operation is a number larger than will fit into its destination field. For a register destination, then, an overflow will occur when the number generated requires more than 31 bits (since the first bit is the sign bit). The overflow condition takes precedence over the others, so that if an overflow occurs, you will not know whether the result is also positive, negative, or zero.

EXAMPLE 5.1

How does the following set of instructions set the condition code?

```
            L      7,NUM1
            S      7,NUM2
            ...
NUM1        DC     F'3'
NUM2        DC     F'9'
```

The subtract instruction sets the condition code to 1, because the result of the subtraction $(3-9)$ leaves a negative number (-6) in register 7.

EXAMPLE 5.2

What is the setting of the condition code after execution of the following instructions?

```
            L      8,NUM
            LCR    8,8
            ...
NUM         DC     F'-3'
```

The condition code is set to 2. After we load NUM into register 8, LCR loads the complement of NUM into register 8; thus register 8 finally receives the positive value 3.

The Branch Instructions (BC and BCR)

Once the condition code is set, branches can be made using the BC or BCR (Branch on Condition) instructions. These instructions test the condition code and branch accordingly. There are several ways to test the condition code with the BC or BCR instructions. One way is to use extended mnemonics, which will be discussed in the next subsection. Another way is to use a mask (M1) as the first operand in the instruction. The mask is a 4-bit binary number, in which each of the 4 bits corresponds to a setting of the condition code.

The first bit in the mask controls the branching if cc = 0

The second bit in the mask controls the branching if cc = 1

The third bit in the mask controls the branching if cc = 2

The fourth bit in the mask controls the branching if cc = 3

The branch instruction causes a branch only when a 1 in the bit mask corresponds to the current setting of the condition code. Thus if the mask is B'0100' and the current setting of the condition code is 1, the branch will take place. If the condition code is 0, 2, or 3 with this mask, no branch will occur.

The mask can be represented a second way, as the decimal equivalent of the binary mask. As an example,

               BC   B'1000',ZERO   and   BC   8,ZERO

are two RX-format branch instructions, causing a branch when the result of the arithmetic operation is zero (or, more generally, when the cc = 0).

The BCR instructions are similar to the BC instructions, but they have a register as their second operand. Thus the following instructions would have the same effect as the preceding ones:

         LA   9,ZERO   followed by   BCR   B'1000',9   or   BCR   8,9

Table 5-2 shows the relationship between the condition code, the mask, and the decimal equivalent of the mask. Each mask shown will cause a branch only for the condition code setting to its left.

Table 5-2 Masks for the Condition Code

Condition Code	Four-Bit Mask	Decimal Equivalent
0	B'1000'	8
1	B'0100'	4
2	B'0010'	2
3	B'0001'	1

More Complicated Masks

Each 1 bit in the mask represents one setting of the condition code under which a branch will occur. We can combine the settings of the bits in the mask to correspond to more complicated conditions. Thus we can also have a mask of B'1100', which represents branching with condition codes of 0 or 1, or B'1110', which represents branching with condition codes of 0, 1, or 2. With a mask of B'0110', for example, we will branch if the condition code is set to 1 or to 2. There are obviously 16 different combinations of settings.

We might choose to branch if the result of the operation is not positive—that is, if it is either negative or zero. In this case, we can set the mask to B'1100', or decimal 12. If we want to branch if the number is anything but zero, we can set the mask to B'0111' or decimal 7. If we want to branch under all conditions, we can set the mask to B'1111' or decimal 15. [Usually the decimal representation includes the 1 bit for the overflow condition, even if such a condition will not occur as a result of executing the instruction. Thus, for instructions which cannot cause overflow, we can use either decimal 6 or 7 (B'0110' or B'0111') for branch if not zero, and similarly 14 or 15 (B'1110' or B'1111') for an "unconditional" branch.]

EXAMPLE 5.3

The following code performs an arithmetic operation, then checks to see what the sign of the result is. If the result is positive, it branches and adds 1 to a counter of positive numbers. Otherwise, it does not branch, but adds 1 to a counter of zero or negative numbers.

```
          SR    7,7              ZERO THE POSITIVE COUNTER
          SR    8,8              ZERO THE NEGATIVE-OR-ZERO COUNTER
          L     4,BIGNUM         LOAD IN BIGNUM
          S     4,LGNUM          SUBTRACT LGNUM FROM IT
          BC    B'0010',POS      TEST CC; IF CONTENTS OF
*                                  REGISTER 4 ARE > 0, BRANCH
*                                  TO POS
NEG       A     8,=F'1'          NOT POSITIVE, SO ADD 1 TO
*                                  NEGATIVE-OR-ZERO COUNTER
          BC    B'1111',DONE     UNCONDITIONAL BRANCH
*                                  IF WE GOT HERE,
*                                  WE DON'T ALSO
*                                  ADD 1 TO REGISTER 7
POS       A     7,=F'1'          POSITIVE, SO ADD 1 TO
*                                  POSITIVE COUNTER
DONE      ...
BIGNUM    DC    F'197'
LGNUM     DC    F'194'
```

Let's trace the example. First we initialize our counter registers to zero. We load 197 into register 4 and then subtract 194 from it, leaving 3 in register 4. The subtract instruction thus sets the condition code to 2. The BC instruction tests the condition code and branches if cc = 2. Since cc = 2, we branch to POS. At POS, we add 1 to register 7, which we are using as our counter of positive numbers. This makes sense, since we have produced a positive number by our subtract operation. When we are finished, register 7 will have the value 1 and register 8 will have the value 0. If our data were different, we might end up with a negative result, follow the other path, and end up with a 1 in register 8. At the first BC instruction, we would not branch to POS, but would instead proceed to NEG, where we would add 1 to register 8, then branch to DONE.

Extended Mnemonics and the Arithmetic Instructions

The third method of testing the condition code is to use extended mnemonics instead of bit masks or decimal values. Extended mnemonics are more like instructions in high-level languages. They allow us to specify when to branch as part of the branch instruction mnemonic itself, rather than as a separate operand. Thus BC B'0111' can be represented as BNZ (Branch on Not Zero), and BC B'0100' can be represented as BM (Branch on Minus). "Minus" stands for negative, while "plus" stands for positive. Table 5-3 shows the extended mnemonics that we can use after arithmetic instructions. Other instructions (to be discussed later in the chapter) will require different extended mnemonics.

Note that the decimal equivalents for BNP, BNM, and BNZ include the 1 bit for overflow. If you do not wish to branch on overflow with these instructions, you have to use BC 12, BC 10, or BC 6, respectively.

Table 5-3 Extended Mnemonics after Arithmetic Instructions

Extended Code (RX or RR)	Meaning	Machine Instruction (RX or RR)	Binary Mask
B or BR	Branch Unconditionally	BC or BCR 15,	B'1111'
BZ or BZR	Branch on Zero	BC or BCR 8,	B'1000'
BP or BPR	Branch on Plus	BC or BCR 2,	B'0010'
BM or BMR	Branch on Minus	BC or BCR 4,	B'0100'
BNZ or BNZR	Branch on Not Zero	BC or BCR 7,	B'0111'
BNP or BNPR	Branch on Not Plus	BC or BCR 13,	B'1101'
BNM or BNMR	Branch on Not Minus	BC or BCR 11,	B'1011'
BO or BOR	Branch on Overflow	BC or BCR 1,	B'0001'
BNO or BNOR	Branch on No Overflow	BC or BCR 14,	B'1110'

EXAMPLE 5.4

The previous example contained the following branch instruction:

BC   B'0010',POS

The following sets of statements do exactly the same thing.

1. LA   5,POS
   BCR   B'0010',5   Binary mask with RR instruction
2. BC   2,POS   Decimal equivalent of B'0010' with RX instruction
3. LA   5,POS
   BCR   2,5   Decimal equivalent of B'0010' with RR instruction
4. BP   POS   Extended mnemonic with RX instruction
5. LA   5,POS
   BPR   5   Extended mnemonic with RR instruction

You may use any of the above options, as you wish. However, most programmers find the extended mnemonics easiest to recognize at a glance. This is important when you are debugging your program or when someone else is trying to analyze what your program does. You will notice that we use extended mnemonics in almost all the examples in later chapters, for just this reason.

5.2 Load and Test Register

The Load and Test Register (LTR) instruction is exactly the same as the LR instruction, except that LTR sets the condition code while LR does not. It sets the condition code according to the rules shown in Table 5-1. (However, LTR never sets the condition code to 3.) LTR is commonly used to load a register from itself, thus changing the contents of no registers, but simply setting the condition code.

EXAMPLE 5.5

Suppose we want to test the value produced as the result of a multiplication instruction, which does not set the condition code. The following code will do the task for us.

```
                L       7,ANUMB
                M       6,BNUMB
                LTR     7,7             TEST RESULT IN REGISTER 7
                BZ      DONTDIV         IF RESULT IS 0, DON'T DIVIDE
                L       5,CNUMB         LOAD DIVIDEND
                M       4,-F'1'         EXTEND THE SIGN TO REGISTER 4
                DR      4,7             DIVIDE 4-5 REGISTER PAIR BY REGISTER 7
                ST      5,ANS           QUOTIENT IN ODD MEMBER OF
*                                       DIVIDEND REGISTER PAIR
                B       DONE            SKIP STORING PARTANS
DONTDIV         ST      7,PARTANS       STORE THE 0 TO SHOW
*                                       WHAT HAPPENED
DONE            ...
ANUMB           DC      F'8'
BNUMB           DC      F'-5'
CNUMB           DC      F'400'
ANS             DS      F
PARTANS         DS      F
```

In this example, we want to multiply ANUMB and BNUMB together, and if the result of that multiplication is not 0, we want to divide CNUMB by the result. This is basically, then, ANS = CNUMB/(ANUMB × BNUMB). IF ANUMB × BNUMB = 0, we will store that result at PARTANS so we know why there is no answer at ANS. We load 8 into register 7, then multiply it by −5, leaving the product in the 6-7 register pair.

This leaves a result of −40 in register 7. Our next step would be a division, but we don't want to divide if the result of the multiplication is 0, since division by 0 is undefined and will cause an error in the program (see Appendix 2). We therefore use LTR to test the contents of register 7. If it contains 0, the LTR will set the condition code to 0. However, since −40 is negative, the condition code is 1, so we do not branch. We load 400 into register 5, then multiply the 4-5 register pair by 1 to extend the sign into register 4. Then we divide the 4-5 pair by the contents of register 7. The quotient ends up in register 5 (the remainder is in register 4), and we store the quotient at ANS.

5.3 Compare Instructions

As is true of the most common use of LTR, the compare instructions have setting the condition code as their only purpose. There are several compare instructions; they vary by the types of data they compare. For example, C and CR (respectively RX and RR instructions) operate on binary full words, and CH (an RX instruction) compares halfwords. CLC, CL, CLR, and CLI (respectively SS, RX, RR, and SI instructions—see Chap. 7) compare logical (unsigned or alphanumeric) data, while CP (an SS instruction) compares packed decimal numbers (see Chap. 8).

The compare instructions set the condition code in a different way from the arithmetic instructions. Table 5-4 lists the settings of the condition code after compare instructions. The condition code is set to 0, 1, or 2, as if the second operand had been subtracted from the first. Compare instructions never set the condition code to 3.

Table 5-4 Condition Code Settings after Compare Instructions

CC Setting	Meaning
0	First operand = second operand
1	First operand < second operand
2	First operand > second operand
3	Condition code never set to 3 by compare

Compare, Compare Register

The Compare (C) instruction takes two operands. The first is a register, and the second is a full word in memory. The operands are considered to be signed numbers, so the leftmost (sign) bits are compared first; then the remaining bits are compared.

EXAMPLE 5.6

To what value is the condition code set by the following set of instructions?

```
        L     6,FIRST
        A     6,NUM
        C     6,SECOND
        ...
FIRST   DC    F'25'
SECOND  DC    F'29'
NUM     DC    F'5'
```

The 25 is loaded into register 6, and 5 is added to it, putting 30 into register 6. This is compared to 29. Since 30 is greater than 29, the condition code is set to 2.

The Compare Register (CR) instruction takes two registers for its operands. Other than that, it works the same way the C instruction does.

EXAMPLE 5.7

To what value is the condition code set by the following set of instructions?

```
        L     8,LEAF
        L     10,TREE
        CR    8,10
        ...
LEAF    DC    F'9'
TREE    DC    F'900'
```

Register 8 holds 9, while register 10 holds 900. The CR instruction compares 9 with 900, and since 9 < 900, sets the condition code to 1. (If we had subtracted 900 from 9, we would have gotten a negative result, which also would have set the condition code to 1.)

Compare Halfword

The Compare Halfword (CH) instruction also compares binary numbers. It compares a full word in a register with a halfword in storage.

EXAMPLE 5.8

(*a*) What two things are actually compared when the following instructions are executed?

```
        L     7,FNUM
        CH    7,HNUM
        ...
FNUM    DC    F'7'
HNUM    DC    H'6'
```

Register 7 is loaded with 00000007, which is then compared with HNUM. HNUM is temporarily expanded [within the arithmetic logical unit (ALU)—the processing part of the machine—but not in memory] by copying the positive sign bit to the left, producing 00000006. Thus 00000007 is compared with 00000006, and the condition code is set to 2.

(*b*) How will the following instructions set the condition code?

```
        L     4,EGG
        CH    4,NOG
        ...
EGG     DC    F'37'
NOG     DC    H'-10'
```

Register 4 is loaded with 00000025_{16}, which is then compared to NOG, which is FFF6. The sign bit of NOG is 1, since hex 'F' is binary '1111', indicating that NOG is negative; its (temporarily extended) value is FFFFFFF6. When the two values are compared, positive 00000025 is greater than negative FFFFFFF6, so the condition code is set to 2.

Table 5-5 Extended Mnemonics after Compare Instructions

Extended Code (RX or RR)	Meaning	Machine Instruction (RX or RR)	Binary Mask
BH or BHR	Branch on First Operand High	BC or BCR 2,	B'0010'
BL or BLR	Branch on First Operand Low	BC or BCR 4,	B'0100'
BE or BER	Branch on First Operand Equal Second	BC or BCR 8,	B'1000'
BNH or BNHR	Branch on First Operand Not High	BC or BCR 13,	B'1101'
BNL or BNLR	Branch on First Operand Not Low	BC or BCR 11,	B'1011'
BNE or BNER	Branch on First Operand Not Equal Second	BC or BCR 7,	B'0111'

Extended Mnemonics after Compare Instructions

The binary mask and its decimal equivalent work the same way for compare instructions as for the arithmetic instructions, but their values and meaning and the extended mnemonics which interpret them are different (see Table 5-5).

Let's look at some examples which use the compare instructions with the branch instructions.

EXAMPLE 5.9

We have three fullword numbers stored at locations A, B, and C. We would like to know if these three numbers can represent the sides of a valid right triangle. Remember the rule for a valid right triangle: $A^2 + B^2 = C^2$, where C is the longest side of the triangle. The following code will use the CR instruction to test whether these numbers represent a right triangle.

```
           L     7,A
           M     6,A          A SQUARED IN REGISTER 7
           L     9,B
           MR    8,9          B SQUARED IN REGISTER 9
           AR    7,9          A SQUARED + B SQUARED
           L     9,C
           M     8,C          C SQUARED IN REGISTER 9
           CR    7,9          COMPARE THE RESULTS
           BNE   INVALID      IF NOT RIGHT TRIANGLE,
*                                BRANCH TO INVALID
           ...
A          DC    F'3'
B          DC    F'4'
C          DC    F'5'
```

The first two instructions load a 3 into register 7 and multiply it by 3, yielding 9 in register 7. The second two load a 4 into register 9 and multiply it by 4, putting 16 in register 9. (Note the two different ways of squaring.) Then we add these two products together, placing 25 in register 7. We no longer need the number in the 8-9 register pair, so we reuse the pair. We load 5 into register 9 and multiply it by 5, leaving 25 in register 9. Now we compare registers 7 and 9. If these three numbers represent a right triangle, the numbers in registers 7 and 9 should be equal, as they are. As a result, we do not branch to INVALID, since the instruction is BNE, branch if first operand is not equal to second operand.

EXAMPLE 5.10

Suppose that we want to find the value of the largest of three numbers, NUM1, NUM2, and NUM3. We can set up the following code to do this, by first comparing two of the three numbers, and then comparing the larger of the two with the third. The largest of the three numbers will be stored at TOPNUM.

One method to do this follows:

```
           L     2,NUM1       LOAD NUM1
           C     2,NUM2       COMPARE WITH NUM2
           BNL   TEST2        IF NUM1>=NUM2, BRANCH TO COMPARE
*                                NUM1 WITH NUM3
           L     2,NUM2       SINCE NUM2>NUM1, LOAD NUM2 TO
*                                CONTINUE
TEST2      C     2,NUM3       COMPARE LARGER WITH NUM3
           BNL   STORE        REGISTER 2 CONTAINS LARGEST
           L     2,NUM3       IF WE GET HERE, NUM3 IS LARGEST
STORE      ST    2,TOPNUM
DONE       ...
NUM1       DC    F'47935'
NUM2       DC    F'31249'
NUM3       DC    F'12045'
TOPNUM     DS    F
```

The code is carefully set up so that we perform as few branches and as few loads as possible, considering the instructions we have available. We have set up the comparisons so that, under the best of circumstances (all three numbers equal), we must load only one number into a register. We have accomplished this by using BNL instead of BH after two of the comparisons. If the two numbers are equal, we branch and reuse the same number for the next comparison. Using the same register throughout also means that we can use one ST instruction and thus fewer branches.

EXAMPLE 5.11

Suppose that we want to translate the following Pascal code into assembly language statements to accomplish the same results. Note that either the THEN clause or the ELSE clause is executed, but not both.

$$\text{if } T - 2 = \text{ANS}$$
$$\text{then } C := C * Y + 8$$
$$\text{else } R := R - 2$$

The assembly language instructions interpret the condition as a comparison and a series of branches, as follows:

```
          L      3,T
          S      3,=F'2'
          C      3,ANS
          BNE    ELSE
THEN      L      7,C
          M      6,Y
          A      7,=F'8'
          ST     7,C
          B      OVER
ELSE      L      7,R
          S      7,=F'2'
          ST     7,R
OVER      ...
```

The instructions at and following the THEN label are executed only if the condition (BNE) is false, that is, if the compared values are equal. Reversing the Pascal condition allows us to use as few branching statements as possible.

EXAMPLE 5.12

Here is a more complicated section of Pascal code, utilizing the logical operator AND. We will translate this into assembly code. Note that the code for the second condition needs to be executed only if the first condition evaluates to true.

$$\text{if } (X - D > 0) \text{ and } (\text{NUM} = K)$$
$$\text{then } B := \text{NUM} + X$$
$$\text{else } B := \text{NUM}$$

The assembly language instructions follow:

```
          L      5,X
          S      5,D
          BNP    ELSE           CC SET BY SUBTRACT INSTRUCTION
          L      6,NUM
          C      6,K
          BNE    ELSE
THEN      L      5,X
          AR     5,6            IF WE GET HERE, REGISTER 6 CONTAINS NUM
          ST     5,B
          B      NEXT
ELSE      L      6,NUM          REGISTER 6 MAY NOT CONTAIN NUM
          ST     6,B
NEXT      ...
```

It is important to note that we cannot assume that register 6 contains NUM at the statement labeled ELSE, while we can make this assumption in the AR statement three statements prior. This is because we may come to the ELSE label by branching before we load NUM into register 6. If, in contrast, we are at the AR statement, we assuredly have already loaded NUM into register 6 in testing the second half of the condition.

EXAMPLE 5.13

Labels can be designated by using explicit notation. This example allows us to branch to different locations depending upon the result of the multiplication instruction. Assume that A and B are both positive.

```
              LA    2,THERE
              L     5,A
              M     4,B
              LTR   4,4           DOES RESULT FIT IN ONE REGISTER?
              BC    7,4(0,2)      NO--SKIP STORING RESULT
              LTR   5,5           IS RESULT IN REGISTER 5 LESS THAN 32 BITS?
              BM    4(0,2)        NO--SKIP STORING RESULT
      THERE   ST    5,RESULT
              D     4,=F'10'
```

If the multiplication results in an answer that fits into the last 31 bits of one register, the ST instruction is executed. Otherwise, there is a branch to THERE+4 (register 2 contains the address of THERE, and we add a displacement of 4 to that address). The divide instruction is at that address, 4 bytes past THERE. [Note that the instruction BNZ THERE+4 would ordinarily be used instead of the instructions LA 2,THERE and BC 7,4(0,2).]

Solved Problems

5.1 Is the branch performed in the following cases or not?

```
    (a)         LA    3,9              (d)           L     8,ONE
                S     3,=F'10'                       S     8,TWO
                BC    B'1000',NEXT                   BC    2,NEXT
                                                     ...
                                        ONE          DC    F'-8'
                                        TWO          DC    F'10'
    (b)         L     9,NUM1           (e)           L     7,NUM
                A     9,NUM2                         S     7,NUM2
                BC    B'1101',NEXT                   BNP   NEGNUM
                ...                                  ...
      NUM1      DC    F'10'             NUM          DC    F'86'
      NUM2      DC    F'-9'             NUM2         DC    F'92'
    (c)         LA    7,50             (f)           L     6,ANUM
                A     7,FIR                          A     6,PNUM
                S     7,SEC                          BNZ   NEWPL
                BC    11,NEXT                        ...
                ...                     ANUM         DC    F'12'
      FIR       DC    F'45'             PNUM         DC    F'-12'
      SEC       DC    F'35'
```

(g)	L	9,F	(h)		LA	7,8
	A	9,C			M	6,NEWN
	A	9,D			LTR	7,7
	BO	ERROR			BM	FIX
	...				...	
F	DC	F'43900'		NEWN	DC	F'6'
C	DC	F'99999'				
D	DC	F'23000'				

(a) No. $9 - 10 = -1$, and B'1000' says branch on zero.

(b) No. $10 + (-9) = 1$, and B'1101' says branch on zero, negative or overflow.

(c) Yes. $50 + 45 - 35 = 60$, and we branch on zero, positive or overflow.

(d) No. $-8 - 10 = -18$, and BC 2 says branch on positive.

(e) Yes. $86 - 92 = -6$ and BNP says branch on negative or zero.

(f) No. $12 + (-12) = 0$, and BNZ says branch on not zero.

(g) No. $43{,}900 + 99{,}999 + 23{,}000 = 166{,}899$, which is not greater than $2^{31} - 1$.

(h) No. $8 \times 6 = 48$, and BM says branch if value is negative.

5.2 What is the difference between BNL and BH? Between BNH and BL? Between BNP and BM? Between BP and BNM?

BNL and BNH branch on equal, while BH and BL do not. BNP and BNM branch on zero, while BM and BP do not.

5.3 What is the difference between BP and BH?

Each is a BC instruction with a mask of 2. But for readability, when the condition code is set by an arithmetic or LTR instruction, it is natural to use BP, while BH is the natural form to use when the condition code is set by a compare instruction.

5.4 Is the branch performed in the following cases or not? Register 5 contains the binary equivalent of decimal 127.

(a)	C	5,NEGNM	(e)		C	5,=F'92'
	BC	B'1011',NEXT			BNH	NEXT
	...					
NEGNM	DC	F'-8004'				
(b)	C	5,CNUM	(f)		C	5,=F'-9'
	BC	B'1000',NEXT			BNE	NEWLOC
	...					
CNUM	DC	F'271'				
(c)	C	5,=F'86'	(g)		C	5,=F'127'
	BC	7,NEXT			BNL	LOC
(d)	L	8,ZERO	(h)		C	5,=F'92'
	CR	5,8			BH	NEW
	BC	4,NEXT				
	...					
ZERO	DC	F'0'				

(a) Yes. $127 > -8004$, and B'1011' says branch unless first operand < second operand.

(b) No. $127 < 271$, and B'1000' says branch if first operand = second operand.

(c) Yes. $127 > 86$, and BC 7 says branch unless first operand = second operand.

(d) No. $127 > 0$, and BC 4 says branch if first operand < second operand.

(e) No. 127 > 92, and BNH says branch if first operand ≤ second operand.
(f) Yes. 127 > −9, and BNE says branch if first operand not equal to second operand.
(g) Yes. 127 = 127, and BNL says branch if first operand ≥ second operand.
(h) Yes. 127 > 92, and BH says branch if first operand > second operand.

5.5 Given the contents of the registers 6, 7, and 8, and storage locations A, B, and D, will the following sets of instructions cause a branch? (Numbers are all in hexadecimal.)

```
                Register 6    FBC20089
                Register 7    0089FBC2
                Register 8    00000031
                A             32000031
                B             0089FBC3
                D             FBC20000
```

(a)	CR 6,7	(e)	CH 7,D	(i)	C 6,D
	BH SECOND		BNH NEXT		BH NEXT
(b)	C 7,B	(f)	C 8,A	(j)	CH 6,D
	BNL NEXT		BL TWO		BNE DONE
(c)	CH 7,B	(g)	CH 8,A	(k)	CH 6,B
	BH NEXT		BL TWO		BE NEXT
(d)	CH 7,B+2	(h)	CH 8,A+2	(l)	CH 8,D+2
	BH NEXT		BE NEXT		BE FUZZ

(a) No. The first value is negative (F is binary 1111), so FBC20089 is less than 0089FBC2.
(b) No. 0089FBC2 is less than 0089FBC3.
(c) Yes. Register 7 contains 0089FBC2, which is greater than 0089, which is the contents of the *halfword* starting at B.
(d) Yes. Register 7 contains 0089FBC2, while the contents of the halfword is FBC3, which is negative.
(e) No. Register 7 contains 0089FBC2, while the halfword at D = FBC2, which is negative.
(f) Yes. 00000031 is less than 32000031.
(g) Yes. Register 8 contains 00000031, while the first two bytes of A = 3200, which is larger.
(h) Yes. 0031 = 0031.
(i) Yes. Both are negative, so FBC20089 is greater than FBC20000. (With negative numbers, greater means closer to zero, and FBC20089 has a smaller magnitude.)
(j) Yes. Register 6 contains FBC20089, which is less than FFFFFBC2.
(k) No. Register 6 contains FBC20089, which is negative and therefore less than 00000089.
(l) No. Register 8 contains 00000031, which is greater than D+2, which is 0000.

5.6 Simplify the following code:

```
          AR   2,6
          BZ   LOC1
          BP   LOC2
LOC1      A    2,Z
          ST   2,SUM
          B    OVER
```

```
         LOC2      LTR     2,2
                   BM      DONE
                   ST      2,SUM
                   B       OVER
         DONE      A       7,LISTVAL
                   ST      7,FINAL
                   B       OVER
         OVER      ...

                   AR      2,6
         *                                 OMIT BZ  LOC1, SINCE IF REGISTER 2
         *                                    CONTAINS 0, LOC1 IS EXECUTED NEXT
         *                                    ANYWAY
                   BP      LOC2
         LOC1      A       2,Z
         *                                 CONDENSE TWO ITERATIONS OF ST  2,SUM
         *                                    AND B  OVER
         *                                 OMIT LTR, SINCE CC ALREADY SET BY AR
         *                                    INSTRUCTION
         *                                 OMIT BM  DONE, SINCE THIS CODE IS
         *                                    EXECUTED ONLY IF REGISTER 2
         *                                    CONTAINS A POSITIVE NUMBER
         LOC2      ST      2,SUM
         *                                 OMIT B OVER SINCE OVER IS NEXT
         *                                    STATEMENT
         *                                 OMIT A  7, LISTVAL AND ST  7,FINAL
         *                                    SINCE NOT EVER EXECUTED
         OVER      ...                     OMIT B  OVER, SINCE OVER IS NEXT ANYWAY
```

5.7 Rewrite the following instructions using decimal format and extended mnenomic format.

    (a)   BC   B'1011',THERE   (c)   BC   B'1000',THERE

    (b)   BC   B'1111',THERE   (d)   BC   B'0111',THERE

		Decimal		*Extended*	
(a)	BC	11,THERE	BNM	THERE	(or BNL)
(b)	BC	15,THERE	B	THERE	
(c)	BC	8,THERE	BE	THERE	(or BZ)
(d)	BC	7,THERE	BNZ	THERE	(or BNE)

5.8 Criticize the style in the following code:

    (a)   A   2,SUM   (b)   C   2,TUE
           BNE   THERE   BNZ   THERE

    Use BNZ in (a) and BNE in (b).

5.9 State what is accomplished by the following code, or write high-level language statements to accomplish the same results.

```
              L     3,D
              M     2,C
              C     3,VALUE
              BNE   ELSE
     THEN     L     7,X
              A     7,Y
              S     7,=F'4'
              ST    7,W
              L     7,X
              S     7,Y
              ST    7,T
              B     OVER
     ELSE     L     7,X
              A     7,Y
              ST    7,W
     OVER     ...
```

```
if C * D = VALUE
   then begin
        W := X + Y - 4;
        T := X - Y
        end
   else W := X + Y
```

5.10 You have to set up an inventory system for a parts distributor. Set up the storage so that at PART you store the (fullword) part number, followed by QUAN, the (fullword) quantity on hand of that part. The inventory system should check the quantity on hand. If it is less than 100, branch to REORDER, where you will store the part number at GETMORE. If it is greater than 2000, go to REDUCE, where you will store the part number at SALEITEM for price reduction. After performing the calculations at REORDER and REDUCE, or if neither is done, the program should continue processing.

```
              L     2,QUAN
              C     2,=F'100'       COMPARE QUANTITY WITH 100
              BL    REORDER         IF < 100, ORDER
              C     2,=F'2000'      COMPARE QUANTITY WITH 2000
              BH    REDUCE          IF > 2000, REDUCE
              B     REST            CONTINUE PROCESSING
     REORDER  L     5,PART          STORE PART NUMBER
              ST    5,GETMORE
              B     REST            CONTINUE PROCESSING
     REDUCE   L     5,PART          STORE PART NUMBER
              ST    5,SALEITEM
     REST     ...
              ...
     PART     DC    F'2976'
     QUAN     DC    F'90'
     GETMORE  DS    F
     SALEITEM DS    F
```

In this program, the quantity, which is stored at QUAN, is compared to 100. It is less, so we branch to REORDER, where we store the number of PART at GETMORE, then branch to REST to continue the program. If the quantity had been 2001, we would not have branched to REORDER but would have checked the quantity against 2000 and branched to REDUCE. A number between 100 and 2000 inclusive would cause a branch to REST.

5.11 Given a number NUM, write code to see if it is evenly divisible by 2.

```
        L       5,NUM
        M       4,=F'1'         EXTEND THE SIGN
        D       4,=F'2'
        LTR     4,4             CHECK VALUE OF REM
        BNZ     NOTDIV          IF REM NOT EQUAL TO 0, NUM IS
*                                 NOT DIVISIBLE BY 2
```

5.12 What happens in the following code? Show what will end up in the registers.

```
        SR      2,2
        SR      3,3
        L       6,NUM
        A       6,=F'123'
        BC      B'0010',POS
        A       3,=F'1'
        B       NEXT
POS     A       2,=F'1'
NEXT    ...
        ...
NUM     DC      F'-302'
```

The first two instructions initialize registers 2 and 3 to zero for use as counters. Register 3 is the zero-or-negative number counter, while register 2 is the positive number counter. Register 6 gets −302, and 123 is added to it, leaving −179 in register 6. BC B'0010' says branch if the result of the arithmetic operation is positive, which it is not, so we don't branch. We add 1 to register 3, then branch to NEXT. At the end, register 6 contains −179, register 3 contains 1, and register 2 contains 0.

5.13 The following code automates a small banking system, adding in deposits and subtracting withdrawals. Modify the code so that it doesn't subtract the withdrawal from the balance if the withdrawal amount is greater than the balance.

```
        L       8,INITDEP
        S       8,WITHD1        TAKE OUT THE WITHDRAWAL
        BM      OVERDRAW        SEE IF OVERDRAWN
        A       8,DEP1
        A       8,DEP2
        S       8,WITHD2        DO IT AGAIN
        BM      OVERDRAW
        A       8,INTEREST
        ST      8,BAL
```

The following code has the appropriate modifications:

```
        L       8,INITDEP
        C       8,WITHD1        COMPARE BAL WITH WITHD1
        BL      OVERDRAW        IF BAL LESS, NOT OK
        S       8,WITHD1        TAKE OUT ONLY IF OK
        A       8,DEP1
        A       8,DEP2
        C       8,WITHD2        DO IT AGAIN
        BL      OVERDRAW
        S       8,WITHD2
        A       8,INTEREST
        ST      8,BAL
```

5.14 What is stored at ANS after execution of the following code?

```
        LH    5,A
        LH    6,C
        SR    5,6
        BNP   STANS
        STH   5,ANS
        B     DONE
STANS   AH    5,B
        STH   5,ANS
DONE    ...
        ...
A       DC    H'12'
B       DC    H'97'
C       DC    H'48'
ANS     DS    H
```

First, register 5 is loaded with 12 and register 6 is loaded with 48. We subtract the 48 in register 6 from the 12 in register 5, leaving −36 in register 5. Since the result of this last operation is not positive, we branch to STANS, where we add 97 to the −36 in register 5, leaving 61 in register 5, which we then store at ANS.

5.15 What is wrong with the following sets of instructions? Write a possible correction for each one.

(a)
```
    LA   4,50
    CR   4,NUM
    BC   B'0000',TOOBIG
```

(b)
```
    L    3,MULT
    M    2,LUNCH
    LTR  3,2
    BNP  MAKEPOS
```

(c)
```
    L    9,=F'60'
    A    9,SOMENUM
    BC   NOWHERE
```

(d)
```
    L    3,NUM
    C    3,F'2'
    BR   DONE
```

(e)
```
    L    3,TRUCKWT
    C    3,OVERWT
    BP   OVER
```

(f)
```
    L    2,ZEBRA
    A    2,HORSE
    BNE  MARE
```

(a) CR requires two registers as operands. In addition, B'0000' will never branch. This is legal, but is not likely to be what we want. Correction:

```
    LA   5,NUM
    LA   4,50
    CR   4,5
    BC   B'0010',TOOBIG
```

(b) The LTR 3,2 loaded whatever was in register 2 into register 3 and wiped out the result of our multiplication, which is probably not what we wanted. Correction:
```
    LTR  3,3
```

(c) BC needs a mask. Correction:
```
    BC   4,NOWHERE
```

(d) The literal is missing its equal sign. BR requires a register as its operand. Correction:

```
    L    3,NUM
    C    3,=F'2'
    B    DONE
```

(e) BP is an extended mnemonic used after arithmetic instructions. While this will work, it is bad style. We want BH here.

(f) BNE is an extended mnemonic after compare instructions. As in (e), this will work, but it is bad style. We want BNZ here.

CHAP. 5] COMPARE AND BRANCH INSTRUCTIONS

5.16 Write all the equivalent ways to branch to SECOND if and only if WORD1 > WORD2, where WORD1 and WORD2 are aligned full words and contain the following hexadecimal values:

        WORD1   345678912
        WORD2   123456789

Start with these two instructions:

    L   8,WORD1
    C   8,WORD2

(a) BC   B'0010',SECOND
(b) BC   2,SECOND
(c) BH   SECOND
(d) LA   9,SECOND
    BCR B'0010',9
(e) LA   9,SECOND
    BCR 2,9
(f) LA   9,SECOND
    BHR 9
(g) Note that instead of BH [part (c)] and BHR [part (f)], we could use BP and BPR, but it would be poor style.

5.17 Given a (fullword) number grade from 0 to 100, write the code to branch to a section of code to process the appropriate letter grade. The grading scale is as follows:

    A   90–100
    B   80–89
    C   70–79
    D   60–69
    F   0–59

```
        L     10,GRADE
        C     10,=F'90'
        BNL   A              90 AND ABOVE IS A
        C     10,=F'80'
        BNL   B              80 TO 89 IS B
        C     10,=F'70'
        BNL   C              70 TO 79 IS C
        C     10,=F'60'
        BNL   D              60 TO 69 IS D
F       ...                  IF WE GET HERE, GRADE IS F
        B     DONE
D       ...                  GRADE IS D
        B     DONE
C       ...                  GRADE IS C
        B     DONE
B       ...                  GRADE IS B
        B     DONE
A       ...                  GRADE IS A
DONE    ...
GRADE   DC    F'83'
```

    The code here is simply a series of tests and branches. The branches cause us to leave the main body of code if we have found our grade, so the later comparisons are not encountered and do not produce multiple answers. For example, the sample grade assigned to GRADE was 83. In this case, the first comparison fails: 83 is lower than 90. At the second comparison, where 83 is compared with 80, we branch to B. At B, we do some processing to indicate the grade, printing a message or doing some assignment of a letter to a field associated with GRADE.

The important thing to remember is not to try to do the actual processing within the main body of code, as this produces many more branches and is thus less efficient. As an example, here is a short segment of this program done very poorly:

```
            L       10,GRADE
            C       10,=F'90'
            BL      CHECKB
            ...                     PROCESS AN 'A'
            B       DONE
CHECKB      C       10,=F'80'
            BL      CHECKC
            ...                     PROCESS A 'B'
            B       DONE
CHECKC      ...
```

This code forces execution of several extra branches for each test, and it is harder to follow. For our 83, we would compare with 90 and branch to CHECKB, compare with 80 and succeed. Then we would process the grade in some way and branch to DONE. In the previous code, we fell through to the next section of code, instead of branching. It is easier to follow the code which simply falls through.

Supplementary Problems

5.18 Will the branch be performed in the following examples?

```
(a)         LA      11,25                   (d)         LA      10,9
            S       11,NEG20                            A       10,NUM8
            BC      B'1100',ERROR                       S       10,NUM9
            ...                                         LPR     9,10
NEG20       F'-20'                                      BC      5,ERROR
                                                        ...
                                            NUM8        DC      F'8'
                                            NUM9        DC      F'9'

(b)         L       9,PNUM                  (e)         L       9,=F'4349872'
            A       9,NNUM                              A       9,=F'3625460'
            M       8,NUMX                              BO      ERROR
            S       9,X
            BC      B'0100',NEXT            (f)         L       6,=F'72'
            ...                                         S       6,BIG
PNUM        DC      F'20'                               A       6,SMALL
NNUM        DC      F'-21'                              A       6,MED
NUMX        DC      F'-3'                               BP      MORE
X           DC      F'36'                               ...
                                            BIG         DC      F'2500'
(c)         LA      7,4                     MED         DC      F'100'
            M       6,=F'2'                 SMALL       DC      F'3'
            S       7,NUM
            BC      4,NEWLOC
            ...
NUM         DC      F'12'
```

(g)	L	7,NMB		(h)	L	8,B
	LTR	7,7			A	8,C
	BNZ	NEW			A	8,D
	...				A	8,E
NMB	DC	F'−8'			BNM	TOTALPOS
					...	
				B	DC	F'14'
				C	DC	F'−29'
				D	DC	F'18'
				E	DC	F'−13'

5.19 Is the branch performed in the following cases? Assume that register 5 holds decimal 184.

(a)	L	2,F	(d)		C	5,NUM2	(g)		L	4,A
	CR	5,2			BC	2,NEXT			CR	5,4
	BC	B'0111',NEXT			...				BE	NEXT
	...			NUM2	DC	F'111'			...	
F	DC	F'182'						A	DC	F'2'
(b)	L	8,G	(e)		L	7,NUM	(h)		L	10,B
	CR	5,8			CR	7,5			CR	5,10
	BC	B'0100',NEXT			BL	NEXT			BH	NEXT
	...				...				...	
G	DC	F'10'		NUM	DC	F'8'		B	DC	F'128'
(c)	C	5,NUM	(f)		L	4,A				
	BC	11,NEXT			CR	5,4				
	...				BH	NEXT				
NUM	DC	F'126'			...					
				A	DC	F'827'				

5.20 Simplify and thus improve the following portions of code, if possible, without changing the meaning.

(a)	BH	HERE	(b)	C	3,=F'0'	(c)	LNR	2,4
	B	THERE					LTR	2,2
HERE	...							

5.21 Criticize the style in the following code.

(a)	LTR	2,2	(b)	C	2=F'0'
	BNE	THERE		BNZ	THERE

5.22 State what is accomplished by the following code, or write high-level language statements to accomplish the same results.

```
            L     3,B
            M     2,C
            C     3,VALUE
            BL    ELSE
            L     7,X
            LCR   7,7
            C     7,Y
            BE    ELSE
   THEN     LPR   7,7
            S     7,Y
            ST    7,T
            B     OVER
   ELSE     L     7,X
            A     7,Y
            ST    7,W
   OVER     ...
```

5.23 A student claimed that LNR must yield a condition code of 1; a second student disagreed. Who is correct? Explain.

5.24 Write code to test whether the value in memory location X is odd or even.

5.25 Write a program to test which is the largest n for which $n!$ will fit (correctly) into a single general-purpose register. [For all $n > 0$, $n!$ means $n \times (n-1) \times (n-2) \times \cdots \times 1$.]

5.26 For each value of d from 1 to 9, determine the largest value of n for which $d \times 10^n$ will fit in one register (with the proper sign).

5.27 Write an assembly language translation for each of the following portions of high-level language code. Assume that all variables are fullword binary.

    (a) if $A > B$ then $Z := 4$;
           $Q := 1$

    (b) if $A > B$ then $Z := 4$
           else $Z := 3$;
           $Q := 1$

    (c) if $A >= B$ then begin
                $Z := 4$;
                $Y := 3$
           end;
           $Q := 1$

    (d) if $(A > B)$ and $(C >= D)$
         then $T := 2$;
         $Q := 1$

    (e) if $(A <= B)$ or $(C <> D)$ ($<>$ means not equal)
         then $T := 2$;
         $Q := 1$

5.28 Write assembly language instructions corresponding to each of the following sequences of high-level language statements. Assume that all variables are fullword binary.

    (a) if $A = B$ then $X := 1$;
         $Y := 7$

    (b) if $A = B$ then $X := 1$
           else $X := 2$;
         $Y := 7$

    (c) if $A = B$ then $X := 1$
           else if $C = D$ then $X := 2$;
         $Y := 7$

    (d) if $A = B$ then $X := 1$
           else if $C = D$ then $X := 2$
                else $X := 3$;
         $Y := 7$

    (e) if $A = B$ then begin
                $X := 1$;
                $Z := 8$;
                $T := 2$
         if $A = B$ then end
            else if $C = D$ then $X := 2$;
         $Y := 7$

    (f) if $A > B$ then $X := A - B$
           else $X := B - A$;
         $Y := 7$

    (g) if $A < B$ then $X := A - B$
           else $X := B - A$;
         $Y := 7$

5.29 At STUD, we have stored a student's ID number (a full word) and at SCORE we have stored the student's test score (also a full word). Write the code that will check to see if the test score is in the "C" range, which is from 70 to 79. If it is, print the student's ID number, using whatever method of printing you have been taught.

5.30 Modify Problem 5.11 so that it tests whether NUM is divisible by 3. Modify the problem again so that it tests whether NUM is divisible by 5. *Hint*: Is there much change?

5.31 You run a truck weighing station. Given the total weight of all the cartons on a truck and the weight of the truck alone, determine whether the truck can cross the bridge. The bridge can hold 27,832 pounds. There are several possibilities to consider in the code: (1) The truck can be completely overweight (too heavy even empty), (2) it can be fine as is, or (3) it can be required to unload some of its cartons. Store a code number (1, 2, 3) at fullword location WTCHK to indicate which case has been encountered. If the truck must unload some cartons, also store the amount of the overweight at fullword location OVERWT.

5.32 Suppose that you have read into CODE either a 1 or a 2. You have also read a number into MONEY. Write the code to do the following: If CODE is 1, add the MONEY amount to TOTAL. If CODE is 2, subtract the MONEY amount from TOTAL.

5.33 Given a fullword number NUMERO, check to see whether it is positive, negative, or zero. There are three variables: POSCT, NEGCT, and ZEROCT. Add one to the variable appropriate to the sign of NUMERO.

5.34 Given a fullword number NUMERO, check to see if it is positive or negative. There are two variables: POSCT and NEGCT. Add 1 to the variable appropriate to the sign of NUMERO. Do not count zeros! This is not the same problem as Problem 5.33.

5.35 Given the following Pascal code, write an equivalent section of assembly language code.

```
var X,Y,Z: integer;
...
    X := 30;
    Y := X*X;
    if X + 2 >= 43
        then Z := X
        else Z := Y
```

5.36 Translate the following high-level language instructions into assembly language instructions. Assume that all variables are fullword binary.

(a) if (A > B) and (A > C)
    then Q := 1;
  D := T

(b) if (A > B) or (A > C)
    then Q := Q + 2;
  D := T

(c) if (A = B) and (C = D)
    then Q := C
    else if Z = 2
        then Z := 3
        else Y := 2;
  D := T

5.37 What possible values may the condition code be set to by (a) LPR? (b) LNR? (c) LCR?

5.38 Simplify:

(a) C   2,TEMP
     BC 15,THERE

(b) AR 2,10
     LTR 2,2
     BC   7,OUT

(c) S   5,NUM
     BP   NEXT
     BM OUT
     BZ   ZERO
  NEXT ...

(d) C   2,ALPHA
     BC B'0100',PLACE
     BC 4,NEXT
     BM OVER

(e) LH   5,SUM
     MR   4,5
     LTR 5,5
     BM   OUCH

(f) LPR 2,7
     BM   OUCH

(g) LNR 2,2
     BO   OUCH

Chapter 6

Arrays and Looping

6.1 Introduction

The code which we have written so far has not been as powerful as it might be. We want to be able to reuse a set of instructions several times to perform the same task over and over—in other words, set up a loop. For example, we want to be able to compare one item with many items in a list, add up numbers in a list, or sort a list of items. In order to expand our programs so that they can accomplish these tasks, we must be able to set up lists, also called *arrays*, and to process arrays by doing address modification and looping.

6.2 The BCT and BCTR Instructions

There are several methods of looping in assembly language. One which is fairly compact and easy to implement uses the Branch on Count (BCT) instruction. If we know how many times we want to repeat a loop, we can use the BCT instruction to count the number of times we repeat the loop.

The BCT instruction is an RX instruction, where the first operand is a register that is loaded with a value equal to the number of times we wish to execute the loop. This counter register is automatically decremented by 1 each time the BCT instruction is executed. The second operand (usually a label) is the location we branch to whenever the new value in the counter register is nonzero. In other words, the BCT instruction counts backward. When the counter register has been decremented to zero, we fall out of the loop. *Note*: If the counter register is initialized to zero or to a negative number, the value will move away from zero, probably resulting in an infinite loop. To summarize, BCT performs the following operations, in this order:

1. Decrements by 1
2. Compares with zero
3. Branches (or does not)

The following code shows the format of a loop using BCT:

```
        LA    5,3           INITIALIZE THE COUNTER TO 3
LOOP    ...
        ...
        BCT   5,LOOP        DECREMENT THE COUNTER. IF COUNTER IS THEN
*                           NONZERO, BRANCH TO LOOP
```

This skeletal loop is equivalent to the following code without BCT:

```
        LA    5,3           INITIALIZE THE COUNTER TO 3
LOOP    ...
        ...
        S     5,=F'1'       DECREMENT THE COUNTER
        BNZ   LOOP          IF IT IS NONZERO, BRANCH TO LOOP
```

Note that the decision on whether or not to branch is done after decrementing.

EXAMPLE 6.1

Suppose that we want to divide 17 by 6 and print the quotient including three digits to the right of the decimal point. With fullword numbers, we cannot produce actual decimal places, but we can generate individual digits of the answer one at a time, by setting up a loop.

Consider the process by which we divide. After we calculate the quotient, we multiply the remainder by 10 and divide it by the divisor to get each decimal place of the answer:

$$\begin{array}{r} 2.833 \\ 6\overline{)17.000} \\ 12 \\ \overline{50} \\ 48 \\ \overline{20} \\ 18 \\ \overline{2} \end{array}$$

In assembly language, we would do this as follows:

```
        LA    9,4           LOOP COUNTER
        L     5,NUM
        M     4,=F'1'       EXTEND THE SIGN
TOP     D     4,DIV         QUOTIENT IN 5, REMAINDER IN 4
        ...
(print contents of register 5 in some manner)
        ...
        LR    5,4           SHIFT REMAINDER TO REGISTER 5
        M     4,=F'10'
        BCT   9,TOP         GO BACK AND DO IT AGAIN
        ...
NUM     DC    F'17'
DIV     DC    F'6'
```

Outside the loop, we set up the counter for the BCT, and then prepare to calculate the quotient and the remainder. The actual division to produce all four digits of the answer is done in the loop, which is why we want to execute the loop four times. Each time through the loop, we do the same thing: divide the value in register 5 by DIV, print the result (by whatever method is available), move the remainder to register 5, and multiply it by 10 to continue the division. The first time through the loop, we divide the number in register 5 by DIV and get a quotient (2) in register 5 and a remainder (5) in register 4. Then we load the value from register 4 into register 5, and multiply the even-odd pair by 10 (why don't we also have to multiply by 1?). This gives us 50 in register 5. Then we encounter the BCT instruction, which causes the value in register 9 to be decremented to 3. Since this is nonzero, we branch to TOP and continue the process. Dividing 50 by 6 leaves a quotient of 8, which we print as the first decimal place, and a remainder of 2, which we shift to register 5 and multiply by 10, leaving 20 in register 5. The BCT decrements register 9 to 2. Since 2 is not zero, we branch to TOP. There we divide 20 by 6, placing a quotient of 3 in register 5 and a remainder of 2 in register 4. After we print the 3 as the second decimal place, shift the 2 to register 5, and multiply it by 10, the BCT decrements register 9 to 1. This is still nonzero, so we again branch to TOP. We repeat the exact same procedure as last time (with the same values), calculating and printing another 3 as the third decimal place. This time, when we encounter the BCT, it decrements register 9 to 0. This value causes us to fall out of the loop.

EXAMPLE 6.2

Suppose that we want to sum the numbers from 1 to 50; that is, in Pascal,

```
SUM := 0;
for I := 1 to 50 do
    SUM := SUM + I
```

Again we can use a BCT to control the loop. Here is the assembly language code to solve the problem:

```
              LA    8,50          LOOP COUNTER
              SR    5,5           SUM := 0
              LA    7,1           FIRST VALUE TO SUM (I := 1)
      TOP     AR    5,7           SUM := SUM + I
              LA    7,1(0,7)      I := I + 1
              BCT   8,TOP         LOOP BACK TO CONTINUE
              ST    5,SUM
```

In this example, register 7 contains the consecutive values from 1 to 50 as we loop through the code. Each value is then added into register 5, which holds the sum as it is accumulated.

This code is quite adequate. However, the order in which we process the values makes no difference in this case, so we can take advantage of the fact that register 8 contains the values from 50 to 1, in that order, and use the following, more efficient section of code:

```
              LA    8,50          LOOP COUNTER
              SR    5,5           SUM := 0
      TOP     AR    5,8           SUM := SUM + I
              BCT   8,TOP         LOOP BACK TO CONTINUE
              ST    5,SUM
```

Here register 8 does double duty, holding the values of I, from 50 to 1, at the same time that it controls the loop as a counter.

We can also put the address of the destination of the branch into a register. If we do this, we must use the BCTR instruction—Branch on Count to Register—which has the RR format. R1 is the counter and R2 holds the address of the destination of the branch. If reg2 is 0 (for example, BCTR 5,0), no branch occurs, no matter what register 5 contains. The use of 0 as the second operand in this instruction is an efficient way to decrement a register by 1.

EXAMPLE 6.3

Sum the numbers from 1 to 50 using BCTR.

```
              LA    7,TOP         PUT ADDRESS OF TOP INTO REGISTER 7
              LA    8,50          LOOP COUNTER
              SR    5,5           SUM := 0
      TOP     AR    5,8           SUM := SUM + I
              BCTR  8,7           LOOP BACK TO CONTINUE
              ST    5,SUM
```

Each time the BCTR instruction is executed, it decrements register 8 by 1 and, if the result is nonzero, causes a branch to the address in register 7, which is the address of TOP.

There are several limitations on the BCT instruction. First, it always decrements by 1 each time through the loop. If we want to count by something other than 1, we must either change the value of the counter register again within the loop, or use another type of instruction to do the work.

EXAMPLE 6.4

Sum the even numbers from 0 to 50, counting by 2 and using BCT.

```
              LA    8,50          INITIALIZE THE COUNTER
              SR    5,5           CLEAR REGISTER 5 FOR SUM
      TOP     AR    5,8           ADD AN EVEN NUMBER TO THE SUM
              BCTR  8,0           DECREMENT COUNTER BY 1 WITHOUT BRANCHING
              BCT   8,TOP         DECREMENT COUNTER BY 1 MORE AND BRANCH TO TOP
*                                   IF NONZERO
```

In this example, we go through the loop 25 times and add only the even numbers. We initialize register 8 to 50; after adding the number 50 into the sum, we decrement register 8 twice: The BCTR instruction reduces the contents to 49, and the BCT then reduces it to 48. We branch back to TOP, where we add in the 48 and continue the process until we have decremented register 8 to 0. The BCTR instruction thus allows us to decrement the counter register by more than 1. We must be careful using this technique, however. If the counter register becomes 0 or negative after the BCTR instruction, as it would if register 8 were initialized to 51 rather than 50, the BCT would decrement the register below 0 and this would become an infinite loop. The solved problems suggest several ways to prevent this from happening.

The second problem with the BCT instruction is that it requires us to count downward rather than upward. This problem can be resolved only by using another looping instruction, such as one of the instructions discussed in Sec. 6.5.

6.3 Arrays

An array is set up in assembly language by joining together several DC statements with a label (typically) on only the first item. An array of five full words (each 4 bytes long) could be declared and initialized as follows:

```
NUMS      DC      F'10'
          DC      F'20'
          DC      F'30'
          DC      F'40'
          DC      F'50'
```

The elements are addressed by their displacements from the beginning of the array. Thus the 10 is at location NUMS, the 20 at location NUMS+4, the 30 at NUMS+8, the 40 at NUMS+12, and the 50 at NUMS+16.

An array can also be declared and initialized on one line:

```
NUMS      DC      F'10,20,30,40,50'
```

This declaration is exactly the same as the one above.

Storage can be reserved for an array using a DS statement, as follows:

```
NUMS      DS      25F
```

This statement reserves 25 consecutive full words at location NUMS, but does not initialize them. Note, however, that the declaration

```
NUMS      DC      3F'5,7'
```

reserves six full words, and initializes them to 5, 7, 5, 7, 5, and 7, respectively.

Figure 6-1 shows how the values in array NUMS are stored. Notice that element 1 is at a displacement of 0 from NUMS, at address NUMS+0, while element 2 is at NUMS+4, etc.

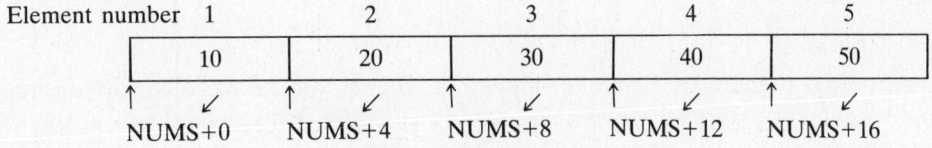

Fig. 6-1 Array NUMS.

The address of the *n*th element of an array is an important quantity. To translate an element of an array from a high-level language into assembly language, one needs to calculate the displacement of the element from the beginning of the array. One easy way is to multiply the number of elements *before* the element in question by the number of bytes per element. One can also calculate the displacement mathematically, as follows. The displacement of the nth element of a one-dimensional array is given by

$$(n - \text{LB}) * \text{ESIZE}$$

where LB stands for lower bound (the subscript of the first element in the array in the high-level language) and ESIZE is the number of bytes per element. For a fullword array starting with element 1, this simplifies to $4(n - 1)$.

EXAMPLE 6.5

Assume that you are given the Pascal declaration

    var   A: array[1..10] of integer

and the corresponding assembly language declaration

    A   DS   10F

(a) Write the assembly language instructions corresponding to the Pascal statement

    X := A[7]

Since $n = 7$, LB $= 1$, and ESIZE $= 4$, the displacement is $(7 - 1) * 4 = 24$. Or, since six elements have been skipped, at 4 bytes each, the displacement is 24 bytes. The assembly language instructions are

    L   2,A+24
    ST   2,X

(b) Write the high-level language statement corresponding to

    L   7,A+16
    ST   7,X

The displacement of 16 bytes means that we have skipped four fullword elements. The element in question must then be A[5]. Thus the Pascal statement is

    X := A[5]

For a two-dimensional array, Pascal and PL/1 store the elements a row at a time. The displacement of the (i, j)th element is given by

$$((i - \text{L1}) * \text{R2} + (j - \text{L2})) * \text{ESIZE}$$

where L1 is the lower bound in the first dimension, L2 is the lower bound in the second dimension, and R2 is the range of the second dimension (upper bound $-$ lower bound $+$ 1). For a fullword array with rows 1 to 3 and columns 1 to 5, this simplifies to $((i - 1) * 5 + (j - 1)) * 4$. For example, the element marked with an x in the 3×5 array shown below has a displacement $4(1 \times 5 + 2) = 28$ bytes from the first element.

Again, counting the number of elements skipped is an easy way to calculate the desired displacement. For the element marked x, seven elements (five in the first row and two in the second) are skipped, corresponding to 28 bytes.

EXAMPLE 6.6

Given the Pascal declaration

    var   ARR: array[1..3,1..5] of integer

CHAP. 6]   ARRAYS AND LOOPING   111

and the corresponding assembly language declaration

$$\text{ARR} \quad \text{DS} \quad 15\text{F}$$

write the assembly language instructions corresponding to the Pascal statement

$$X := A[3,4]$$

Assume that the data type integer in a Pascal implementation uses fullword memory locations. The displacement of ARR[3,4] from ARR[1,1] is 52 bytes, corresponding to 13 elements skipped (see the o's in the table below).

o	o	o	o	o
o	o	o	o	o
o	o	o	x	

Alternatively, we can solve using the equation, with

$$i = 3 \quad j = 4 \quad L1 = 1 \quad L2 = 1 \quad R2 = 5 - 1 + 1 = 5 \quad \text{ESIZE} = 4$$

Thus the displacement is $((3-1) * (5) + (4-1)) * 4 = 52$:

$$\text{L} \quad 3,\text{ARR}+52$$
$$\text{ST} \quad 3,\text{X}$$

It is usually easier to determine the number of elements skipped.

Like structures in PL/1 or records in Pascal or COBOL, arrays in assembly language may be heterogeneous. A heterogeneous array is a list of records consisting of different data types. For an example of this, see Sec. 7.6.

While it is possible to address elements in an array by explicitly specifying their displacement at each use, it is awkward and time-consuming, especially for large arrays. Suppose we wanted to add up the five numbers in the NUMS array shown in Fig. 6-1. To address the elements by their displacements, we would have to use something like the following series of instructions:

```
        L       5,NUMS
        A       5,NUMS+4
        A       5,NUMS+8
        A       5,NUMS+12
        A       5,NUMS+16
```

Now suppose that the array contained 500 numbers instead of only five. Clearly this is not a good method to use to solve the problem of adding 500 numbers. Instead, we would like to take advantage of the fact that each element in an array occupies a constant number of bytes (in array NUMS, 4 bytes). Therefore, the displacement of each consecutive element in an array differs from the displacement of the previous element by that number of bytes (in array NUMS, the second element has a displacement of 4 from NUMS, the third element has a displacement of 8 from NUMS). As we go through a loop, we keep track of the address of the current element of the array. Then we can easily modify this address to refer to the next element of the array. This is called address modification.

6.4 Address Modification

Address modification means changing the address referred to in an instruction. If we know that we want to sum 100 full words starting at NUMS, we can modify or change the address that the add instruction calculates, so that it first addresses NUMS, then NUMS+4, then NUMS+8, then NUMS+12, etc., up to NUMS+396, which is the location of the hundredth number. This address modification can be done in two ways. One is by modifying an index register, and the other is by modifying a base register.

Index Register Modification (with an Implied Base Register)

An index register holds the number of bytes that we must add to the base address of the array to get the address of the element we are interested in. The method which is easiest to conceptualize uses an index register and an implied base register. This means that we take advantage of the fact that the addresses of all symbolic variables in the program are calculated from the address in the base register for the entire program. Suppose that we begin by saying

```
            BALR   12,0
            USING  *,12
```

Then, if we write

```
            L      3,NUMS
```

the assembler will provide the base register (12) and the displacement of NUMS from the address in register 12. It will assume that there is no index register, and will use 0 in the machine language code for this instruction. However, we may, in addition, specify an index register. The format is

```
            L      3,NUMS(5)
```

In this load instruction, NUMS is the name of the array and 5 is the index register. The base register and the displacement of NUMS from the base address are obtained from the location of NUMS, already calculated, just as they would be if we had simply written L   3,NUMS. The index register, supplied in the instruction, is assembled into the machine instruction. This instruction is the equivalent of writing

```
            L      3,"displacement of NUMS"(5,12)
```

Remember from Chap. 4 that the effective address is given by the sum of the following:

Base register contents

Index register contents

Displacement

(If the base and/or index register is given as 0, the value 0 is added, not the contents of register 0.)

We can use the index register as a means of processing an array. To add 100 full words starting at location NUMS, we would first put 0 into a register, and then use that register as the index register for the add instruction.

```
            SR     5,5
            A      3,NUMS(5)
```

Here, register 5 is being initialized and then used in the add instruction as the index register for the array NUMS. When register 5 contains 0, the add instruction refers to the value at the address of NUMS+0—that is, the value at NUMS. We can refer to the number at NUMS+4 by adding 4 to the contents of register 5:

```
            LA     5,4(0,5)     REGISTER 5 IS THE BASE REGISTER
*                               FOR THIS INSTRUCTION
```

A reminder: This instruction says to take the contents of base register 5, add 4 to it, and store the result in register 5. If register 5 contains 0 before this instruction, then after this instruction has been executed, register 5 will contain 4.

If we continue to add 4 to the contents of register 5, register 5 will contain consecutively 8, 12, etc. Each time we thus increment the value in register 5, we have the means of accessing the value of another number in the NUMS array. We can use this result to help in our summing. If we reuse the add instruction, A 3,NUMS(5), with the new contents of register 5, we will be addressing consecutive elements in array NUMS. Each time through the loop we increment the index register by the size of one element in the array.

EXAMPLE 6.7

Let's see how to add together three full words stored at locations NUMS, NUMS+4, and NUMS+8 by changing an index register.

```
        SR    3,3              CLEAR REGISTER 3 FOR SUM
        SR    5,5              PUT 0 INTO INDEX REGISTER 5
        A     3,NUMS(5)        ADD VALUE AT NUMS+0 INTO REGISTER 3
        LA    5,4(0,5)         INCREMENT INDEX REGISTER
        A     3,NUMS(5)        ADD CONTENTS OF LOCATION NUMS+4 INTO REG 3
        LA    5,4(0,5)         INCREMENT INDEX REGISTER
        A     3,NUMS(5)        ADD CONTENTS OF LOCATION NUMS+8 INTO REG 3
        ST    3,SUM            STORE THE RESULT
```

This works, but actually is less efficient than the following:

```
        L     3,NUMS
        A     3,NUMS+4
        A     3,NUMS+8
```

In addition, the first piece of code would take more time to write. So what have we saved? If you look at the last five instructions in the code in Example 6.7, you can see that two instructions are repeated:

```
        LA    5,4(0,5)
        A     3,NUMS(5)
```

To add more numbers, we would repeat these two instructions for each new number. Therefore, if we could set up a loop to repeat these two instructions, we could save ourselves a lot of work. In fact, we can use a branch instruction to set up the loop.

EXAMPLE 6.8

Here we will modify Example 6.7 by using an unconditional branch to set up a loop which modifies an index register. The code is still incomplete (you should easily be able to tell what is wrong).

```
        SR    3,3              CLEAR REGISTER 3 FOR SUM
        SR    5,5              ZERO OUT REGISTER 5 FOR INDEX REGISTER
LOOP    A     3,NUMS(5)        ADD A NUMBER INTO THE SUM
        LA    5,4(0,5)         INCREMENT THE INDEX REGISTER
        B     LOOP             RETURN TO LOOP TO ADD IN ANOTHER NUMBER
        ST    3,SUM            STORE THE RESULT
```

This example uses an unconditional branch which has a major flaw—it sets up an infinite loop.

In this example, register 5 is initially set to 0. Then the first number is added into register 3 from the address in NUMS(5), which is the address of NUMS plus the contents of register 5, which is now 0, so the number is added from NUMS+0 or NUMS. Then register 5 is incremented by 4, so that it contains 4. At the top of the loop, the number from NUMS+4 is added into register 3. We increment register 5 to 8, branch back to add in the number from NUMS+8, and then increment register 5 to 12. Unfortunately, we will continue doing this forever, or until we are kicked off the machine for using too much time.

Despite the flaw in this code that prevents ever reaching the ST 3,SUM statement, note that outside the loop is the proper place to store the sum which is computed within a loop. To store the value each time through the loop would be extremely wasteful.

We must add to this section of code one of several available ways to exit from the loop. One way is to calculate the final value which the index register should hold, then compare the contents of the index register with the final value each time through the loop. For example, if we want to add up the three full words at NUMS, then the final value in the index register before the branch is last executed will be 12. Figure 6-2 shows why.

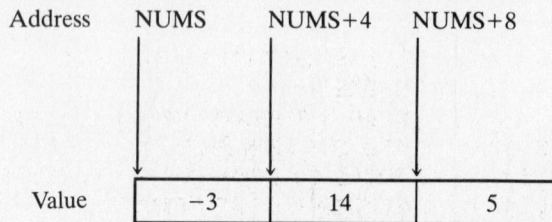

Fig. 6-2 View of storage showing addresses in the array NUMS.

After we have added the third number and incremented the index register the third time, the index register contains 12, which is the number of bytes from NUMS to next address in storage. The value 12 is the one which we will use as the limit. When the current value in the index register is less than 12, we want to branch back to the top of the loop; when the current value in the index register is equal to 12, we don't want to branch. Example 6.9 shows how we can use this idea to get rid of the infinite loop in Example 6.8.

EXAMPLE 6.9

The following code demonstrates looping by changing an index register (complete):

```
         SR    3,3           CLEAR REGISTER 3 FOR SUM
         SR    5,5           REGISTER 5 IS THE INDEX REGISTER
LOOP     A     3,NUMS(5)     ADD A NUMBER TO THE SUM
         LA    5,4(0,5)      INCREMENT THE INDEX REGISTER
         C     5,=F'12'      COMPARE INDEX VALUE WITH THE FINAL
*                              VALUE IT SHOULD HOLD
         BL    LOOP          IF REGISTER 5 IS LOW, BRANCH TO LOOP
         ST    3,SUM         STORE THE RESULT
```

We can also do the test slightly differently. Rather than compare the index with the first value we don't want to use, we can compare it with the last value we do want to use. Then the test at the bottom of the loop will be to see whether the index value currently calculated is less than or equal to the limit value. If it is less than or equal to the limit (not higher than the limit), we will branch; if it is higher, we will fall out of the loop (proceed to the next statement after the branch statement). Example 6.10 shows this variation.

EXAMPLE 6.10

The following code demonstrates looping by changing an index register—second version (complete):

```
         SR    3,3           CLEAR REGISTER 3 FOR SUM
         SR    5,5           ZERO OUT REGISTER 5 FOR INDEX REGISTER
LOOP     A     3,NUMS(5)     ADD A NUMBER TO THE SUM
         LA    5,4(0,5)      INCREMENT THE INDEX REGISTER
         C     5,=F'8'       COMPARE INDEX VALUE WITH THE LIMIT VALUE
         BNH   LOOP          IF REGISTER 5 IS NOT HIGH, BRANCH TO LOOP
         ST    3,SUM         STORE THE RESULT
```

Another method is to set up a counter in the loop. We initialize the counter to zero. Each time through the loop, we add 1 to the counter. We can then test the value of the counter. If we want to add three numbers, for example, we want to branch to the top of the loop if the counter is less than 3. A simple way to set up a counter is to use a register as a counter register and increment that register each time through the loop. The incrementing may be done with a load address statement.

EXAMPLE 6.11

The following code demonstrates looping by modifying an index register and using a counter:

```
            SR    3,3           CLEAR REGISTER 3 FOR SUM
            SR    2,2           COUNTER
            SR    5,5           ZERO OUT REGISTER 5 FOR INDEX REGISTER
LOOP        A     3,NUMS(5)     ADD IN THE NUMBER
            LA    5,4(0,5)      INCREMENT THE INDEX REGISTER
            LA    2,1(0,2)      INCREMENT THE COUNTER
            C     2,=F'3'       COMPARE THE COUNTER WITH THE FINAL VALUE
            BL    LOOP          BRANCH AS LONG AS COUNTER IS LOW
            ST    3,SUM         STORE THE RESULT
```

In this example, we add the number at location NUMS into the sum. Then we increment the index register to 4 to prepare for the next pass through the loop. Next, we count the number of times we have gone through the loop by incrementing the value of the counter to 1, and then test the value of the counter. Register 2 (the counter) holds the value 1, so we branch to the top of the loop and add in the number at NUMS+4. We increment the index register to contain 8; then we increment the counter to 2, to indicate that we have added in two numbers. Again we test the value of the counter. Register 2 contains 2, which is less than 3, so we branch again and add the value at NUMS+8 into the sum. Again we increment the index register to 12 and increment the counter to 3, indicating that we have added in three numbers. This time, however, when we test the value of the counter, we see that it is no longer less than 3. We have added in all three numbers, so we do not branch, but instead fall out of the loop.

Of course, this is very close to the action of the BCT instruction, which we can use for the same purpose (see Example 6.12).

EXAMPLE 6.12

Sum the three numbers from array NUMS using BCT (and an index register):

```
            LA    2,3           INITIALIZE THE COUNTER REGISTER
            SR    5,5           ZERO OUT THE INDEX REGISTER
            SR    3,3           CLEAR REGISTER 3 FOR SUM
LOOP        A     3,NUMS(5)     ADD A NUMBER INTO SUM
            LA    5,4(0,5)      INCREMENT THE INDEX REGISTER
            BCT   2,LOOP        DECREMENT REGISTER 2; IF THE RESULT IS
*                                 NONZERO, BRANCH TO LOOP
            ST    3,SUM         STORE THE RESULT
```

The BCT instruction performs the actions of counting, comparing, and branching, which were done by separate instructions in Example 6.11. Otherwise, the action of this loop is the same as in the preceding example.

Let's contrast the difference between the displacement of NUMS and the value in the index register. The displacement of NUMS is the number of bytes between the base address and the starting address of array NUMS. The value in the index register is the difference in bytes between the current element in array NUMS and the starting address of array NUMS (see Fig. 6-3).

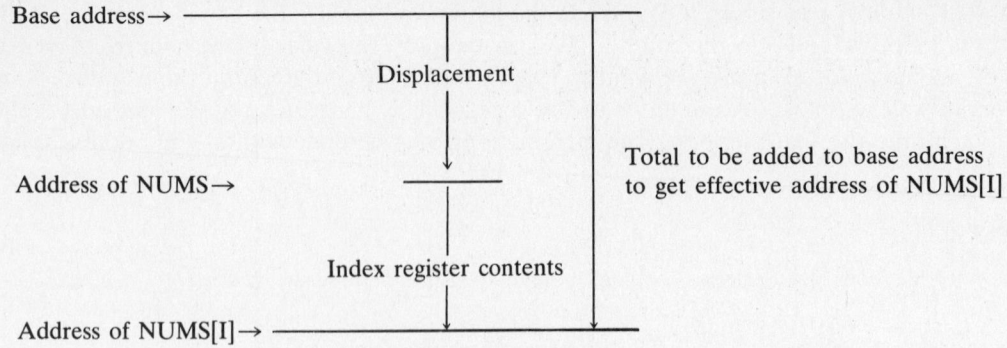

Fig. 6-3 Address of symbolic element NUMS[I].

Using an Index Register with an Explicit Base Register

There is another way to use an index register that is a bit more complex. This method is to use an index register with an explicit base register. In this technique, we do not simply use the name of the array and allow the assembler to provide the base register and displacement. Instead, we explicitly set up a base register to hold the address of the first element in the array. We also use an index register to help pinpoint the current element. Although there is a base address for the entire program, it is often useful to calculate addresses from some position farther down in the program. For example, you might give directions to someone in one of two ways: (1) drive south for 43 blocks, or (2) drive south to 2 blocks past the railroad tracks (which happen to be 41 blocks from here).

EXAMPLE 6.13

Let's again add together the three full words in the NUMS array, this time using an index register with an explicit base register.

```
         LA    5,NUMS         REGISTER 5 IS THE BASE REGISTER
         SR    3,3            ZERO OUT THE SUM
         SR    9,9            ZERO OUT THE INDEX REGISTER
LOOP     A     3,0(9,5)       ADD IN THE NUMBER AT THE ADDRESS
*                             CALCULATED BY ADDING TOGETHER THE
*                             CONTENTS OF THE BASE REGISTER (5)
*                             AND THE INDEX REGISTER (9)
         LA    9,4(0,9)       INCREMENT THE INDEX REGISTER
         C     9,=F'8'        COMPARE THE CONTENTS OF THE INDEX
*                             REGISTER WITH THE FINAL VALUE
         BNH   LOOP           BRANCH IF INDEX REGISTER IS NOT HIGH
         ST    3,SUM          STORE THE RESULT
```

In this example, we use both an explicit base register and an index register. This complicates the example a bit, because we use two registers. Register 5 is set up as the base register; it always contains the address of NUMS. Register 9, the index register, at any given moment contains the difference in bytes between the current array element and the base address. The index register is incremented each time through the loop. When it contains 0, the add instruction takes the value from location NUMS+0—that is, NUMS. Then the index register contains 4, and the add instruction takes a value from location NUMS+4. After the next increment, the index register contains 8, and we add from location NUMS+8. At that point, the index register is incremented to contain 12. This time the comparison shows the index register to be high, and we do not branch back to the top of the loop.

Note that we use LA 9,4(0,9), with 9 in the position of the base register. This is because 9 is the base register for the LA instruction, even though it is the index register for the add instruction. A register can be used as both an index register and a base register in the same program. Alternatively, we could have written LA 9,4(9,0), which would produce the same result.

Base Register Modification

We can also process an array by modifying the contents of a base register. With this approach, the base register will be modified to hold the address of the current element each time through the loop.

To use a base register to add 100 full words starting at location NUMS, we would first put the address of NUMS into a register, and then use that register as the base register for the add instruction, in explicit notation:

```
        LA    5,NUMS
        A     3,0(0,5)
```

Here, register 5 is being initialized and then used in the add instruction as the base register for the array NUMS. We can refer to the number at NUMS+4 by adding 4 to the contents of register 5, just as we did when register 5 was used as an index register:

```
        LA    5,4(0,5)      REGISTER 5 IS THE BASE REGISTER
*                           FOR THIS INSTRUCTION
```

If register 5 contains the address of NUMS before this instruction, then after this instruction has been executed, register 5 will contain the address of NUMS+4—the address of the second number on the list. If we continue to add 4 to the contents of register 5, register 5 will contain consecutively the addresses NUMS+8, NUMS+12, etc. Each time we thus increment the address in register 5, we have the means of accessing the value of another number in the NUMS array. If we use the add instruction, A 3,0(0,5), in a loop, and increment the contents of register 5 by the value 4 each time, we will be addressing consecutive elements in array NUMS.

EXAMPLE 6.14

Let's modify Example 6.10 so that it uses only a base register.

```
        SR    3,3           CLEAR REGISTER 3 FOR SUM
        LA    5,NUMS        REGISTER 5 IS BASE REGISTER
LOOP    A     3,0(0,5)      ADD A NUMBER INTO THE SUM
        LA    5,4(0,5)      INCREMENT THE BASE REGISTER
        C     5,=A(NUMS+8)  COMPARE BASE ADDRESS WITH THE ADDRESS
*                           LITERAL, ADDRESS OF NUMS+8
        BNH   LOOP          IF REGISTER 5 IS NOT HIGH, BRANCH TO LOOP
        ST    3,SUM         STORE THE RESULT
```

In this example, register 5 is the base register, which contains, consecutively, the addresses of NUMS+0, NUMS+4, NUMS+8, and NUMS+12. The final value, the one which will cause us to terminate the loop, is the address of NUMS+12, the next address after the array in storage.

EXAMPLE 6.15

Let's rewrite Example 6.12 using only a base register.

```
        LA    2,3           INITIALIZE THE LOOP COUNTER REGISTER
        LA    5,NUMS        *REGISTER 5 IS BASE REGISTER
        SR    3,3           CLEAR REGISTER 3 FOR SUM
LOOP    A     3,0(0,5)      *ADD IN THE NUMBER
        LA    5,4(0,5)      INCREMENT THE BASE REGISTER
        BCT   2,LOOP        BRANCH AS LONG AS REGISTER 2 IS NONZERO
        ST    3,SUM         STORE THE RESULT
```

In this example, the only instructions which have changed are the ones which have been marked with an asterisk in the Comment field.

6.5 The BXLE and BXH Instructions

The BXLE (Branch on Index Register Low or Equal) and BXH (Branch on Index Register High) instructions solve both the problems raised by the BCT instruction. These instructions allow an increment of any value to be built into the looping instruction. They also allow us to count either upward or downward. BXLE and BXH differ only in the circumstances under which they branch.

The BXLE and BXH instructions have RS (register-storage) format. The formats are as follows:

Assembly language	BXLE	R1,R3	D2(B2)
Machine language	op code	R1 R3	B2 D2
	1 byte	1 byte	2 bytes

R1 is the index register. R3, if even, stands for an even-odd register pair. The three registers hold the values that control the operation of the loop. R1 is the index register—the register which is incremented at each execution of the loop. The even register of the even-odd register pair contains the increment; the odd register contains the final value against which the index register is compared. If R3 is specified as an odd register, it serves as both the increment and the final value. (For example, this could be used for decrementing by −4 to −4.) Operand 2 is the address to branch to when the index register value has not exceeded the final value.

The BXLE and BXH statements work as follows. All the registers have been initialized before the loop. When the BXLE (or BXH) instruction is encountered, the following things happen. First, the index register is incremented by the amount of the increment. Second, the index register is compared to the register holding the final value. Third,

For BXLE: If the index register is less than or equal to the final value, we branch to the address specified by the second operand.

For BXH: If the index register is higher than (but not equal to) the final value, we branch to the address specified by the second operand.

EXAMPLE 6.16

Sum the numbers from 0 to 20 that are divisible by 5.

```
            SR      4,4             INDEX
            LA      6,5             INCREMENT
            LA      7,20            LIMIT
*                                   THE ABOVE INSTRUCTIONS SET UP THE LOOP
            SR      3,3             SUM=0
TOP         AR      3,4             ADD IN THE NUMBER
            BXLE    4,6,TOP         INCREMENT AND BRANCH
            ST      3,SUM           STORE THE SUM
```

This is a simple example of BXLE. Since we want to use only the numbers between 0 and 20 that are divisible by 5, we would like to be able to increment by 5, and BXLE is most suitable for this. First, we set up the loop, initializing the index register to 0, the increment register to 5, and the limit register to 20. We zero out register 3 to use for the sum, then enter the loop. We add the first value in the index register into the sum; since it is 0, register 3 contains 0. Then we encounter the BXLE, which causes the contents of the increment register, register 6, to be added to the index register, register 4. This puts a 5 in register 4. Then the contents of the index register are compared with the contents of the limit register, register 7. Since 5 is less than 20, we branch to TOP. There, we again add the contents of the index register into the sum; this time, we add 5 into register 3. Again the BXLE causes the contents of 6 to be added to the index, register 4, and register 4 contains 10. This is the next number which is divisible by 5. Since 10 is less than 20, we branch to TOP, where the 10 is added into register 3, giving its contents the value 15. Then the BXLE causes another 5 to be added into register 4, which then contains 15. Since 15 is less than 20, we again branch and add the 15 into the sum, giving register 3 the value 30. Again, we increment the index register by the amount of the increment, giving register 4 the value 20; since this is equal to the value in the limit register, we again branch to TOP and add 20 into register 3, which then contains 50. At the BXLE, this time, the index register is incremented to 25, which is greater than the upper limit of 20, so we do not branch to TOP.

Now let's apply the BXLE instruction to array processing.

EXAMPLE 6.17

Suppose we have an array NUMS which contains 30 fullword numbers, and we want to compare each number in the array with 75. We will count the number of 75s we find. In order to process the array, we must use either an index register or a base register. We will first illustrate the use of BXLE with an index register for processing the array.

```
            SR      5,5             INDEX REGISTER
            LA      8,4             INCREMENT
            LA      9,116           UPPER LIMIT (120-BYTE ARRAY; LAST NUMBER WE
*                                       WANT IS AT NUMS+116)
            SR      2,2             COUNTER OF 75S
TOP         L       7,NUMS(5)       GET THE NUMBER TO COMPARE
            C       7,=F'75'        IS IT 75?
            BNE     NEXT            BRANCH IF NOT
            LA      2,1(0,2)        YES--COUNT IT
NEXT        BXLE    5,8,TOP         INCREMENT AND BRANCH
            ST      2,COUNT
            ...
NUMS        DC      F'3,89,...'
```

Register 8 is the increment register; it contains 4, which is the number of bytes in each array element. Register 9 contains the upper limit, 116. There are 30 numbers in the array, so the entire array occupies 120 bytes. Since the first number begins at NUMS+0, the last number begins at NUMS+116.

Each time through the loop, we will add the value of the increment—4—to register 5. Thus register 5 will consecutively contain the values 0, 4, 8, 12, . . . , 116. Each time through the loop, we will load a number into register 7 from the address indicated as NUMS(5), and then compare that number with 75. If the number is equal to 75, we count it and continue with the BXLE; otherwise we simply continue with the BXLE. When register 5 contains 0, we will load the number at NUMS+0; then the BXLE adds the contents of register 8 to register 5, incrementing register 5 to 4. The new index value is less than the limit value of 116, so we branch to TOP, load into register 7 the number at NUMS+4, and compare this number with 75. Again, the BXLE increments register 5 by adding to it the contents of register 8, giving register 5 the value 8; since 8 is less than 116, we branch. At TOP, we load into register 7 the value at NUMS+8. We continue this process until register 5 is incremented to 116. This time, we branch to TOP because the value in register 5 is equal to the upper limit. We load a final number into register 7 from NUMS+116, comparing the number in register 7 with 75, and then the BXLE increments register 5 to 120, causing us to fall out of the loop.

Here is an example showing the use of BXLE with an index and a base register for processing the array.

EXAMPLE 6.18

Revise Example 6.17 so that it uses a base register, together with an index register, for processing the array.

```
          LA    6,NUMS           BASE REGISTER
          SR    5,5              INDEX REGISTER
          LA    8,4              INCREMENT
          LA    9,116            UPPER LIMIT (120-BYTE ARRAY; LAST NUMBER WE
*                                    WANT IS AT NUMS+116)
          SR    2,2              COUNTER OF 75S
TOP       L     7,0(5,6)         GET THE NUMBER TO COMPARE
          C     7,=F'75'         IS IT 75?
          BNE   NEXT             BRANCH IF NOT
          LA    2,1(0,2)         YES--COUNT IT
NEXT      BXLE  5,8,TOP          INCREMENT AND BRANCH
          ST    2,COUNT
          ...
NUMS      DC    F'3,89,...'
```

The difference between this example and the preceding one is that register 6 is being used as a base register for the array. We do not specifically increment the base register each time through the loop. Instead, we use a combination of base register (6) and index register (5) to calculate the address of the current element in the NUMS array.

We can also use BXLE while processing the array by modifying the contents of a base register. When using instructions which do not contain an index register (see Chap. 8), it is necessary to use this method for processing an array.

EXAMPLE 6.19

Revise Example 6.17 so that it uses a base register (but no index register) for addressing the array

```
          LA    5,NUMS           BASE REGISTER FOR ARRAY
          LA    8,4              INCREMENT
          LA    9,NUMS+116       UPPER LIMIT (120-BYTE ARRAY; LAST
*                                    NUMBER WE WANT IS AT NUMS+116)
          SR    2,2              COUNTER OF 75S
TOP       L     7,0(0,5)         GET THE NUMBER TO COMPARE
          C     7,=F'75'         IS IT 75?
          BNE   NEXT             BRANCH IF NOT
          LA    2,1(0,2)         YES--COUNT IT
NEXT      BXLE  5,8,TOP
          ST    2,COUNT
          ...
NUMS      DC    F'3,89,...'
```

Note that register 5 holds the addresses of each of the array elements in turn, from the base address of the array (address of NUMS) to the limit address (address of NUMS+116), which is held in register 9. Also note that register 5 is referred to as the base register in the load instruction but as the index register in the BXLE instruction.

The BXH instruction differs from the BXLE instruction only in the condition under which we branch. This instruction causes a branch when the index register is higher than the limit register. Thus, in most cases, this instruction is used when decrementing.

EXAMPLE 6.20

We will set up a BXH loop to approximate the action of this PL/1 DO loop:

```
      SUM=0;
LOOP: DO I=N TO 50 BY -2;
          SUM=SUM+I;
      END LOOP;
```

This loop requires us to decrement from N to 50. The index will thus have to start at N; the increment value will be −2, and the final value will be either 48 or 49, depending on whether N is even or odd. (We want it to branch when the index is 50, so we set the limit to 49. BXH does not branch when the values are equal, as BXLE does.)

```
            SR      7,7             CLEAR REGISTER 7 FOR SUM
            L       6,N             INDEX REGISTER
            L       2,=F'-2'        INCREMENT (DECREMENT)
            LA      3,49            LIMIT VALUE
TOP         AR      7,6             ADD INDEX TO SUM
            BXH     6,2,TOP         DECREMENT AND BRANCH
            ST      7,SUM           STORE THE RESULT
```

Since we are decrementing from the larger to the smaller value, we initialize the index register to N. Each time we execute the BXH instruction, we add the increment to the index register. Since the increment is negative, this has the effect of decrementing the index register by 2. We branch to TOP as long as the index register contains a value higher than the limit. Thus we branch when register 6 contains $N, N-2, \ldots, 50$; however, we do not branch when register 6 contains 48 or 49. Note the difference in how to set the limit in a BXLE loop and a BXH loop.

This BXH loop differs from a Pascal FOR loop or a PL/1 DO loop in a significant way. In these high-level language loops, the test against the final value is done at the top of the loop rather than at the bottom. It is possible to be more accurate in representing a FOR loop or DO loop, as shown in Example 6.21.

EXAMPLE 6.21

Set up a BXH loop to accomplish the same action as this Pascal FOR loop:

```
SUM := 0;
for I := 1 to N do
    SUM := SUM + I
```

In order to simulate the FOR loop, we will use the BXH at the top of the loop. As is true of the FOR loop, if the index is higher than the final value, we will branch out of the loop. If the initial value is higher than the final value, we will never enter the loop at all. We will need an unconditional branch at the bottom of the loop to represent the automatic transfer back to the top of the loop in Pascal.

```
            SR      9,9             CLEAR REGISTER 9 FOR SUM
            SR      5,5             INDEX REGISTER--INITIAL VALUE OF ZERO
*                                   COMPENSATES FOR AUTOMATIC INCREMENT BY BXH
            LA      6,1             INCREMENT
            L       7,N             LIMIT
LOOP        BXH     5,6,OUT         INCREMENT AND TEST
            AR      9,5             ADD INDEX INTO SUM
            B       LOOP            AUTOMATICALLY BRANCH BACK
OUT         ST      9,SUM
```

This loop does exactly what the equivalent Pascal loop did. In Pascal, as in PL/1 and other languages (but not in FORTRAN), the first time we encounter a loop header, the index is given the initial value; then that value is tested against the final value, and either we branch out of the loop immediately or the loop is performed with the initial value of the index. When we encounter a loop header subsequently, the index is incremented and then tested.

The adjustment of the initial value of the index register in the assembly language program requires comment. The BXH and BXLE instructions do not operate in the same way as the header of a DO loop or a FOR loop. Every time we execute the BXH instruction in Example 6.21, the index register is incremented by the value in the increment register. In order to process the loop beginning with a 1 in register 5, we must initialize register 5 to 0. (As a general case, we can load in the value of the index and then subtract from it the value of the increment—see Example 6.22.) Then the BXH increases register 5 to 1 and tests it against N. If the value in register 5 is not greater than N, we do not branch to OUT, but instead process the body of the loop. The instruction B   LOOP automatically sends us back to the top where we again increment register 5 and test. When register 5 is incremented to N, we again enter the body of the loop, but when it is incremented to N + 1, we branch to OUT.

EXAMPLE 6.22

Represent the following Pascal FOR loop with a BXH-controlled loop.

```
SUM := 0;
for I := INIT to FIN do
    SUM := SUM + I
```

In the general case, we do not know a specific value for INIT. Therefore, we must load INIT and subtract 1 (the increment) from it to compensate for the initial increment in the BXH.

```
          SR    2,2         SUM := 0
          L     3,INIT      INDEX
          LA    8,1         INCREMENT
          L     9,FIN       LIMIT VALUE
          SR    3,8         COMPENSATE FOR INITIAL INCREMENT
TOP       BXH   3,8,OUT     INCREMENT AND TEST
          AR    2,3         SUM := SUM + I
          B     TOP         BRANCH BACK
OUT       ST    2,SUM
          ...
```

We load the initial value into the index register. Before encountering the BXH instruction, we subtract the value of the increment register from the index register. Because of this, when we execute the BXH instruction the first time, the index register will be incremented back up to the initial value, INIT. Note that we assume that the increment is +1, since Pascal has another form of the FOR loop (for INDEX := INIT downto FIN) to be used when the increment is −1.

Solved Problems

6.1 What value should be in the index register (register 2) for the instruction

$$L \quad 4, ARRAY(2)$$

to load (a) the first element of fullword array ARRAY? (b) the ninth element? (c) the fortieth element? (d) the Nth element?

(a) 0   (b) 32   (c) 156   (d) 4N − 4

6.2 What element in the fullword array ARRAY will be loaded by the instruction

$$L \quad 4, ARRAY(2)$$

if the contents of register 2 are as follows.

(a) 100   (b) 52   (c) 76   (d) 0   (e) 4N

(a) twenty-sixth   (b) fourteenth   (c) twentieth   (d) first   (e) (N + 1)th

CHAP. 6] ARRAYS AND LOOPING 123

6.3 How would the answers to Problems 6.1 and 6.2 be changed if ARRAY were composed of halfword elements?

The answers to Problem 6.1 would be divided by 2. The answers to Problem 6.2 would be the following.

(a) fifty-first   (b) twenty-seventh   (c) thirty-ninth   (d) first   (e) $(2N+1)$th

6.4 Simplify and thus improve the following portions of code.

(a) L   7,X+0   (b) L   2,X(0)   (c) LA   2,X
                                                A   3,8(4,2)

(a) L   7,X
(b) L   2,X   When the index register value is zero, the value zero is used, not the contents of register 0.
(c) A   3,X+8(4)   Note the form of this instruction. X+8 specifies that the assembler use the displacement for X+8, and (4) specifies the index register. It would not be correct to use X(4)+8.

6.5 Arrays in high-level languages are implemented in different ways, depending on the language and the machine on which it is to be used. Most high-level languages have an integer data type; in Pascal and FORTRAN, this is called INTEGER; in PL/1 it is called FIXED; in COBOL it is indicated by a PIC 9 format. In most languages, the integer data type occupies 4 bytes in memory, exactly as does an assembly language full word. In other languages, particularly Pascal on microcomputers, the integer data type occupies only 2 bytes, or a halfword. [PL/1, for example, has three integer data types: FIXED DECIMAL, which causes the value to be stored as a decimal number rather than as a binary number; FIXED BINARY(31,0), which causes the value to be stored as a full word; and FIXED BINARY(15,0), which causes the value to be stored as a halfword.]

Assume that we have used the following declarations in Pascal and assembly language, and that the implementation of the Pascal integer data type is 4 bytes.

```
var A: array [1..100] of integer;      A   DS   100F
    B: array [1..100] of integer;      B   DS   100F
    C: array [1..100] of integer       C   DS   100F
```

Assume that values have already been stored in these arrays. All other variables are of type integer (4 bytes) in Pascal and fullword fixed binary in assembly language. Finally, assume that a value has already been stored in N and that this value is such that a subscript range error will not be produced.

Convert the following Pascal statements to assembly language.

(a) X := A[36]   (h) X := A[3] + A[19]
(b) X := A[23]   (i) X := A[N]
(c) X := A[16] + A[40] (j) X := A[N − 1]
(d) X := A[72] + A[37] (k) X := A[N + 2]
(e) X := A[29] + A[84] + A[57]   (l) A[5] := B[44]
(f) X := A[25] + B[17] (m) A[41] := B[92] + B[73]
(g) X := A[60] + A[7] + A[1]

(a) For A[36], skip 35 elements at 4 bytes per element, or 140 bytes:

L   2,A+140
ST 2,X

124 ARRAYS AND LOOPING [CHAP. 6

(b)   L   2,A+88
       ST   2,X

(c)   L   2,A+60
       A   2,A+156
       ST   2,X

(d)   L   2,A+284
       A   2,A+144
       ST   2,X

(e)   L   2,A+112
       A   2,A+332
       A   2,A+224
       ST   2,X

(f)   L   2,A+96
       A   2,B+64
       ST   2,X

(g)   L   2,A+236
       A   2,A+24
       A   2,A
       ST   2,X

(h)   L   2,A+8
       A   2,A+72
       ST   2,X

(i)   L   3,N
       BCTR 3,0
       M   2,=F'4'
       L   5,A(3)
       ST   5,X

(j)   L   3,N
       S   3,=F'2'
       MH   3,=H'4'
       L   5,A(3)
       ST   5,X

(k)   L   3,N
       A   3,=F'1'
       MH   3,=H'4'
       L   5,A(3)
       ST   5,X

(l)   L   2,B+172
       ST   2,A+16

(m)   L   2,B+364
       A   2,B+288
       ST   2,A+160

6.6 Convert the following from assembly language to a high-level language.

(a)   L   2,A+40
       ST   2,X

(b)   L   2,A+188
       ST   2,X

(c)   L   2,A+64
       ST   2,X

(d)   L   2,A+124
       A   2,A+204
       ST   2,X

(e)   L   2,A+72
       A   2,A+236
       ST   2,X

(f)   L   2,A+28
       A   2,A+332
       ST   2,X

(g)   L   2,A+152
       A   2,A+92
       S   2,A+248
       ST   2,X

(h)   L   2,A+304
       A   2,A+276
       S   2,A+88
       A   2,A+168
       ST   2,X

(i)   L   3,N
       M   2,=F'4'
       A   3,=F'4'
       L   2,B(3)
       ST   2,X

(j)   L   3,N
       M   2,=F'4'
       L   2,B(3)
       A   3,=F'8'
       A   2,A(3)
       ST   2,A−4(3)

(k)   L   3,N
       M   2,=F'4'
       L   2,A+4(3)
       A   2,A−4(3)
       ST   2,A(3)

(a)   40 bytes, or 10 elements, have been skipped; hence element 11 is loaded: X := A[11]
(b)   X := A[48]
(c)   X := A[17]

(d) X := A[32] + A[52]
(e) X := A[19] + A[60]
(f) X := A[8] + A[84]
(g) X := A[39] + A[24] − A[63]
(h) X := A[77] + A[70] − A[23] + A[43]
(i) X := B[N + 2]
(j) A[N + 2] := B[N + 1] + A[N + 3]
(k) A[N + 1] := A[N + 2] + A[N]

6.7 Trace the following loops. What are the contents of the registers at the end of each segment?

```
(a)          LA    5,LOC
      TOP    L     3,0(0,5)
             LA    5,4(0,5)
             LTR   3,3
             BP    TOP
             ...
      LOC    DC    F'2,9,8,-3,-7,10'

(b)          SR    9,9
             LA    8,FILE
      LOOP2  A     9,0(0,8)
             LA    8,4(0,8)            ADD SETS THE CC; LA DOES NOT
             BNP   LOOP2
             ...
      FILE   DC    F'0,-8,-6,4,12,-8'

(c)          SR    5,5
             SR    9,9
             LA    7,NUMS
      BEGIN  L     3,0(0,7)
             M     2,=F'1'
             D     2,=F'2'
             LTR   2,2
             BNZ   ODD
             A     9,0(0,7)
      ODD    LA    7,4(0,7)
             LA    5,1(0,5)
             C     5,=F'5'
             BNH   BEGIN
             ...
      NUMS   DC    F'2,13,8,0,7,-3'
```

	Register	Contents	Register	Contents
(a)	5	A(LOC+16)	3	−3
(b)	8	A(FILE+20)	9	2
(c)	5	6	9	10
	7	A(NUMS+24)	3	−1

6.8 Write an RR instruction which decrements register 3 by 1 and then proceeds to the next instruction.

BCTR   3,0

6.9 Criticize the following loop, designed to be executed N/2 times.

```
                L       3,N
LOOP            ...
                S       3,=F'1'
                BCT     3,LOOP
```

If N is odd, the loop will be an infinite loop, because the BCT instruction will act on even values only, and, after decrementing, will never find zero.

6.10 How can the difficulty in Problem 6.9 be resolved?

If N is odd, this code changes it to an even value by truncation on division, and then restores the value of N for use within the loop.

```
                L       3,N
                M       2,=F'1'
                D       2,=F'2'         IF N IS ODD, CHANGE IT TO AN EVEN
                M       2,=F'2'            NUMBER BY TRUNCATION
LOOP            ...
                S       3,=F'1'
                BCT     3,LOOP
```

The following better code simply tests the value of N after the subtract instruction.

```
                L       3,N
LOOP            ...
                S       3,=F'1'         IF RESULT OF SUBTRACTION IS ZERO OR
                BNP     OUT                NEGATIVE, LEAVE LOOP
                BCT     3,LOOP
OUT             ...
```

If the value of N is not used within the loop, we can simply divide N by 2, obtaining an even value by truncation. No further tests or extra subtractions are then necessary.

```
                L       3,N
                M       2,=F'1'
                D       2,=F'2'
LOOP            ...
                BCT     3,LOOP
```

6.11 Add the odd numbers from 0 to 50, using BCT to control the loop.

```
                LA      8,50            INITIALIZE THE COUNTER
                SR      6,6             CLEAR REGISTER 6 FOR SUM
TOP             BCTR    8,0             DECREMENT COUNTER BY 1 WITHOUT BRANCHING
                AR      6,8             ADD AN ODD NUMBER INTO THE SUM
                BCT     8,TOP           DECREMENT COUNTER BY 1 MORE AND BRANCH
*                                          TO TOP
                ST      6,SUM
```

6.12 Write a program segment which will add the first N elements of a halfword array HWA, and place the result in the full word SUM.

```
         L      2,N              COUNTER
         SR     3,3              SUM
         SR     4,4              INDEX
LOOP     AH     3,HWA(4)
         LA     4,2(0,4)         INCREMENT INDEX REGISTER BY 2
         BCT    2,LOOP
         ST     3,SUM
```

6.13 Write a program segment to set the first N elements of the halfword array HWA equal to the corresponding elements of the fullword array FWA.

We can use either of the following:

```
         L      3,N
         SR     2,2              HWA INDEX
         SR     4,4              FWA INDEX
LOOP     L      5,FWA(4)
         STH    5,HWA(2)
         LA     4,4(0,4)         INCREMENT FWA INDEX BY 4
         LA     2,2(0,2)         INCREMENT HWA INDEX BY 2
         BCT    3,LOOP
```

or

```
         LA     2,2              INCREMENT
         L      3,N
         MH     3,=H'2'          2N
         SR     3,2              2N − 2 = LIMIT
         SR     4,4              INDEX FOR FWA
         SR     5,5              INDEX FOR HWA
LOOP     L      6,FWA(4)
         STH    6,HWA(5)
         LA     4,4(0,4)         INCREMENT FWA INDEX
         BXLE   5,2,LOOP         INCREMENT HWA INDEX AND BRANCH
```

6.14 How can we increment a BCT loop by +1? That is, perform a Pascal loop such as

for I := −10 to −1 do

The last two instructions in the loop will be

```
         A      7,=F'2'          INCREASE BY 2
         BCT    7,LOOP           DECREASE BY 1
```

6.15 Write a program to count the number of odd and the number of even numbers in a list of full words NUMS. Assume that there are 50 full words at NUMS.

```
         SR     8,8              EVEN COUNTER
         SR     9,9              ODD COUNTER
         LA     10,50            LOOP COUNTER
         LA     7,NUMS           BASE
TOP      L      3,0(0,7)
         M      2,=F'1'          FIND REMAINDER
         D      2,=F'2'             WHEN DIVIDED BY 2
         LTR    2,2
         BNZ    ODD
         LA     8,1(0,8)         COUNT EVENS
         B      NEXT
ODD      LA     9,1(0,9)         COUNT ODDS
NEXT     LA     7,4(0,7)
         BCT    10,TOP
```

6.16 At TRAIN is a list of N fullword code numbers of train routes. At PASNGRS is a list of N full words representing the number of passengers riding each of the corresponding trains on a given day. Write a program to process the parallel arrays and determine which train route had the highest number of passengers on that day.

```
            L       11,PASNGRS          HIGHEST SO FAR IN REGISTER 11
            SR      8,8                 INDEX OF HIGHEST SO FAR IN
*                                           REGISTER 8
            LA      7,N                 LOOP COUNTER
            BCTR    7,0                 N-1 COMPARISONS
            LA      4,4                 INDEX REGISTER
FIND        L       10,PASNGRS(4)       GET NEXT PASNGRS AMOUNT
            CR      10,11               COMPARE WITH HIGH
            BNH     ENDLOOP             IF NOT HIGHER, BRANCH
            LR      11,10               CHANGE HIGHEST NUMBER OF
*                                           PASSENGERS
            LR      8,4                 CHANGE HIGHEST TRAIN
ENDLOOP     LA      4,4(0,4)            INCREMENT INDEX REGISTER
            BCT     7,FIND
            L       7,TRAIN(8)
            ST      7,MOST              STORE NUMBER OF HIGHEST
*                                           TRAIN
            ...
N           DC      F'4'                4 TRAINS
TRAIN       DC      F'5,44,3,7'
PASNGRS     DC      F'1234,960,3620,210'
MOST        DS      F
```

6.17 Write a program to search for the first number 44 in a list FILE which consists of 40 fullword numbers. Use an index register to process the list.

One possible method follows:

```
            LA      7,40                COUNTER
            SR      5,5                 INDEX REGISTER
FILL        L       4,FILE(5)
            C       4,=F'44'
            BE      GOTIT
            LA      5,4(0,5)            INCREMENT INDEX REGISTER
            BCT     7,FILL
            B       NOTHERE             IF WE GET PAST BCT, THERE IS NO 44
GOTIT       ST      5,LOC               INDEX FOR LOCATION OF FIRST 44
            ...
NOTHERE     ...
```

6.18 At location NUMS there are 50 full words. Write the code to determine how many of them are positive and how many are negative.

(a) Use an index register.
(b) Use only a base register.

```
(a)         LA      9,50
            SR      2,2                 POSITIVE COUNTER
            SR      3,3                 NEGATIVE COUNTER
            SR      5,5                 INDEX REGISTER
```

```
        TOP     L       4,NUMS(5)
                LTR     4,4
                BZ      NEXT
                BP      POS
                LA      3,1(0,3)        COUNT NEGATIVE
                B       NEXT
        POS     LA      2,1(0,2)        COUNT POSITIVE
        NEXT    LA      5,4(0,5)        INCREMENT INDEX
                BCT     9,TOP
(b)             LA      9,50
                SR      2,2             POSITIVE COUNTER
                SR      3,3             NEGATIVE COUNTER
                LA      5,NUMS          BASE REGISTER
        TOP     L       4,0(0,5)
                LTR     4,4
                BZ      NEXT
                BP      POS
                LA      3,1(0,3)        COUNT NEGATIVE
                B       NEXT
        POS     LA      2,1(0,2)        COUNT POSITIVE
        NEXT    LA      5,4(0,5)        INCREMENT BASE
                BCT     9,TOP
```

6.19 Write a program segment to process a loop with BXLE or BXH at the bottom of the loop, but still not entering the loop if the index is initially past the limit. The loop should add up the numbers from 1 to N. Compare the efficiency of your segment with the algorithm illustrated in Examples 6.19 and 6.20.

The following loop has one fewer instruction to execute N times, at the expense of execution of one or two additional instructions before the loop. If N is large, this version is more efficient. Note: Do not store the contents of register 9 each time through the loop. It would be very wasteful to do so.

```
                SR      9,9             SUM
                LA      5,1             INDEX
                LR      6,5             INCREMENT = 1
                L       7,N             LIMIT
                CR      5,7
                BH      OUT
        LOOP    AR      9,5
                BXLE    5,6,LOOP
        OUT     ST      9,SUM
```

6.20 For each of the following tasks, state whether it matters if we loop up or down through the array. That is, would the following Pascal loops yield different results?

        for I := 1 to N do   versus   for I := N downto 1 do

If it matters, explain why.

(a) To set each of the first $N-1$ values in an array equal to the following value.

(b) To sum N elements of an array.

(c) To set each of the first N elements of array A equal to the values of the corresponding elements of array B.

(d) To add a constant to each of the first N elements of an array.

(e) To add the subscript value to each of the first N elements of an array—that is, to perform $A[I] := A[I] + I$.

(a) Yes. If you replace a value before it is copied, you will lose the original value.
(b) No   (c) No   (d) No   (e) No

In most of these cases a BCT loop might do just as well as a BXLE loop.

6.21 Rewrite Example 6.16 using BXH at the top of the loop instead of BXLE at the bottom.

```
          L     4,=F'-5'      INDEX
          LA    6,5           INCREMENT
          LA    7,20          LIMIT
*                             THE ABOVE INSTRUCTIONS SET UP THE LOOP
          SR    3,3           SUM = 0
TOP       BXH   4,6,OUT       INCREMENT AND BRANCH
          AR    3,4           ADD IN THE NUMBER
          B     TOP
OUT       ST    3,SUM         STORE THE SUM
```

6.22 Simplify and thus improve the following portion of code:

```
          BL    CHANGE
          BXLE  7,10,LOOP
          B     CHECK
CHANGE    L     2,X(7)
          ST    6,X(7)
          ST    2,X+4(7)
          BXLE  7,10,LOOP
CHECK     ...


          BNL   NOCHANGE
          L     2,X(7)
          ST    6,X(7)
          ST    2,X+4(7)
NOCHANGE  BXLE  7,10,LOOP
CHECK     ...
```

6.23 A and B are 21-element fullword arrays. Write code to set A[1] to the value of B[2], A[2] to the value of B[3], ..., A[N − 1] to B[N], ..., A[20] to B[21]. Use only one changing register for addressing array elements.

```
          LA    11,76         LIMIT
          LA    10,4          INCREMENT
          SR    7,7           INDEX
LOOP      L     2,B+4(7)
          ST    2,A(7)
          BXLE  7,10,LOOP
```

6.24 Convert the following loops from Pascal to assembly language. Use a BXLE or BXH instruction to close the loop. Use fullword arrays. For simplicity, assume that each loop will be executed at least once. In place of I, use an index register value to control looping.

(a) SUM := 0;
    for I := 1 to N do
        SUM := SUM + A[I]

(b) SUM := 0;
    I := 1;
    while I <= N do
        begin
            SUM := SUM + A[I];
            I := I + 3
        end

(c) for I := 2 to N do
        A[I] := A[I+1] + A[I-1]

(d) for I := N downto 1 do
        A[I] := A[I] + A[I+1]

(e) I := K+1;
    while I <= N-1 do
        begin
            A[I] := B[I] + C[I];
            I := I + 2
        end

(f) I := 1;
    while I <= N do
        begin
            for J := I+1 to N+1 do
                if A[J] > B[J]
                    then A[J] := B[I] + C[J];
            I := I + 3
        end

(g) for I := 1 to N do
        A[I] := A[I] * I

```
(a)          L     11,N
             M     10,=F'4'
             S     11,=F'4'
             L     10,=F'4'
             SR    7,7              CLEAR INDEX REGISTER
             SR    5,5              SUM = 0
     LOOP    A     5,A(7)           SUM IN REGISTER 5
             BXLE  7,10,LOOP
             ST    5,SUM

(b)          L     11,N
             MH    11,=H'4'         4N
             SH    11,=H'4'         4N - 4 FOR UPPER LIMIT
             L     10,=F'12'        INCREMENT BY 12 BYTES FOR 3 ELEMENTS
             SR    7,7              INDEX VALUE OF FIRST ELEMENT (4I - 4)
             SR    5,5              SUM = 0
     LOOP    A     5,A(7)           SUM IN REGISTER 5
             BXLE  7,10,LOOP
             ST    5,SUM
```

Instead of storing I, we merely hold the index value, $4I - 4$, in register 7. Therefore, we initialize register 7 to zero, and then increment it by 12 each time through the loop until we pass the limit, $4N - 4$.

```
(c)          L     11,N
             M     10,=F'4'
             S     11,=F'4'
             L     10,=F'4'
             L     7,=F'4'          SET INDEX FOR A[2]
     LOOP    L     3,A+4(7)
             A     3,A-4(7)
             ST    3,A(7)
             BXLE  7,10,LOOP
```

(d)
```
            L      10,=F'-4'
            L      11,=F'-4'        LIMIT = -4
            L      7,N
            MH     7,=H'4'          4*N
            S      7,=F'4'          4*N-4
    LOOP    L      3,A(7)
            A      3,A+4(7)
            ST     3,A(7)
            BXH    7,10,LOOP
```

(e)
```
            L      11,N
            M      10,=F'4'
            S      11,=F'8'         4*N-8
            L      10,=F'8'         INCREMENT = 8
            L      7,K
            MH     7,=H'4'          INDEX REGISTER = 4*K
    LOOP    L      3,B(7)
            A      3,C(7)
            ST     3,A(7)
            BXLE   7,10,LOOP        ALTERNATIVELY WE COULD USE BXH 7,11,
    *                               LOOP AND SAVE REGISTER 10
```

(f)
```
            L      11,N
            LR     9,11
            M      10,=F'4'
            S      11,=F'4'         LIMIT FOR I
            L      10,=F'12'        INCREMENT FOR I
            MH     9,=H'4'          LIMIT FOR J
            L      8,=F'4'          INCREMENT FOR J
            SR     7,7              INITIALIZE I
    OUTER   LR     5,7
            A      5,=F'4'          INITIALIZE J
    INNER   L      3,A(5)
            C      3,B(5)
            BNH    ENDLOOP
            L      3,B(7)
            A      3,C(5)
            ST     3,A(5)
    ENDLOOP BXLE   5,8,INNER
            BXLE   7,10,OUTER
```

(g)
```
            L      11,N
            L      10,=F'1'         INCREMENT FOR I
            L      8,=F'1'          REGISTER 8 HOLDS I
            SR     7,7              CLEAR INDEX REGISTER
    LOOP    L      3,A(7)           LOAD A[I]
            MR     2,8
            ST     3,A(7)
            A      7,=F'4'          ADVANCE INDEX REGISTER
            BXLE   8,10,LOOP        ADVANCE AND TEST I
```

Supplementary Problems

6.25 Write a portion of assembly language code corresponding to the following Pascal code:

```
I := 1;
while I <= N-1 do
   begin
      ARRAY[I] := 2 * ARRAY[I+1];
      if I mod 4 = 0
         then I := I + 2
         else I := I + 1
   end
```

6.26 Suppose that we have used the following two-dimensional array declarations in Pascal and in assembly language, assuming that the data type integer in this implementation of Pascal is 4 bytes long:

var D: array [1..10,1..20] of integer;	D	DS	200F
E: array [1..5,1..8] of integer;	E	DS	40F
S: array [1..100] of integer	S	DS	100F

Convert the following Pascal statements to assembly language.

(a) D[2,3] := S[5]   (e) E[2,7] := E[1,8]
(b) S[50] := D[7,5]   (f) D[5,7] := D[7,5]
(c) E[3,2] := D[3,2]   (g) S[23] := D[3,6] + E[3,2]
(d) D[5,9] := D[7,4]   (h) E[2,6] := S[73] + D[8,13]

6.27 Using the same declarations as in Problem 6.26, convert the following assembly language instructions to a high-level language.

(a) L   2,S+40   (d) L   3,D+48
     ST 2,D+144   ST 3,D+124
(b) L   3,D+252   (e) L   3,D+436
     ST 3,S+160   A   3,E+92
                              ST 3,S+348
(c) L   3,D+280
     ST 3,E+72

6.28 Suppose that we have used the assembly language definitions

C	DS	160F
D	DS	40F

corresponding to the Pascal declarations

var C: array [1..10,1..16] of integer;
    D: array [1..8,1..5] of integer

Write the assembly language statements corresponding to the following Pascal statements.

(a) V := C[5,7]   (b) W := C[7,5]

Write the Pascal statements corresponding to the following assembly language instructions.

(c) L   7,D+104   (d) L   7,D+76
     ST 7,P   ST 7,Q

6.29 There are 75 fullword numbers starting at SPOT. Write a program to determine how many of them are greater than 15.

6.30 There are an unknown number of full words at location B. Write a program to add up the numbers. Stop when you find a negative number.

6.31 There are two lists of 25 full words, one at X and one at Y. There are also 25 full words of storage at Z. Write a program to add each full word at X to the corresponding full word at Y and store the result at the corresponding full word at Z. In other words, perform the following matrix addition:

for I := 1 to 25 do
    Z[I] := X[I] + Y[I]

(a) Solve the problem using index register(s).
(b) Solve the problem using only base register(s).
(c) Solve the problem using BXLE.

6.32 Find the (integer) average of the 35 fullword numbers at location STOR.

6.33 There are 50 fullword numbers at LOC. Write a program segment to sum the positive numbers in the list.

6.34 Write a portion of assembly language code corresponding to the following Pascal loop, in which the array has a lower bound of zero:

for I := 0 to N do
    SUM := SUM + ARRAY[I]

6.35 Write assembly language code corresponding to the following Pascal code:

for I := 1 to 10 do
    A[I] := A[I] + A[3]

6.36 Write a BCT loop which decrements by 3, avoiding the difficulty in Problem 6.9.

6.37 Rewrite Problem 6.17 without using BCT. Use a counter and compare it with a final value.

6.38 Modify the answers to Problem 6.18 to determine how many numbers are zero as well.

6.39 There is a list of 30 fullword numbers at B and a list of 30 fullword numbers at D. Write a program to compare the corresponding elements in the two arrays and store the larger of each pair at the corresponding position in array MAXARR. In other words, perform the following:

for I := 1 to 30 do
    if B[I] > D[I]
       then MAXARR[I] := B[I]
       else MAXARR[I] := D[I]

6.40 Write a portion of assembly language code corresponding to the following:

for I := 1 to N do
    ARRAY[I] := I

(a) for all fullword variables, (b) for all halfword variables, (c) for I and N full words and ARRAY halfwords.

6.41 Write a portion of assembly language code corresponding to the following Pascal loop, where the FW array is full word and the HW array is halfword:

FWSUM := 0;
HWSUM := 0;
for I := 1 to N do
    begin
       FWSUM := FWSUM + FW[I];
       HWSUM := HWSUM + HW[I]
    end

CHAP. 6] ARRAYS AND LOOPING 135

6.42 Consider Problems 6.9 and 6.10. Which is easier to use for a loop with increment other than −1, BCT or one of BXLE or BXH? Explain.

6.43 Modify your answer to Problem 6.23 so that it also changes the value of A[21] to the value of B[1].

6.44 Suppose that we have used the Pascal declaration

var G: array [1..8,1..14] of integer

Write the assembly language instructions corresponding to the following loops in Pascal.

(a) SUM1 := 0;
    for I := 1 to 8 do
        SUM1 := SUM1 + G[I,6]

(b) SUM2 := 0;
    for J := 1 to 14 do
        SUM2 := SUM2 + G[4,J]

(c) SUM3 := 0;
    for I := 1 to 8 do
        SUM3 := SUM3 + G[I,I]

6.45 Suppose that we have used the declarations

TEST	DS	500F
TESTAV	DS	100F
CLASSAV	DS	5F

corresponding to the Pascal declarations

var TEST: array [1..100,1..5] of integer;
    TESTAV: array [1..100] of integer;
    CLASSAV: array [1..5] of integer

All other variables are of data type integer in Pascal and fullword fixed binary in assembly language. The array TEST holds 5 test scores for each of N students in a class. We want to compute the (integer) average for each student in the class and store it in the array TESTAV. Also, we want to compute the class average (integer) for each test and store it in the array CLASSAV. Assume that data are already stored in N and in the first N rows of TEST. This calculation is performed by the following Pascal statements:

```
for I := 1 to N do
    begin
      SUM := 0;
      for J := 1 to 5 do
          SUM := SUM + TEST[I,J];
      TESTAV[I] := SUM div 5
    end;
for J := 1 to 5 do
    begin
      SUM := 0;
      for I := 1 to N do
          SUM := SUM + TEST[I,J];
      CLASSAV[J] := SUM div N
    end
```

Convert this portion of a program to assembly language.

6.46 At location NUM there is a list of 15 numbers. Sort the numbers in ascending order (a) using a linear sort or (b) using a bubble sort.

6.47 Write the code to sum up the 25 halfword numbers at location HW. (a) Use BCT with an index register. (b) Use BCT with only a base register. (c) Use BXLE.

Chapter 7

Character String Manipulation

7.1 Representation of Character Strings

Character strings are stored in the IBM 370 using 1 byte per character. Each character is encoded using an 8-bit code called EBCDIC (extended binary coded decimal interchange code), as shown in Table 7-1. We shall use two hexadecimal digits instead of the 8-bit binary representation for each character. Not every 8-bit byte represents a printable character. Note that the EBCDIC character representation of numbers is different from their representation in binary 2's complement notation. Thus the digit 9 is represented in binary as 1001, while the character '9' is represented as 11111001 (F9).

Note that hexadecimal 40 represents a blank. Any byte which has no entry in Table 7-1 is not an EBCDIC character (and may print as a blank or as something else). In this text, we will often denote a blank by ƀ, a b with a slash through it.

Table 7-1 EBCDIC Representation of Characters

Decimal Value	Hexa-decimal Value	Character	Decimal Value	Hexa-decimal Value	Character
64	40	blank	96	60	-
74	4A	¢	97	61	/
75	4B	.	107	6B	,
76	4C	<	108	6C	%
77	4D	(	109	6D	_
78	4E	+	110	6E	>
79	4F	|	111	6F	?
80	50	&			
90	5A	!	122	7A	:
91	5B	$	123	7B	#
92	5C	*	124	7C	@
93	5D	)	125	7D	'
94	5E	;	126	7E	=
95	5F	¬	127	7F	"
			192	C0	{
129	81	a	193	C1	A
130	82	b	194	C2	B
131	83	c	195	C3	C
132	84	d	196	C4	D
133	85	e	197	C5	E
134	86	f	198	C6	F
135	87	g	199	C7	G
136	88	h	200	C8	H
137	89	i	201	C9	I

Table 7-1 (continued)

Decimal Value	Hexa-decimal Value	Character	Decimal Value	Hexa-decimal Value	Character
			208	D0	}
145	91	j	209	D1	J
146	92	k	210	D2	K
147	93	l	211	D3	L
148	94	m	212	D4	M
149	95	n	213	D5	N
150	96	o	214	D6	O
151	97	p	215	D7	P
152	98	q	216	D8	Q
153	99	r	217	D9	R
161	A1	~	224	E0	\
162	A2	s	226	E2	S
163	A3	t	227	E3	T
164	A4	u	228	E4	U
165	A5	v	229	E5	V
166	A6	w	230	E6	W
167	A7	x	231	E7	X
168	A8	y	232	E8	Y
169	A9	z	233	E9	Z
			240	F0	0
			241	F1	1
			242	F2	2
			243	F3	3
			244	F4	4
			245	F5	5
			246	F6	6
			247	F7	7
			248	F8	8
			249	F9	9

7.2 Declaration of Character Strings

In Define Storage (DS) or Define Constant (DC) statements, the letter C is used to denote character strings just as the letter F is used to denote fullword binary numbers. But since character strings may vary in length, the length may be specified in the declaration. Each byte can hold one character. Thus CL3 means character string of length 3 bytes. If no length is specified, the length is taken from the initial value. An initial value can be specified by enclosing it in single quotes. If an initial value is given with a CL format which specifies a length different from the length of the value, the value is truncated on the right or padded with blanks on the right to the declared length. If neither a length nor an initial value is specified, the default length of 1 byte will be used. There are no boundary requirements for character strings.

EXAMPLE 7.1

Table 7-2 Examples of Character String Definitions

	Definition		Stored Value	Remarks
A	DC	CL3'ABC'	ABC	
B	DC	C'ABC'	ABC	Length taken from initial value
C	DC	CL3'AB'	AB⌿	Padded with blank
D	DC	CL3'ABCDE'	ABC	Truncated on the right
E	DC	CL3'123'	123	The characters may be digits
F	DC	CL4' ;,*'	⌿;,*	The characters may be blanks or punctuation marks
G	DC	3C'*'	***	Three asterisks
H	DC	CL3'*'	*⌿⌿	Only one asterisk
I	DS	CL3	none	3 bytes reserved
J	DS	CL3'ABC'	none	3 bytes reserved
K	DS	C'ABC'	none	3 bytes reserved
L	DS	C	none	1 byte reserved (by default)
M	DC	C''''	'	Two successive single quotes within the enclosing single quotes must be used to get one quote into a string

At times we may wish to specify the contents of a byte in hexadecimal or binary format. X or B formats are used for this purpose. The X or B format may be followed by a number in hexadecimal or binary format, respectively, in single quotation marks. We may even use the X and B formats to represent characters, so the following declarations are equivalent:

A	DC	C'A'	
A	DC	X'C1'	C1 is the hexadecimal equivalent of A
A	DC	B'11000001'	11000001 is the binary equivalent of X'C1' or C'A'

We can also specify a length when using an X or B format, as in XL3 or BL3. The number designated in each case is the number of *bytes* of memory reserved. If a length is given which does not match an initial value in a DC statement, the value is truncated on the left or zeros are inserted on the left to make it match the declared length. Note the difference between these formats and the C format, in which truncation is done at the right, or blanks (not zeros) are inserted at the right. (In effect, the X and B formats treat initial values like numbers.)

EXAMPLE 7.2

The definitions in the accompanying table yield the values (in hexadecimal) shown at the right. Notice that some of the values do not represent printable characters (or blanks).

	Definition		Hexadecimal Value Stored	Comment
X1	DC	XL3'C4D6'	00C4D6	Zeros inserted
X2	DC	XL3'C2D6D3D6'	D6D3D6	C2 truncated
X3	DC	XL1'C'	0C	1 zero inserted
B1	DC	BL2'11000110'	00C6	1 byte of zeros inserted
B2	DC	BL2'1111011111100000111010010'	C1D2	F7 is lost from the left
B3	DC	BL1'11'	03	6 bits of 0 are inserted to yield 00000011

7.3 Move Character (MVC)

The major character string instructions are MVC, MVI, CLC, and CLI. MVC and CLC are examples of a new type of instruction, called a *single-length SS* (*storage-to-storage*) *instruction*. (Another type of SS instruction is introduced in Chap. 8.)

SS instructions are 6 bytes long and specify two operands in memory. Since they are designed to deal with operands of various lengths, these SS instructions specify the length of the operands in addition to their locations. The formats of this type of SS instruction, where L designates the length of the operands, are as follows:

```
Assembly language    OPCODE   D1(L,B1),D2(B2)
Machine language      OP    L    B1 D1   B2 D2
                    1 byte 1 byte 2 bytes 2 bytes
```

No index register may be specified. The second byte of the machine language instruction is used to specify the number of bytes on which the instruction operates. (If no length is specified in the assembly language program, the default number of bytes used in an SS instruction is the declared length of the first operand.) The length that can be specified in an SS instruction ranges from 1 to 256 bytes (00 to FF in the machine language instruction). (In order to fit $256 = 100_{16}$ into two hexadecimal digits, the actual value stored in the machine language instruction for any length is 1 less than the actual length.)

The MVC instruction allows us to move data from one location in storage to another, without going through registers. Despite the name (move), Move Character *copies* the specified number of bytes starting at the address of the second operand into that same number of bytes starting at the address of the first operand, 1 byte at a time. Also despite the name (Move *Character*), the instruction operates on any memory contents. The bytes in memory do not have to represent valid characters; they may represent digits or special codes or garbage. No check is made of the contents of either memory location.

EXAMPLE 7.3

Given the declaration

```
A    DC    CL4'FROG'
B    DC    CL4'POND'
```

the instruction

```
MVC    A(4),B
```

will give A the value of 'POND'. B will remain 'POND'.

The instruction can also work on part of a memory location.

EXAMPLE 7.4

If LOC1 contains 'ABCDEFG' and LOC2 contains '123456789', then

```
MVC    LOC1(6),LOC2
```

will give LOC1 the value '123456G' by moving the 6 bytes containing the characters 123456 from LOC2 to LOC1, replacing the 6 bytes ABCDEF. The instruction

```
MVC    LOC2(3),LOC1
```

operating on the original values, would change LOC2 to 'ABC456789'.

We can change a string at a position past its beginning.

EXAMPLE 7.5

The instructions in the accompanying table, each operating on the initial contents of LOC1 and LOC2 given above, would yield the values shown at the right.

Instruction		LOC1	LOC2
MVC	LOC1+2(3),LOC2	AB123FG	123456789
MVC	LOC1+2(3),LOC2+3	AB456FG	123456789
MVC	LOC2+2(7),LOC1	ABCDEFG	12ABCDEFG
MVC	LOC1(7),LOC2+1	2345678	123456789

Explicit notation may also be used with MVC. Consider the same two memory locations and their contents. We load the addresses of LOC1 and LOC2 into registers 3 and 4, respectively.

$$LA \quad 3,LOC1$$
$$LA \quad 4,LOC2$$

Then the instruction MVC 0(7,3),0(4)
is the same as MVC LOC1(7),LOC2

In this explicit instruction, register 3 is the base register for LOC1, register 4 is the base register for LOC2, and 7 is the length. The displacement for each operand is 0.

EXAMPLE 7.6

Each of the four symbolic move instructions in Example 7.5 is rewritten in explicit notation, with registers 3 and 4 containing the addresses of LOC1 and LOC2, respectively.

Symbolic		Explicit		Displacements
MVC	LOC1+2(3),LOC2	MVC	2(3,3),0(4)	2 from LOC1, 0 from LOC2
MVC	LOC1+2(3),LOC2+3	MVC	2(3,3),3(4)	2 from LOC1, 3 from LOC2
MVC	LOC2+2(7),LOC1	MVC	2(7,4),0(3)	2 from LOC2, 0 from LOC1
MVC	LOC1(7),LOC2+1	MVC	0(7,3),1(4)	0 from LOC1, 1 from LOC2

The results of the explicit moves are exactly the same as those of the corresponding moves shown in Example 7.5, again using the original values of each memory location for each instruction.

We may also use a character string literal. For example,

$$MVC \quad LOC1(3),=C'CAT'$$

will change the 3 bytes at LOC1 to CAT.

It is possible that the two operands of MVC overlap, in which case it is necessary to remember that the actual move is done one character at a time, from left to right.

EXAMPLE 7.7

Consider LOC1, again containing ABCDEFG.

$$MVC \quad LOC1(5),LOC1+1$$

ABCDEFG
/////
BCDEFFG
Unchanged

This instruction copies the B from location LOC1+1 to the first byte of LOC1, the C from LOC1+2 to the second byte of LOC1, etc.

The result in Example 7.7 is what we would expect. But what happens with the following?

    MVC LOC1+1(5),LOC1

The character in the first byte is copied into the second byte; then the character in the second byte is copied into the third byte; etc. But that new character in the second byte is the copy of the first byte. As the instruction is executed, the following intermediate results are produced:

    ABCDEFG

    AACDEFG After the first byte is moved

    AAADEFG After the second byte is moved

    AAAAEFG After the third byte is moved

    AAAAAFG After the fourth byte is moved

    AAAAAAG After the fifth byte is moved

This approach can be used to fill an entire string with blanks.

```
                MVC     LINE(121),BLANK
                ...
        BLANK   DC      C' '
        LINE    DS      CL121
```

This can be used to clear a line for printing, but will work only if BLANK immediately precedes LINE in memory. The first character (a blank) is moved from BLANK to the first byte in LINE. The next character is moved from BLANK+1 (which happens to be LINE+0) to LINE+1. But that character has just previously been changed to a blank, so LINE+1 becomes a blank. The next step is to copy the new blank from LINE+1 into LINE+2, and the process is repeated for the entire 121-byte LINE. Here is a picture of a portion of the affected memory locations. Note that 40 is the hexadecimal representation for blank.

	LINE+0	LINE+1	LINE+2	LINE+3	LINE+4
40	?	?	?	?	?
BLANK	BLANK+1	BLANK+2	BLANK+3	BLANK+4	BLANK+5

This also illustrates that MVC copies the specified number of bytes, regardless of the declared length of the variable to be copied, even if this means copying from storage locations assigned to another variable.

7.4 Logical Comparisons

Compare Logical Character

The word "logical" in the Compare Logical Character (CLC) instruction means that the data are treated as unsigned or logical data, as opposed to arithmetic or numerical data. The leading bit does not serve as a sign bit. The data are regarded as unsigned binary numbers. The CLC instruction compares values of two storage locations, treating each value as if it were simply a string of bits. CLC is an SS instruction, with formats the same as those of MVC. CLC does not change the value of any memory location; like other compare instructions, it merely sets the condition code, as follows:

	Condition Code
First operand equal to second	0
First operand lower	1
First operand higher	2

You might ask how the letter A might be less than B or greater than a semicolon. It is possible because each character is represented in the computer in binary code; the IBM 370 system uses EBCDIC, which represents characters as shown in Table 7-1. (Note that hexadecimal 40 represents a blank.)

Since each byte is represented by a pair of hexadecimal digits, comparison of two characters is actually a comparison of their (unsigned) numeric representations, and thus one can be less than or greater than the other. Note in this regard that the representation of a blank (40) is less than that of any printable character. This code was carefully constructed so that sorting in ascending order with letters yields alphabetization, and with digits produces increasing size. The hexadecimal representation of A is C1; the hexadecimal representation of B is C2; therefore A < B. Note that since the digits are represented by F0 through F9, they are "greater than" the letters in this code.

EXAMPLE 7.8

Given the following declarations, the condition code is set as shown at the right by each of the instructions (a) through (f). Remember that the length, if not supplied, is taken from the declared length of the first operand.

```
        A    DC    C'A'
        B1   DC    C'B'
        B2   DC    C'B'
        C1   DC    C'1'
        C2   DC    C'2'
        Z    DC    C'Zb:'
```

(a)	CLC	A,B1	1	('A' is less than 'B')
(b)	CLC	B1,B2	0	('B' is equal to 'B')
(c)	CLC	C1,C2	1	('1' is less than '2')
(d)	CLC	C1,Z	2	('1' is greater than 'Z'—see Table 7-1)
(e)	CLC	A,Z+1	2	('A' is greater than ' ')
(f)	CLC	A,Z+2	2	('A' is greater than ':'—see Table 7-1)

Using CLC, we need make only one comparison to test two strings in their entirety. It is not necessary to compare one character at a time. Suppose LOC1 contains ABCDEFG and LOC3 contains ABCDEF9.

```
                CLC    LOC1(7),LOC3
```

sets the condition code to 1, since the first operand is lower. (ABCDEF is the same in both strings, but G is lower than 9; see Table 7-1.)

EXAMPLE 7.9

The value to which the condition code will be set for each of the following instructions is shown to the right of the instruction. Assume that LOC4 contains ABCDE1G and LOC5 contains ABCDD2G.

(a)	CLC	LOC4(4),LOC5	0	(The first 4 bytes, the only ones being compared, are the same.)
(b)	CLC	LOC4(7),LOC5	2	(E in the fifth byte is greater than D.)
(c)	CLC	LOC4+4(3),LOC5	2	(E1G > ABC)
(d)	CLC	LOC4+5(2),LOC5+5	1	(1G < 2G)

Character Literals

Both MVC and CLC may be used with a literal:

$$\text{MVC} \quad \text{LOC(3),=C'ABC'}$$
$$\text{CLC} \quad \text{LOC(3),=C'ABC'}$$

Either of these instructions would cause a literal memory location to be established and assigned a value 'ABC'. This value would then be copied to LOC by the MVC instruction, or compared with LOC by the CLC instruction.

EXAMPLE 7.10

What is stored at LOC4 (currently ABCDE1G) after execution of the following instruction?

$$\text{MVC} \quad \text{LOC4(4),=C'XYZbb'}$$

The instruction establishes a 5-byte memory location for the literal, and copies the first 4 bytes from that literal into LOC4, yielding XYZbE1G.

Compare Logical and Compare Logical Register

Two instructions which are related to CLC are Compare Logical (CL) and Compare Logical Register (CLR). Both compare logical data and set the condition code, just as CLC does. However, CL is an RX instruction in which the first operand is a register and the second is a full word in memory. CLR is an RR instruction in which both operands are registers. In each case, the length of each operand is exactly 4 bytes.

We can load character string data or other logical data into registers using the L operation. It is then possible to compare numeric data without regard to sign using these instructions (negative numbers will be larger than positive numbers since their first bit is 1).

EXAMPLE 7.11

Assume that you are running a lottery. Each entrant selects five different numbers in the range 1 through 32. We store the five choices in a single word by storing a 1 in the bit position corresponding to each number selected (left to right). Thus the word contains exactly 5 ones and 27 zeros. For example, if the choices were 1, 2, 4, 6, and 32, the word would be

$$11010100000000000000000000000001$$

To win, the entrant must select all five numbers correctly. To find the winning entries, we compare the winning choices (in WINNING) with each entry. Since the bits are logical data (no bit represents a sign), we can use a logical comparison.

```
            L     4,WINNING
            CL    4,ENTRY
            BE    WINNER
            ...
ENTRY       DC    B'11010100000000000000000000000001'   (OR X'D4000001')
```

If all bits of an entry match the winning number, the ticket is a winner.

7.5 Immediate Instructions

Move Immediate

Move Immediate (MVI) and Compare Logical Immediate (CLI) are examples of still another type of instruction, called an *SI instruction*. SI instructions are called *immediate* instructions because the instruction contains the value of the second operand as immediate data—data within the instruction itself—instead of specifying its location. These instructions operate on 1 byte of data, and the instruction contains the value of the second operand and the location of the first operand. The formats for the SI instructions are as follows:

$$\text{Assembly language} \quad \text{OPCODE} \quad D1(B1),I2$$
$$\text{Machine language} \quad \underbrace{\text{OP}}_{1 \text{ byte}} \quad \underbrace{\text{I2}}_{1 \text{ byte}} \quad \underbrace{\text{B1 D1}}_{2 \text{ bytes}}$$

MVI copies 1 byte of data from the instruction into the location specified by the first operand, and CLI compares 1 byte of data of the instruction with the byte specified by the first operand.

The usual ways of writing such instructions are

MVI	LOCATION,C'Q'	symbolic
MVI	0(7),C'Q'	explicit

Several points about these instructions should be noted:

1. No length is stated. The instructions operate on only 1 byte.
2. No equal sign is included in the second operand, which is the immediate data. The equal sign is used for literals, which are memory locations with names provided by the assembler (e.g., .LIT0001). An SI instruction does not use a memory location for its second operand; the second operand is included in the machine language instruction (I2).
3. There is no index register. (See the effect of the lack of an index register in Sec. 7.6.)

In the assembly language program, I2 may be expressed in several different formats:

As a character, with C
As a pair of hexadecimal digits, with X
As an 8-bit binary number, with B
As an unsigned decimal number, with no designation

For example, all of the following would have the same effect:

MVI	LOC,C'Q'	
MVI	LOC,X'D8'	D8 is the hexadecimal equivalent of Q (see Table 7-1)
MVI	LOC,B'11011000'	11011000 is the binary equivalent of hexadecimal D8
MVI	LOC,216	216 is the decimal equivalent of hexadecimal D8

The first two of these representations are by far the most common.

EXAMPLE 7.12

Consider this memory location, whose address has been placed in register 2:

LOC6   DC   CL5'ABCDE'

Execution of the following instructions, each operating on this original value, will produce the results shown in the right-hand column.

CHARACTER STRING MANIPULATION

	Instructions		Results
(a)	MVI	LOC6,C'1'	1BCDE
(b)	MVI	LOC6,X'F1'	1BCDE [same as (a)]
(c)	MVI	LOC6+2,C'1'	AB1DE
(d)	MVI	3(2),C'1'	ABC1E
(e)	MVI	0(2),C'1'	1BCDE [same as (a)]
(f)	MVI	0(2),B'11110001'	1BCDE [same as (a)]
(g)	MVI	0(2),241	1BCDE [same as (a)]

Compare Logical Immediate

The Compare Logical Immediate (CLI) instruction compares 1 byte of the specified memory location (operand 1) to the value in I2, setting the condition code as usual for compare instructions. (Zero means the first operand is equal to the second; 1 means the first operand is lower than the second; 2 means the first operand is higher than the second.)

EXAMPLE 7.13

The value of the condition code set by each of the following instructions, using memory location LOC7 and register 3, is shown in the right-hand column. Assume the following DC and LA statements:

```
        LA    3,LOC7
        ...
LOC7    DC    C'VWXYZ'
```

	Instruction		CC setting	Comment
(a)	CLI	LOC7,C'V'	0	V = V
(b)	CLI	LOC7,X'E6'	1	E6 represents W
(c)	CLI	LOC7+1,X'E6'	0	E6 represents W
(d)	CLI	0(3),C'W'	1	V < W
(e)	CLI	3(3),C'W'	2	Y > W

A summary of compare instructions is presented in Table 7-3.

Table 7-3 Summary of Compare Instructions*

Assembly Mnemonic	Instruction Type	Length Compared (Bytes)	Type of Comparison	Operands
C	RX	4	Numeric	Register and memory
CH	RX	2	Numeric	Register and memory
CR	RR	4	Numeric	2 registers
CL	RX	4	Logical	Register and memory
CLR	RR	4	Logical	2 registers
CLC	SS	1–256	Logical	2 memory locations
CLI	SI	1	Logical	Memory and instruction
CLCL†	RR	1 or more	Logical	2 memory locations
CP†	SS	1–16	Packed†	2 memory locations

*See also Chaps. 8 and 12.
†See Sec. 7.7.

7.6 Arrays of Character Strings

We can have an array of character strings, declared similarly to an array of full words. Here are three string arrays, STRARR1, STRARR2, and STRARR3, each of which can hold 10 strings of length 20.

```
STRARR1   DS    10CL20              TEN 20-BYTE STRINGS
STRARR2   DC    CL20'ABC'
          DC    CL20'1234'
          DC    CL20'XYZ'
          DC    CL20'DDT'
          DC    CL20'ABC NBC CBS'
          DC    CL20'THE RAIN IN SPAIN'
          DC    CL20'MACHINE LANGUAGE'
          DC    CL20'ASSEMBLY LANGUAGE'
          DC    CL20'HIGH LEVEL'
          DC    CL20'PROGRAMMING'
STRARR3   DS    CL200               TEN 20-BYTE STRINGS OR TWENTY 10-BYTE
*                                     STRINGS, ETC.
ANS1      DS    CL20
ANS2      DS    CL20
ANS3      DS    CL20
```

What does the declaration for STRARR1 actually do? It sets up 200 bytes of memory with a single name. We can accomplish the same effect with the declaration for STRARR3. In either case, we can use the memory space for our 10-element array (or for other purposes). The declaration for STRARR2 sets up the array explicitly and gives it values at the same time.

EXAMPLE 7.14

What would be the effect of the following instructions, using the declarations above?

```
          MVC   STRARR1(200),STRARR2
          MVC   STRARR3(200),STRARR2
          MVC   ANS1(20),STRARR1+20
          MVC   ANS2(20),STRARR2+20
          MVC   ANS3(20),STRARR3+20
```

The first two instructions copy the contents of STRARR2 to STRARR1 and STRARR3. The last three instructions show that we can access any element of the array, element 2 for example, by indicating the number of bytes of displacement from the beginning of the array. There is no essential difference between the declarations of STRARR1 and STRARR3.

Looping through an Array of Strings

Since there is no index register in an SS-type instruction, looping through an array of character strings requires changing the base register for that instruction, using explicit notation.

EXAMPLE 7.15

Write code which will cause a branch to FOUND if the characters ABC are the first three characters in any of the elements in STRARR2, declared at the beginning of this section.

```
          LA    7,STRARR2           BASE REGISTER
          LA    10,10               COUNTER
LOOP      CLC   0(3,7),=C'ABC'
          BE    FOUND
          LA    7,20(0,7)           INCREMENT BASE REGISTER
          BCT   10,LOOP
```

Here register 7 is the base register for the instruction, which will contain consecutively the addresses STRARR2, STRARR2+20, STRARR2+40, ..., STRARR2+180. Three bytes from each address are compared with ABC, and the base address is incremented each time through the loop.

EXAMPLE 7.16

How should the code of the preceding example be amended if the branch is to be executed for a string consisting of ABC followed by 17 blanks?

```
         LOOP    CLC    0(20,7),=CL20'ABC'
```

The length of the first operand must be changed to 20 bytes. Moreover, the literal (or memory location) which is set up must also be 20 bytes, in order to avoid comparing some of the characters from the next memory location.

Arrays of Heterogeneous Data

We can set up an array of heterogeneous data, as is done by a structure in PL/1 or a record in COBOL or Pascal. If we have both character data and fixed binary data, the latter should be on proper boundaries in order to be efficiently loaded for arithmetic purposes. If we declare the arithmetic data explicitly as full words, the declaration automatically sets up the memory location on the fullword boundary.

EXAMPLE 7.17

Write code to add the fullword numbers, corresponding to weights, in the following array:

```
1BC400   ARRAY   DC    F'120'
1BC404           DC    CL10'CARROTS'
1BC410           DC    F'100'
1BC414           DC    CL10'POTATOES'
1BC420           DC    F'55'
1BC424           DC    CL10'RICE'
1BC430           DC    F'75'
1BC434           DC    CL10'FLOUR'
```

The following code represents one method:

```
         SR      2,2              INITIALIZE FOR SUM
         SR      7,7              INDEX REGISTER
         LA      10,4             COUNTER
LOOP     A       2,ARRAY(7)
         LA      7,16(0,7)        INCREMENT (FULLWORD BOUNDARY REQUIRES 16 BYTES)
         BCT     10,LOOP
         ST      2,SUM
```

The first array element, the weight of CARROTS, lies on a fullword boundary (1BC400) because it is declared F. It takes 4 bytes. The character string takes 10 bytes. The next element cannot start at the next byte (1BC40E), because it is not on a fullword boundary; thus it skips 2 bytes and starts on the next fullword boundary (1BC410). The number of bytes occupied by each two-part element is 16, and that is the increment needed for the looping.

This example illustrates that the knowledge of boundary requirements is important even if the assembler automatically fixes the memory location on the proper boundary. The next few paragraphs also illustrate this point.

Suppose we wish to set up an array like the one in the preceding example, but containing 50 or even 500 elements. It would be time-consuming to declare each element individually. But if the data can be entered in some way other than by initialization in DC statements, we can set up memory locations as follows:

```
         ARRAY   DS    50CL16
```

This declaration will set up fifty 16-byte memory locations. It does not matter that we have declared the memory locations character and intend to use part of them for fullword binary numbers. We can use the memory for any purpose that we want! We intend to use the first 4 bytes of each element for a full word and the next 10 bytes for a character string. We intend to waste the last 2 bytes of each element. The only difficulty with this declaration is that the first byte of the first element might not happen to be on a fullword boundary. In order to ensure that it is on a fullword boundary, we will declare it immediately after another fullword (or double-word) declaration. If there is no such declaration, we can enter one—a dummy declaration. We will waste at most 3 bytes of memory to do so, if we use this format:

```
DUMMY      DS     0F
ARRAY      DS     50CL16
```

The DUMMY statement requires the assembler to set up zero full words. The assembler aligns DUMMY on a fullword boundary, and reserves zero bytes (for zero full words). Since the next declaration is that of our array, we can be sure that the array starts on a fullword boundary.

Suppose that we want our array to have the 10-byte character string first, then the full word. We can still use the same declarations, but will set our index register initially to 12 and use the last 4 bytes of each element for the full word. We still waste 2 bytes in each element, but now they are somewhere in the middle.

Element 1			Element 2			
Full word	10 bytes	2 bytes wasted	Full word	10 bytes	2 bytes wasted	...

↓ Fullword boundary   ↓ Fullword boundary

EXAMPLE 7.18

Write code to add the first 10 full words of an array of records, each consisting of a 10-byte character string followed by a full word. Use the declarations above.

```
        SR      2,2                 SUM
        LA      7,12                INDEX AT FIRST FULL WORD
        LA      10,16               INCREMENT STILL 16
        LA      11,156              LIMIT (12 BYTES PAST START OF LAST ELEMENT)
LOOP    A       2,ARRAY(7)
        BXLE    7,10,LOOP
        ST      2,SUM
```

What if we have a 3-byte character string, then a full word, then a 9-byte character string in each element? How can we set up a 50-element array so that it wastes the fewest bytes?

```
DUMMY      DS     0F
DUMMY2     DS     CL1
ARRAY      DS     50CL16
```

We set up the array starting 1 byte past a fullword boundary. The 3-byte character string brings the full word to the fullword boundary. The 9-byte string then uses up the last 9 bytes of the 16 bytes allocated to the array element. The next element has a 3-byte string to start, making the next full word start on a fullword boundary. A diagram of this set up is shown in Fig. 7-1. We have set up the array wasting 1 byte for DUMMY2 plus as many bytes as are required to get DUMMY to its fullword boundary. A maximum of 4 bytes is wasted, which is not bad for a 50-element array (or a 500-element array, if we had wanted one).

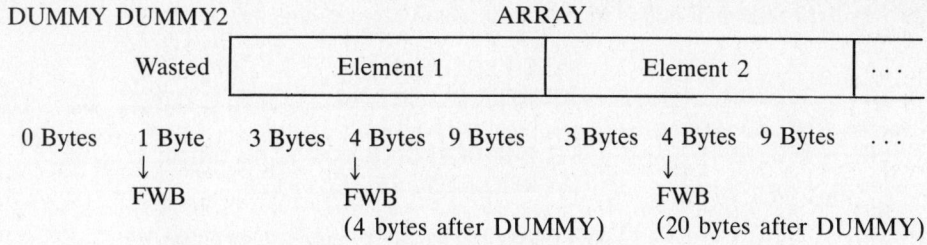

Fig. 7-1 Arranging full words on fullword boundaries (FWB).

EXAMPLE 7.19

Set up a loop to add the full words in the ARRAY of Fig. 7-1.

```
        LA    7,3              INDEX REGISTER
        LA    10,50            COUNTER
        SR    2,2              INITIALIZE 2 FOR SUM
LOOP    A     2,ARRAY(7)
        LA    7,16(0,7)        INCREMENT INDEX REGISTER
        BCT   10,LOOP
        ST    2,SUM
```

The only difference between this and Example 7.17 is the initial value of the index register (and the counter).

Looping through a Character String

How can we write a program segment to tell if the letter B occurs at least once in a character string 200 bytes long? (See also the TRT instruction, Sec. 13.3.) We may use the instruction CLI with each byte in turn, until we either find a B or exhaust the string. But there is no index register in an SI-type instruction, so we will again use a special base register to address each character. We simply treat the character string as an array of records of length 1 byte each.

EXAMPLE 7.20

Suppose STRING is defined as follows and is filled with characters in some manner.

                STRING   DS   CL200

The following program segment searches for a B in STRING and loads a message for printing into a memory location called RESULT. It sets up an index register, which is then used to set up a base register for the SI instruction.

```
          SR    7,7              INDEX REGISTER
          LA    9,200            COUNTER
LOOP      LA    6,STRING(7)      LOADS ADDRESS OF CURRENT BYTE
*                                  INTO REGISTER 6
          CLI   0(6),C'B'
          BE    FOUND            STOP LOOKING IF YOU FIND ONE B
          LA    7,1(0,7)         INCREMENT TO NEXT BYTE
          BCT   9,LOOP
NOTFOUND  MVC   RESULT(27),=CL27'THERE IS NO B IN THE STRING'
          B     OUT
FOUND     MVC   RESULT(27),=CL27'THERE IS AT LEAST ONE B'
OUT       ...
```

Another way to do the same job is to modify the base register directly.

```
           LA     7,STRING        BASE REGISTER
           LA     9,200           COUNTER
LOOP       CLI    0(7),C'B'
           BE     FOUND           STOP LOOKING IF YOU FIND ONE B
           LA     7,1(0,7)        INCREMENT BASE REGISTER
           BCT    9,LOOP
NOTFOUND   MVC    RESULT(27),=CL27'THERE IS NO B IN THE STRING'
           B      OUT
FOUND      MVC    RESULT(27),=CL27'THERE IS AT LEAST ONE B'
OUT        ...
```

The second method saves a register, but the first method makes it easier to keep track of the position in the string where the first B was found.

EXAMPLE 7.21

To tell if there were a sequence 'ABC' in the 200-byte string, you could amend either of these segments by using CLC instead of CLI and specifying the string to be 3 bytes long. You would also have to change the messages and change the counter to 198 since the string 'ABC' cannot start at the 199th or 200th byte of a 200-byte string. (If the string ended in 'A' and the next variable in memory started with 'BC', a limit of 200 would yield a result "THERE IS AT LEAST ONE ABC" when there actually is not. If the string were at the end of the memory allocated to your program, you would get an error.) Note that it would be wrong to change the increment to 3 as well, since the sequence ABC might begin at any position.

```
           LA     7,STRING        INDEX REGISTER
           LA     9,198           COUNTER
LOOP       CLC    0(3,7),=C'ABC'
           BE     FOUND           STOP LOOKING IF YOU FIND ONE ABC
           LA     7,1(0,7)        INCREMENT
           BCT    9,LOOP
NOTFOUND   MVC    RESULT(29),=CL29'THERE IS NO ABC IN THE STRING'
           B      OUT
FOUND      MVC    RESULT(29),=CL29'THERE IS AT LEAST ONE ABC'
OUT        ...
```

7.7 Move Character Long and Compare Logical Character Long

Move Character (MVC) and Compare Logical Character (CLC) are limited to character strings up to 256 bytes in length. Two instructions, Move Character Long (MVCL) and Compare Logical Character Long (CLCL), can be used with strings of any length. These instructions are RR type, with each of the two operands being the even register of a different even-odd pair. For MVCL, the four registers involved hold five pieces of information:

1. The even register of operand 1 (R1) holds the address of the destination string.
2. The odd register of that pair (R1+1) designates the length of the destination string.
3. The even register of operand 2 (R2) holds the address of the source string (which will be copied).
4. The last 24 bits of the odd register of the second operand (R2+1) hold the length of the source string.
5. Since the lengths of the two strings may be different, the first 8 bits of R2+1 contain a character which will be used to fill up the destination field in case the source field is shorter. Copies of this *fill* character will be added to the right of the destination field until the specified length is totally filled. For now, the fill character will be X'00'. Later we will introduce instructions to insert another value as the fill character. See the IC instruction in

Sec. 11.4 or the SLL instruction in Sec. 11.2. On the other hand, if the source field is longer than the destination field, only enough characters to fill the destination field will be copied.

The CLCL instruction uses the registers in the same way as the MVCL instruction and compares the two strings specified. There is no "source" or "destination" since neither string is changed. The fill character is used to pad the shorter of the two operands for the purpose of comparison.

EXAMPLE 7.22

Execution of the following code will accomplish the results explained below.

```
         LA    2,Q
         LA    3,2000       LOADS X'000007D0' INTO REGISTER 3;
*                           Q IS 2000 BYTES LONG
         LA    4,P
         LA    5,1500       LOADS X'000005DC' INTO REGISTER 5;
*                           P IS 1500 BYTES LONG
         MVCL  2,4
```

Fifteen hundred bytes of memory beginning at P will be copied into the first 1500 bytes starting at Q. The next 500 bytes of Q will be filled with hexadecimal zeros, since the first two hexadecimal digits of register 5 are 00.

EXAMPLE 7.23

Suppose the last instruction in the previous sequence of instructions were MVCL 4,2. What would be the result of execution?

In this case, the first 1500 bytes of memory starting at Q would be copied into the memory location starting at P.

Solved Problems

7.1 Write the binary representation produced in memory by each of the following declarations:

```
         CHAR     DC     C'E4'
         XFORM    DC     X'E4'
```

The binary representation is

```
         CHAR     1100 0101 1111 0100
         XFORM    1110 0100
```

7.2 What value is stored in memory (in character format) by each of the following declarations?

(a) A   DC   C'XYZ'   (c) C   DC   CL3'XY'
(b) B   DC   CL3'XYZ'   (d) D   DC   CL3'XYZW'

(a) XYZ   (b) XYZ   (c) XYb̸   (d) XYZ

7.3 Rewrite in X format:

```
         A    DC    CL3'A'
```

The C format is automatically padded with blanks on the right as necessary, but the X format is not.

```
         A    DC    XL3'C14040'
```

152   CHARACTER STRING MANIPULATION   [CHAP. 7

7.4 How many bytes of memory are reserved by each of the following declarations?

A	DC	C'ABCD'		E	DC	B'101'
B	DC	X'ABCD'		F	DC	CL3'ABCD'
C	DC	B'11100001'		G	DC	XL3'ABCD'
D	DC	X'ABC'				

     A   4   (four letters in C format)
     B   2   (four hexadecimal digits, half byte each)
     C   1   (8 bits)
     D   2   (three hexadecimal digits, and a zero to make a whole number of bytes)
     E   1   (3 bits plus 5 bits of zero, for a full byte)
     F   3   (CL3 determines the number of bytes reserved)
     G   3   (XL3 determines the number of bytes reserved)

7.5 Which of the following cannot be declared in character format?

     A   DC   B'00000000'
     B   DC   X'00'
     C   DC   XL3'F3'

None of them can be declared in character format, since each has at least 1 hexadecimal byte 00, which does not represent any printable character.

7.6 Give the EBCDIC representations of

(a) '0' (zero)   (c) 'Q'   (e) '/'   (g) ' '
(b) 'O' (letter)   (d) '7'   (f) '{'

(a) F0   (b) D6   (c) D8   (d) F7   (e) 61   (f) C0   (g) 40

7.7 Arrange the following strings in increasing order as they would be arranged by a SORT program using CLC.

(a) WORD♭TWO   (e) WORD♭♭TWO
(b) ♭WORD♭TWO   (f) WORD,♭TWO
(c) SECONDONE   (g) 1WORD
(d) SECOND   (h) 1♭WORD

Blanks precede punctuation, which precedes letters, which precede digits (see Table 7-1).

$$b < d < c < e < a < f < h < g$$

7.8 What key on a terminal has the lowest EBCDIC representation?

The space bar.

7.9 What are the contents in character format of each memory location after the following declarations?

(a) A   DC   C'ABC'   (e) E   DC   X'D6'
(b) B   DC   X'F0C5E9'   (f) F   DC   X'F0'
(c) C   DC   B'11011001'   (g) G   DC   CL1'ABC'
(d) D   DS   B'11000001'

(a) ABC   (e) O (letter)
(b) 0EZ   (f) 0 (zero)
(c) R   (g) A (1 byte only)
(d) garbage (DS statement)

7.10 What is the new value of the operands produced by each of the following instructions? Use the following declarations before each instruction. (Assume that STRING and STR2 occupy consecutive bytes of memory.)

    STRING   DC   C'ABCDEFG'
    STR2   DC   C'12345'

(a) MVC   STRING+2(4),STR2
(b) MVC   STR2,STRING   DEFAULT LENGTH
(c) MVC   STRING+4(3),STR2
(d) MVC   STRING+6(3),STR2   OVERLAP
(e) MVC   STRING(7),STRING+2
(f) MVC   STRING+2(4),STRING   OVERLAP

(a) STRING is AB1234G
(b) STR2 is ABCDE
(c) STRING is ABCD123
(d) STRING is ABCDEF1; STR2 is 23345
(e) STRING is CDEFG12 (12 is from STR2)
(f) STRING is ABABABG

7.11 In a portion of text 240 bytes beyond PARAGRAF, you have two sentences in memory whose order you want to reverse. In performing the interchange, it will be helpful to declare TEMP to be 70 bytes long. Write code to do this if (a) each sentence is 60 bytes long, (b) the first sentence is 70 bytes and the second is 50 bytes, and (c) the first sentence is 50 bytes and the second is 70 bytes.

(a) MVC   TEMP(60),PARAGRAF+240
     MVC   PARAGRAF+240(60),PARAGRAF+300
     MVC   PARAGRAF+300(60),TEMP
(b) MVC   TEMP(70),PARAGRAF+240
     MVC   PARAGRAF+240(50),PARAGRAF+310
     MVC   PARAGRAF+290(70),TEMP
(c) MVC   TEMP(50),PARAGRAF+240
     MVC   PARAGRAF+240(70),PARAGRAF+290
     MVC   PARAGRAF+310(50),TEMP

7.12 In a portion of text 240 bytes beyond PARAGRAF, you have two sentences in memory. You replace it by the second, and insert a third sentence THIRD after that. Write code to do this if (a) each sentence is 60 bytes long, (b) the first and third sentences are 70 bytes each and the second is 50 bytes, and (c) the first and third sentences are 50 bytes each and the second is 70 bytes.

(a) MVC   PARAGRAF+240(60),PARAGRAF+300
     MVC   PARAGRAF+300(60),THIRD
(b) MVC   PARAGRAF+240(50),PARAGRAF+310
     MVC   PARAGRAF+290(70),THIRD
(c) MVC   PARAGRAF+240(70),PARAGRAF+290   THE LAST 20 BYTES OVERLAP
     MVC   PARAGRAF+310(50),THIRD

7.13 Write machine language instructions corresponding to each of the following assembly language instructions. Assume that STR1 and STR2 are each 30 bytes long, that they are declared in sequence, and that the displacement of STR1 is 0A0 (hexadecimal). The base register is 12.

        STR1   DS   CL30
        STR2   DS   CL30

(a) MVC   STR1(20),STR2   (f) MVC   160(20,12),190(12)
(b) MVC   STR1(20),STR1+1   (g) MVC   160(20,12),161(12)
(c) MVC   STR1(4),STR2+20   (h) MVC   160(4,12),210(12)
(d) MVC   STR1(256),STR1+1   (i) MVC   160(256,12),161(12)
(e) MVC   STR2+2(3),STR2   (j) MVC   192(3,12),190(12)

(a) D213C0A0C0BE   (d) D2FFC0A0C0A1
(b) D213C0A0C0A1   (e) D202C0C0C0BE
(c) D203C0A0C0D2

Parts (f) through (j) are the same as (a) through (e), respectively. Note that the length in assembly language instructions is the actual length, while in the machine language instructions the hexadecimal value is 1 less than the actual length. The reason for this machine language value is highlighted in part (d), where the length 256 can be stored in two hexadecimal digits.

7.14 What will be the new value of the first operand after execution of each of the following instructions? Use the initial values of the strings for each part.

    STR1   DC   C'ABCDE'
    STR2   DC   C'12345'
    STR3   DC   C'WXYZ'
    STR4   DC   CL5'LMN'
    STR5   DC   CL2'123'

(a) MVC   STR1(4),STR2   (h) MVC   STR3(5),STR4
(b) MVC   STR1(5),STR4   (i) MVC   STR5(2),STR2+3
(c) MVC   STR1(3),STR2+2   (j) MVC   STR2+1(2),STR1+4
(d) MVC   STR1+1(3),STR2+4   (k) MVC   STR3(8),STR2
(e) MVC   STR1(3),STR2   (l) MVC   STR5(1),STR2+4
(f) MVC   STR3(2),STR2+1   (m) MVC   STR2+2(2),STR3+4
(g) MVC   STR2+1(3),STR2

(a) STR1 = '1234E'
(b) STR1 = 'LMN♭♭'   Note that the declaration of STR4 as CL5 adds blanks.
(c) STR1 = '345DE'
(d) STR1 = 'A5WXE'
(e) STR1 = '123DE'
(f) STR3 = '23YZ'
(g) STR2 = '11115'
(h) STR3 = 'LMN♭'   STR4 = '♭MN♭♭'
(i) STR5 = '45'   The declared length of STR5 is only 2 bytes.
(j) STR2 = '1E145'
(k) STR3 = '1234'   STR4 = '5123♭'
(l) STR5 = '52'
(m) STR2 = '12LM5'

7.15 What is wrong with the following statement?

$$\text{MVC} \quad \text{A(10),=C'POTATOES'}$$

The length to be moved exceeds the length of the literal, so 2 bytes of whatever follows this literal will be used. To correct this problem, use =CL10'POTATOES'.

7.16 Write one instruction for each of the following. Assume each variable to be full word. ARR and BRR are arrays of 21 elements.

(a)   A := B
(b)   ARR := BRR
(c)   for I := 1 to 20 do
         ARR[I] := BRR[I + 1]

(a)   MVC   A(4),B   (b)   MVC   ARR(84),BRR   (c)   MVC   ARR(80),BRR+4

7.17 What is the difference between CL and CLC, since they both compare bits?

CL compares the contents of a 4-byte memory location with the value in a register. CLC compares two portions of memory (of some length specified in the instruction). CL is an RX instruction and can therefore be used with an index register; CLC, an SS instruction, cannot be used in this way.

7.18 In order to arrange two strings in alphabetical order, is it necessary for the programmer to set up a loop to compare each character in the strings from left to right?

No. CLC compares the strings automatically for the entire length specified (from left to right).

7.19 Suppose that you want to find the address of an element in the array STRARR2 (declared at the beginning of Sec. 7.6) in which the first 4 bytes are ABCb.

(a) Why is CL easier to use for this purpose than CLC?
(b) Write the code to perform this calculation using CL.
(c) Why can't you use a CL instruction to see if the element is 'ABC' followed by 17 blanks?

(a) With CL you can use an index register, which makes coding easier.

(b)
```
        L     4,=CL4'ABCb'
        SR    7,7
        LA    10,10
LOOP    CL    4,STRARR2(7)
        BE    FOUND
        LA    7,20(0,7)
        BCT   10,LOOP
```

(c) CL compares 4 bytes, not 20 bytes. To see if the next 16 bytes were blank would require four more CL instructions.

7.20 To what value would the condition code be set by each of the following instructions, using these declarations?

```
STR1    DC    C'ABCDE'
STR2    DC    C'12345'
STR3    DC    C'WXYZ'
STR4    DC    CL5'ABC'
STR5    DC    CL2'123'
```

(a) CLC   STR1(4),STR2   (h) CLC   STR3(5),STR4
(b) CLC   STR1(5),STR4   (i) CLC   STR5(2),STR2+3
(c) CLC   STR1(3),STR2+2   (j) CLC   STR2+1(2),STR1+4
(d) CLC   STR1+1(3),STR2+4   (k) CLC   STR3(8),STR3
(e) CLC   STR1(3),STR2   (l) CLC   STR5(1),STR2+4
(f) CLC   STR3(2),STR2+1   (m) CLC   STR2+2(2),STR3+4
(g) CLC   STR2+1(3),STR2

(a) 1   (f) 1   (k) 0
(b) 2   (g) 2   (l) 1
(c) 1   (h) 2   (m) 2
(d) 1   (i) 1
(e) 1   (j) 2

7.21 The answer to Problem 7.19 (c) used the instruction

L   4,=C'ABC␢'

but there is no guarantee that the literal =C'ABC␢' will be on a fullword boundary. How can this program be modified to avoid this problem?

Change

L   4,=C'ABC␢'   to   L   4,CONS

and declare CONS using

                    DS   0F
            CONS   DC   C'ABC␢'

7.22 Using CLC instead of CLI, rewrite the instructions in Example 7.13.

(a) CLC   LOC7(1),=C'V'   (d) CLC   0(1,3),=C'W'
(b) CLC   LOC7(1),=X'E6'   (e) CLC   3(1,3),=C'W'
(c) CLC   LOC7+1(1),=X'E6'

7.23 State what, if anything, is wrong with each of the following instructions.

(a) MVI   LOC(1),C' '   (g) MVI   LOC(2),C'AB'
(b) MVI   LOC,=C'Q'   (h) MVI   LOC+2(2),=X'F0F1'
(c) MVI   LOC,C' '   (i) MVI   0(0,2),27
(d) MVI   LOC,=C' '   (j) MVI   LOC,200
(e) MVI   LOC,X'Q'   (k) MVI   LOC,2
(f) MVI   LOC,C'F3'   (l) MVI   LOC+2,C'Q'

(a) No length or index register may be included in an SI instruction.
(b) Immediate data is not written with an equal sign. An equal sign indicates a literal.
(c) Valid. (A blank is as valid a character as any other.)
(d) No literal may be included in an SI instruction.
(e) Q is not a hexadecimal digit. C'Q' would be valid.
(f) Only 1 byte is stored in the machine language instruction. Perhaps X'F3' was intended.
(g) No length or index register may be specified, and only 1 byte may be used in the instruction.

CHAP. 7] CHARACTER STRING MANIPULATION 157

(h) No length or index register or literal may be included, and the length must be 1 byte. This instruction is in the format of the MVC instruction.

(i) No length or index register may be specified. (Incidentally, the decimal value does not correspond to any printable character, but it does not have to.)

(j) Valid. (The hexadecimal equivalent is C8, corresponding to the character H.)

(k) Valid. (The character does not have to be printable for the instruction to be valid.)

(l) Valid. (The byte for the first operand need not be the first byte in a memory location.)

7.24 What is the new value of LINE produced by the following set of instructions?

```
           MVI     LINE,C'*'
           MVC     LINE+1(7),LINE
           ...
LINE       DS      CL8
```

LINE is ********

7.25 What is the value of STR (in character format) after execution of each of the following instructions?

```
                    STR    DC    C'ABC'
```

(a) MVI STR,C'E' (c) MVI STR,B'11000101'
(b) MVI STR,X'C5' (d) MVI STR,197

STR is EBC in each case.

7.26 To what value is the condition code set by each of the following instructions? Use the following declarations. Assume they are in this order with no intervening variables.

```
STR1       DC      C'ɮABC'
STR2       DC      C'ABCɮ'
STR3       DC      C'BBC'
STR4       DC      C'AZZ'
STR5       DC      CL3'ABCD'
STR6       DC      CL4'ABCD'
```

(a) CLC STR3(3),STR4   (f) CLI STR2,C' '
(b) CLC STR1(4),STR2   (g) CLI STR2,C'1'
(c) CLC STR1+1(3),STR2   (h) CLC STR3(4),STR4
(d) CLC STR2+1(1),STR3+1 (i) CLC STR5(4),STR6
(e) CLC STR2+1(2),STR3

(a) 2   (e) 2
(b) 1   (40 < C1)   (f) 2
(c) 0 (3 bytes of STR2 are used) (g) 1
(d) 0   (h) 2
(i) 1 (STR5 is 3 bytes long, so the fourth byte is the first byte of STR6; ABCA is less than ABCD.)

7.27 In each of the following instructions, what will be the new value of the string which is changed? Use the initial values of the strings for each part. If a nonprintable character is present, use hexadecimal format.

```
STR1    DC    C'ABCDE'
STR2    DC    C'12345'
STR3    DC    C'WXYZ'
STR4    DC    CL5'LMN'
STR5    DC    CL2'123'
```

(a)	MVI	STR1,C'Q'		(k)	MVI	STR1,X'F0'
(b)	MVI	STR2,C'P'		(l)	MVI	STR3,B'10000101'
(c)	MVI	STR3,C'R'		(m)	MVI	STR4,B'11001001'
(d)	MVI	STR4,C'S'		(n)	MVI	STR4+1,C'A'
(e)	MVI	STR5,C'1'		(o)	MVI	STR3,X'00'
(f)	MVI	STR1+3,C'Q'		(p)	MVI	STR1,B'11110000'
(g)	MVI	STR2+2,C'Q'		(q)	MVI	STR1+1,B'11000011'
(h)	MVI	STR5+1,C'T'		(r)	MVI	STR1+2,C'M'
(i)	MVI	STR1+7,C'?'		(s)	MVI	STR4+2,X'E2'
(j)	MVI	STR2,X'C1'		(t)	MVI	STR2+2,B'00000000'

(a)	QBCDE	(f)	ABCQE	(k)	0BCDE	(p)	0BCDE
(b)	P2345	(g)	12Q45	(l)	eXYZ	(q)	ACCDE
(c)	RXYZ	(h)	1T	(m)	IMNbb	(r)	ABMDE
(d)	SMNbb	(i)	12?45 (STR2)	(n)	LANbb	(s)	LMSbb
(e)	12	(j)	A2345	(o)	X'00E7E8E9'	(t)	X'F1F200F4F5'

7.28 To what value will the condition code be set by each of the following sequences? A, B, C, D, E, F, and G are declared CL1.

(a)	MVI	A,C'A'	(e)	MVI	E,C'O'	(letter)
	CLI	A,X'A'		CLI	E,C'0'	(zero)
(b)	MVI	B,X'F0'	(f)	MVC	F(2),=CL2'C1'	
	CLI	B,C'0'		CLC	F(2),=XL2'C1'	
(c)	MVI	C,X'F0'	(g)	MVC	G(2),=BL2'11'	
	CLI	C,C' '		CLC	G(2),=XL2'3'	
(d)	MVI	D,X'00'	(h)	MVC	F(2),=C'C1'	
	CLI	D,C'0'		CLC	F=X'C1'	

(a)	2	(c)	2	(e)	1	(g)	0
(b)	0	(d)	1	(f)	2	(h)	2

In part (e), look carefully at the immediate data. The operand for the MVI instruction is the letter O, while that for the CLI instruction is zero. Note that in parts (f) through (h), the actual location filled and/or compared is larger than the variable F or G.

7.29 Write the instruction which will determine whether the letter 'M' is in position 3 of the variable TITLE.

CLI   TITLE+2,C'M'

7.30 What, if anything, is wrong with the following statements? Write the correct statements.

(a)   CLI   FIRST,C'CAT'

Assume the declaration FIRST   DC   C'MAN'.

(b)   L   5,ABCS
       CLR   5,LETTERS

Assume that the variables ABCS and LETTERS are unsigned full words.

(c)
```
            L       8,CAT
            CL      8,DOG
            ...
   ALIGN    DS      0F
   CAT      DC      C'CATS'
   DOG      DC      C'DOGS'
```

(d)
```
            CLI     TOWEL,=C'F'
            ...
   TOWEL    DC      C'TERRY'
```

(a) CLI uses 1 byte of immediate data, not 3. Either of the following might have been intended:

       CLI   FIRST,C'C'   or   CLC   FIRST(3),=C'CAT'

(b) CLR requires two register operands. Two possible corrections are as follows:

```
         L    5,ABCS              L    5,ABCS
         L    8,LETTERS     or    CL   5,LETTERS
         CLR  5,8
```

(c) This is legal.

(d) CLI requires a byte of immediate data. The equal sign creates a literal instead. Correction:

       CLI   TOWEL,C'F'

7.31 Write a program segment to count the number of commas in STRING, which is 30 bytes long. (See also the TRT instruction, Sec. 13.3.)

```
            SR      2,2             COUNT=0
            LA      7,STRING        INDEX
            LA      10,30           COUNTER
   LOOP     CLI     0(7),C','       IS THIS BYTE A COMMA?
            BNE     NOT
            LA      2,1(0,2)        INCREMENT COUNTER
   NOT      LA      7,1(0,7)        INCREMENT INDEX
            BCT     10,LOOP
            ST      2,COUNT
```

7.32 Suppose STRING1 through STRING10 are declared sequentially and are 30 bytes each. Write a program segment to determine the number of the string that has the most commas, and store its number in BIGGEST. (See also the TRT instruction, Sec. 13.3.) If more than one STRING is tied for first place, store the number of the first of them at BIGGEST.

The inner loop determines how many commas there are in each string by looping through each character in the string. The outer loop loops through all the strings finding the one with the most commas.

```
               SR     3,3            BIGGEST = 0
               ST     3,BIGGEST      ZERO INDICATES NO COMMAS FOUND
               LA     8,10           OUTER LOOP COUNTER
               LA     7,STRING1      BASE REGISTER FOR BOTH LOOPS
       OUTER   LA     10,30          INNER LOOP COUNTER
               SR     2,2            EACH STRING COUNT = 0
       INNER   CLI    0(7),C','      IS THIS BYTE A COMMA?
               BNE    NOT
               LA     2,1(0,2)       INCREMENT COUNTER
       NOT     LA     7,1(0,7)
               BCT    10,INNER
               CR     2,3
               BNH    ENDOUT         IF EQUAL TO BIGGEST SO FAR, DON'T CHANGE
               LR     3,2            CHANGE VALUE OF BIGGEST IN REGISTER 3
               LA     4,11           CALCULATE NUMBER OF STRING WITH
               SR     4,8               MOST SO FAR
               ST     4,BIGGEST      STORE NUMBER OF STRING WITH MOST SO FAR
       ENDOUT  BCT    8,OUTER
```

7.33 Suppose you want an array of 50 Pascal records or PL/1 structures, each consisting of a full word and then a 20-byte character string. Show how to declare this data structure.

Since the first byte of each element is on a fullword boundary, we can use the first 4 bytes to store full words for loading, etc.

```
               DS     0F             SETS BOUNDARY ALIGNMENT
       RECORDS DS     50CL24         RESERVES FIFTY 24-BYTE PORTIONS OF
       *                                MEMORY
```

7.34 Suppose you want an array of 50 Pascal records or PL/1 structures, each consisting of a full word and then a 21-byte character string. Show how to declare this data structure.

```
               DS     0F             SETS BOUNDARY ALIGNMENT
       RECORD  DS     50CL28         RESERVES FIFTY 28-BYTE PORTIONS OF MEMORY
       *                             THE FIRST BYTE OF EACH ELEMENT IS
       *                             ON A FULL-WORD BOUNDARY
```

Use the first 4 bytes of each element for the full word, the next 21 bytes for the character string, and "waste" the last 3 bytes to ensure proper alignment. It is possible to set up a dummy area properly aligned and to move each record into this area before using the full word. This procedure saves the inefficiency of the wasted bytes at a cost of execution of extra instructions.

7.35 What value is stored in memory (in character format) by each of the following declarations?

(a) A   DC   CL12' '   (d) D   DC   12C'*'
(b) B   DC   12C' '   (e) E   DC   3C'$9'
(c) C   DC   CL12'*'   (f) F   DC   3CL2'$9'

(a) 12 blanks   (d) 12 '*'s
(b) 12 blanks   (e) $9$9$9
(c) * followed by 11 blanks   (f) $9$9$9

CHARACTER STRING MANIPULATION

7.36 How many bytes of storage are reserved in each case?

(a) A   DC   3C'AB'   (e) E   DS   3CL3
(b) B   DC   3CL2'AB'   (f) F   DC   3X'C1C2C5'
(c) C   DC   3CL3'AB'   (g) G   DC   3XL3'C1C2C3'
(d) D   DC   3C'A'   (h) H   DC   3XL3'0123'

(a) 6   (b) 6   (c) 9   (d) 3   (e) 9   (f) 9   (g) 9   (h) 9

7.37 A student has an assembly language array of records called ARRAY, each containing a (fullword) number and an 8-byte description consisting of capital letters, digits, and blanks only.

```
NUMELEM   DC    F'
ARRAY     DC    F'...           ELEMENT 1
          DC    CL8'...
          DC    F'...           ELEMENT 2
          DC    CL8'...
          DC    F'...           ELEMENT 3
          ...
```

(a) Write a portion of a program to add up the numbers in the array. Assume ARRAY is declared immediately after a full word NUMELEM containing the number of elements in the array.

(b) Write a portion of a program to add up those numbers contained in records in which the initial letter of the description is A.

(c) Write a portion of a program to add up those numbers contained in records in which the initial letter of the description is a letter (not a digit) which follows I in the alphabet.

(d) Write a portion of a program to add up those numbers contained in records in which any letter of the description is the letter A.

```
(a)            SR    7,7           INDEX
               L     10,NUMELEM    COUNTER
               LA    5,ARRAY
               SR    2,2           SUM, INITIALLY ZERO
       LOOP    A     2,0(7,5)
               LA    7,12(0,7)     INCREMENT REGISTER 7
               BCT   10,LOOP
               ST    2,SUM
(b)            SR    7,7           INDEX
               L     10,NUMELEM    COUNTER
               LA    5,ARRAY
               SR    2,2           SUM, INITIALLY ZERO
       LOOP    LA    3,4(7,5)      4 BYTES PAST START OF ARRAY ELEMENT
               CLI   0(3),C'A'
               BNE   CONT
               A     2,0(7,5)
       CONT    LA    7,12(0,7)     INCREMENT REGISTER 7
               BCT   10,LOOP
               ST    2,SUMA
```

```
        (c)             SR      7,7              INDEX
                        L       10,NUMELEM       COUNTER
                        LA      5,ARRAY
                        SR      2,2              SUM, INITIALLY ZERO
                LOOP    LA      3,4(7,5)
                        CLI     0(3),C'I'
                        BNH     CONT             ALL LETTERS J THROUGH Z ARE HIGHER
      *                                             THAN I
                        CLI     0(3),C'Z'
                        BH      CONT             DIGITS ARE HIGHER THAN Z
                        A       2,0(7,5)
                CONT    LA      7,12(0,7)
                        BCT     10,LOOP
                        ST      2,SUMJTOZ
        (d)             SR      7,7              INDEX (4-BYTE DISPLACEMENT)
                        L       10,NUMELEM       COUNTER
                        LA      5,ARRAY
                        SR      2,2              SUM, INITIALLY ZERO
                OUTER   LA      3,4(7,5)
                        LA      4,8              COUNT
                INNER   CLI     0(3),C'A'
                        BNE     INCONT
                        A       2,0(7,5)
                        B       OUTCONT
                INCONT  LA      3,1(0,3)
                        BCT     4,INNER
                OUTCONT LA      7,12(0,7)
                        BCT     10,OUTER
                        ST      2,SUMB
```

7.38 How would Problem 7.37(a) be changed if there were a 4-byte code introduced in each record, followed by the full word and the description (for a total of 16 bytes in each element)?

```
        NUMELEM DC      F'...
        ARRAY   DC      CL4'...          ELEMENT 1
                DC      F'...
                DC      CL8'...
                DC      CL4'...          ELEMENT 2
                ...
```

The setup for the loop would be changed as follows:

```
                LA      7,4              INDEX, STARTING AT THE FULL WORD OF
      *                                     ELEMENT 1
                LA      7,16(0,7)        INCREMENT INDEX BY 16
```

7.39 (a) Show the declaration that you would use for an array RECORD like the array ARRAY in Problem 7.37 but having no initial values.

(b) Write code to initialize the numbers in the RECORD array by modifying values from a fullword array NUMS in the following way. Each number in RECORD is I more than the corresponding number in NUMS, where I is the subscript. That is,

$$RECORD[1] := NUMS[1] + 1;$$
$$RECORD[2] := NUMS[2] + 2$$
$$\ldots$$

(c) Repeat part (b), except do not add I to RECORD[I]. Use MVC instead of L and ST.

```
(a)     NUMELEM  DC   F'30'
        RECORD   DS   30CL12           EACH ON A FULLWORD BOUNDARY
(b)              LA   7,RECORD         INDEX FOR RECORD
                 L    10,NUMELEM       COUNTER
                 LA   2,NUMS           INDEX FOR NUMS
                 LA   5,1              I = 1
        LOOP     L    4,0(0,2)         NUMS[I] IN 4
                 AR   4,5              ADD I
                 ST   4,0(0,7)
                 LA   5,1(0,5)         INCREMENT I
                 LA   2,4(0,2)         INCREMENT NUMS INDEX
                 LA   7,12(0,7)        INCREMENT RECORD INDEX
                 BCT  10,LOOP
```

(c) For the fourth through the eighth instructions, substitute

```
        LOOP     MVC  0(4,7),0(2)
```

7.40 How would the answer to Problem 7.38 be changed if the CODE were only 2 bytes long?

No change. The 2 bytes following CODE are skipped so that each number is on a full-word boundary for later use in addition. (There is no boundary requirement for MVC.) The CODE goes in the first 2 bytes of each element, and the second 2 bytes are "wasted" so that the number in each element is on a fullword boundary.

7.41 Trace the following loop. What are the contents of the registers at the end of the program segment?

```
                 LA   3,LIST+8
        TOP      L    4,0(0,3)
                 C    4,=F'16'
                 BE   FOUND
                 LA   3,12(0,3)
                 C    3,=A(LIST+32)
                 BL   TOP
                 ...
        FOUND    ...
        DUMMY    DS   0F
        LIST     DC   CL5'JOHN'
                 DC   F'12'
                 DC   CL5'NANCY'
                 DC   F'14'
                 DC   CL5'FRANK'
                 DC   F'16'
```

Register 3: A(LIST+32); register 4: 14.

7.42 (a) How can a record or structure with 15 elements, each having a 3-byte character string, a fullword number, and a 9-byte character string, be declared so as to occupy the least amount of space and yet have the fullword numbers on fullword boundaries? (b) How can the full words be totaled?

```
            (a)         DS      0F
                        DS      CL1         1 BYTE WASTED TO PUT WORD ON BOUNDARY
            RECORD      DS      15CL16
            (b)         SR      3,3         TOTAL
                        LA      10,15       COUNT
                        LA      7,RECORD
            LOOP        A       3,3(0,7)    7 IS BASE REGISTER
                        LA      7,16(0,7)   INCREMENT BASE REGISTER
                        BCT     10,LOOP
```

7.43 Write a program segment to check to see if the item 'POTATOES' is present in an array FOODS declared DS 15CL10. If it is present, branch immediately to a portion of code labeled FOUND.

```
                    LA      7,FOODS
                    LA      8,15                    COUNTER
        LOOP        CLC     0(10,7),=CL10'POTATOES'
                    BE      FOUND
                    LA      7,10(0,7)
                    BCT     8,LOOP
```

7.44 Write a program to search for the name ROBERT JONES in a list PEOPLE which consists of 15 records, each having a fullword ID number followed by a 20-character name. Move his name to location PERSON.

```
                    LA      8,PEOPLE
                    LA      10,15                       COUNTER
        COMP        CLC     4(20,8),=CL20'ROBERT JONES'
                    BE      FOUND
                    LA      8,24(0,8)                   INCREMENT RECORD ARRAY
                    BCT     10,COMP
                    B       DONE
        FOUND       MVC     PERSON(20),4(8)             4 BYTES BEYOND ID NUMBER
                    ...
        DONE        ...
                    ...
        PERSON      DS      CL20
        PEOPLE      DC      F'1234'
                    DC      CL20'JOAN SMITH'
                    DC      F'1987'
                    DC      CL20'ROBERT JONES'
                    ...
```

7.45 There are 30 records at FILE. Each is 40 bytes long and consists of the following: a fullword identification number, a 20-byte name, and a 16-byte address. Example:

```
            FILE    DC      F'1243'
                    DC      CL20'POCAHONTAS'
                    DC      CL16'BLACK FOREST'
```

Write a program segment to find the record of EINSTEIN, ALBERT. Move his ID to FOUNDID, and print out the name and address of that record. (Use whatever method of printing you have learned.)

(a) Assume that the records are in random order.

(b) Assume that the records are in alphabetical order.

(a)
```
            LA     8,30                               COUNT
            LA     7,FILE
    LOOP    CLC    4(20,7),=CL20'EINSTEIN, ALBERT'
            BE     FOUND
            LA     7,40(0,7)                          INCREMENT ONE RECORD
            BCT    8,LOOP
    NOTHERE ...
            ...
    FOUND   MVC    FOUNDID(4),0(7)
            ...
```

(b) We can quit if we find a name past EINSTEIN in alphabetical order. Thus we merely add

$$BH \quad NOTHERE$$

before or after the BE FOUND instruction of part (a).

7.46 Write a program segment to sum the weights of the foods in a 50-element array, in which each element consists of the weight of the food in pounds stored in a halfword, plus the name of the food stored in a 10-byte character string. Declare the array without using 50 DS and DC statements. The first element might be

$$150 \quad RICE$$

A possible solution follows:

```
            SR     7,7                    INDEX REGISTER
            LA     10,50                  COUNTER
            SR     2,2                    SUM IN 2
    LOOP    AH     2,FOOD(7)
            LA     7,12(0,7)
            BCT    10,LOOP
            ST     2,TOTALWT
            ...
    DUMMY   DS     0H
    FOOD    DS     50CL12                 FIRST 2 BYTES ARE WEIGHT, LAST 10 TYPE
```

7.47 Using the array of Problem 7.46, write a program segment to place in a 10-byte memory location MOST the name of the food which is present in greatest weight.

```
            LA     7,FOOD             INDEX WITH ADDRESS OF FIRST ELEMENT
            LA     10,50              COUNTER
            SR     2,2                WILL HOLD LARGEST WEIGHT SO FAR
    LOOP    CH     2,0(0,7)           CHECK FOR MOST SO FAR
            BNL    ENDLOOP            DON'T CHANGE UNLESS ELEMENT IS HIGHER
            LH     2,FOOD(7)          CHANGE GREATEST WEIGHT SO FAR
            MVC    MOST(10),2(7)      CHANGE NAME (2 BYTES PAST ADDRESS IN 7)
    ENDLOOP LA     7,12(0,7)          INCREMENT
            BCT    10,LOOP
            ...
    MOST    DC     CL10' '
```

7.48 At TRAIN is a list of one-character names of train routes. The number of routes is stored in NUMEL. At PASNGRS is a list of full words representing the number of passengers riding each of the corresponding trains on a given day. Write a program to process the parallel arrays and determine which train route had the highest number of passengers on that day.

```
              LA      5,TRAIN
              LA      6,PASNGRS
              MVC     HI(4),0(6)        HIGHEST NUMBER SO FAR
              MVC     MOST(1),0(5)      HIGHEST TRAIN SO FOR
              L       7,NUMEL           NUMBER OF ELEMENTS IN ARRAYS
              BCTR    7,0               ONE FEWER COMPARISON
    FIND      LA      5,1(0,5)          INCREMENT TRAIN
              LA      6,4(0,6)          INCREMENT NUMBER
              CLC     0(4,6),HI         NUMBER OF PASSENGERS IS ALWAYS
    *                                       NEGATIVE
              BNH     ENDLOOP
              MVC     HI(4),0(6)        SUBSTITUTE HIGH VALUE
              MVC     MOST(1),0(5)      SUBSTITUTE HIGH TRAIN
    ENDLOOP   BCT     7,FIND
              ...
    NUMEL     DC      F'4'
    TRAIN     DC      C'FEAN'
    PASNGRS   DC      F'1234,960,3620,210'
```

7.49 Assume that you are writing the code for an automated banking machine. Write a program that will branch according to a one-character code which will be read into CODE. The code can be 'N', meaning new account, 'D', meaning deposit, 'W', meaning withdrawal, or 'B', meaning balance inquiry.

```
              CLI     CODE,C'N'
              BE      NEWACCT
              CLI     CODE,C'D'
              BE      DEPOSIT
              CLI     CODE,C'W'
              BE      WITHDRAW
              CLI     CODE,C'B'
              BE      BALANCE
    ERROR     ...                       IF WE GET HERE, BAD CODE
                                        SKIP OTHER TRANSACTIONS
              B       DONE
    NEWACCT   ...
              B       DONE
    DEPOSIT   ...
              B       DONE
    WITHDRAW  ...
              B       DONE
    BALANCE   ...
    DONE      ...                       NO BRANCH NEEDED HERE;
    *                                   DONE IS NEXT
```

7.50 A credit card company has a list of 1402 lost or stolen credit cards. Each card that is reported stolen is added to the end of the list. Each card has a 16-digit identification number. Write a program segment to determine if a card presented for authorization from a customer is on the list of lost or stolen cards. Start searching (linear search) at the end of the list, since the last cards stolen are the ones most likely to be presented.

The declarations that we will use are:

```
LOSTSTOL  DS    1500CL16
CARDPRES  DS    CL16
          DS    F
```

Before the following segment is encountered, these variables will have been initialized. For example, the number lost, N, will be 1402.

```
          L     7,NUMLOST
          LR    5,7                      CALCULATE  A(LOSTSTOL)+16N-16=
          M     4,=F'16'                 THE ADDRESS OF THE
          S     5,=F'16'                 LAST ELEMENT OF
          LA    8,LOSTSTOL               THE ARRAY AND PLACE IN
          AR    8,5                      REGISTER 8
LOOP      CLC   CARDPRES(16),0(8)        COMPARE WITH ARRAY ELEMENT
          BE    FOUND
          S     8,=F'16'
          BCT   7,LOOP
NOTFOUND  ...
          ...
FOUND     ...
```

Register 7 is initialized to the number of lost cards for use in looping. That same number is multiplied by 16, and 16 is subtracted from the product, since the last element of the array is $16(N-1)$ bytes away from the first element. That value is added to the address of the first element to get the address of the last element. In a loop, each card number in turn is compared with the number of the card presented, and if they are the same, execution branches to the location FOUND. Otherwise, the address register is decremented by 16 to the address of the preceding element, and the looping continues. If no branch to FOUND ever occurs, execution passes normally to NOTFOUND.

Supplementary Problems

7.51 Rewrite each declaration in character format:

```
           A    DC    X'C1D2E3'
           B    DC    X'F0F1F2'
           C    DC    XL3'F94040'
```

7.52 What value is stored in memory (in character format) by each of the following declarations?

(a) A DC C'A'   (d) D DC C'AA'
(b) B DC X'C1'   (e) E DC X'C1C1'
(c) C DC B'11000001'   (f) F DC B'1100000111000001'

7.53 Discuss what would happen to the number NUM declared below if numbers in B format were padded with zeros on the right. Would such a result be desirable? Explain why padding with zeros occurs on the left in B and X format declarations. Why, then, can character format data be padded on the right?

```
           NUM   DC   B'11'
```

7.54 What printable character, if any, is represented by each of these hexadecimal values?

(a) C5   (b) D7   (c) D0   (d) 5B   (e) 20   (f) 40

7.55 What happens to the character string C'AAAA' if it is loaded into a register and has 1 added to it, and then is stored?

```
        L    2,LETTERS
        A    2,=F'1'
        ST   2,LETTERS
```

7.56 In a portion of text 240 bytes beyond PARAGRAF, you have two sentences in memory. You want to delete the second sentence, replace it with the first, and insert a third sentence before that. Write code to do this if (a) each sentence is 60 bytes long, (b) the first sentence is 50 bytes and the second and third are 70 bytes each, and (c) the first sentence is 70 bytes and the second and third are 50 bytes each.

7.57 What would be the effect of execution of each of the following instructions on the original contents of STR1 and STR2, declared as follows with no intervening variables?

```
        STR1    DC    C'ABCD'
        STR2    DC    C'12345'
```

(a) MVC   STR1,STR2   DEFAULT LENGTH
(b) MVC   STR2,STR1   OVERLAPPING
(c) MVC   STR1+2,STR2

7.58 What, if anything, is wrong with each of the following instructions?

(a) MVC   LOC(8),=C'ABCDE'   (c) MVC   LOC(8),=XL8'ABCDEFGH'
(b) CLC   LOC(8),=X'ABCDEF12'   (d) MVC   LOC(8),=XL8'ABCDEF12'

7.59 What tells you how the condition code is set by execution of the following instruction? Explain fully.

```
        CLC   WORD(4),=C'F'
        ...
        WORD  DC    CL10'FROG'
```

7.60 What, if anything, is wrong with the following instruction?

```
        CLC   5,=F'TOP'
```

7.61 Explain how the MVC instruction can be substituted for any MVI instruction. Since this is true, what is the use of having MVI?

7.62 To what value is the condition code set by each of the following instructions? Use the following declarations.

```
        STRING1   DC    C'ABC'
        STRING2   DC    C'ABC'
        STRING3   DC    C'DEF'
        STRING4   DC    C'ABCD'
        STRING5   DC    X'C1C2C3C4'
```

(a) CLC   STRING1(3),STRING2   (d) CLI   STRING1,C'A'
(b) CLC   STRING1(4),STRING2   (e) CLC   STRING1+2(3),STRING1
(c) CLI   STRING1+2,C'C'   (f) CLC   STRING4(4),STRING5

7.63 To what value is the condition code set by each of the following CLI instructions? Each part uses the originally declared values.

```
        LETTER   DC    CL1'A'
        WORD     DC    CL10'FROG'
```

(a) CLI   WORD,C'F'   (c) MVI   LETTER,C'.'
                                                                           CLI   LETTER,X'4B'

(b) CLI   WORD+6,C'.'   (d) MVI   WORD,C'.'
                                                                           CLI   WORD,X'4B'

7.64 To what value will the condition code be set by the execution of each of the following instructions? Use these declarations:

STR1	DC	C'ABCDE'
STR2	DC	C'12345'
STR3	DC	C'WXYZ'
STR4	DC	CL5'LMN'
STR5	DC	CL2'123'

(a) CLI   STR1,C'Q'   (d) CLI   STR4,C'S'
(b) CLI   STR2,C'P'   (e) CLI   STR5,C'1'
(c) CLI   STR3,C'R'   (f) CLI   STR1+3,C'Q'

7.65 Write code to count the number of times the string 'ABC' begins any string in an array STRINGS, which contains 50 strings, each 100 characters long.

7.66 Write a program segment to count the number of times the three-character sequence 'THE' appears in STRING, which is declared 30 bytes long.

7.67 Write code to count the number of times the string 'ABC' occurs in any string in an array STRINGS, which contains 50 strings, each 100 characters long.

7.68 Write code to count the number of times the string 'ABC' ends any string in an array STRINGS, which contains 50 strings, each 100 characters long.

7.69 Write a program segment to count the number of occurrences of the word 'THE' in STRING, which is 45 bytes long. For example, the string

            'ONE MUST BATHE BEFORE GOING TO THE THEATER'

has one 'THE' in it which is a separate word. Note that the letters 'THE' occur in 'BATHE' and 'THEATER' but are not to be counted. Assume that all the letters are capital, and that there is no punctuation. *Warning*: You must count all occurrences of the word 'THE', including the special cases in which it is the first or last word in the string.

7.70 Consider the following declarations of B:

(i)   A   DS   F   (ii)   A   DS   F
       B   DS   F   B   DS   CL4

(a) State precisely and fully what each declaration of B does.
(b) What kinds of values (what formats) may be placed in B in each case? Explain.
(c) If an initial value of zero were given in a DC statement for B, would the same memory contents result?

7.71 Why is knowledge of fullword boundary requirements important for a programmer despite the fact that the assembler assigns addresses for F statements automatically?

7.72 Repeat Problem 7.42 using halfword memory locations for the integers.

7.73 Use a bubble sort to arrange the first 10 elements of the array in Problem 7.46 (a) in order of weight and (b) in alphabetical order. Be sure to keep the proper weight with each food.

7.74 Write a portion of assembly language to arrange ten 20-character strings into alphabetical order using a bubble sort procedure (compare Chap. 6).

7.75 At GRADES is a list of a student's letter grades in each of four courses. At CREDITS are listed four full words representing the number of credits for each course.

$$\text{GRADES} \quad \text{DC} \quad \text{C'B,A,D,D'}$$
$$\text{CREDITS} \quad \text{DC} \quad \text{F'3,4,2,3'}$$

For example, the first course is a three-credit course in which the student received a grade of B. Assume that an A is valued at 4 points, B at 3 points, C at 2 points, D at 1 point. Determine whether the student is on academic probation (has an average under 2).

7.76 Write machine language instructions corresponding to the assembly language instructions given below. The base register is register 12, and it contains 1BC042. The address of OUT is 1BC144, and that of VAR1 is 1BC244.

```
        MVC     VAR1(6),VAR2
        CLC     VAR1+4(3),VAR3
        BL      OUT
        MVI     VAR1+3,X'C3'
        MVI     VAR2,C'C'
OUT     ...
VAR1    DC      C'ABCDEFGH'
VAR2    DC      CL4'147'
VAR3    DC      CL3'ZZZ'
```

7.77 Write machine language instructions corresponding to these assembly language instructions:

```
        MVC     0(7,9),3(6)
        MVI     7(9),B'11110000'
        CLI     255(9),X'D2'
        CLCL    2,4
        CLR     4,3
```

Chapter 8

Packed Decimal Numbers

8.1 Introduction

In this chapter, packed decimal numbers will be introduced. Chapter 9 will deal with more advanced concepts involving packed decimal numbers, including packed decimal numbers with fractional parts and conversion of packed decimal numbers to fixed binary format and to character string format.

8.2 Packed Decimal Number Format

In addition to the binary numbers we have discussed up to now, numbers may be stored in the memory of the IBM 370 system in a form called *packed decimal*. In this case, each decimal digit is represented by its 4-bit binary representation, and two decimal digits are stored per byte. It is important to observe that we are not converting the entire number from decimal to binary. Instead, each decimal digit is independently coded in binary. Thus decimal 57 becomes 0101 0111 (binary 5 binary 7) rather than 111001 (binary 57).

EXAMPLE 8.1

Using 4 bits to represent each of the digits in (decimal) 328, we would write 0011 0010 1000. In contrast, the binary representation of 328 is 0001 0100 1000.

The packed decimal representation does not use complements for negative numbers. Instead, we always store the sign and magnitude of the number, with the sign placed in the rightmost hexadecimal digit (rightmost half byte) of the number. The hexadecimal digits A through F are used to represent the sign; any of the letters A, C, E, or F can be used to represent a plus sign, and either B or D can be used to represent a minus sign.

Packed Decimal Number	Decimal Interpretation
123A	+123
9F	+9
123B	−123
76543C	+76,543
0C	0
33D	−33

Results produced by packed decimal instructions use C for plus and D for minus. The assembler assigns these same values for plus and minus, respectively, to values established in DC statements and literals.

There are several advantages and several disadvantages to the use of packed decimal numbers as opposed to fixed binary numbers. The advantages include:

1. Ability to handle large numbers (up to 31 decimal digits).
2. Less conversion on input/output (see Chap. 9).
3. Greater programmer familiarity with decimal numbers.
4. More accurate representation of fixed-point numbers, as for dollars and cents.

The disadvantages include:

1. Inefficient use of space. Binary numbers use only 1 bit for the sign, rather than the 4 bits used by packed decimal. Moreover, binary numbers use fewer bits to store the same values, in general. For example, a nine-digit number which would occupy 31 bits (a full word) as a binary number requires 5 bytes in packed decimal format.
2. Slower execution of operations, since a memory location rather than a register serves as the first operand in packed decimal operations.
3. The fact that packed decimal numbers cannot be used for addresses. The numbers in registers (index register and base register) are always binary.

8.3 Declaration (Definition) of Packed Decimal Numbers

Just as the letter F is used to denote fullword binary numbers in declarations and literals, the letter P is used to denote packed decimal numbers. Packed decimal numbers may have any length from 1 to 16 bytes; therefore, the length may be specified in the definition. Thus PL3 means packed decimal of length 3 bytes. Since each byte can hold two hexadecimal digits, a decimal number with n digits will require $(n+1)/2$ bytes, or $\frac{1}{2}$ byte for the sign and $\frac{1}{2}$ byte for each decimal digit. Here is an example of a PL3 number with five digits and a sign.

12	34	5C

A five-digit decimal number will require a memory location at least 3 bytes long. A 16-byte packed number (the maximum) consists of 31 decimal digits and a sign.

Packed variables, like fullword variables, can be defined as constants (DC) or merely defined to reserve space (DS). If an initial value is specified which has a length different from the defined length, the number is padded with zeros on the left or truncated on the left to match the defined length. If we do not specify a length in a DC statement, the length will be taken by default from the initial value. If neither a length nor an initial value is specified, the default value of 1 byte will be used. Every memory location consists of a whole number of bytes; no half bytes are reserved. Thus a four-digit number requires 3 bytes (and will have a leading zero). There are no boundary requirements for packed decimal numbers. (See Table 8-1 for examples.)

Table 8-1 Definition of Packed Decimal Numbers

	Definition		Stored Value	Remarks
A	DC	PL3'12345'	12345C	
B	DC	P'12345'	12345C	Length taken from initial value
C	DC	PL4'12345'	0012345C	Padded with zeros
D	DC	PL3'123456'	23456C	The 1 is truncated
E	DC	PL3'−12345'	12345D	
F	DC	P'0'	0C	The assembler uses the plus sign
G	DC	P'−9'	9D	
H	DC	P'1234'	01234C	A whole number of bytes
I	DS	PL3	None	3 bytes reserved
J	DS	PL3'12345'	None	3 bytes reserved
K	DS	P'12345'	None	3 bytes reserved
L	DS	P	None	1 byte reserved (by default)

8.4 Packed Decimal Operations and Formats

Packed decimal instructions take two operands, both of which are in memory. The mnemonics for packed instructions are the following:

AP	Add Packed
SP	Subtract Packed
ZAP	Zero and Add Packed
MP	Multiply Packed
DP	Divide Packed
CP	Compare Packed

Add Packed

A typical packed decimal instruction might look as follows:

$$AP \quad C(4),B(3)$$

Here the operation is Add Packed (AP), the operands are the packed decimal numbers C and B, and the numbers 4 and 3 in parentheses indicate that C has a length of 4 bytes and B has a length of 3 bytes. The packed decimal instructions are SS-type instructions. Because the two operands may have different lengths, both lengths may be specified in the assembly language instruction. (In this regard, these SS instructions, called *two-length SS instructions*, differ from those we discussed in Chap. 7.) In assembly language, the length of each operand is put in parentheses after the operand. If the length is not specified, the assembler will use the length specified in the declaration of the symbol. In machine language, the second byte of the instruction is split into two 4-bit fields to specify the lengths of the two operands. These instructions are 6 bytes long and have the following formats:

```
Assembly language   OPCODE    D1(L1,B1),D2(L2,B2)
Machine language    OP   L1 L2   B1 D1    B2 D2
                    1    1       2 bytes  2 bytes
                    byte byte
```

In the object code, the values of fields L1 and L2 are each stored as a number 1 less than the length specified in the assembly language instruction. This allows a length of up to 16 bytes to be specified in one hexadecimal digit. Thus

$$AP \quad 4(8,10),8(16,10)$$

will be processed into the following object code:

$$FA \quad 7F \quad A004 \quad A008$$

Note that in the second byte, the first length (8) is stored as 7 and the second length (16) is stored as F. There is no index register available in SS-type instructions. Its absence causes complications in using arrays of packed decimal numbers (Sec. 8.8).

In each operation except CP, the first operand is changed.

EXAMPLE 8.2

Using the declarations in Table 8-1, which will also be used in the next few examples, let us see how one of these instructions works.

$$AP \quad A(3),B(3)$$

AP A(3),B(3) takes the first 3 bytes at B and adds them to the first 3 bytes at A. Thus, the value of B (+12,345) is added to that of A (+12,345), and the result (+24,690) is stored in A.

EXAMPLE 8.3

What happens when the following instruction is executed?

$$\text{AP} \quad \text{C(4),B(3)}$$

The 3-byte number beginning at B is added to the 4-byte number beginning at C, and the answer is placed in C. Thus C becomes +24,690, which is stored as 0024690C.

EXAMPLE 8.4

Let's see what happens in this case:

$$\text{AP} \quad \text{A,B}$$

Since no lengths are included, the assembler uses the lengths in the declarations of A and B. Therefore, the first 3 bytes at B are added to the first 3 bytes at A, which is exactly the same result as with AP A(3),B(3), and the effect is the same as in the previous example.

EXAMPLE 8.5

What happens in the following case?

$$\text{AP} \quad \text{A(3),C(4)}$$

The answer 24690C is placed in A. It doesn't matter that the length of C is greater than the length of A, as long as the answer will fit in A.

The location to be operated on may be specified using an expression.

EXAMPLE 8.6

Let's see what happens when we do this:

$$\text{AP} \quad \text{A(3),C+1(3)}$$

The number starting at C+1 (the second through fourth bytes of C, 12345C) is added to A, yielding A (24690C). The same result would have been obtained by AP A,C because the leading byte of C contains 2 zeros. However, this format can sometimes result in the loss of information.

EXAMPLE 8.7

What is the effect of the following instruction?

$$\text{AP} \quad \text{A(3),B+1(2)}$$

The value 345C is added to A, yielding 12690C in A. The first byte of B, containing 12, is completely ignored, since the instruction specifies the 2 bytes from B+1.

EXAMPLE 8.8

Numbers to be added or subtracted must be valid packed decimal numbers. That is, the rightmost hexadecimal digit must be a sign (A − F) and the rest must be decimal digits. Thus the following would cause an error:

$$\text{AP} \quad \text{A(2),B(3)}$$

This is an error because the 2 bytes starting at A do not have a sign as the last half byte; therefore this number is not a valid packed decimal number.

EXAMPLE 8.9

An error would also result if the following instruction were executed:

$$\text{AP} \quad \text{A,C+1}$$

The length of C is 4 (from Table 8-1), so the assembler supplies a length of 4 for the second operand. Thus this instruction is the same as

AP   A,C+1(4)

and the use of 4 bytes starting at C+1 puts a sign digit in the middle of a number, which is illegal.

00	12	34	5C	23	45	6C
C	C+1	C+2	C+3	D	D+1	D+2

The number specified, 12 34 5C 23, is not a legal packed decimal number.

Subtract Packed

The Subtract Packed (SP) operation works in exactly the same way that Add Packed works, except, of course, that the second operand is subtracted from the first. Both AP and SP set the condition code in exactly the same manner that A and S do:

Result	*Condition Code*
Zero	0
Negative	1
Positive	2
Overflow	3

An overflow occurs if the answer is too big to be held in the first operand.

8.5 Zero and Add Packed

The special instruction Zero and Add Packed (ZAP) is used to initialize a packed decimal variable. It zeros the first operand and adds the value of the second operand to that zero. In effect, it copies the second operand into the first. It also sets the condition code, just as the other arithmetic operations do. The instruction ZAP A,B copies the value of B into A. If the lengths of the operands are different, it truncates the result on the left or pads it with zeros on the left.

EXAMPLE 8.10

Consider the instruction

```
        ZAP    A(3),B(2)
        ...
A       DC     PL3'123'
B       DC     PL2'444'
```

The instruction copies the value of B into A, so A gets the value 00444C and B stays 444C. Since the length of the operands need not be the same, ZAP does more than merely copy the second operand into the first. It truncates on the left or pads with zeros on the left. It also sets the condition code.

EXAMPLE 8.11

This is how we zero a packed decimal memory location:

```
        ZAP    A(3),=P'0'
```

This instruction zeros A and then adds zero to it, yielding a final result of zero in A and setting the condition code to zero. This also guarantees that the zero in A will have packed decimal format.

8.6 Multiplication and Division of Packed Numbers

There are special rules for multiplication and division of packed decimal numbers just as there are for fullword numbers.

Multiply Packed

In multiplication, the answer is placed in the first operand location; therefore, there must be enough space available at that location for the answer. This leads to the following limitations:

1. The first operand must have at least as many leading zeros as the total number of digits in the second operand (including the sign). This is a requirement of the IBM 370 and is more zeros than are logically necessary. It follows that the product will always have at least one leading zero (see Example 8.12).
2. The second operand cannot exceed 8 bytes, nor can it exceed the length of the first operand. These are also requirements of the IBM 370 which are not logically necessary.

EXAMPLE 8.12

Here is how multiplication works:

```
        MP      A(4),B(2)
        ...
A       DC      PL4'999'        0000999C
B       DC      PL2'999'        999C
```

Here B holds the largest number that will fit in 2 bytes, and A holds the largest number which will fit into 4 bytes, with sufficient leading zeros so that it can be multiplied by B. The result in A is 0998001C. Despite the fact that we used the largest numbers permitted, we still got a leading zero in the answer.

EXAMPLE 8.13

We will determine which of the following multiplications are legal, using the following definitions:

```
A       DC      PL4'123'        0000123C
B       DC      PL3'123'        00123C
C       DC      PL2'123'        123C
```

(a) MP   A(4),C(2)
(b) MP   A(4),B(3)
(c) MP   A(4),B+1(2)
(d) MP   A+1(3),B+1(2)
(e) MP   A+1(3),C+1(1)
(f) MP   B(3),C(1)
(g) MP   A(4),B(5)

(a) This is legal. The 4 zeros are sufficient for the entire number C.
(b) This is not legal. There are only 4 leading zeros in A, but B has six digits (including the sign).
(c) This is legal. There are enough leading zeros in A for the second operand, which is specified to be the last 2 bytes of B.
(d) This is not legal. There is only 1 leading byte of zeros in A+1, but the number at B+1 has three digits and a sign.
(e) This is legal. However, the value of the second operand is not the value of C.
(f) This is not legal. The second operand is not a legal packed decimal number, since it does not have a sign.
(g) This is not legal. The second operand exceeds the first in length. Also, the second operand is not a valid packed decimal number.

Often the requirement of leading zeros forces us to make adjustments to accomplish a multiplication.

EXAMPLE 8.14

Suppose we want to multiply A by B, putting the answer in A.

    A   DC   PL3'123'
    B   DC   PL3'111'

The problem is that A does not have enough leading zeros to make the multiplication legal, even though the nonzero portion of the answer will fit into the 3 bytes of A. That is, the answer, 13653, is small enough to fit into A, but A is not long enough to be used to do the MP operation directly. To solve the problem, we use a temporary memory location.

```
         ZAP    TEMP,A
         MP     TEMP,B
         ZAP    A,TEMP
         ...
TEMP     DS     PL8
```

A copy of A is made at TEMP, with extra leading zeros. This is then multiplied by B. When TEMP is ZAPped into A, the leading zeros are truncated.

EXAMPLE 8.15

Show how to multiply A times B, placing the result in B.

    A   DC   PL3'123'
    B   DC   PL4'3'

We can do this very simply:

    MP   B(4),A(3)

In this example, B (0000003C) has sufficient leading zeros to hold the entire six digits of A (including sign), so no temporary location is needed.

Now show how to multiply A times B, placing the result in B, using these declarations:

    A   DC   PL3'123'
    B   DC   PL3'1'

In this example, B (00001C) does not have sufficient leading zeros to hold the entire six digits of A (including sign), so a temporary location is needed, despite the fact that multiplication by 1 will not increase the number of digits in the answer.

```
         ZAP    TEMP(6),B(3)
         MP     TEMP(6),A(3)
         ZAP    B(3),TEMP(6)
```

Mathematically, the number of digits in a product cannot exceed the sum of the numbers of digits in the two operands. Therefore, it is sufficient to use a TEMP whose length is the sum of the lengths of A and B.

Divide Packed

The Divide Packed (DP) operation divides the first operand by the second operand and places both the quotient and the remainder in the space occupied by the first operand. Thus, after the Divide Packed operation has been executed, the first operand holds two numbers (the quotient and the remainder), which are stored with the remainder following the quotient. The remainder has the same length as the divisor (second operand), and the remaining bytes of the first operand hold the quotient. The following rules apply to Divide Packed:

1. The length of the divisor cannot exceed 8 bytes and must be less than the length of the first operand.
2. The length of the quotient will be the length of the first operand minus the length of the second operand.

EXAMPLE 8.16

Using the following declarations, we see how DP works:

	Declaration		Value Stored in Memory
A	DC	PL3'48'	00 04 8C
B	DC	PL1'5'	5C
C	DC	PL2'5'	00 5C

If we divide A by B,

        DP   A,B

the new value stored in A is

      00 9C   3C
      Quotient   Remainder

But if we divide the original value of A by C (with DP A,C), since C has length 2 bytes, the new value in A will be

      9C   00 3C
    Quotient   Remainder

Since 2 bytes are used for the remainder, the quotient is only 1 byte long. Of course, if we know that C is a single-digit number, we can write

        DP   A,C+1(1)

which will produce the same result as DP A,B. If we do not know that the quoteint will fit into 1 byte, we have to use a temporary location to perform the division. Thus if we want to divide D by C and place the result in D, we can use the declarations

    D   DC   PL3'123'
    TEMP DS   PL5

and the instructions

    ZAP   TEMP,D
    DP   TEMP,C
    ZAP   D,TEMP(3)

Note that after DP, the quotient is the first 3 bytes of TEMP, so we must specify the length in the last instruction. If we did not specify the length, the assembler would use 5 bytes from the declaration of TEMP, and there would be an error because the data is not a valid packed decimal number. (The sign of the quotient is in the middle of the 5 bytes.)

EXAMPLE 8.17

Suppose that A and B are packed decimal numbers, where A has length 7 bytes and B has length 3 bytes. After dividing A by B, we put the quotient in QUOT and the remainder in REM.

    DP   A(7),B(3)
    ZAP   QUOT,A(4)   QUOTIENT IS IN THE FIRST 4 BYTES OF A
    ZAP   REM,A+4(3)   REMAINDER IS IN BYTES 5, 6, AND 7 OF A

8.7 Compare Packed

The Compare Packed (CP) instruction may be used to set the condition code. The settings are analogous to those set by all other compare operations:

Condition Code	Result
0	First operand equal to second
1	First operand lower
2	First operand higher

The condition code can be tested with a mask or with extended mnemonics (see Chap. 5). For example, if A is equal to or greater than B, the instructions

    CP   A,B   or   CP   A,B
    BC   10,THERE   BNL   THERE

will cause a branch to THERE. CP will set the condition code to 0 or 2, which will match one of the 1 bits in the mask (B'1010'), causing the branch to be executed.

8.8 Arrays of Packed Decimal Numbers

Arrays of packed decimal numbers are defined as follows:

```
ARR1    DC   PL3'1,2,3,6,5,4'    An initialized, six-element array
ARR2    DS   5PL3                A five-element array, uninitialized
ARR3    DC   2PL3'10,20'         A four-element array, with values 10, 20, 10, and 20
ARR4    DC   PL3'7'              A three-element array
        DC   PL3'11'
        DC   PL3'-22'
```

Listing values as in the definition of ARR1 reserves a number of memory spaces and puts a value in each. Alternatively, the number of elements may be explicitly stated before the P (as in ARR2). Doing both of these multiplies the number of explicit elements by the replication factor (see ARR3). These rules are similar to those for fixed binary arrays (see Chap. 6). ARR4 explicitly defines each value in its own DC statement.

Accessing each element in an array of packed decimal numbers is slightly different from the corresponding act for a fixed binary array, because (1) the length of packed decimal numbers is not always 4 bytes, and (2) there is no index register in SS-type instructions. These differences mean that we must frequently use explicit notation with packed decimal instructions. Remember that we can use explicit notation for either or both of the operands of a packed decimal instruction. For example, if A is 3 bytes long with a displacement (in hexadecimal) of 0A0, and D is 2 bytes long with a displacement (in hexadecimal) of 0AA, the following two instructions are equivalent (assuming that the base register is 12):

                                                  Lengths
                                              ↙   ↘
    AP   A(3),D(2)   AP   160(3,12),170(2,12)
                                              ↖   ↗
                                              Displacements
                                              (in decimal)

Care must be exercised in interpreting packed decimal notation. In particular, A(3) means different things in an SS-type instruction and an RX-type instruction, even if A is a packed decimal variable in each. For example, compare the following instructions:

Instruction	Type	Format
AP B,A(3)	SS	D1(L1,B1),D2(L2,B2)
LA 2,A(3)	RX	R1,D2(X2,B2)

The 3 in the AP instruction is a length (in this case, L2). The 3 in the LA instruction, however, refers to X2, an index register. The type of instruction determines the nature of the parts of the operand(s).

For example, looping through an array to calculate its sum requires modifying the base register of the instruction. This forces us to use explicit notation for the second operand of our AP instruction. We must set up a base register for this instruction and get the address of each of the array elements into that register one at a time. Suppose we want to add each element of a 10-element array to a variable called SUM, which is first initialized to zero. Then we use the following instruction in a loop:

```
        AP      SUM,0(3,8)
                     ↗  ↖
                Length   Base register for this instruction
```

We can set up a base register for this instruction in one of two ways.

Method 1

Use an RX instruction which uses an index register that can be incremented:

```
        LA      8,ARR(7)
```

Register 7 is the index register of this RX instruction, and register 8 will be the base register for the SS instruction and will contain the address of the current element.

EXAMPLE 8.18

Using method 1, let's sum a 10-element array of 3-byte packed decimal numbers.

```
        ZAP     SUM,=P'0'       INITIALIZE SUM
        SR      7,7             INDEX IN 7
        LA      10,10           COUNTER
LOOP    LA      8,ARR(7)        ADDRESS OF CURRENT ELEMENT IN REGISTER 8
*                               REGISTER 7 IS INDEX REG IN THIS RX INSTRUCTION
        AP      SUM,0(3,8)      LENGTH 3, BASE 8
        LA      7,3(0,7)        INCREMENT REGISTER 7 BY 3 (3-BYTE NUMBERS)
        BCT     10,LOOP
```

Method 2

Load the address of the first element of the array into the "base" register, and increment it to the address of the last element of the array.

```
        ZAP     SUM,=P'0'       INITIALIZE SUM
        LA      7,ARR           7 IS THE BASE REGISTER FOR AP
        LA      10,10           10 ELEMENTS
LOOP    AP      SUM,0(3,7)      7 IS BASE FOR AP
        LA      7,3(0,7)        INCREMENT BASE REGISTER BY 3 BYTES
        BCT     10,LOOP
```

EXAMPLE 8.19

Suppose that A and B are each arrays of 10 packed decimal numbers of length 3 and we want to add B(I) to A(I) for each I. Here are two ways to do this.

First, we use an index register:

```
           SR    7,7              INITIALIZE INDEX REGISTER
           LA    10,10            INITIALIZE COUNTER
LOOP       LA    8,A(7)           8 IS THE BASE REGISTER FOR A
           LA    9,B(7)           9 IS THE BASE REGISTER FOR B
           AP    0(3,8),0(3,9)    ADD B(I) TO A(I)
           LA    7,3(0,7)         INCREMENT THE INDEX REGISTER
           BCT   10,LOOP
```

Our second approach increments the base registers:

```
           LA    8,A              8 IS THE BASE REGISTER FOR A
           LA    9,B              9 IS THE BASE REGISTER FOR B
           LA    10,10            INITIALIZE COUNTER
LOOP       AP    0(3,8),0(3,9)    ADD B(I) TO A(I)
           LA    8,3(0,8)         INCREMENT BASE REGISTER FOR A
           LA    9,3(0,9)         INCREMENT BASE REGISTER FOR B
           BCT   10,LOOP
```

EXAMPLE 8.20

Modify Example 8.19 so that the elements of A have length 5 and the elements of B have length 3. First we use two index registers, one for A and the other for B:

```
           SR    6,6              INITIALIZE INDEX REGISTER FOR A
           SR    7,7              INITIALIZE INDEX REGISTER FOR B
           LA    10,10            INITIALIZE COUNTER
LOOP       LA    8,A(6)           8 IS THE BASE REGISTER FOR A
           LA    9,B(7)           9 IS THE BASE REGISTER FOR B
           AP    0(5,8),0(3,9)    ADD B(I) TO A(I)
           LA    6,5(0,6)         INCREMENT INDEX REGISTER FOR A
           LA    7,3(0,7)         INCREMENT INDEX REGISTER FOR B
           BCT   10,LOOP
```

It is much easier to modify the approach which increments the base registers, because we have to change only the increment for the base register for A and the length of A in the AP instruction:

```
           LA    8,A              8 IS THE BASE REGISTER FOR A
           LA    9,B              9 IS THE BASE REGISTER FOR B
           LA    10,10            INITIALIZE COUNTER
LOOP       AP    0(5,8),0(3,9)    ADD B(I) TO A(I)
           LA    8,5(0,8)         INCREMENT BASE REGISTER FOR A
           LA    9,3(0,9)         INCREMENT BASE REGISTER FOR B
           BCT   10,LOOP
```

Solved Problems

8.1 Give the decimal value of each of the following packed decimal numbers.

(a) 123C   (c) 123F   (e) 0C   (g) 000C
(b) 123A   (d) 123D   (f) 0D   (h) 0023456C

(a)–(c) +123   (d) −123   (e)–(g) 0   (h) 23,456

8.2 Write the hexadecimal representation of the following decimal numbers in two ways: first as halfword fixed binary numbers and then as packed decimal numbers. Use as few bytes as possible for the latter.

(a) 100 (b) −100 (c) 4095 (d) 0

	Hexadecimal Representation of Binary Number	Hexadecimal Representation of Packed Decimal Number
(a)	0064	100C
(b)	FF9C	100D
(c)	0FFF	04095C
(d)	0000	0C

8.3 Can a 3-byte packed number hold more than three digits?

Yes. It can hold five digits (plus a sign digit, making 6 half bytes).

8.4 What is the value of each of the following numbers in memory (in packed decimal notation)?

(a) PL3'999'   (d) PL3'987654'
(b) PL3'−999' (e) PL3'0'
(c) P'999'   (f) PL3'−0'

(a) 00999C
(b) 00999D
(c) 999C
(d) 87654C (9 has been truncated)
(e) 00000C
(f) 00000D (the assembler assigns D for minus zero, notwithstanding that the value is also equal to +0)

8.5 With the following declaration, what is the value in memory of A? How many bytes of memory are used for A?

A   DC   P'10000'

The value is

10000C   3 bytes of memory are assigned

8.6 Show the final value in TEMP after execution of each of the following instructions, using the definitions

```
FIRST    DC    PL3'12'
SECOND   DC    PL4'−20'
BIG      DC    P'123456789098765'
TEMP     DS    PL6
```

(a) ZAP TEMP,FIRST   (g) ZAP TEMP,=P'0'
(b) ZAP TEMP,SECOND   ZAP TEMP+2(4),FIRST+1(2)
(c) ZAP TEMP,BIG   (h) ZAP TEMP,=P'0'
(d) ZAP TEMP,BIG+4(4)   ZAP TEMP+1(3),FIRST
(e) ZAP TEMP,BIG+2(6)   (i) ZAP TEMP,BIG+3(5)
(f) ZAP TEMP,=P'0'   ZAP TEMP(3),FIRST+2(1)

(a) 00000000012C   (f) 00000000000C
(b) 00000000020D   (g) 00000000012C
(c) 56789098765C OVERFLOW (h) 0000012C000C
(d) 00009098765C   (i) 00002C98765C
(e) 56789098765C

8.7 Explain what is wrong with the following code:

```
FIRST    DC    PL5'2000'
SECOND   DC    PL4'200'
ANSWER   DS    PL4
TEMP     DS    PL8
```

(a) ZAP   TEMP,FIRST   (d) ZAP   ANSWER,FIRST
    DP   TEMP,SECOND   DP   ANSWER,SECOND
    ZAP   ANSWER,TEMP

(b) MP   FIRST,SECOND   (e) DP   FIRST, SECOND

(c) ZAP   TEMP,FIRST
    MP   TEMP,SECOND
    ZAP   FIRST(3),TEMP(3)

(a) DP places two packed decimal numbers in TEMP—a quotient and a remainder. ZAP will work only if a valid packed decimal number (and only one) is the second operand. [Use ZAP   ANSWER,TEMP(4) to get the quotient into ANSWER.]

(b) FIRST does not have 4 bytes of leading zeros, required for multiplication by a 4-byte second operand. [Use MP   FIRST,SECOND+2(2).]

(c) The first 3 bytes of TEMP contain no sign digit, so this ZAP will not work. [Use ZAP   FIRST(5),TEMP+5(3) or ZAP   FIRST(5),TEMP(8).]

(d) Because the remainder requires 4 bytes (as many as are in SECOND), there are no bytes for the quotient, which is not allowed. [Use DP   ANSWER,SECOND+2(2).]

(e) Because the remainder requires 4 bytes (as many as are in SECOND), there is only 1 byte for the quotient, which is insufficient for 010C. [Use DP   FIRST,SECOND+2(2).]

8.8 Write the instructions to ZAP the remainder into REM and the quotient into QUOT after each of the following sequences of instructions. (The variables have previously been initialized.)

```
TWO     DS    PL2
THREE   DS    PL3
FOUR    DS    PL4
FIVE    DS    PL5
QUOT    DS    PL4
REM     DS    PL4
TEMP    DS    PL10
```

(a) DP   TEMP,TWO   (d) DP   TEMP,FIVE+1(4)
(b) DP   TEMP,THREE   (e) DP   TEMP,FIVE
(c) DP   TEMP,FOUR+1(3)

(a) ZAP   QUOT,TEMP(8)   (d) ZAP   QUOT,TEMP(6)
    ZAP   REM,TEMP+8(2)   ZAP   REM,TEMP+6(4)
(b) ZAP   QUOT,TEMP(7)   (e) ZAP   QUOT,TEMP(5)
    ZAP   REM,TEMP+7(3)   ZAP   REM,TEMP+5(5)
(c) ZAP   QUOT,TEMP(7)
    ZAP   REM,TEMP+7(3)

8.9 State whether the branch(es) occur(s) in each of the following cases.

```
A       DC      P'123'
B       DC      P'-123'
C       DC      PL1'123'
D       DC      PL6'-7077'
```

(a) CP   A,B   (d) CP   A,C
    BH   THERE   BE   THERE
(b) SP   A,B   (e) CP   B,D+4(2)
    BM   THERE   BH   THERE
(c) AP   A,B   (f) AP   A,D+4(2)
    BP   THERE   BP   THERE
    BM   HERE

(a) Yes.
(b) No (A contains +246).
(c) Neither produces a branch (addition results in 0).
(d) No (C contains 3C, since it has a length of 1 byte).
(e) No ($-123 < -077$, and the last 2 bytes of D contain 077D).
(f) Yes ($+123 - 077 > 0$).

8.10 Write code to divide D by B and branch to THERE if the quotient is positive. Use the declarations from the preceding problem.

```
        DP      D,B
        CP      D(4),=P'0'
        BH      THERE
```

8.11 Write a program segment to determine the average of the values in an 11-element 5-byte packed decimal array PARRAY, and store the answer in AVE.

```
            LA      10,11               COUNTER
            LA      7,PARRAY
            ZAP     SUM,=P'0'           INITIALIZE SUM
LOOP        AP      SUM,0(5,7)          ELEMENT LENGTH 5 BYTES, BASE REGISTER 7
            LA      7,5(0,7)            INCREMENT BASE REGISTER
            BCT     10,LOOP
            DP      SUM(7),=P'11'
            ZAP     AVE(5),SUM(5)       QUOTIENT IS FIRST 5 BYTES
            ...
PARRAY      DS      11PL5
SUM         DS      PL7
AVE         DS      PL5
```

8.12 Write a program segment to determine how many of the elements in the array of Problem 8.11 differ by more than 25 from the average and to store that number in COUNT. Assume that the average has already been computed and stored in AVE.

```
                LA    10,11               LOOP COUNTER
                LA    7,PARRAY
                SR    2,2                 COUNT OF NUMBERS > 25 AWAY
        LOOP    ZAP   TEMP,AVE
                SP    TEMP,0(5,7)
                CP    TEMP,=P'-25'        IF TEMP LOWER, NUMBER IS MORE THAN 25 AWAY
                BNL   NOTLOW
                LA    2,1(0,2)            INCREMENT COUNT
                B     ENDLOOP
        NOTLOW  CP    TEMP,=P'25'         IF TEMP HIGHER, NUMBER IS MORE THAN 25 AWAY
                BNH   ENDLOOP
                LA    2,1(0,2)            INCREMENT COUNT
        ENDLOOP LA    7,5(0,7)            INCREMENT BASE REGISTER
                BCT   10,LOOP
```

8.13 To change the sign of a number in a register you use the instruction LCR. Is there a comparable instruction for packed decimal numbers? Show two methods that you could use to change the sign of a packed decimal number.

There is no single instruction. Either of the following sequences of instructions might do:

```
        ZAP   TEMP,=P'0'
        SP    TEMP,NUM
        ZAP   NUM,TEMP
or
        ZAP   TEMP,NUM
        MP    TEMP,=P'-1'    TEMP MUST HAVE 1 BYTE OF LEADING ZEROS
        ZAP   NUM,TEMP
```

8.14 Write a program segment to sum a fullword binary array and a 3-byte decimal array within the same loop. For example,

```
for I = 1 to N do
    begin
        BINSUM := BINSUM + BARRAY[I];
        DECSUM := DECSUM + DARRAY[I]
    end
```

One possible solution follows:

```
                ZAP   DECSUM,=P'0'        INITIALIZE DECIMAL SUM
                SR    2,2                 BINSUM IN 2
                SR    7,7                 INDEX IN 7
                LA    10,4                INCREMENT FOR BINSUM IN 10
                L     11,N                N
                MH    11,=H'4'            4N
                SH    11,=H'4'            4N - 4
                LA    9,DARRAY            BASE ADDRESS FOR DECIMAL ARRAY
        LOOP    A     2,BARRAY(7)         ADD BINARY ELEMENT
                AP    DECSUM,0(3,9)       ADD DECIMAL ELEMENT
                LA    9,3(0,9)            INCREMENT DECIMAL REGISTER
                BXLE  7,10,LOOP           INCREMENT BINARY REGISTER,
        *                                 AND CONTROL LOOPING
                ST    2,BINSUM
```

Here is another possible solution:

```
              ZAP   DECSUM,=P'0'     INITIALIZE DECIMAL SUM
              SR    2,2              BINSUM IN 2
              SR    7,7              INDEX IN 7
              L     11,N             COUNTER
              LA    9,DARRAY         BASE ADDRESS FOR DECIMAL ARRAY
      LOOP    A     2,BARRAY(7)      ADD BINARY ELEMENT
              AP    DECSUM,0(3,9)    ADD DECIMAL ELEMENT
              LA    9,3(0,9)         INCREMENT DECIMAL REGISTER
              LA    7,4(0,7)         INCREMENT BINARY REGISTER
              BCT   11,LOOP
              ST    2,BINSUM
```

8.15 Problem 7.50 checked a credit card number against a list of lost or stolen credit cards.

(a) Would holding the list as packed decimal data be more efficient?

(b) Can the data be held as fullword numbers?

(c) Would leading zeros in some of the numbers present any problems?

Explain each answer fully.

(a) Holding the card numbers as packed decimal numbers would require much less memory, since a 16-digit number can be held in a 9-byte packed decimal memory location. About 10,000 bytes of memory is saved for 1400 elements. However, in general, the card numbers could not utilize characters other than the digits 0 through 9 [see parts (b) and (c)]. Either Compare Packed or Compare Logical Character could be used.

(b) The numbers could not be held in fullword memory locations, since they are too long.

(c) Leading zeros would cause no problem, since each identification number is 16 digits long. (If different card numbers were represented with different numbers of digits, such as 0007, 007, and 7, there would be a problem, since the computer could not distinguish among these three values if they were held as packed decimal numbers.)

Supplementary Problems

8.16 Write machine language instructions corresponding to the assembly language instructions given below. The base register is register 12, and it contains the base address 1BC042. The address of VAR1 is 1BC244.

```
              ZAP   NUM3(4),NUM1(3)
              AP    NUM2+3(1),NUM1+1(2)
              ZAP   TEMP,NUM2
              DP    TEMP,NUM1
              ZAP   VAR1,TEMP(5)
              ZAP   VAR2,TEMP+5(3)
              ...
      VAR1    DC    PL4'123'
      VAR2    DC    PL3'-887'
      NUM1    DC    PL3'1000'
      NUM2    DC    PL4'-1'
      NUM3    DS    PL5
      TEMP    DS    PL8
```

CHAP. 8] PACKED DECIMAL NUMBERS 187

8.17 Write machine language instructions corresponding to the assembly language instructions given below.

```
ZAP    0(4,6),0(3,7)
AP     0(5,2),4(16,5)
DP     0(8,6),202(4,4)
ZAP    0(3,3),0(4,7)
ZAP    0(4,7),4(4,7)
```

8.18 What is the effect of the following sequence of code?

```
        L     2,NUM1
        A     2,=F'1'
        ST    2,ANS
        ...
        DS    0F
NUM1    DC    PL4'100'
ANS     DS    PL4
```

8.19 An overflow occurs when an attempt is made to ZAP a number into a memory location which is not long enough to hold it, causing loss of the most significant digits. A and B have previously been initialized. Which of the following portions of code will branch to ERROR when A * B will not fit in A?

```
             A       DS    PL3
             B       DS    PL3
             TEMP    DS    PL8
```

```
(a)  ZAP    TEMP,A          (b)  ZAP    TEMP,A
     MP     TEMP,B               MP     TEMP,B
     ZAP    A,TEMP+5(3)          ZAP    A,TEMP
     BO     ERROR                BO     ERROR
```

8.20 What is accomplished by the following code? Show the values in memory as each instruction is executed.

```
            ZAP    QUOT(8),DIVID
            DP     QUOT(8),DIVIS
            ...
DIVID       DC     PL5'2021'
DIVIS       DC     PL3'101'
QUOT        DS     PL5
REM         DS     PL3
```

8.21 What is wrong with the following instruction, designed to initialize SUM to zero?

```
            SP     SUM,SUM
            ...
SUM         DS     PL5
```

8.22 Write a program segment to sum the first N elements of a 100-element, 3-byte packed decimal array.

8.23 Write a program segment to sum the elements with odd subscripts of a 100-element array of 3-byte packed decimal numbers.

8.24 Write a program segment to sort the elements of a 25-element packed decimal array with 3-byte elements. Use a bubble sort or some other type of sort procedure to get the elements into ascending order.

8.25 Write a program segment to count the number of elements in a 50-element packed decimal array which exceed the value in the prior element. Assume that each element is 3 bytes long. Thus the array

1 3 2 7 3	would have 2 as its answer
1 3 3 2 19	would have 2 as its answer
10 9 8 7 6	would have 0 as its answer

8.26 Write a program segment to do the following for an 11-element array of 3-byte packed decimal numbers. Starting from the first element in the array, set the new value of each of the first 10 elements to 3 more than the as-yet-unchanged value of the next element.

8.27 Write a program segment to do the following for an 11-element array of 3-byte packed decimal numbers. Starting from the last element in the array, set the new value of each of the first 10 elements to 3 more than the final value of the next element.

8.28 Write a program segment to sum the elements of a 25-element packed decimal array and sum separately a 25-element, fullword fixed binary array. Do both summations in one loop. The packed decimal array elements are 3 bytes each. Place the first answer in SUMPACK and the second in SUMBIN.

8.29 Write a program segment to sum the elements of two 25-element packed decimal arrays. The first array has 3-byte elements, and the second has 5-byte elements. Sum the two arrays separately in one loop, yielding two answers.

8.30 An array consists of 25 elements, each containing a 15-byte character string and a 3-byte packed decimal number. Write a program segment to place the character string corresponding to the highest packed decimal number into a memory location called MAXSTR. If there is more than one element with the highest number, use the first.

8.31 What is the effect of execution of the following MP instructions?

```
          MP    DUMMY(6),A(3)
          MP    B-3(6),A(3)
          ...
DUMMY     DC    X'000000'
B         DC    PL3'123'
A         DC    PL3'456'
```

8.32 For a set of variables with base register 12 and the following displacements, write the explicit version of each instruction given and also write its machine language translation.

Displacement
(Hexadecimal)

		AP	A(3),D(2)
		AP	A(3),C(4)
		AP	A(3),C+2(2)
		AP	B(3),D+1(1)
		...	
0A0	A	DS	PL3
0A3	B	DS	PL3
0A6	C	DS	PL4
0AA	D	DS	PL2

Chapter 9

Advanced Packed Decimal Concepts

9.1 Introduction

Chapter 8 presented packed decimal arithmetic (formats, arithmetic operations, and the compare instruction). So far, however, only integral packed decimal numbers have been considered; therefore this chapter will discuss fractional packed decimal numbers. It will also consider conversions of packed decimal numbers to fixed binary and zoned (character string) numbers.

9.2 Fractional Packed Decimal Numbers

The computer doesn't keep track of the decimal point in fractional packed decimal numbers. Consequently, it is the responsibility of the programmer to keep track of how many decimal places each packed decimal number has.

In definition statements and literals, a decimal point in a packed decimal number is ignored by the assembler. Thus these two statements generate the same initial value in memory:

```
         X      DC      PL3'123'
         X      DC      PL3'1.23'
```

It is often a good technique to include a decimal point in such statements as a reminder to the programmer of how many decimal places each variable is supposed to have.

It is useful to review briefly the number of decimal places required and/or produced in arithmetic operations with fractional decimal numbers. In multiplication, the number of decimal places in the product is the sum of the numbers of decimal places in the factors. For example, if A has two decimal places and B has one, their product will have three. If we want to store the value of the product with more or fewer decimal places than these rules specify, then it is necessary to add or truncate digits in the answer. Suppose we want PROD with four decimal places equal to A times B. On the computer, this might be programmed as follows:

```
              ZAP     PROD,A
              MP      PROD,B          PROD HAS THREE DECIMAL PLACES
              MP      PROD,=P'1.0'    PROD NOW HAS FOUR DECIMAL PLACES
              ...
        A     DC      PL3'1.26'       TWO OF THE FIVE DIGITS ARE AFTER THE DECIMAL
        *                                     POINT
        B     DC      PL3'50.0'       ONE OF THE DIGITS IS AFTER THE DECIMAL POINT
        PROD  DS      PL10
```

Similarly, in division, the number of decimal places in the quotient is the number of decimal places in the dividend minus the number in the divisor. The remainder always has the same number of decimal places as the dividend. Thus if 1.23124 is divided by 1.23, the quotient is 1.001 and the remainder is 0.00001. (It is unusual to talk about remainders with numbers having decimal places, but the computer does not know that the numbers have decimal places, and it keeps a remainder anyway.)

EXAMPLE 9.1

```
              1001 → 1.001        2        Quotient is 2
    1.23)1.23124         0.2)0.5
        1 23                4
        ────                ─
         0124               1        Remainder cannot be greater
          123                        than the dividend; it is 0.1, not 1
          ───
            1
```

If we want to store the value of the quotient with fewer digits than these rules specify, we can simply perform the division and then adjust (truncate or round) the answer. But if we want more digits in the quotient, we have to adjust the dividend so that the quotient will have the correct number of digits. (Adjusting the answer after division would append zeros to the quotient rather than develop more digits of the quotient.)

EXAMPLE 9.2

We wish to divide DIVIDEND, which is 6 bytes long and has two decimal places, by DIVISOR, which is 3 bytes long and has one decimal place. QUOTIENT is 3 bytes long and has two decimal places. The code presented first gives an answer with a last digit of zero no matter what values are divided. The second section of code gives a more accurate value.

			First Operand Value	Answer
	ZAP	TEMP,DIVIDEND	000000000000001234C	
	DP	TEMP,DIVISOR	0000000000024C00034C	
	ZAP	QUOTIENT,TEMP(7)	0000000000024C	
	MP	QUOTIENT,=P'1.0'	0000000000240C	2.40
	...			
TEMP	DS	PL10		
DIVISOR	DC	PL3'5.0'		
DIVIDEND	DC	PL6'12.34'		
QUOTIENT	DS	PL7		

The more accurate code is as follows:

	ZAP	TEMP,DIVIDEND	000000000000001234C	
	MP	TEMP,=P'1.0'	000000000000012340C	
	DP	TEMP,DIVISOR	0000000000246C00040C	
	ZAP	QUOTIENT,TEMP(7)	0000000000246C	2.46
	...			
TEMP	DS	PL10		
DIVISOR	DC	PL3'5.0'		
DIVIDEND	DC	PL6'12.34'		
QUOTIENT	DS	PL7		

Notice that in Example 9.2 we have written the literal as =P'1.0'. This produces the same effect as the literal =P'10', but it indicates to the reader that our intention is simply to produce one more decimal place in the product or one more decimal place in the quotient.

The rules for addition and subtraction are different. The number of decimal places in each number to be added or subtracted must be the same (the decimal points must be aligned) before the operation. How should we add or subtract two numbers with different numbers of decimal places? Merely adding or subtracting ignores the fact that the decimal points must be aligned. The A and B from above should be added as follows:

```
   1.26
  50.0
  ─────
  51.26
```

but merely using an AP instruction would add them in the following way:

$$\begin{array}{r} 126 \\ 500 \\ \hline 626 \end{array}$$

The technique which must be used to align the decimal points is to add digits to the number with fewer decimal places so that the numbers of decimal places are equal. Then add or subtract the numbers, and, finally, truncate if necessary to get the desired number of decimal places in the answer. Here is how we would do the previous addition:

1.26	stays as	1.26	held in the computer as	126
50.0	changes to	50.00	held in the computer as	5000
	the sum is	51.26	held in the computer as	5126

If the answer is to be stored in a variable with fewer than two decimal places, then the answer must be shortened.

For our calculation of A + B, the question, then, is how to increase the number of digits of B and later how to decrease the number of digits in the answer. There are three algorithms for such changes:

1. Multiply or divide the number by 10, 100, 1000, etc., to change the variable to the appropriate number of digits.
2. Use Shift and Round Packed (SRP) to shift the proper number of decimal digits (Sec. 9.3).
3. Use move operations to effect the same results, using MVC (Chap. 7) for even numbers of digits and MVO (Sec. 9.5) for odd numbers of digits. It may also be necessary to use MVZ and/or MVN (Sec. 9.4) in either case.

EXAMPLE 9.3

Using packed decimal multiplication and division, we show how to subtract A (with two decimal places) from B (with one decimal place) to yield DIFF (with one decimal place).

```
                ZAP     TEMP,B
                MP      TEMP,=P'1.0'    MULTIPLIES BY 10 (DECIMAL POINT IGNORED)
                SP      TEMP,A          TWO DECIMAL PLACES
                DP      TEMP,=P'1.0'    ONE DECIMAL PLACE
                ZAP     DIFF,TEMP(4)    DIVISION BY 10 (2 BYTES) LEFT THE
*                                       QUOTIENT IN THE FIRST 4 BYTES OF TEMP
                ...
A               DC      PL3'1.26'
B               DC      PL3'50.0'
DIFF            DS      PL3
TEMP            DS      PL6
```

The value of B is lengthened before addition or subtraction, and the answer is later truncated. Do not merely truncate A to one decimal place to align the decimal points and avoid the later truncation of the answer, or you may introduce the following type of error:

	Correct		Incorrect
B	50.00	B	50.0
A	− 1.26	A	− 1.2
	48.74 → 48.7		48.8

The use of a temporary location to perform arithmetic is quite common with packed decimal instructions, but we may be able to avoid it by using one of the other approaches described below.

9.3 Shift and Round Packed

Shift and Round Packed (SRP) is an SS-type instruction with the following formats:

Assembly language	SRP	D1(L,B1),D2(B2),I3
Machine language		OP L1 I3 B1 D1 B2 D2
		1 1 2 2
		byte byte bytes bytes

The first operand is the memory location (including its length), the second is the direction and number of decimal places to shift, and the third indicates whether to round or not. (Rounding applies to right shifts only.) For example, consider

$$\text{SRP} \quad B(5),2,0$$

This simple instruction will move B two digits to the left within its memory location, and will not attempt to round the result. Thus if B starts out as

$$00\ 12\ 34\ 56\ 7C$$

execution of this operation will result in B having the value

$$12\ 34\ 56\ 70\ 0C$$

The condition code is set by SRP, with the following results:

Condition Code	Value of First Operand
0	Zero
1	Negative
2	Positive
3	Overflow

Thus the instruction in the preceding example sets the condition code to 2, for positive.

The SRP operation can be more complex. The operands work as follows:

1. The first operand denotes the memory position which will be operated on. If no length is specified in the assembly language instruction, the declared length will be used. The first operand will be shifted either right or left by a certain number of decimal digits (half bytes), leaving the sign digit in its original position. If a left shift is done, zeros will be added at the end of the number (before the sign). If a left shift would cause a loss of significant digits, an interruption occurs, and the condition code is set to 3. If a right shift is done, the last digit(s) will be lost, and rounding or truncation will occur.

2. The second operand (displacement plus base register contents) designates the number of digits to be moved, and whether it will be a left or right shift. If the second operand has a value from 1 to 32, then a left shift of that number of digits will be performed. Since the maximum length of a packed decimal number is 16 bytes, no shift of more than 32 digits is ever needed. Right shifts are specified by using a value between 33 and 64. The second operand is 64 minus the number of places to be shifted to the right. For example, to shift B two places to the right, the second operand is $64-2=62$. We can code this as either

$$\text{SRP} \quad B,62,0 \quad \text{or} \quad \text{SRP} \quad B,64-2,0$$

The second form might eliminate errors in mental arithmetic. SRP uses only the last 6 bits of the second operand. This number will always be in the range from 0 to 63.

EXAMPLE 9.4

If we use the definition

$$B \quad DC \quad PL5'1234' \quad (000001234C)$$

the execution of

$$\text{SRP} \quad B(5),2,0$$

will change B to 000123400C. Similarly, execution of

$$\text{SRP} \quad B(5),62,0$$

will change the original value of B to 000000012C.

3. The third operand determines whether truncation or rounding will be done if a right shift is involved. The third operand, I3, is a single decimal digit which, before truncation, is added to the leftmost digit in the portion to be dropped. If I3 plus that digit causes a carry, the last digit not dropped is raised by one unit. The usual values for I3 are 0 for truncation, and 5 for normal rounding. In a left shift, the value of I3 is ignored, but I3 still must be specified in the instruction.

EXAMPLE 9.5

Round to integers the following 3-digit numbers, representing numbers with one decimal place each: 117, 114, 197.

$$\begin{array}{ccc} 117 & 114 & 197 \\ +\ 5 & +\ 5 & +\ 5 \\ \hline 122 & 119 & 202 \\ \uparrow & \uparrow & \uparrow \\ \text{dropped} & \text{dropped} & \text{dropped} \end{array}$$

Thus 117 rounds to 12, 114 rounds to 11, and 197 rounds to 20.

Note that when rounding occurs, the digit I3 is added to the absolute value of the number. Thus if 137B is shifted one place to the right and I3 is 5, the result is 014B.

$$\begin{array}{cc} -137 & 137B \\ 5 & 5 \\ \hline -142\ \text{which rounds to }-14 & \overline{142B}\ \text{which rounds to 14B} \end{array}$$

CAUTION: Just because SRP has the word ROUND in its mnemonic does not mean that it has to round every time it is used. It never rounds on a left shift, no matter what value I3 has. In addition, it has the capability of truncation on shifting right, and truncation is probably used more than rounding in execution of computer programs.

EXAMPLE 9.6

Suppose NUMBER is a 5-byte packed decimal number containing 001234567C. What would be the value in NUMBER after each of the following instructions is executed?

(a) SRP NUMBER(5),2,0
(b) SRP NUMBER(5),62,0
(c) SRP NUMBER(5),62,5
(d) SRP NUMBER(5),60,5

(a) 123456700C The digits have been shifted two places to the left. No rounding is ever involved in a left shift.

(b) 000012345C The digits have been shifted two places to the right. No rounding is done, since 0 was added to the 6 before truncation.

(c) 000012346C The digits have been shifted two places to the right. The 5 was rounded to 6 as follows:

$$\begin{array}{r} 1234567 \\ 5 \\ \hline 1234617 \end{array}$$ 5 added to leftmost digit of the portion dropped

These digits were truncated after the 5 was added. The value of I3 caused the last digit retained to be rounded up to the next higher value.

(d) 000000123C The number has been shifted four places to the right. Normal rounding was done, but the result does not show it, since the leftmost digit dropped (4) was less than 5.

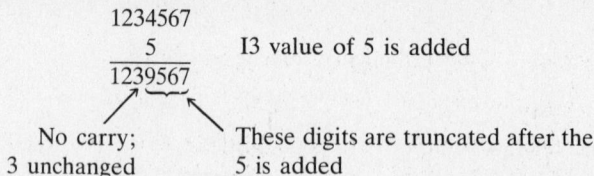

If the number is negative, rounding will produce a more negative number. To round −12.57 to one decimal place, the computer must drop one digit from the right. Thus −1257 will be rounded to −126 by a shift of one digit right.

```
                NEGNUM    01257D
SRP  NEGNUM(3),63,5  produces  00126D
```

The second operand consists of the base register contents plus a displacement. Often, as in the preceding examples, the base register is omitted, and the machine language uses 0, meaning to add 0 instead of the contents of register 0 to the stated displacement. If a nonzero value of B2 is included, the contents of register B2 are added to the displacement. Thus, a second operand of 3(7), where register 7 contains the value 2, would produce a left shift of five digits. A second operand of 61(7) would instead produce a right shift of one digit:

```
From displacement               61
From base register contents      2
Hence right shift of one digit  63
```

EXAMPLE 9.7

Suppose NUMBER is a 5-byte packed decimal number containing 001234567C and register 7 contains the value 2. Let's examine the value in NUMBER after each of the following instructions is executed.

(a) SRP NUMBER(5),2(0),0
(b) SRP NUMBER(5),0(7),0
(c) SRP NUMBER(5),62(7),0
(d) SRP NUMBER(5),2(7),0

(a) 123456700C The digits are shifted two places to the left. This example is the same as Example 9.6(a), except that the base register (0) is shown explicitly. As usual, the value 0 for a base register means to use 0, not the contents of register 0.

(b) 123456700C The number is shifted two digits to the left, corresponding to the value 2 in register 7 plus the 0 displacement.

(c) 001234567C The −2 displacement (64 − 62) right plus the +2 register contents yields 0, or no shift. (62 + 2 = 64, which in binary is 1000000. Since the last 6 bits are zeros, no shift is done.) The condition code is set, but nothing else happens.

(d) 345670000C The number is shifted four digits to the left. The condition code is set to 3, for overflow, since significant digits have been lost from the left end.

EXAMPLE 9.8

What happens in SRP depends on the last 6 bits of the sum of the displacement and base register contents.

```
     L    2,=F'-3'       PUTS FFFFFFFD IN REGISTER 2
     SRP  SUM,1(2),0     USES LAST 6 BITS OF FFFFFFFE (111110₂ = 62₁₀),
*                        HENCE SHIFTS TWO DIGITS RIGHT
     LA   2,65
     SRP  SUM,0(2),0     SHIFTS ONE DIGIT LEFT (LAST 6 BITS 000001)
```

Together with ZAP, which can add or delete bytes at the left of a number, SRP can be used to position any valid packed number anywhere in a second packed number field.

CHAP. 9] ADVANCED PACKED DECIMAL CONCEPTS 195

EXAMPLE 9.9

Let's rework Example 9.3, this time using SRP.

```
        ZAP     TEMP(4),B(3)
        SRP     TEMP(4),1,0       ADD ONE 0 AT THE RIGHT
        SP      TEMP(4),A(3)
        SRP     TEMP(4),63,0      TRUNCATE ONE DIGIT FROM THE RIGHT
        ZAP     DIFF(3),TEMP(4)
        ...
A       DC      PL3'1.26'
B       DC      PL3'50.0'
DIFF    DS      PL3
TEMP    DS      PL4
```

It is still necessary to use a TEMP in this example. Even though the final answer might fit into DIFF (as it does with this pair of numbers), the expanded result before the final SRP operation might not fit (as in the next example). In the following code, the value of TEMP is given in the fourth column.

```
        ZAP     TEMP(4),B(3)      0055555C
        SRP     TEMP(4),1,0       0555550C   (WOULD NOT FIT IN DIFF)
        SP      TEMP(4),A(3)      0543205C
        SRP     TEMP(4),63,0      0054320C
        ZAP     DIFF(3),TEMP(4)   0054320C   (DIFF BECOMES 54320C)
        ...
A       DC      PL3'123.45'
B       DC      PL3'5555.5'
DIFF    DS      PL3
TEMP    DS      PL4
```

When the variable to be extended in digits has sufficient leading zeros to prevent overflow, a temporary memory location may not be needed for an SRP operation. For example, to add C, with two decimal places, to B, with one decimal place, and store the result in B, use the following code:

```
        SRP     B(3),1,0          ADD A DIGIT
        AP      B(3),C(2)
        SRP     B(3),63,0         TRUNCATE THE LAST DIGIT
```

9.4 Move Zone and Move Numeric

Two instructions move half bytes of an operand to a second operand. Move Zone (MVZ) and Move Numeric (MVN) are both single-length SS-type instructions, like MVC (Chap. 7). Instead of moving entire bytes as MVC does, MVZ and MVN move only half of each byte in the specified string.

MVZ moves the first half of each byte.

MVN moves the second half of each byte.

The use of the word "zone" stems from operations on zoned decimal numbers (Sec. 9.6), where the first half of each byte is the zone and the second half is the numeric portion. But it must be emphasized that these operations can also be used to move half bytes of packed decimal numbers or any other data.

EXAMPLE 9.10

```
        MVZ     A(4),B
        ...
A       DC      X'11223344'
B       DC      X'88776655'
```

This MVZ instruction works as follows. The left half of each of 4 bytes starting at B is copied to the left half of the 4 bytes starting at A. Thus A becomes 81726354, while B remains 88776655:

$$
\begin{array}{ll}
B & 88\ 77\ 66\ 55 \\
& \downarrow\ \downarrow\ \downarrow\ \downarrow \\
A & 11\ 22\ 33\ 44 \\
\text{New A} & 81\ 72\ 63\ 54
\end{array}
$$

EXAMPLE 9.11

MVN works similarly, but uses the right half bytes. Assume the declarations from Example 9.10.

MVN   A(4),B

Starting with the same values in A and B, the MVN operation copies to A the right half bytes from the 4 bytes starting at B. Thus A becomes 18273645, and B remains unchanged.

EXAMPLE 9.12

The contents of A and B are as follows:

$$
\begin{array}{ll}
A & 40\ 40\ 40\ 40\ 4A \\
B & 12\ 34\ 56\ 78\ 90
\end{array}
$$

Using these values for each part, let's look at the value of the first operand after execution of each of the following instructions.

(a)   MVZ   A(5),B
(b)   MVN   A(5),B
(c)   MVZ   A(1),B
(d)   MVZ   A+4(1),B+4
(e)   MVZ   A+4(1),B
(f)   MVN   B+1(2),A+3

In (a), there is a simple copying of all the left half bytes from one memory location to the left half bytes of the other memory location. In (b), the right half bytes are moved.

(a)   A becomes 10 30 50 70 9A
(b)   A becomes 42 44 46 48 40

In (c), only one half byte is moved.

(c)   A becomes 10 40 40 40 4A

In (d) through (f), the first operand starts after the beginning of the memory location, as do the second operands in (d) and (f). Moreover, fewer than 5 half bytes are copied.

(d)   A becomes 40 40 40 40 9A
(e)   A becomes 40 40 40 40 1A
(f)   B becomes 12 30 5A 78 90

We may use MVC with MVN and MVZ to multiply or divide decimal numbers by any even power of 10. This procedure may be more efficient than using packed multiplication or division.

EXAMPLE 9.13

Multiply A by 100. (The question marks represent garbage, and the value of TEMP is given in the comment field.)

```
        MVC   TEMP(3),A            00 12 3C ??
        MVN   TEMP+2(1),=X'00'     00 12 30 ??
        MVZ   TEMP+3(1),=X'00'     00 12 30 0?
        MVN   TEMP+3(1),A+2        00 12 30 0C
        ...
A       DC    PL3'1.23'            00 12 3C
TEMP    DS    PL4                  ?? ?? ?? ??
```

TEMP now holds a value 100 times that in A, corresponding to addition of two zeros after the decimal point (1.2300). (A is 00123C; TEMP is 0012300C.) Another way to accomplish this task is as follows:

```
        ZAP   TEMP,=P'0'           00 00 00 0C
        MVC   TEMP(3),A            00 12 3C 0C
        MVN   TEMP+2(1),=X'00'     00 12 30 0C
        MVN   TEMP+3(1),A+2        00 12 30 0C
```

9.5 Move with Offset

The Move with Offset (MVO) instruction is also used to adjust the number of decimal places in packed decimal numbers. The SRP instruction, discussed in Sec. 9.3, does the same task more simply, but it is an IBM 370 instruction, not available on the IBM 360.

Move Character moves entire bytes, but not half bytes. MVZ and MVN move half bytes (one digit), but do not shift by an odd number of half bytes. To get each digit to shift an odd number of half bytes, we need the instruction MVO (Move with Offset). MVO is a two-length SS-type instruction. The formats are as follows

```
Assembly language    MVO    D1(L1,B1),D2(L2,B2)
Machine language     OP    L1 L2   D1 B1    D2 B2
                    1 byte 1 byte  2 bytes  2 bytes
```

The length of each operand is reduced by 1 for the machine language instruction, in order that the maximum value (16) can fit into one hexadecimal digit (F). If the lengths are not stated explicitly, the default values (the values declared for the variables) are used.

MVO copies a number from a sending field (second operand) to a receiving field (first operand), moving each half byte $\frac{1}{2}$ byte to the left. Padding or truncation of the first operand, if any, occurs at the left. Overlap of the first and second operands is legal but dangerous.

EXAMPLE 9.14

Suppose A and B are 3-byte packed decimal numbers, A having the value +123, and we execute the instruction

$$\text{MVO} \quad B(3),A(3)$$

This instruction yields in B

$$01 \ 23 \ C?$$

(The question mark represents whatever was present before execution of the instruction.) Let's look at this in more detail.

```
B before    | ?? | ?? | ?? |

A           | 00 | 12 | 3C |

B after     | 01 | 23 | C? |
```

The net effect of such a move of $\frac{1}{2}$ byte is multiplication by 10. However, MVO alone is not sufficient to carry out a multiplication since the sign half byte ends up in the wrong place. MVZ and MVN or MVI are necessary to adjust the last byte, as shown in the next example.

EXAMPLE 9.15

Adjust the last byte of the number in the previous example so that B represents a proper packed decimal number.

		B	0123C?
MVZ	B+2(1),=X'00'		01230?
MVN	B+2(1),A+2		01230C

By adjusting the lengths of the sending and receiving fields (second and first operands), one can multiply or divide by any odd power of 10.

EXAMPLE 9.16

Let's look at the contents of C and A after the following instruction is executed.

    MVO   C(5),A(3)

C is 5 bytes long, and A is 3 bytes long. Here the source (A) is shorter than the destination (C). C is filled from the right, and the leading bytes are filled with zeros.

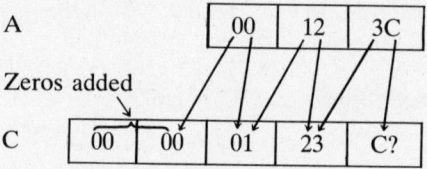

EXAMPLE 9.17

Consider another example, in which the second operand is longer than the first.

    MVO   D(2),A(3)

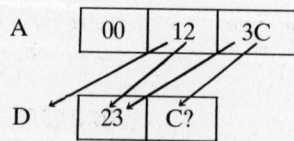

Since D is filled from the right, the 1 at the left is truncated.

EXAMPLE 9.18

We can use MVO to copy A to C, moving the hexadecimal digits 3 half bytes to the left, in the following manner:

    MVO   C(4),A(3)

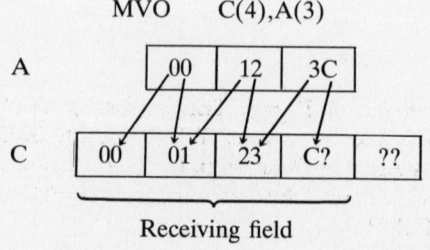

C is 5 bytes long, but A is copied into the first 4 bytes only, leaving the last byte unchanged. The last 2 bytes of C may then be adjusted to yield a number 1000 times the value of A:

	MVC	C+3(1),=X'00'	C becomes 00 01 23 00 ??
	MVZ	C+4(1),=X'00'	C becomes 00 01 23 00 0?
	MVN	C+4(1),A+2	C becomes 00 01 23 00 0C

EXAMPLE 9.19

A value can be divided by 10, with truncation, using MVO.

```
        MVO    D(2),A(2)
        ...
A       DC     PL3'123'
D       DS     PL2
```

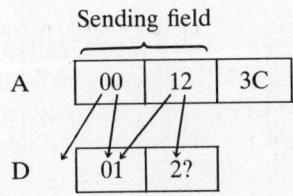

MVO copies 2 bytes of A to D, moving each digit a half byte to the left. The third byte of A is not part of the second operand. The job is completed with a Move Numeric:

```
        MVN    D+1(1),A+2
```

D | 01 | 2C |

EXAMPLE 9.20

In Example 9.3, we used packed multiplication and division to subtract two numbers (A and B) with different numbers of decimal places. We will now do the same job, this time using MVO.

```
        MVO    TEMP(4),B(3)         ADD ONE ZERO
        MVZ    TEMP+3(1),=X'00'     REPLACE OLD SIGN WITH ZERO
        MVN    TEMP+3(1),B+2        COPY OLD SIGN
        SP     TEMP(4),A(3)
        MVO    DIFF(3),TEMP(3)      OMIT LAST DIGIT OF TEMP
        MVN    DIFF+2(1),TEMP+3     COPY SIGN
        ...
A       DC     PL3'1.26'
B       DC     PL3'50.0'
DIFF    DS     PL3
TEMP    DS     PL4
```

The MVO instruction copies the value of B into TEMP, making TEMP equal to 000500C?. The MVZ instruction converts the old sign of B into a 0, making TEMP equal to 0005000?. The MVN instruction copies the sign into its proper place from the original location in B. TEMP is now ready for the subtraction operation. To truncate the extra decimal place, we move the first 3 bytes of TEMP into DIFF, then copy the sign into its proper place from its location in TEMP.

9.6 Number Conversions

Zoned Number Format

When numbers are read from input, they are in the form of characters (Chap. 7). Generally, we want to convert these numbers to other formats so that we can do arithmetic on them. There are several steps in the conversion process, depending on what type of number we want as a result. If we later want to print the results of our computations, we must convert back to character format. Figure 9-1 shows these conversions diagrammatically. Each one will be discussed in the sections which follow.

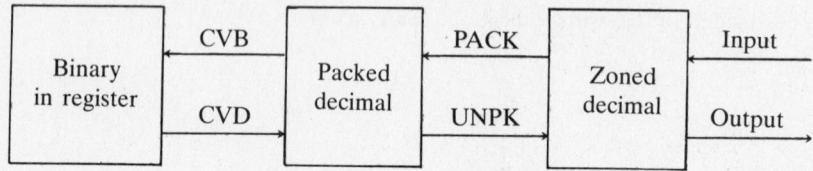

Fig. 9-1 Number conversions.

Representation of numbers in character form is called *zoned decimal* representation, and numbers composed of one or more of these characters are called *zoned numbers*. In zoned decimal format, each character occupies 1 byte of memory. The first hexadecimal digit of each byte is called the *zone*. The zone of each byte except the last of a zoned decimal number is an F. The last half of each byte, called the *numeric*, is the decimal digit itself.

Decimal digit	0	1	2	3	4	5	6	7	8	9
Representation	F0	F1	F2	F3	F4	F5	F6	F7	F8	F9

The zone of the last byte of a zoned number represents the sign of the number, with A, C, E, or F meaning positive and B or D meaning negative. Thus we could represent +123 and −123 as follows:

$$+123 \quad F1F2C3$$
$$-123 \quad F1F2D3$$

Note that if we interpret these 3 bytes as EBCDIC character strings, they would be 12C and 12L, respectively.

Pack

The PACK instruction is used to convert from zoned decimal numbers to packed decimal numbers. It is a two-length SS-type instruction. PACK reverses the order of the hexadecimal digits in the last byte and removes the zones from the other bytes, "packing" the digits into a smaller space.

EXAMPLE 9.21

Suppose the value of the variable ZONED is

$$F1F2F3F4F5$$

The instruction

$$\text{PACK} \quad \text{PACKED(3),ZONED(5)}$$

does the following:

ZONED	F1	F2	F3	F4	F5	
	↓	↓	↓	↓	✗	
PACKED	1	2	3	4	5F	→ 12345F

The result in PACKED is 12345F. As usual, the first operand is changed. Also as usual, truncation or padding with zeros occurs on the left.

The PACK operation ignores all zones in a number except for the one in the last byte. Moreover, the sign digits C and F both have the same meaning in a packed decimal number—positive. Thus the following instructions both yield the same 3-byte RESULT, +12,345.

      PACK   RESULT,=C'ABCDE'
      PACK   RESULT,=C'12345'

```
C1 C2 C3 C4 C5      F1 F2 F3 F4 F5
 ↓  ↓  ↓  ↓  ↓       ↓  ↓  ↓  ↓  ↓
 1  2  3  4 5C       1  2  3  4 5F
```

EXAMPLE 9.22

Let's see how we can interpret INDATA (read from input) which has the magnitude of A in bytes 1 through 5 and the magnitude of B in bytes 11 through 15. If either A or B is a negative number, it will have a minus sign in the next byte (6 or 16). We will show how to get A and B into APACK and BPACK, with the proper sign. The format of INDATA might be

        12345−   12345   or   99   179−

```
         PACK    APACK,INDATA(5)
         CLI     INDATA+5,C'-'
         BNE     NEXT1
         MVN     APACK+2(1),=X'0D'
NEXT1    PACK    BPACK,INDATA+10(5)
         CLI     INDATA+15,C'-'
         BNE     NEXT2
         MVN     BPACK+2(1),=X'0D'
NEXT2    ...
         ...
APACK    DS      PL3
BPACK    DS      PL3
INDATA   DS      CL80
```

Unpack

The converse of the PACK instruction is the unpack (UNPK) instruction. It converts a packed number to a zoned number by reversing the last byte and supplying an F as the zone for each of the other digits. Again, truncation or padding with zeros is done on the left.

EXAMPLE 9.23

The instruction

        UNPK   ZONED(5),PACKED(3)

does the following:

```
PACKED(3)   | 1  | 2  | 3  | 4  | 5F |
              ↓    ↓    ↓    ↓    ↓
ZONED(5)    | F1 | F2 | F3 | F4 | F5 |
```
becomes

The result is F1F2F3F4F5.

We must be able to determine how many bytes are required for these conversions.

A five-digit zoned number requires 3 bytes when it is packed.

        F1F2F3F4F5 → 12345F

A four-digit zoned number requires 3 bytes when it is packed.

$$F1F2F3F4 \rightarrow 01234F$$

In general, a zoned number with n digits requires $(n + 1)/2$ bytes when it is packed if n is odd, and $(n + 2)/2$ bytes when it is packed if n is even.

The PACK and UNPK operations do not check the format of either of the operands. For example, if the second operand of a PACK instruction is not a valid zoned number, the instruction operates on whatever is there, most likely producing garbage. However, no interruption (Appendix 2) or error is produced by either the PACK or the UNPK instruction. Neither instruction sets the condition code.

EXAMPLE 9.24

Suppose we execute the following PACK instruction. What will be the resulting contents of the first operand?

```
        PACK    GAR(3),BAGE(4)
        ...
BAGE    DC      X'CACBCCCD'
GAR     DS      PL3
```

After the instruction has been executed,

BAGE(4)

GAR(3)

Padded with 0

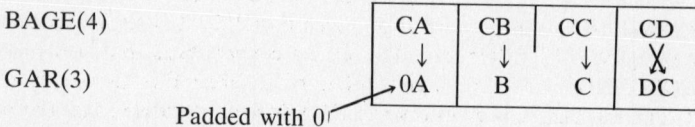

GAR will contain 0ABCDC. No check will have been made to see that BAGE is not a valid packed number.

Packed to Binary and Binary to Packed Number Conversions

Convert to Binary

A packed decimal number may be converted to binary and placed in a register using the Convert to Binary (CVB) operation. CVB is an RX instruction which requires that the second operand be a packed number of double-word length placed on a double-word boundary.

EXAMPLE 9.25

Let's see what is accomplished by

$$\text{CVB} \quad 7,\text{DW}$$

Suppose DW is declared by

```
DW      DS      D           DOUBLE WORD ON A DOUBLE-WORD BOUNDARY
```

and the current contents of DW are

00	00	00	00	00	00	16	0C

Then the instruction CVB 7,DW converts the value in DW into binary and puts the result into register 7. Thus this instruction puts 000000A0, the binary equivalent of 160, into register 7.

Convert to Decimal

The converse of the CVB instruction is Convert to Decimal (CVD), which is also an RX instruction and also requires a double-word memory location as its second operand. It converts a binary number in a register to a packed decimal number, changing the value of the second operand.

EXAMPLE 9.26

Suppose register 4 holds 00000011, corresponding to decimal 17. The following instruction places decimal 17 into PNUM:

```
        CVD    4,PNUM
        ...
PNUM    DS     D
```

EXAMPLE 9.27

Let's convert a zoned decimal number START, which contains F1F2F5, into a fixed binary number in register 7. We will add 1 to it and then convert the answer back to a zoned decimal number, ANS.

```
        PACK   PNUM(8),START(3)    PACK INTO 8-BYTE PNUM
        CVB    7,PNUM              8-BYTE NUMBER REQUIRED FOR CVB
        A      7,=F'1'             ADD 1 TO BINARY NUM IN 7
        CVD    7,PNUM              WE CAN REUSE PNUM
        UNPK   ANS(3),PNUM(8)      UNPK PNUM INTO ZONED ANS
        ...
START   DC     C'125'              CHARACTER (ZONED) FORMAT
ANS     DS     CL3
PNUM    DS     D
```

Although the PACK instruction has no requirements for the length of the first operand, we provided PNUM with 8 bytes so that it would be a double word as required by CVB. It is an 8-byte number on a double-word boundary, because we declared it D. After the addition, we convert back to decimal, reusing PNUM. Finally, we unpack PNUM to ANS. ANS will have a zone of C rather than F in its last byte, because the machine instructions always produce the sign C for positive packed decimal numbers, and the value of ANS is +126.

9.7 Input/Output

The details of I/O vary from installation to installation, so they cannot be discussed here. We will assume that a record has already been read from input as a string of characters, and we will discuss the handling of this record. Similarly, we will produce a string of characters to be printed, but will not discuss the printing of that record.

For output, the usual record length is 133 characters or 121 characters, depending on the number of columns which the line printer is able to print. The programmer moves character strings to portions of an output line, which may be declared as follows:

```
        OUTPUT    DS    CL121
```

When the string is ready, some sort of print instruction is used to accomplish the actual printing. (The method of printing output depends on the installation.)

However, there are several problems involved in preparation of numeric data for printing. First, the last digit of a packed decimal number prints as a letter (A through I for C1 through C9, J through R for D1 through D9) if the number is simply unpacked and printed. In addition, leading zeros must be suppressed.

EXAMPLE 9.28

The packed decimal number 128C when it is unpacked yields the zoned number F1F2C8. This prints as 12H, since C8 is the representation of H.

To get the correct value to print, the zone of the last digit must be changed to F. This will cause loss of the sign information, which must be preserved in some other way. If the number is negative, some indication—a minus sign or "CR" for "credit balance"—should be included in the output line. If the number contains decimal places, a decimal point must be printed.

Preparing the data for printing can be done using UNPK plus numerous move instructions. To suppress leading zeros, we may use the Edit or Edit with Mark instructions (Sec. 9.8).

EXAMPLE 9.29

To print the packed number 128C stored in PNUM, we may do the following:

```
        UNPK    ZON(3),PNUM(2)
        MVZ     ZON+2(1),=X'F0'
```

Now ZON is F1F2F8, which will print as 128. If we want to save the sign information, we must do the following:

```
        UNPK    ZON(4),PNUM(2)
        CP      PNUM,=P'0'
        BNL     POS
        MVI     ZON,C'-'
POS     MVZ     ZON+3(1),=X'F0'
```

Now the number will print as 0128 if positive and as −128 if negative.

9.8 Edit and Edit with Mark

The Edit (ED) and Edit with Mark (EDMK) instructions each operate on a packed decimal number and yield a zoned decimal number in a format ready for output. Their place in the scheme of number conversions is shown in Fig. 9-2. Among the things which can be done by Edit and Edit with Mark are the following:

1. Suppression of leading zeros.
2. Inclusion of the decimal point and commas for long numbers (e.g., 33,456.50).
3. Inclusion of a minus sign in the proper place, a CR sign, or another indication of a negative value.
4. Inclusion of a floating dollar sign (floating means that the $ appears immediately before the first significant digit, which yields $1.98 or $1000.98 but not $ 1.98).
5. Automatic conversion of the last byte of a zoned number to print as a digit.
6. Inclusion of asterisks or other symbols to produce a number such as $***1.23, for check protection.

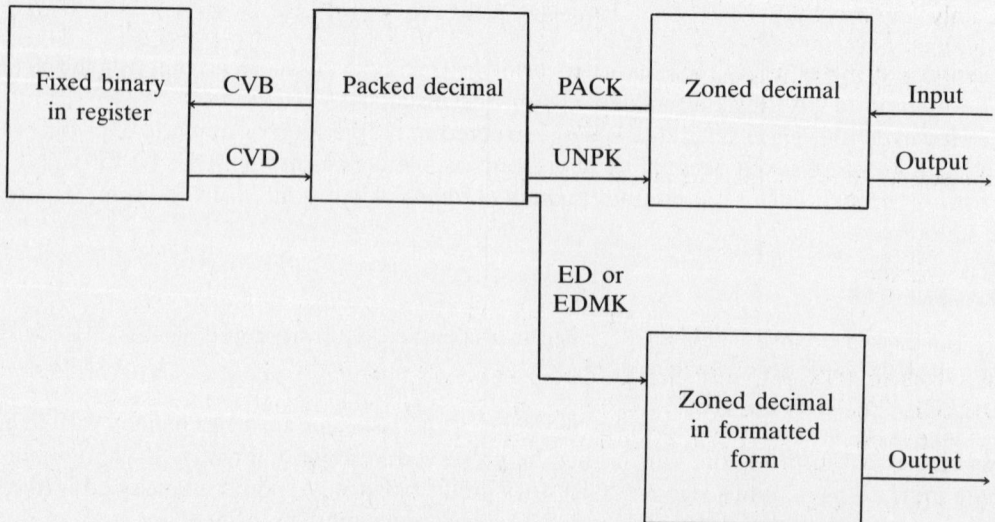

Fig. 9-2 Number conversions, including Edit and Edit with Mark.

EXAMPLE 9.30

Here is an exercise to show why the Edit and Edit with Mark instructions are important:

(a) Write the packed decimal representation for a 4-byte number with a value +12345 which has been calculated by the computer.
(b) How would that number ordinarily be printed by a human?
(c) What zoned decimal number would result from UNPK on this packed number?
(d) What characters would result if that zoned decimal number were printed?
(e) What jobs should the Edit instruction do which UNPK does not do?

(a) 0012345C   (The sign digit generated by packed decimal instructions is C for positive numbers.)
(b) 12,345   (The comma might sometimes be omitted, especially with values less than 10,000.)
(c) F0F0F1F2F3F4FC5
(d) 001234E   (C5 is the EBCDIC representation of E.)
(e) Replace leading zeros with blanks, introduce the comma, and fix up the zone of the last digit.

Such powerful instructions are necessarily somewhat complex, so we will take up their features one at a time.

The ED instruction is a single-length SS-type instruction with two operands. The first operand is the string to be operated on, called the *pattern*. The second is the source string, which must be in packed decimal form. The programmer writes the pattern to control the way the numbers should appear when printed. Thus the pattern includes special characters (hexadecimal 20 or 21) which will be replaced by the actual digits from the source. Other characters, called *message characters*, may include a decimal point, a plus sign, commas for numbers which may be greater than 999, and other symbols or letters (such as CR). The ED instruction replaces the special symbols with digits, replaces leading zeros with blanks or other specified characters, and performs other tasks.

The pattern is composed largely of the hexadecimal characters 20 and 21. Each 20 (called the *digit selector*) or 21 (called the *significance starter*) selects the next digit from the source and, if the digit is significant, copies it as a zoned digit into its own place in the pattern. The first byte of the pattern is called the *fill character*—the character which is to replace leading zeros. If blanks are to replace leading zeros, hexadecimal 40 (blank) is used as the fill character. Other characters in the pattern are the hexadecimal codes for decimal point, comma, etc. The other characters do not select a digit from the source.

To build a pattern to turn a 3-byte positive packed decimal number into printable form, we need five digit selectors—20 or 21—one for each digit. (Since 21 has a special use, explained later, we will use only 20 here.) We also need a 40 as the fill character, which causes leading zeros to be replaced by blanks.

Here is the declaration for the pattern:

                PATTERN   DC   X'402020202020'

If the source (the number we want to convert to printable form) is

                SOURCE   01025C

the instruction

                ED   PATTERN(6),SOURCE

will act as follows. ED will change the bytes at location PATTERN according to what appears at SOURCE. The 40 in the pattern will remain a leading blank. The first 20 in the pattern "selects" the first digit from the source—0. Since this digit is a leading 0, it is replaced in the pattern by 40 (blank). The next 20 "selects" the 1, and F1 replaces that 20 in the pattern. The next digit is 0, but it is not a leading 0, so the next 20 is converted to F0. Notice the difference between this 0 and the leading 0; this 0 will be printed. The 2 and 5 from the source cause the last two 20s to be converted to F2 and F5, respectively.

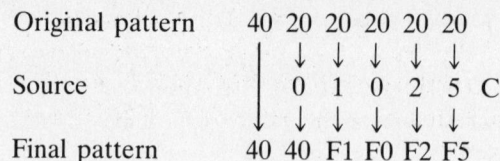

Printing this pattern would yield

 ƀƀ1025

where ƀ is a blank. If the first two digits of the source had been 0, both would have been replaced by blanks. In fact, until the ED instruction encounters the first nonzero character in SOURCE, all leading 0s and all message characters in PATTERN are changed to the fill character.

Let's change the format to include a decimal point followed by two decimal digits. We need a 40 as the fill character—which causes leading zeros to be replaced by blanks—and a decimal point (4B). Here is the declaration for the pattern:

PATTERN   DC   X'402020204B2020'

If the source (the number we want to convert to printable form) is

SOURCE   01025C

the instruction

ED   PATTERN(7),SOURCE

will act as in the previous example until it reaches 4B. The 4B does not select any digit from the source (it is not 20 or 21), and is therefore left unchanged in the pattern. Then the last two 20s select the 2 and 5 and are converted to F2 and F5, respectively.

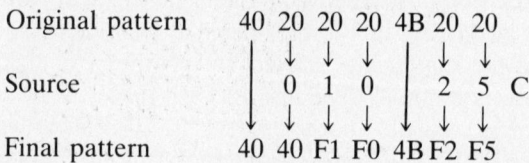

Printing this pattern would yield

 ƀƀ10.25

where ƀ is a blank.

EXAMPLE 9.31

Using the pattern 402020204B2020, what would be printed if the source were 00123C?

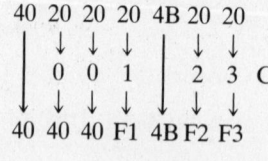

which would print as   ƀƀƀ1.23

Using the pattern above, what would be printed if the source were 00013C?

```
40 20 20 20 4B 20 20
 ↓  ↓  ↓     ↓  ↓
 0  0  0     1  3  C
 ↓  ↓  ↓  ↓  ↓  ↓
40 40 40 40 40 F1 F3
```

which would print as   ƀƀƀƀƀ13

Note in this example that the decimal point is converted to the fill character and is not printed.

We say that the first nonzero digit is the first *significant digit*. When the ED instruction encounters a significant digit, it turns on a bit called the *significance indicator*. When the significance indicator is on, all zeros are transformed into F0 rather than into the fill character, and all message characters remain. When the significance indicator is off, (leading) zeros and message characters are changed to the fill character.

What would happen with the above pattern if the source were equal to zero? All the zeros would be leading zeros, and all would be turned to blanks. Even the decimal point would be converted to a blank, since no prior significant digits were found. The pattern would wind up all 40s, which would print as blanks. What would we ordinarily want printed? Either .00 or, better, 0.00, with one digit before the decimal point, even if it is zero. To tell the pattern to stop suppressing leading zeros at some point, we use the symbol 21 instead of 20. The 21 artificially turns on the significance indicator, and thus is called the *significance starter*. The 21 acts first as a digit selector, and only *afterward* turns on the significance indicator. Thus, the 21 acts just like the 20, but in addition it stops replacement of characters with fill characters in the *next* byte.

EXAMPLE 9.32

What pattern should we use if we want at least one digit to the left of the decimal point in our 3-byte, two-decimal-place number?

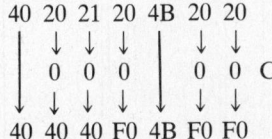

Our packed number is

This will yield

The 21 selects the second zero, which is replaced by the fill character. Then it turns on the significance indicator, which causes the third zero (in the *next* byte) to be replaced by F0 instead of by the fill character.

The 21 symbol stops suppression of characters (leading zeros, decimal points, etc.) at the next byte of pattern. If the pattern had been

$$40\ 20\ 20\ 21\ 4B\ 20\ 20$$

and the packed number were zero, the decimal point would have been the first character not replaced with the fill character, yielding

$$40\ 40\ 40\ 40\ 4B\ F0\ F0$$

which prints as ｂｂｂｂ.00

EXAMPLE 9.33

Suppose that we want to print the amount on a check. The maximum amount payable is 9999.99. We want the amount to have at least one digit to the left of the decimal point even if the amount is less than $1. We want a comma for values $1000 or larger. The dollar sign is preprinted on the check. In order to prevent alteration of the check, we will insert asterisks (*) before the first printed digit. Write a PATTERN to accomplish this purpose. The smallest and largest amounts should print as follows:

$$****0.00$$
$$9,999.99$$

The pattern is declared as follows:

        PATTERN   DC   X'5C206B2021204B2020'   6B IS COMMA; 5C IS ASTERISK.

Note that we must be careful to print only the last 8 bytes of PATTERN after editing, so that we print only what was requested and not the fill character itself.

Notice that the pattern is changed as it is used. If the ED instruction is used in a loop, the pattern must be reestablished (by an MVC instruction) each time through the loop before the ED instruction is executed.

EXAMPLE 9.34

```
LOOP           ...
         MVC   PATTERN(8),TEMPLATE
         ED    PATTERN(8),0(4)        EXPLICIT NOTATION,
*                                     USED JUST AS IN OTHER INSTRUCTIONS
*                                     print the PATTERN, or move the
*                                     PATTERN to the output line
         BCT   ...
               ...
PATTERN  DS    CL8
TEMPLATE DC    X'40202021204B2020'
```

The value in TEMPLATE is the value of the pattern desired. After the first time the ED instruction is executed, the value in PATTERN is not what is needed for the next execution of the ED instruction, so the original pattern is reloaded from TEMPLATE. We can also simply MVC the pattern to a section of the output line and edit that section before printing the line.

```
         MVC   LINE+10(8),TEMPLATE
         ED    LINE+10(8),PNUM
               ...
LINE     DS    121C
TEMPLATE DC    X'40202021204B2020'
```

EXAMPLE 9.35

Let's see what would happen if the pattern in Example 9.32 were reused without being reloaded. The pattern has been changed to 40 40 40 F0 4B F0 F0. Since there are no digit selectors in this pattern, no digits would be selected from the source. The significance indicator would not be turned on, and all the bytes would be interpreted as message characters and changed to the fill character.

When the ED instruction reaches the sign of the packed decimal number, it reacts as follows:

A positive sign turns off the significance indicator. Thus ED changes all further message characters (if any) to fill characters.

A negative sign does not affect the significance indicator. Thus all further message characters remain as is.

Many commercial applications use the letters CR to denote credit balance for charge customers. A positive amount means that the customer owes the store money, which is the usual situation, but a negative amount means a credit balance. Stores want to print an indication such as CR rather than a minus sign, which might confuse customers. The CR can be included in the pattern as message characters. For a 3-byte source, we can use a pattern such as this:

    FORMAT   DC   X'402021204B202040C3D9'   (C3 IS C, D9 IS R)

The value 01234D will cause the CR to print:

```
Pattern   40 20 21 20 4B 20 20 40 C3 D9
               ↓  ↓  ↓     ↓  ↓
Value           0  1  2     3  4 (D
               ↓  ↓  ↓     ↓  ↓
Result    40 40 F1 F2 4B F3 F4 40 C3 D9
```

The D leaves the significance indicator on, and the rest of the characters print. The result prints as

    ҍҍ12.34ҍCR

The same pattern

with a positive number

yields

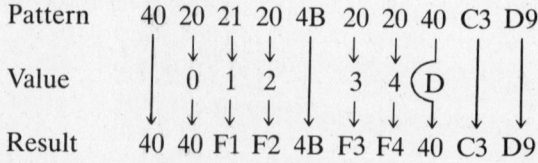

The C turns off the significance indicator, so the message characters are converted to the fill character. The result prints as

$$\text{bb}12.34\text{bbb}$$

Any negative balance will thus be printed with the letters CR after it, indicating a credit balance. Of course, any message desired (up to 256 characters total for the pattern) may be included. When a long message is desired, it is usually easier to set up the format in two parts, one hexadecimal and one character:

```
           FORMAT   DC   X'402021204B202040'
                    DC   C'CREDIT--DO NOT PAY'
```

Edit with Mark

How can we place a dollar sign or a minus sign next to the first digit to be printed, when we don't know in advance how many digits will be printed? We must use the Edit with Mark (EDMK) instruction. Edit with Mark does exactly the same things that Edit (ED) does, but it performs one additional task as well. It loads the address of the first significant digit in the pattern into the last 24 bits of register 1. We can then use this address to place the dollar sign or minus sign in the proper position.

EXAMPLE 9.36

What value will be loaded into register 1 by the following EDMK instruction?

```
                    EDMK   PATTERN(6),SOURCE
                    ...
           SOURCE   DC     PL3'103'              00103C
1BCA00     PATTERN  DC     X'402020202020'
```

The first significant digit is the 1 in SOURCE, whose corresponding byte in PATTERN has an address 1BCA03, which is the value placed in register 1 by EDMK.

However, if the character 21 (rather than a significant digit) turns on the significance indicator, then register 1 is not changed. No address is loaded into register 1 by EDMK. In this case, though, we know which byte will be the first significant digit: the one following the 21. Thus, prior to executing the EDMK instruction, we can take the precaution of loading into register 1 the address of the byte following the 21 in the pattern. When the EDMK has completed execution, one of two things will be true: (1) The 21 will have turned on the significance indicator, in which case the address that we previously put into register 1 will be the address of the first nonfill character. (2) A significant digit will have turned on the significance indicator and will have replaced the address that we put into register 1 by the address of that significant digit. The programmer can then use the address in register 1 to place a dollar sign or a minus sign adjacent to the first printed digit.

EXAMPLE 9.37

Here is code which will place a dollar sign immediately to the left of a printed balance, producing

$1.00 or $1000.00 or $0.10   but not $ 1.00 or $.10

Assume that the value to be printed is 3 bytes long and that we want at least one digit to the left of the decimal point.

```
           LA     1,PATTERN+3           THE BYTE AFTER THE 21
           EDMK   PATTERN(10),VALUE
           S      1,=F'1'               ADDRESS OF BYTE BEFORE THE FIRST DIGIT
           MVI    0(1),C'$'             REPLACES BLANK WITH $
           ...
PATTERN    DC     X'402021204B202040C3D9'
VALUE      DS     PL3
```

Note that we must reduce the address in register 1 by 1 before execution of the MVI instruction, or we will replace the first significant digit with the dollar sign. A more efficient way to reduce the contents of register 1 by 1 is the instruction BCTR 1,0. BCTR decrements by 1, but with a zero second operand, no branch will occur.

We can move a minus sign to the beginning of a number using this same technique. Of course, we must check the sign before doing so. This is easy since ED and EDMK set the condition code to 0 for zero, to 1 for a negative number, and to 2 for a positive number.

```
          LA     1,PATTERN+3
          EDMK   PATTERN(7),VALUE
          BNM    POS
          BCTR   1,0                DECREMENTS REGISTER 1, BUT DOES NOT BRANCH
          MVI    0(1),C'-'
POS       ...
          ...
PATTERN   DC     X'402021204B2020'
```

A special character, hexadecimal 22, known as a *field separator*, restarts the process from scratch so that more than one value can be edited by one Edit or Edit with Mark instruction. Thus a pattern

            PATTERN   DC   X'402021204B2020222021204B2020'

could be used for two 3-byte packed numbers. The byte represented by 22 is replaced by the fill character, and the significance indicator is turned off. Therefore, the next number is examined for leading zeros as the first number was.

EXAMPLE 9.38

Assume that we use the pattern shown above to print the following two variables, defined in sequence:

            VAL1   DC   PL3'1234'
            VAL2   DC   PL3'5678'

Use the instruction

            ED   PATTERN(14),VAL1

The digits will be selected as follows:

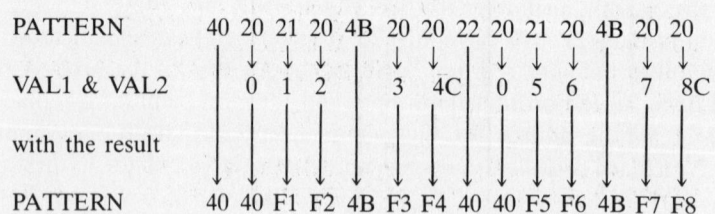

Since VAL2 was defined immediately after VAL1 in memory, its digits were used by the ED instruction to change the second half of PATTERN.

Solved Problems

9.1 What is the difference in initial values in memory of (a) A, B, and C? (b) A, D, and E?

```
A      DC    PL3'1.00'
B      DC    PL3'10.0'
C      DC    PL3'100'
D      DC    PL3'1.0'
E      DC    PL3'1'
```

(a) They are all the same, 00100C.

(b) A is 00100C, D is 00010C, and E is 00001C.

9.2 Using the following declarations, show how each of the additions may be performed using packed decimal multiplication and division.

```
A      DC    PL3'1.234'      THREE DECIMAL PLACES
B      DC    PL2'0.01'       TWO DECIMAL PLACES
C      DC    PL5'1234.1'     ONE DECIMAL PLACE
ANS    DS    PL3             ONE DECIMAL PLACE
ANS2   DS    PL4             NO DECIMAL PLACES
TEMP   DS    PL8
```

(a) ANS = A + B   (c) ANS = B + C   (e) ANS2 = A + C
(b) ANS = A + C   (d) ANS2 = A + B   (f) ANS2 = B + C

```
(a)  ZAP   TEMP(8),B(2)
     MP    TEMP(8),=P'1.0'      10 × B (THREE DECIMAL)
     AP    TEMP(8),A(3)         THREE DECIMAL PLACES
     DP    TEMP(8),=P'1.00'     ONE DECIMAL PLACE
     ZAP   ANS(3),TEMP(6)       QUOTIENT IN FIRST 6 BYTES
(b)  ZAP   TEMP(8),C(5)
     MP    TEMP(8),=P'1.00'     THREE DECIMAL PLACES
     AP    TEMP(8),A(3)         THREE DECIMAL PLACES
     DP    TEMP(8),=P'1.00'     ONE DECIMAL PLACE (IN FIRST 6 BYTES)
     ZAP   ANS(3),TEMP(6)
(c)  ZAP   TEMP(8),C(5)
     MP    TEMP(8),=P'1.0'      TWO DECIMAL PLACES
     AP    TEMP(8),B(2)         TWO DECIMAL PLACES
     DP    TEMP(8),=P'1.0'      ONE DECIMAL PLACE (IN FIRST 6 BYTES)
     ZAP   ANS(3),TEMP(6)
(d)  ZAP   TEMP(8),B(2)
     MP    TEMP(8),=P'1.0'      10 × B (THREE DECIMAL PLACES)
     AP    TEMP(8),A(3)         THREE DECIMAL PLACES
     DP    TEMP(8),=P'1.000'    NO DECIMAL PLACES
     ZAP   ANS2(4),TEMP(5)      QUOTIENT IN FIRST 5 BYTES
(e)  ZAP   TEMP(8),C(5)
     MP    TEMP(8),=P'1.00'     THREE DECIMAL PLACES
     AP    TEMP(8),A(3)         THREE DECIMAL PLACES
     DP    TEMP(8),=P'1.000'    NO DECIMAL PLACES (IN FIRST 5 BYTES)
     ZAP   ANS2(4),TEMP(5)
```

(f)
```
     ZAP   TEMP(8),C(5)
     MP    TEMP(8),=P'1.0'      TWO DECIMAL PLACES
     AP    TEMP(8),B(2)         TWO DECIMAL PLACES
     DP    TEMP(8),=P'1.00'     NO DECIMAL PLACES (IN FIRST 6 BYTES)
     ZAP   ANS2(4),TEMP(6)
```

9.3 Write assembly language code to multiply A by B and put the result into C. A, B, and C are declared PL4. A has one decimal place, B has two decimal places, and C has three decimal places.

```
            ZAP   TEMP,A       TEMP HAS ONE DECIMAL PLACE
            MP    TEMP,B       TEMP HAS THREE DECIMAL PLACES
            ZAP   C,TEMP       C HAS THREE DECIMAL PLACES
            ...
     TEMP   DS    PL8
```

9.4 Write assembly language code to multiply A by B and put the result into C. A, B, and C are declared PL4. A and B have two decimal places; C has three decimal places.

```
            ZAP   TC,A         TC HAS TWO DECIMAL PLACES
            MP    TC,B         TC HAS FOUR DECIMAL PLACES
            DP    TC,=P'1.0'   TC(6) HAS THREE DECIMAL PLACES
            ZAP   C,TC(6)
            ...
     TC     DS    PL8
```

9.5 Write assembly language code to divide C by A and put the result into B. A, B, and C are declared PL4. A and B have one decimal place, and C has three decimal places.

```
            ZAP   TB,C         TB HAS THREE DECIMAL PLACES
            DP    TB,A         TB(4) HAS TWO DECIMAL PLACES
            ZAP   TB,TB(4)     TB HAS TWO DECIMAL PLACES
            DP    TB,=P'1.0'   TB(6) HAS ONE DECIMAL PLACE
            ZAP   B,TB(6)
            ...
     TB     DS    PL8
```

9.6 In an SRP operation, can the contents of B2 (the base register for the second operand) ever be negative?

Yes. The instruction uses the last 6 bits of the effective address (the displacement plus the contents of the base register) no matter what their value.

9.7 What will be the contents of each memory location after execution of each set of operations on the original memory contents?

```
            VAR   DC   PL4'1046'    (0001046C)
```

(a)	SRP	VAR,2,0		(f)	LA	2,3
					SRP	VAR,2(2),0
(b)	SRP	VAR,62,0		(g)	L	2,=F'−3'
					SRP	VAR,3(2),0
(c)	SRP	VAR,63,0		(h)	L	2,=F'−63'
					SRP	VAR,65(2),0
(d)	SRP	VAR,63,5		(i)	L	2,=F'−4'
					SRP	VAR,2(2),0
(e)	LA	2,3				
	SRP	VAR,0(2),0				

(a) 0104600C
(b) 0000010C
(c) 0000104C
(d) 0000105C
(e) 1046000C
(f) 4600000C (Significant digits lost, causing interruption)
(g) 0001046C
(h) 0104600C
(i) 0000010C

9.8 Write an SRP instruction (or series of instructions) to change the number in the first column in each part to the number in the second column. Use VAR as the name of your variable. VAR is declared PL3.

	First Column	*Second Column*	
(a)	00012C	00120C	
(b)	12345C	34500C	(Use TEMP to avoid an interruption)
(c)	12345C	00123C	

(a)	SRP	VAR,1,0			
(b)	ZAP	TEMP(4),VAR			
	SRP	TEMP(4),2,0			
	ZAP	VAR,TEMP+1(3)			
(c)	SRP	VAR,62,5	or	SRP	VAR,62,0

9.9 Repeat Problem 9.2 using the Shift and Round Packed operation instead of packed decimal multiplication and division.

(a)	ZAP	ANS(3),B(2)	
	SRP	ANS(3),1,0	10 × B
	AP	ANS(3),A(3)	
	SRP	ANS(3),62,0	TRUNCATE TO ONE DECIMAL PLACE
(b)	ZAP	TEMP(8),C(5)	
	SRP	TEMP(8),2,0	THREE DECIMAL PLACES (TOO BIG FOR ANS)
	AP	TEMP(8),A(3)	
	SRP	TEMP(8),62,0	TRUNCATE TO ONE DECIMAL PLACE
	ZAP	ANS(3),TEMP(8)	

```
        (c)  ZAP   TEMP(8),C(5)
             SRP   TEMP(8),1,0        TWO DECIMAL PLACES (TOO BIG FOR ANS)
             AP    TEMP(8),B(2)
             SRP   TEMP(8),63,0       TRUNCATE TO ONE DECIMAL PLACE
             ZAP   ANS(3),TEMP(8)
        (d)  ZAP   ANS2(4),B(2)
             SRP   ANS2(4),1,0        10 × B
             AP    ANS2(4),A(3)
             SRP   ANS2(4),61,0       TRUNCATE TO NO DECIMAL PLACES
        (e)  ZAP   TEMP(8),C(5)
             SRP   TEMP(8),2,0        THREE DECIMAL PLACES (TOO BIG FOR ANS)
             AP    TEMP(8),A(3)
             SRP   TEMP(8),61,0       TRUNCATE TO NO DECIMAL PLACES
             ZAP   ANS2(4),TEMP(8)
        (f)  ZAP   TEMP(8),C(5)
             SRP   TEMP(8),1,0        TWO DECIMAL PLACES (TOO BIG FOR ANS)
             AP    TEMP(8),B(2)
             SRP   TEMP(8),62,0       TRUNCATE TO NO DECIMAL PLACES
             ZAP   ANS2(4),TEMP(8)
```

Note that we do not need TEMP in parts (a) and (d) because ANS and ANS2 are large enough to hold B after it is shifted one digit.

9.10 In an SRP operation, can D2 (the displacement of the second operand) ever be negative?

No, a displacement can never be negative.

9.11 What is the effect of each of the following?

```
  (a)  L    3,=F'-30'          (b)  L    3,=F'-9'
       SRP  NUM(7),33(3),0          SRP  NUM(7),7(3),0
```

(a) A shift of three digits to the left (33 − 30 = 3).

(b) The second operand has a value FFFFFFFE, so the last 6 bits are 111110, which corresponds to 62. Therefore, there will be a shift of two digits to the right.

9.12 What is the result of execution of each of the following instructions on the initial value of PACKED or on the initial value of ZONED?

```
                    PACKED   DC   PL4'12345'
                    ZONED    DC   CL4'6789'
```

```
  (a)  MVZ   PACKED(1),=X'11'      (d)  MVN   ZONED+3(1),=X'88'
  (b)  MVN   PACKED(1),=X'11'      (e)  MVZ   PACKED+3(1),=X'00'
  (c)  MVZ   ZONED+3(1),=X'88'
```

(a) 1012345C   (d) F6F7F8F8
(b) 0112345C   (e) 0012340C
(c) F6F7F889

9.13 Use MVZ to change the value of ZONED to 'STUV'.

```
                    ZONED    DC   CL4'2345'
```

Since ZONED is F2F3F4F5, we need to change only the zones:

```
             MVZ   ZONED(4),=X'E0E0E0E0'
```

CHAP. 9] ADVANCED PACKED DECIMAL CONCEPTS 215

9.14 In each part, the contents of FINAL resulting from an MVO operation on SOURCE are shown, along with the desired result in FINAL. Provide instructions to change what is there to what is desired. Both memory locations are declared PL4. *Note*: X in the last half byte of the value desired means the appropriate sign (C or D), and the question marks in the present value represent garbage.

	Present	Desired
(a)	012345D?	0123450D
(b)	012345D?	0123450X
(c)	2345D???	2345000D
(d)	0001234?	0001234X
(e)	??2345D?	0023450D
(f)	?234567?	0234567X

(a) MVI   FINAL+3,X'0D'
(b) MVZ   FINAL+3(1),=X'00'
     MVN   FINAL+3(1),SOURCE+3
(c) MVC   FINAL+2(2),=X'000D'
(d) MVN   FINAL+3(1),SOURCE+3
(e) MVI   FINAL,X'00'
     MVI   FINAL+3,X'0D'
(f) MVZ   FINAL(1),=X'00'
     MVN   FINAL+3(1),SOURCE+3

9.15 What will be contents of FIRST produced by each of the following instructions acting on the original memory contents? Show each unknown digit with a question mark.

SECOND   DC   PL4'−12345'   (0012345D)
FIRST   DS   PL4

(a) MVO   FIRST(4),SECOND(4)
(b) MVO   FIRST(3),SECOND(4)
(c) MVO   FIRST(4),SECOND(3)
(d) MVO   FIRST+1(3),SECOND(4)
(e) MVO   FIRST(4),SECOND+1(3)
(f) MVO   FIRST+1(3),SECOND+1(3)

(a) 012345D?
(b) 2345D???
(c) 0001234?
(d) ??2345D?
(e) 012345D?
(f) ??2345D?

9.16 What will be produced in FINAL by the following sets of code, all acting on the original memory contents? Both variables are declared PL4.

INITIAL   DC   PL4'1234567'

(a) MVO   FINAL(4),INITIAL(4)
     MVN   FINAL+3(1),=X'0F'
(b) MVC   FINAL(3),INITIAL
     MVI   FINAL+3,X'0F'
(c) MVC   FINAL(3),INITIAL
     MVZ   FINAL+3(1),=X'00'
     MVN   FINAL+3(1),INITIAL+3
(d) MVO   FINAL(4),INITIAL(3)
     MVN   FINAL+3(1),INITIAL+3
(e) MVO   FINAL(3),INITIAL(4)
     MVZ   FINAL+2(2),=X'0000'
     MVN   FINAL+2(2),=X'F00F'

(a) 234567CF
(b) 1234560F
(c) 1234560C
(d) 0123456C
(e) 4567000F

9.17 Repeat Problem 9.2 using MVO and/or MVC instead of packed decimal multiplication and division.

(a)	MVO	ANS(3),B(2)	10 × B (YIELDING 0001C?)
	MVZ	ANS+2(1),=X'00'	FIX LAST BYTE
	MVN	ANS+2(1),B+1	FIX LAST BYTE (YIELDING 00010C)
	AP	ANS(3),A(3)	
	MVN	ANS+1(1),ANS+2	COPY SIGN TO SECOND BYTE
	ZAP	ANS(3),ANS(2)	DELETE THIRD BYTE
(b)	ZAP	TEMP(7),C(5)	PLACE C IN BYTES 3 THROUGH 7 OF TEMP
	MVN	TEMP+6(1),=X'00'	
	MVZ	TEMP+7(1),=X'00'	
	MVN	TEMP+7(1),C+4	COPY SIGN FROM C
	AP	TEMP(8),A(3)	
	MVN	TEMP+6(1),TEMP+7	COPY SIGN
	ZAP	ANS(3),TEMP(7)	ZAP SHORTENED NUMBER
(c)	MVO	TEMP(8),C(5)	
	MVZ	TEMP+7(1),=X'0F'	TWO DECIMAL PLACES
	MVN	TEMP+7(1),C+4	COPY SIGN
	AP	TEMP(8),B(2)	
	MVO	ANS(3),TEMP(7)	ONE DECIMAL PLACE
	MVN	ANS+2(1),TEMP+7	COPY SIGN
(d)	MVO	TEMP(8),B(2)	10 × B (YIELDING 00000000000001C?)
	MVZ	TEMP+7(1),=X'00'	FIX LAST BYTE
	MVN	TEMP+7(1),B+1	YIELDING 0000000000000010F
	AP	TEMP(8),A(3)	
	MVO	ANS2(4),TEMP(6)	TRUNCATE THREE DIGITS
	MVN	ANS2+3(1),TEMP+7	COPY SIGN
(e)	ZAP	TEMP(7),C(5)	
	MVN	TEMP+6(1),=X'00'	
	MVZ	TEMP+7(1),=X'00'	
	MVN	TEMP+7(1),C+4	COPY SIGN FROM C
	AP	TEMP(8),A(3)	
	MVO	ANS2(4),TEMP(6)	TRUNCATE THREE DIGITS
	MVN	ANS2+3(1),TEMP+7	COPY SIGN
(f)	MVO	TEMP(8),C(5)	PLACE C IN BYTES 3 THROUGH 7 OF TEMP
	MVZ	TEMP+7(1),=X'0F'	TWO DECIMAL PLACES
	MVN	TEMP+7(1),C+4	COPY SIGN
	AP	TEMP(8),B(2)	
	MVN	TEMP+6(1),TEMP+7	COPY SIGN
	ZAP	ANS2(4),TEMP(7)	TRUNCATE DIGITS TO NO DECIMAL PLACES

9.18 Write an MVO instruction to place into TEMP a value which (after fixing up with MVN and/or MVZ) will lead to (a) multiplication of VAR by 10, (b) multiplication of VAR by 1000, (c) division of VAR by 10, and (d) division of VAR by 1000.

Use the declarations

	VAR	DS	PL4
	TEMP	DC	PL6'0'

(a)	MVO	TEMP(6),VAR(4)		(c)	MVO	TEMP(6),VAR(3)
(b)	MVO	TEMP(5),VAR(4)		(d)	MVO	TEMP(6),VAR(2)

9.19 Write an instruction, similar to the ones in the preceding problem, to place in TEMP a number which will lead to division of VAR by 100.

                MVC   TEMP+3(3),VAR

9.20 If you pack a 9-byte source, how many bytes will it occupy with no padding or truncation?

    5 bytes.

9.21 If you unpack a 4-byte source, how many bytes will it occupy with no padding or truncation?

    7 bytes.

9.22 What is the value of TARGET after execution of each of the following instructions, using the original values for each part?

                SOURCE   DC   C'1234L'
                TARGET   DC   PL3'0'

(a) PACK   TARGET,SOURCE
(b) PACK   TARGET(2),SOURCE(4)
(c) PACK   TARGET(1),SOURCE+4(1)

(a) 12343D
(b) 234F0C (truncated)
(c) 3D000C

9.23 What is the value of TARGET after execution of each of the following instructions, using the original values for each part?

              SOURCE   DC   C'ABCDEJKL'
              TARGET   DC   PL8'0'   (000000000000000C)

(a) PACK   TARGET,SOURCE   (d) PACK   TARGET(3),SOURCE(5)
(b) PACK   TARGET(7),SOURCE   (e) PACK   TARGET(7),SOURCE(7)
(c) PACK   TARGET,SOURCE(5)

(a) 000000012345123D   (d) 12345C000000000C
(b) 0000012345123D0C   (e) 0000001234512D0C
(c) 000000000012345C

9.24 What value is produced in TARGET by each of the following instructions executed on the original values?

              SOURCE   DC   XL3'F1F2'
              TARGET   DC   PL3'0'

(a) PACK   TARGET,SOURCE
(b) PACK   TARGET(3),SOURCE(2)
(c) PACK   TARGET(1),SOURCE+2(1)

(a) 00012F   Note that SOURCE is initialized to 00F1F2—padded with 2 zeros on the left.
(b) 00001F   Padded with 3 zeros on the left.
(c) 2F000C   Note that TARGET is initialized to 00000C.

9.25 What value is produced in TARGET by each of the following instructions executed on the original values?

>   SOURCE   DC   X'ABCDEF'
>   TARGET   DC   CL5'1'

(a) UNPK   TARGET,SOURCE
(b) UNPK   TARGET(4),SOURCE(2)
(c) UNPK   TARGET(3),SOURCE(2)

(a) FAFBFCFDFE
(b) F0FAFBDC40   Note that TARGET was initialized to '1ɸɸɸɸ'.
(c) FAFBDC4040   Note that TARGET was initialized to '1ɸɸɸɸ'.

9.26 What result is produced by

>   UNPK   ANS(5),=X'12345C'

The last byte is reversed, and an F is added as the zone for each of the other bytes.

>   F1 F2 F3 F4 C5

9.27 What result is produced by the following.

(a) UNPK   ANS(3),=X'12345C'
(b) UNPK   ANS(6),=X'12345C'

(a) F3 F4 C5   Truncated at the left.
(b) F0 F1 F2 F3 F4 C5   Padded at the left.

9.28 In the following pair of instructions, NUM has a parenthesized length in one operand but not in the other. Explain why.

>   PACK   NUM(8),LINE(5)
>   CVB   2,NUM

CVB is an RX instruction which automatically operates on a double word, so the length cannot be provided. If we wrote

>   CVB   2,NUM(8)

the 8 would refer to an index register.

9.29 What will be the contents of each memory location after execution of each set of operations on the original memory contents?

```
INITIAL   DC   PL4'-123456'
SIGN      DS   CL1
FINAL     DS   CL7
OUTLINE   DC   CL121' '
```

(a) UNPK   FINAL,INITIAL
(b) UNPK   FINAL,INITIAL
    MVZ   FINAL+6(1),=C'0'

```
        (c)             MVI     SIGN,C' '
                        UNPK    FINAL,INITIAL
                        MVZ     FINAL+6(1),=C'0'
                        CP      INITIAL,=P'0'
                        BNL     OUT
                        MVI     SIGN,C'-'
                OUT     MVC     OUTLINE+1(8),SIGN
```

(a) FINAL is F0F1F2F3F4F5D6.

(b) FINAL is F0F1F2F3F4F5F6 (C'0' is X'F0').

(c) FINAL is F0F1F2F3F4F5F6; SIGN is C'-' (X'60'); OUTLINE is 4060F0F1F2F3F4F5F6 followed by 112 blanks. (The MVC involves 8 bytes starting at SIGN and including FINAL.)

9.30 (a) State the effect of PACK on the zoned forms of the following character strings (read from input):

'   456'

'000456'

(b) Does the input have to have leading zeros rather than leading blanks?

(c) Would there be any difference between '   ' (six blanks) and '000000'?

(a)
Character	Zoned Value	Packed Value
' 456'	404040F4F5F6	0000456F
'000456'	F0F0F0F4F5F6	0000456F

(b) No. Zeros (F0) or blanks (40) both pack to the same value, except when they occur as the last digit.

(c) The number '000000' would yield 0000000F; the same number of blanks would yield 00000004, and an illegal packed decimal number would result.

9.31 A 30-byte memory location called DATA (read from input) has values for VAL1, VAL2, and VAL3 in bytes 2 through 6, 12 through 16, and 22 through 26, respectively. If any of these numbers is negative, a minus sign appears in byte 1, 11, or 21. Write assembly language instructions to sum these values. Use P1, P2, and P3 (declared PL3) as the packed decimal memory locations.

```
                PACK    P1,DATA+1(5)
                CLI     DATA,C'-'
                BNE     CONT
                MVN     P1+2(1),=X'0D'
        CONT    PACK    P2,DATA+11(5)
                CLI     DATA+10,C'-'
                BNE     CONT2
                MVN     P2+2(1),=X'0D'
        CONT2   PACK    P3,DATA+21(5)
                CLI     DATA+20,C'-'
                BNE     CONT3
                MVN     P3+2(1),=X'0D'
        CONT3   ZAP     SUM,P1
                AP      SUM,P2
                AP      SUM,P3
```

9.32 A line read from input contains 'WXYZ' instead of '6789' as expected by the programmer. During execution of which instruction, if either, would an error or interruption occur?

```
            PACK    NUM(8),LINE(4)
            CVB     2,NUM
            ...
NUM         DS      D
LINE        DS      CL80
```

PACK never checks the contents of the second operand; it merely removes zones of all but the last byte and reverses the hexadecimal characters in the last byte. If there is to be an error, it must be in CVB, which requires a valid packed decimal number as a second operand. In this case, however, the second operand is a valid packed decimal number and just happens to be what the programmer expected.

$$\text{WXYZ} \quad \text{E6 E7 E8 E9}$$
$$6 \quad 7 \quad 8 \quad 9\text{E}$$

Since the digit E corresponds to positive, as does F, the value +6789 is placed into NUM for later conversion to binary in register 2. There is no execution error. (There may be a logical error, of course.)

9.33 A line read from input has '.,;:' instead of '6789' as expected by the programmer. During execution of which instruction, if any, would an error or interruption occur?

```
            PACK    NUM(8),LINE(4)
            CVB     2,NUM
            ...
NUM         DS      D
LINE        DS      CL80
```

PACK never checks the contents of the second operand; it merely removes zones of all but the last byte and reverses the hexadecimal characters in the last byte. If there is to be an error, it must be in CVB, which requires a valid packed decimal number as a second operand. In this case, the hexadecimal representation for '.,;:' is

$$\text{4B 6B 7A 5E}$$

which is packed to $\quad$ 00 00 00 00 00 0B BA E5

This value will give an error when the CVB operation is executed, because the result of the PACK operation is not a valid packed decimal operand.

9.34 (a) Assume that you want an 80-byte memory location called LINEOUT to contain the words listed below in the positions indicated, together with their accompanying values. Decimal points are to be placed in columns 35 and 56. NUM, PRI, and AMT are zoned decimal numbers, having lengths 4, 6, and 7, respectively.

NUMBER	PRICE		AMOUNT	
2–7	11–14	21–25	31–34.36–37	41–46	51–55.57–58
	NUM		PRI		AMT

Put the four digits of NUM in bytes 11 through 14; put the first four digits of PRI in bytes 31 through 34 and the next two digits of PRI in bytes 36 and 37; put the first five digits of AMT in bytes 51 through 55 and the last two digits of AMT in bytes 57 and 58. Columns 35 and 56 contain decimal points. Write instructions to put these values in these locations efficiently, leaving all other bytes of LINEOUT blank.

(b) Repeat part (a), but do as much of the work as possible with DC statements.

(a) MVI   LINEOUT,C' '
     MVC   LINEOUT+1(79),LINEOUT   BLANKS LINEOUT
     MVC   LINEOUT+1(6)=C'NUMBER'
     MVC   LINEOUT+20(5),=C'PRICE'
     MVC   LINEOUT+40(6),=C'AMOUNT'
     MVC   LINEOUT+10(4),NUM
     MVC   LINEOUT+30(4),PRI
     MVI   LINEOUT+34,C'.'
     MVC   LINEOUT+35(2),PRI+4
     MVC   LINEOUT+50(5),AMT
     MVI   LINEOUT+55,C'.'
     MVC   LINEOUT+56(2),AMT+5

(b) Use these declarations:

     LINEOUT DC   C' '
              DC   CL6'NUMBER'
              DC   CL3' '
     OUTNUM   DS   CL4
              DC   CL6' '
              DC   C'PRICE'
              DC   CL5' '
     INTPRI   DS   CL4   INTEGER PART OF PRICE
              DC   C'.'
     DECPRI   DS   CL2   DECIMAL PART OF PRICE
              DC   CL3' '
              DC   C'AMOUNT'
              DC   CL4' '
     INTAMT   DS   CL5   INTEGER PART OF AMOUNT
              DC   C'.'
     DECAMT   DS   CL2   DECIMAL PART OF AMOUNT
              DC   CL22' '

Then use these instructions:

     MVC   OUTNUM(4),NUM
     MVC   INTPRI(4),PRI
     MVC   DECPRI(2),PRI+4
     MVC   INTAMT(5),AMT
     MVC   DECAMT(2),AMT+5

9.35 A value for VAL1 read from input is in columns 1 through 5 of INDATA, and a value for VAL2 is in columns 11 through 14. Both numbers are integers, and either one or both could be negative. If either or both are negative, a minus sign will be located in columns 6 and/or 15. Write code to place the two numbers in printable format, right justified in columns 21 through 27 and 31 through 37 in OUTLINE, and their sum in columns 41 through 47. Suppress leading zeros and print a minus sign in front of every negative number.

```
            PACK  VAL1(4),INDATA(5)
            PACK  VAL2(4),INDATA+10(4)
            CLI   INDATA+5,C'-'
            BNE   NEXT1
            MVN   VAL1+3(1),=X'0D'
   NEXT1    CLI   INDATA+14,C'-'
            BNE   NEXT2
            MVN   VAL2+3(1),=X'0D'
```

```
       NEXT2     ZAP   SUM(4),VAL1
                 AP    SUM(4),VAL2
                 MVC   PATTERN(8),TEMPLATE
                 LA    1,PATTERN+7
                 EDMK  PATTERN(8),VAL1
                 BNM   NEXT3
                 BCTR  1,0
                 MVI   0(1),C'-'
       NEXT3     MVC   OUTLINE+20(7),PATTERN+1
                 MVC   PATTERN(8),TEMPLATE
                 LA    1,PATTERN+7
                 EDMK  PATTERN(8),VAL2
                 BNM   NEXT4
                 BCTR  1,0
                 MVI   0(1),C'-'
       NEXT4     MVC   OUTLINE+30(7),PATTERN+1
                 MVC   PATTERN(8),TEMPLATE
                 LA    1,PATTERN+7
                 EDMK  PATTERN(8),SUM
                 BNM   NEXT5
                 BCTR  1,0
                 MVI   0(1),C'-'
       NEXT5     MVC   OUTLINE+40(7),PATTERN+1
                 ...
       VAL1      DS    PL4
       VAL2      DS    PL4
       SUM       DS    PL4
       PATTERN   DS    XL8
       TEMPLATE  DC    X'4020202020202120'
       INDATA    DS    CL80
       OUTLINE   DC    CL121' '
```

9.36 A value for VAL1 read from input is in columns 1 through 4 of INDATA, and a value for VAL2 is in columns 11 through 14. Each number has one decimal place and either one or both could be negative. If either or both are negative, a minus sign will be located in columns 5 and/or 15. Write code to place the two numbers in printable format, right justified in columns 21 through 29 and 31 through 39 in OUTLINE, and their sum in columns 41 through 49. There is no decimal point in the INPUT record.

```
                 PACK  VAL1(3),INDATA(4)
                 PACK  VAL2(3),INDATA+10(4)
                 CLI   INDATA+4,C'-'
                 BNE   NEXT1
                 MVN   VAL1+2(1),=X'0D'
       NEXT1     CLI   INDATA+14,C'-'
                 BNE   NEXT2
                 MVN   VAL2+2(1),=X'0D'
       NEXT2     ZAP   SUM(3),VAL1
                 AP    SUM(3),VAL2
                 MVC   PATTERN(9),TEMPLATE
                 LA    1,PATTERN+6
                 EDMK  PATTERN(9),VAL1
                 BNM   NEXT3
                 BCTR  1,0
                 MVI   0(1),C'-'
```

```
        NEXT3     MVC     OUTLINE+20(9),PATTERN
                  MVC     PATTERN(9),TEMPLATE
                  LA      1,PATTERN+6
                  EDMK    PATTERN(9),VAL2
                  BNM     NEXT4
                  BCTR    1,0
                  MVI     0(1),C'-'
        NEXT4     MVC     OUTLINE+30(9),PATTERN
                  MVC     PATTERN(9),TEMPLATE
                  LA      1,PATTERN+6
                  EDMK    PATTERN(9),SUM
                  BNM     NEXT5
                  BCTR    1,0
                  MVI     0(1),C'-'
        NEXT5     MVC     OUTLINE+40(9),PATTERN
                  ...
        VAL1      DS      PL3
        VAL2      DS      PL3
        SUM       DS      PL3
        PATTERN   DS      XL9
        TEMPLATE  DC      X'4040206B2021204B20'
        INDATA    DS      CL80
        OUTLINE   DC      CL121' '
```

9.37 A value for VAL1 read from input is in columns 1 through 5 of INDATA, and a value for VAL2 is in columns 11 through 14. VAL1 has one decimal place and VAL2 has two decimal places, and either one or both could be negative. If either or both are negative, a minus sign will be located in columns 6 and/or 15. Write code to place the two numbers in printable format, right justified in columns 21 through 29 and 31 through 39 in OUTLINE, and their sum in columns 41 through 49. There is no decimal point in the INPUT record.

```
                  PACK    VAL1(3),INDATA(5)
                  PACK    VAL2(3),INDATA+10(4)
                  CLI     INDATA+5,C'-'
                  BNE     NEXT1
                  MVN     VAL1+2(1),=X'0D'
        NEXT1     CLI     INDATA+14,C'-'
                  BNE     NEXT2
                  MVN     VAL2+2(1),=X'0D'
        NEXT2     ZAP     SUM(4),VAL1
                  SRP     SUM(4),1,0
                  AP      SUM(4),VAL2
                  MVC     PATTERN1(9),TEMPLAT1
                  LA      1,PATTERN1+6
                  EDMK    PATTERN1(9),VAL1
                  BNM     NEXT3
                  BCTR    1,0
                  MVI     0(1),C'-'
```

```
         NEXT3     MVC   OUTLINE+20(9),PATTERN1
                   MVC   PATTERN1(9),TEMPLAT2
                   LA    1,PATTERN1+5
                   EDMK  PATTERN1(9),VAL2
                   BNM   NEXT4
                   BCTR  1,0
                   MVI   0(1),C'-'
         NEXT4     MVC   OUTLINE+30(9),PATTERN1
                   MVC   PATTERN2(10),TEMPLAT3
                   LA    1,PATTERN2+6
                   EDMK  PATTERN2(10),SUM
                   BNM   NEXT5
                   BCTR  1,0
                   MVI   0(1),C'-'
         NEXT5     MVC   OUTLINE+40(9),PATTERN2+1
                   ...
         VAL1      DS    PL3
         VAL2      DS    PL3
         SUM       DS    PL4
         PATTERN1  DS    XL9
         PATTERN2  DS    XL10
         TEMPLAT1  DC    X'4040206B2021204B20'
         TEMPLAT2  DC    X'4040402021204B2020'
         TEMPLAT3  DC    X'4020206B2021204B2020'
         INDATA    DS    CL80
         OUTLINE   DC    CL121' '
```

9.38 Write patterns to use to edit the following variables as specified. All values may be assumed to be positive.

	Variable Name	Length	Number of Decimal Places	Commas Wanted?
(a)	VAL1	PL3	None	Yes
(b)	VAL2	PL4	None	Yes
(c)	VAL3	PL4	One	Yes
(d)	VAL4	PL5	One	Yes
(e)	VAL5	PL7	Two	No

(a) XL7'4020206B202120'

(b) XL10'40206B2020206B202120'

(c) XL10'402020206B2021204B20'

(d) XL13'4020206B2020206B2021204B20'

(e) XL15'402020202020202020202021204B2020'

9.39 Write a pattern to edit a ZIP code, such as 97141 or 00603.

XL6'F02120202020'   or   XL6'F02020202020'

Note that F0 is used as the fill character to guarantee that all leading zeros will be printed. However, care must be taken not to print the fill character itself, so that you don't have a six-digit ZIP code.

9.40 Write a pattern to edit a social security number in the format

123-45-6789

F0 is used as the fill character, in case the first digit is zero. The 21 turns on the significance indicator for the second character and is needed to prevent replacing the first hyphen with a zero in case the first three digits are zero. As in Problem 9.39, the fill character must not be printed after the edit instruction.

XL12′F02120206020206020202020′

9.41 TEMPLATE, declared below, is at address 1BC001. It will be used by EDMK to edit a dollar amount and to place a dollar sign just before the first significant digit. What address should be loaded into register 1 to prepare for the possibility that the value edited will be less than $1? Assume that we want at least one whole number digit even if the value is less than $1.

    1BC001   TEMPLATE   DC   XL10′4020206B2021204B2020′

TEMPLATE+6 which is

1BC007

9.42 What difference, if any, would there be in the operation of the following patterns?

402021204B2020   402021214B2121

The effect of the operation is the same using these two patterns. Once the significance indicator is turned on, the 21 acts just the same as the 20.

9.43 (a) What happens if an edit instruction runs out of digits in the second operand before it runs out of digit selectors (20 or 21)?

(b) What happens if the instruction runs out of pattern before it runs out of digits?

(a) The instruction continues, using whatever follows the second operand in memory. An interruption may occur if this does not correspond to decimal digits.

(b) It changes the pattern present and ignores the extra digits.

9.44 How many bytes of 20 or 21 should there be in a pattern to edit a PL4 packed decimal number?

Seven.

9.45 What values will be placed in LOC1 and LOC2 by the following portion of assembly language code? PNUM1 and PNUM2 contain 00123C and 23456C, respectively.

```
        ED    TEMPLATE(6),PNUM1
        MVC   LOC1(6),TEMPLATE
        ED    TEMPLATE(6),PNUM2
        MVC   LOC2(6),TEMPLATE
        ...
TEMPLATE DC   XL6′402020202120′
```

LOC1 will contain ⌿⌿⌿123. LOC2 will contain nothing but fill characters. The second of the edit instructions acted on TEMPLATE with no 20 or 21 bytes in it because the bytes had already been changed by the first edit instruction. The significance indicator was never turned on, and the fill character replaced all the "message characters."

9.46 What will be the final value of PATTERN after execution of the following instructions on PNUM, declared PL3, or PNUM2, declared PL2?

	Instruction		PATTERN	Value of PNUM or PNUM2
(a)	ED	PATTERN(9),PNUM	40202020202040C3D9	12345
(b)	ED	PATTERN(9),PNUM	40202020202040C3D9	−12345
(c)	ED	PATTERN(7),PNUM	40202020202040C3D9	12345
(d)	ED	PATTERN(9),PNUM2	40202020202040C3D9	123

(a) ƀ12345ƀƀƀ

(b) ƀ12345ƀCR

(c) ƀ12345ƀCR   (The part of pattern corresponding to CR was not changed because it was not part of the first operand.)

(d) ƀ123garbage   (When the digits are exhausted, garbage will be produced.)

9.47 Describe the most logical attributes of each operand in the following set of instructions:

```
PACK   TARGET1,SOURCE1
UNPK   TARGET2,SOURCE2
ED     PATTERN,SOURCE3
```

Because of the way they are used we can assume the following attributes:

TARGET1	Packed decimal
SOURCE1	Zoned decimal
TARGET2	Zoned decimal
SOURCE2	Packed decimal
PATTERN	Hexadecimal
SOURCE3	Packed decimal

9.48 Suppose each of the credit cards of Problem 8.15 has a letter or a digit as the final character after 15 digits. Would holding the data as packed decimal numbers still be possible? Explain.

Yes, it is still possible. The "numbers" would have to be defined as character strings and then packed. When the card number is packed, the two hexadecimal digits of the last character are interchanged, but both halves are still retained. Thus it is still possible to distinguish two numbers which differ only in their last characters. It would be necessary to use Compare Logical Character in this case. The Compare Packed instruction could not be used, since the last bytes of the numbers are ambiguous. For example, the last bytes 6E (packed from 'W'), 6C (packed from 'F'), or 6F (packed from '6') would not be distinguished by Compare Packed.

9.49 Suppose each of the credit cards of the preceding problem has a letter A through I as the first character, followed by 14 digits and a final character. Would holding the data as packed decimal numbers interfere with the identification process? Explain.

Packing such numbers would yield a digit 1 through 9 as the first digit, which is okay. However, if letters from different thirds of the alphabet were used, they could not be distinguished, since A (X'C1') and J (X'D1') would both pack to 1; B (X'C2'), K (X'D2'), and S (X'E2') would all pack to 2; etc. Thus, no programming advantage would be gained by using an initial letter in place of a digit. In fact, there would be one fewer possible value—0 through 9 is 10 values while A through I is 9 values. However, there might be a psychological advantage for customers who do not like to remember so many digits.

9.50 A supermarket chain holds its pricing data in a 100-element array of records, with each record composed of 32 bytes as follows:

CHAP. 9] ADVANCED PACKED DECIMAL CONCEPTS 227

Bytes	15	10	1	2	4
Format	BRAND NAME	TYPE	SIZE CODE	RETAIL PRICE	EST. UNITS SOLD
Example	BRAND X	PEAS	2	040	40000
Declaration	CL15	CL10	PL1	PL2'X.XX'	PL4'XXXXXXX'

Write code to discount the retail price of all BRAND X merchandise by 15 percent, storing the new price in the proper place in the array. If the price turns out to include a fraction of a cent, use SRP to round the price up to the next whole cent if the fraction is 0.3 cent or above.

The declarations are as follows:

```
                PRICINFO    DS    100CL32
                TEMP        DS    PL6
```

The code is as follows:

```
          LA    7,PRICINFO
          LA    8,100                    COUNT
LOOP      CLC   0(15,7),=CL15'BRAND X'   CHECK ID
          BNE   ENDLOOP
          ZAP   TEMP(6),26(2,7)          PUT PRICE IN TEMP
          MP    TEMP(6),=P'0.85'
          SRP   TEMP(6),64-2,7
          ZAP   26(2,7),TEMP
ENDLOOP   LA    7,32(0,7)                INCREMENT REGISTER 7
          BCT   8,LOOP
          ...
```

The address of the array is loaded into register 7 and the number of elements into register 8. The first 15 bytes of the element is compared with 'BRAND X'. If the name is not 'BRAND X', execution branches to the end of the loop. If the name is 'BRAND X', the price, which starts 26 bytes beyond the start of the record, is ZAPped into TEMP, multiplied by 85, and then divided by 100. The SRP instruction divides by 100 by shifting two digits to the right. It adds 7 to the first digit to be dropped. Thus, if that digit is 2, no carry will occur and the price will not be rounded up. If the digit is 3 or more, addition of 7 will cause a carry and rounding up will occur. The value in TEMP is placed back in the array in its proper place, and the looping continues.

9.51 Write code to calculate the estimated total discount of the preceding problem if the number of units of each BRAND X product estimated to be sold is actually sold.

Additional declarations are as follows:

```
                DISCOUNT    DS    PL12
                TOTDISC     DS    PL4
```

The code is as follows:

```
          ZAP   TOTDISC(4),=P'0'         INITIALIZE TOTAL TO ZERO
          LA    7,PRICINFO
          LA    8,1000                   COUNT
LOOP      CLC   0(15,7),=CL15'BRAND X'
          BNE   ENDLOOP
          ZAP   DISCOUNT(8),26(2,7)      SAVE REGULAR PRICE
          ZAP   TEMP(6),26(2,7)
          MP    TEMP(6),=P'0.85'
          SRP   TEMP(6),64-2,7
          ZAP   26(2,7),TEMP(6)
          SP    DISCOUNT(8),TEMP(6)      SUBTRACT DISCOUNT PRICE
          MP    DISCOUNT(8),28(4,7)      MULTIPLY BY ESTIMATED
*                                           NUMBER SOLD
          AP    TOTDISC(4),DISCOUNT(8)
ENDLOOP   LA    7,32(0,7)                INCREMENT REGISTER 7
          BCT   8,LOOP
          ...
```

This problem requires the following additions. TOTDISC is initialized to zero. If the name is 'BRAND X', the regular price is saved in DISCOUNT, and the discounted price is later subtracted from it to yield the actual discount for each unit. This value is multiplied by the estimated number to be sold to get the estimated total discount for the item, which is added to TOTDISC. Both TEMP and DISCOUNT must have sufficient bytes to ensure enough leading zeros to allow for packed decimal multiplication.

Supplementary Problems

9.52 Trace Problem 9.2(a), using the values A = 1.234 and B = 0.67.

9.53 Rework Example 9.9 without using TEMP. Test your program segment using the following values, and comment on the usefulness of TEMP: (a) A = 12.00 and B = 6.0, (b) A = 923.00 and B = 1000.0.

9.54 Trace Problem 9.9(a), using the values A = 1.234 and B = 0.67.

9.55 Rework Example 9.20 without using TEMP. Test your program segment using the following values, and comment on the usefulness of TEMP: (a) A = 12.00 and B = 6.0, (b) A = 923.00 and B = 1000.0.

9.56 Trace Problem 9.17(a), using the values A = 1.234 and B = 0.67.

9.57 In Problem 9.17(a), assume that you know that B is positive. Simplify the coding somewhat, using an MVI instruction.

9.58 Write a loop in which an SRP instruction causes a shift of (a) one digit left the first time through the loop, two digits left the second time through the loop, and three digits left the third time through the loop; (b) one digit left the first time through the loop, no shift the second time through the loop, and one digit right the third time through the loop.

9.59 What is the maximum length of the first operand for each of the following?

(a) MVO (b) MVC (c) MVN (d) PACK (e) ED

9.60 Which of the instructions of the prior problem are single-length SS-type instructions and which are two-length instructions?

9.61 Write the machine language code for the second byte of the instructions in the prior two problems using (1) the maximum length for each operand, (2) 1 byte for each operand, and (3) 2 bytes for each operand. How do single-length and two-length instructions differ in this regard?

9.62 It is possible to write SS-type instructions in assembly language with a zero length for the operand(s), which is translated into machine code with zero in the second byte (not 1 less than the assembly language length). If such machine language instructions were executed, what length would be used for the operand(s)? (One reason for writing zero-length SS instructions is presented in Sec. 13.4.)

9.63 The EX instruction (see Sec. 13.4) allows us to change the length of an SS machine language instruction during execution. Why is it necessary to know that machine language instructions store a value 1 less than the desired length?

9.64 Suppose that a number is declared PL4 and has two digits to the right of the decimal point. You want to suppress leading zeros. What pattern would you use (a) if you want to print at least one leading zero to the left of the decimal point, such as 0.02, (b) if you do not want any leading zeros to the left of the decimal point but you want the decimal point to be printed no matter what the number, such as .02?

CHAP. 9] ADVANCED PACKED DECIMAL CONCEPTS 229

9.65 Show how these assignments can be made. Be sure to produce the correct number of decimal places in the answer.

A	DC	PL3'2.00'	TWO DECIMAL PLACES
B	DC	PL4'3.000'	THREE DECIMAL PLACES
C	DC	PL5'5.5555'	FOUR DECIMAL PLACES

(a) A = B   (b) A = C   (c) B = C   (d) C = A

9.66 Government pay checks are sometimes drawn with the amount in the format:

____dollars ____cents

Show how to divide up the 5-byte packed decimal number PAY into packed decimal DOLLARS and CENTS for this format, in two different ways.

9.67 Write machine language instructions corresponding to the assembly language instructions given below. The base register is register 12 and it contains 1BC042. The address of VAR1 is 1BC244.

```
              ZAP   NUM3(4),NUM1(3)
              AP    NUM2+3(1),NUM1+1(2)
              ZAP   TEMP,NUM2
              DP    TEMP,NUM1
              ZAP   VAR1,TEMP(5)
              ZAP   VAR2,TEMP+5(3)
              ...
VAR1   DC    PL4'12.3'
VAR2   DC    PL3'-88.7'
NUM1   DC    PL3'10.00'
NUM2   DC    PL4'-0.1'
NUM3   DS    PL5
TEMP   DS    PL8
```

9.68 Write machine language instructions corresponding to the assembly language instructions after the Load Address instructions given below.

```
              LA    6,VAR1
              LA    7,VAR2
              LA    2,NUM1
              LA    5,NUM2
              LA    3,NUM3
              LA    4,TEMP
              ZAP   0(4,6),0(3,7)
              AP    0(5,2),4(16,5)
              DP    0(8,6),202(4,4)
              ZAP   0(3,3),0(4,7)
              ZAP   0(4,7),4(4,7)
              ...
VAR1   DC    PL4'12.3'
VAR2   DC    PL3'-88.7'
NUM1   DC    PL3'10.00'
NUM2   DC    PL4'-0.1'
NUM3   DS    PL5
TEMP   DS    PL8
```

9.69 (a) Write a program segment which will divide DIVIDEND, with two decimal places, by DIVISOR, with one decimal place, to get QUOTIENT, with two decimal places. Trace your segment using the values DIVIDEND = 22.00 and DIVISOR = 3.0.

(b) What answer would you have obtained if you divided first then multiplied by =P'1.0'?

Chapter 10

Subprograms

10.1 Introduction

Writing subprograms is an effective way (1) to modularize a program, (2) to perform the same operations repeatedly on the same or different variables, (3) to use library programs to reduce work. Subprograms are executed on call. That means that to execute a subprogram, we must branch to it, and after the subprogram has finished execution, it must branch back. If the same subprogram is called more than once from the same program, it must branch back to the correct address each time. One subprogram can be called from several different programs, and it must be able to return correctly to each one.

A list of variables, called *parameters*, is generally sent to the subprogram. The subprogram must receive the correct parameters each time it is called. The first parameter of a subprogram might represent one variable one time the subprogram is called, but another variable the next time it is called.

A subprogram may be classified as either a *function* or a *subroutine*. A function is designed to return one value to the calling program. A subroutine does not return a value, but typically it alters the values of its parameters while it is executing. A function may also alter the values of its parameters (although it is often considered bad style to have a function do so). These two types of subprograms are more alike than different, but their differences will be highlighted in this chapter.

Since one of the reasons for using subprograms is to apportion the programming work among several programmers, it should be easy for a programmer to use a subprogram written by someone else. To this end, a set of standard conventions has been established for the linkage of subprograms. If both the calling program and the subprogram follow these conventions, the person who writes the calling program can call the subprogram without having to be familiar with the details of what happens inside the subprogram. Since registers 0, 1, 13, 14, and 15 are used for subprogram linkage, it is best to avoid using them for other purposes, if possible. [There are, however, other uses for register 1: for example TRT (Sec. 13.3) and EDMK (Sec. 9.8).]

Table 10-1 Tasks of the Calling Program and the Called Program

Calling Program	Called Program	Register Involved	Section
Branch to the subprogram		15	10.3
Specify the address to which the subprogram is to return	Return to the address specified by the calling program	14	10.3
Send parameters to the subprogram	Receive parameters from the calling program	1	10.5
Receive the value returned by a function	A function subprogram returns a value	0	10.8
Provide an area in memory in which the subprogram can save the contents of the registers	Save the original contents of the registers before reusing the registers, and then restore the original contents before returning	13	10.6
	Establish addressability	Usually 11 or 12	10.7

10.2 Control Sections

Each of the programs that we have written so far has consisted of one control section. A *control section* is the smallest entity that can be relocated independently of other control sections. Consequently, a control section may be assembled independently of other control sections, and then various control sections may be linked together to run as a single program. The advantages of writing programs in different control sections include the possibility that different programmers can write and test different control sections independently of one another. In fact, one can assemble them independently, saving the object codes and linking them together to make a complete machine language program at execution time.

Each control section begins with a pseudo-instruction—either START or CSECT. The control section containing the main program can use either of these; each other control section must use CSECT. Every control section in a program must have a different name in the Name field (although the main program does not require a name).

Typically, we will use START with the main program and CSECT with any other control sections. Thus the first statement in a control section may look like the following:

       MAIN   START 0   or   SUB1   CSECT

Each control section is ended by another CSECT pseudo-instruction or the END statement. Note that the END statement signifies the end of the material to be assembled at one time, so we do not use an END between control sections which are assembled together. (See Fig. 10-1.)

There can be one or more subprograms (perhaps including a main program) in one control section. Subprograms within the same control section as the main program are referred to as *internal* subprograms. Subprograms in different control sections are called *external* subprograms. Typically, each control section will include a BALR and a USING instruction to establish addressability. In fact, each subprogram might do so. Since each control section has its own addressability, it cannot refer to the symbolic name of a variable defined in another control section. Furthermore, there can be no duplication of names within a section of code assembled as a unit, even if it consists of more than one control section. However, if two control sections are assembled independently, the names used in each are completely independent and thus may be duplicates (except for the names of the control sections themselves). In order to maintain addressability of literals within each of the control sections, the programmer must use LTORG (Sec. 4.11) to group the literals at the end of the current control section.

```
MAIN     START 0             NAME1    CSECT
...                          ...
...                          ...
NAMEA    CSECT               NAME2    CSECT     Ends first control
...                          ...                section, begins second
...                          ...
NAMEB    CSECT               NAME3    CSECT     Ends second control
...                          ...                sections, begins third
...                          ...
END                          END                Ends third control
                                                section and signifies
                                                the end of the material
                                                being assembled at this time
                                                (only one END is permitted
                                                for each assembly)
```

Fig. 10-1 Control sections.

10.3 Branching to and Returning from a Subprogram

A given subprogram may be executed several times within a calling program. Each time, execution must branch back to the proper place—the instruction after the call to the subprogram. These links are accomplished by use of the BALR (or BAL) instruction in the calling program and the BR instruction in the subprogram.

Branch and Link, and Branch and Link Register

Branch and Link (BAL) and Branch and Link Register (BALR) are related. BAL is an RX instruction, and BALR is an RR instruction. In general, they both do the following two tasks:

1. Load the address of the *next* instruction into the register specified as the first operand.
2. Branch to the address designated by the second operand (with the exception noted after Example 10.1).

EXAMPLE 10.1

In each of the following program segments, the BAL or BALR instruction loads the address of HERE into register 9 and then branches to THERE.

```
(a)            BAL    9,THERE
      HERE     ...
                ...
      THERE    ...
(b)            LA     7,THERE
               BAL    9,0(0,7)
      HERE     ...
                ...
      THERE    ...
(c)            LA     7,THERE
               BALR   9,7
      HERE     ...
                ...
      THERE    ...
```

When the second operand of BALR is zero, no branch occurs. (This is also the case with BCR and BCTR.) We have been using this feature of BALR since Chap. 2 to establish base addresses.

Naturally, BAL can do the same things as BALR, as we illustrated in Example 10.1, but it is less flexible than BALR. The normal way to use BAL is to use a symbolic second operand, such as in BAL 14,THERE. However, in that case the second operand of BAL must be an address within the range of addressability of the current USING pseudo-instruction. When the program is assembled, the assembler must be able to determine the base register and displacement for the address. This is impossible to do for a name in another control section. With BALR, the register which holds the destination of the branch may hold any address, even that of another control section. Therefore, we will use BALR exclusively in the programs in this book.

The BALR instruction will perform two of the tasks mentioned in Sec. 10.1; namely, it will branch to the subprogram and save the address to which to return.

By convention, register 14 is used to hold the return address and register 15 is used to hold the address of the subprogram. Thus, when all other instructions in preparation for the subprogram have been accomplished, the address of the subprogram is placed in register 15 and the instruction

```
              BALR    14,15
```

is used to transfer control to the subprogram. This instruction first loads the address of the next instruction into register 14, and then it branches to the address in register 15. Each time execution of a subprogram ends, control should return to the next instruction after the call that passed control to the subprogram. Hence that next address is the return address from the subprogram. When the subprogram has completed its work, it will return by branching to the address found in register 14.

There are some subroutines, including some supplied by the operating system, which change register 15, so we cannot count on finding the address of the subroutine in register 15 when control returns to the calling program. Therefore, it is good practice for the calling program to reload register 15 with the address of the subroutine before each call, even if it did nothing in between to alter the contents of this register.

Loading register 15 is best accomplished by using an address constant. The name of the subprogram is the constant, and an A or a V is used to signify "the address of." The symbol A is used for addresses of subprograms within the same control section, and V is used for addresses of subprograms in different control sections.

```
          L       15,ADSUB       USING ONE OF THE FOLLOWING DECLARATIONS FOR ADSUB
          ...
ADSUB     DC      A(SUB)         THE SYMBOL A IS FOR ADDRESSES IN SAME CSECT
```

or

```
ADSUB     DC      V(SUB)         THE SYMBOL V IS FOR ADDRESSES IN DIFFERENT CSECTS
```

Note that parentheses rather than quotation marks are used around the constant name.

A literal might also be used:

```
          L       15,=A(SUB)     FOR SUBPROGRAMS IN SAME CSECT
```

or

```
          L       15,=V(SUB)     FOR OTHER SUBPROGRAMS
```

A Load Address instruction cannot be used to load the address of a subprogram in another control section, nor can it be used for a subprogram which occurs before the current base address. Only for a program which is within the range of addressability of the calling program could we use this instruction:

```
                  LA      15,SUB      DO NOT USE
```

The use of an address constant is still the preferred style even in this case.

EXAMPLE 10.2

The following declarations prepare an address constant for an internal subprogram named AVERAGE and one for an external subprogram named DEVIATN:

```
ADAVG     DC      A(AVERAGE)
ADDEV     DC      V(DEVIATN)
```

When the subprogram is ready to return, it must branch to the address in register 14, which is the address of the instruction following the call (put there by BALR 14,15). This can be done by the instruction BR 14.

We recognize the BR 14 instruction as the instruction that we have been using since Chap. 2 to halt execution of our main programs. It turns out that a main program is actually a subprogram of the operating system, and BR 14 in the main program branches back to the operating system, halting execution of our program. Since the operating system has entered an address for this purpose into register 14 at the start of execution, we must be careful to save that piece of information before our first call to a subprogram. Otherwise, we will not know what address to branch to in order to halt execution. Thus we save the contents of register 14 before our first call to a subprogram:

```
                    ST    14,SAVEADD
```

We then reload that address after return from the last subprogram and before we halt execution:

```
                    L     14,SAVEADD
                    BR    14
```

(In subprograms, the return address is saved and reloaded in a different way. See Sec. 10.6.)

10.4 Load Multiple and Store Multiple

Two instructions which are particularly useful in subprogram linkage are discussed in this section. While the use of these instructions is not limited to subprograms, they perform specific tasks that arise in calling subprograms.

Until now, we have been able to load or store only one register at a time. Load Multiple (LM) and Store Multiple (STM) allow us to operate on more than one register at a time. LM copies full words from consecutive memory locations to consecutive registers, and STM copies the information in the other direction. Load Multiple and Store Multiple are RS-type instructions. Their formats are as follows:

Assembly language	OPCODE	R1,R3,D2(B2)
Machine language	OP	R1 R3 B2 D2
	1 byte	1 byte / 2 bytes

No index register may be used. The number of full words copied is determined by the number of registers from R1 through R3 inclusive. The number of full words in memory is the same as the number of registers. For example, the instruction

```
                    LM    2,4,START
```

loads registers 2, 3, and 4 (three registers) with the three full words at START, START+4, and START+8.

```
                    STM   2,4,START
```

stores the information from registers 2, 3, and 4 into memory locations START, START+4, and START+8, respectively.

For the purpose of LM and STM, the register numbers may be thought to be cyclic, with register 0 following register 15. This is sometimes called *wraparound*. Thus, if R3 is lower than R1, all the registers starting at R1 through register 15 and those starting at register 0 through R3 will be used.

EXAMPLE 10.3

The instruction

```
                    LM    14,2,BEGIN
```

will load

Register 14 from memory location BEGIN
Register 15 from memory location BEGIN+4
Register 0 from memory location BEGIN+8
Register 1 from memory location BEGIN+12
Register 2 from memory location BEGIN+16

Thus LM and STM may be used to copy as many as 16 full words between consecutive (fullword) memory locations and consecutive registers, starting at any register number.

EXAMPLE 10.4

The final values in all changed registers and memory locations after execution of each of the following instructions are shown at the right. In each part, assume that registers 0 through 15 hold the values 0 through 15, respectively, and memory locations A1 through A18 are full words which hold the values 10, 20, 30, ..., 180, respectively.

(a) LM   2,4,A1   reg2 holds 10   reg3 holds 20   reg4 holds 30
(b) LM   2,4,A11   reg2 holds 110   reg3 holds 120   reg4 holds 130
(c) STM 7,8,A8   A8 holds 7   A9 holds 8
(d) STM 2,4,A8   A8 holds 2   A9 holds 3   A10 holds 4
(e) STM 14,2,A5   A5 holds 14   A6 holds 15   A7 holds 0
                    A8 holds 1   A9 holds 2
(f) LM   14,12,A1 reg14 holds 10   reg15 holds 20   reg0 holds 30
                    reg1 holds 40 ... reg12 holds 150

As usual, the memory location may be expressed in explicit notation.

EXAMPLE 10.5

Using the same initial contents as in the previous example, the following instructions produce the final values shown at the right.

(a) LA   13,A1
     LM   14,12,0(13)   reg14 holds 10   reg15 holds 20 ... reg12 holds 150
(b) LA   13,A1
     LM   14,12,12(13) reg14 holds 40   reg15 holds 50
                        reg0 holds 60   ... reg12 holds 180

Among other uses, these instructions are used to save register contents in a subprogram and to restore the contents at the end of the subprogram. The last LM in Example 10.5 is, for reasons which will be discussed in Sec. 10.6, the format usually used in this case. The format for STM is similar:

$$\text{STM} \quad 14,12,12(13)$$

10.5 Passing Parameters

One of the most important tasks of a subprogram is to accept the parameters (if any) from the calling program. The list of parameters can vary from call to call, and therefore we must identify the memory locations corresponding to the parameters. Each parameter is in memory, and thus each has an address by which it may be identified.

In general, the programmer who writes a subprogram knows the number of parameters it receives and the attributes of each (fixed binary full word, packed decimal of length 5, 10-element array of character strings of length 15, etc.). The main program passes parameters to the subprogram by giving the subprogram their addresses.

The standard convention for passing parameters is for the calling program to load into register 1, and for the subprogram to find there, the address of a list which contains the addresses of the parameters. For example, if the main program wishes to use X, T, and S as parameters, it can set up a list of addresses as follows:

$$\text{ADLIST} \quad \text{DC} \quad A(X,T,S)$$

This list is an array of three fullword addresses: the address of X is stored at ADLIST, followed by the address of T at ADLIST+4, and the address of S at ADLIST+8.

The calling program loads the address of this list of addresses into register 1:

LA   1,ADLIST

It is not the *contents* at ADLIST that are loaded into register 1, but the *address* of ADLIST. From that address, the subprogram can find the addresses and thereafter the values of the parameters.

EXAMPLE 10.6

Let's use the following declarations to determine (as precisely as possible) what values would be loaded into register 1 by each of the following instructions.

```
1BC440   X        DC    F'8'
1BC444   Y        DC    F'4'
1BC448   ADLIST   DC    A(X,Y)
```

(a) LA 1,ADLIST   (d) L   1,=A(ADLIST)
(b) L   1,ADLIST   (e) L   1,=A(X,Y)
(c) LA 1,=A(ADLIST)   (f) LA 1,=A(X,Y)

The values loaded are as follows:

(a) 1BC448 (the address of ADLIST)
(b) 1BC440 (the value at ADLIST+0, which is the address of X)
(c) 1BC450 or higher (the address of the literal)
(d) 1BC448 (the correct value obtained in a poor way)
(e) 1BC440 (the address of X)
(f) 1BC450 or higher (the address of the literal)

Suppose that there are two fullword parameters, X and Y. The subprogram may get the values of X and Y into registers 8 and 9 by the following sequence of instructions:

```
LM   2,3,0(1)     LOADS ADDRESS OF X INTO 2, ADDRESS OF Y INTO 3
L    8,0(0,2)
L    9,0(0,3)
```

The LM instruction loads into register 2 the value at the address in register 1 and loads into register 3 the value at the memory location 4 bytes beyond the address in register 1. The values at those memory locations are the addresses of X and Y, respectively. In summary:

Memory Location	Value	Loaded into
ADLIST	Address of X	Register 2
ADLIST+4	Address of Y	Register 3

The instruction L 8,0(0,2) then loads register 8 with the contents of the memory location whose effective address is the contents of register 2 (plus 0 plus 0). Since the address of X is in register 2, the value of X is loaded into register 8. The value of Y is loaded into register 9 in a similar way by the second instruction.

Explicit notation is used for parameters. The actual names cannot be used since the same parameter may refer to different memory locations on different calls to the subprogram, even from the same calling program. Moreover, there is no need to set up another memory location to hold the parameter.

The procedure for passing parameters to subprograms might seem cumbersome at first, but it uses only one register to transfer to the subprogram all the information necessary about the parameters, no matter how many parameters there are or how complicated they might be.

EXAMPLE 10.7

Here is how the values of four fullword parameters R, S, T, and U (passed in this order) can be loaded into registers 6, 7, 8, and 9 in a subprogram.

```
        LM      2,5,0(1)        ADDRESSES IN REGISTERS 2 THROUGH 5
        L       6,0(0,2)        VALUE OF R IN REGISTER 6
        L       7,0(0,3)        VALUE OF S IN REGISTER 7
        L       8,0(0,4)        VALUE OF T IN REGISTER 8
        L       9,0(0,5)        VALUE OF U IN REGISTER 9
```

If the address of a full word or halfword parameter will no longer be needed after its value has been loaded, the value may even be loaded into the register which held the address, replacing the address:

```
        LM      2,3,0(1)        ADDRESS OF X IN 2, ADDRESS OF Y IN 3
        L       3,0(0,3)        VALUE OF FULL WORD Y NOW IN 3
```

Note that since the address of X is in register 2, to refer to X we must use the explicit notation 0(0,2). Thus, if we want to change the value of X, we may not write ST 5,X. Instead, we write ST 5,0(0,2).

If the parameters are character strings, packed decimal numbers, or some other nonbinary format, there is little difference from the case where the parameters are in binary format; the address of the parameter is included in the address list. The called program must use instructions suitable to the attributes of the parameters, but the linkage between the subroutine or function and the calling program is essentially the same.

EXAMPLE 10.8

Here is how the values of four 3-byte packed decimal parameters R, S, T, and U (passed in this order) can be loaded into memory locations SUBR, SUBS, SUBT, and SUBU in a subprogram.

```
        LM      2,5,0(1)        ADDRESSES IN REGISTERS 2 THROUGH 5
        ZAP     SUBR,0(3,2)     VALUE OF R IN SUBR
        ZAP     SUBS,0(3,3)     VALUE OF S IN SUBS
        ZAP     SUBT,0(3,4)     VALUE OF T IN SUBT
        ZAP     SUBU,0(3,5)     VALUE OF U IN SUBU
```

EXAMPLE 10.9

Let's see how we can load the values from an array. Assume that the parameter list consists of the addresses of N (a single element telling how many elements of the array ARR to access) and ARR (an array of 10 full words). Once we load the address of ARR into a register, we can use that register as the base register to access the elements in the array.

```
        LM      2,3,0(1)        ADDRESS OF N IN REGISTER 2, ADDRESS OF ARR IN
                                  REGISTER 3
*       L       2,0(0,2)        VALUE OF N WILL BE LOOP COUNTER
TOP     L       4,0(0,3)        VALUE OF ONE ELEMENT IN REGISTER 4
        ...
        LA      3,4(0,3)        INCREMENT REGISTER 3 FOR NEXT ELEMENT
        BCT     2,TOP
```

We have two warnings on this process: First, if you do not use LM to load addresses from the parameter list, you must be careful to use L rather than LA. LA 2,0(0,1) will copy the address of the LIST from register 1 into register 2. On the other hand, L 2,0(0,1) will correctly load the value of the first element in the parameter list (i.e., the address of the first parameter) into register 2.

As a second warning, note that we cannot get addresses for ARR by incrementing register 1. Incrementing register 1 moves us through the list of addresses of parameters (see Example 10.10).

EXAMPLE 10.10

Suppose we have set up the following variables and parameter list. Note that D is an array of four full words.

```
A       DC      F'10'
C       DC      F'4'
D       DC      F'3,4,5,9'
LIST    DC      A(A,B,C,D)
B       DC      F'2'
```

In SUB, we want to access all the parameters. If we use individual load instructions rather than Load Multiple, we can write:

```
L       2,0(0,1)        ADDRESS OF A IN REGISTER 2
L       3,4(0,1)        ADDRESS OF B IN REGISTER 3
L       4,8(0,1)        ADDRESS OF C IN REGISTER 4
L       5,12(0,1)       ADDRESS OF D IN REGISTER 5
```

Now we want to access the elements of the D array. We cannot write

```
L       6,16(0,1)
```

to access the second element of D. What we would load into register 6 with that instruction is *not* the address of the next element in D, but the value of B. Why? Because B is the next word in memory after LIST. Instead, we must access the elements of D through register 5, which contains the address of D:

```
L       6,0(0,5)        LOADS THE FIRST ELEMENT OF D
L       6,4(0,5)        LOADS THE SECOND ELEMENT OF D
...
```

Note especially that parameters are located in memory. If a subprogram is called within a loop and the control variable is one of the parameters, we have an additional problem. The control variable of a loop is usually held only in a register, but the parameter passed to a subprogram must be in memory. In this case, we must continually update the current value of the control variable in memory and in the register. Let us consider the following high-level language loop:

```
for I := 1 to 10 do
    SUB (X,I)
```

The control variable I will be changed by the looping process, but the parameter passed to the subprogram is the address of I in memory. After each change in value by the looping process, we must store the new value of I in memory. Since in some languages the looping is affected by a change in the value of the control variable within the loop, we must reload the register after each return from the subprogram.

```
        LA      7,1             INDEX
        LR      10,7            INCREMENT OF 1 (NO ARRAY TO WORRY ABOUT)
        LA      11,10           LIMIT
        LA      1,ADLIST
        ...
LOOP    ST      7,I             UPDATE MEMORY WITH CURRENT VALUE OF I
        L       15,ADSUB        RELOAD REGISTER 15 FOR EACH CALL
        BALR    14,15           CALL SUB
        L       7,I             UPDATE REGISTER 7 WITH CURRENT VALUE OF I
        BXLE    7,10,LOOP       INCREMENT VALUE OF I IN REGISTER 7
```

10.6 Saving Register Contents

When a program calls a subprogram, control of execution shifts to the subprogram. When control of execution reverts to the calling program, the programmer expects that the contents of the registers are the same as they were when the subprogram was called (with the exception of register 0 if the subprogram was a function—see Sec. 10.8). In particular, the programmer assumes that the base register is not changed. How can the subprogram guarantee that the register contents will not be disturbed and yet have registers with which to work? The first thing that it does is to save the register contents in a specially declared area in memory, and just before returning control to the calling program, it reloads the registers from those memory locations.

By convention, the calling program establishes an 18-fullword SAVE area and places the address of that area in register 13. Using the STM instruction, the subprogram uses the last 15 full words of this array to store the contents of registers 14, 15, and 0 through 12 (see Fig. 10-2). (Use of one of the other three full words of this array will be discussed in Sec. 10.8.) Just before returning control to the calling program, a subroutine reloads all 15 of these registers, using the LM instruction. The instructions are as follows. In the calling program:

```
        LA      13,SAVE
        ...
SAVE    DS      18F
```

(Some programmers initialize the SAVE area to 0, using

```
        SAVE    DC      18F'0'
```

so that a later dump will show immediately whether the SAVE area has ever been used.) In a subroutine SUBR:

```
SUBR    STM     14,12,12(13)
        ...
        LM      14,12,12(13)
        BR      14
```

Full word	Contents	Relative address
1		SAVE+0
2		SAVE+4
3		SAVE+8
4	Register 14	SAVE+12
5	Register 15	SAVE+16
6	Register 0	SAVE+20
7	Register 1	SAVE+24
8	Register 2	SAVE+28
9	Register 3	SAVE+32
10	Register 4	SAVE+36
11	Register 5	SAVE+40
12	Register 6	SAVE+44
13	Register 7	SAVE+48
14	Register 8	SAVE+52
15	Register 9	SAVE+56
16	Register 10	SAVE+60
17	Register 11	SAVE+64
18	Register 12	SAVE+68

Fig. 10-2 The SAVE area.

In a subprogram, the first instruction stores the contents of registers 14 through 12. It starts storing them at a position 12 bytes past the address in register 13.

Here is an analysis of the STM instruction:

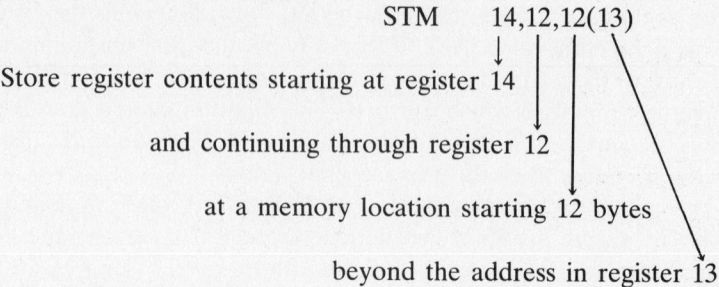

From Fig. 10-2, it is apparent that the register 14 contents will be stored in the fourth full word of the SAVE area, SAVE+12. The contents of each of the subsequent registers are in subsequent memory locations. At the end of the subroutine, the registers are reloaded from the same memory locations, using the instruction LM 14,12,12(13). (See Sec. 10.8 for the method used in a function.)

If a calling program calls several subprograms, it can use the same SAVE area for each call, since it cannot issue another call until control has returned to it from the previous call. It is a good practice to leave the address of the SAVE area in register 13, and use the instruction

```
        LA    13,SAVE
```

only once, early in the program.

You will note that thus far we have not mentioned saving the contents of register 13. There is no use burying the treasure map with the treasure. We need the value in register 13 to find the SAVE area. In Sec. 10.9, we will discuss saving the contents of register 13 when necessary.

10.7 Establishing Addressability

Each external subprogram must establish addressability by setting up a base register to hold the base address for the subprogram. Each internal subprogram should also do so. This task is done by

```
        BALR  12,0
        USING *,12
```

exactly as in the main program. (A different register may be used.) These two instructions follow the Store Multiple instruction, so that the contents of the previous base register are saved before the contents are replaced. Here is an example showing the first three lines of the typical subprogram:

```
NAME    STM   14,12,12(13)
        BALR  12,0
        USING *,12
```

These instructions are necessary to permit calculation of local addresses within the subprogram. They need not be used in subprograms in which there are no symbolic variables and no named instructions (other than the program name), such as LOOP, to which to branch. They are less obviously necessary in internal subprograms, but they still should be used.

EXAMPLE 10.11

Here is a complete example, showing a main program and subprogram, with addressing in both.

```
MAIN        START   0
            BALR    12,0
            USING   *,12
            ST      14,RETADD
            LA      13,SAVE
            LA      1,LIST
            L       15,ADSUB
            BALR    14,15
            ...
            L       14,RETADD
            BR      14
A           DS      F
            ...
LIST        DC      A(A,B,C,D)
SAVE        DC      18F'0'
ADSUB       DC      A(MIDDLE)
RETADD      DS      F
*
*    TO RETURN THE MIDDLE VALUE (NOT HIGHEST, NOT LOWEST)
*       OF THE FIRST THREE PARAMETERS (A, B, C) AS THE FOURTH (D)
MIDDLE      STM     14,12,12(13)
            BALR    12,0
            USING   *,12
            LM      2,5,0(1)
            L       6,0(0,2)        A IN 6
            L       7,0(0,3)        B IN 7
            CR      6,7
            BH      AHIGH
            ST      7,HI            B IS HIGHER
            ST      6,LO            A IS LOWER
            B       CONTINUE
AHIGH       ST      6,HI            A IS HIGHER
            ST      7,LO            B IS LOWER
*       FIRST TWO PARAMETERS NOW IN HI AND LO
CONTINUE    L       6,0(0,4)
            C       6,HI            C HIGHEST?
            BNH     CHECKLOW        NO
            L       6,HI            YES
            B       RETURN
CHECKLOW    C       6,LO            C LOWEST?
            BNL     RETURN          NO
            L       6,LO            YES
RETURN      ST      6,0(0,5)        STORE D
            LM      14,12,12(13)
            BR      14
HI          DS      F
LO          DS      F
            END
```

10.8 Returning a Value from a Function

Now, suppose the programmer wants the subprogram to be a function. A function has the role of returning one value to the calling program. If the value returned is a fixed binary number, the standard convention requires that it be returned in register 0. Therefore, the subprogram must place the value in register 0, and the calling program must look for it there. However, restoring the original contents of the registers using LM 14,12,12(13) would cause the contents placed in register 0 by the subprogram to be lost. Therefore, we must use a different method. When a function restores the original contents of the registers, it does so in two parts:

```
FUNC      STM    14,12,12(13)
          ...
*   LOAD THE VALUE TO BE RETURNED
*      INTO REGISTER 0
          ...
          LM     14,15,12(13)
          LM     1,12,24(13)
          BR     14
```

Register 14 and 15 are loaded from the two full words starting 12 bytes beyond SAVE, and registers 1 through 12 are reloaded from the 12 full words starting at SAVE+24 (see Fig. 10-2). By restoring registers 14 and 15, and then 1 through 12, it leaves in register 0 the value to be returned. The calling program can then retrieve that value. (Of course, before the call, the calling program should not put anything which is needed into register 0, or that value will be lost.)

In cases in which the value to be returned to the calling program is not in binary format (full word or halfword), the value itself cannot be returned in a register. In these cases, the value returned in register 0 is the address of the value to be returned. The calling program must then extract the value, knowing that the address is in register 0. This will take an extra step since register 0 cannot be used as an index register or a base register. The calling program must therefore load the address from register 0 to another register to be able to access the value stored at the address.

EXAMPLE 10.12

Suppose that a function has returned in register 0 the address of a 20-byte character string which the calling program wants to move to LINE for printing. The instruction

```
          MVC    LINE+10(20),0(0)    ILLEGAL
```

will not work. Instead we may use the following:

```
          LR     5,0                 COPY THE ADDRESS INTO AN ACCESSIBLE
*                                       REGISTER
          MVC    LINE+10(20),0(5)    USE THAT REGISTER AS THE BASE REGISTER
```

EXAMPLE 10.13

Write the portion of a main program which calls a function MAX to determine the value of the largest number in a 10-element array of packed decimal numbers of length 3 bytes each, and stores that value in MAXIMUM.

```
          LA     1,ADLIST
          LA     13,SAVE
          L      15,ADMAX
          BALR   14,15
          LR     4,0                 LOAD ADDRESS OF MAX VALUE INTO REGISTER 4
          ZAP    MAXIMUM(3),0(3,4)   EITHER MVC OR ZAP CAN BE USED
          ...
```

```
ADLIST    DC    A(ARRAY,N)
ARRAY     DS    10PL3
MAXIMUM   DS    PL3
SAVE      DS    18F
ADMAX     DC    A(MAX)
N         DC    F'10'
```

EXAMPLE 10.14

Write the function MAX for the preceding example.

```
MAX       STM   14,12,12(13)
          BALR  12,0
          USING *,12
          LM    2,3,0(1)        ADDRESSES OF ARR AND N IN 2 AND
*                                3, RESPECTIVELY
          ZAP   BIG(3),0(3,2)   FIRST ELEMENT IN LOCAL VARIABLE BIG
          L     4,0(0,3)        N IN 4
LOOP      CP    BIG,0(3,2)
          BNL   ENDLOOP
          ZAP   BIG,0(3,2)      REPLACE BIG WITH CURRENT ELEMENT
ENDLOOP   LA    2,3(0,2)        INCREMENT REGISTER 2
          BCT   4,LOOP
          LA    0,BIG           PLACE ADDRESS OF ANSWER INTO REGISTER 0
          LM    14,15,12(13)
          LM    1,12,24(13)
          BR    14
BIG       DS    PL3
```

10.9 Subprograms Which Call Other Subprograms

When a subprogram (SUB1) calls another subprogram (SUB2), it must establish its own SAVE area in which SUB1 will store the register contents of the calling subprogram (SUB1). The address of this SAVE area must be put into register 13. (SUB2 might be called by many programs; it expects to find the address of the proper SAVE area in register 13 for each call.) But if the calling subprogram puts the address of its own SAVE area in register 13, what happens to the address already there—the address of the SAVE area of the program which called it? The calling subprogram must store that address before it loads the address of its own SAVE area. It will reload the original register 13 contents just before reloading all the other registers to return to its own calling program. The conventional place to store the SAVE area address originally sent to a subprogram is in the second full word of the subroutine's own SAVE area. Thus the sequence of instructions is as follows:

```
          STM   14,12,12(13)
          BALR  12,0
          USINC *,12
          ST    13,SAVESUB+4
          LA    13,SAVESUB
          ...
* CALLS TO OTHER SUBPROGRAMS
          ...
          L     13,SAVESUB+4    RELOADS ORIGINAL SAVE AREA ADDRESS
          LM    14,12,12(13)    USES ORIGINAL SAVE AREA ADDRESS
          BR    14              RETURNS FROM "MIDDLE" SUBPROGRAM
SAVESUB   DC    18F'0'
```

If a subprogram does not call other subprograms, it does not need a SAVE area of its own, and it does not have to store (and reload) the address of the SAVE area of the calling program in register 13, since it will not need to use that register. However, it is good practice to store this information anyway for two reasons:

1. The subprogram might use a system macro which calls a system subprogram and thus would have its registers changed.
2. Later revisions of the program might require the storage of register 13 anyway.

Since the operating system uses the same conventions in calling our main program that we use in calling subprograms, we may use the standard STM instruction for registers 14 through 12 and ST for 13 in our main program, just as we do in our subprograms. There are macros to do the storing and reloading of the registers, and many programmers use the same macros in the main program as in the subprograms. (See Chap. 14 for these macros.)

An additional complication involving parameters may arise when a subprogram calls another subprogram. If one of the parameters to be passed by this subprogram is one of the parameters which was passed to it, the address of that parameter is not known when the program is assembled. In general, this address is not even the same each time the subprogram is called. In this case, the address of this parameter must be placed in the address list during execution of the subprogram.

EXAMPLE 10.15

Consider the following high-level language program segment:

```
PROCEDURE SUB (VAR X,Y,Z: INTEGER);
  ...
     SUBSUB (Y,X)
  ...
```

The first and second parameters of three parameters passed to SUB are to be the second and first parameters sent by SUB to SUBSUB. The address list is handled as follows:

```
           LM    2,4,0(1)      ADDRESS OF FIRST PARAMETER IS IN REGISTER 2
*                              ADDRESS OF SECOND PARAMETER IS IN REGISTER 3
           ST    3,ADLIST      PUTS SECOND PARAMETER ADDRESS AT ADLIST
           ST    2,ADLIST+4    PUTS FIRST PARAMETER ADDRESS AT ADLIST+4
           LA    1,ADLIST
           ...
ADLIST     DS    2A
```

The same memory location ADLIST may be used for multiple calls to this or other subprograms. The contents of the array are merely updated for each new call.

A subprogram may also send local variables to another subprogram, along with parameters.

EXAMPLE 10.16

Suppose SUB calls SUB2, sending it LOC, a local variable, and PAR, a variable sent to it as the second parameter from its calling program. Then SUB can include PAR in its ADLIST as follows:

```
           LM    2,3,0(1)
           ST    3,ADLIST+4
           ...
ADLIST     DC    A(LOC)
           DS    A
LOC        DS    F
```

Solved Problems

10.1 What is the effect of BR 14 in a main program?

The instruction branches to the address in register 14. If the programmer has not loaded anything into register 14, it contains an address placed there by the operating system (OS). This causes a branch back to the OS, terminating the program. In effect, the main program is a subprogram of the operating system.

10.2 (a) In the main program, the register 14 contents may be stored with an instruction such as ST 14,SAVE14. Why is that instruction not used in subprograms?

(b) Explain why the instruction STM 14,12,12(13) can be used at the beginning of a main program in place of the ST 14 instruction.

(a) In subprograms, the register 14 contents (as well as the contents of 14 other registers) are stored with the Store Multiple instruction.

(b) The main program is a subprogram of the operating system, which uses the standard linkage conventions.

10.3 What is the difference between

$$\text{BAL} \quad 12,*+4 \quad \text{and} \quad \text{BALR} \quad 12,0$$

BAL 12,*+4 would load the address of the next machine instruction into register 12, then branch to the next instruction (since BAL is a 4-byte instruction). Branching to the next instruction has the same effect as not branching. BALR 12,0 also loads the address of the next instruction into register 12, but does not branch. The big difference between these two instructions is that the second operand of BAL 12,*+4 requires that a base address already be established, while BALR 12,0 can be used to establish a base register.

10.4 Assume that registers 0 through 14 hold the values 0, −1, −2, ..., −14, respectively, and register 15 holds the base address. State what values are stored, and the memory locations where they are stored, by each of the following instructions.

(a) STM   2,4,THERE   (c) STM   4,7,THERE+4
(b) STM   14,2,THERE   (d) STM   15,0,THERE+12

(a) THERE holds −2, THERE+4 holds −3, THERE+8 holds −4.
(b) THERE holds −14, THERE+4 holds the base address, THERE+8 holds 0, THERE+12 holds −1, THERE+16 holds −2.
(c) THERE+4 holds −4, THERE+8 holds −5, THERE+12 holds −6, THERE+16 holds −7.
(d) THERE+12 holds the base address, THERE+16 holds 0.

10.5 Assume that LOCATION is an array of 18 fullword numbers, holding the values 0, 100, 200, ..., 1700, and that register 13 holds the base address. What registers are loaded and what values are placed in these registers as a result of the following instructions?

(a) LM   2,3,LOCATION   (c) LM   14,12,LOCATION+12
(b) LM   14,1,LOCATION   (d) LM   1,12,LOCATION+24

(a) Register 2 holds 0, register 3 holds 100.
(b) Register 14 holds 0, register 15 holds 100, register 0 holds 200, register 1 holds 300.
(c) Register 14 holds 300, register 15 holds 400, register 0 holds 500, ..., register 12 holds 1700.
(d) Register 1 holds 600, register 2 holds 700, ..., register 12 holds 1700.

10.6 What disadvantages would there be to passing to a subprogram the addresses of all the parameters instead of passing the address of the parameter list?

There might be too many parameters to hold at once in registers.

10.7 Explain why parameters are not declared in a subprogram.

The purpose of declarations (DS and DC) in assembly language programs is to set aside memory locations for variables. However, the memory locations for the parameters have already been established. Moreover, the formal parameters may represent different actual parameters each time the subprogram is called.

10.8 If a program calls a function once and a subroutine twice, how many SAVE areas should it set up? How many times should it load the address of each area?

One SAVE area will do, and its address need be loaded only once.

10.9 A program calls a function once and a subroutine twice. How many times should it load register 15?

Three times, once for each call.

10.10 Write machine language code corresponding to the following assembly language instructions. Assume that the address of the SUB instruction is 1AA000 in each part.

```
(a)  SUB     STM    14,12,12(13)
             BALR   12,0
             USING  *,12
             LM     2,4,0(1)
             L      5,0(0,2)
             A      5,0(0,3)
             ST     5,0(0,4)
(b)  SUB     STM    14,12,12(13)
             BALR   12,0
             USING  *,12
             ST     13,SAVESUB+4
             LA     13,SAVESUB
             L      15,ADFUNC
             LM     2,3,0(1)
             ST     3,ADLIST+4
             ...
     *                              ADDRESS OF ADLIST IS 1AA1AC
     ADLIST  DC     A(T)
             DS     F
     ADFUNC  DC     A(FUNC)
     T       DS     F
     SAVESUB DC     18F'0'
```

(a) 90EC D00C   (b) 90EC D00C
    05C0   05C0
    98241000   50D0C1BA   (The base address is 1AA006.)
    58502000   41D0C1B6
    5A503000   58F0C1AE
    50504000   98231000
                   5030C1AA

10.11 What would be the effect of execution of the following program, in which the second subprogram is called from the main but there is no BALR instruction in that subprogram?

```
MAIN       START  0
           BALR   12,0
           USING  *,12
           ...
*  CALL TO SUB2
           ...
SUB1       STM    14,12,12(13)
           BALR   11,0
           USING  *,11
           ...
SUB2       STM    14,12,12(13)
           LM     2,3,0(1)
           ST     2,ADDLIST
           ...
```

The USING instruction in SUB1 tells the assembler during assembly that it may use register 11 as the base register for subsequent instructions. During execution, there will be garbage in register 11 if SUB2 is called from the MAIN program. If register 11 is used as the base register, there is no telling what will happen, but probably an interruption will occur at every statement which requires a base address.

10.12 Write a function which returns the sum of 2 plus the product of its two fullword parameters. Assume that the resulting value fits into one register.

```
FUNC       STM    14,12,12(13)
           BALR   12,0
           USING  *,12
           LM     2,3,0(1)
           L      5,0(0,2)         FIRST PARAMETER IN 5
           M      4,0(0,3)         PRODUCT IN 5
           A      5,=F'2'          SUM IN 5
           LR     0,5              SUM IN 0, FOR RETURN
           LM     14,15,12(13)     RELOAD REGISTERS 14 AND 15
           LM     1,12,24(13)      RELOAD REGISTERS 1 THROUGH 12
*                                  DO NOT TOUCH REGISTER 0
           BR     14               RETURN
```

10.13 Write a main program which follows the calculations described by the pseudocode in each of the following parts.

   (a) A = 7
        B = 6
        CALL SUB (A,B,C)   (SUB GIVES C A VALUE)
        A = A + 1
        B = B + 2
        C = C + 3
        CALL SUB (C,A,B)
        ...

   (b) A = 7
        B = 6
        C = FUNC (A,B)   (Call FUNC. The value returned by FUNC is stored in C.)
        A = A + 1
        B = B + 2
        C = C + 3
        B = FUNC (C,A)
        ...

(a) It is clear that we need the addresses of two address lists—one containing the addresses of A, B, and C and the other the addresses of C, A, and B. We can define two such address lists, or we can define one address list containing both sequences, as follows:

$$\text{ADLIST} \quad \text{DC} \quad \text{A(C,A,B,C)}$$

Then ADLIST is the address of the list A(C,A,B) and ADLIST+4 is the address of the list A(A,B,C).

```
MAIN      START  0
          BALR   12,0
          USING  *,12
          LA     2,7
          ST     2,A
          LA     2,6
          ST     2,B
          ST     14,SAVE14
          LA     1,ADLIST+4    A(A,B,C)
          LA     13,SAVE
          L      15,ADSUB
          BALR   14,15
          L      2,A
          A      2,=F'1'
          ST     2,A
          L      2,B
          A      2,=F'2'
          ST     2,B
          L      2,C
          A      2,=F'3'
          ST     2,C
          LA     1,ADLIST      A(C,A,B)
          L      15,ADSUB
          BALR   14,15
          ...
A         DS     F
B         DS     F
C         DS     F
SAVE      DC     18F'0'
ADLIST    DC     A(C,A,B,C)
ADSUB     DC     A(SUB)
SAVE14    DS     A
```

(b) The only differences between parts (a) and (b) are the following: (1) Part (b) uses ST 0,C after the first BALR 14,15, and it uses ST 0,B after the second. (2) ADLIST may be shortened to A(C,A,B). (3) Register 15 is loaded with ADFUNC [DC A(FUNC)]. Of course, the comments should also be changed.

10.14 In the second call to SUB in Problem 10.13 (a), is the initial value of B used? Is the statement B = B + 2 then useful? Explain.

SUB presumably does not use the initial value of the third parameter, since C had no meaningful value the first time SUB was called. We can deduce that the third parameter is sent only to have its value set in SUB. (It is said to be an output parameter.) Therefore, the initial value of B on the second call is ignored by SUB. Thus the incrementing statement B = B + 2 serves no purpose; the final value of B is set by SUB without regard to the value set by the statement B = B + 2.

10.15 Write a subroutine which adds 1 to its first parameter, 2 to its second parameter, and 3 to its third parameter. The parameters are all declared full word.

```
SUB     STM     14,12,12(13)
        BALR    12,0
        USING   *,12
        LM      2,4,0(1)
        L       5,0(0,2)        FIRST PARAMETER IN 5
        A       5,=F'1'         SUM IN 5
        ST      5,0(0,2)        STORE
        L       5,0(0,3)        SECOND PARAMETER IN 5
        A       5,=F'2'         SUM IN 5
        ST      5,0(0,3)        STORE
        L       5,0(0,4)        THIRD PARAMETER IN 5
        A       5,=F'3'         SUM IN 5
        ST      5,0(0,4)        STORE
        LM      14,12,12(13)    RELOAD REGISTERS
        BR      14              RETURN
```

10.16 Write a subroutine which adds 4 to every value in the 30-element binary, fullword array which is its only parameter.

```
SUB     CSECT
        STM     14,12,12(13)
        BALR    12,0
        USING   *,12
        L       2,0(0,1)        ADDRESS OF ARRAY IN 2
        LA      4,30            COUNTER
LOOP    L       5,0(0,2)        LOAD ELEMENT
        A       5,=F'4'         ADD 4
        ST      5,0(0,2)        STORE ELEMENT
        LA      2,4(0,2)        INCREMENT BASE REGISTER
        BCT     4,LOOP
        LM      14,12,12(13)    RELOAD REGISTERS
        BR      14              RETURN
```

10.17 Write a subroutine which adds 10 to each element of a 15-member packed decimal array of length PL4.

```
ADD10   STM     14,12,12(13)
        BALR    12,0
        USING   *,12
        L       2,0(0,1)        ADDRESS OF ARRAY IN REGISTER 2
        LA      4,15            LOOP COUNTER
LOOP    AP      0(4,2),=P'10'   CHANGE EACH MEMORY LOCATION IN TURN
        LA      2,4(0,2)        INCREMENT REGISTER 2
        BCT     4,LOOP
        LM      14,12,12(13)
        BR      14
```

10.18 Write a function PROD which returns the product of the 10 elements of a packed decimal array declared PL3.

```
        PROD    CSECT
                STM     14,12,12(13)
                BALR    12,0
                USING   *,12
                L       2,0(0,1)         ADDRESS OF ARRAY IN REGISTER 2
                ZAP     PRODUCT,=P'1'    INITIALIZE PRODUCT
                LA      4,10             LOOP COUNTER
        LOOP    MP      PRODUCT,0(3,2)
                LA      2,3(0,2)         INCREMENT REGISTER 2
                BCT     4,LOOP
                LA      0,PRODUCT        PLACE ADDRESS OF ANSWER IN
        *                                    REGISTER 0
                LM      14,15,12(13)
                LM      1,12,24(13)
                BR      14
        PRODUCT DS      PL15
```

10.19 Write a function which returns the highest value in the 30-element binary, fullword array which is its only parameter.

```
        FUNC    STM     14,12,12(13)
                BALR    12,0
                USING   *,12
                L       2,0(0,1)         ADDRESS OF ARRAY IN 2
                LA      10,29            COUNTER
                L       0,0(0,2)         LOAD FIRST ELEMENT IN 0, HIGHEST SO FAR
        LOOP    C       0,4(0,2)         COMPARE ELEMENT
                BNL     ENDLOOP
                L       0,4(0,2)         LOAD HIGHER ELEMENT IN 0, HIGHEST SO FAR
        ENDLOOP LA      2,4(0,2)         INCREMENT ADDRESS IN 2: NEXT ELEMENT
                BCT     10,LOOP
                LM      14,15,12(13)     RELOAD REGISTERS 14 AND 15
                LM      1,12,24(13)      RELOAD REGISTERS 1 THROUGH 12
        *                                DO NOT TOUCH REGISTER 0
                BR      14               RETURN
```

10.20 Write the portion of a main program which will call a function BESTDEPT to return the address of the name of the department with the highest sales in a department store. The department names are stored in an array NAME, and their total sales are stored in a parallel array SALES. NAME is declared CL15, and SALES is declared PL5. The number of departments is stored in a full word N. Also write the function BESTDEPT.

```
                LA      1,ADLIST
                LA      13,SAVE
                L       15,ADBEST
                BALR    14,15
                LR      3,0              LOAD ADDRESS OF BEST DEPT INTO REG 3
                MVC     BEST(15),0(3)    REG 3 CAN BE USED AS A BASE REGISTER
                ...
        ADLIST  DC      A(SALES,NAME,N)
        SALES   DS      10PL5
        NAME    DS      10CL15
        BEST    DS      CL15
        SAVE    DC      18F'0'
        ADBEST  DC      V(BESTDEPT)
        N       DC      F'10'
```

```
        BESTDEPT  CSECT
                  STM     14,12,12(13)
                  BALR    12,0
                  USING   *,12
                  LM      2,4,0(1)        ADDRESSES OF SALES, NAME AND
*                                           N IN 2,3,4, RESPECTIVELY
                  ZAP     BIG,0(5,2)      FIRST ELEMENT IN LOCAL VARIABLE BIG
                  LR      0,3             ADDRESS OF FIRST ELEMENT
                  L       4,0(0,4)        N IN 4
        LOOP      CP      BIG,0(5,2)
                  BNL     ENDLOOP
                  ZAP     BIG,0(5,2)      REPLACE BIG WITH CURRENT ELEMENT
                  LR      0,3             REPLACE WITH ADDRESS OF BIGGER ELEMENT
        ENDLOOP   LA      2,5(0,2)        INCREMENT REGISTER 2
                  LA      3,15(0,3)       INCREMENT REGISTER 3
                  BCT     4,LOOP
                  LM      14,15,12(13)
                  LM      1,12,24(13)
                  BR      14
        BIG       DS      PL5
```

10.21 (*a*) You have, in a main program, a list of identification numbers and names in the following format:

```
        LIST      DC      F'7890'
                  DC      CL20'PETER COOPER'
                  DC      F'5678'
                  DC      CL20'JACK BENNY'
                  ...
```

There are a total of 10 sets of identification numbers and names on the list. Write a function to find the identification number '2345' in this list and return the address of the name associated with that number. Send the list and the identification number '2345' as arguments to the function. Assume that the identification number appears once and only once.

(*b*) How would this function change if each name preceded the identification number in the array LIST, as follows?

```
        LIST      DC      CL20'PETER COOPER'
                  DC      F'7890'
                  DC      CL20'JACK BENNY'
                  DC      F'5678'
                  ...
```

(*c*) Write all the statements in the main program that are necessary to call the function you wrote in part (*a*). Follow all conventions, and show the declarations. (You need not recopy the entire LIST.)

```
        (a)  FIND     STM     14,12,12(13)
                      BALR    12,0
                      USING   *,12
                      LM      2,3,0(1)
                      L       4,0(0,3)        ID IN 4
                      LA      5,10            COUNTER
```

```
          LOOP     C       4,0(0,2)         COMPARE CURRENT ELEMENT
                   BE      OUT
                   LA      2,24(0,2)        INCREMENT
                   BCT     5,LOOP
          OUT      LA      0,4(0,2)         LOAD ADDRESS OF NAME
                   LM      14,15,12(13)
                   LM      1,12,24(13)
                   BR      14
```

(b) The main changes are in the statements labeled LOOP and OUT:

```
          LOOP     C       4,20(0,2)
                   ...
          OUT      LR      0,2
```

In addition, the declaration for LIST must be aligned on a fullword boundary to guarantee that each identification number is 20 bytes beyond the start of each record:

```
          LIST     DS      0F
                   DS      CL20'PETER COOPER'
```

(c)
```
                   LA      1,ADDLIST
                   LA      13,SAVEMAIN
                   L       15,ADFUNC
                   BALR    14,15
                   ST      0,ADNAME
                   ...
          ADDLIST  DC      A(LIST,IDNUM)
          ADFUNC   DC      A(FIND)
          SAVEMAIN DC      18F'0'
          IDNUM    DC      F'2345'
          ADNAME   DS      A
                   ...
```

10.22 (a) Write a function, as in Problem 10.21(a), to search the same array, LIST, for a person with the name 'MARK WILSON' (sent as the second parameter). Return the address of the record with that name. If the name does not appear, return zero.

(b) As in part (a), search for the name 'MARK WILSON' but return the identification number associated with that name.

```
(a)  FINDNAME STM     14,12,12(13)
              BALR    12,0
              USING   *,12
              LM      2,3,0(1)         A(ARRAY) IN 2; A(NAME) IN 3
              LA      4,10             COUNTER
     LOOP     CLC     0(20,3),4(2)     COMPARE CURRENT ELEMENT TO NAME
              BE      OUT
              LA      2,24(0,2)        INCREMENT REGISTER 2
              BCT     4,LOOP
              SR      0,0              IN CASE NAME NOT FOUND
              B       RETURN
     OUT      LR      0,2              LOAD ADDRESS OF RECORD
     RETURN   LM      14,15,12(13)
              LM      1,12,24(13)
              BR      14
```

(b) Change the LR 0,2 instruction to L 0,0(0,2).

CHAP. 10] SUBPROGRAMS

10.23 Write a function that receives a parameter N, plus N additional parameters, say, A, B, C, ..., each a fullword number. The function should return the average of the N additional numbers.

We will load N into register 10. Then we will initialize register 6 to contain LIST plus 4, which is the address where the address of A is stored. Each time through the loop, we will load the address of one of the parameters [A(A), A(B), etc.] into register 7, then add the value of the parameter to the sum which is contained in register 5.

Address	Value
LIST	A(N)
LIST+4	A(A)
LIST+8	A(B)
LIST+12	A(C)
...	

In the calling program:

```
        LA      1,LIST
        ...
LIST    DC      A(N,A,B,C,D,E,F,G)
```

In the subprogram:

```
AVER    STM     14,12,12(13)
        BALR    12,0
        USING   *,12
        L       9,0(0,1)        ADDRESS OF N
        L       10,0(0,9)       VALUE OF N IN 10; LOOP COUNTER
        SR      5,5             SUM=0
        LA      6,4(0,1)        ADDRESS OF THE ADDRESS OF THE FIRST
*                                 NUMBER IN THE PARAMETER ADDRESS LIST
*                                 TO BE ADDED: BASE ADDRESS FOR THE
*                                 REST OF THE ADDRESSES
LOOP    L       7,0(0,6)        ADDRESS OF A VALUE
        A       5,0(0,7)        ADD IN THE VALUE
        LA      6,4(0,6)        INCREMENT THE BASE REGISTER TO THE ADDRESS
*                                 OF THE ADDRESS OF THE NEXT PARAMETER
        BCT     10,LOOP
        M       4,=F'1'
        D       4,0(0,9)        DIVIDE SUM BY N
        LR      0,5             VALUE TO RETURN
        LM      14,15,12(13)
        LM      1,12,24(13)
        BR      14
```

10.24 Write a subroutine to multiply two packed decimal numbers sent as parameters, and put the product in the memory location associated with a third parameter. The first two parameters are declared PL3; the third is PL6.

```
MULTPACK STM    14,12,12(13)
         BALR   12,0
         USING  *,12
         LM     2,4,0(1)
         ZAP    0(6,4),0(3,2)
         MP     0(6,4),0(3,3)
         LM     14,12,12(13)
         BR     14
```

Note that the BALR and USING statements were not required in this subroutine, because no symbolic variables or statement names were used. However, it is good practice to include these instructions in all subroutines for uniformity and possible later revision.

10.25 Write an assembly language subprogram which accepts three fullword parameters X, Y, and Z, and which uses three local variables U, V, and W. It performs the calculations described by the following pseudocode, including two calls to another subprogram:

```
U = X + Y
CALL OTHERSUB (U,V)
CALL OTHERSUB (V,W)
Y = V
Z = U + V + W
RETURN
```

The code follows:

```
SUB       STM    14,12,12(13)
          BALR   12,0
          USING  *,12
          ST     13,SAVESUB+4
          LA     13,SAVESUB
          LM     2,4,0(1)
          L      2,0(0,2)          X IN REGISTER 2
          L      5,0(0,3)          Y IN REGISTER 5
          AR     2,5
          ST     2,U
CALL1     LA     1,ADLIST1
          L      15,ADOTHER
          BALR   14,15
CALL2     LA     1,ADLIST2
          L      15,ADOTHER
          BALR   14,15
RET2      L      7,V
          ST     7,0(0,3)          STORE Y
          A      7,U
          A      7,W
          ST     7,0(0,4)          STORE Z
RETM      L      13,SAVESUB+4
          LM     14,12,12(13)
          BR     14
U         DS     F
V         DS     F
W         DS     F
SAVESUB   DC     18F'0'
ADLIST1   DC     A(U,V)
ADLIST2   DC     A(V,W)
ADOTHER   DC     A(OTHERSUB)
```

10.26 Write an assembly language translation of this PL/1 function, which calls a subroutine. The function has two arguments, X and Y, and a local variable, A, all of which are full words. It returns a fullword integer.

```
FUNC: PROC(X,Y) RETURNS (FIXED BIN(31,0));
      DCL (X,Y,A)    FIXED BIN(31,0);
      CALL SUB(X,Y,A);
      RETURN (A-X);
    END FUNC;
```

The assembly language translation follows:

```
FUNC      STM    14,12,12(13)
          BALR   12,0
          USING  *,12
          ST     13,SAVEF+4
          LA     13,SAVEF
          LM     2,3,0(1)
          STM    2,3,ADLIST
          LA     1,ADLIST
          L      15,ADSUB
          BALR   14,15
          L      0,A              VALUE OF A WAS SET IN SUBROUTINE
          S      0,0(0,2)         A - X
          L      13,SAVEF+4
          LM     14,15,12(13)
          LM     1,12,24(13)
          BR     14
A         DS     F
SAVEF     DC     18F'0'
ADLIST    DS     2A
          DC     A(A)
ADSUB     DC     A(SUB)
```

10.27 Write an assembly language subprogram which accepts three fullword parameters X, Y, and Z, and which uses four local variables T, U, V, and W. It performs the calculations described by the following pseudocode, including four calls to a function FUNC:

U = X + Y
V = X − Y
T = 2 * FUNC (U,V)
W = FUNC (T,U) + FUNC (T,V)
Y = FUNC (T,W) ** 2   ** MEANS EXPONENTIATION
Z = T + W
RETURN

The assembly language translation follows:

```
SUB       STM    14,12,12(13)
          BALR   12,0
          USING  *,12
          ST     13,SAVESUB+4
          LA     13,SAVESUB
          LM     2,4,0(1)
          L      5,0(0,2)         X IN REGISTER 5
          L      6,0(0,3)         Y IN REGISTER 6
          LR     7,5
          AR     7,6
          ST     7,U              U = X + Y
          SR     5,6
          ST     5,V              V = X - Y
USE1      LA     1,ADLIST1
          L      15,ADDFUNC
          BALR   14,15
RET1      AR     0,0              2 * FUNC(U,V)
          ST     0,T
```

```
         USE2       LA    1,ADLIST2
                    L     15,ADDFUNC
                    BALR  14,15
         RET2       LR    2,0            FUNC(T,U) IN 2
         USE3       LA    1,ADLIST3
                    L     15,ADDFUNC
                    BALR  14,15
         RET3       AR    0,2            FUNC(T,U) + FUNC(T,V)
                    ST    0,W
         USE4       LA    1,ADLIST4
                    L     15,ADDFUNC
                    BALR  14,15
         RET4       LR    9,0            FUNC(T,W) IN 9
                    MR    8,9
                    ST    9,0(0,3)       STORE Y
                    L     2,T
                    A     2,W
                    ST    2,0(0,4)       STORE Z
         RETM       L     13,SAVESUB+4
                    LM    14,12,12(13)
                    BR    14
         T          DS    F
         U          DS    F
         V          DS    F
         W          DS    F
         SAVESUB    DC    18F'0'
         ADLIST1    DC    A(U,V)
         ADLIST2    DC    A(T,U)
         ADLIST3    DC    A(T,V)
         ADLIST4    DC    A(T,W)
         ADDFUNC    DC    A(FUNC)
```

10.28 Using standard linkage conventions, write the portion of an assembly language main program that does the following:

    Calls SUB with parameters A, B, and D
    Calls SUB with parameters D, 15, and E
    Calls SUB with parameters 23, E, and F

A through F are fullword binary numbers, with A, B, and C initialized to 83, 91, and 27, respectively. The program does the following:

```
         MAIN       START 0
                    BALR  12,0
                    USING *,12
                    ST    14,ADD14
                    LA    13,SAVEMAIN
         CALL1      LA    1,ADLIST1
                    L     15,ADSUB
                    BALR  14,15
         CALL2      LA    1,ADLIST2
                    LA    2,15
                    ST    2,DUMMY
                    L     15,ADSUB
                    BALR  14,15
```

```
        CALL3     LA    1,ADLIST3
                  LA    2,23
                  ST    2,DUMMY
                  L     15,ADSUB
                  BALR  14,15
                  ...
                  L     14,ADD14
                  BR    14
        A         DC    F'83'
        B         DC    F'91'
        C         DC    F'27'
        D         DS    F
        E         DS    F
        F         DS    F
        SAVEMAIN  DC    18F'0'
        DUMMY     DS    F
        ADLIST1   DC    A(A,B,D)
        ADLIST2   DC    A(D,DUMMY,E)
        ADLIST3   DC    A(DUMMY,E,F)
        ADSUB     DC    A(SUB)
        ADD14     DS    F
```

10.29 Convert the following portion of a main program to assembly language. Use standard linkage conventions. A through E are fullword binary numbers, with A and B initialized to 48 and 172, respectively. The program calls two functions, F and G. The program sets C, D, and E equal to values as follows:

$$C = F(A) + G(B)$$
$$D = F(B) + G(A) + G(C)$$
$$E = F(C) * G(D) + (F(D)) ** 2 \quad (** \text{ means exponentiation})$$

```
        MAIN      START 0
                  BALR  12,0
                  USING *,12
                  ST    14,ADD14
                  LA    13,SAVEMAIN
        USE1      LA    1,ADDPAR        A(A)
                  L     15,ADDF
                  BALR  14,15
        RETURN1   LR    2,0             F(A) IN 2
        USE2      LA    1,ADDPAR+4      A(B)
                  L     15,ADDG
                  BALR  14,15
        RETURN2   AR    2,0             F(A) + G(B) IN 2
                  ST    2,C             C = F(A) + G(B)
        USE3      LA    1,ADDPAR+4      A(B)
                  L     15,ADDF
                  BALR  14,15
        RETURN3   LR    2,0             F(B)
        USE4      LA    1,ADDPAR        A(A)
                  L     15,ADDG
                  BALR  14,15
```

```
         RETURN4    AR     2,0              F(B) + G(A) IN 2
         USE5       LA     1,ADDPAR+8       A(C)
                    L      15,ADDG
                    BALR   14,15
         RETURN5    AR     0,2              F(B) + G(A) + G(C) IN 0
                    ST     0,D              D = F(B) + G(A) + G(C)
         USE6       LA     1,ADDPAR+8       A(C)
                    L      15,ADDF
                    BALR   14,15
         RETURN6    LR     3,0              F(C) IN 3
         USE7       LA     1,ADDPAR+12      A(D)
                    L      15,ADDG
                    BALR   14,15
         RETURN7    MR     2,0              F(C) * G(D) IN 3
         USE8       LA     1,ADDPAR+12      A(D)
                    L      15,ADDF
                    BALR   14,15
         RETURN8    LR     5,0              F(D)
                    MR     4,5              (F(D))**2
                    AR     3,5              F(C) * G(D) + (F(D))**2 IN 3
                    ST     3,E              E = F(C) * G(D) + (F(D))**2
                    ...
                    L      14,ADD14
                    BR     14
         A          DC     F'48'
         B          DC     F'172'
         C          DS     F
         D          DS     F
         E          DS     F
         ADD14      DS     F
         SAVEMAIN   DC     18F'0'
         ADDPAR     DC     A(A,B,C,D)
         ADDF       DC     A(F)
         ADDG       DC     A(G)
```

10.30 Using standard linkage conventions, write the portion of an assembly language main program that does the following:

  Calls SUB with parameters A, B, and D
  Calls SUB with parameters D, B+D and E
  Calls SUB with parameters B, D+E, and F

A through F are fullword binary numbers, with A, B, and C initialized to 38, 195, and −42, respectively. The program does the following:

```
         MAIN       START  0
                    BALR   12,0
                    USING  *,12
                    ST     14,ADD14
                    LA     13,SAVEMAIN
         CALL1      LA     1,ADLIST1
                    L      15,ADSUB
                    BALR   14,15
```

```
        RET1    L     2,B
                A     2,D
                ST    2,DUMMY       DUMMY HOLDS B + D
        CALL2   LA    1,ADLIST2
                L     15,ADSUB
                BALR  14,15
        RET2    L     2,D
                A     2,E
                ST    2,DUMMY
        CALL3   LA    1,ADLIST3
                L     15,ADSUB
                BALR  14,15
                ...
                L     14,ADD14
                BR    14
        A       DC    F'38'
        B       DC    F'195'
        C       DC    F'-42'
        D       DS    F
        E       DS    F
        F       DS    F
        SAVEMAIN DC   18F'0'
        DUMMY   DS    F
        ADLIST1 DC    A(A,B,D)
        ADLIST2 DC    A(D,DUMMY,E)
        ADLIST3 DC    A(B,DUMMY,F)
        ADSUB   DC    A(SUB)
        ADD14   DS    F
```

10.31 Convert the following portion of a main program to assembly language. Use standard linkage conventions. A through E are fullword binary numbers, with A and B initialized to 5 and 98, respectively. The program calls two functions, F and G. The program sets C, D, and E equal to values as follows:

$$C = F(A) + G(A + B)$$
$$D = F(A * B) + G(F(B))$$
$$E = F(A * D - B) * G(F(A * C) + F(D))$$

```
        MAIN    START 0
                BALR  12,0
                USING *,12
                ST    14,ADD14
                LA    13,SAVEMAIN
        USE1    LA    1,ADLIST      A(A)
                L     15,ADDF
                BALR  14,15
        RETURN1 LR    2,0           F(A)
                L     3,A
                A     3,B
                ST    3,DUMMY       A+B IN DUMMY
        USE2    LA    1,ADLIST+4    A(DUMMY)
                L     15,ADDG
                BALR  14,15
```

```
         RETURN2   AR      2,0                F(A) + G(A+B)
                   ST      2,C
                   L       3,A
                   M       2,B
                   ST      3,DUMMY            A*B IN DUMMY
         USE3      LA      1,ADLIST+4         A(DUMMY)
                   L       15,ADDF
                   BALR    14,15
         RETURN3   LR      2,0                F(A*B)
         USE4      LA      1,ADLIST+8         A(B)
                   L       15,ADDF
                   BALR    14,15
         RETURN4   ST      0,DUMMY            F(B) IN DUMMY
         USE5      LA      1,ADLIST+4         A(DUMMY)
                   L       15,ADDG
                   BALR    14,15
         RETURN5   AR      0,2                F(A*B) + G(F(B)) IN 0
                   ST      0,D
                   L       3,A
                   M       2,D
                   S       3,B
                   ST      3,DUMMY            (A*D-B) IN DUMMY
         USE6      LA      1,ADLIST+4         A(DUMMY)
                   L       15,ADDF
                   BALR    14,15
         RETURN6   LR      2,0                F(A*D-B)
                   L       5,A
                   M       4,C
                   ST      5,DUMMY            A*C IN DUMMY
         USE7      LA      1,ADLIST+4         A(DUMMY)
                   L       15,ADDF
                   BALR    14,15
         RETURN7   LR      3,0                F(A*C)
         USE8      LA      1,ADLIST+12        A(D)
                   L       15,ADDF
                   BALR    14,15
         RETURN8   AR      0,3                F(A*C) + F(D) IN 0
                   ST      0,DUMMY            F(A*C) + F(D) IN DUMMY
         USE9      LA      1,ADLIST+4         A(DUMMY)
                   L       15,ADDG
                   BALR    14,15
                   LR      1,0
                   MR      0,2
                   ST      1,E                E = F(A*D-B) * G(F(A*C) + F(D))
                   ...

                   L       14,ADD14
                   BR      14
         A         DC      F'5'
         B         DC      F'98'
         C         DS      F
         D         DS      F
         E         DS      F
```

```
            SAVEMAIN  DC    18F'0'
            ADLIST    DC    A(A,DUMMY,B,D)
            ADDF      DC    A(F)
            ADDG      DC    A(G)
            ADD14     DS    F
            DUMMY     DS    F
```

10.32 Convert the following portions of main programs to assembly language. Use standard linkage conventions.

(a) A is an array of 100 full words, and K and SUM are full words. Assume that FUNC is a function which does not change the value of its parameters and that the array is initialized.

$$SUM := 0;$$
$$\text{for } K := 1 \text{ to } 100 \text{ do}$$
$$SUM := SUM + FUNC(K, A[K])$$

(b) How would the answer to part (a) change if the argument K were not passed to FUNC? That is,

$$SUM := SUM + FUNC(A[K])$$

(a)

```
PARTA     START  0
          BALR   12,0
          USING  *,12
          ST     14,ADD14
          LA     1,ADDPAR
          LA     13,SAVEMAIN
          ...                      INITIALIZE A
          SR     2,2               INITIALIZE SUM
          SR     11,11             INITIALIZE K
          LA     10,A
LOOP      LA     11,1(0,11)        INCREMENT K
          ST     11,K
          ST     10,ADDPAR+4
          L      15,ADDFUNC
          BALR   14,15
RETURN    AR     2,0               SUM IN REGISTER 2
          LA     10,4(0,10)        INCREMENT ADDRESS OF A[K]
          C      11,=F'100'
          BL     LOOP
          ST     2,SUM
          ...
          L      14,ADD14
          BR     14
A         DS     100F
SUM       DS     F
ADDPAR    DC     A(K,A)
ADDFUNC   DC     A(FUNC)
K         DS     F
ADD14     DS     F
SAVEMAIN  DC     18F'0'
```

(b) The only changes from part (a) are the following:

(1)	ADDPAR	DC	A(A)	delete K from address list
(2)		ST	10,ADDPAR	delete '+4'
(3)		ST	11,K	is deleted
(4)	K	DS	F	is deleted

Supplementary Problems

10.33 Assume that LOCATION is an array of 18 fullword numbers, holding $0, 100, 200, \ldots, 1700$. What registers are loaded and what values are placed in them as a result of the following instructions?

(a)   LA   13,LOCATION
       LM   2,3,0(13)

(b)   LA   13,LOCATION
       LM   14,12,0(13)

(c)   LA   13,LOCATION
       LM   14,12,12(13)

(d)   LA   13,LOCATION
       LM   1,12,24(13)

10.34 The contents of which register are conventionally stored at the memory location SAVE+20?

10.35 The third word in the SAVE area is sometimes used to store the address of the prior program's SAVE area, in order to aid debugging. How could that help?

10.36 Assume that the initial values in registers 2 through 11 are 2 through 11, respectively, when the program calls a subprogram. What are the values after return from execution of the subprogram?

10.37 Would the following instruction work to establish a base address?

                 LA   12,*+4

10.38 What instruction having to do with program linkage is missing from the following subprogram?

```
SUBPRO    STM     14,12,12(13)
          BALR    12,0
          USING   *,12
          LM      2,3,0(1)
          LA      13,SAVESUB
          LA      1,ADLIST
          ...     ...              INSTRUCTIONS NOT DEALING WITH LINKAGE
          L       15,ADDSUB2
          BALR    14,15
          AR      0,7
          ST      0,0(0,2)
          L       13,SAVESUB+4
          LM      14,12,12(13)
          BR      14
```

10.39 Is the subprogram of Problem 10.38 a function or a subroutine? What is the called subprogram? How can you tell?

10.40 Which one(s) of registers 1, 13, and 15 is (are) conventionally loaded in the calling program with the load instruction, and which one(s) is (are) loaded with the Load Address instruction?

CHAP. 10] SUBPROGRAMS

10.41 A program calls a function once and a subroutine twice. How many times should it expect to find a value in register 0?

10.42 A program calls a function once and a subroutine twice. Can you tell how many different address lists for parameters it should set up? What different possibilities exist?

10.43 Write object code for the following subprogram. Are the BALR and USING instructions required? Explain.

```
*  SUBPROGRAM           REPLACES THE VALUE OF THE FIRST
*                       PARAMETER WITH THE SUM OF THE OTHER
*                       TWO PARAMETERS
SUB    STM    14,12,12(13)
       BALR   12,0
       USING  *,12
       LM     2,4,0(1)
       L      5,0(0,3)
       A      5,0(0,4)
       ST     5,0(0,2)
       LM     14,12,12(13)
       BR     14
```

10.44 Write machine language code for each instruction preceded by a line in the leftmost column below.

```
                1BC040   MAIN    START  0
                1BC040           BALR   12,0
                1BC042           USING  *,12
                1BC042           LA     1,ADLIST
_____         1BC046           LA     13,SAVE
_____         1BC04A           L      15,ADFUNC
_____         1BC04E           ST     14,RETADD
_____         1BC052           BALR   14,15
                                 ...
_____         1BC100           BR     14
                1BC104   A       DC     F'135'
                1BC108   B       DC     F'-13'
                1BC10C   ADLIST  DC     A(A,B)
                1BC114   SAVE    DC     18F'0'
                1BC15C   ADFUNC  DC     A(FUNC)
                1BC160   RETADD  DS     F
                                 ...
                1BC188   FUNC    STM    14,12,12(13)
                1BC18C           BALR   11,0
_____         1BC18E           USING  *,11
                1BC18E           LM     2,3,0(1)
                1BC192           L      7,0(0,2)
                1BC196           A      7,0(0,3)
                1BC19A           ST     7,X
_____         1BC19E           MR     6,7
                1BC1A0           A      7,X
_____         1BC1A4           A      7,X          X*X + 2*X
_____         1BC1A8           LR     0,7
                                 ...
                1BC1C0   X       DS     F
```

10.45 (a) What would be the difference in Problem 10.44 if the BALR and USING instructions in FUNC had used register 12 instead of register 11?

(b) How would the answer to part (a) differ if those instructions had been omitted entirely?

10.46 What instruction having to do with subprogram linkage is missing from the following subprogram?

```
SUBPRO   STM    14,12,12(13)
         BALR   12,0
         USING  *,12
         LM     2,3,0(1)
         ST     13,SAVESUB+4
         LA     13,SAVESUB
         LA     1,ADLIST
         ...
         L      15,ADSUB
         BALR   14,15
         AR     0,7
         ST     0,0(0,2)
         ...    ...              INSTRUCTIONS NOT DEALING WITH LINKAGE
         LM     14,15,12(13)
         LM     1,12,24(13)
         BR     14
```

10.47 What extra instruction is present in the following subprogram, which does not call another subprogram?

```
SUBPRO   STM    14,12,12(13)
         BALR   12,0
         USING  *,12
         LM     2,3,0(1)
         ...    ...              INSTRUCTIONS NOT DEALING WITH LINKAGE
         L      13,SAVESUB+4
         LM     14,12,12(13)
         BR     14
SAVESUB  DC     18F'0'
```

10.48 State the function of each instruction in the following portion of a program:

```
         L       15,ADSUB
         LA      13,SAVEMAIN
         LA      1,ADLISTM
         ST      14,RETADD
         BALR    14,15
         ...
         L       14,RETADD
         BR      14
SAVEMAIN DC      18F'0'
RETADD   DS      F
ADSUB    DC      A(SUBPRO)
ADLISTM  DC      A(X,Y)
         ...
*
```

```
        SUBPRO    STM     14,12,12(13)
                  BALR    12,0
                  USING   *,12
                  LM      2,3,0(1)
                  ST      13,SAVESUB+4
                  LA      13,SAVESUB
                  L       15,ADFUNC
                  LA      1,ADLIST
                  STM     2,3,ADLIST
                  ...     ...              NOT DEALING WITH LINKAGE
                  BALR    14,15
                  AR      0,7
                  L       13,SAVESUB+4
                  LM      14,15,12(13)
                  LM      1,12,24(13)
                  BR      14
        SAVESUB   DC      18F'0'
        ADLIST    DS      2A
        ADFUNC    DC      A(FUNC)
```

10.49 Arrange each of the sets of instructions in the proper order in which they would be found in a typical subprogram. (There might be other instructions between them.) If they are already in order, leave them alone.

(a) STM   14,12,12(13)
     LM   14,12,12(13)

(b) ST   13,SAVESUB+4
     L   13,SAVESUB+4

(c) ST   13,SAVESUB+4
     LA   13,SAVESUB

(d) STM   14,12,12(13)
     BALR 12,0

(e) STM   14,12,12(13)
     LM   14,12,12(13)
     ST   13,SAVESUB+4
     L   13,SAVESUB+4
     LA   13,SAVESUB

(f) LM   14,15,12(13)
     SR   0,7
     BR   14
     BALR 14,15
     LM   1,12,24(13)

(g) LM   2,4,0(1)
     L   5,0(0,2)

10.50 Assume X and Y are passed to a subprogram by LIST   DC   A(X,Y). The subprogram passes X as the first parameter and T, a local variable, as second parameter to another subprogram. Show three different ways the address list can be prepared in these circumstances.

10.51 A student uses the statement LA   13,SAVE+4 instead of L   13,SAVE+4 just before reloading the other registers with LM   14,12,12(13). What effects would this error cause?

10.52 Write a function which returns the sum of its three fullword parameters. Assume that the value fits into one register.

10.53 If the LM   14,15,12(13) instruction had been omitted from the program in Problem 10.52, what effect would the omission have had? Explain.

10.54 Write a subroutine SUB which does each of the following.

(a) Accepts three fullword parameters X, Y, and Z, uses local variables A, B, and C, and executes the following pseudocode:

```
A = X - Y
B = X - Z
C = Y - Z
IF (A > B) AND (A > C) THEN X = X + A
IF (B > A) AND (B > C) THEN Y = Y + B
IF (C > A) AND (C > B) THEN Z = Z + C
RETURN
```

    (b) Accepts two parameters X and Y, and subtracts 1 from each parameter which is initially odd.

    (c) Accepts three parameters X, Y, and Z, and adds 5 to the value of the smallest of them.

    (d) Accepts three parameters X, Y, and Z, and executes the following pseudocode:

```
IF X > Y THEN BEGIN
              TEMP = X
              X = Y
              Y = TEMP
              END
IF Y > Z THEN BEGIN
              TEMP = Y
              Y = Z
              Z = TEMP
              END
IF X > Y THEN BEGIN
              TEMP = X
              X = Y
              Y = TEMP
              END
RETURN
```

10.55 Assuming that all variables are fullword binary, write a function FUNC which does the following.

    (a) Accepts three parameters X, Y, and Z, and returns the absolute value of the difference between the two closest. That is, it follows this pseudocode:

```
DIFF = ABS (X - Y)     (ABS means absolute value)
IF DIFF > ABS (X - Z) THEN DIFF = ABS (X - Z)
IF DIFF > ABS (Y - Z) THEN DIFF = ABS (Y - Z)
RETURN (DIFF)
```

    (b) Accepts two parameters and returns the square of the difference between them.

    (c) Accepts two parameters N and X, and returns X to the Nth power. Assume both X and N to be positive integers and that the answer will fit into one register.

10.56 Which main programs in Problems 10.13 and 10.28 through 10.32 could be used with which subprograms in Problems 10.54 and 10.55? Explain.

10.57 Write a function MAX which accepts a variable number of fullword parameters and returns the value of the largest. The minimum number of parameters is two. The last address in the address list is indicated by a 1 in bit 0 (the first bit). Thus if the address of the last parameter is 1BC104, then the last word in the parameter list would be 801BC104.

10.58 A main program has a 21-element array NAME of salesperson's names (25 bytes each) and a second 21-element array SALES of total sales (full word). Each element of SALES is the amount sold by the person in the corresponding element of NAME. Write a main program to place the name of the salesperson who sold the most units in TOPSELLR, and the number of units that salesperson sold in BIG. Use a function MOST to determine which sales figure was greatest and to return the index in the SALES array of that sales figure. This will be $4N - 4$, where N is the subscript of the element corresponding to that sales figure in the array, and each sales figure is 4 bytes long.

10.59 Write an assembly language subprogram which accepts three fullword parameters X, Y, and Z, and which performs three calls to another subprogram:

CALL OTHERSUB (X,Y)
CALL OTHERSUB (Y,Z)
CALL OTHERSUB (X,Z)
RETURN

10.60 Write an assembly language function FUNC which accepts three fullword parameters X, Y, and Z, and which uses three local variables U, V, and W. It performs the calculations described by the following pseudocode, including three calls to another subprogram:

U = X + Y
CALL OTHERSUB (X,Y,V)
CALL OTHERSUB (V,U,W)
U = Z − V ∗ W
CALL OTHERSUB (U,X,Z)
RETURN (V − U ∗ Z)

10.61 How could you prepare an address list, ADLIST, for Problem 10.57, in which the fourth parameter is to be the final parameter?

10.62 Write a subroutine to print a list of names, each 30 bytes long. Arguments to the subroutine are the array of names and the number of elements in the array which are to be printed.

10.63 Consider the following portion of a program, which has been assembled as a unit:

```
WRONG1   CSECT
         BALR  12,0
         USING *,12
         ...
FIRST    L     3,=F'1'
         ...
X        DC    F'7'
WRONG2   CSECT
         BALR  12,0
         USING *,12
         ...
SECOND   L     9,=F'1'
         LA    10,X
         ...
         END
```

(a) Where will the literal pool be placed for this portion of a program if no LTORG pseudo-instruction has been used?
(b) What effect will the placement of the literal pool have on this portion of a program?
(c) Would the problem be corrected if LTORG were used in WRONG1 but not in WRONG2?
(d) How many literals (=F'1') will be defined by the method mentioned in part (c)?
(e) Why won't the LA 10,X statement in WRONG2 execute properly?

Chapter 11

Bit and Byte Manipulation

11.1 Introduction

The instructions presented in this chapter deal with manipulation of individual bits and bytes. The shift operations (Sec. 11.2) move the set of bits in a register or an even-odd register pair a specified number of bit positions to the left or right. The logical operations presented in Sec. 11.3 also work on bits, yielding an answer which depends only on the corresponding bits in each of the two operands. Test under Mask (Sec. 11.4) allows testing of certain bits of information within a specified byte. The remaining operations discussed in the chapter deal with bytes of information rather than bits. Insert Character and Store Character (Sec. 11.5) copy single bytes from register to memory or vice versa. Insert Character under Mask, Store Character under Mask, and Compare Logical Character under Mask (Sec. 11.6) move or compare from 1 to 4 bytes of information.

11.2 Shift Operations

The shift operations move bits within registers. There are different instructions depending on whether we want to

1. Shift right or left
2. Shift single or double—that is, use one register or an even-odd pair
3. Shift arithmetic (with special treatment for the sign bit) or logical

Two options in each of three choices leads to $2^3 = 8$ different shift instructions:

SLL	Shift Left Logical
SRL	Shift Right Logical
SLDL	Shift Left Double Logical
SRDL	Shift Right Double Logical
SLA	Shift Left Arithmetic
SRA	Shift Right Arithmetic
SLDA	Shift Left Double Arithmetic
SRDA	Shift Right Double Arithmetic

The first letter in each instruction, S, signifies shift. The second letter indicates the direction of the shift, left or right. The last letter signifies logical or arithmetic (pronounced ar·ith·*met*·ic). If the shift is a double register shift, a D appears before the last letter; if no D is present, a single shift is indicated. The shift instructions take two operands. The first operand is the register to shift. (In a double shift, it is the even register of an even-odd pair.) The second operand is the number of bits to shift (0 through 63).

Logical Shifts

Let us examine the logical operations first. In general, logical operations treat the number as a string of bits rather than as a signed number. The instruction

SLL   2,1

CHAP. 11] BIT AND BYTE MANIPULATION 269

states that each bit in register 2 is to be shifted one place to the left. The leftmost bit is lost, and a zero is inserted at the right.

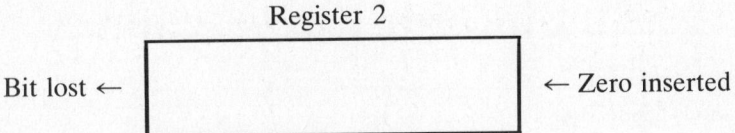

If the original contents of register 2 were

1010 1111 0000 1111 0000 1111 0000 1010

then the new contents after execution of this instruction would be

0101 1110 0001 1110 0001 1110 0001 0100

If the instruction were to require a shift of 2 bits on the original contents of register 2 (SLL 2,2), 2 bits would be lost at the left and 2 zeros would be inserted at the right. The result would be

1011 1100 0011 1100 0011 1100 0010 1000

EXAMPLE 11.1

Let's determine the contents of register 2 in hexadecimal after execution of each of the following instructions. The initial hexadecimal contents of register 2 are AB106F74.

(a) SLL   2,4
(b) SLL   2,1

(a) B106F740   Four bits (one hexadecimal digit) are lost from the left, and 4 bits of zero are inserted at the right. This is clear, since we have shifted a half byte, or one entire hexadecimal digit.

(b) 5620DEE8   Since this operation affects less than a half byte, we must look at each bit separately to understand what is happening:

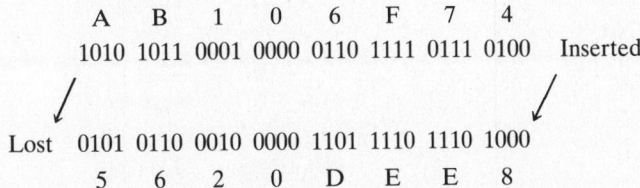

The shift instructions operate on bits, not hexadecimal digits. In part (a), the shift happened to be a shift of 4 bits, equivalent to one hexadecimal digit, and the answer was easy. In part (b), we have to expand the hexadecimal notation to bits in order to understand a shift of only one bit position. Later we reconvert the answer to hexadecimal as required by the question.

A logical shift to the right merely shifts the bits in the other direction. Bits are lost at the right and zeros are inserted at the left. Acting on the value

0101 1110 0001 1110 0001 1110 0001 0100

the instruction SRL   2,1 would yield

0010 1111 0000 1111 0000 1111 0000 1010

A right shift of 2 bits acting on the original contents of register 2 (SRL   2,2) would produce

0001 0111 1000 0111 1000 0111 1000 0101

EXAMPLE 11.2

Now let's look at the shifts in Example 11.1, this time shifting to the right instead of to the left. We assume that the initial contents of register 2 are

$$AB106F74$$

(a) SRL 2,4   yields 0AB106F7

(b) SRL 2,1   yields 558837BA

Double Shifts

Double register shifts involve the 64 bits of an even-odd pair of registers. The first operand is specified by the number of the even register. The two registers are treated as a contiguous string of 64 bits. Bits which are shifted from the left end of the odd register are shifted into the right end of the even register, or vice versa. The outer ends of the even-odd pair are affected just like the ends of one register in a single register shift. The top half of Fig. 11-1 illustrates a right double shift, and the bottom half illustrates a left double shift.

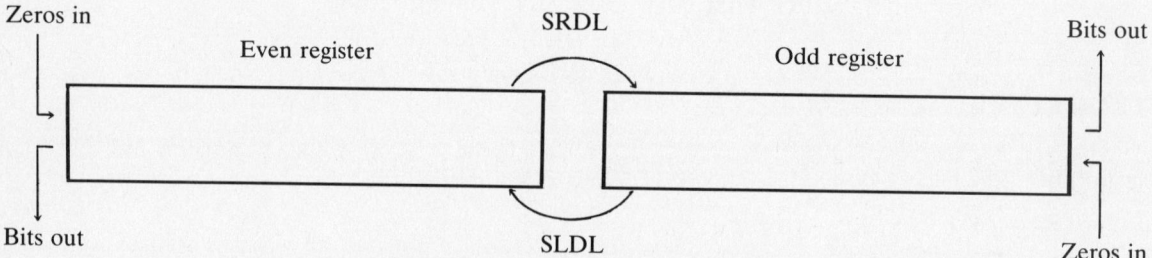

Fig. 11-1 Logical double register shifts.

EXAMPLE 11.3

Let's see the effect on the contents of registers 2 and 3 of execution of the instruction

$$\text{SRDL} \quad 2,4$$

Suppose that the original contents of register 2 in hexadecimal are the following:

	Register 2	Register 3
	ABC1D2E7	65F0139C
The result is	0ABC1D2E	765F0139

The C has been lost from the right (corresponding to the loss of 4 bits), and a hexadecimal zero (4 bits of zero) has been inserted at the left, just as in a single register shift. In this double register shift, the 7 (0111) has been shifted from register 2 to register 3. In effect, the even-odd pair has been treated as a single unit for the purpose of this instruction.

SLDL works the same way, but in the opposite direction. SLDL 2,4 acting on the original contents of registers 2 and 3, which are

	Register 2	Register3
	ABC1D2E7	65F0139C
produces	BC1D2E76	5F0139C0

Bit shifts are frequently done within the even-odd register pair.

EXAMPLE 11.4

Suppose that we wish to count the number of 1 bits in a 4-byte string. We can load the string into the odd register and count the bits by shifting them, one at a time, into the even register.

```
                LA      6,32            LOOP COUNTER
                L       3,TEST          STRING TO TEST
                SR      7,7             COUNTER OF 1 BITS
TOP             SR      2,2             CLEAR EVEN REGISTER
                SLDL    2,1             SHIFT A BIT INTO REGISTER 2
                AR      7,2             ADD BIT TO COUNTER
*                                       (ONLY 1 BITS WILL CAUSE A CHANGE)
                BCT     6,TOP
```

The bit string to be shifted in a two-register shift can be placed in either the even register or the odd register, depending on how one plans to use it.

EXAMPLE 11.5

Find the sum of all the odd values in an array ARR of 10 full words.

```
                SR      7,7             INDEX
                LA      10,10           COUNTER
                SR      4,4             SUM
LOOP            L       2,ARR(7)
                SRDL    2,1             SHIFT RIGHTMOST BIT TO REGISTER 3
                LTR     3,3             NEGATIVE MEANS ODD VALUE
                BNM     ENDLOOP
                A       4,ARR(7)        ADD ODD VALUE TO SUM
ENDLOOP         LA      7,4(0,7)        INCREMENT INDEX REGISTER
                BCT     10,LOOP
                ST      4,SUM
```

Arithmetic Shifts

Arithmetic shifts differ from logical shifts in that they preserve the sign bit. Essentially, only the rightmost 31 bits are involved in a single register shift or 63 bits in a double register shift. In an arithmetic shift to the left, as in a logical shift to the left, zeros are inserted at the right. But bits are lost from the position next to the sign bit, and the sign bit is unchanged. The instruction

$$SLA \quad 2,2$$

does the following:

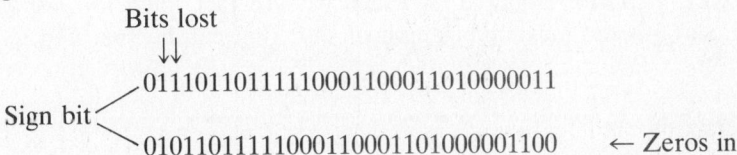

Arithmetic shifts set the condition code. If any bit different from the sign bit is shifted out by a left shift, the condition code is set to 3 for overflow. (Otherwise the condition code is set to 0, 1, or 2, depending upon whether the value remaining is zero, negative, or positive.) In arithmetic shifts to the right, bits are lost from the right, as in logical shifts to the right. But instead of zeros being inserted on the left, copies of the sign bit (either zero or one) are inserted. For example,

$$SRA \quad 2,2$$

does the following:

```
                                    Bits lost
                                       ↓↓
                    10111100001110101100011101000111

becomes             11101111000011101011000111010001
                       ↑↑
                Sign bit copied
```

272   BIT AND BYTE MANIPULATION   [CHAP. 11

EXAMPLE 11.6

Let's see the result of execution of each of the following instructions on register 2, initially containing hexadecimal A7107F39.

(a) SLA 2,4   (b) SRA 2,4

(a)
```
         A    7    1    0    7    F    3    9
        1010 0111 0001 0000 0111 1111 0011 1001
        ‾‾‾‾
        Lost
                                              Added
                                              ‾‾‾‾
        1111 0001 0000 0111 1111 0011 1001 0000
         F    1    0    7    F    3    9    0
```

Despite the fact that 4 bits are being shifted, we still must consider the first hexadecimal digit as being composed of 4 separate bits. The first bit is the sign bit and is not affected by the shift. The next 4 bits are lost, leaving 1111 as the first 4 bits of the result. Each of the other hexadecimal digits is moved one place (4 bits) to the left, and 4 bits of 0 (one hexadecimal 0) are inserted at the right.

(b)   FA7107F3

```
        A    7   ...        original value
        1010 0111 ...
        ↑
        Inserted

        1111
        ↓
        1111 1010 0111 ...
         F    A    7   ...   resulting value
```

Four bits of 1 are inserted to the right of the sign bit. The first three of these, together with the sign bit, yield a hexadecimal F. The fourth, together with the next 3 bits, yields a hexadecimal A, and each of the other hexadecimal digits is shifted one digit to the right. The 9 is shifted out.

The shift instructions are all RS type [normally R1,R3,D2(B2)], in which R3 is always ignored. The assembly language format is thus R1,D2(B2). B2 is very seldom used, and the machine language translation generally has zeros for both R3 and B2. Thus the machine language instruction corresponding to SLL 2,1, for example, is 89200001. (In fact, only the last 6 bits of its second operand are used, so 63 is the maximum length of shift that can be specified.)

11.3 Logical Operations

Logical operations work on a bit from each of two operands to yield a bit in the answer. Actually, groups of bits from each operand yield a group of bits in the answer, but the result for each particular pair of bits depends only on that pair, not on any others in the operands. That is, if execution is proceeding on two 8-bit operands, each of the 8 bits in the answer depends only on the corresponding two bits of the operand.

First operand	10100110
Second operand	10111000
Result of a certain operation	10100000

For example, the third bit in the answer gets its value from only the third bit of each operand.

There are four types of logical instructions: RX, RR, SS, and SI. RR and RX logical instructions operate on 32-bit groups, SS instructions operate on 1- to 256-byte groups, and SI instructions operate on 8-bit groups. More specifically, these types of instructions have the following operands:

BIT AND BYTE MANIPULATION

1. In an RX instruction, the first operand is a register and the second is a 32-bit memory location.
2. In an RR instruction, both operands are registers.
3. In a single-length SS instruction, both operands are memory locations ranging from 1 to 256 bytes in length. (The two operands have equal lengths. Note that the number of bytes must be specified for an SS instruction.)
4. In an SI instruction, the first operand is a single byte in memory and the second is a byte within the instruction.

For each of these four instruction types, there are three logical operations:

AND
OR
EXCLUSIVE-OR

Thus there are 12 different logical instructions. Table 11-1 shows the 12 operation codes. No matter where the operands are located, the result is placed in the first operand without changing the second.

Table 11-1 Logical Operators

Operation	RX	RR	SS	SI
AND	N	NR	NC	NI
OR	O	OR	OC	OI
EXCLUSIVE OR	X	XR	XC	XI

For example,

N is aNd

OR is Or Register

XC is eXclusive or Character

NI is aNd Immediate

The AND Operations

The AND operations yield a result of 1 in each bit where both operands have a value of 1; otherwise they yield a result of 0. Table 11-2 shows the results of the AND operations.

Table 11-2 The AND Operations (N, NR, NC, NI)

```
                    Second Operand
                      0   1
                     _____
        First    0 |  0   0
        Operand  1 |  0   1   Result
```

It is useful to note that any bit ANDed with zero yields zero; any bit ANDed with 1 yields the bit unchanged, and any bit ANDed with itself is also unchanged.

The OR Operations

The OR operations yield a result of 1 in each bit where either operand has a value of 1; only if both operands have a value of zero is the result 0. Table 11-3 shows the results of the OR operations.

Table 11-3 The OR Operations (O, OR, OC, OI)

	Second Operand	
	0	1
First Operand 0	0	1
First Operand 1	1	1

Result

It is useful to note that any bit ORed with zero yields the bit unchanged; any bit ORed with 1 yields 1, and any bit ORed with itself is also unchanged.

The EXCLUSIVE OR Operations

The EXCLUSIVE OR operations yield a result of 1 in each bit where either operand, *but not both*, has a value of 1; if the bits are the same in the two operands, the result is 0. Table 11-4 shows the results of the EXCLUSIVE OR operations.

Table 11-4 The EXCLUSIVE OR Operations (X, XR, XC, XI)

	Second Operand	
	0	1
First Operand 0	0	1
First Operand 1	1	0

Result

It is useful to note that any bit EXCLUSIVE ORed with 0 yields the bit unchanged; any bit EXCLUSIVE ORed with 1 yields the bit with the complement value, and any bit EXCLUSIVE ORed with itself yields 0.

EXAMPLE 11.7

Identify the type of instruction for each of the following:

(*a*) O   (*b*) OR   (*c*) XI   (*d*) NC

(*a*) An RX instruction

(*b*) An RR instruction

(*c*) An SI instruction

(*d*) A single-length SS instruction

EXAMPLE 11.8

The results of the following operations, each using this original value in LOC, are shown at the right. Note that these are all SI instructions.

```
                LOC   DC   B'10101100'
(a)  NI   LOC,B'11100111'     10100100
(b)  OI   LOC,B'11100111'     11101111
(c)  XI   LOC,B'11100111'     01001011
```

EXAMPLE 11.9

Here are several logical operations. Let's see the result (value and location) of each instruction operating on the original contents of the following registers and memory locations.

```
Register 9    1011 1011 1001 0000 1111 0111 1000 1100
Register 10   1100 0111 1110 0110 1001 1110 1010 1101
Location L1   1101 0010
Location L2   1000 1111 1010 1100 0000 1111 0110 0101
```

(a) NI   L1,B'11110000'
(b) OR   9,10
(c) XC   L1(1),L2
(d) O   10,L2

(a) L1 is changed to 11010000.
(b) Register 9 is changed to 1111 1111 1111 0110 1111 1111 1010 1101.
(c) L1 is changed to 01011101.
(d) Register 10 is changed to 1100 1111 1110 1110 1001 1111 1110 1101.

EXAMPLE 11.10

Explain the effect of each of the following. Note that you do not need to know the initial values for L1 or register 2 to answer.

(a) OI   L1,B'11111111'
(b) NI   L1,B'11111111'
(c) OI   L1,B'00000000'
(d) NI   L1,B'00000000'
(e) OI   L1,X'FF'
(f) NI   L1,X'00'
(g) N   2,=X'00000000'
(h) XR   2,2
(i) N   2,=F'0'
(j) OI   L1,X'0F'

(a) All 1s (anything ORed with 1 is 1).
(b) No change (anything ANDed with 1 is itself).
(c) No change (anything ORed with 0 is itself).
(d) All 0s (anything ANDed with 0 is 0).
(e) Same as part (a).
(f) Same as part (d).
(g) All 0s in register 2 [see part (i)].
(h) All 0s in register 2 (anything XORed with itself is 0).
(i) All 0s in register 2 [same as part (g), but better style because of alignment].
(j) First 4 bits unchanged; last 4 bits are 1111.

EXAMPLE 11.11

Determine the value produced by the following operations, each using these original values in hexadecimal:

Register 9   A037421F
Register 10   D3167AB3
Location L1   EE
Location L2   13069F2D

(a) NI   L1,X'C1'
(b) NI   L1,C'A'
(c) OR   9,10
(d) OC   L1(1),L2
(e) XI   L2+2,X'AA'

(a) L1: X'C0'

(b) L1: X'C0'   [same as part (a); C'A' is X'C1']

(c) 9: X'F3377ABF'

(d) L1: X'FF'   (13 is used from L2)

(e) L2+2: X'35'   (L2+2 was 9F)

Uses of Logical Instructions

When do we use these instructions? Use AND when we want to change bits to 0; use OR to change bits to 1; use XOR to exchange bits from 0 to 1 and vice versa.

EXAMPLE 11.12

After execution of UNPK (Chap. 9), a zoned decimal number ZON has a C as the zone of its last byte (e.g., F7F6C2). How can we change the C to F without using MVZ?

Since 1s are needed, use an OR operation,

$$\text{OI} \quad \text{ZON+2,X'F0'}$$

The F is ORed with C, producing 1111 (F). The 0 is ORed with the decimal digit, leaving it unchanged.

EXAMPLE 11.13

Change the value of the 5-byte packed decimal number PNUM to its absolute value, using a logical operation.

We may use either

	OI	PNUM+4,B'00001111'	(or use X'0F')
or	NI	PNUM+4,B'11111110'	(or use X'FE')

Either instruction leaves the first half of the last byte unchanged. The OI changes the sign digit to F. The NI instruction changes the sign B to A or D to C by converting the last bit to 0. (It also changes F to E, which does not matter, and it leaves A, C, and E unchanged.)

EXAMPLE 11.14

A 32-question true-false test has the correct answers at KEY and a student's answers at ANS. (A 1 bit means true; 0, false.) How could we determine which answers are correct and which are incorrect?

```
        L       2,KEY
        X       2,ANS           INCORRECT ANSWERS PRODUCE 1 BITS
```

EXAMPLE 11.15

An unsigned number with a value between 0 and 255 inclusive is stored in the last byte of a full word, FW. Show how to get that value into register 2.

```
            L       2,FW
            N       2,ANDVAL
            ...
DUMMY       DS      0F
ANDVAL      DC      X'000000FF'
```

11.4 Test under Mask

The function of the Test under Mask (TM) instruction is to set the condition code, depending on the value of certain selected bits. It is an SI instruction, whose first operand is 1 byte in memory. The byte of immediate data in the instruction, called the *mask*, specifies which bits in memory are to be tested. Bits in the byte in memory corresponding to bits with values of 1 in the mask are tested. Bits in the memory location corresponding to 0 bits in the mask are ignored. The condition code is set as follows:

	Condition Code
All bits in the mask are 0	0
All selected memory bits are 0	0
All selected memory bits are 1	3
Some selected memory bits are 0 and some selected memory bits are 1	1

EXAMPLE 11.16

Suppose that LOCATION holds 10100101. Determine how the condition code is set by each of the following.

(a)   TM   LOCATION,B'00000111'   cc = 1

The last 3 bits of LOCATION are tested. Some are 0 and some are 1.

(b)   TM   LOCATION,B'10000001'   cc = 3

The first and last bits of LOCATION are tested. Both are 1.

(c)   TM   LOCATION,B'01011010'   cc = 0

Bits 2, 4, 5, and 7 of LOCATION are tested. All are 0.

(d)   TM   LOCATION,B'00000000'   cc = 0

None of the bits of LOCATION is tested. The condition code is set to zero no matter what value is in LOCATION.

EXAMPLE 11.17

We can use TM in the following manner to determine if FW, a full word in memory, is negative or not.

               TM   FW,B'10000000'   ONLY FIRST BIT IS TESTED

A condition code setting of 3 indicates a 1 is the first bit of FW, which means that it is negative.
This use of TM differs from LTR in that the value is in memory and not in a register. Also LTR distinguishes between zero and positive, which this use of TM does not do. Finally, the TM instruction sets the condition code to 3 if the number is negative, while LTR sets it to 1 under this condition.

EXAMPLE 11.18

We can also use TM to determine if FW, a full word in memory, is odd or even.

                     TM   FW+3,B'00000001'

If the condition code is set to 0, the number is even, if it is set to 3, the number is odd, since the last bit of a binary number is 0 for an even number and 1 for an odd number.

EXAMPLE 11.19

We can use TM to look at hexadecimal values. Here we will determine if the last hexadecimal digit in a 3-digit character string CHAR is 'F', '0', or some other value.

                     TM   CHAR+2,X'0F'

A condition code of 3 signifies that the last hexadecimal digit is F, a condition code of 0 signifies that it is 0, a condition code of 1 signifies some other value.

EXAMPLE 11.20

Suppose a company offers eight insurance plans to its employees. It keeps track of each employee's selected plan in a bit string BENEFIT. A 1 bit in a selected position means that the employee carries that type of insurance.

(a) To find which employees have the HMO insurance plan, represented by the sixth bit, the company can test each employee's BENEFIT string:

      TM BENEFIT,B'00000100'

(b) To find out if the employee carries any of the plans, use

      TM BENEFIT,B'11111111'

A condition code of zero indicates that the employee carries none of the plans.

Since the only function of Test under Mask is to set the condition code, it is reasonable to expect a conditional branch instruction to follow the TM instruction. The availability of extended mnemonic instructions for use after TM makes these branching instructions easier to use. The extended mnemonics after TM are the following:

BO or BOR	Branch if all Ones	BC or BCR	1,
BM or BMR	Branch if Mixed	BC or BCR	4,
BZ or BZR	Branch if all Zeros	BC or BCR	8,
BNO or BNOR	Branch if Not all Ones	BC or BCR	14,
BNM or BNMR	Branch if Not Mixed	BC or BCR	11,
BNZ or BNZR	Branch if Not all Zeros	BC or BCR	7,

EXAMPLE 11.21

Test a full word FW in memory and branch to ODD if FW is odd.

```
        TM    FW+3,B'00000001'    TESTS LAST BIT OF FW+3
        BO    ODD                 BRANCHES IF ALL THE BITS TESTED ARE 1
```

11.5 Insert Character and Store Character

The Insert Character (IC) and Store Character (STC) instructions copy 1 single byte from memory to a register or from a register to memory, respectively. The last 8 bits (the low-order byte) of a register are changed by IC or copied by STC, without affecting any of the other bits.

Despite the names of the instructions, each may copy any information in a byte, not necessarily a printable character. There is no boundary requirement on the position in memory that the byte is copied from or to. Both IC and STC are RX instructions. Neither instruction sets the condition code.

EXAMPLE 11.22

Suppose register 2 contains hexadecimal AB1743F0. Memory location LOC contains hexadecimal 12.

```
        IC    2,LOC    would change register 2 to AB174312
        STC   2,LOC    would change LOC to F0
```

11.6 The ICM, STCM, and CLM Instructions

Insert Character under Mask (ICM), Store Character under Mask (STCM), and Compare Logical Character under Mask (CLM) are all RS instructions. ICM and STCM, like IC and STC, permit copying bytes of information between a register and a storage location. However, ICM and STCM permit changing or copying *any or all* of the 4 bytes in the register. ICM copies bytes from sequential bytes in memory to selected bytes in a register. STCM copies selected bytes from a register into sequential bytes of memory. CLM performs a logical comparison of selected bytes in a register with sequential bytes in memory and sets the condition code. These three instructions operate on any bytes of data, printable or not, despite the word "character" in its name.

CHAP. 11] BIT AND BYTE MANIPULATION

These instructions have the format R1,M3,D2(B2). The first operand is the register, and D2(B2) specifies the memory location. M3 is a 4-bit mask which tells the computer how many bytes and which bytes of the register are to be used. Each bit, left to right, represents its corresponding byte in the register. For example, the value of the first bit of the mask indicates what is to happen to the first (leftmost) byte of the register. A 1 bit means copy (or compare); a 0 bit means do not copy or compare. The number of 1 bits in the mask is the number of bytes to be copied or compared. Decimal values may be used to denote the value of the mask.

Mask		Copy or Compare	Number of Bytes
Decimal	Binary		
10	1010	First and third bytes	2
1	0001	Last byte	1
14	1110	First 3 bytes	3
7	0111	Last 3 bytes	3
15	1111	All 4 bytes	4

If the mask is zero, no bytes are copied or compared. If the mask is 15, all bytes are used. An ICM, STCM, or CLM instruction with a mask of 15 might be used where L, ST, or CL should not be used because of boundary restrictions.

EXAMPLE 11.23

What is the value in register 7 after execution of the following instructions? In each part assume that register 7 contains hexadecimal ABCDEF12 and LOC holds hexadecimal 99887766. Remember, ICM copies sequential bytes in memory into selected bytes in a register.

(a) ICM   7,B'0001',LOC
(b) ICM   7,2,LOC
(c) ICM   7,8,LOC
(d) ICM   7,15,LOC
(e) ICM   7,10,LOC

(a) ABCDEF99   (fourth byte affected)
(b) ABCD9912   (third byte affected)
(c) 99CDEF12   (first byte affected)
(d) 99887766   (all bytes affected)
(e) 99CD8812   (first and third bytes of register affected; first and second bytes of LOC used)

Note that adjacent bytes in memory are involved despite the fact that the 8-bit segments in the register may not be adjacent.

EXAMPLE 11.24

Calculate the value of LOC after execution of the following instructions. Register 7 contains AABBCCDD. LOC contains hexadecimal 11223344. Remember, STCM copies selected bytes from a register into sequential bytes in memory.

(a) STCM   7,B'0100',LOC
(b) STCM   7,B'1001',LOC
(c) STCM   7,3,LOC+1
(d) STCM   7,13,LOC
(e) STCM   7,7,LOC

(a) BB223344
(b) AADD3344
(c) 11CCDD44
(d) AABBDD44
(e) BBCCDD44

Note that adjacent bytes in memory are affected in parts (b) through (e), whether or not adjacent 8-bit segments in the register are involved.

ICM and CLM also set the condition code. In fact, the sole function of CLM is to set the condition code. ICM sets the condition code as follows:

	Condition Code
Mask is 0	0
All inserted bits are 0	0
First bit inserted is 1	1
First bit (but not all bits) inserted is 0	2

CLM sets the condition code like all other compare instructions:

	Condition Code
Selected bytes all equal	0
Selected field of first operand low	1
Selected field of first operand high	2

EXAMPLE 11.25

The condition code is set as shown at the right by the following instructions, assuming that LOC contains AABB1122 and register 8 contains 1122BBAA.

CLM	8,B'1100',LOC+2	cc = 0	
CLM	8,B'1001',LOC	cc = 2	(11AA > AABB)
CLM	8,B'0011',LOC	cc = 2	(BBAA > AABB)
CLM	8,B'1000',LOC+3	cc = 1	(11 < 22)

Solved Problems

11.1 What are the results of the following instructions given that register 8 contains hexadecimal 357AD184 for each part?

(a) SLL 8,3   (e) SLL 8,4
(b) SRL 8,7   (f) SRL 8,1
(c) SLL 8,10   (g) SLL 8,5
(d) SRL 8,2   (h) SRL 8,6

First, convert the hexadecimal number into its binary equivalent.

(a) Register 8 = 357AD184 =

3	5	7	A	D	1	8	4
0011	0101	0111	1010	1101	0001	1000	0100

SLL   8,3 yields

1010	1011	1101	0110	1000	1100	0010	0000
A	B	D	6	8	C	2	0

It is important to note that in a logical shift the fill bits are always zero. The final answer is $ABD68C20_{16}$.

(b) For the SRL instruction, the procedure is essentially the same. First, we convert, and then we shift. Register 8 = 357AD184 =

3	5	7	A	D	1	8	4
0011	0101	0111	1010	1101	0001	1000	0100

SRL   8,7 yields

0000	0000	0110	1010	1111	0101	1010	0011
0	0	6	A	F	5	A	3

Again remember that all fill bits are zero. The final answer is $006AF5A3_{16}$.

(c) $EB461000_{16}$ (f) $1ABD68C2_{16}$
(d) $0D5EB461_{16}$ (g) $AF5A3080_{16}$
(e) $57AD1840_{16}$ (h) $00D5EB46_{16}$

11.2 What are the results of the following instructions given that register 9 contains hexadecimal 001E9DF4 for each part?

(a) SRA   9,6   (e) SRA   9,8
(b) SLA   9,5   (f) SLA   9,10
(c) SRA   9,1   (g) SRA   9,7
(d) SLA   9,4   (h) SLA   9,12

(a) For the SRA instruction, again convert the number to binary form. Register 9 = 001E9DF4 =

0	0	1	E	9	D	F	4
0000	0000	0001	1110	1001	1101	1111	0100

and then shift the required number of places, in this case, six. Thus, SRA   9,6 yields

0000	0000	0000	0000	0111	1010	0111	0111
0	0	0	0	7	A	7	7

or $00007A77_{16}$. If the sign bit were a 1, the fill bits would have been 1s. If Register 9 = CBA98765 =

C	B	A	9	8	7	6	5
1100	1011	1010	1001	1000	0111	0110	0101

then the instruction SRA   9,6 would yield

1111	1111	0010	1110	1010	0110	0001	1101
F	F	2	E	A	6	1	D

(b) For the SLA instruction the procedure is very similar. Convert the number to binary form. Register 9 = 001E9DF4 =

0	0	1	E	9	D	F	4
0000	0000	0001	1110	1001	1101	1111	0100

and the shift SLA   9,5 yields

0000	0011	1101	0011	1011	1110	1000	0000
0	3	D	3	B	E	8	0

or $03D3BE80_{16}$. During a left arithmetic shift, if any bit shifted out is not the same as the sign bit, a condition code of 3 is set (fixed-point overflow) and a program interrupt may occur.

(c) $000F4EFA_{16}$
(d) $01E9DF40_{16}$
(e) $00001E9D_{16}$
(f) $7A77D000_{16}$
(g) $00003D3B_{16}$
(h) $69DF4000_{16}$. Fixed-point overflow, because bit 0 is a 0, while bit 11 (which should be shifted out) is a 1. Bits 1 through 10 are 0, which causes no problem. However, bit 11 is a 1 bit, different from the sign bit, so the condition code is set to 3.

11.3 Multiplication by a power of 2 can be accomplished by a left arithmetic shift operation, as long as significant digits are not lost. Division can be accomplished by right arithmetic shifts, but with rounding down. Show what this last statement means by dividing 11 and -11 by 2 by using shift operations.

$$\cdots 0000\ 0000\ 1011 \xrightarrow{SRA} \cdots 0000\ 0000\ 0101 \qquad 11 \to 5$$

$$\cdots 1111\ 1111\ 0101 \xrightarrow{SRA} \cdots 1111\ 1111\ 1010 \qquad -11 \to -6$$

The positive number (11/2 = 5.5) is rounded down (truncated) to 5; the negative number ($-11/2 = -5.5$) is rounded down to -6 (not truncated to -5).

11.4 A class was asked to find the median of a fullword array with an odd number of elements, N. After the array has been sorted, they can address the median by using an index register which contains the value 4 * (N/2) (where N/2 is computed using integer arithmetic). Which, if any, of the following portions of code correctly computes this value?

(a) L   7,N   (d) L   7,N   (f) L   7,N
     SRA 7,1   SRL 7,1   SLL 7,2
     SLA 7,2   SLL 7,2   SRL 7,1
(b) L   7,N   (e) L   7,N   (g) None of these
     SLA 7,1   SLL 7,1
(c) L   7,N
     SLA 7,2
     SRA 7,1

(a) and (d) accomplish the purpose. Truncation in the division must be done before the multiplication. Logical shifts have the same effect as arithmetic shifts for a small positive number, such as the number of elements in an array.

11.5 If the original contents of register 2 are AB106F74, what would be the contents of register 2 after execution of this shift?

                            SRL   2,3

Register 2 would contain

                            15620DEE

11.6 What is accomplished by each of the following special-use instructions?

(a) SLL   2,32   (b) SRL   2,32   (c) SRDA   2,32

Both (a) and (b) zero register 2; (c) moves the contents of register 2 into register 3, leaving copies of the sign bit in register 2.

11.7 Comment on the following shift instruction as preparation for the divide instruction.

```
        L       2,DIVIDEND
        SRDA    2,32
        D       2,DIVISOR
```

We load the dividend into register 2 rather than register 3. By executing a double register right arithmetic shift, we put the dividend into register 3, where it must be located for division. At the same time, because we have used an arithmetic shift, we fill register 2 with copies of the sign bit, as required. This set of instructions works perfectly (and is more efficient than multiplication of the odd register contents by the literal =F'1').

11.8 What are the contents of register 2 after each of the following shift instructions has been executed? Do parts (a) through (c) four times each, once for each of the initial contents shown below:

(1) FF0FFFFF   (2) 7FFFFFFF   (3) BFFFFFFF   (4) 40000000

(a) SLA   2,1   (b) SLL   2,1   (c) SLA   2,4

	(1)	(2)	(3)	(4)
(a)	FE1FFFFE	7FFFFFFE	FFFFFFFE	00000000
(b)	FE1FFFFE	FFFFFFFE	7FFFFFFE	80000000
(c)	F0FFFFF0	7FFFFFF0	FFFFFFF0	00000000

11.9 State the effect of each of the following shifts. Comment explicitly on the new location of the old values and the position and values of any bits shifted in.

(a) SRDL   2,32   (c) SLDL   2,32

(b) SRDA   2,32   (d) SLDA   2,32

(a) Zeros will be shifted into register 2, and the old value from register 2 will have been shifted to register 3.

(b) The sign bit of register 2 will have been copied to the other 31 bits of register 2 and to the first bit of register 3. The original values from the last 31 bits of register 2 are now in the last 31 bits of register 3.

(c) The old value from register 3 is now in register 2, and register 3 has been filled with zeros.

(d) The sign bit in register 2 has been preserved, but the last 31 bits of register 2 have been lost, along with the first bit of register 3. The last 31 bits from register 3 are now in register 2, and register 3 has been filled with zeros.

11.10 The largest shift allowed by the assembler is 63 bits. Justify this limitation.

A double register contains only 64 bits.

11.11 What effect, if any, would the following pair of instructions have on the contents of register 2 if they were executed sequentially? Explain.

$$\text{SLL} \quad 2,1$$
$$\text{SRL} \quad 2,1$$

The instructions set the leftmost bit in register 2 to zero, leaving the other 31 bits unchanged. Whatever was in that position would be lost during execution of the left shift, and replaced by a zero during execution of the right shift.

11.12 Show how the number of 0 bits in register 3 (perhaps representing correct answers on a 32-question true-false test) can be determined.

```
        LA    7,32            LOOP CONTROL
        LR    6,7             TOTAL POSSIBLE RIGHT ANSWERS IN 6
LOOP    SR    2,2             ZERO REGISTER 2
        SLDL  2,1             SHIFT NEXT BIT TO REGISTER 2
        SR    6,2             SUBTRACT 1 IF ANSWER IS WRONG (BIT=1)
        BCT   7,LOOP
        ST    6,COUNT
```

or

```
        LA    7,32            LOOP CONTROL
        SR    6,6             COUNT IN 6
LOOP    LTR   3,3             CHECK FIRST BIT
        BM    LOOPEND
        LA    6,1(0,6)        ADD 1 IF 0 IN FIRST BIT
LOOPEND SLL   3,1
        BCT   7,LOOP
        ST    6,COUNT
```

11.13 What is contained in the even-odd register pair after execution of each instruction? In each case, assume that the original contents of the registers are as follows:

Register 6 = FFE12558   Register 7 = FFE85521

(a) SLDA 6,4   (e) SLDA 6,8
(b) SRDA 6,9   (f) SRDA 6,5
(c) SLDA 6,6   (g) SLDA 6,2
(d) SRDA 6,3   (h) SRDA 6,7

In the SLDA instruction, convert both the even and odd registers. Register 6 = FFE12558 =

F	F	E	1	2	5	5	8
1111	1111	1110	0001	0010	0101	0101	1000

Register 7 = FFE85521 =

F	F	E	8	5	5	2	1
1111	1111	1110	1000	0101	0101	0010	0001

and shift the required number of places.

(a) After execution of SLDA 6,4, register 6 =

1111	1110	0001	0010	0101	0101	1000	1111
F	E	1	2	5	5	8	F

or FE12558F$_{16}$, and register 7 =

1111	1110	1000	0101	0101	0010	0001	0000
F	E	8	5	5	2	1	0

or FE855210$_{16}$. Note that the two registers are treated as a double word so the first bit may be shifted in the odd register but not in the even one.

(b) The SRDA is about the same as the SRA. Convert the registers. Register 6 = FFE12558 =

F	F	E	1	2	5	5	8
1111	1111	1110	0001	0010	0101	0101	1000

Register 7 = FFE85521 =

F	F	E	8	5	5	2	1
1111	1111	1110	1000	0101	0101	0010	0001

After execution of SRDA 6,9, register 6 =

1111	1111	1111	1111	1111	0000	1001	0010
F	F	F	F	F	0	9	2

or FFFFF092$_{16}$, and register 7 =

1010	1100	0111	1111	1111	0100	0010	1010
A	C	7	F	F	4	2	A

or AC7FF42A$_{16}$. Again remember that the first bit of the odd register can be changed. Imagine the two registers as a double word in memory.

(c) Register 6 = F849563F$_{16}$; register 7 = FA154840$_{16}$.
(d) Register 6 = FFFC24AB$_{16}$; register 7 = 1FFD0AA4$_{16}$.
(e) Register 6 = E12558FF$_{16}$; register 7 = E8552100$_{16}$.
(f) Register 6 = FFFF092A$_{16}$; register 7 = C7FF42A9$_{16}$.
(g) Register 6 = FF849563$_{16}$; register 7 = FFA15484$_{16}$.
(h) Register 6 = FFFFC24A$_{16}$; register 7 = B1FFD0AA$_{16}$.

11.14 What are the contents of the even-odd register pair after execution of each instruction? Assume that the contents of register 6 = ADEF0147 and the contents of register 7 = B0AC7191.

(a) SRDL 6,7   (e) SRDL 6,4
(b) SLDL 6,3   (f) SLDL 6,10
(c) SRDL 6,6   (g) SRDL 6,2
(d) SLDL 6,5   (h) SLDL 6,8

The double logical shifts are simpler than their arithmetic counterparts. It is just straight shifting—there is no sign bit.

(a) Register 6 = $015BDE02_{16}$; register 7 = $8F6158E3_{16}$.
(b) Register 6 = $6F780A3D_{16}$; register 7 = $85638C88_{16}$.
(c) Register 6 = $02B7BC05_{16}$; register 7 = $1EC2B1C6_{16}$.
(d) Register 6 = $BDE028F6_{16}$; register 7 = $158E3220_{16}$.
(e) Register 6 = $0ADEF014_{16}$; register 7 = $7B0AC719_{16}$.
(f) Register 6 = $BC051EC2_{16}$; register 7 = $B1C64400_{16}$.
(g) Register 6 = $2B7BC051_{16}$; register 7 = $EC2B1C64_{16}$.
(h) Register 6 = $EF0147B0_{16}$; register 7 = $AC719100_{16}$.

11.15 What are the results of the following instructions? For each part, start with the following initial hexadecimal contents of the registers and memory locations: register 7 = A0CB59E3; register 11 = F91FE478; A = 4CAC1354; B = 000459D7.

(a) N   7,A   (h) NC   A(2),B
(b) N   11,B   (i) NC   A+2(2),B+1
(c) NR   7,11   (j) NI   A,X'1C'
(d) N   7,B   (k) NI   B+3,X'AA'
(e) N   11,A   (l) NC   A(2),B+2
(f) NR   7,7   (m) NI   A+2,X'F0'
(g) NC   A(4),B   (n) NC   B+2(2),B

First, change the operands into bit strings from hexadecimal numbers.

(a) Register 7 = A0CB59E3 =

A	0	C	B	5	9	E	3
1010	0000	1100	1011	0101	1001	1110	0011

A = 4CAC1354 =

4	C	A	C	1	3	5	4
0100	1100	1010	1100	0001	0011	0101	0100

and then AND yields

0000	0000	1000	1000	0001	0001	0100	0000
0	0	8	8	1	1	4	0

or 00881140_{16}.

(b) 00044050_{16}

(c) $A00B4060_{16}$

(d) $000059C3_{16}$

(e) $480C0050_{16}$

(f) $A0CB59E3_{16}$

(g) 00041154_{16}

(h) 00041354_{16}

(i) The NC instruction acts on the number of bytes specified in the first operand field

$$A+2(2) = \begin{array}{|c|c|c|c|} \hline 1 & 3 & 5 & 4 \\ \hline 0001 & 0011 & 0101 & 0100 \\ \hline \end{array}$$

$$B+1(2) = \begin{array}{|c|c|c|c|} \hline 0 & 4 & 5 & 9 \\ \hline 0000 & 0100 & 0101 & 1001 \\ \hline \end{array}$$

and ANDs only those bytes:

0000	0000	0101	0000
0	0	5	0

The rest of the word stays the same, resulting in $A = 4CAC0050_{16}$.

(j) The NI instruction ANDs the byte indicated in storage at A

$$A = \begin{array}{|c|c|} \hline 4 & C \\ \hline 0100 & 1100 \\ \hline \end{array}$$

with the byte of immediate data

1	C
0001	1100

yielding

0000	1100
0	C

The rest of the word stays the same, resulting in $A = 0CAC1354_{16}$.

(k) 00045982_{16}

(l) 48841354_{16}

(m) $4CAC1054_{16}$

(n) 00040004_{16}

11.16 What are the results of the following instructions? For each part, start with the following initial hexadecimal contents of the registers and memory locations: register 3 = AAAACCCC; register 5 = 0F0F0F0F; E = 0FCA0FF0; M = A0F0A0F0.

(a)	O	3,E		(h)	OC	E(4),M
(b)	O	5,M		(i)	OI	E+2,X'AC'
(c)	OR	3,5		(j)	OC	M+2(2),E
(d)	O	3,M		(k)	OI	E,X'7E'
(e)	O	5,E		(l)	OC	E+2(2),M+1
(f)	OR	5,3		(m)	OI	M+3,X'BF'
(g)	OR	5,5		(n)	OC	E(2),M+2

For the O instructions, first change the operands from hexadecimal numbers into bit strings.

(a) Register 3 = AAAACCCC =

A	A	A	A	C	C	C	C
1010	1010	1010	1010	1100	1100	1100	1100

E = 0FCA0FF0 =

0	F	C	A	0	F	F	0
0000	1111	1100	1010	0000	1111	1111	0000

and OR as usual

1010	1111	1110	1010	1100	1111	1111	1100
A	F	E	A	C	F	F	C

to get $AFEACFFC_{16}$.

(b) $AFFFAFFF_{16}$
(c) $AFAFCFCF_{16}$
(d) $AAFAECFC_{16}$
(e) $0FCF0FFF_{16}$
(f) $AFAFCFCF_{16}$
(g) $0F0F0F0F_{16}$
(h) The OC instruction acts on the number of bytes specified in the first operand.

E(4) =

0	F	C	A	0	F	F	0
0000	1111	1100	1010	0000	1111	1111	0000

M(4) =

A	0	F	0	A	0	F	0
1010	0000	1111	0000	1010	0000	1111	0000

and OR as usual:

1010	1111	1111	1010	1010	1111	1111	0000
A	F	F	A	A	F	F	0

Thus the answer is $AFFAAFF0_{16}$.

(i) The OI instruction ORs the byte indicated in storage at E+2:

$$E+2 = \begin{array}{|c|c|} \hline 0 & F \\ \hline 0000 & 1111 \\ \hline \end{array}$$

with the byte of immediate data

$$\begin{array}{|c|c|} \hline A & C \\ \hline 1010 & 1100 \\ \hline \end{array}$$

yielding

$$\begin{array}{|c|c|} \hline 1010 & 1111 \\ \hline A & F \\ \hline \end{array}$$

The rest of the word stays the same, resulting in $E = 0FCAAFF0_{16}$.

(j) $A0F0AFFA_{16}$

(k) $7FCA0FF0_{16}$

(l) $0FCAFFF0_{16}$

(m) $A0F0A0FF_{16}$

(n) $AFFA0FF0_{16}$

11.17 What are the results of the following instructions? For each part, start with the following initial hexadecimal contents of the registers and memory locations: register 4 = 149ADE07; register 10 = B0AC1365; C = 1432A78E; D = 224431A0.

(a) X   4,C   (h) XC   C(2),D+2
(b) X   10,D   (i) XI   D+3,X'C7'
(c) XR   4,10   (j) XC   C+2(2),D+1
(d) X   4,D   (k) XI   C,X'FB'
(e) X   10,C   (l) XC   D+2(2),C
(f) XR   10,4   (m) XI   C+2,X'BD'
(g) XR   4,4   (n) XC   C(4),D

For the EXCLUSIVE OR instructions, first change the operands from hexadecimal numbers to bit strings.

(a) Register 4 = 149ADE07 =

1	4	9	A	D	E	0	7
0001	0100	1001	1010	1101	1110	0000	0111

C = 1432A78E =

1	4	3	2	A	7	8	E
0001	0100	0011	0010	1010	0111	1000	1110

and EXCLUSIVE OR as usual:

0000	0000	1010	1000	0111	1001	1000	1001
0	0	A	8	7	9	8	9

to get $00A87989_{16}$.

(b) $92E822C5_{16}$

(c) $A436CD62_{16}$

(d) $36DEEFA7_{16}$

(e) $A49EB4EB_{16}$

(f) $A436CD62_{16}$

(g) 00000000_{16}

(h) The XC instruction acts on the number of bytes specified in the first operand.

$$C(2) = \begin{array}{|c|c|c|c|} \hline 1 & 4 & 3 & 2 \\ \hline 0001 & 0100 & 0011 & 0010 \\ \hline \end{array}$$

$$D+2(2) = \begin{array}{|c|c|c|c|} \hline 3 & 1 & A & 0 \\ \hline 0011 & 0011 & 1010 & 0000 \\ \hline \end{array}$$

and EXCLUSIVE OR as usual:

$$\begin{array}{|c|c|c|c|} \hline 0010 & 0101 & 1001 & 0010 \\ \hline 2 & 5 & 9 & 2 \\ \hline \end{array}$$

to get $2592A78E_{16}$.

(i) The XI instruction EXCLUSIVE ORs the byte indicated in memory at D+3:

$$D+3 = \begin{array}{|c|c|} \hline A & 0 \\ \hline 1010 & 0000 \\ \hline \end{array}$$

with the byte of immediate data

$$\begin{array}{|c|c|} \hline C & 7 \\ \hline 1100 & 0111 \\ \hline \end{array}$$

yielding

$$\begin{array}{|c|c|} \hline 0110 & 0111 \\ \hline 6 & 7 \\ \hline \end{array}$$

The rest of the word stays the same, resulting in 22443167_{16}.

(j) $1432E3BF_{16}$

(k) $EF32A78E_{16}$

(l) 22442592_{16}

(m) $14321A8E_{16}$

(n) $3676962E_{16}$

11.18 Which instruction(s) from this chapter has (have) the same effect as LA 4,0?

(a) XR 4,4   This instruction zeros out register 4 because if you EXCLUSIVE OR 2 equal bits, you get a zero. Since this instruction EXCLUSIVE ORs every bit with itself, all XORed bits will be equal and the resulting bits will all be zero, making the whole register zero.

(b) N 4,=F'0'   or   N 4,=X'00000000'   Anything ANDed with 0 is 0, so the entire register will be changed to zeros.

(c) ICM 4,B'1111',=X'00000000'   Zeros are inserted into every byte (every mask bit is 1) from the literal, which contains only zeros.

(d) SLL 4,32   or   SRL 4,32

11.19 What will be the value of the condition code after execution of each instruction if the contents of BYT1 = 11010101?

(a)	TM	BYT1,B'10010111'		(f)	TM	BYT1,B'00101010'
(b)	TM	BYT1,B'10010001'		(g)	TM	BYT1,B'11111111'
(c)	TM	BYT1,B'00001000'		(h)	TM	BYT1,B'11110000'
(d)	TM	BYT1,B'10101010'		(i)	TM	BYT1,B'00000000'
(e)	TM	BYT1,B'11010101'				

(a) cc = 1 because the tested bits are mixed.
(b) cc = 3 because the tested bits are all 1.
(c) cc = 0 because the tested bit is zero.
(d) cc = 1 because the tested bits are mixed.
(e) cc = 3 because the tested bits are all 1.
(f) cc = 0 because the tested bits are all zero.
(g) cc = 1 because the tested bits are mixed.
(h) cc = 1 because the tested bits are mixed.
(i) cc = 0 because all mask bits are zero. It should be noted that since the mask is '00000000' the condition code will be zero because there are no tested bits.

11.20 Logical operations can be used as an efficient way to change and manipulate certain bytes or words. If register 7 contains some arbitrary value, for example, B0ACACE2, what operation(s) and what operand(s) would you use to obtain the following results in register 7?

(a) Obtain the 1's complement of the register: 4F53531D.

(b) Retain the fifth through seventh hexadecimal digits, changing all others to zeros: 0000ACE0.

(c) Retain the first four hexadecimal digits, changing the others to zeros: B0AC0000.

(d) If the number is even, make the number odd by logically adding 1 to the last digit (adding 1 to the magnitude without regard to the sign): B0ACACE3. Remember that when you AND something with zero you get zero, and when you OR a number with 1, you get a 1.

(e) Change the first three and last hexadecimal digits to zero, the fourth digit to F, and leave the others alone: 000FACE0.

(f) Change every even hexadecimal digit to the next higher magnitude odd digit (logical addition): B1BDBDF3.

(g) Use logical operations to change all digits but the last to zero, and change the last to 5: 00000005.

(a)		X	7,=X'FFFFFFFF'		(e)	O	7,=X'000F0000'
						N	7,=X'000FFFF0'
(b)		SLL	7,16		(f)	O	7,=X'11111111'
		SRL	7,20				
		SLL	7,4				
	or	N	7,=X'0000FFF0'				
(c)		SRL	7,16		(g)	O	7,=X'00000005'
		SLL	7,16			N	7,=X'00000005'
	or	N	7,=X'FFFF0000'				
	or	ICM	7,B'0011',=X'00000000'				
(d)		O	7,=X'00000001'				

11.21 Suppose a teacher has four students in class and gives them a true-and-false test with 32 questions. The students' answers (1-true; 0-false) are stored starting at ANS in 32-bit strings aligned on fullword boundaries. The answer key is equal to hexadecimal F5A19FC2. That is, questions 1 through 4 are true; 5 is false, 6 is true, 7 is false, 8 is true, etc. Write a program segment to compute each student's score.

```
              SR    4,4            INDEX
              LA    2,4            OUTER LOOP CONTROL
              L     5,KEY
OUTER         LA    3,32           MAXIMUM SCORE IN REGISTER 3
              L     7,ANS(4)       STUDENT ANSWER
              XR    7,5            CORRECT ANSWERS ARE 0 BITS,
*                                    INCORRECT 1 BITS
              LR    9,3            INNER LOOP CONTROL
INNER         SR    6,6
              SLDL  6,1            SHIFT 1 BIT FROM REGISTER 7
              SR    3,6            SUBTRACT THE BIT FROM SCORE
*                                    (BIT=1 MEANS WRONG;
*                                     BIT=0 MEANS RIGHT)
              BCT   9,INNER
              ST    3,CORRECT(4)   STORE EACH STUDENT'S SCORE
              LA    4,4(0,4)       INCREMENT INDEX REGISTER
              BCT   2,OUTER
              ...
DUMMY         DS    0F
ANS           DC    B'...'
              DC    B'...'
              DC    B'...'
              DC    B'...'
KEY           DC    X'F5A19FC2'
CORRECT       DS    4F
```

The following program segment might be employed instead:

```
              LA    8,4            OUTER LOOP COUNTER
              SR    6,6            INDEX
OUTER         SR    7,7            ACCUMULATED SCORE
              L     2,KEY
              L     4,ANS(6)       STUDENT ANSWERS
              LA    9,32           INNER LOOP COUNTER
INNER         SR    3,3
              SR    5,5
              SRDL  2,1
              SRDL  4,1
              CR    3,5            COMPARE EACH ANSWER WITH KEY
              BNE   CONTINUE
              LA    7,1(0,7)       INCREMENT COUNT OF CORRECT ANSWERS
CONTINUE      BCT   9,INNER
              ST    7,CORRECT(6)
              LA    6,4(0,6)       INCREMENT INDEX
              BCT   8,OUTER
```

11.22 STCM 2,B'0011',HW has the same effect as STH 2,HW, but their "reverse" instructions ICM 2,B'0011',HW and LH 2,HW have different results. Explain.

LH puts copies of the sign bit into the first half of the register, whereas ICM leaves the first half unchanged.

CHAP. 11] BIT AND BYTE MANIPULATION 293

11.23 How could you get the 3 bytes at B3 into the first, second, and fourth bytes of register 2, with zero in the third byte of register 2, (a) without any insert instruction? (b) with ICM? (c) with IC?

```
(a)         L     2,B3            GARBAGE IN LAST 8 BITS
            SRDL  2,16            IF REGISTER 3 HAS USEFUL INFOR-
      *                           MATION, IT SHOULD BE STORED FIRST,
      *                           LATER RELOADED
            SLL   2,8
            SLDL  2,8
(b)         SR    2,2             ZERO THIRD QUARTER (AND OTHERS)
            ICM   2,B'1101',B3    INSERT FIRST, SECOND, AND FOURTH
(c)         IC    2,B3            REGISTER 2:  __ __ __ B3
            SLL   2,8                           __ __ B3 00
            IC    2,B3+1                        __ __ B3 B3+1
            SLL   2,16                          B3 B3+1 00 00
            IC    2,B3+2                        B3 B3+1 00 B3+2
```

11.24 To what value is the condition code set by each of the following instructions, using the following initial values in hexadecimal for each part?

    Register 6   ABCD1234
    Location LOC   12ABCD34

(a) CLM 6,B'0010',LOC   (d) CLM 6,B'0101',LOC+2
(b) CLM 6,B'0001',LOC+3   (e) CLM 6,B'1010',LOC+1
(c) CLM 6,B'1100',LOC+1

(a) cc = 0   (d) cc = 0
(b) cc = 0   (e) cc = 2
(c) cc = 0

11.25 Which of the byte instructions introduced in this chapter—IC, STC, ICM, STCM, CLM—set the condition code?

    ICM and CLM

11.26 What ICM instruction performs the same action as IC 7,LOC?

    ICM   7,B'0001',LOC

11.27 To load into register 3 the 4 bytes starting at B4, which lies 2 bytes beyond a fullword boundary, L 3,B4 would violate the boundary alignment restriction. Show how to avoid this problem (a) without any insert character instructions, (b) with ICM.

(a)

		Register 2		Register 3	
		First 2 Bytes	Last 2 Bytes	First 2 Bytes	Last 2 Bytes
LM	2,3,B4−2	Garbage 0000	B4 B4+1 Garbage	B4+2 B4+3 B4+1	Garbage B4+2 B4+3
SRDL	2,16				

(b) ICM   3,B'1111',B4

11.28 Compare the extended mnemonics after TM with those after arithmetic instructions. Do the initials mean the same things in the two cases? Do the same initials produce the same object code in the two cases?

We are using the same mnemonic as before, but giving the initials new meanings. For example, BO always means BC with a mask of B'0001' (or 1), but when we use it after TM, we call it Branch on All Ones instead of Branch on Overflow.

Supplementary Problems

11.29 What instructions from this chapter can be used to subtract two binary numbers without using S, SH, or SR? The program must compute first the 1's complement and then the 2's complement of one of the numbers and add that result to the other number.

11.30 Write a program to multiply two positive binary numbers without using M, MH, or MR. Use the following algorithm. First, initialize a counter to 32; second, place one of the numbers in the odd register of an even-odd pair. Now, in a loop going from 1 to 32 (once for each bit), do the following: check the rightmost bit of the odd register to see if it is 1. If it is, add the second number to the contents of the even register. Then shift both registers one place to the right. Increment the count and check to see if you reached 32. If you did, end; if you didn't, branch back to the top of the loop. Upon completion of the loop, the product will be in the odd register of the even-odd register pair.

11.31 Write a program to divide two positive binary numbers without using D, DR, S, or SR. Use the following algorithm: First, initialize a counter to 32. Second, find the 2's complement of the divisor and then load the dividend into the odd register of an even-odd pair and zero out the even register. Now perform the following series of instructions in a loop going from 1 to 32 (one for each bit). Shift both registers left one place without changing the sign bit. Next add the 2's complement of the divisor to the even register. If the result of that operation is minus, restore the previous value of the even register. If the result of that operation isn't minus, put a 1 in the last bit of the odd register and leave the rest of the register unchanged. After the test, increment the counter and check it against 32. Upon completion of the loop, the even register will contain the quotient and the odd register will contain the remainder.

11.32 Without knowing what is initially in register 10, describe in words how the bits will be changed in register 10 after each of the following operations.

(a)   NR   10,10   (b)   OR   10,10   (c)   XR   10,10

Chapter 12

Floating-Point Operations

12.1 Introduction

Floating-point notation, also known as scientific notation, can be used to express numbers with very large or very small magnitudes. The number of miles to a distant star, the estimated national debt in the year 2000, and the radius of a hydrogen atom nucleus are examples of such numbers. Using base 10, such numbers may be written as follows:

$$7.0 \times 10^{17} \quad 1.0 \times 10^{12} \quad 4 \times 10^{-12}$$

The coefficient is a decimal number which is multiplied by the exponential part of the number, which consists of a base (in this case, 10) and an exponent. The value of the number is the product of the coefficient and the exponential part.

$$\underbrace{2.0}_{\text{Coefficient}} \times \underbrace{10}_{\text{Base}}{}^{\underbrace{14}_{\text{Exponent}}}$$

A positive exponent tells how many places we must move the decimal point to the right to obtain the number in decimal form; a negative exponent tells how many places to the left.

$$1.23 \times 10^2 = 123 \quad 123 \times 10^{-2} = 1.23$$

Accuracy of Numeric Results

Floating-point numbers are used primarily in mathematical and scientific calculations. As stated in Chap. 9, when we want to use packed decimal notation to represent noninteger numbers, we have to keep track of the number of decimal places in each number. This is usually quite easy when we are dealing with dollars and cents, but it can become extremely difficult in complicated mathematical calculations. The problem is that we have to know where the decimal point will be in every intermediate result. When we are solving a problem by hand, we typically shorten the result after each operation to a relatively few digits and retain an indication of where the decimal point lies. This is what the computer does in floating-point calculations.

Even when we perform as simple an operation as dividing 2 by 3 (in base 10), the exact result requires infinitely many digits. Therefore, we have to decide how many digits to keep. It is typical to select a certain number of digits, say 10, and keep that number of significant digits in all the numbers throughout the calculation. All intermediate results and the answer are shortened to this accuracy. Thus, it is typical that we incur rounding errors in shortening numbers to the specified accuracy, and the floating-point numbers are approximations for the values we are trying to compute. We can get more accuracy by using more digits.

EXAMPLE 12.1

The fact that truncation is performed explains why some high-level language calculations give incorrect results. Suppose we wish to calculate

$$X = (A/B) * C \quad \text{where } A = 1, B = 3, \text{ and } C = 3$$

The answer (with noninteger arithmetic) is stored as 0.999999 in many languages. The division yields an answer such as 0.333333; the "real" answer would have an infinite number of decimal places. Multiplication of the intermediate answer, shortened by truncation, yields the final result, which is not exactly correct. Although the small difference may not always be important, it is easy to see that the following statement might give a very misleading result:

IF X = A THEN ...

When using floating-point variables, it is safer to compare the absolute value of the difference (X − A) to some appropriately small value:

IF ABS(X − A) < 0.00001 THEN ...

The IBM 370 system provides operations dealing with floating-point numbers having two different levels of accuracy: a short form, using 32 bits, having an accuracy of about 6 to 8 decimal digits, and a long form, using 64 bits, having an accuracy of about 15 to 17 decimal digits.

12.2 Format of Floating-Point Numbers

In Sec. 12.1, we introduced the general concept of floating-point numbers. The representation of such numbers in the IBM 370 is different from the representation we have discussed, because the 370 uses hexadecimal instead of decimal numbers. Floating-point numbers occupy either 32 or 64 bits (a full word or a double word). We refer to the 32-bit format as *short* or *single precision*, and to the 64-bit format as *long* or *double precision*. In either case, the number is represented as a hexadecimal fraction times a power of 16_{10}. In Table 12-1, several decimal integers and their hexadecimal values in fixed-point and floating-point form are shown.

Table 12-1 Some Decimal Numbers and Their Hexadecimal Equivalents

Decimal	Hexadecimal (Fixed Point)	Hexadecimal (Floating Point)
16	10	0.10×16^2
256	100	0.10×16^3
2	2	0.20×16^1
100	64	0.64×16^2
1,000	3E8	$0.3E8 \times 16^3$
10,000	2710	0.271×16^4

Table 12-2 Some Decimal Fractions and Their Hexadecimal Equivalents

Decimal	Hexadecimal (Fixed Point)	Hexadecimal (Floating Point)
0.5	0.8	0.8×16^0
0.25	0.4	0.4×16^0
0.125	0.2	0.2×16^0
0.0625	0.1	0.1×16^0
0.03125	0.08	0.8×16^{-1}
0.75	0.C	$0.C \times 16^0$
0.1	0.19999A	$0.19999A \times 16^0$
0.2	0.333333	0.333333×16^0
0.3	0.4CCCCD	$0.4CCCCD \times 16^0$
0.4	0.666666	0.666666×16^0

Floating-point numbers need not be integers. Some fractional decimal numbers are shown with their hexadecimal equivalents in Table 12-2. Note that 0.5 is 5/10, which is equal to 8/16, so $0.5_{10} = 0.8_{16}$, etc.

Decimal numbers may be converted to the form in which they will be represented as follows:

1. Change the number to hexadecimal.
2. Move the hexadecimal point to the left of the first nonzero digit, and adjust the power of 16 appropriately. This form is called *normalized form* (see the next section for more details). For example,

$$16_{10} \to 10_{16} \to 0.10 \times 16^2$$

Floating-point numbers are stored in the computer as follows:

1. The first bit (bit 0) is the sign bit. A minus sign is represented by 1 and a plus sign by 0. Complement notation is *not* used for floating-point numbers.
2. The next 7 bits (bits 1 through 7) represent the value of the exponent. With 7 bits, 128 different values may be represented. By adding 64 to the value we wish to represent (this is called *excess-64 notation*), we make the values 0 through 63 (hexadecimal 00 through 3F) represent negative values of the exponent, the value 64 (hexadecimal 40) represent a zero exponent, and the values 65 through 127 (hexadecimal 41 through 7F) represent positive exponents. [Note the difference between the sign of the number (bit 0) and the sign of the exponent.] To determine the hexadecimal value to use for the exponent, given its decimal value, first add 64_{10} to the exponent and then convert the sum to hexadecimal (or convert the exponent to hexadecimal and then add 40_{16}).
3. The remaining bits (bits 8 through 31, or 8 through 63) represent the fractional part of the number, in hexadecimal. Thus, the fraction contains 6 hexadecimal digits in the short form or 14 hexadecimal digits in the long form.

EXAMPLE 12.2

The decimal number -120 is represented in 32 bits of memory as follows:

Decimal	Hexadecimal	Normalized form
-120_{10} →	-78_{16} →	-0.78×16^2

The exponent will be stored as

$$2_{10} + 64_{10} = 66_{10} = 42_{16} \quad \text{or} \quad 2_{16} + 40_{16} = 42_{16}$$

$$\underbrace{1\ \overbrace{100\ 0010}^{\text{Exponent } (42_{16})}}_{\substack{\uparrow \\ \text{Sign bit} \\ \text{(negative)}}}\ \underbrace{0111\ 1000\ 0000\ 0000\ 0000\ 0000}_{\substack{\text{Fractional part} \\ (780000_{16})}}$$

As long as the number is represented in binary, the representation is easily understandable. If the number is represented in hexadecimal, the first 8 bits can cause some confusion, because the first bit represents one thing (the sign) and the next 7 bits represent something else (the exponent). However, the first 4 bits (the sign bit and the first 3 exponent bits) are combined into 1 hexadecimal digit. If a floating-point number is represented in hexadecimal, merely converting it into binary before trying to interpret it can save much confusion, especially at first.

EXAMPLE 12.3

The following floating-point numbers, represented in hexadecimal, are interpreted as decimal numbers:

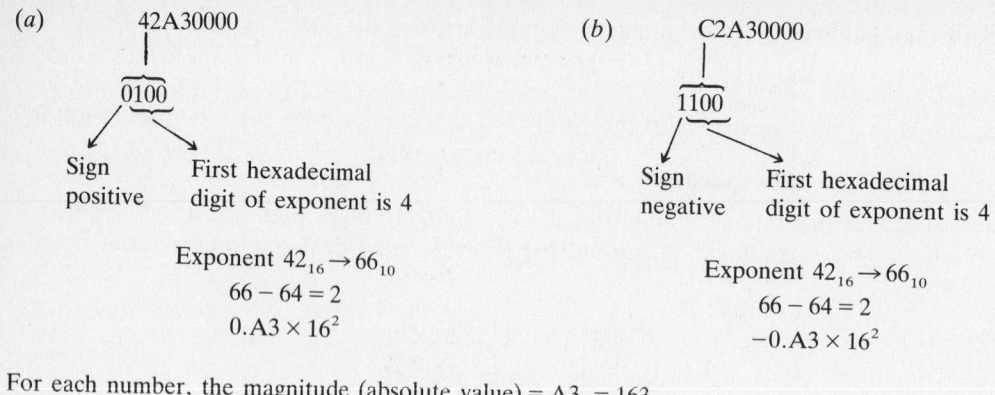

For each number, the magnitude (absolute value) = A3. = 163_{10}.

$+163$ $\qquad\qquad\qquad\qquad\qquad\qquad\qquad\qquad$ -163

The second number differs from the first only in its sign. The number in part (b) is negative.

To convert the fractional part of a decimal number to hexadecimal, repeatedly multiply the fraction by 16 and accumulate the integer parts of the answer to the right of the hexadecimal point (and to the right of the integers already obtained). Repeat until the fraction is zero or until sufficient digits are obtained. For example, convert 0.25 to hexadecimal as follows:

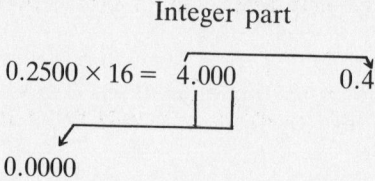

Convert 0.1000_{10} to hexadecimal:

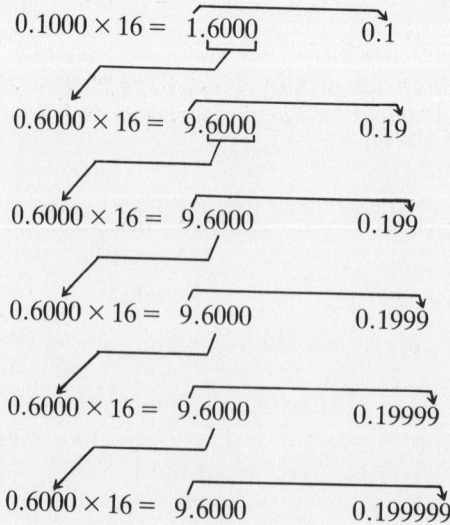

It is easy to see that we will continue to add 9s so long as we repeat the calculation. Since the computer retains 6 (or 14) hexadecimal digits in floating-point numbers, we will stop here.

Convert 0.2525 to hexadecimal:

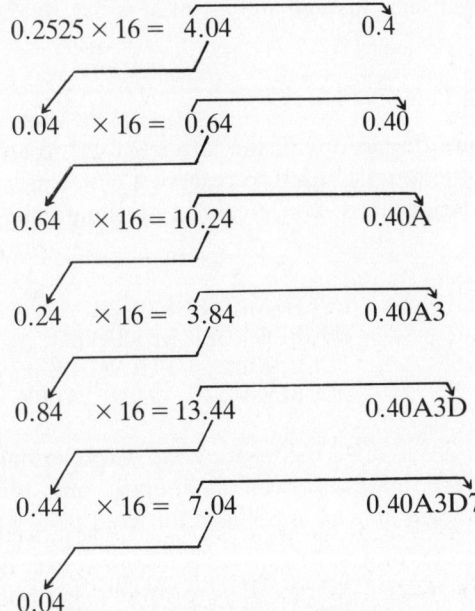

We now have a fraction 0.04, which we had above. Continued processing will cause the same succession of digits to be produced (to yield 40A3D70A3D70A3 for a long floating-point number).

Normalization

There are alternative ways in which to write a floating-point number. For example, all the following represent the same number:

$$20 \times 10^3 = 2 \times 10^4 = 0.2 \times 10^5$$

Scientists use as a standard notation a decimal portion with one whole number digit in the coefficient. That is, 2×10^4 is in "standard exponential form." Similarly, there is one "normal" way to hold a floating-point number in the IBM 370 system. A number is said to be *normalized* if:

1. The number is zero and all digits are zero, or
2. The number is nonzero and the first hexadecimal digit of the fractional part (after the first two hexadecimal digits which comprise the sign and exponent) is nonzero

EXAMPLE 12.4

Which of the following floating-point numbers are normalized?

(a) 40103000
(b) 41000000
(c) 00000000
(d) 40000000
(e) 41030100
(f) 3F273130
(g) 00100000

(a), (c), (f), and (g) are normalized.

(b) has a value of zero (0.0×16^1), but its exponential part is nonzero.
(d) has a value of zero (0.0×16^0), but its exponential part is nonzero.
(e) has a zero digit as the first digit of the fraction 0.0301×16^1.

300 FLOATING-POINT OPERATIONS [CHAP. 12

The usual floating-point operations produce normalized answers automatically. (Special addition and subtraction operations which leave the answer unnormalized are discussed in Sec. 12.6.)

12.3 Declaration of Floating-Point Numbers

Floating-point numbers are declared with the letter E used to reserve a 32-bit memory location on a fullword boundary and the letter D used to reserve a 64-bit memory location on a double-word boundary. As usual, the declarations are given in decimal; the assembler converts them to hexadecimal.

```
FPSHORT   DS    E              FULL WORD RESERVED
FPLONG    DS    D              DOUBLE WORD RESERVED
FP32      DC    E'+123.5'      FULL WORD, WITH VALUE +123.5
FP64      DC    D'-123.5'      DOUBLE WORD, WITH VALUE -123.5
```

In addition, constants themselves may incorporate an exponential part using the letter E for exponent. This is true in declarations as well as literals, and for long- as well as short-form floating-point numbers. (This form may even be used for fixed binary and packed decimal numbers.)

```
HUGE      DC    E'1E20'        1 × 10 TO THE 20TH
TINY      DC    E'1E-20'       1 × 10 TO THE MINUS 20TH
VAST      DC    D'1E20'        A MORE ACCURATE REPRESENTATION THAN HUGE
*                              OF 10 TO THE 20TH POWER
```

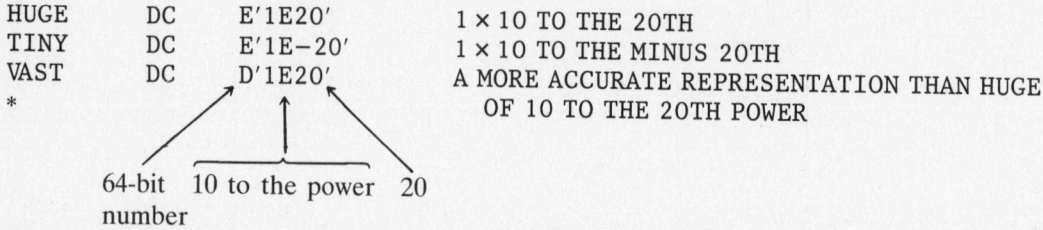

As is evident once again, just because a memory location is declared with one format, D for example, does not mean that it cannot be used for data in other formats. We used D format in Chap. 9 to reserve space for use in conversions between packed decimal numbers and fixed binary numbers in a register. The D reserved 8 bytes on a double-word boundary, which was exactly what was needed. Furthermore, in Sec. 12.6, we will encounter a situation in which it is convenient to use X format for a double-word floating-point number.

12.4 Floating-Point Registers and Floating-Point Instructions

In addition to the general-purpose registers (GPRs) that we have been using so far, there are four 64-bit floating-point registers (FPRs), numbered 0, 2, 4, and 6. There are two kinds of floating-point instructions. Those whose operands are short floating-point numbers have mnemonics including the letter E, while those whose operands are long floating-point numbers have mnemonics including the letter D. These letters differentiate floating-point instructions, which use the floating-point registers, from fixed binary instructions, which use the general-purpose registers. Table 12-3 presents fixed binary instructions in the left-hand column, together with the corresponding floating-point instructions in the rightmost two columns. There are also other floating-point instructions which do not correspond directly to fixed binary instructions. Some of these will be introduced in Sec. 12.6.

The instructions including a D deal with 64-bit operands, each of which is either in a floating-point register or in a double word in memory. These instructions produce a 64-bit result. For example, the instruction

```
                    LD    2,X
```

loads the 64-bit number starting at X into the entire 64 bits of floating-point register 2.

Table 12-3 Floating-Point Instructions Analogous to Fullword Instructions

Instruction	Fixed Binary	Short Floating Point	Long Floating Point
Load	L	LE	LD
Add	A	AE	AD
Subtract	S	SE	SD
Multiply	M	ME	MD
Divide	D	DE	DD
Store	ST	STE	STD
Load Register	LR	LER	LDR
Add Register	AR	AER	ADR
Subtract Register	SR	SER	SDR
Multiply Register	MR	MER	MDR
Divide Register	DR	DER	DDR
Load Positive	LPR	LPER	LPDR
Load Negative	LNR	LNER	LNDR
Load Complement	LCR	LCER	LCDR
Load and Test	LTR	LTER	LTDR
Compare	C	CE	CD
Compare Register	CR	CER	CDR

The instructions including an E deal with short floating-point (32-bit) operands, each of which is either in a full word in memory or in the left half of a floating-point register. The result produced is a short floating-point number. For example,

```
        LE    2,X
```

loads the 32-bit number starting at address X into the first 32 bits of floating-point register 2. The last 32 bits of the register remain unchanged. An exception to this rule is the ME instruction, which multiplies two short floating-point numbers but yields a long floating-point number (64 bits) as its result.

Coding addition and subtraction of floating-point numbers is similar to the coding for fixed binary arithmetic. Coding multiplication and division of floating-point numbers is simpler than coding the corresponding fixed binary operations, because the floating-point operations use only one register. Division yields a quotient but no remainder.

EXAMPLE 12.5

Here are a high-level language statement and the assembly language instructions corresponding to it. All the variables are in short floating-point format, and are declared E.

$$X = (A + B)/C$$

which corresponds to

```
        LE    0,A
        AE    0,B
        DE    0,C           (A+B)/C
        STE   0,X
```

We note that floating-point register 0 can be used for all purposes, unlike general-purpose register 0. Also note that the division operation need not be preceded by multiplication, and that no special register or even-odd pair is required. The quotient is given in floating-point register 0; no remainder is calculated.

If 64-bit (long) floating-point numbers were involved, each instruction would have had a D in place of the E: LD, AD, DD, and STD. The variables would have been declared D.

Floating-Point Arrays

Floating-point arrays are handled much like fixed binary arrays. The values of the elements are processed in floating-point registers. Note, however, that the base and index registers, used to locate the floating-point operands in memory, are still general-purpose registers.

EXAMPLE 12.6

Sum a 10-element, short floating-point array FPARR   DS   10E, and place the answer in SUM   DS   E.

```
        SR      7,7             INDEX IN GPR 7
        LA      10,4            INCREMENT IN GPR 10
        LA      11,36           LIMIT IN GPR 11    (4*N-4)
        SER     0,0             INITIALIZE FPR 0 FOR SUM
LOOP    AE      0,FPARR(7)
        BXLE    7,10,LOOP
        STE     0,SUM
```

EXAMPLE 12.7

Sum a 10-element, long floating-point array FPARR   DS   10D, and place the answer in SUM   DS   D. Find the average of the array and place it in AVG   DS   D.

```
        SR      7,7             INDEX IN GPR 7
        LA      10,8            8-BYTE INCREMENT IN GPR 10
        LA      11,72           LIMIT IN GPR 11    (8*N-8)
        SDR     0,0             INITIALIZE FPR 0 FOR SUM
LOOP    AD      0,FPARR(7)
        BXLE    7,10,LOOP
        STD     0,SUM
        DD      0,=D'10'        DIVISOR MUST BE FLOAT
        STD     0,AVG
        ...
FPARR   DC      D'1,3,1E2,-5,4,3,2,1,0,-1'
SUM     DS      D
AVG     DS      D
```

12.5 Floating-Point Arithmetic

Rules for Arithmetic Operations with Exponential Numbers

Before the computer handling of floating-point numbers is considered, it is important to consider the rules for floating-point operations in ordinary algebra.

Addition and Subtraction

For numbers in exponential form to be added or subtracted, the numbers must have the same base and exponent.

EXAMPLE 12.8

$$\begin{array}{cc} 2.5 \times 10^5 & 7.5 \times 10^{14} \\ +1.3 \times 10^5 & -1.1 \times 10^{14} \\ \hline 3.8 \times 10^5 & 6.4 \times 10^{14} \end{array}$$

If the exponents are originally not the same, we must change one or more so that they are the same. We can change the format of a number while leaving its value unchanged by multiplying and dividing the number by a given power of 10. We multiply either the coefficient or the exponential part, and divide the other. For example,

$$2 \times 10^3 = (2 \times 10) \times \left(\frac{10^3}{10}\right) = 20 \times 10^2$$

or

$$2 \times 10^3 = \left(\frac{2}{10}\right) \times (10^3 \times 10) = 0.2 \times 10^4$$

(Note that multiplying exponential numbers involves addition of the exponents; see the next subsection.)

EXAMPLE 12.9

Add 2.5×10^6 and 1.0×10^5.

$$\begin{array}{c} 2.5 \times 10^6 \\ + 1.0 \times 10^5 \end{array} \quad \text{must be changed to} \quad \begin{array}{c} 2.5 \times 10^6 \\ + 0.10 \times 10^6 \\ \hline 2.6 \times 10^6 \end{array} \quad \text{or} \quad \begin{array}{c} 25 \times 10^5 \\ + 1 \times 10^5 \\ \hline 26 \times 10^5 \end{array}$$

An equivalent change of format can be done in hexadecimal by multiplication and division by a given power of 16. Actually, to add or subtract numbers with different exponents, the computer divides the coefficient of the number with the lower exponent by the power of 16 which is sufficient to make the lower exponent equal to the larger. It then multiplies the exponential part of the lower number by that power of 16.

$$\begin{array}{c} 0.11 \times 16^3 \\ + 0.20 \times 16^2 \end{array} \rightarrow \begin{array}{c} 0.11 \times 16^3 \\ + 0.020 \times 16^3 \end{array}$$

Divided by 16^1 Multiplied by 16^1

$$16^2 \times 16^1 = 16^3$$
$$2 + 1 = 3$$

Multiplication and Division

In contrast to addition and subtraction, when numbers in exponential notation are multiplied or divided, the exponents do not have to be the same. (The base, of course, must be the same.) The coefficient of the product of numbers in exponential form is obtained by multiplying the coefficients. The exponent of the product is obtained by adding the exponents.

$$(2 \times 10^3) \times (4 \times 10^6) = 8 \times 10^9$$

$$\underbrace{}_{2 \times 4} \quad \underbrace{}_{3 + 6}$$

The coefficient of the quotient of two such numbers is the quotient of the coefficients. The exponent of the quotient is the exponent of the numerator minus the exponent of the denominator.

$$\frac{4.5 \times 10^7}{1.5 \times 10^3} = 3.0 \times 10^4$$

$$\underbrace{}_{4.5/1.5} \quad \underbrace{}_{7-3}$$

Exponentiation

Raising an exponential number to a power is equivalent to multiplying the number by itself many times. To compute X^N, we can begin with 1 and multiply N times by X. For example, $X^3 = 1 \times X \times X \times X$. Therefore, the coefficient of the result is obtained by raising the coefficient to the power. The exponent is obtained by multiplying the exponent by the power:

$$(2 \times 10^4)^3 = 8 \times 10^{12}$$

with 2^3 below the coefficient and 4×3 below the exponent.

Floating-Point Arithmetic in the Computer

We now consider the details of floating-point arithmetic. We have seen that to add or subtract numbers with different exponents we must first write the numbers with the same exponent. Then we perform the addition or subtraction, and finally we normalize the answer if necessary. Thus, floating-point addition and subtraction consist of the following three steps, all done automatically by the computer:

1. The number with the smaller exponent is shifted to the right K places, where K is the difference between the exponents.
2. The coefficients are added or subtracted.
3. The result is normalized if necessary, and the coefficient is shortened to 6 (or 14) hexadecimal digits.

EXAMPLE 12.10

Add the following pairs of floating point numbers:

(a) 421735AC
    +42593945

(b) 428735AC
    +42A93945

(c) 421735AC
    +C2173456

(d) 421735AC
    +40152000

(a) *Step 1.* The exponents are the same, so no shifting is needed.
   Step 2. Add the coefficients:

   .1735AC
   .593945
   .706EF1

   Step 3. The result is already normalized. The answer is 42706EF1.

(b) *Step 1.* Again, the exponents are the same, so no shifting is needed.
   Step 2. Add the coefficients:

   .8735AC
   .A93945
   1.306EF1

   Step 3. We have found that the sum is $16^2 \times 1.306\text{EF1}_{16}$. To make the coefficient a fraction, we shift it one place to the right and compensate by increasing the exponent by 1. This yields $16^3 \times .1306\text{EF1}$. Since we can keep only 6 hexadecimal digits in the coefficient, we truncate it to six places, getting .1306EF. Thus the answer is 431306EF.

(c) *Step 1.* The exponents are the same, so no shifting is needed.
   Step 2. Since the second number is negative, we subtract the fractions.

   .1735AC
   −.173456
   .000156

   Step 3. We have found that the answer is $16^2 \times .000156$. To normalize this number, we shift the coefficient three places to the left and compensate by decreasing the exponent by 3. This yields $16^{-1} \times .156000$, so the answer is 3F156000.

(d) *Step 1.* Since the exponents differ by 2, the number with the smaller exponent (the second number) must be shifted two places to the right. This yields .001520, and the exponent is increased by 2.
Step 2. Add the coefficients:

$$\begin{array}{r} .1735AC \\ .001520 \\ \hline .174ACC \end{array}$$

Step 3. No normalization is required. The answer is 42174ACC.

In part (d) of Example 12.10, we had to shift one of the coefficients to the right. When this happens, the IBM 370 retains one extra digit of the number. This digit is called the *guard digit*, and it may be shifted into the answer if postnormalization (normalization of the answer) is required. This procedure is illustrated in the next example.

EXAMPLE 12.11

Add the following pairs of floating point numbers:

(a) 421735AC   (b) 421735AC   (c) 421005AC
    +401525E2   +C01525E2   +C01525E2

(a) *Step 1.* The number with the smaller exponent (the second number) must be shifted two places to the right. Since we retain only one guard digit, the 2 is dropped, and we get .001525E.
Step. 2. Add the coefficients:

$$\begin{array}{r} .1735AC_0 \\ +.001525E \\ \hline .174AD1E \end{array}$$

Step 3. The answer is $16^2 \times .174AD1E$. We must shorten the coefficient to six places by truncating the E, so the answer is 42174AD1.

(b) *Step 1.* Again the second number is shifted two places to the right, and only 1 guard digit is retained. This yields .001525E.
Step 2. Since the second number is negative, we subtract the magnitudes of the coefficients:

$$\begin{array}{r} .1735AC_0 \\ -.001525E \\ \hline .1720862 \end{array}$$

Step 3. Again the answer must be shortened to 6 hexadecimal digits, so the answer is 42172086. Note that the last digit is 1 smaller than it would have been if we had not retained the guard digit.

$$\begin{array}{r} .1735AC \\ -.001525 \\ \hline .172087 \end{array}$$

(c) *Step 1.* Again the second number must be shifted two places to the right, retaining only 1 guard digit. As in part (b), this yields .001525E.
Step 2. Again the signs are opposite, so we must subtract the absolute values:

$$\begin{array}{r} .1005AC_0 \\ -.001525E \\ \hline .0FF0862 \end{array}$$

Step 3. The answer is $16^2 \times .0FF0862$. We normalize it by shifting the coefficient one place to the left, and decreasing the exponent by 1. This yields $16^1 \times .FF0862$, and the answer is 41FF0862. Note that the guard digit has been shifted into the answer.

EXAMPLE 12.12

Trace what happens as the following sequence of operations is executed:

```
        LE    6,A
        AE    6,B
        ...
A   DC    E'3E4'
B   DC    E'6E2'
```

The operation which the computer will perform may be done by a human as follows:

			Decimal	Hexadecimal
LE	6,A	A	30000	7530
AE	6,B	B	600	258
		Result	30600	7788

The computer handles the calculation in floating-point format as follows:

	Normalized format		Adjusted format	
A	44753000	→	44753000	A is unchanged
B	43258000		440258000	B must have the same exponent
		Result	44778800	

The exponents must be the same before addition. The 43258000, corresponding to $258_{16} = 600_{10}$, is changed to 44025800, then added to 44753000.

12.6 Instructions Which Yield Unnormalized Answers

There are instructions for addition and subtraction of floating-point numbers which generally do not normalize the final answer. It is a bit unusual for the programmer to wish to leave the answer unnormalized, but sometimes there is a good reason to do so. (The instructions for conversion of a floating-point number to a fixed binary number and vice versa use numbers in unnormalized format, for example.) The unnormalized instructions are listed in Table 12-4. The letter U fairly obviously refers to unnormalized, and is used for short floating-point instructions. For double-length unnormalized instructions, "double U" is required—that is, W. It should also be noted that load and store instructions do not normalize, but merely copy the format of the sending operand.

Table 12-4 Unnormalized Floating-Point Instructions

Instruction	Short	Long
Add Unnormalized	AU	AW
Add Register Unnormalized	AUR	AWR
Subtract Unnormalized	SU	SW
Subtract Register Unnormalized	SUR	SWR

The instructions listed in Table 12-4 will not shift the answer to eliminate zeros before the first significant digit of the coefficient, but they will shift if necessary to ensure that the coefficient is a fraction. For example, if floating-point register 0 holds 41900000 in the first 32 bits, the instruction

$$\text{AUR} \quad 0,0 \quad \text{UNNORMALIZED ADDITION}$$

will produce 42120000 in the first 32 bits, since

$$0.9_{16} + 0.9_{16} = 1.2_{16}$$

There is no place for an integer 1 in the register, so the 1.2 coefficient is shifted to 0.12 and the exponent is increased by 1, just as it would be in a normalized instruction. In contrast, in the subtraction

$$\begin{array}{r} 41123456 \\ -\ 41123123 \\ \hline 41000333 \end{array}$$

SU would produce 41000333, and SE would produce 3E333000.

EXAMPLE 12.13

To add a number to a second number with an exponent 4E, the fraction of the original number must be shifted (4E − exponent) places. How far would the instruction AW 2,UZERO shift each of the following values of X, where UZERO, an unnormalized form of zero, is defined as shown?

```
DUMMY    DS    0D
UZERO    DC    X'4E00000000000000'
```

(a) $X = 1_{10} = 1_{16} = 0.1_{16} \times 16^1 = 41100000$
(b) $X = 4096_{10} = 1000_{16} = 0.1_{16} \times 16^4 = 44100000$
(c) $X = 1/16_{10} = 0.1_{16} = 0.1_{16} \times 16^0 = 40100000$

(a) to make 16^1 (41) equal to 16^{14} (4E), the exponent must be increased by 13 units. The number is shifted 13 places:

$$4E00000000000001$$

(b) To make 16^4 (44) equal to 16^{14} (4E), the exponent must be increased by 10 units. The number is shifted 10 places:

$$4E00000000001000$$

(c) To make 16^0 (40) equal to 16^{14} (4E), the exponent must be increased 14 units. The number is shifted 14 places:

$$4E000000000000001$$
↖
Truncated

That is, the fractional part is truncated. The value of the number is shifted completely out of the register. This yields an unnormalized zero.

Conversion of a Floating-Point Number to a Fixed Binary Number

This type of conversion takes advantage of the fact that the fractional part of a floating-point number is in the same binary format as a positive fixed binary number. The strategy is to move the fraction to the second half of a floating-point register, store the register contents in a double word, and copy the second half of that double word into a fixed binary (fullword) memory location. The instructions involve unnormalized addition using an unnormalized form of zero.

EXAMPLE 12.14

We want to convert X, a floating-point number, to a fullword binary number, N. We assume that the value of X will fit into a fullword binary number. The algorithm that we will use is to move the fraction of a floating-point number into the right half of the register as if it were an integer with a hexadecimal point at the end and with an exponent of 16^0. However, in a floating-point register, the hexadecimal point is assumed to be after the second hexadecimal digit, 14 digits to the left. To compensate for shifting the fraction to the right, while retaining the appropriate value, we must change the exponent to 16^{14}, or 4E. To get such an exponent, we merely add 0×16^{14}. We will use the following declarations. Note that UZERO is equal to zero because its fraction is zero. No matter what its exponent, anything multiplied by zero is zero.

```
D          DS    D
UZERO      DC    X'4E00000000000000'    ZERO IN UNNORMALIZED FORMAT
X          DS    E
N          DS    F
```

The instructions follow:

```
           SDR   2,2        ZERO FLOATING-POINT REGISTER 2
           LE    2,X        THE FIRST HALF OF REGISTER 2 CONTAINS X
           AW    2,UZERO    DOES NOT CHANGE VALUE, BUT SHIFTS X TO THE
*                              RIGHT HALF OF THE REGISTER
*                              THE FIRST HALF CONTAINS 4E000000 OR CE000000
*                              THE LAST HALF CONTAINS THE ABSOLUTE VALUE OF X
           STD   2,D        COPY INTO MEMORY
           L     2,D+4      COPY SECOND HALF INTO GPR 2
           LTDR  2,2        CHECK SIGN OF ORIGINAL NUMBER
           BNM   STOR
           LCR   2,2        CHANGE SIGN IF ORIGINAL NUMBER NEGATIVE
STOR       ST    2,N        STORE FINAL RESULT
```

Solved Problems

12.1 Convert the following decimal numbers to short (hexadecimal) floating-point format.

(a) 100 (d) −100 (g) 0.50
(b) 514 (e) −4096 (h) 0.125
(c) 1008 (f) −50 (i) −0.25

(a) $100_{10} = 64_{16} = 0.64_{16} \times 16^2$; coefficient $= 0.64_{16}$; Representation of exponent $= 2 + 40_{16} = 42_{16}$; final representation: 42640000

(b) 43202000

(c) 433F0000

(d) This is the same problem as part (a), except that the sign is negative. The sign bit, together with the representation of the exponent, $42_{16} = 100\ 0010_2$, yields the first byte: $1100\ 0010_2 = C2_{16}$. Final representation: C2640000

(e) C4100000

(f) C2320000

(g) $0.50_{10} = 0.80_{16}$ (see Table 12-2); $0.80_{16} = 0.80_{16} \times 16^0$; Representation of exponent $= 0 + 40_{16} = 40_{16}$; final representation: 40800000

(h) 40200000

(i) C0400000

12.2 Convert the following numbers in short floating-point format to decimal format.

(a) 41600000 (d) C3111000 (g) 3F800000
(b) 41A00000 (e) C2AA0000 (h) 3E400000
(c) C1F00000 (f) 43100000 (i) CF100000

(a) Exponent = 1; coefficient = 0.6_{16}; $0.6_{16} \times 16^1 = 6_{16} = 6_{10}$
(b) 10
(c)
$$C1_{16} = \underbrace{1}_{\text{Sign minus}} \underbrace{100\ 0001}_{\text{Representation of exponent} = 41_{16}}{}_2$$

.F $\times 16^1 = F_{16} = 15_{10}$. The value is -15.
(d) -273
(e) -170
(f) 256
(g) 3F represents $3F_{16} - 40_{16} = -1$; $0.8_{16} \times 16^{-1} = 0.08_{16} = 8/256 = 0.03125$
(h) Approximately 9.765×10^{-4}
(i) Approximately -7.206×10^{16}

12.3 Write in hexadecimal short floating-point format (a) the largest positive number that can be expressed, (b) the smallest (negative) number that can be expressed, (c) the number with the largest magnitude, and (d) the smallest positive number that can be expressed as a normalized short floating-point number.

(a) 7FFFFFFF
(b) FFFFFFFF
(c) 7FFFFFFF or FFFFFFFF (equal magnitude)
(d) 00100000

12.4 A student writes two statements to zero general purpose registers 4, 5, and 6 and put 1 into register 7:

$$\text{LM} \quad 4,5,=D'0'$$
$$\text{LM} \quad 6,7,=D'1'$$

The first one does exactly what she wanted, but the second one does not. Explain these results. What values (in hexadecimal) appear in registers 6 and 7?

The first LM instruction sets up a literal of double-word length, and initializes it to zero (making it all zeros). The second sets up a literal and initializes it to 41100000 00000000 (in floating-point format). The value in register 6 is 41100000, while that in register 7 is 00000000.

12.5 Explain why no DC statements were used with D formats in prior chapters, despite the fact that D memory locations were mentioned or actually used.

The values would have been initialized in floating-point format, which would have been inappropriate for their use in earlier chapters.

12.6 Add the hexadecimal values for decimal 0.100 and 0.100 (from Table 12-2). Is the sum the same as the value for 0.200 in the table? Explain. Compare the sum of 0.100 and 0.300 to the value for 0.400. Generalize your answer.

In these and many other cases, the sum of the two fractions is slightly greater than the equivalent value for the decimal sum, because of rounding errors.

12.7 Trace the contents of floating-point register 6 as the following sequences of operations are executed.

(a)	LE	6,A	(c)	LE	6,E
	AE	6,B		ME	6,F
	...			...	
A	DC	E'33'	E	DC	E'3E4'
B	DC	E'43'	F	DC	E'−5E−1'
(b)	LE	6,T	(d)	LE	6,G
	SE	6,D		DE	6,H
	...			...	
T	DC	E'−66'	G	DC	E'1'
D	DC	E'1E2'	H	DC	E'−0.5'

(a)	LE	6,A	42210000	Exponents of the numbers and the answer are all the same.
	* B is		422B0000	
	AE	6,B	424C0000	
(b)	LE	6,T	C2420000	T and the answer $[(-66)-(100)]$ are both negative, so the first bit is 1.
	* D is		42640000	
	SE	6,D	C2A60000	
(c)	LE	6,E	44753000	The value 3E4 represents $3 \times 10^4 = 30{,}000$, which has a hexadecimal equivalent of $7530_{16} = 0.753 \times 16^4$.
	* F is		C0800000	$-5E-1$ signifies $-5 \times 10^{-1} = -0.5 = -0.5 \times 10^0$. The exponents are added $(4+0=4)$, and the coefficients are multiplied. The product is $-1.5 \times 10^4 = -15{,}000$. The hexadecimal representation of its absolute value is $3A98 = 0.3A98 \times 16^4$.
	ME	6,F	C43A9800	The sign of the answer is negative. The exponents need not be the same.
(d)	LE	6,G	41100000	The exponents are subtracted, and the fractions are divided.
	* H is		C0800000	
	DE	6,H	C1200000	The sign of the answer is negative. The exponents need not be the same.

12.8 What is the value in scientific notation of each of the following expressions?

(a) $(2 \times 10^3)^2$ (b) $(3 \times 10^4) + (3 \times 10^3)$ (c) $(3 \times 10^{-4})/(3 \times 10^{-3})$

(a) 4×10^6 (b) 3.3×10^4 (c) 1×10^{-1}

12.9 What value will remain in register 2 after execution of each of the following sets of instructions?

(a)		L	2,FLOAT2	(b)		LE	2,FLOAT2
		L	4,FLOAT1			LE	4,FLOAT1
		SR	2,4			SER	2,4
		...				...	
	FLOAT1	DC	E'1'		FLOAT1	DC	E'1'
	FLOAT2	DC	E'2'		FLOAT2	DC	E'2'

(c) Would boundary requirements be a problem for either set of instructions?

(a) General-purpose register 2 holds 00100000, which is the difference between 41200000 and 41100000.

(b) Floating-point register 2 holds 41100000, corresponding to 1.

(c) There is no problem with boundary alignment, since numbers in E format are full words on fullword boundaries.

12.10 What is the difference between each of the following pairs of instructions?

(a) SER   0,0   and   SDR   0,0
(b) LCER   0,0   and   LCDR   0,0

(a) SER zeros the first half of the register and leaves the second half unchanged; SDR zeros the entire register.

(b) There is no effective difference, since the two operands are the same. Each merely changes the sign of the value. It does not matter if the first half or the entire register is copied into itself.

12.11 Floating-point register 2 contains 40123456789ABCDE. What will be its contents after each of the following instructions is executed?

(a) SER   2,2   (b) LCER   2,2   (c) LCDR   2,2

(a) 00000000789ABCDE   Last half unchanged
(b) C0123456789ABCDE
(c) C0123456789ABCDE

12.12 Floating-point register 2 contains 40123456789ABCDE. What will be its contents after each of the following instructions is executed?

```
DUMMY    DS    0D
UNUM1    DC    X'4200000000000000'
UNUM2    DC    X'3F00000000000000'
```

(a) AU   2,UNUM1   (c) AE   2,UNUM1   (e) AW   2,UNUM2
(b) AW   2,UNUM1   (d) AD   2,UNUM1

(a) 42001234789ABCDE   Last half of register unchanged.
(b) 4200123456789ABC
(c) 40123450789ABCDE   Last half of register unchanged.
(d) 40123456789ABCD0   Only one guard digit is available.
(e) 40123456789ABCDE   No change. The value of UNUM2 is altered before the addition, since it has the smaller exponent. The sum has the exponent of the original number.

12.13 To what value would the condition code be set by the following CE instruction? Explain fully. (Refer to Table 12-2, if necessary.)

```
         LE    0,POINT1
         AE    0,POINT1
         CE    0,POINT2
         ...
POINT1   DC    E'0.1'
POINT2   DC    E'0.2'
```

The value in memory for POINT1 corresponds to 0.19999A; therefore, the value in floating-point register 2 corresponds to 0.333334, whereas that for POINT2 is 0.333333. Therefore, the value in the register is higher, and the condition code is set to 2. It should be emphasized that testing floating-point numbers with nonzero fractional parts for equality is perilous.

12.14 Floating-point register 0 contains 0000000000000000 and floating-point register 2 contains 40123456789ABCDE. What will be the contents of register 0 after each of the following instructions is executed on the original register contents?

(a) SER   0,2   (b) LCER   0,2   (c) LCDR   0,2

(a) C012345600000000   (b) C012345600000000   (c) C0123456789ABCDE

12.15 Write a high-level language statement which corresponds to the following assembly language segment. N is a full word with a value between 10 and 90, and ARR is a short floating-point array of 100 elements with bounds 1 and 100.

```
        L     3,N
        SLA   3,2
        LE    0,ARR(3)
        A     3,=F'4'
        SE    0,ARR(3)
        STE   0,ARR-8(3)
```

This represents ARR[N] := ARR[N+1] − ARR[N+2]

12.16 In mathematics, we can add exponential numbers by changing either exponent.

$$\begin{array}{c} 1. \times 10^3 \\ + 2. \times 10^2 \end{array} \quad \text{can be changed to} \quad \begin{array}{c} 1.0 \times 10^3 \\ + .2 \times 10^3 \end{array} \quad \text{or} \quad \begin{array}{c} 10. \times 10^2 \\ + 2. \times 10^2 \end{array}$$

What method does the computer choose? Why?

The computer shifts the coefficient to the right and increases the exponent of the number with the lower exponent. It cannot shift the coefficient to the left, since all coefficients are held as fractions and their leftmost digits are significant digits.

12.17 Show that the guard digit is useful in the following example:

$$\begin{array}{c} C010001D \\ + 41100011 \end{array}$$

With guard digit

C1010001D
41100011
410F000F3 → 40F000F3

Without guard digit

C1010001
41100011
410F0010 → 40F00100

12.18 Suppose that N is a fullword fixed binary number and X is a short floating-point number. Write the instructions that will compute X to the Nth power, and store the result in POWER. You may assume that X and N are not both zero.

```
             LE    0,=E'1'       INITIALIZE POWER TO 1
             L     2,N
             LPR   3,2           NUMBER OF TIMES TO MULTIPLY = |N|
             BZ    STO           IF N=0, POWER=1
      LOOP   ME    0,X
             BCT   3,LOOP
             LTR   2,2           IF N POSITIVE, WE HAVE THE ANSWER
             BP    STO
             LE    2,=E'1'       IF N NEGATIVE, TAKE RECIPROCAL
             DER   2,0
             LER   0,2
      STO    STE   0,POWER       STORE FULLWORD PRECISION
```

12.19 Write the instructions to compute $N!$, where $0! = 1$ and for every positive integer K

$$K! = 1 \times 2 \times 3 \times \cdots \times K$$

You are given a fullword fixed binary number N. If N is negative, branch to ERROR. Otherwise, compute $N!$ as a short floating-point number FACT.

```
              LE    0,=E'1'          INITIALIZE FACT TO 1
              L     2,N
              LTR   2,2
              BM    ERROR
              BZ    STO
              LER   2,0              FP REGISTER 2
     LOOP     MER   0,2
              AE    2,=E'1'
              BCT   2,LOOP           GP REGISTER 2
     STO      STE   0,FACT
              ...
     ERROR    ...
```

12.20 You can compute the sine of x from the infinite series

$$\sin x = x - \frac{x^3}{3!} + \frac{x^5}{5!} - \frac{x^7}{7!} + \cdots$$

Write the instructions which will perform this calculation using short floating-point arithmetic. You may stop when adding a term to the sum does not change the sum. In other words, you stop when we have exceeded the maximum possible precision of the answer.

```
              SER   0,0              SUM
              LE    2,X              TERM
              LE    4,=E'1'          SUBSCRIPT OF THE TERM
     LOOP     STE   0,SIN
              AER   0,2
              ME    2,X
              ME    2,X              NOW MULTIPLIED BY X * X
              AE    4,=E'1'          ADD 1 TO GET NEXT TERM OF FACTORIAL
              DER   2,4
              AE    4,=E'1'          ADD 1 AGAIN, TO GET TO NEXT TERM
              DER   2,4              DIVIDE BY NEXT PART OF FACTORIAL
              LCER  2,2              CHANGE SIGN OF TERM
              CE    0,SIN            DOES LAST TERM MAKE ANY DIFFERENCE?
              BNE   LOOP
```

12.21 If two normalized positive numbers are subtracted, in which direction might it be necessary to shift the result to normalize the answer?

Left.

12.22 Explain the difference between having a definition of a normalized number that requires the first hexadecimal digit of the coefficient to be nonzero and a definition of a normalized number that requires the first bit of the coefficient to be nonzero. Which of these definitions does the IBM 370 use?

The first hexadecimal digit after the exponent must be nonzero if the hexadecimal definition is used, as it is on the IBM 370. Thus 40100000 is considered to be normalized even though the first bits after the exponent are zeros:

$$\underbrace{0100\ 0000}_{\text{Exponent}}\ \underset{\uparrow}{0001}\ 0000\ 0000\ 0000\ 0000\ 0000$$

Exponent Start of coefficient

12.23 (a) Write a program segment which will average the N elements of a long floating-point array, where N is a fullword binary number.

(b) Amend the program to average the N elements of a short floating-point array, where N is a fullword binary number.

(a)
```
            SR      7,7                     INDEX IN GPR 7
            LA      10,8                    8-BYTE INCREMENT IN GPR 10
            L       11,N                    LIMIT TO GO INTO GPR 11:
*                                             8N - 8
            SLA     11,3                    8N
            SR      11,10                   8N - 8
            SDR     0,0                     INITIALIZE FPR 0 FOR SUM
            SDR     2,2                     COUNT = 0
    LOOP    AD      0,FPARR(7)
            AD      2,=D'1'                 INCREMENT COUNT IN FLOAT
            BXLE    7,10,LOOP
            STD     0,SUM
            DDR     0,2                     DIVISOR MUST BE FLOAT
            STD     0,AVG
            ...
    FPARR   DC      D'1,3,1E2,-5,4,3,2,1,0,-1'
    SUM     DS      D
    AVG     DS      D
```

(b)
```
            SR      7,7                     INDEX IN GPR 7
            LA      10,4                    4-BYTE INCREMENT IN GPR 10
            L       11,N                    LIMIT TO GO INTO GPR 11:
*                                             4N - 4
            SLA     11,2                    4N
            SR      11,10                   4N - 4
            SER     0,0                     INITIALIZE FPR 0 FOR SUM
            SER     2,2                     COUNT = 0
    LOOP    AE      0,FPARR(7)
            AE      2,=E'1'                 INCREMENT COUNT IN FLOAT
            BXLE    7,10,LOOP
            STE     0,SUM
            DER     0,2                     DIVISOR MUST BE FLOAT
            STE     0,AVG
            ...
    FPARR   DC      E'1,3,1E2,-5,4,3,2,1,0,-1'
    SUM     DS      E
    AVG     DS      E
```

12.24 Suppose that N is a fullword binary number and X and Y are equivalent arrays of short floating-point numbers. An important calculation in matrix theory is to compute the sum of products defined by

$$P := X[1] * Y[1] + X[2] * Y[2] + \cdots + X[N] * Y[N]$$

Write the assembly language instructions that will perform this calculation. Assume that N and the arrays are already initialized.

```
              L      11,N
              BCTR   11,0            N-1
              SLA    11,2            4*(N-1)    LIMIT
              LA     10,4
              SER    0,0             INITIALIZE SUM (SINGLE WORD PRECISION)
              SR     7,7             INDEX
    LOOP      LE     2,X(7)
              ME     2,Y(7)
              AER    0,2             ADD, SINGLE WORD PRECISION
              BXLE   7,10,LOOP
              STE    0,P
```

12.25 In order to improve the accuracy of the result calculated in Problem 12.24, it is common to modify the calculation slightly. We want to compute the products X[i] * Y[i] to full accuracy, then sum these products as long floating-point numbers. The final result is shortened to a short floating-point number and stored in P. How would you modify the answer to Problem 12.24 to accomplish this?

Use SDR 0,0 to initialize register 0, and change AER 0,2 to ADR 0,2. (The ME instruction always produces a long floating-point result.)

12.26 Suppose that we want to compute the square root of A, where A is a short floating-point number. If A is positive, we can generate a sequence of points, $x[0], x[1], x[2], \ldots$, which converges to the square root of x. We generate these points by selecting any positive number for $x[0]$ and generating $x[1], x[2], \ldots$, from the relation

$$x[n+1] = \frac{x[n] + A/x[n]}{2}$$

In theory, this will generate a sequence of points that will become arbitrarily close to the square root of A, but, in practice, the accuracy of the result will be limited by rounding errors. To use this algorithm, we can set $x[0] = 1$ and stop adding terms when n is at least 2 and $x[n] \geq x[n+1]$. Write instructions that will compute the square root of A and store the result in SQRT. If $A = 0$, the answer is zero. If A is negative, branch to ERROR. A convenient way to divide a floating-point number by 2 is to use the instruction HER. This is an RR instruction which halves the value of the second operand and places the result in the first operand.

```
              LE     0,A
              LTER   2,0
              BM     ERROR
              BZ     STO
              AE     2,=E'1'
              HER    2,2             HALVES VALUE IN 2
    LOOP      LER    0,2
              LE     2,A
              DER    2,0
              AER    2,0
              HER    2,2
              CER    2,0
              BL     LOOP
    STO       STE    0,SQRT
              ...
    ERROR     ...
```

12.27 NUM is a 50-element short floating-point array; SQUARE is a 50-element long floating-point array. N is a fullword binary number. Write a program segment to place the square of each of the first N elements of NUM into the corresponding element of SQUARE.

```
            SR      7,7             INDEX FOR NUM
            LA      10,4            INCREMENT
            L       11,N
            BCTR    11,0            N−1
            SLA     11,2            4N−4=LIMIT
            SR      8,8             INDEX FOR SQUARE
   LOOP     LE      2,NUM(7)
            MER     2,2
            STD     2,SQUARE(8)
            LA      8,8(0,8)        INCREMENT INDEX FOR SQUARE
            BXLE    7,10,LOOP
```

12.28 NUM is a 50-element short floating-point array; SQUARE is a 50-element long floating-point array. Write a program segment to put the product of NUM[I] times NUM[I+1] into SQUARE[I] for the first 49 elements of SQUARE, and to put NUM[50] times NUM[1] into SQUARE[50].

```
            SR      7,7             INDEX
            LA      10,4            INCREMENT
            LA      11,192          LIMIT (FOR ELEMENT 49)
            SR      8,8             INDEX FOR DOUBLE WORD
   LOOP     LE      2,NUM(7)
            ME      2,NUM+4(7)
            STD     2,SQUARE(8)
            LA      8,8(0,8)        INCREMENT REGISTER 8
            BXLE    7,10,LOOP       INCREMENT REGISTER 7
            LE      2,NUM+196
            ME      2,NUM
            STD     2,SQUARE+392
```

12.29 Explain the difference between the mnemonics U and W as opposed to E and D.

U and W signify short and long floating point, respectively, but they also indicate that the answer is not to be normalized. E and D require normalization of the answer.

12.30 Convert N, a binary fullword number, to X, a short floating-point number.

```
            L       2,N
            LPR     3,2
   *                                ABSOLUTE VALUE; FLOATING-POINT
                                      IS NOT IN COMPLEMENT NOTATION
            MVC     D(8),UZERO
            ST      3,D+4           CHANGE SECOND HALF OF D
            LD      2,D             UNNORMALIZED VALUE IN FPR 2
            AD      2,=D'0'         NORMALIZE THE VALUE IN FPR 2
            LTR     2,2             TEST THE ORIGINAL VALUE OF N
   *                                  FOR SIGN (GPR 2)
            BNM     STOR
            LCER    2,2             CHANGE SIGN OF X
   STOR     STE     2,X             STORE FIRST 32 BITS OF FPR 2
            ...
   D        DS      D
   UZERO    DC      X'4E00000000000000'
```

12.31 Write the instructions to compute the remainder when A is divided by B. Assume that A, B, and the remainder are all short floating-point numbers. To compute the remainder, let Q be the integer part of the quotient A/B. Then

$$R = A - B \times Q$$

```
          LE    0,A
          DE    0,B
          AU    0,UZERO     MOVES FRACTIONAL PORTION OF ANSWER OUT OF
*                             REGISTER (LEAVES RIGHT HALF UNCHANGED)
          ME    0,B         MULTIPLY, USING LEFT HALF OF REGISTER ONLY
          LCER  0,0
          AE    0,A
          STE   0,R
          ...
DUMMY     DS    0E
UZERO     DC    X'46000000'
```

Supplementary Problems

12.32 What is the difference, if any, in the magnitude of the value stored in each pair of numbers?

(a) DC E'12.3'   DC D'12.3'

(b) DC E'12.3'   DC P'12.3'

(c) DC E'12.3'   DC F'12.3'

(d) DC E'1.0E4'   DC F'1.0E4'

12.33 Repeat Problem 12.6 using long floating-point numbers. Does your answer change? Explain the improvement, if any.

12.34 The algorithm described in Problem 12.26 will converge rapidly if $x[0]$ is close to the square root of A, but it will take longer if $x[0]$ is far from the square root of A. To speed up the program, we would like to make a better choice for $x[0]$. Since the square root of 16^{2K} is 16^K, a reasonable choice for $x[0]$ is a number whose exponent is half the exponent of A. Modify the answer to Problem 12.26 so that $x[0]$ is a number whose coefficient is the same as the coefficient of A and whose exponent is half the exponent of A (truncated, if necessary).

12.35 Write a function which uses the algorithm of Problem 12.26 or that of the preceding problem to compute the square root of a short floating-point number.

12.36 Write a subroutine which finds the roots of a quadratic equation. The parameters, A, B, C, ROOT1, and ROOT2, are all short floating-point numbers. The formula to find the roots of a quadratic equation is

$$X = (-B \pm \sqrt{(B*B - 4*A*C)})/(2*A)$$

12.37 In certain cases, we can produce more accurate values for the roots of a quadratic equation by evaluating the discriminant $B*B - 4*A*C$ in long floating-point arithmetic, even though the rest of the calculation (including the square root) is performed in short floating-point arithmetic. Rewrite the subroutine that you wrote for Problem 12.36 to incorporate this approach. The parameters are still short floating-point numbers, but the discriminant is to be calculated using long floating-point arithmetic. Then it is shortened to a short floating-point number before its square root is computed. The rest of the calculation uses short floating-point arithmetic.

12.38 Write a subprogram to place in SQUARE, a long floating-point memory location, the square of NUM, a fullword binary number. *Hint:* If necessary, see Problem 12.30.

12.39 Write a program to place into each of the first 10 elements of SQUARE, a long floating-point array, the squares of the corresponding elements of NUM, an array of fullword numbers. Use the subprogram you wrote for the preceding problem.

12.40 Write a main program to place into each element of SQUARE, a long floating-point array, the squares of the corresponding elements of NUM, an array of halfword numbers.

12.41 Would it be easier to convert the square of a full word or the square of a halfword number into a floating-point number? Explain.

Chapter 13

Advanced Instructions

13.1 Introduction

Chapter 13 deals with several powerful instructions which are extremely useful in computer science. The Translate (TR) instruction (Sec. 13.2) allows translation of each character in a string to any specified character. The Translate and Test (TRT) instruction (Sec. 13.3) searches for a specified character or characters in a string. The Execute (EX) instruction (Sec. 13.4) allows execution of other instructions with certain parameters set during execution instead of being fixed at the time the program is assembled. Such powerful instructions are necessarily a bit complex.

13.2 Translate

The Translate (TR) instruction is designed to change a source string into a result string one character at a time. The TR instruction is a single-length SS-type instruction in which the first operand is the source string. It may be from 1 to 256 characters long, and the characters need not be printable. Execution of the TR instruction changes the first operand into the resulting string, one character at a time. The second operand is not changed. Execution of the instruction continues until the first operand is exhausted. The second operand is a table of values. Each character in the source string identifies a location in the table which holds the character to use in the source string.

The instruction works in the following manner. Each byte in the source string is individually used as a displacement into the table. The TR instruction adds the value of the source character (in hexadecimal) to the address of the table, and it translates that source character into the value found at that address. That is, the byte at the resulting address is selected and substituted into the source string in place of the source byte. The byte fetched from the table is called the *function byte*.

EXAMPLE 13.1

```
            TR      STRINGA(4),TABLE
            TR      STRINGB(4),TABLE
            ...
TABLE       DC      C'GROFAL'
STRINGA     DC      X'03010200'
STRINGB     DC      X'03050400'
```

STRINGA is translated as follows. The first byte, 03, is added to the address of TABLE, producing the address of TABLE+3. The byte at TABLE+3 is 'F' (hexadecimal C6), which is substituted into STRINGA to replace the 03:

C6010200

Next, the 01 is added to the address of TABLE, and the byte there—character 'R' or hexadecimal D9—is substituted into STRINGA in place of the 01:

C6D90200

Then the third byte—02—selects the byte at TABLE+2—letter 'O' or hexadecimal D6—which is substituted in STRINGA:

C6D9D600

Finally, the fourth byte—00—generates the address of TABLE+0. The byte there is the letter 'G', or hexadecimal C7. STRINGA is thus changed into 'C6D9D6C7', or 'FROG'. Similarly, STRINGB is converted to 'FLAG'.

Note that the source bytes are hexadecimal values, no matter whether they are expressed as characters, hexadecimal values, full words, etc.

EXAMPLE 13.2

```
        TR      STRING(4),TABLE
        ...
STRING  DC      X'100A110C'
TABLE   DC      X'01C9D4C1E2110A0B0C0DF1E6E8C41923F9C1'
```

Here the values at STRING are hexadecimal digits which differ from their decimal counterparts. STRING is translated as follows:

Hexadecimal		Decimal	Byte at
10	→	16	TABLE+16 → F9
0A	→	10	TABLE+10 → F1
11	→	17	TABLE+17 → C1
0C	→	12	TABLE+12 → E8

STRING becomes X'F9F1C1E8' or character '91AY'.

EXAMPLE 13.3

Suppose we write the following:

```
        TR      SRC(3),TABLE
        ...
SRC     DC      C'ABC'
TABLE   DC      X'...'
```

How long should TABLE be?

The source string, SRC, has source bytes 'A' (hexadecimal C1 or decimal 193), 'B' (hexadecimal C2 or decimal 194), and 'C' (hexadecimal C3 or decimal 195). This means that they will seek function bytes from TABLE+193, TABLE+194, and TABLE+195. Since there must be values at these addresses, TABLE in this case must be at least 196 bytes long.

Table 13-1 Sample TR Table*

```
TABLE   DC      X'000102030405060708090A0B0C0D0E0F'
        DC      X'101112131415161718191A1B1C1D1E1F'
        DC      X'202122232425262728292A2B2C2D2E2F'
        DC      X'303132333435363738393A3B3C3D3E3F'
        DC      X'404142434445464748494A4B4C4D4E4F'
        DC      X'505152535455565758595A5B5C5D5E5F'
        DC      X'606162636465666768696A6B6C6D6E6F'
        DC      X'707172737475767778797A7B7C7D7E7F'
        DC      X'808182838485868788898A8B8C8D8E8F'
        DC      X'909192939495969798999A9B9C9D9E9F'
        DC      X'A0A1A2A3A4A5A6A7A8A9AAABACADAEAF'
        DC      X'B0B1B2B3B4B5B6B7B8B9BABBBCBDBEBF'
        DC      X'C0C1C2C3C4C5C6C7C8C9CACBCCCDCECF'
        DC      X'D0D1D2D3D4D5D6D7D8D9DADBDCDDDEDF'
        DC      X'E0E1E2E3E4E5E6E7E8E9EAEBECEDEEEF'
        DC      X'F0F1F2F3F4F5F6F7F8F9FAFBFCFDFEFF'
```

*This table changes no values.

Since there are 256 possible values for a byte, each of which might be translated, the table is normally 256 characters long. A sample table is shown in Table 13-1.

The character zero ('0') has an EBCDIC representation X'F0' or decimal 240 (Table 7-1), and the first character in the sixteenth row of the TABLE (the byte at TABLE+240 in Table 13-1) is the one which will be used to replace any '0' in the first operand of a TR instruction using this table as second operand. If we do not want zero to be changed, we put X'F0' at that location. If we want zero changed to some other character, we put the EBCDIC representation of that character at location TABLE+240.

EXAMPLE 13.4

Perhaps the simplest "secret" code results from changing each letter of a string (except 'Z') into the next letter of the alphabet, and changing 'Z' into 'A'. Encoding a message in this simple manner would change

MESSAGE

into NFTTBHF. Here are the last four rows of the table which will encode the source by changing each of the letters 'A' to 'Y' to the next letter ('B' to 'Z') in the alphabet and by changing 'Z' to 'A' (leaving alone all characters which are not capital letters):

```
        DC    X'C0C2C3C4C5C6C7C8C9D1CACBCCCDCECF'
        DC    X'D0D2D3D4D5D6D7D8D9E2DADBDCDDDEDF'
        DC    X'E0E1E3E4E5E6E7E8E9C1EAEBECEDEEEF'
        DC    X'F0F1F2F3F4F5F6F7F8F9FAFBFCFDFEFF'
```

Since C0, D0, and E0 do not represent capital letters, the table represents them by characters which are the same as their source characters. The same is true for all the characters of the last row, all the characters of the last six columns (two hexadecimal digits per column), and E1 (as well as the 12 rows not shown here). At the address corresponding to each letter from 'A' to 'Y' is stored the code for the next letter of the alphabet. For example, the letter 'A' is hexadecimal C1 or decimal 193, and the character found at TABLE+193 is hexadecimal C2, corresponding to 'B'. Each 'I' (C9) will be changed to 'J' (D1), and each 'R' (D9) will be changed to 'S' (E2), etc. 'Z' will be changed to 'A'. The nonalphabetic character E1 is not changed.

To translate 'MESSAGE' by the code referred to above, we use the TABLE of Example 13.4 and the instruction

```
            TR    STRING(7),TABLE
            ...
    STRING  DC    C'MESSAGE'
```

Each of the seven characters of 'MESSAGE' is in turn translated into the next letter of the alphabet, yielding 'NFTTBHF'.

Another frequent use of TR is to rearrange the characters in a string. If we wish to reverse the characters in a 10-byte string, for example, we can use

```
            TR    PATTERN(10),STRING-1
            ...
    PATTERN DC    X'0A090807060504030201'
    STRING  DC    C'ABCDEFGHIJ'
```

or

```
            TR    PATTERN(10),STRING
            ...
    PATTERN DC    X'09080706050403020100'
    STRING  DC    C'ABCDEFGHIJ'
```

In the first case, 10 ($0A_{16}$) is added to the address of STRING−1, yielding STRING+9. The character at that address ('J') replaces the 0A in PATTERN. Then 9 is added to STRING−1, yielding STRING+8. The character there ('I') replaces the 09 in PATTERN. This procedure is carried out for 10 bytes, producing the reversed string 'JIHGFEDCBA'. If you trace the second TR instruction, you will see that it produces the same result.

The pattern is destroyed by execution of the TR instruction, so if it is to be used again, it should be copied before each execution. For example, MVC   PATTERN(10),TEMPLATE would reinitialize PATTERN if TEMPLATE were declared as X'09080706050403020100'.

EXAMPLE 13.5

We will write instructions to move the eleventh through fifteenth characters in a 20-character string STRING to the second through sixth bytes of a 10-character string RESULT. We will also put the first character in STRING in the tenth byte of RESULT, and make each of the other characters of RESULT blank.

```
        TR      RESULT(10),STRING-1
        ...
RESULT  DC      X'000B0C0D0E0F00000001'
BLANK   DC      X'40'
STRING  DC      CL20'MARTHA WASHINGTON'
```

This instruction works as follows:

1. Zero (00) bytes beyond STRING−1 is a blank (40). Every place in RESULT where 00 appears, the blank will replace it.

2. Eleven (0B) bytes beyond STRING−1 is the eleventh character of STRING ('H'), which replaces the second byte of RESULT. The twelfth through fifteenth characters ('INGT') are treated in the same way.

3. The tenth character of RESULT is found 1 (01) byte beyond STRING−1; that is, it is at STRING. RESULT thus becomes 'bHINGTbbbM'.

EXAMPLE 13.6

The TR instruction can be used with explicit notation:

```
        LA      7,A-10
        LA      2,B
        TR      3(4,2),5(7)
                D1 length B1  D2 B2
A       00 01 02 03 04 05 06 07 08 09 0A 0B 0C 0D 0E 0F
B       13 14 12 13 14 12 11 13 14
```

The text to translate starts at B+3 and is 4 bytes long. The table begins at A−10+5 = A−5. Hence the first function byte is at A−5+19 = A+14. Since this byte contains 0E, the first byte of B is replaced by 0E. Similarly, the 14 is replaced by 0F, the 12 by 0D, and the 11 by 0C. The final value of B is thus

```
B       13 14 12 0E 0F 0D 0C 13 14
```

13.3 Translate and Test

The Translate and Test (TRT) instruction has the same format as TR, with a table as the second operand, but its purpose and function are quite different. Its purpose is to search for, without changing, any specified character or characters in its first operand. The programmer specifies which characters are to be searched for by inserting a nonzero character in the second operand. Typically, most of the characters in the second operand will be zeros (X'00'), and the nonzero characters will be the hexadecimal representations of the characters for which we are searching. Since the values in the second operand are repeated so much, it is easier to construct the table for TRT than for TR.

EXAMPLE 13.7

Suppose we want a table to use to search for a period (X'4B'). TABLE could be declared as follows:

```
TABLE   DC     75X'00'           HEXADECIMAL 4B = DECIMAL 75
        DC     X'4B'             A NONZERO CHARACTER
        DC     180X'00'
```

The nonzero value (4B) is placed in the seventy-sixth character position of the TABLE. Hexadecimal 4B is decimal 75, so there are 75 characters (including X'00') before 4B in the table, all of which are set to zero. Since 256 different character values can be represented by 1 byte each, there are 256 characters in the table, and the remaining 180 are all zero also.

TRT searches its first operand one character at a time, from left to right. As soon as it locates a character corresponding to a nonzero entry in the table, it stops searching. Otherwise, it stops after exhausting the entire first operand. If it does not find any character corresponding to a nonzero entry in the table, it sets the condition code to zero and does nothing else. If it finds a nonzero character in the table corresponding to one of the characters of the first operand, it does the following:

1. It stops searching.
2. It sets the condition code to 1 if the character is found before the last byte of the first operand, or to 2 if the character is found at the last byte of the first operand.
3. It loads the address of the byte found (in the first operand) into the last 24 bits of register 1, without changing the first 8 bits.
4. It loads the value from the table into the last 8 bits of register 2, without changing the first 24 bits.

In no case does TRT change either the first or the second operand.

In Example 13.7, locating a period in the string tested will cause hexadecimal 4B to be placed in register 2. Examining the contents of register 2 will show what was found. Instead of using the value 4B for period, which is equal to its EBCDIC value, we could use any nonzero value. For example, if we wished to determine whether a punctuation mark or a digit came first in a string, we could use 01 for all punctuation marks and 02 for all digits. Then, examining the value in register 2 would tell us which class of characters came first in the string.

These instructions can be written in explicit format. Explicit notation might be useful to locate a substring consisting of more than one character. If the address of STRING is in register 3, the following TRT statements are equivalent:

```
        TRT    STRING(20),TABLE          TRT    0(20,3),TABLE
```

EXAMPLE 13.8

Is the letter immediately after the first 'A' in STRING a 'B'? If not (or if there is no 'A'), place a zero in register 0. If the first occurrence of 'A' is followed immediately by a 'B', place in register 0 the number corresponding to the position of the 'A' in the string. For example, if the string is

```
XABC     place 2 in register 0
XXAB     place 3 in register 0
XXXX     place 0 in register 0
AXB0     place 0 in register 0
```

```
        SR     1,1                ZERO REGISTER 1
        TRT    STRING(20),TABLE   LOOK FOR AN 'A'
        BZ     RETZERO            IF CC = 0, 'A' NOT FOUND
        CLI    1(1),C'B'          LOOK 1 BYTE BEYOND THE ADDRESS IN
                                     REGISTER 1
```

```
            BNE     RETZERO                 IF NOT EQUAL, 'B' NOT THERE
            S       1,=A(STRING-1)
* ADDRESS OF 'A' IN REGISTER 1 MINUS ADDRESS OF STRING, PLUS 1. (IF 'A' IS
* FIRST CHARACTER, THE ADDRESS IN REGISTER 1 MINUS THE ADDRESS OF STRING
* IS ZERO. WE WANT THE VALUE 1 THERE, SO WE SUBTRACT 1 LESS)
            LR      0,1
            B       DONE
            ...
RETZERO     LA      0,0
DONE        ...
TABLE       DC      193X'00'
            DC      X'C1'                   SEARCHING FOR 'A'
            DC      62X'00'
```

13.4 The Execute Instruction

In the preceding section, we learned how to translate and test a 3-byte string or an 80-byte string. But we cannot yet translate an n-byte string, where n is a variable. In the same manner, we cannot Move Character (Chap. 7) a variable number of bytes or PACK two operands (Chap. 9) of variable numbers of digits (bytes), etc. In each of these examples, we want to specify the length at the time the instruction is executed. Note that it is easy to modify an address by placing the address that we want in a register and using explicit notation for the instruction. But we cannot use a register to specify the length. The Execute (EX) instruction allows us to modify another instruction temporarily and execute that modified instruction.

The Execute instruction is an RX instruction. The first operand is a register of which only the last 8 bits will be used. The second operand is the location [symbolic name or explicit notation: D2(X2,B2)] of another instruction. This other instruction is placed with the DS and DC statements, so that it won't be executed independently of the EX instruction. Here is an example:

```
            EX      7,TRTA
            ...
STRING      DC      CL5'ABCDE'
TRTA        TRT     STRING(0),TABLE
```

Execution of the EX instruction does the following:

1. Makes a copy of the named instruction.
2. Logically ORs (Chap. 11) the last 8 bits of the first operand (R1) with bits 8 through 15 (the second byte) of the copy of the named instruction. (The named instruction is not changed in memory.)
3. Executes the instruction produced in step 2.
4. Returns control to the instruction after the EX instruction, unless the named instruction causes a branch.

The second byte of the named instruction generally is set to zero by the programmer, so that the logical OR produces the value in the last 8 bits of R1.

EXAMPLE 13.9

Suppose we wish to TR n bytes of STRING (up to 256 bytes), where n is contained in a variable named N which is a fullword binary memory location.

```
          LA     5,STRING
          L      7,N
          BCTR   7,0                  THE VALUE IN THE MACHINE LANGUAGE
*                                     INSTRUCTION MUST BE 1 LESS THAN
*                                     THE LENGTH
          EX     7,EXECTR
          MVC    LINE(20),STRING
          ...
EXECTR    TR     0(0,5),TABLE         LENGTH OF FIRST OP = 0
STRING    DC     CL20'...'
LINE      DS     CL121
```

The instruction to be executed

$$\text{EXECTR} \quad \text{TR} \quad 0(0,5),\text{TABLE}$$

is translated into machine language as follows:

```
        DC    00    5000...
        ↑     ↑     ↗ ⌒
        op    L    B1 D1 B2 D2
        code
```

Bits 0 through 7 hold the op code. Bits 8 through 15 hold the length, 0. (If the assembly language length is 0, then 0 rather than -1 is used in the machine language instruction.) The other 4 bytes contain B1 D1 B2 D2.

No matter what type of instruction is to be executed, the Execute instruction always modifies bits 8 through 15, the second byte. In an SS instruction, that byte holds the length(s). In this case, EX 7,EXECTR logically ORs the 0 in the second byte of the EXECTR instruction with the value in the last 8 bits of register 7. This operation produces the value from register 7 in the second byte of the copy of EXECTR. Then this modified instruction is executed. The MVC instruction is executed next.

In an SI instruction, bits 8 through 15 contain the immediate data.

EXAMPLE 13.10

Show how to move either a dollar sign ($) or a minus sign ($-$) to a number which has been formatted with EDMK. Use '$' if the number is positive and '$-$' if the number is negative. (Note: It is easier simply to use two MVI instructions to perform this task.)

```
          LA       1,PATTERN+6
          EDMK     PATTERN(8),PNUM
          BCTR     1,0
          BM       NEG
          ICM      B'0001',4,=C'$'
          B        NEXT
NEG       ICM      B'0001',4,=C'-'
NEXT      EX       4,EXMVI
          ...
PNUM      DC       PL4'...'
PATTERN   DC       X'4020202020212020'
EXMVI     MVI      0(1),X'00'
```

If PNUM is negative, the minus sign is ORed with X'00' in the MVI instruction. Otherwise the dollar sign is used.

Solved Problems

13.1 Can TRT be used to search for X'00'? Explain how if it can, or why not if it cannot.

Yes. Place a nonzero byte in the first byte of the table.

13.2 TRT cannot place a certain character in register 2. Which one? Why not?

X'00', which indicates that the character is not sought.

13.3 Devise a method to translate a 30-byte source string in the following way. The first occurrence of each capital letter is translated to the next letter in the alphabet (with wraparound, so 'Z' becomes 'A'). The next occurrence of the same letter is translated to the following letter, etc. Do not translate any other characters. Thus 'AA*ABA' would result in 'BC*DCE', while 'ZFZ' would become 'AGB'.

The algorithm that will be used is the following: Translate 1 byte at a time. Then amend the table by changing the byte just used to the next successive character. A second table will be used for this second step.

```
                MVC     CHANGING(256),PERMANET    COPY TABLE
                LA      3,30                      LOOP CONTROL
                LA      4,SOURCE                  ADDRESS OF CURRENT BYTE
                LA      5,CHANGING                ADDRESS OF TABLE TO CHANGE
        LOOP    SR      7,7                       CLEAR REGISTER 7
                IC      7,0(0,4)                  PLACE CHARACTER VALUE IN 7
                TR      0(1,4),CHANGING           CHANGE BYTE IN SOURCE
                AR      7,5                       ADDRESS OF BYTE IN CHANGING
                TR      0(1,7),PERMANET           CHANGE BYTE IN CHANGING
                LA      4,1(0,4)                  INCREMENT BYTE IN SOURCE
                BCT     3,LOOP
                ...
        SOURCE   DC     CL30'AA*ABA...'
        CHANGING DS     CL256
        PERMANET DC     CL256'...the table from Example 13.4...'
```

13.4 Write a portion of program to decode the string encoded in Example 13.4.

Use the TABLE of Table 13-1 with the thirteenth through the fifteenth lines changed as follows:

```
        DC      X'C0E9C1C2C3C4C5C6C7C8CACBCCCDCECF'
        DC      X'D0C9D1D2D3D4D5D6D7D8DADBDCDDDEDF'
        DC      X'E0E1D9E2E3E4E5E6E7E8EAEBECEDEEEF'
```

13.5 Write a portion of a program to determine if there is a sequence 'AB' in a certain 20-byte string.

```
                LA      3,STRING          3 HOLDS STARTING
        *                                   ADDRESS
                LA      7,19              7 HOLDS LENGTH MINUS 1
                LA      9,STRING+18       9 HOLDS END ADDRESS
        LOOP    EX      7,TRTINSTR        EXECUTE
                BZ      NOTFOUND          IF CC=0, 'A' NOT FOUND
                CLI     1(1),C'B'         LOOK 1 BYTE PAST THE
        *                                   ADDRESS IN REGISTER 1
```

CHAP. 13]   ADVANCED INSTRUCTIONS   327

```
                BE       FOUND              IF EQUAL, 'B' IS THERE
                LR       7,9                UPDATE LENGTH
                SR       7,1                UPDATE LENGTH
                LA       3,1(0,1)           UPDATE STARTING
*                                            ADDRESS PAST 'A'
                B        LOOP
NOTFOUND        ...
FOUND           ...
TABLE           DC       193X'00'
                DC       X'C1'              SEARCHING FOR 'A'
                DC       62X'00'
STRING          DC       CL20'ABCDE12345ZYXWU98765'
TRTINSTR        TRT      0(0,3),TABLE
```

13.6 What should be the maximum value of any character in the first operand of the following instruction, if the instruction is to work correctly?

```
           TR      FIRSTOP,=X'F0F1F2F3F4F5F6F7F8F9'
```

What does execution of this instruction do?

The largest value should be hexadecimal 9. The instruction changes hexadecimal 0 through 9 to character 0 through 9, respectively.

13.7 For the following TABLE, describe the limitations on the first operand of the TR instruction, and describe the effect of execution of the TR operation.

```
                TR       FIRSTOP,TABLE
                ...
TABLE           DS       XL240
                DC       X'F9F8F7F6F5F4F3F2F1F0'
                DS       XL6
```

The first operand cannot exceed 256 bytes. This table is designed to work with EBCDIC digits only. The operation changes the decimal numbers (in character format) from 0 through 9 into character format 9 through 0, respectively. It would change any other values to garbage.

13.8 Describe how to amend TABLE in Table 13-1 in order to use it in a TR instruction which will (a) change all capital O's to zeros, (b) change all lowercase letters to the corresponding capital letters, (c) change brackets ([ ]) to angle brackets (< >), and (d) change all lowercase L's to 1s.

(a) Change 'D6' to 'F0'

(b) Change '81' through '89' to 'C1' through 'C9'
Change '91' through '99' to 'D1' through 'D9'
Change 'A2' through 'A9' to 'E2' through 'E9'

(c) Change 'AD' and 'BD' to '4C' and '6E', respectively

(d) Change '93' to 'F1'

13.9 Write a program segment to change an 80-character line of text from capital to lowercase letters except for the first letter of the line and the one letter which occurs immediately after the one period followed by a blank.

```
         TR    LINE+1(79),UPTOLO
         TRT   LINE(80),FINDPER
         CLI   1(1),C' '           IS NEXT BYTE BLANK?
         BNE   ERROR
         TR    2(1,1),LOTOUP       CAPITALIZE SECOND
*                                  BYTE AFTER PERIOD
         ...
ERROR    ...
         ...
UPTOLO   DC    XL16'copy Table 13-1 except for lines 13 through 15'
         ...
               XL16'C0818283848586878889CACBCCCDCECF'
               XL16'D0919293949596979899DADBDCDDDEDF'
               XL16'E0E1A2A3A4A5A6A7A8A9EAEBECEDEEEF'
         ...
LOTOUP   DC    XL16'copy Table 13-1 except for lines 9 through 11'
               XL16'80C1C2C3C4C5C6C7C8C98A8B8C8D8E8F'
               XL16'90D1D2D3D4D5D6D7D8D99A9B9C9D9E9F'
               XL16'A0A1E2E3E4E5E6E7E8E9AAABACADAEAF'
         ...
FINDPER  DC    75X'00'
         DC    X'4B'               PERIOD
         DC    180X'00'
```

13.10 Construct a TR table to reverse the alphabet—that is, to replace every 'A' in a string by 'Z', every 'B' by 'Y', every 'a' by 'z', etc.

Use Table 13-1 with lines 9 through 11 and 13 through 15 amended as follows:

```
         DC    XL16'80A9A8A7A6A5A4A3A2998A8B8C8D8E8F'
         DC    XL16'90989796959493929 1899A9B9C9D9E9F'
         DC    XL16'A0A18887868584838281AAABACADAEAF'
         ...
         DC    XL16'C0E9E8E7E6E5E4E3E2D9CACBCCCDCECF'
         DC    XL16'D0D8D7D6D5D4D3D2D1C9DADBDCDDDEDF'
         DC    XL16'E0E1C8C7C6C5C4C3C2C1EAEBECEDEEEF'
```

13.11 Using Table 7-1 as necessary, construct a TRT table to locate the following.

(a) character zero   (e) hexadecimal 7A
(b) letter O   (f) either 'Q' or 'Z'
(c) comma   (g) either colon or semicolon
(d) hexadecimal DA

```
(a) 240X'00'         (c) 107X'00'      (e) 122X'00'          (g) 94X'00'
    X'F0'   ZERO         X'6B'             X'7A'                 X'5E'   ;
    15X'00'              148X'00'          133X'00'              27X'00'
(b) 214X'00'         (d) 218X'00'      (f) 216X'00'              X'7A'   :
    X'D6'    O           X'DA'             X'D8'    Q            133X'00'
    41X'00'              37X'00'           16X'00'
                                           X'E9'    Z
                                           22X'00'
```

13.12 (a) What decimal value should you put in the last 8 bits of R1 to execute (EX) a single-length SS instruction in which the length is 17 bytes?

(b) What decimal value should you put in the last 8 bits of R1 to execute a two-length SS instruction in which the first length is 5 bytes and the second length is 4 bytes?

(a) The value 16 should be used, because it is 1 less than the length required.

(b) Hexadecimal 43 is needed since *each* length is reduced by 1. This value corresponds to decimal 67, which is the value to be entered into R1.

13.13 A student mistakenly used Table 13-1 for the second operand in a TRT instruction. Was an error message produced? What most likely did occur?

No error message was produced. The first character in the first operand is "found" (unless that first character was X'00'). Its address is placed in register 1 and its value in register 2.

13.14 A student mistakenly used the following TRT table for a TR instruction. Was an error message produced? What most likely did occur?

```
TRTTABLE  DC    200X'00'
          DC    X'C1'
          DC    55X'00'
```

No error message was produced. All H's were changed to A's and everything else was changed to X'00'.

13.15 Since the capital letters and the digits are in the last four rows of Table 13-1, could the format of these four rows be changed from X to C?

No. The first byte, the last 6 bytes in lines 13 through 15, and the last 6 bytes in line 16 are not printable, and thus have no character equivalents.

13.16 Write a TRT instruction to find the address of the first occurrence of the character 'T' in the table in Example 13.4.

```
          SR    1,1
          TRT   TRTABLE(256),NEWTABLE   ADDRESS IS IN REGISTER 1
          ...
NEWTABLE  DC    227X'00'
          DC    X'E3'
          DC    28X'00'
```

13.17 (a) What change does execution of the following TR instruction cause?

(b) From what address does the first character take its value?

```
          TR    PATTERN(5),LOCATION
          ...
PATTERN   DC    X'0503010402'
LOCATION  DC    C'b12345'
```

(a) PATTERN is changed to C'53142'

(b) LOCATION+5

13.18 Write the declaration for a TRT table designed to locate the first occurrence of either an arithmetic operator (+, −, *, /) or a punctuation mark (any period, comma, question mark, colon, semicolon, apostrophe, or quotation mark). Show how such a table might be used.

```
TABLE   DC      75X'00'
        DC      X'01'        4B    PERIOD
        DC      2X'00'
        DC      X'02'        4E    PLUS SIGN
        DC      13X'00'
        DC      X'02'        5C    ASTERISK
        DC      X'00'
        DC      X'01'        5E    SEMICOLON
        DC      X'00'
        DC      X'02'        60    MINUS SIGN
        DC      X'02'        61    SLASH
        DC      9X'00'
        DC      X'01'        6B    COMMA
        DC      3X'00'
        DC      X'01'        6F    QUESTION MARK
        DC      10X'00'
        DC      X'01'        7A    COLON
        DC      2X'00'
        DC      X'01'        7D    APOSTROPHE
        DC      X'00'
        DC      X'01'        7F    DOUBLE QUOTE
        DC      128X'00'
```

The table could be used as follows:

```
        TRT     STRING(50),TABLE
        CLM     2,B'0001',=X'01'
        BH      ARITH
PUNCT   ...
        ...
ARITH   ...
```

The TRT instruction will place 01 in register 2 if a punctuation mark comes first, or 02 in register 2 if an arithmetic sign comes first.

13.19 Write a TR instruction that will place the first five characters of a 10-byte IN string into the last 5 bytes of a 20-byte OUT string, and the last five characters of IN into the first 5 bytes of OUT. The middle 10 characters of OUT are to be blanks.

```
        TR      OUT,BLANK
        ...
OUT     DC      X'060708090A0000000000000000000102030405'
BLANK   DC      C' '
IN      DS      10C
```

13.20 A student who wanted to test for the string 'AB' in an 80-character STRING declared BLANK DC 80C' ' immediately after STRING. Explain how this declaration could simplify the coding of the program.

The student could use TRT with a length of 80 instead of an EX instruction varying the length of the TRT instruction. Since the 80 characters beyond STRING could not possibly contain an 'A', there is no possibility that a string 'AB' could be found that is not in STRING.

13.21 Write a TRT instruction and table that can locate whichever is first on an 80-character input line—an equal sign or an open parenthesis.

```
              TRT     INLINE(80),EQORPAR
              ...
INLINE   DS    CL80
EQORPAR  DC    77X'00'
         DC    X'4D'              OPEN PARENTHESIS
         DC    48X'00'
         DC    X'7E'              EQUAL SIGN
         DC    129X'00'
```

The TRT instruction stops when either symbol is found. The rightmost 8 bits of register 2 will contain whichever function byte was found.

13.22 Write a program segment that will use TRT to find the length of a string in INPTLINE. The string is delimited by a dollar sign ($) on either side. Then use TR to encode the string by changing each character to the next, each digit to the next, 'Z' to 'A', and '9' to '0', using the table from Example 13.4, with the last line amended to

$$\text{F1F2F3F4F5F6F7F8F9F0FAFBFCFDFEFF}$$

For example,

```
Columns    1 2 3 4 5 6 7 8 9 10 11 12 13 ... 79 80
Given              $ A 3 B 2 Z 6 $
Produced           $ B 4 C 3 A 7 $
```

```
              SR    1,1                CLEAR FIRST BYTE OF REGISTER 1
              TRT   INPTLINE(80),DSIGN
              LR    3,1                ADDRESS OF FIRST $
              LA    3,1(0,3)           NEXT BYTE
              TRT   0(80,3),DSIGN      ADDRESS OF SECOND $
              SR    1,3
              BCTR  1,0                REDUCE TO MACHINE LENGTH
              EX    1,TRX
              ...
INPTLINE DS   CL80
DSIGN    DC   91X'00'
         DC   X'5B'                    DOLLAR SIGN
         DC   164X'00'
TRX      TR   0(0,3),TABLE
              ↑   ↑
           Length  Base register (where to begin)
        (ORed with value
         in register 1)
```

13.23 An 80-byte string INPUT contains a string of characters enclosed in single quotes. Write a program segment that will find the letter 'A' within the portion of INPUT that is within the quotation marks. A maximum of one such 'A' exists within the quotes, and no 'A' outside the quotes is to be considered.

	TRT	INPUT(80),QUOTE	FIND FIRST SINGLE QUOTE
	LA	3,1(0,1)	STARTING ADDRESS OF INCLUDED STRING
	TRT	0(80,3),QUOTE	FIND SECOND SINGLE QUOTE
	SR	1,3	ACTUAL LENGTH OF INCLUDED STRING
	BCTR	1,0	LENGTH FOR MACHINE CODE
	EX	1,TRTX	FIND 'A' IN INCLUDED STRING
	...		
TRTX	TRT	0(0,3),A	
QUOTE	DC	125X'00'	
	DC	X'7D'	SINGLE QUOTE
	DC	130X'00'	
A	DC	193X'00'	
	DC	X'C1'	
	DC	62X'00'	
INPUT	DS	CL80	

Supplementary Problems

13.24 Suppose we have used the definitions

C	DS	CL3
D	DS	CL5
TABLE	DC	XL10'A7B3C9D4E3F9A0BFC4D8'
	DC	XL10'E2F0A4B6CFDEE1F2A8B0'

What are the contents of C and D (in hexadecimal) after each of the following pairs of instructions is executed? In each case, assume that before the instructions are executed the contents of C and D are as follows:

$$C \quad 03 \ 07 \ 0E$$
$$D \quad 01 \ 09 \ 0B \ 04 \ 06$$

(a) TR   C(3),TABLE   (b) TR   C(2),TABLE   (c) TR   C(3),TABLE+2
    TR   D(5),TABLE   TR   D+1(3),TABLE   TR   D(5),TABLE+4

13.25 Suppose that X is a fullword binary number. Write assembly language instructions to produce a character string HEX which shows the hexadecimal representation of X. Use the following definitions:

X	DS	F
HEX	DS	CL8
TABLE	DC	CL16'0123456789ABCDEF'

If you need any other variables, show the definitions for them.

13.26 Suppose that we have read 80 columns from input into a character string called LINE. Columns 21 through 29 of LINE contain a number which we want to place into X, where X is defined by

$$X \quad DS \quad PL5$$

If the number is negative, the sign is represented by the character "−" immediately to the left of the first nonzero digit. Use TRT to find the minus sign, if there is one, and then pack the number into X. Assume that TABLE contains 256 bytes, where all bytes are zero except for the byte corresponding to the character "−".

13.27 Assume that you have read 80 bytes from input. You know that the input string contains two numbers, and you want to store the first of these numbers in A and the second in B. Both A and B are defined to be packed decimal numbers of length 6. There are only two numbers in the input string, but you don't know where either of them starts or how long either of them is. They are separated by a comma and some number of blanks. Neither of the numbers is negative. Use the TRT and the EX instructions to locate and pack these numbers. Describe the table(s) you need.

13.28 Write a program segment to change an 80-character line of text from capitals to lowercase except for the first letter of the line and every letter which occurs immediately after a period or question mark followed by a blank.

13.29 Write a program segment using TM (Chap. 11) and EX to determine which insurance plans an employee has. The employee's plans are represented by a bit string FLAG. A 1 means that the employee has a particular plan, and a 0 indicates that the employee does not have a plan. The possible plans are stored in an array CO containing eight strings, each 4 bytes long:

```
CO      DC      CL4'GHI'
        DC      CL4'HIP'
        DC      CL4'BLCR'
        DC      CL4'MDAD'
        DC      CL4'PRUD'
        DC      CL4'AETN'
        DC      CL4'HART'
        DC      CL4'TRAV'
```

If there is a 1 in the rightmost bit of FLAG, the segment should print TRAV; if there is a 1 in the leftmost bit, the segment should print GHI.

13.30 Write a function MAX like the one presented in Example 10.14, but which accepts as an additional parameter the length of the packed decimal array.

Chapter 14

Macros and Conditional Assembly

14.1 Introduction

In assembly language programming, certain operations are performed over and over again. While it is possible to write the instructions to perform these operations each time, it is easier and less conducive to error to write the set of instructions once and to use this module whenever it is needed. Subprograms are used this way, as are macro instructions, known as *macros*.

Though a macro has some similarity to a subprogram, it is not the same. A subprogram is assembled once and stored in memory once; each time it is called, the program branches to the code for the subprogram and executes that code (see Fig. 14-1). The instructions that form the subprogram can be reused several times.

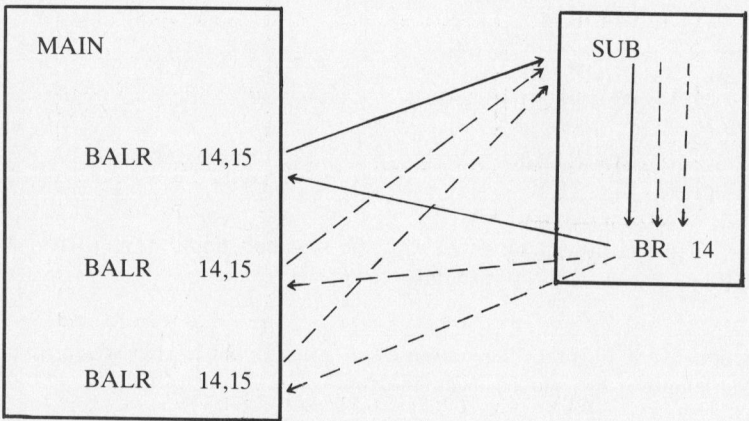

Fig. 14-1 Flow of control in three calls to a subroutine.

A macro instruction is written once, but the actual code is stored in memory each time the macro is invoked during assembly. When the macro is invoked, the instructions that comprise the macro are physically inserted into the program at the point of call (see Fig. 14-2). If a macro is invoked once, the instructions will be stored in memory once; if it is invoked three times, the instructions will appear in memory three times; if it is never invoked, the instructions will never appear in memory at all. The macro is simply a pattern or template to show which instructions should appear whenever the macro is invoked.

One advantage to using macros is convenience. The details of input/output are complicated and vary from one installation to another. If you have done any I/O on your system, by now you have already encountered some macros which have been written to make these tasks easier. In Assembler G and Assembler H, some of these are OPEN, CLOSE, GET, and PUT. In SPASM (a single-pass student assembler), they are READCARD, PRINTOUT, and PRINTLIN. In ASSIST, another student assembler, they are XREAD, XPRNT, XDECI, and XDECO. Your assembler may have others. In addition, there are SAVE and RETURN macros for subprogram linkage.

Whatever macros you have used, you have probably noticed that the code generated by using one of them is not 2, 4, or 6 bytes long, as is the code for other instructions. Instead, many bytes of machine code have been inserted into memory. These are the instructions which make up the macro. When you write your own macros, you will see more clearly how this works, but essentially a macro instruction is like a statement in a high-level language. Each macro invocation generates many machine instructions.

A subprogram may seem to have an advantage over a macro, since the subprogram's code exists in memory only once. However, a macro is much more flexible than a subprogram. Macros permit program modification at assembly time. Through conditional assembly, a programmer can write a macro that will generate one set of assembly language instructions under one set of conditions and another set of instructions under another set of conditions. This feature can be used to generate code that is very efficient, yet which would be too time-consuming for a programmer to enter manually. Second, using a macro can save the overhead involved in branching to a subprogram and loading and storing registers.

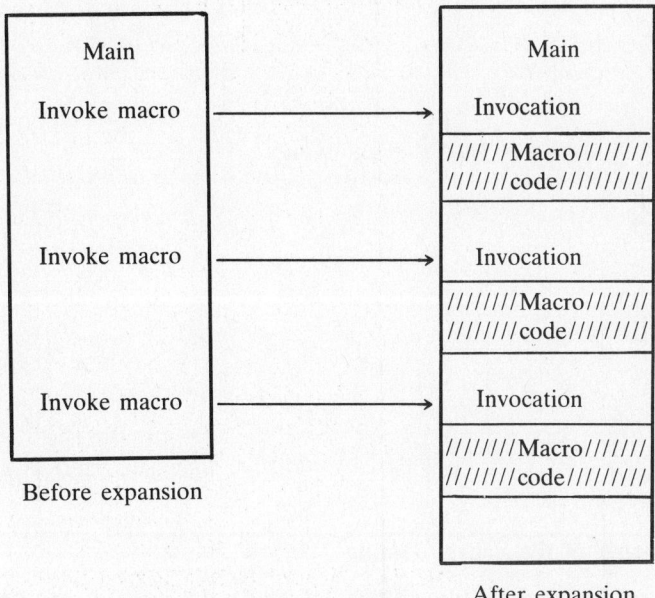

Fig. 14-2 Three invocations of a macro.

14.2 Simple Macros

Macro definitions appear at the very start of the source code, before the START or CSECT statement and before all executable code, including the BALR and USING statements. Several macro definitions may appear in succession in a program. However, although one macro may invoke another macro, no macro definition can be contained in another macro definition.

There are several parts to a macro, as shown in Example 14.1.

EXAMPLE 14.1

Let's look at a simple macro to see the placement of its several parts.

Operation Field	Operand Field	Name of Macro Part
MACRO		Header
ADD		Prototype—what the macro will look like when it is invoked
AR	2,3	Model statements—the statements that will be generated by the macro; also
AR	2,4	known as the body of the macro
MEND		Trailer—macro end

Macro expansion, also known as macro generation, is done as part of assembly, but before the assembler assigns any addresses or assembles any of the rest of the program. Each macro call is replaced by the model statements in the macro definition.

When invoked, the macro in Example 14.1 will generate the two model statements to be stored in memory and later executed. The action which it will perform at execution time is to add up the contents of registers 2, 3, and 4. This macro can be invoked in the calling program in the following manner:

```
        L       3,A
        L       4,B
        L       2,C
        ADD
```

At assembly time, this is expanded into the following:

```
        L       3,A
        L       4,B
        L       2,C
        ADD
+       AR      2,3
+       AR      2,4
```

The model statements generated are indicated by the plus signs, inserted by the assembler.

Controlling the Appearance of the Source Listing

If you have used system macros like OPEN or CLOSE, you probably have noticed that no statements are printed on your program listing as a result of invoking these macros. The printing of the generated statements is controlled by inserting one of the following statements into the program, starting in the Operation field:

       PRINT   NOGEN   suppresses printing of the generated statements

or   PRINT   GEN   causes generated statements to print

Any comments included in a macro definition in the normal manner (placing them in the Comment field, or making an entire line a comment by putting an asterisk in column 1) will appear in the source listing if the macro expansion is itself printed. It is possible, however, to insert into a macro a comment line that will not be printed with the macro expansion. This is done by placing a period (.) in column 1, before the *, which moves to column 2, as shown below:

*   THIS COMMENT LINE WILL BE PRINTED WITH THE MACRO EXPANSION
.*   THIS COMMENT LINE WILL NOT BE PRINTED WITH THE MACRO EXPANSION

It is also possible to print a message from a macro even if PRINT NOGEN is invoked. This is done by using MNOTE. MNOTE may be used to generate a comment in the source listing. It is usually used to print a message in the source listing if there is an error during macro expansion. MNOTE appears in the Operation field. Its format in some assemblers is the following:

       MNOTE n,'a character string message to be printed'

where n can be given a value that indicates the severity of the error. In other assemblers, the format is the following:

       MNOTE   'a character string message to be printed'

14.3 Symbolic Parameters

The macro introduced in Example 14.1 is not particularly useful, since all it does is add the contents of registers 2, 3, and 4. However, it is possible to make a macro more widely applicable by sending it parameters, called *symbolic parameters*. Symbolic parameters are simply placeholders placed in the macro definition. The real values will be substituted when the macro is invoked. If there are no symbolic parameters, as in Example 14.1, no substitution will be done.

The name of a symbolic parameter must start with an ampersand (&), followed by up to seven alphanumeric characters, starting with a letter. Symbolic parameters cannot start with &SYS, since this prefix is reserved for system variables (see Sec. 14.4). Thus legal names for a symbolic parameter might be &NAME, &R2, &COUNTER, or &REG4. Here is the prototype of the macro in Example 14.1, revised to accept parameters:

Name field	Operation field	Operand field
&NAME	ADD	&R1,&R2,&R3

This macro receives four parameters, &NAME, &R1, &R2, and &R3. &NAME will be matched with a label placed on the macro invocation; the other parameters will be matched up, left to right, with the parameters used in the Operand field of the macro invocation. Example 14.2 shows the complete macro from Example 14.1, revised to use symbolic parameters.

EXAMPLE 14.2

```
        MACRO
&NAME   ADD    &R1,&R2,&R3
&NAME   AR     &R1,&R2
        AR     &R1,&R3
        MEND
```

The symbolic parameters are identified in the prototype and then used in the model statements. Thus the label parameter &NAME is used in the first model statement, as are the symbolic parameters &R1 and &R2. The symbolic parameters &R1 and &R3 are used in the second model statement. Depending on the values sent in the invocation, this version of the macro can add up the contents of any three registers.

The invocation provides the actual parameters to be matched up with the symbolic parameters. It is important to note that the parameters are passed by name, not by value or by reference. That is, the assembler makes a character substitution of the actual parameters for the symbolic parameters.

The macro in Example 14.2 could be invoked by the calling program in something like the following manner:

```
        BL     HERE
        L      6,A
        L      7,B
        L      8,C
HERE    ADD    6,7,8
```

(Note that & is omitted in the parameters in the invocation.) In this case, the macro would be expanded to the following at assembly time:

```
        BL     HERE
        L      6,A
        L      7,B
        L      8,C
  HERE  ADD    6,7,8
 +HERE  AR     6,7
 +      AR     6,8
```

There are several things to note about this expansion. First of all, let's see how the matchup of parameters works, using the parameter 6 as an example. The 6 is matched up with &R1. Wherever the symbolic parameter &R1 appears in the model statements, the number 6 will be substituted. During the process of assembly, when this substitution is done, the assembler makes a character substitution of one symbol for the other, without paying attention to whether the symbol is appropriate for the position in which it is used. If, instead of 6, the first parameter were T, the assembler would generate the model statement AR T,7. Only when it tried to assemble the instruction would the error be detected.

Second, a few points about the label are in order. It is not necessary to put a label on the prototype or to use a label in the macro; the label facility is available in case one wishes to branch to a statement within the macro. A regular label without an ampersand cannot be placed on the appropriate statement within the macro, because the same label would appear each time the macro was invoked. If the macro were invoked more than once, this would create more than one instruction with the same name. Also, when a label is used, it is not necessarily attached to the first of the model statements; it is placed on whichever statement will be branched to. Finally, it appears that there are two statements with the label HERE after the macro has been expanded. However, the macro invocation is not stored in memory and has no address. Only the model statements appear in memory and have addresses; thus the label is attached only to the model statement. Even if the prototype has a label, we may choose to omit the label in some or all invocations of the macro.

A symbolic parameter doesn't have to represent a register. A symbolic parameter may be a variable, a constant, a literal, or a character string. Note, however, that no checking for the validity of the operands is done during macro expansion. Example 14.3 shows some of the other alternatives available.

EXAMPLE 14.3

```
        MACRO
&LAB    MULT    &Z,&Y,&BASE
&LAB    STM     4,5,SAVE
        L       5,&Z
        M       4,&Y
        ST      5,0(0,&BASE)
        LM     4,5,SAVE
        MEND
```

The invocation for this macro could be something like the following:

```
        LA      7,RESULT
NEXT    MULT    A,=F'35',7
```

This example multiplies the first two parameters, A and the literal 35, and stores the result at the address provided in the third parameter, register 7, which contains the address of RESULT.

The statements generated by this macro would be the following:

```
+NEXT   STM     4,5,SAVE
+       L       5,A
+       M       4,=F'35'
+       ST      5,0(0,7)
+       LM      4,5,SAVE
```

Note that this macro uses registers 4 and 5. Since the programmer may not expect any change in the contents of these registers, the macro must store their contents before using them and reload their contents at the end. SAVE must be declared within the program unit in which the macro is invoked.

EXAMPLE 14.4

It would also be possible to use the following variant on the above example, sending the even register as one of the operands:

```
        MACRO
&LAB    MULT    &Z,&Y,&REG,&BASE
&LAB    L       &REG+1,&Z
        M       &REG,&Y
        ST      &REG+1,0(0,&BASE)
        MEND
```

The invocation for this macro could be something like the following, where register 4 is now a parameter:

```
        LA      7,RESULT
NEXT    MULT    A,=F'35',4,7
```

The statements generated by this macro would be the following:

```
+NEXT   L       4+1,A
+       M       4,=F'35'
+       ST      4+1,0(0,7)
```

The macro does not need to save the registers, since the calling program knew which registers would be used for multiplication. In particular, note that only one of the two registers of the even-odd pair need be sent, since the other can be generated by &REG+1. This produces the instruction L   4+1,A. This format, though unusual in appearance, is entirely legal anywhere in an assembly language program.

A macro might not use all its parameters at each call. In that case, it can be invoked with one or more of its parameters omitted. This can be accomplished by using the null string in place of the parameter in the invocation. Here is a macro invocation which sends values to match only the first, second, and fourth parameters.

```
LOC     ADD     NUM1,NUM2,,NUM4
```

The null string (a string of length zero) is used in place of the third parameter. Notice that this is not the same as a blank (NUM2,' ',NUM4), which is a string of length 1 and which would be actually used by the macro. Even worse, if we used a blank without quotation marks (NUM2, ,NUM4), then NUM4 would be considered to be a comment.

Concatenation

A macro can be made more useful by adding the facility of concatenation (joining), using symbolic parameters. Since a symbolic parameter is simply a string of symbols, it can be concatenated with other strings of symbols to produce different instructions or operands. This enables the macro to produce different code at each call, depending on its parameters.

EXAMPLE 14.5

Suppose we want to add together three variables, which are all either halfword, full word, or short or long floating-point numbers. We want to use the same macro to perform the addition in each case. In fact, we want to use not only the same macro but exactly the same model statements. Here is code which will add &A, &B, and &C and store the results at &A. &T tells the type of the other parameters.

```
            MACRO
&LABEL      ADD     &T,&A,&B,&C
&LABEL      L&T     2,&A
            A&T     2,&C
            A&T     2,&B
            ST&T    2,&A
            MEND
```

Placing a symbolic parameter to the right of another string of characters causes the two strings to be concatenated together. Depending on the value of &T, the string L&T will generate one of the following four instructions: L, LH, LE, or LD.

The macro is invoked in one of the following ways:

```
ONE     ADD     E,W,Y,Z     SHORT FLOATING POINT
TWO     ADD     D,F,G,L     LONG FLOATING POINT
THREE   ADD     H,M,N,J     HALFWORD
FOUR    ADD     ,R,S,U      FULL WORD
```

The first parameter is matched up with &T and provides the letter that is concatenated to the load, add, and store instructions to determine which type of operation they will perform. When &T is E, the macro generates LE, AE, and STE instructions; when &T is D, it produces LD, AD, and STD; when &T is H, it produces LH, AH, and STH. What about fullword numbers? The macro should just generate L, A, and ST. This can be done as in invocation FOUR, where we send a null operand to match &T. The null operand is indicated by a comma, which reserves its place (otherwise R would be matched with &T, S with &A, and U with &B, leaving nothing to be matched with &C). The value of &T is thus null; nothing is concatenated with the L, the A, and the ST, generating the appropriate instructions.

Note that we have selected register 2 in which to perform the addition, so that the instructions can be used for floating-point numbers as well as binary numbers. Instead, we could have used a symbolic parameter to represent the register number. Then we could have sent a value (a register number) on each invocation.

In order to concatenate a symbolic parameter to the left of another string, before an alphanumeric character or a left parenthesis, we must add another symbol. Suppose that we want to generate an RR instruction, such as LDR or LER. Attempting to concatenate by using L&TR would lead the assembler to try to concatenate L with symbolic parameter &TR. Therefore, we must insert a symbol to separate the symbolic parameter from the symbols concatenated to its right. The symbol used is a period. The instruction L&T.R becomes LDR when &T is D and LER when &T is E. It is also possible to use the null string in a concatenation between two symbols. When &T is null, L&T.R becomes LR.

Sublists

In a macro, we can also use as a parameter a sublist, which looks like an array. To create a sublist, we enclose the names of several parameters within a pair of parentheses. Then, within the macro, the elements of the sublist can be referred to by using subscripts designating the position of the element in the sublist. In Example 14.6, we rewrite Example 14.5 using a sublist.

EXAMPLE 14.6

```
            MACRO
&LABEL      ADD     &T,&Z
&LABEL      L&T     2,&Z(1)
            A&T     2,&Z(3)
            A&T     2,&Z(2)
            ST&T    2,&Z(1)
            MEND
```

Here is a possible invocation of this macro:

```
ONE       ADD    E,(W,X,Y)        SHORT FLOATING POINT
```

The sublist is enclosed within parentheses. The parameter E is matched up with &T, and the sublist is matched up with &Z. W becomes &Z(1), X becomes &Z(2), and Y becomes &Z(3). The macro expansion would be the following:

```
ONE       LE     2,W
          AE     2,Y
          AE     2,X
          STE    2,W
```

Notice that there is no period before the open parenthesis in the operands &Z(1), etc. The period is not used because this is not an example of concatenation. In the expansion of the macro, the parentheses disappear when the whole operand is replaced by one of the items in the sublist. If this were concatenation, the parentheses would remain in the expanded operand.

14.4 System Macros and System Variables

SAVE and RETURN Macros

Two simple system macros are the SAVE and RETURN macros. These do not have to be written by the user. Instead, they are provided by the system. They are used to save the registers at the beginning of a subroutine and to restore the registers and return to the calling program at the end of a subroutine. Typically, these macros are also used in a main program, since the main program is a subroutine called by the operating system.

The SAVE macro invocation usually appears as follows:

```
SAVE      (14,12)
```

The values in the sublist are the first and last registers to be saved by the STM statement it generates (the DS is for alignment on a halfword boundary):

```
+         DS     0H
+         STM    14,12,12(13)
```

Note that the SAVE macro assumes that register 13 contains the address of the save area to be used. At the beginning of an assembly language program, the operating system places the address of its save area into register 13. Therefore, before calling another subroutine, the programmer should save the contents of register 13, as shown in Chap. 10. Then, before invoking the RETURN macro, the programmer should restore the contents of register 13, also as shown in Chap. 10. Also notice that the macro supplies the displacement beyond register 13 appropriate for the first register specified.

The RETURN macro invocation usually appears as follows:

```
RETURN    (14,12)
```

The values in the sublist are the first and last registers to be loaded by the LM statement it generates. Like the SAVE macro, it supplies register 13 and the appropriate displacement for the first register specified. It also generates the statement returning control to the calling program. The statements generated by this invocation are shown below:

```
+         LM     14,12,12(13)
+         BR     14
```

System Variables

There are three system variables which can be useful—&SYSDATE, &SYSTIME, and &SYSDNX. &SYSDATE provides the date on which the program was assembled as an 8-byte string in the format mm/dd/yy. &SYSTIME provides the time of day the program was assembled as an

8-byte string in the format hh:mm:ss, using a 24-hour clock. Thus a program could use the following declarations in a macro:

```
DATE      DC     C'&SYSDATE'
TIME      DC     C'&SYSTIME'
```

If the program were assembled on Dec. 15, 1988, at 2:31 p.m., DATE would have the value '12/15/88' and TIME would have the value '14:31:00'.

&SYSNDX provides a four-digit number which increases by 1 for each macro expansion. This provides the facility for avoiding duplicate labels in the generated code. If placed in the Name field concatenated with another symbolic parameter or with a string, &SYSNDX will cause a different name to be used for each macro expansion. For example, suppose we use LP&SYSNDX as a label on a model statement. The first time the macro is expanded, &SYSNDX will have the value 0001, and the label will be LP0001. The next time, &SYSNDX will have the value 0002 and the label will be LP0002. If the same macro contains two different labels using &SYSNDX, such as L&SYSNDX and P&SYSNDX, each will start at 0001, generating L0001 and P0001 the first time, L0002 and P0002 the second time. The value of &SYSNDX does not change within a given macro expansion.

14.5 Keyword Parameters

The symbolic parameters which we have used so far can also be called *positional parameters*. That is, the value which each parameter takes on during macro expansion is determined by the position of the parameter in the prototype and of the value in the invocation.

If some of the parameters to a macro rarely change from one invocation to another, there is a better option. There is another kind of parameter, called a *keyword parameter*, whose value is determined not by its position, but by a keyword associated with the value both in the prototype and in the invocation. A normal or default value is specified in the prototype as follows:

```
          MACRO
&NAME     MULT   &NUM1,&NUM2,&REG=2
```

Here, the default value for keyword parameter &REG is 2. A value must be specified for a keyword parameter in the invocation only if the new value differs from the default; otherwise, the default value is used. Thus, if no different register is specified for &REG in the invocation for MULT, it will have the value 2. An invocation which uses the default value for this macro would be the following:

```
HERE      MULT   X,Y
```

The macro would produce instructions to multiply X and Y using the 2-3 register pair. If the keyword is given a new value in the invocation, the new value overrides the default value. Should we wish to use a different register pair at a later time, the invocation which changes the keyword parameter might be the following:

```
TOP       MULT   R,S,REG=4
```

The macro would produce instructions to multiply R and S using the 4-5 register pair. Note that in the invocation, the & is omitted from the name of the keyword; in all other respects it must have the same name as in the prototype.

It is also possible to give a keyword parameter a null value as the default. This means that, if no value is supplied in the invocation, the parameter has a null value. This is specified in the prototype in the following manner:

```
&NAME     ADD    &NUM,&NUM2,&T=
          L&T    2,&NUM
          A&T    2,&NUM2
```

In this case, since &T specifies the type of the operands, a null value for &T would mean that we are adding fullword variables. An invocation that intended to use the null value would send parameters to match only &NUM and &NUM2.

If a macro uses both positional and keyword parameters, the positional parameters should appear first in the prototype and the invocation (this is required for some assemblers).

14.6 Set Symbols

Macros can use symbols other than symbolic parameters. In particular, they use *set symbols*. Set symbols follow the same naming conventions as symbolic parameters, but differ from symbolic parameters in a major way. A symbolic parameter takes on a value—essentially, a character string—at assembly time, when the macro is invoked. Once established for a given macro invocation, the value of a symbolic parameter can't be changed. In contrast, set symbols are true variables. They also take on values—numeric, character, or boolean—at assembly time; however, these values can be changed within the macro as it is being assembled. Set symbols are temporary storage areas and have no validity at execution time. Set symbols are used to help create the assembly language statements needed by the current invocation of the macro. They can be used to do looping during macro expansion, or to create new variable names or varying versions of assembly language instructions during macro expansion.

Global versus Local Set Symbols

There are six different kinds of set symbols—two classes of three types each. The classes are local and global set symbols. Local set symbols, like local variables in a subprogram, have meaning only within a given macro invocation. If &CT starts at 1 and is incremented to 5 by the end of the macro, it starts at 1 again when the macro is next invoked. If the same name is used for a local set symbol in two different macros, they are two different set symbols. Global set symbols, in contrast, retain their value from one macro invocation to the next; they can be used to communicate between macro invocations (and between different macros). If global &CT starts at 1 and is incremented to 5 by the end of a macro, it starts at 5 the next time a macro that uses it is invoked. If the same name is used for a global set symbol in two different macros, it is the same set symbol. Global set symbols can even be used entirely outside a macro by declaring them after all macro definitions and before all regular assembly language statements.

The three types of set symbols apply to both local and global set symbols. They may be type A, B, or C set symbols. Set symbols must be declared after the prototype statement and before the model statements. The declaration for set symbols is LCL for local set symbols, and GBL for global set symbols. To this is appended A, B, or C, depending on the type (see Table 14-1). All global set symbols must be declared before any local set symbols. Here are some sample declarations:

```
         GBLA      &COUNTER
         GBLB      &FLAG
         GBLC      &ERRMSG,&NAME
         LCLA      &NUM,&CT,&T
         LCLB      &SWITCH
         LCLC      &MSG
```

Table 14-1 Kinds of Set Symbols

	Local	Global	Type of Value	Value Set By
A	LCLA	GBLA	Arithmetic	SETA
B	LCLB	GBLB	Boolean (1 for true, 0 for false)	SETB
C	LCLC	GBLC	Character	SETC

The declaration of a set symbol does not give it a value. That is done by the SET statement, which is again followed by A, B, or C, depending on the type of the set symbol (see Table 14-1). Set symbols can be assigned values anywhere within the macro definition.

Here are some sample statements giving values to a few of the set symbols declared above:

```
&CT      SETA    4
&MSG     SETC    'NO NUMBERS TO AVERAGE'
&FLAG    SETB    1
&CT      SETA    &CT+1
```

Type A Set Symbols

Type A set symbols can be given values which are self-defining terms, symbolic parameters whose values are self-defining terms, attributes L' or N' (see Sec. 14.7), or other set symbols. The elements which make up the value may be expressions using the arithmetic operators +, −, *, /, or parentheses. The operators follow normal precedence rules—multiplication and division, followed by addition and subtraction. Arithmetic operations produce integer results without leading zeros. (In division, the quotient is truncated.) A constant used on the right-hand side of a SETA cannot be signed. A SETA symbol which is not initialized explicitly is initialized to 0 by default. Here are some examples.

```
&CT      SETA    3              Value = 3    Self-defining term
&NUM     SETA    &NUM+&CT       Value = 3    Set symbols connected by +; &NUM initialized
                                              to 0 by default; &CT set to 3 in prior statement
&DISP    SETA    5              Value = 5    Self-defining term
&QUOT    SETA    &DISP/&CT      Value = 1    Truncation
&CT      SETA    −1                          Illegal
```

Set symbols may be concatenated to symbolic parameters or to other set symbols to create new names. The symbol & at the beginning of an identifier indicates either a symbolic parameter or a set symbol. The assembler recognizes two of these identifiers placed together as concatenation. At assembly time, the value of the set symbol will be converted to a character string without leading zeros, and then concatenated (as is done with symbolic parameters). If the set symbol has a negative numeric value, the absolute value of the set symbol will be used.

Example 14.7 shows some of the ways in which the features of set symbols can be used.

EXAMPLE 14.7

```
         MACRO
&NAME    MOVE    &TO,&FROM
         LCLA    &A,&B,&C,&D
&A       SETA    10
&B       SETA    12
&C       SETA    &A−&B
&D       SETA    &A+&B
&NAME    ST      2,SAVE
         L       2,&FROM&C
&D       SETA    &D+1
         ST      2,&TO&D
         L       2,SAVE
         MEND
```

Before we look at the invocation, let's examine the values given to the set symbols. &A gets an initial value of 10, and &B becomes 12. The value of &C is &A−&B, or 10−12, or −2. The value of &D is &A+&B, or 10+12, or 22. Later the value of &D is changed to &D+1, or 23.

The invocation of this macro is the following:

```
HERE     MOVE    FIELDA,FIELDB
```

The expansion of the macro is the following:

```
+HERE    ST      2,SAVE
+        L       2,FIELDB2
+        ST      2,FIELDA23
+        L       2,SAVE
```

FIELDB2 is produced by the concatenation of &FROM (which has the value FIELDB) with &C, which has the value −2. The absolute value of &C is used in the concatenation. FIELDA23 is produced by the concatenation of &TO (which has the value FIELDA) with &D, which has just been incremented to 23. The concatenations (&FROM&C and &TO&D) allow the generation of assembly language statements using different variable names each time. Of course, FIELDB2 and FIELDA23 must have been declared within the program unit which invoked the macro call.

Set symbols have values that are used during assembly rather than during execution. Therefore, they are used to control what happens during assembly. If a variable like SAVE, which is to be used at execution time, is used in a macro, as in Example 14.7, SAVE must be declared within the program unit which invoked the macro call.

Note that the set symbols do not appear within the macro expansion. Set symbols have meaning only at the time the macro is being expanded.

Type B and Type C Set Symbols

Type B set symbols can be given a value of 1 or 0, or a logical expression (see Sec. 14.7). If not explicitly initialized, a SETB symbol is initialized to 0 by default.

Type C set symbols can be given a value which is a character expression, a T′ attribute (see Sec. 14.7), a SETA symbol, or a character expression which has been produced through concatenation of other strings, including set symbols and symbolic parameters. All values assigned to type C set symbols must be enclosed in quotation marks, since the string produced after expansion will then be a character string. A blank can be concatenated into a string, as can boolean values and arithmetic values and operators. A period or an apostrophe can be included by using two consecutively. If not explicitly initialized, a SETC symbol is initialized to ′′ (a string of length 0) by default. The maximum length of a type C set symbol is 256 characters.

EXAMPLE 14.8

Here are some examples of type C set symbols. Assume that &PARAM is a symbolic parameter with the value 'LINE'.

			Value	Type of Value Given
&CT	SETA	7	7	
&CHAR	SETC	'DOG'	'DOG'	A string
&STR	SETC	'&CT'	'7'	A SETA symbol
&OPND	SETC	'&PARAM.(&CT)'	'LINE(7)'	A concatenated character expression
&PET	SETC	'&CHAR&STR'	'DOG7'	A concatenated character expression
&BLANK	SETC	'&CHAR &STR'	'DOG 7'	A blank is embedded
&ARITH	SETC	'&CT+1'	'7+1'	A string—no arithmetic is performed
&DOTS	SETC	'&CHAR..&CT'	'DOG.7'	Double period produces period in final string
&APOS	SETC	'&CHAR''''S'	'DOG''S'	Quadruple apostrophe produces double apostrophe in final string
&CT	SETA	&CT−8	−1	
&CH	SETC	'&CHAR&CT'	'DOG1'	Uses absolute value of SETA symbol in concatenation

Substrings

It is possible to take a substring of a symbolic parameter. If &PARAM is the name of a symbolic parameter, then '&PARAM'(f,n) will take a substring of the value of &PARAM that starts in position f and continues for n characters. If &PARAM is matched up with CHARVAL, declared as DC CL6'SUBWAY', then '&PARAM'(2,3) will have the value 'HAR', '&PARAM'(1,2) will have the value 'CH', and '&PARAM'(1,6) will have the value 'CHARVA'. Both f and n must always have values which are in the range from 1 to 256, and which have validity for the string in question. That is, no attempt may be made to access positions beyond the length of the string. Note that the parenthesized subscripts go outside the quotation marks defining the string whose substring is to be taken.

The values obtained by the substring operation may be used as values for SETC symbols, used in logical expressions (see Sec. 14.7), and used in concatenation to form other strings. Here are some examples of their use:

			Value
&PARAM			'CHARVAL'
&SUB	SETC	'&PARAM'(2,3)	'HAR'
&NEW	SETC	'&PARAM'(4,1).'EG'	'REG'
	MVC	LINE(5),=C'&PARAM'(5,3).'UE'	'VALUE'

14.7 Conditional Assembly

Conditional assembly is a very powerful feature of assembly language which allows branching and looping within assembly language statements at assembly time. This feature can be used to produce code which is tailor-made for a given problem. For example, suppose that we want the sum of the first few elements of an array. The most efficient code would be a Load, a few Adds, and a Store. This suggests that it would be desirable to have a set of macros, with each macro adding the first N elements of an array for different values of N. Instead, using conditional assembly, we can write a single macro which will allow us to specify how many elements we want added (see Example 14.9).

With conditional assembly, there may be looping involved, but it will be done at assembly time, not at execution time. At first, one might not see the difference here, because student programs are typically assembled each time they are run. However, in the real world, programs are assembled until they are correct; then they are not assembled again unless changes must be made. Thus a loop at assembly time may be performed once, while the more efficient object code which results may be executed thousands of times.

Branching

There are three branch operators in conditional assembly. AIF is a conditional branch. It is used in the following format:

Operation field	*Operand field*
AIF	(logical expression)sequence symbol

A logical expression is a comparison of two values—e.g., set symbols, symbolic parameters, or constants, or any of these combined with arithmetic operators—using one of the following operators:

EQ	Equal
NE	Not equal
GT	Greater than
LT	Less than
GE	Greater than or equal
LE	Less than or equal

A sequence symbol is like a label, but one that has validity only during macro expansion. A sequence symbol begins with a period followed by a letter and then from zero to six additional letters or digits.

Here is an example of an AIF statement as it might appear within a macro:

```
        AIF     (&A LT &B).NEXT
```

Notice that there is no space between the parenthesized logical expression and the sequence symbol. This statement says to test the logical expression. If it is true, that is, if &A is less than &B, it will cause a branch to the statement labeled .NEXT in the Name field.

Logical expressions can be quite complex, using up to 18 relational expressions and up to five levels of parentheses. In addition, they may use the logical operators AND, OR, and NOT. Logical expressions are evaluated using normal precedence of operations—NOT has the highest precedence, then AND, then OR. Expressions in the innermost parentheses are evaluated first. A signed number cannot be used as the right-hand side of a relational expression. Here is a more complex example:

```
        AIF     ((&A+1 LT &B*&C) AND (&T EQ 'E')).LOOP
```

A type B set symbol can take on the value of a logical expression. If one part of a logical expression doesn't vary, it is possible to use a SETB symbol for the nonvarying part and save testing it each time. Here is an example:

```
&SWITCH SETB    (&SORT EQ &LIM)
        AIF     ((&CT LT 9) AND NOT &SWITCH).LOOP
```

A second type of branching statement is AGO, which is an unconditional branch. It has the following format:

```
        AGO     sequence symbol
```

As a specific example,

```
        AGO     .LOOP
```

Whenever this statement is encountered, it will cause a branch to the statement labeled .LOOP in the Name field.

The third kind of branching statement does not actually cause a branch. It is the ANOP, or No Operation, statement. The ANOP statement causes no operation to be performed, but it can be labeled. Since a statement cannot be labeled with both a sequence symbol and a symbolic parameter label or a regular label, inserting an ANOP with a label before the target allows the target to be labeled in two ways. (See Example 14.10.)

Conditional assembly depends heavily upon the use of set symbols, since their values can be changed during macro expansion. Example 14.9 shows the use of both conditional assembly and set symbols.

EXAMPLE 14.9

Let's write a macro which will sum a variable number of consecutive full words in memory, without using a loop at execution time. The macro will produce a series of Add statements instead.

```
        MACRO
&NAME   ADD     &START,&CT
        LCLA    &DISP
&DISP   SETA    4
&NAME   ST      2,SAVE
        L       2,&START
.LOOP   A       2,&START+&DISP
&DISP   SETA    &DISP+4
        AIF     (&DISP LT 4*&CT).LOOP
        ST      2,SUM
        L       2,SAVE
        MEND
```

Here &START is the first full word in the list of numbers to be summed. &CT is the number of elements to be summed. They are symbolic parameters. &DISP is a set symbol which consecutively holds 4, 8, 12, ..., 4*&CT. The logical expression in the AIF statement says "If &DISP is less than 4 times the number of elements, branch to .LOOP." This branching causes the Add model statement to be generated again, using a new value of &DISP, and causes &DISP to be incremented again. Let's see what happens if the invocation is the following:

```
HERE    ADD    NUM,6
```

The macro expansion is the following:

```
HERE    ST     2,SAVE
        L      2,NUMS
        A      2,NUMS+4
        A      2,NUMS+8
        A      2,NUMS+12
        A      2,NUMS+16
        A      2,NUMS+20
        ST     2,SUM
        L      2,SAVE
```

With branching comes the possibility of performing different types of operations within a macro, and having the macro end in different places. The MEXIT instruction allows the macro to end at some place other than the MEND statement, if one branch should terminate while the other does not. In addition, there are several useful tests that can be performed to determine which segment of code should be expanded.

A method of branching that can be used anywhere in a program, but that is especially useful in a macro because it doesn't require a label, is the following:

$$B \quad *+n$$

where n is the number of bytes from the beginning of the branch instruction to the beginning of the destination of the branch (see Example 14.10).

Attributes and Tests

There are several attributes of symbolic parameters that can be tested within a logical expression to determine the direction of a branch. The important attributes are type, number, length, and count. Two further attributes are scaling and integer, which have to do with the number of significant digits and the location of the decimal point in fixed and floating-point constants. We will not discuss these two attributes.

Type

The test for type is done by placing T' before the name of the symbolic parameter whose type is to be tested; for example, T'&A. This test returns a single character which represents the type of the symbolic parameter. Some of the possible types are the following:

A	Address constant or symbol	I	Machine instruction
C	Character constant or symbol	M	Macro instruction
D	Long floating-point constant or symbol	N	Self-defining term
E	Short floating-point constant or symbol	P	Packed decimal constant or symbol
F	Fullword constant or symbol	O	Omitted operand
X	Hexadecimal constant		

For example, if the value of &A is NUM, declared DC F'23', then T'&A has the value 'F'. This can be tested as follows:

```
        AIF    (T'&A EQ 'C').CHAR
```

The value returned from the type test is a character. In order to test it, it must be compared with a character in quotation marks. Since T'&A is not equal to 'C', no branch to .CHAR will be made. If &A had been a character constant, T'&A would have returned 'C', which would have caused the logical expression to be true, and the branch to .CHAR would have been made.

Number

The test for number permits testing the number of elements in a sublist. This can be used to control the number of times a conditional assembly loop is executed. The test for number is performed by placing N' before the name of a symbolic parameter, for example, N'&NUMS.

The test for number returns an integer corresponding to the number of elements in the sublist. If &NUMS has the value (W,Y,Z), then N'&NUMS has the value 3; if &NUMS has the value (W,,R), with the second operand omitted, N'&NUMS still returns 3, since it counts the number of commas and adds 1. If &NUMS is not a sublist, the number of elements is 1, and if the operand is omitted entirely (as we did with the value for &T in Example 14.5), the value returned is 0.

EXAMPLE 14.10

To see how the test for number is used, let's write a macro to find the maximum of a variable number of arguments, sent in as elements of a sublist, and to put the largest value in the variable MAXNUM, also sent as a parameter. The macro might receive anything from two to five numbers in the sublist. The macro invocation statement with four numbers as arguments would look something like this:

```
HERE      MAX     (NUM1,NUM2,NUM3,NUM4),MAXNUM
```

Here is the macro.

```
          MACRO
&NAME     MAX     &NUMS,&MAX
          LCLA    &CT
&CT       SETA    1
          AIF     (&CT GE N'&NUMS).ERR
          B       S&SYSNDX+4
S&SYSNDX  DS      F
          ST      2,S&SYSDNX
          MVC     &MAX.(4),&NUMS(&CT)
.LOOP     ANOP
&CT       SETA    &CT+1
          L       2,&NUMS(&CT)
          C       2,&MAX
          BNH     *+8
          ST      2,&MAX
          AIF     (&CT LT N'&NUMS).LOOP
          L       2,S&SYSNDX
          MEXIT
.ERR      MNOTE   'TOO FEW ARGUMENTS SENT'
          MEND
```

Here is the first expansion:

```
 HERE     MAX    (NUM1,NUM2,NUM3,NUM4),MAXNUM
+         B      S0001+4
+S0001    DS     F
+         ST     2,S0001
+         MVC    MAXNUM(4),NUM1
+         L      2,NUM2
+         C      2,MAXNUM
+         BNH    *+8
+         ST     2,MAXNUM
```

```
+         L      2,NUM3
+         C      2,MAXNUM
+         BNH    *+8
+         ST     2,MAXNUM
+         L      2,NUM4
+         C      2,MAXNUM
+         BNH    *+8
+         ST     2,MAXNUM
+         L      2,S0001
```

This macro uses the number of elements in the sublist to control the number of iterations of the conditional assembly loop, as well as to determine whether or not there is an error in the number of arguments sent to the macro. The set symbol &CT counts iterations of the loop, and is also used as the subscript of the elements in the sublist. The logical expression compares the current value of &CT with the number of elements in the sublist, determined by N'&NUMS. At the bottom of the loop, the value of &CT is always equal to the number of elements that have been compared. As long as &CT is less than the number of elements in the sublist, we will loop. When it is equal to N'&NUMS, we have finished.

Note these things about this macro. First, ANOP has been used to place a label on a statement that already has the name &CT in the Name field. Second, MNOTE has been used to produce an error message, if necessary, in the program listing. Third, the macro itself generates a fullword variable in which to save the contents of register 2. Since this is done each time the macro is invoked, the macro uses &SYSNDX to create a unique variable name each time. Moreover, since the declaration appears among executable instructions, we need to include B S&SYSNDX+4 to prevent execution of the DS statement.

After the first MVC, this macro will generate a series of load, compare, branch, and store statements. During execution, BNH *+8 causes a branch past the Store instruction to the next Load instruction so that we execute a Store instruction only when the value in register 2 is greater than MAXNUM. If, at any point, the value loaded into register 2 is greater than the value at MAXNUM, the store statement will be executed. Note that conditional assembly cannot be used to determine whether or not to generate the store statement, since the need for the store statement will be determined by the values in register 2 and at MAXNUM, which can be checked only during execution.

Length

The test for length of a symbolic parameter returns a number corresponding to the length explicitly associated with the symbol in the DC or DS statement. The test is performed by placing L' next to the name of the symbolic parameter, as in L'&STR.

EXAMPLE 14.11

Suppose &STR is a symbolic parameter associated with the variable

```
CHAR      DC     CL16'A LOT OF LETTERS'
```

L'&STR will return the value 16. This can be used as follows:

```
&SUB      SETA   L'&STR
          MVC    LINE(&SUB),&STR
```

Here the length attribute returns a value that is used to specify how many characters the MVC operation will be expected to move.

It is possible to test the length attribute in a logical expression as well. Here is an example:

```
          AIF    (L'&STR GT 16).ERR
```

The length attribute can also be used in arithmetic expressions and even outside of macro definitions.

Count

The count attribute tests the number of characters in the name of a variable symbol. If symbolic parameter &SYM is matched up with the variable ALPHA   DC   CL3'ABC', then the count attribute K'&SYM will return 5, for the number of characters in the name ALPHA. In contrast, the length attribute, L'&SYM, would return the value 3, for the length of the string 'ABC'. Both length and count return integer values which can be assigned to SETA set symbols. The count attribute can be useful in substring manipulation.

Other Tests

Since the name of a symbolic parameter is a character string, it is also possible to use the name as part of a test. Suppose we want to write a macro AVG to average the numbers in a sublist. In this example, the numbers can be either full word or short floating point, and the type is indicated by the first parameter, which is either E or null. In other words, the prototype is

```
&TOP       AVG     &T,&NUMS
```

Two possible invocations might be the following:

```
TOP        AVG     E,(ENUM1,ENUM2,ENUM3)
NEXT       AVG     ,(FNUM1,FNUM2,FNUM3,FNUM4)
```

The addition part of the macro can use the same model statements for both the fullword and the floating-point numbers. However, the division must be performed using different instructions, and there must be a branch. The test which could be used is the following:

$$\text{AIF} \quad (\text{'\&T' EQ 'E'}).\text{FLOAT}$$

This tests the value of the string &T, which has the character value of 'E' or ''. If it has the value 'E', we want to branch to the section of code that performs floating-point division; otherwise, we want to generate the section of code that performs fullword division. The full macro is shown in Example 14.12.

EXAMPLE 14.12

Assume that we do not know how many elements are in the sublist.

```
           MACRO
&NAME      AVG     &T,&NUMS
           LCLA    &COUNT
&COUNT     SETA    1
           STM     2,3,SAVE
           STE     2,SAVEE
           S&T.R   2,2
.LOOP      A&T     2,&NUMS(&COUNT)
&COUNT     SETA    &COUNT+1
           AIF     (&COUNT LE N'&NUMS).LOOP
&COUNT     SETA    &COUNT-1
           AIF     ('&T' EQ 'E').FLOAT
           SRDA    2,32
           D       2,=F'&COUNT'
           ST      3,QUOT
           AGO     .RESTOR
.FLOAT     DE      2,=E'&COUNT'
           STE     2,FLQUOT
.RESTOR    LM      2,3,SAVE
           LE      2,SAVEE
           MEND
```

The instruction S&T.R expands into SER or SR, depending on the value of &T, and the appropriate register 2 is then zeroed and used for the addition.

This macro branches in several ways. It compares &COUNT and the number of elements in the sublist to control the number of iterations of the addition loop. When &COUNT becomes greater than the number of elements that have been summed, the loop terminates. At that point, the macro decrements &COUNT to compensate for the extra increment and uses &COUNT to create a literal for the division. Then the macro uses the value of &T to determine whether to perform fullword division or short floating-point division. The AGO instruction guarantees that the registers will be saved after either division is performed. Alternatively, the macro could end as follows:

```
           ST      3,QUOT
           LM      2,3,SAVE
           MEXIT
.FLOAT     DE      2,=E'&COUNT'
           STE     2,FLQUOT
           LE      2,SAVEE
           MEND
```

With this approach, we could also save one of the ST instructions at the beginning by instead writing the following:

```
           AIF     ('&T' EQ 'E').SKIP
           STM     2,3,SAVE
           AGO     .NEXT
.SKIP      STE     2,SAVEE
.NEXT      S&T.R   2,2
```

Solved Problems

14.1 Write a macro ADDER that adds two fullword numbers and stores them at the location of the first number. The macro receives as parameters the register in which to do the addition, and the two operands.

```
           MACRO
&NAME      ADDER   &REG,&OP1,&OP2        ADDS TWO NUMBERS AND STORES
*                                          THEM IN FIRST OPERAND
&NAME      L       &REG,&OP1             LOAD OPERAND 1
           A       &REG,&OP2             ADD OPERAND 2
           ST      &REG,&OP1             STORE THE RESULT
           MEND
```

14.2 Write a macro ADDER2 that adds two numbers of the same type—F, E, D, or H—and stores them at the location of the first number. The macro receives as parameters the type of number, the register in which to do the addition, and the two operands.

```
           MACRO
&NAME      ADDER2  &TYPE,&REG,&OP1,&OP2  ADDS TWO NUMBERS OF SAME TYPE
&NAME      L&TYPE  &REG,&OP1             LOAD OPERAND 1
           A&TYPE  &REG,&OP2             ADD SECOND OPERAND
           ST&TYPE &REG,&OP1             STORE RESULT
           MEND
```

14.3 Write a macro USE to set up the BALR and USING statements for a program. The macro receives one parameter, the number of the register to be used as the base register.

```
                MACRO
&NAME           USE     &USEREG            SETS UP BASE REGISTER
&NAME           BALR    &USEREG,0
                USING   *,&USEREG
                MEND
```

14.4 Write a macro PROC to generate the statements necessary to save registers and establish addressability at the beginning of a subroutine. Its parameters are the base register for the subroutine and the name of the subroutine's SAVE area.

```
                MACRO
&NAME           PROC    &USING,&SAVNAM     MACRO TO SET UP THE
*                                            INITIATION OF A SUBROUTINE
&NAME           STM     14,12,12(13)       STORE REGISTERS 14, 15, 0 THROUGH 12
                BALR    &USING,0           SET UP NEW BASE REGISTER
                USING   *,&USING
                ST      13,&SAVNAM+4       STORE ADDRESS OF CALLING
*                                            SAVEAREA IN SUBROUTINE SAVEAREA
                MEND
```

14.5 (a) Write a macro RETURN to generate the statements necessary to return from a function. Its only parameter is the name of the function's SAVE area.

(b) Show how to call the system RETURN macro to return from a function.

```
(a)             MACRO
&NAME           RETURN  &SAVNAM            MACRO TO RETURN FROM A FUNCTION
&NAME           L       13,&SAVNAM+4       LOAD ADDRESS OF CALLING
*                                            PROGRAM'S SAVE AREA
                LM      14,15,12(13)       RESTORE REGISTERS 14 AND 15 WITH
*                                            THE INFORMATION WHICH WAS
*                                            PRESENT AT CALL TO SUBROUTINE
                LM      1,12,24(13)        RESTORE REGISTERS 1 THROUGH 12
                BR      14                 BRANCH BACK TO CALLING PROGRAM
                MEND
(b)
                LM      14,15,12(13)
                RETURN  (1,12)
```

It is necessary to write the first LM statement out instead of writing RETURN(14,15) since each call to RETURN produces a BR 14 instruction as well as an LM instruction.

14.6 Write the macro MULT with parameters A, B, C, REG, and OVER. MULT computes the product A * B using the even-odd pair of registers specified by REG. (REG must be even.) If the product can be represented in a full word, the product is stored in C. But if the product cannot be stored in a full word, the macro leaves C unchanged and branches to the address specified by the parameter OVER.

```
                MACRO
&HERE           MULT    &A,&B,&C,&REG,&OVER
&HERE           L       &REG+1,&A
                M       &REG,&B
                SLDA    &REG,32
                BO      &OVER
                ST      &REG,&C
                MEND
```

14.7 Write the macro MOD with fullword parameters A, B, and C and parameter REG. If B is not zero, MOD computes the remainder when A is divided by B, and stores the remainder in C. It uses the even-odd pair of registers specified by REG. (REG must be even.) On the other hand, if B is zero, MOD stores A in C.

```
            MACRO
&HERE       MOD     &A,&B,&C,&REG
&HERE       L       &REG,&B
            LTR     &REG,&REG
            L       &REG,&A
            BZ      *+12
            SRDA    &REG,32
            D       &REG,&B
            ST      &REG,&C
            MEND
```

14.8 Write the macro POWER with fullword parameters A, B, and N and parameters REG1 and REG2. If N is positive, POWER computes A to the Nth power, using the even-odd pair of registers designated by REG1 and the single register REG2. (REG1 must be even.) The result is stored in B. If N is zero, 1 is stored in B, and if N is negative, 0 is stored in B. Assume that the power will fit into one register.

```
            MACRO
&HERE       POWER   &A,&B,&NUM,&REG1,&REG2
&HERE       L       &REG2,&NUM
            SR      &REG1+1,&REG1+1
            LTR     &REG2,&REG2
            BM      *+20
            LA      &REG1+1,1
            BZ      *+12
            M       &REG1,&A
            BCT     &REG2,*-4
            ST      &REG1+1,&B
            MEND
```

14.9 Write the macro FLPOWER with parameters Z, Y, K, FPR, and GPR. FLPOWER computes Z to the Kth power and stores the result in Y. Here K is a fullword number, while Z and Y are short floating-point numbers. FPR and GPR specify a floating-point register and a general-purpose register, respectively, which can be used for the calculation. Assume that Z is not zero if K is zero or negative.

```
            MACRO
&HERE       FLPOWER &Z,&Y,&K,&FPR,&GPR
&HERE       L       &GPR,&K
            LE      &FPR,=E'1'
            LPR     &GPR,&GPR
            BZ      *+34
            ME      &FPR,&Z
            BCT     &GPR,*-4
            STE     &FPR,&Y
            L       &GPR,&K
            LTR     &GPR,&GPR
            BP      *+12
            LE      &FPR,=E'1'
            DE      &FPR,&Y
            STE     &FPR,&Y
            MEND
```

or

```
               MACRO
&HERE          FLPOWER   &Z,&Y,&K,&FPR,&GPR
&HERE          L         &GPR,&K
               LE        &FPR,=E'1'
               LTR       &GPR,&GPR
               BM        *+20
               BZ        *+26
               ME        &FPR,&Z
               BCT       &GPR,*-4
               B         *+14
               LPR       &GPR,&GPR
               DE        &FPR,&Z
               BCT       &GPR,*-4
               STE       &FPR,&Y
               MEND
```

14.10 Define macros to perform (a) fixed-to-float and (b) float-to-fixed conversions. (See Chap. 12.) Assume that D and UZERO, shown below, are defined globally.

```
               D         DS        D
               UZERO     DC        X'4E00000000000000'
```

(a)
```
               MACRO
&HERE          FLOAT     &Z,&NUM,&GPR,&FPR
&HERE          L         &GPR,&NUM
               LPR       &GPR,&GPR
               MVC       D(8),UZERO
               ST        &GPR,D+4
               LD        &FPR,D
               AD        &FPR,=D'0'
               L         &GPR,&NUM
               LTR       &GPR,&GPR
               BNM       *+6
               LCER      &FPR,&FPR
               STE       &FPR,&Z
               MEND
```

(b)
```
               MACRO
&HERE          FIXED     &NUM,&Z,&GPR,&FPR
&HERE          SDR       &FPR,&FPR
               LE        &FPR,&Z
               AW        &FPR,UZERO
               STD       &FPR,D
               L         &GPR,D+4
               LTER      &FPR,&FPR
               BNM       *+6
               LCR       &GPR,&GPR
               ST        &GPR,&NUM
               MEND
```

14.11 (a) Rewrite the answer to Problem 14.1 so that it uses a keyword parameter instead of a symbolic parameter for the register number.

(b) How will the invocation look if the default value of the keyword parameter is used?

(c) How will the invocation look if the default value of the keyword parameter is not used?

(a)
```
         MACRO
&NAME    ADDER   &OP1,&OP2,&REG=2        ADDS TWO NUMBERS AND STORES
*                                            THEM IN FIRST OPERAND
&NAME    L       &REG,&OP1               LOAD OPERAND 1
         A       &REG,&OP2               ADD OPERAND 2
         ST      &REG,&OP1               STORE THE RESULT
         MEND
```
(b) MAC   ADDER A,B
(c) MAC   ADDER A,B,REG=3

14.12 Write a macro CALL that does the setup to call a subroutine, including setting up and naming the parameter list. CALL receives as parameters the name of the subroutine, the name of the calling program's save area, and a sublist of the parameters.

```
           MACRO
&NAME      CALL    &SUBNAME,&SAVNAM,&PARLIST
*
*                                          SETS UP THE CALL TO A
                                              SUBROUTINE
           LCLA    &PAR,&PARLEN
&PAR       SETA    1
&PARLEN    SETA    N'&PARLIST
&NAME      LA      13,&SAVNAM             LOAD INTO REGISTER 13 THE
*                                            ADDRESS OF THE SAVEAREA
           B       C&SYSNDX               BRANCH AROUND TABLE STORAGE
P&SYSNDX   DS      0F
.LOOP      DC      A(&PARLIST(&PAR))      LOOP SETS UP PARAMETER LIST
&PAR       SETA    &PAR+1
           AIF     (&PAR LE &PARLEN).LOOP
C&SYSNDX   LA      1,P&SYSNDX             ADDRESS OF TABLE IN REGISTER 1
           L       15,=A(&SUBNAME)        ADDRESS OF SUB IN REGISTER 15
           BALR    14,15                  BRANCH TO SUBROUTINE AND SAVE
*                                            ADDRESS OF NEXT INSTRUCTION
           MEND
```

14.13 Write a macro ADDLIST that sums a group of numbers from a sublist and stores the sum at the location of the first number in the sublist. The numbers can be of types F, E, or D. The macro receives as parameters the type of the numbers, a sublist, and the number of the register in which to do the addition. The register should be 0, 2, 4, or 6.

```
           MACRO
&NAME      ADDLIST &T,&LIST,&REG          SUMS A GROUP OF NUMBERS
*                                            FROM A LIST
           LCLA    &COUNT
&COUNT     SETA    1
&NAME      S&T.R   &REG,&REG              CLEAR OUT REGISTER
.AGAIN     A&T     &REG,&LIST(&COUNT)     ADD THE NEXT NUMBER
&COUNT     SETA    &COUNT+1               INCREMENT COUNTER
           AIF     (&COUNT LE N'&LIST).AGAIN   CHECK IF FINISHED
.STORE     ST&T    &REG,&LIST(1)          STORE THE RESULT
           MEND
```

14.14 (*a*) Why can't the macro shown as the answer to Problem 14.13 be used to sum halfword numbers?

(*b*) How could we change the answer so that we could use the macro for halfword or floating-point numbers (but not for fullword numbers)?

(*a*) The macro cannot be used to sum halfword numbers because if &T had the value H, the instruction generated by S&T.R would be SHR, which is not a valid instruction.

(*b*) Change the S&T.R instruction to this: L&T &REG,=&T'0'.

14.15 Using conditional assembly, write a macro POWERS to generate code to perform exponentiation of fullword numbers by repeated multiplication. The macro receives as parameters the name of the fullword variable to be raised to a power, the power it is to be raised to (expressed as a number like 3, not a variable name), the even member of an even-odd register pair in which to do the multiplication, and the location at which to store the answer. Our objective is to produce a sequence of multiply instructions rather than a loop. Assume that the power is at least 0 and that the answer will fit into one register.

```
               MACRO
&NAME          POWERS  &NUM,&POW,&REG,&ANS      GENERATES CODE TO PERFORM
*                                                 EXPONENTIATION BY
*                                                 REPEATED MULTIPLICATION
               LCLA    &TIMES
&TIMES         SETA    0
&NAME          LA      &REG+1,1                 LOAD 1 INTO ODD REGISTER
*                                                 IN CASE POWER IS 0
.AGAIN         AIF     (&TIMES GE &POW).FIN     CHECK IF DONE
               M       &REG,&NUM                MULTIPLY NUMBER
&TIMES         SETA    &TIMES+1                 INCREMENT COUNTER
               AGO     .AGAIN                   RETURN TO TRY AGAIN
.FIN           ST      &REG+1,&ANS              STORE ANSWER
               MEND
```

14.16 Write a main program that uses the macro USE (Problem 14.3), then calls a subroutine POWER twice, using the macro CALL (Problem 14.12). POWER computes the cube of the first argument and stores the result in the second argument. It uses the macros PROC (Problem 14.4), POWERS (Problem 14.15), and the system RETURN macro.

```
MAC2        START    0
            USE      12
            ST       14,REGSAVE
            CALL     POWER,SAVEAREA,(10,PW)
            CALL     POWER,SAVEAREA,(PW,ANS)
            L        14,REGSAVE
            BR       14
SAVEAREA    DS       18F
PW          DS       F
ANS         DS       F
REGSAVE     DS       F
*
POWER       PROC     12,SAV2
            L        2,0(0,1)
            ST       2,NUM
            L        2,4(0,1)
            POWERS   NUM,3,6,ANSWER
```

```
              L      0,ANSWER
              ST     0,0(0,2)
              L      13,SAV2+4
              RETURN (14,12)
SAV2          DS     2F
NUM           DS     F
ANSWER        DS     F
              END
```

14.17 Rewrite the macro MAX from Example 14.10 so that it can find the largest of a sublist of either fullword binary numbers or short floating-point numbers. The type is indicated by the first parameter, which is either E or null. The macro will place the largest number in another variable sent in as the last argument.

```
              MACRO
&NAME         MAX    &T,&NUMS,&MAX
              LCLA   &CT
&CT           SETA   1
              AIF    (&CT GE N'&NUMS).ERR
              B      S&SYSNDX+4
S&SYSNDX      DS     F
              ST&T   2,S&SYSNDX
              MVC    &MAX.(4),&NUMS(&CT)
.LOOP         ANOP
&CT           SETA   &CT+1
              L&T    2,&NUMS(&CT)
              C&T    2,&MAX
              BNH    *+8
              ST&T   2,&MAX
              AIF    (&CT LT N'&NUMS).LOOP
              L&T    2,S&SYSNDX
              MEXIT
.ERR          MNOTE  'TOO FEW ARGUMENTS SENT'
              MEND
```

Supplementary Problems

14.18 Write a macro CVC to convert numbers from binary to zoned decimal format, suitable for printing. You may assume that the number is positive.

14.19 Write a macro CONVB to convert numbers from zoned decimal format to binary.

14.20 Rewrite the answer to Problem 14.8 using conditional assembly. The macro should generate one set of instructions if N is positive and another if N is zero. It will be difficult to test whether N is negative, so you may omit this possibility. In order to determine the value of N at assembly time, N must be sent in as a constant, such as 3 or 0.

14.21 Rewrite the answer to Problem 14.9 using conditional assembly. The macro should generate one set of instructions if N is positive, another if N is negative, and a third if N is zero. In order to determine the sign of N at assembly time, N must be sent in as a self-defining term (a literal such as =F'3' or a constant such as 3).

14.22 Write a macro to divide one halfword number by another, placing the quotient in &HWQUOT and the remainder in &HWREM.

Appendix 1

Assembly and Machine Language Instructions and Formats[1]

A.1.1 Selected Assembly Language Instructions and Formats

In the following table, an asterisk (*) indicates that the instruction sets the condition code.

Name	Mnemonic	Op Code	Format	Operands
Add*	A	5A	RX	R1,D2(X2,B2)
Add Register*	AR	1A	RR	R1,R2
Add Packed*	AP	FA	SS	D1(L1,B1),D2(L2,B2)
Add Halfword*	AH	4A	RX	R1,D2(X2,B2)
Add Logical*	AL	5E	RX	R1,D2(X2,B2)
Add Logical Register*	ALR	1E	RR	R1,R2
And*	N	54	RX	R1,D2(X2,B2)
And Register*	NR	14	RR	R1,R2
And Immediate*	NI	94	SI	D1(B1),I2
And Character*	NC	D4	SS	D1(L,B1),D2(B2)
Branch and Link	BAL	45	RX	R1,D2(X2,B2)
Branch and Link Register	BALR	05	RR	R1,R2
Branch on Condition	BC	47	RX	M1,D2(X2,B2)
Branch on Condition Register	BCR	07	RR	M1,R2
Branch on Count	BCT	46	RX	R1,D2(X2,B2)
Branch on Count Register	BCTR	06	RR	R1,R2
Branch on Index High	BXH	86	RS	R1,R3,D2(B2)
Branch on Index Low or Equal	BXLE	87	RS	R1,R3,D2(B2)
Compare*	C	59	RX	R1,D2(X2,B2)
Compare Register*	CR	19	RR	R1,R2
Compare Packed*	CP	F9	SS	D1(L1,B1),D2(L2,B2)
Compare Halfword*	CH	49	RX	R1,D2(X2,B2)
Compare Logical*	CL	55	RX	R1,D2(X2,B2)
Compare Logical Register*	CLR	15	RR	R1,R2
Compare Logical Character*	CLC	D5	SS	D1(L,B1),D2(B2)
Compare Logical Immediate*	CLI	95	SI	D1(B1),I2
Compare Logical Long*	CLCL	0F	RR	R1,R2
Compare Logical Character under Mask*	CLM	BD	RS	R1,M3,D2(B2)
Convert to Binary	CVB	4F	RX	R1,D2(X2,B2)
Convert to Decimal	CVD	4E	RX	R1,D2(X2,B2)
Divide	D	5D	RX	R1,D2(X2,B2)
Divide Register	DR	1D	RR	R1,R2
Divide Packed	DP	FD	SS	D1(L1,B1),D2(L2,B2)

---

[1] Appendix 1 is adapted with permission from the IBM System 370 Reference Summary.

Name	Mnemonic	Op Code	Format	Operands
Edit*	ED	DE	SS	D1(L,B1),D2(B2)
Edit with Mark*	EDMK	DF	SS	D1(L,B1),D2(B2)
Exclusive Or*	X	57	RX	R1,D2(X2,B2)
Exclusive Or Register*	XR	17	RR	R1,R2
Exclusive Or Immediate*	XI	97	SI	D1(B1),I2
Exclusive Or Character*	XC	D7	SS	D1(L,B1),D2(B2)
Execute	EX	44	RX	R1,D2(X2,B2)
Insert Character	IC	43	RX	R1,D2(X2,B2)
Insert Character under Mask*	ICM	BF	RS	R1,M3,D2(B2)
Load	L	58	RX	R1,D2(X2,B2)
Load Register	LR	18	RR	R1,R2
Load Address	LA	41	RX	R1,D2(X2,B2)
Load Halfword	LH	48	RX	R1,D2(X2,B2)
Load Multiple	LM	98	RS	R1,R3,D2(B2)
Load and Test Register*	LTR	12	RR	R1,R2
Load Complement Register*	LCR	13	RR	R1,R2
Load Negative Register*	LNR	11	RR	R1,R2
Load Positive Register*	LPR	10	RR	R1,R2
Move Immediate	MVI	92	SI	D1(B1),I2
Move Character	MVC	D2	SS	D1(L,B1),D2(B2)
Move Character Long	MVCL	0E	RR	R1,R2
Move Numeric	MVN	D1	SS	D1(L,B1),D2(B2)
Move with Offset	MVO	F1	SS	D1(L1,B1),D2(L2,B2)
Move Zone	MVZ	D3	SS	D1(L,B1),D2(B2)
Multiply	M	5C	RX	R1,D2(X2,B2)
Multiply Register	MR	1C	RR	R1,R2
Multiply Halfword	MH	4C	RX	R1,D2(X2,B2)
Multiply Packed	MP	FC	SS	D1(L1,B1),D2(L2,B2)
Or*	O	56	RX	R1,D2(X2,B2)
Or Register*	OR	16	RR	R1,R2
Or Immediate*	OI	96	SI	D1(B1),I2
Or Character*	OC	D6	SS	D1(L,B1),D2(B2)
Pack	PACK	F2	SS	D1(L1,B1),D2(L2,B2)
Set Program Mask	SPM	04	RR	R1
Shift and Round Packed*	SRP	F0	SS	D1(L1,B1),D2(B2),I3
Shift Left Double Arithmetic*	SLDA	8F	RS	R1,D2(B2)
Shift Left Double Logical	SLDL	8D	RS	R1,D2(B2)
Shift Left Arithmetic*	SLA	8B	RS	R1,D2(B2)
Shift Left Logical	SLL	89	RS	R1,D2(B2)
Shift Right Double Arithmetic*	SRDA	8E	RS	R1,D2(B2)
Shift Right Double Logical	SRDL	8C	RS	R1,D2(B2)
Shift Right Arithmetic*	SRA	8A	RS	R1,D2(B2)

Name	Mnemonic	Op Code	Format	Operands
Shift Right Logical	SRL	88	RS	R1,D2(B2)
Store	ST	50	RX	R1,D2(X2,B2)
Store Character	STC	42	RX	R1,D2(X2,B2)
Store Character under Mask	STCM	BE	RS	R1,M3,D2(B2)
Store Halfword	STH	40	RX	R1,D2(X2,B2)
Store Multiple	STM	90	RS	R1,R3,D2(B2)
Subtract*	S	5B	RX	R1,D2(X2,B2)
Subtract Register*	SR	1B	RR	R1,R2
Subtract Halfword*	SH	4B	RX	R1,D2(X2,B2)
Subtract Logical*	SL	5F	RX	R1,D2(X2,B2)
Subtract Logical Register*	SLR	1F	RR	R1,R2
Subtract Packed*	SP	FB	SS	D1(L1,B1),D2(L2,B2)
Supervisor Call	SVC	0A	RR	I
Test under Mask*	TM	91	SI	D1(B1),I2
Translate	TR	DC	SS	D1(L,B1),D2(B2)
Translate and Test*	TRT	DD	SS	D1(L,B1),D2(B2)
Unpack	UNPK	F3	SS	D1(L1,B1),D2(L2,B2)
Zero and Add Packed*	ZAP	F8	SS	D1(L1,B1),D2(L2,B2)

Floating-Point Instructions

Name	Mnemonic	Op Code	Format	Operands
Add Normalized, Long*	AD	6A	RX	R1,D2(X2,B2)
Add Normalized Register, Long*	ADR	2A	RR	R1,R2
Add Normalized, Short*	AE	7A	RX	R1,D2(X2,B2)
Add Normalized Register, Short*	AER	3A	RR	R1,R2
Add Unnormalized, Long*	AW	6E	RX	R1,D2(X2,B2)
Add Unnormalized Register, Long*	AWR	2E	RR	R1,R2
Add Unnormalized, Short*	AU	7E	RX	R1,D2(X2,B2)
Add Unnormalized Register, Short*	AUR	3E	RR	R1,R2
Compare, Long*	CD	69	RX	R1,D2(X2,B2)
Compare Register, Long*	CDR	29	RR	R1,R2
Compare, Short*	CE	79	RX	R1,D2(X2,B2)
Compare Register, Short*	CER	39	RR	R1,R2
Divide, Long	DD	6D	RX	R1,D2(X2,B2)
Divide Register, Long	DDR	2D	RR	R1,R2
Divide, Short	DE	7D	RX	R1,D2(X2,B2)
Divide Register, Short	DER	3D	RR	R1,R2
Halve, Long	HDR	24	RR	R1,R2
Halve, Short	HER	34	RR	R1,R2
Load and Test Register, Long*	LTDR	22	RR	R1,R2
Load and Test Register, Short*	LTER	32	RR	R1,R2

Name	Mnemonic	Op Code	Format	Operands
Load Complement Register, Long*	LCDR	23	RR	R1,R2
Load Complement Register, Short*	LCER	33	RR	R1,R2
Load, Long	LD	68	RX	R1,D2(X2,B2)
Load Register, Long	LDR	28	RR	R1,R2
Load Negative Register, Long*	LNDR	21	RR	R1,R2
Load Negative Register, Short*	LNER	31	RR	R1,R2
Load Positive Register, Long*	LPDR	20	RR	R1,R2
Load Positive Register, Short*	LPER	30	RR	R1,R2
Load, Short	LE	78	RX	R1,D2(X2,B2)
Load Register, Short	LER	38	RR	R1,R2
Multiply, Long	MD	6C	RX	R1,D2(X2,B2)
Multiply Register, Long	MDR	2C	RR	R1,R2
Multiply, Short to Long	ME	7C	RX	R1,D2(X2,B2)
Multiply Register, Short to Long	MER	3C	RR	R1,R2
Store, Long	STD	60	RX	R1,D2(X2,B2)
Store, Short	STE	70	RX	R1,D2(X2,B2)
Subtract Normalized, Long*	SD	6B	RX	R1,D2(X2,B2)
Subtract Normalized Register, Long*	SDR	2B	RR	R1,R2
Subtract Normalized, Short*	SE	7B	RX	R1,D2(X2,B2)
Subtract Normalized Register, Short*	SER	3B	RR	R1,R2
Subtract Unnormalized, Long*	SW	6F	RX	R1,D2(X2,B2)
Subtract Unnormalized Register, Long*	SWR	2F	RR	R1,R2
Subtract Unnormalized, Short*	SU	7F	RX	R1,D2(X2,B2)
Subtract Unnormalized Register, Short*	SUR	3F	RR	R1,R2

A.1.2 Machine Language Formats

The most widely used machine language formats are listed in Table A-1.

Table A-1 Machine Language Formats

Type	First Halfword		Second Halfword		Third Halfword	
Bits	0–7	8–15	16–19	20–31	32–35	36–47
RR	op code	R1 R2				
RX	op code	R1 X2	B2	D2		
RS	op code	R1 R3	B2	D2		
SI	op code	I2	B1	D1		
SS						
Single-length	op code	L	B1	D1	B2	D2
Two-length		L1 L2/I3	B1	D1	B2	D2

A.1.3 Condition Code Settings

Condition Code Setting	0	1	2	3
Mask Bit Value (decimal)	8	4	2	1

Arithmetic Instructions

Add, Add Halfword	0	<0	>0	Overflow
Add Normalized (Float)	0	<0	>0	....
Add Packed	0	<0	>0	Overflow
Add Unnormalized (Float)	0	<0	>0	....
Edit, Edit with Mark	0	<0	>0	....
Load and Test	0	<0	>0	....
Load and Test (Float)	0	<0	>0	....
Load Complement	0	<0	>0	Overflow
Load Complement (Float)	0	<0	>0	....
Load Negative	0	<0	....	....
Load Negative (Float)	0	<0	....	....
Load Positive	0	....	>0	Overflow
Load Positive (Float)	0	....	>0	....
Shift and Round Packed	0	<0	>0	Overflow
Shift Left Double/Single	0	<0	>0	Overflow
Shift Right Double/Single	0	<0	>0	....
Subtract, Subtract Halfword	0	<0	>0	Overflow
Subtract Normalized (Float)	0	<0	>0	....
Subtract Packed	0	<0	>0	Overflow
Subtract Unnormalized (Float)	0	<0	>0	....
Zero and Add Packed	0	<0	>0	Overflow

Compare Instructions

Compare, Compare Halfword	Equal	1st op low	1st op high	
Compare Logical	Equal	1st op low	1st op high	
Compare Packed	Equal	1st op low	1st op high	
Compare (Float)	Equal	1st op low	1st op high	

Miscellaneous Instructions

And	0	Not 0	....	....
Add Logical	0, no carry	Not 0, no carry	0, carry	Not 0, carry
Exclusive Or	0	Not 0	....	....
Insert Character under Mask	All 0	1st bit 1	1st bit 0	....
Move Character Long	Count equal	Count low	Count high	Overlap
Or	0	Not 0	....	....
Subtract Logical	....	Not 0, no carry	0, carry	Not 0, carry
Test and Set	0	1	....	....
Test under Mask	All 0s	Mixed	....	All 1s
Translate and Test	0	Incomplete	Complete	....

ASSIST Instructions (See Appendix 2)

XREAD	Success	EOF	....	
XDECI	0	<0	>0	No number

Appendix 2

Input/Output

A.2.1 Carriage Control

Carriage control characters are used to determine where a line is printed on the page. A character in column 1 of the output line tells the printer how many line feeds to insert. The following carriage control characters are provided:

	' ' (blank)	Single space
	'0' (zero)	Double space (1 blank line)
	'−'	Triple space (2 blank lines)
	'+'	No space (overprint)
	'1'	New page

A.2.2 SPASM I/O Instructions

SPASM is a system, useful for students learning IBM 370 assembler, which, among other things, provides statements (actually macros) for ease of input and output. The statements we will discuss are PRINTOUT, READCARD, and PRINTLIN.

PRINTOUT

PRINTOUT allows students to print out values of various memory locations and registers (but not arrays). The Operation field contains PRINTOUT, and one or more operands are used. For variables in memory, the name of the variable is used. For general-purpose registers, the register number is used. For floating-point registers, the numbers 16 through 19 are used for registers 0, 2, 4, and 6, respectively. An asterisk in the Operand field of PRINTOUT halts execution of the program. The format of PRINTOUT is as follows:

PRINTOUT	X	Prints out the value of X
PRINTOUT	A,B,C,2,16,*	Prints out the values of the variables A, B, and C plus the values in general-purpose register 2 and floating-point register 0, then halts execution of the program

PRINTOUT prints the values of its operands in the formats shown in Table A-2. For variables, the format selected by PRINTOUT is the one declared in the DC or DS statement for that variable.

Table A-2 Format of Output Printed by PRINTOUT

Variable Type		PRINTOUT Format
F	Full word in memory	Decimal (with minus sign if appropriate)
H	Halfword in memory	Decimal (with minus sign if appropriate)
P	Packed decimal	Hexadecimal (decimal digits and letter for sign)
E	Short floating point	Hexadecimal
D	Long floating point	Hexadecimal
C	Character	Character
General-purpose register		Hexadecimal and decimal
Floating-point register		Hexadecimal

READCARD

The READCARD instruction allows reading input from a line of data or a data card. The format is

$$\text{READCARD} \quad \text{INAREA,LOCN}$$

where INAREA is the start of the 80-byte memory location into which the input will be read. The second operand, which is optional, is the location to which to branch if the end of file has been reached. For example, if the instruction were

```
          READCARD  INLOC,EOF
          ...
EOF       ...
          ...
INLOC     DS        CL80
```

then all 80 columns of the input line would be stored at INLOC (which should be declared at least CL80). When the computer attempts to read data from input, but the end of file has been reached, the program will branch to the instruction labeled EOF.

PRINTLIN

The PRINTLIN instruction permits printing a line of data from a memory location. Its format is as follows:

$$\text{PRINTLIN} \quad \text{LINE,length}$$

Here, LINE is the area in memory to be printed, and the optional second operand is the number of columns to be printed. If no length is specified, a full 121-column line is printed. The information to be printed must have moved to this area prior to execution of the PRINTLIN instruction. The first character of the output line is reserved for carriage control, so a carriage control character should be moved to, or stored at, the first byte of LINE before execution of PRINTLIN. Note that with PRINTLIN it is not necessary to print a full 121-character line. Here is an example of the use of PRINTLIN:

```
          MVC       LINE(121),BLANK       BLANKS OUT LINE AND PROVIDES
*                                         BLANK FOR CARRIAGE CONTROL
          MVC       LINE+40(40),HEADING   CENTERS HEADING ON LINE
          PRINTLIN  A,13
          PRINTLIN  LINE
          ...
BLANK     DC        X'40'
LINE      DS        121C
HEADING   DC        CL40'THIS IS A HEADING TO ILLUSTRATE PRINTLIN'
A         DC        CL13' A SHORT LINE'    NOTE BLANK FOR CARRIAGE CONTROL
```

This will print A SHORT LINE, followed on the next line by the heading centered in a line of blanks. Note that 121 bytes will be printed by the second PRINTLIN statement no matter how long LINE is declared.

A.2.3 ASSIST I/O Instructions

ASSIST is a system, useful for students learning IBM 370 assembler, which, among other things, provides instructions (actually macros) for ease of input and output. The instructions we will discuss are XREAD, XPRNT, XDECI, and XDECO.

XREAD

The XREAD instruction allows reading input from a line of data or a data card. The format is

                XREAD   INAREA,length

where INAREA is the memory location into which the input will be read. The second operand is the number of columns from the 80-column line of input that will be stored at INAREA. For example, if the instruction were

```
          XREAD  INLOC,50
          ...
INLOC     DS     CL50
```

then the first 50 columns of the input line would be stored at INLOC (which should be declared of the appropriate size).

The XREAD instruction also sets the condition code. It sets the condition code to 0 to indicate that it has successfully read a record; it sets the condition code to 1 to indicate that the end of file has been reached and that no record has been read.

XPRNT

The XPRNT instruction permits printing a line of data from a memory location. Its format is as follows:

                XPRNT   LINE,length

Here, LINE is the area in memory to be printed, and the second operand is the number of columns to be printed. The information to be printed must have been moved to this area prior to execution of the XPRNT instruction. The first column of the output line is reserved for carriage control, so a carriage control character should be moved to, or stored at, the first column of LINE before execution of XPRNT. Note that with XPRNT it is not necessary to print a full 133-character line (or 121-character line, depending on your system). Here is an example of the use of XPRNT:

```
*         MVC    LINE(100),BLANK        BLANKS OUT LINE AND PROVIDES
                                        BLANK FOR CARRIAGE CONTROL
          MVC    LINE+45(40),HEADING    CENTERS HEADING ON LINE
          XPRNT  LINE,100
          ...
BLANK     DC     X'40'
LINE      DS     100C
HEADING   DC     CL40'THIS IS A HEADING TO ILLUSTRATE XPRNT'
```

This will print the heading centered in a line of blanks.

XDECI and XDECO

Numbers are read from input in character form and must be printed out in character form. However, they cannot be processed in that form, but must be converted to another form for arithmetic manipulation. Since these conversions are too complicated for a student just beginning to study assembly language programming, the ASSIST system provides relatively simple statements to do the conversions. XDECI converts a number from character form to binary form, placing the result in a register. XDECO converts a number in a register to character form suitable for printing.

The format of the XDECI instruction is as follows:

                XDECI   reg,locn

Locn is the memory location which contains the number in character form to be converted; reg is the register into which the resulting binary number will be placed. The character number may have from one to nine digits; it may include a plus or minus sign immediately preceding the first digit. Here is an example:

```
        XDECI  3,CNUM
        ...
CNUM    DC     C'17'
```

CNUM has the value F1F7, which will be converted to hexadecimal 11 and placed in register 3.

In addition, the XDECI instruction can be used to convert a series of character numbers from a given location. As part of its operation, the instruction places into register 1 the address of the first nondigit following the number which it has converted to binary. Then this address can be used in explicit notation to find the location of the next number to convert, and so forth.

Suppose we have this line of data:

```
         Column 10    14     36
                 ↓     ↓      ↓
                32    45     21
```

The following set of instructions will place the binary representation of 32 in register 3, the binary representation of 45 in register 4, and the binary representation of 21 in register 5.

```
        XREAD  INAREA,50
        XDECI  3,INAREA
        XDECI  4,0(0,1)
        XDECI  5,0(0,1)
```

The XDECI instruction skips over leading blanks to find a character number to convert.

The XDECI instruction also sets the condition code according to the value of the number it has converted:

Condition Code	Meaning
0	Number = 0
1	Number < 0
2	Number > 0
3	No number to convert

The XDECO instruction is almost the reverse of the XDECI instruction. It converts a number from binary to character form, suitable for printing. The format of the XDECO instruction is as follows:

XDECO   reg,locn

Reg is the register which contains the binary number to be converted; locn is the memory location into which the converted number will be placed. The character form of the number is right-justified in a field of 12 bytes; a minus sign is provided, if necessary, and leading blanks are supplied.

To print on one line the numbers converted in the XDECI example above, we can use the following code:

```
        MVC    LINE(133),BLANK
        XDECO  3,LINE+10        NUMBER IS FROM LINE+10 TO LINE+21
        XDECO  4,LINE+25        NUMBER IS FROM LINE+25 TO LINE+36
        XDECO  5,LINE+40        NUMBER IS FROM LINE+40 TO LINE+51
        XPRNT  LINE,133
        ...
BLANK   DC     X'40'
LINE    DS     133C
```

A.2.4 The SNAP Macro

Some assemblers automatically provide a dump of the registers and memory (a complete listing in hexadecimal of the contents of the portion of memory that was used by the program) at the end of execution of the program. Other assemblers provide this information only if there is an execution error in the program. Furthermore, sometimes a programmer may want to see a dump of the memory at some intermediate point in the execution of the program, as an aid to debugging the program.

There is a system macro, called SNAP, which can be used to provide a dump of any portion of memory (and the registers, if desired), at any selected points in the program.

To invoke the SNAP macro, one line must be added to the JCL (job control language). In the GO step, following

```
//GO.SYSIN DD *
```

and any input data used by the program, add the following line to identify the output file:

```
//SOKDUMP DD SYSOUT=A
```

Among the DC statements, add the following statement identifying the DUMPIT file:

```
DUMPIT    DCB    DSORG=PS,RECFM=VBA,MACRF=(W),BLKSIZE=882,             C
                 LRECL=125,DDNAME=SOKDUMP
```

Note several things about this statement. The full statement may not fit in 72 columns. If not, use a continuation line. Remember that a continuation line is indicated by adding some nonblank character (in this case, C) in column 72 of the first line, and that the continuation line must begin in column 16.

Next, in the program itself, do the following things. The file DUMPIT must be opened and closed. Somewhere near the beginning of the program, add the following statement (starting in the Operation field):

```
        OPEN    (DUMPIT,OUTPUT)
```

Somewhere toward the end of the program, close the file, using the following statement, again starting in the Operation field:

```
        CLOSE   (DUMPIT)
```

Now, put labels on the first and last statements for which you wish to see a memory dump. These bracket the area of memory which will be dumped. If you wish to see a dump of the entire program, put labels on the first and last statements of the program. Use these labels to replace the words BEGIN and LAST in the SNAP statement, which has the following form (starting in the Operation field):

```
        SNAP    ID=123,STORAGE=(BEGIN,LAST),PDATA=(REGS),DCB=DUMPIT
```

The SNAP statement itself is inserted in the program wherever you wish to take a "snapshot" of the contents of memory. Use a different number to replace 123 (in ID=123) each time you use the SNAP statement. This number serves to identify the dumps when they are printed. The section STORAGE=(BEGIN,LAST) identifies the portion of memory which will be dumped, from label BEGIN to label LAST. The section PDATA=(REGS) is optional, and, if specified, indicates that the contents of the registers should be dumped as well. The final statement simply identifies the file that has been used.

Appendix 3

Interrupts

Programs are run on the IBM 370 under control of the operating system (OS). The machine may be in either of two states, called *problem state* and *supervisor state*. Typically there are several programs in memory at the same time, and the operating system cycles through them, giving each of them a little bit of CPU time. This gives the appearance of having all the programs running simultaneously, each on a slower CPU. When the OS branches to a program to execute it, it puts the machine into problem state. When the machine is in problem state, a user program is running. When the machine is in supervisor state, the OS is in control, choosing which program to run, etc.

There are certain instructions that can be executed only by the OS, These instructions are called *privileged instructions*. Privileged instructions can be executed only in supervisor state. Since the only way to put the machine into supervisor state is to give control to the OS, only the OS can execute privileged instructions.

All I/O instructions are privileged instructions. This means that the OS, rather than the programmer, is responsible for handling all the details of I/O. For this reason, we have not discussed any of the I/O instructions in this book.

The commonest way for the OS to get control of the machine is through an *interrupt*. An interrupt may be caused by various exceptional circumstances, such as overflow, division by zero, or an invalid address, which are almost always errors in the program. The interrupt is a branch to a fixed point in the OS. When an interrupt occurs, the OS determines what caused the interrupt and decides what action to take. For example, it may print an error message and then either halt execution of the program or allow the program to continue, perhaps skipping the instruction that caused the difficulty.

There are quite a few different conditions that can cause interrupts. The ones we are concerned with occur when the machine finds that it is impossible to execute an instruction and produce the correct answer. This usually indicates that there is an error in the program. Examples of conditions that cause interrupts are:

Overflow: The answer is too large to fit into the space provided.

Zero divisor: If the divisor is zero, the answer is undefined.

Invalid data: The data for a packed decimal number is not in valid packed decimal format.

Invalid operation code: This usually means that we have erroneously branched into the data.

Invalid address: The effective address is outside the range of addresses allocated to the program by the OS.

In addition to these exceptional cases, there is an instruction called a Supervisor Call (SVC) which forces an interrupt and allows the problem program to request certain actions (such as I/O) from the OS.

It is possible for various interrupts to be masked off. There is a mask with 1 bit for each type of interrupt. These mask bits specify whether or not the interrupt is allowed to occur. A 0 bit suppresses the interrupt, while a 1 bit allows it to occur. For four of the interrupts, the mask bits can be set by the instruction Set Program Mask (SPM), which is not privileged. The other interrupts can be masked off only by the OS. The interrupts which can be masked off by SPM are:

Fixed-point overflow
Decimal overflow
Exponent underflow
Significance

The various bits that describe the status of the machine are collected into a 64-bit Program Status Word (PSW) on the IBM 360 and into several control registers on the IBM 370. Error messages often print the contents of the PSW in 16 hexadecimal digits (numbered 0 through 15). The parts of the PSW that are helpful in debugging programs are as follows:

Hexadecimal digit(s)	Bits	PSW Part
4–7	16–31	Interrupt code
8	32–33	Instruction length code
8	34–35	Condition code
9	36–39	Program mask
10–15	40–63	Address of next instruction

In particular, the last six hexadecimal digits of the PSW are the address of the next instruction to be executed. Since an interrupt occurs while executing the current instruction, this address is usually the address of the instruction after the instruction which caused the interrupt, and it can thus be used to locate the error.

Some interrupt codes useful for the beginning assembly language programmer are given in Table A-3.

Table A-3 Interrupt Codes

0001	Operation exception
0002	Privileged operation exception
0003	Execute exception
0004	Protection exception
0005	Addressing exception
0006	Specification exception
0007	Data exception
0008	Fixed-point overflow exception
0009	Fixed-point divide exception
000A	Decimal overflow exception
000B	Decimal divide exception
000C	Exponent overflow exception
000D	Exponent underflow exception
000E	Significance exception
000F	Floating-point divide exception

For example, if the PSW is

$$\ldots 000C7F1AB24C$$

a floating-point overflow has occurred. (The code for floating-point overflow is 000C.) The next instruction is at address 1AB24C. Thus the fifth through eighth hexadecimal digits indicate what happened, and the last six hexadecimal digits indicate where it happened.

Answers to Selected Supplementary Problems

Chapter 1

1.25 (a) 242 (d) 3967 (g) 3942 (j) 64207
(b) 3950 (e) 243 (h) 3903 (k) 3944
(c) 4067 (f) 61454 (i) 4061 (l) 4071

1.30
```
2)109           10)1101101
  ) 54  1          ) 110110  1
  ) 27  0          )  11011  0
  ) 13  1          )   1101  1
  )  6  1          )    110  1
  )  3  0          )     11  0
  )  1  1          )      1  1
       0  1               0  1
```

1.31 Step 1   64 is the largest power of 2 in 109
Step 2   109 − 64 = 45   1
Step 3   45 − 32 = 13   11
         13 < 16   110
         13 − 8 = 5   1101
         5 − 4 = 1   11011
         1 < 2   110110
         1 − 1 = 0   1101101

1.33 No. The first 1 in the 32-bit number is a sign bit, but the first 1 in the 64-bit number is a significant bit. The numbers are not negatives of one another.

1.36 (a) 1010 1010 1010 1010
(b) 0000 0000 0000 0000
(c) 1111 1011 1111 1111
(d) 0001 0000 0000 0000

1.37 The magnitude of each of the numbers is too large to fit into 16 bits. Parts (b) and (c) seem to fit into 16 bits; however, the first of those 16 bits would be considered the sign bit in the 16-bit number, while it was a significant digit in the 32-bit number.

1.38 (a) FFFFABCD   (e) 00001234
(b) FFFF8010   (f) FFFFC104
(c) FFFFCCCD   (g) 00007F5F
(d) FFFF80AC   (h) FFFF9031

1.39 When one divides a binary number by 10000 (equivalent to decimal 16), the remainder one gets is merely the last 4 bits:

```
                              10110 ←quotient
                     10000)101101110
                           10000
                           ‾‾‾‾‾
                            11011
                            10000
                            ‾‾‾‾‾
                            10111
                            10000
                            ‾‾‾‾‾
                             1110 ←remainder
```

The quotient is the original dividend with those last 4 bits removed. Hence dividing repeatedly by 10000 yields the last 4 bits, equivalent to the last hexadecimal digit, and the next 4 bits are produced by the next division, etc. Four bits are removed from the right each time, and can be converted to the single hexadecimal digit corresponding to them. This procedure explains why it is necessary to begin at the right when converting binary to hexadecimal in the procedure of Sec. 1.7.

```
                                          Remainders
                      10000)101101110        ↙
                          )    10110   1110 = E
                          )        1   0110 = 6
                                   0      1 = 1
```

The hexadecimal equivalent is 16E.

1.41
```
       60)20000
       60)  333   20
       60)    5   33
              0    5     Answer 5/33/20, or 5 hours, 33 minutes, 20 seconds
```

The largest power of 60 in 20000 is 3600 (60^2).

Step 2: $20{,}000 - 5 \times 3600 = 2000$ 5
       $2000 - 33 \times 60 = 20$ 5/33
       $20 - 20 \times 1 = 0$ 5/33/20

1.42
```
       A)7A32         2)7A32
        ) C38   2      )3D19   0
        ) 138   8      )1E8C   1
        )  1F   2      ) F46   0
        )   3   1      ) 7A3   0
             0  3      ) 3D1   1
                       ) 1E8   1
                       )  F4   0
                       )  7A   0
                       )  3D   0
                       )  1E   1
                       )   F   0
                       )   7   1
                       )   3   1
                       )   1   1
                            0  1
```

The decimal value, 31,282, is produced by dividing by 10; the binary value, 111 1010 0011 0010, is produced by dividing by 2.

Chapter 2

2.24 (a) L   3,N
              S   3,=F'7'

ANSWERS TO SELECTED SUPPLEMENTARY PROBLEMS

2.28 (a)
L	3,C	
S	3,D	C − D
ST	3,ANS	C − D
L	4,A	
S	4,B	A − B
S	4,ANS	A − B − (C − D)
ST	4,ANS	NEW ANS

2.34 The BR statement stops execution of the program, whereas the END statement stops the assembly of the program.

2.37 (a) 2 (d) 15,000,000 (g) 0
(b) 1 (e) 5,000,000
(c) 10,000,000 (f) −5,000,000

Chapter 3

3.61 (a) B2D05E00

(b) 32

(c) No. The first bit is 1, which would be interpreted as a sign bit. Thus the answer would be interpreted as some negative number (−1,294,967,296) instead of 3,000,000,000.

3.62 A large value (>2 billion) can be stored in two memory locations and later reloaded to be divided by another number.

3.63 Since the result is undefined, an error message is produced by the system, and the machine proceeds to the next instruction.

3.64 (a) Register 4: −1 (FFFFFFFF); register 5: −1,604,378,624 (the 2's complement of A05F2000 is 5FA0E000)

(b) Negative

(c) Quotient: FFFFC155; remainder: FFFECCE0

3.65 Only the first 2 bytes of the full word are used.

3.66 The 4 bytes starting at HW are used for the divisor, which in this case would have the hexadecimal value 00020003, equivalent to decimal 131,075.

3.67
L	3,A
L	4,B
ST	3,B
ST	4,A

3.71 The first three should give the correct answer, unless the product bc is greater than the value that can be held in one register. The fourth method will often result in dividing by zero. If $a > bc$, then the result of the first division is zero, because we get only the integer part of the answer. Division by zero is illegal.

3.72 A will hold 1, and B will hold 2.

3.74 Since x has m digits in base B,
$$B^{m-1} \leq x < B^m$$
Similarly,
$$B^{n-1} \leq y < B^n$$
Then
$$B^{m+n-2} \leq xy < B^{mn}$$
If $xy > B^{m+n-1}$, then it has $m + n$ digits; otherwise it has $m + n - 1$ digits.

3.75 (a) Q = 3, R = 2   (f) Q = −7, R = 2
(b) Q = 6, R = 18   (g) Q = −5, R = 3
(c) Q = 0, R = 8   (h) Q = 8, R = −12
(d) Q = −15, R = −3   (i) Q = 3, R = −8
(e) Q = −2, R = −5

Chapter 4

4.30 The op code.

4.31 The op code tells the type of instruction, which tells its length. When the length is added to the current address, that gives the address of the next instruction.

4.33 Accessing elements in an array is a familiar example.

4.34 There is no difference, since the contents of each register are added. In other instruction types, the error would make a difference.

4.35 R1 occupies a half byte. If there were more than 16 general-purpose registers, the number would require more than one hexadecimal digit, and R1 would take more room.

4.36 No. The base register in an explicit instruction may be any register (except 0). For example, in A 2,0(3,7) the base register is 7. Presumably, register 7 has been loaded (perhaps using LA) with the address of interest.

4.37 Machine language: X2 B2 D2; assembly language: D2(X2,B2). X2 and B2 are in the same order in each.

4.38 No. The machine language is the same whether the 0 is put into the assembly language instruction or not.

4.40 B   1AA35C
C   1AA35E
D   1AA360
E   1AA364
F   1AA368   BOUNDARY REQUIREMENT
G   1AA370   BOUNDARY REQUIREMENT

4.41 Put the D's first, then the F's, then the H's. Then there would be a minimum of wasted space. (That is how the assembler locates literals.)

ANSWERS TO SELECTED SUPPLEMENTARY PROBLEMS 375

4.42 What these statements place in memory (if anything) is not a legal instruction, except by sheer coincidence. A program interruption will almost always result.

4.43 The op code tells the computer what type of instruction is involved.

4.45
    LH   3,A+2   ANY REGISTER (ODD OR EVEN), SECOND HALF OF A
    MH   3,B+2   SECOND HALF OF B
    STH   3,X+2   SECOND HALF OF X

4.46 FFFFFFEB   (*Note:* The MH 2,B instruction uses the first 2 bytes of B, namely FFFF, equivalent to -1, not -32.)

4.47 The reference may be after the DS or DC statement; it must have a positive displacement, but displacement is measured from the USING statement and not from the instruction which contains the name.

4.48
    MH   3,NUMINCLS+2
    ST   3,ANSWER

4.50
(*a*) 1BD300   (4 bytes before 1BD304)
(*b*) 1BD300   (The literal would not have been there)
(*c*) 1BE2FC   (The calculation is shown below)

1000F denotes 1000 full words, which require 4000 bytes, FA0 in hexadecimal. The address of ARRAY would have been 1BD35C, and the address following ARRAY would have been as follows:

$$\begin{array}{r} 1BD35C \\ +\quad FA0 \\ \hline 1BE2FC \end{array}$$

The base address is 1BC402, so the displacement of the literal would be $1BE2FC - 1BC402 = 1EFA_{16} = 7930_{10}$. This displacement is greater than the maximum value permitted for any displacement.

Chapter 5

5.20 (*a*)   BNH   THERE
        HERE   ...

(*b*)   LTR   3,3

(*c*)   LNR   2,4   (LNR sets the condition code; there is no need for LTR)

5.21 (*a*) Use BNZ in (*a*) and BNE in (*b*).

(*b*) If you use compare, use BNE, but better still, use LTR 2,2 instead of C 2,=F'0' and keep the BNZ.

5.23 The second student is correct. The condition code could be set to zero if the original contents of the register were zero.

5.27

(*a*)				(*b*)		
	L	2,A			L	2,A
	C	2,B			C	2,B
	BNH	OUT			BNH	ELSE
THEN	L	2,=F'4'		THEN	L	2,=F'4'
	ST	2,Z			ST	2,Z
OUT	L	2,=F'1'			B	OUT
	ST	2,Q		ELSE	L	2,=F'3'
					ST	2,Z
				OUT	L	2,=F'1'
					ST	2,Q

ANSWERS TO SELECTED SUPPLEMENTARY PROBLEMS

```
         (c)           L     2,A          (e)           L     2,A
                       C     2,B                        C     2,B
                       BL    OUT                        BNH   THEN
               THEN    L     2,=F'4'                    L     2,C
                       ST    2,Z                        C     2,D
                       L     2,=F'3'                    BE    OUT
                       ST    2,Y              THEN      L     2,=F'2'
               OUT     L     2,=F'1'                    ST    2,T
                       ST    2,Q              OUT       L     2,=F'1'
                                                        ST    2,Q
         (d)           L     2,A
                       C     2,B
                       BNH   OUT
                       L     2,C
                       C     2,D
                       BL    OUT
               THEN    L     2,=F'2'
                       ST    2,T
               OUT     L     2,=F'1'
                       ST    2,Q
```

```
5.28  (f)  L    2,A        (g)  L    2,A
           S    2,B             S    2,B
           LPR  2,2             LNR  2,2
           ST   2,X             ST   2,X
           L    3,=F'7'         L    3,=F'7'
           ST   3,Y             ST   3,Y
```

Note that the high-level language statement could have been written more efficiently using the absolute value function.

5.37 (a) 0, 2, or 3   (b) 0 or 1   (c) 0, 1, 2, or 3

Chapter 6

```
6.25              SR    7,7             INDEX REGISTER
                  L     11,N
                  M     10,=F'4'        4 * N
                  S     11,=F'8'        4 * N - 8 = INDEX FOR ELEMENT N - 1
         LOOP     L     3,ARRAY+4(7)    LOAD ELEMENT I + 1
                  AR    3,3             DOUBLE VALUE
                  ST    3,ARRAY(7)      STORE ELEMENT I
                  LR    5,7             INDEX VALUE IN 5
                  LA    5,4(0,5)        INCREMENT BY 4 TO 4 * I
                  M     4,=F'1'         4 * I IN 5
                  D     4,=F'16'        IF I IS DIVISIBLE BY 4, 4 * I IS
         *                                  DIVISIBLE BY 16
                  LTR   4,4             IS THERE A REMAINDER?
                  BNZ   ELSE
         THEN     LA    7,4(0,7)        INCREMENT BY 4 EXTRA IF NO REMAINDER
         ELSE     LA    7,4(0,7)        INCREMENT BY 4 (MORE)
                  CR    7,11            CHECK FOR COMPLETION OF LOOPING
                  BNH   LOOP
```

ANSWERS TO SELECTED SUPPLEMENTARY PROBLEMS

6.26 (a) L   2,S+16   (d) L   2,D+492   (g) L   2,D+180
         ST 2,D+88   ST 2,D+352   A   2,E+68
                                                                                                                ST 2,S+88

      (b) L   2,D+496   (e) L   2,E+28   (h) L   2,S+288
         ST 2,S+196   ST 2,E+56   A   2,D+608
                                                                                                                ST 2,E+52

      (c) L   2,D+164   (f) L   2,D+496
         ST 2,E+68   ST 2,D+344

6.27 (a) D[2,17] := S[11]   (d) D[2,12] := D[1,13]
      (b) S[41] := D[4,4]   (e) S[88] := D[6,10] + E[3,8]
      (c) E[3,3] := D[4,11]

6.28 (a) L   2,C+280   (c) P := D[6,2]
         ST 2,V
      (b) L   2,C+400   (d) Q := D[4,5]
         ST 2,W

6.38 (a)
```
              LA     9,50
              SR     2,2
              SR     3,3
              SR     7,7
              SR     5,5           INDEX REGISTER
       TOP    L      4,NUMS(5)
              LTR    4,4
              BNM    NOTN
              LA     3,1(0,3)
              B      NEXT
       NOTN   BZ     ZERO
              LA     2,1(0,2)
              B      NEXT
       ZERO   LA     7,1(0,7)
       NEXT   LA     5,4(0,5)      INCREMENT INDEX
              BCT    9,TOP
```
      (b)
```
              LA     9,50
              SR     2,2           POSITIVE COUNTER
              SR     3,3           NEGATIVE COUNTER
              SR     7,7           COUNTER OF ZEROS
              LA     5,NUMS        BASE REGISTER
       TOP    L      4,0(0,5)
              LTR    4,4
              BNM    NOTN
              LA     3,1(0,3)      COUNT NEGATIVE
              B      NEXT
       NOTN   BZ     ZERO
              LA     2,1(0,2)      COUNT POSITIVE
              B      NEXT
       ZERO   LA     7,1(0,7)      COUNT ZERO
       NEXT   LA     5,4(0,5)      INCREMENT BASE
              BCT    9,TOP
```

6.44

(a)
```
                LA      4,G
                LA      3,20            REGISTER 3 HOLDS INDEX FOR
        *                                 G[1,6] TO SKIP FIVE ELEMENTS
                SR      2,2             REGISTER 2 HOLDS SUM
                LA      8,8             REGISTER 8 HOLDS LOOP COUNTER
        LOOP    A       2,0(3,4)
                LA      3,56(0,3)       INCREMENT 14 ELEMENTS, 56 BYTES,
        *                                 TO NEXT ROW
                BCT     8,LOOP
                ST      2,SUM1
```

(b)
```
                LA      4,G
                LA      3,168
                SR      2,2
                LA      8,14
        LOOP    A       2,0(3,4)
                LA      3,4(0,3)
                BCT     8,LOOP
                ST      2,SUM2
```

(c)
```
                LA      4,G
                SR      3,3             REGISTER 3 HOLDS INDEX
                SR      2,2             REGISTER 2 HOLDS SUM
                LA      8,8             REGISTER 8 HOLDS LOOP COUNTER
        LOOP    A       2,0(3,4)
                LA      3,60(0,3)
                BCT     8,LOOP
                ST      2,SUM3
```

6.45

```
                LA      11,TESTAV       11 HOLDS ADDRESS OF TESTAV ELEMENT
                L       9,N             9 HOLDS COUNT FOR OUTER LOOP
                LA      10,TEST         10 HOLDS ADDRESS OF ELEMENT OF TEST
        LOOP1   SR      3,3             3 WILL HOLD SUM
                LA      5,5             5 HOLDS COUNT FOR INNER LOOP
        LOOP2   A       3,0(0,10)
                LA      10,4(0,10)      INCREMENT ADDRESS OF ELEMENT OF TEST
                BCT     5,LOOP2
                M       2,=F'1'
                D       2,=F'5'
                ST      3,0(0,11)       STORE TESTAV[I]
                LA      11,4(0,11)      INCREMENT ADDRESS OF TESTAV
                BCT     9,LOOP1
        *                               NEXT SET OF NESTED LOOPS
                SR      8,8             8 HOLDS INDEX
                LA      9,5             9 HOLDS COUNT FOR OUTER LOOP
                LA      11,CLASSAV      11 HOLDS ADDRESS FOR CLASSAV
        LOOP3   SR      3,3             3 HOLDS SUM
                LA      10,TEST
                L       5,N
        LOOP4   A       3,0(8,10)
                LA      10,20(0,10)     INCREMENT TEST[I,J] ADDRESS BY 20
                BCT     5,LOOP4
                M       2,=F'1'
                D       2,N
                ST      3,0(8,11)       STORE CLASSAV[I]
                LA      8,4(0,8)        INCREMENT INDEX REG
                BCT     9,LOOP3
```

Chapter 7

7.51 A   C'AKT'
        B   C'012'
        C   C'9bb' or CL3'9'   (padded with blanks on right)

7.52 (a)–(c)   The character A is stored in each case.

        (d)–(f)   The string AA is stored in each case.

7.53 If NUM were padded with zeros on the right, you would get 11000000, which is the binary equivalent of 192 rather than 3. By padding with zeros on the left, you preserve the numeric values of binary and hexadecimal numbers. Character strings, in contrast, have no meaningful numeric value.

7.54 (a) E   (b) P   (c) }   (d) $ (e) None   (f) Blank

7.55 The string is changed to AAAB. (The last byte of the original string, which was represented by 11000001, has been changed to 11000010.)

7.56 (a)   MVC   PARAGRAF+300(60),PARAGRAF+240
            MVC   PARAGRAF+240(60),THIRD

        (b)   MVC   PARAGRAF+310(50),PARAGRAF+240
            MVC   PARAGRAF+240(70),THIRD

        (c)   MVC   TEMP(70),PARAGRAF+240
            MVC   PARAGRAF+290(70),TEMP
            MVC   PARAGRAF+240(50),THIRD

You cannot MVC PARAGRAF+290(70),PARAGRAF+240, or the last 20 bytes of the first sentence will be overwritten by the first 20 before they are moved. See the discussion following Example 7.7. Another way is as follows:

            MVC   PARAGRAF+340(20),PARAGRAF+290
            MVC   PARAGRAF+290(50),PARAGRAF+240
            MVC   PARAGRAF+240(50),THIRD

7.57 (a) STR1 would contain 1234. Four bytes are moved, corresponding to the declared length of STR1.

        (b) STR2 would contain ABCDA. Five bytes are moved: the ABCD from STR1 and the A then present as the first byte of STR2.

        (c) STR1 is AB12. STR2 is 34345. Four bytes are moved, corresponding to the declared length of STR1. (The +2 does not affect the default value.)

7.58 (a), (b) The length to be moved or compared exceeds the length of the literal, so some bytes of whatever follows the literal will be used. Note for part (b) that these are hexadecimal digits, two per byte, not characters.

        (c) G and H are not legal hexadecimal characters.

        (d) Fine. (The literal is padded with 8 hexadecimal zeros on the left.)

7.59 The instruction sets up a 1-byte literal memory location, containing the letter F. If the following three characters in memory happen to be ROG the condition code will be set to zero. Otherwise, the contents of those 3 bytes determine which operand is "lower."

7.60 CLC is an SS instruction, requiring two operands in memory, and F is inappropriate for character string 'TOP'.

7.61 For MVI LOC,C'X' use MVC LOC(1),=C'X'. The MVC instruction sets up a literal memory location, uses 2 extra bytes of memory for the instruction itself, and must take time to access the literal memory location, making the MVC form less efficient.

7.62 (a) 0
    (b) 1   (The 4 bytes starting at STRING1 are ABCA; at STRING2 they are ABCD.)
    (c) 0
    (d) 0
    (e) 2   (The 3 bytes starting at STRING1+2 are CAB.)
    (f) 0   (The X format value is the hexadecimal equivalent of ABCD.)

7.63 (a) 0   (b) 1 [blank (40) is less than period (4B)]   (c) 0   (d) 0

7.64 (a) 1   (c) 2   (e) 0
    (b) 2   (d) 1   (f) 1

7.70 (a) (i) The declaration reserves 4 bytes of memory. Because B was declared F, it is on a fullword boundary. (ii) The declaration reserves 4 bytes of memory. Because B was placed immediately after a fullword declaration, it is also on a fullword boundary.
    (b) The memory location declared for B in (ii) can be used for any purpose that the location declared in (i) can be used for, and vice versa.
    (c) No. The digits will be stored as fixed binary for the F format and as characters for the C format.

7.76 D205C202C20A
D502C206C20E
4740C102
92C3C205
92C3C20A

7.77 D20690006003
92F09007
95D290FF
0F24
1543

Chapter 8

8.18 ANS holds −100. The value loaded into register 2 is 0000100C. The Add instruction treats this as a binary number, and produces 0000100D as its sum. This is equivalent to −100 in packed decimal format.

8.19 (a) There is no use in checking for an overflow in this sequence. Since only 3 bytes of TEMP are transferred into a 3-byte field, there can be no overflow even if the bytes of TEMP which were not moved contain some nonzero digits.
    (b) If a check is desired, we should ZAP the entire TEMP value. If TEMP holds sufficient leading zeros, or if no check on overflow is required, each part accomplishes the same thing [but part (b) is easier to write].

8.20 The quotient of the DP operation is placed in QUOT and the remainder in REM with no further ZAP operations required.

	QUOT	REM
After ZAP	00 00 00 00 00	02 02 1C
After DP	00 00 00 02 0C	00 00 1C

8.21 For SP, the second operand must contain a valid packed decimal number, even if our intention is to subtract whatever is there from itself. Since SUM has not been initialized, it is not necessarily a packed decimal number. If it is not, an error will result.

8.32

	AP	160(3,12),170(2,12)	FA21C0A0C0AA
	AP	160(3,12),166(4,12)	FA23C0A0C0A6
	AP	160(3,12),168(2,12)	FA21C0A0C0A8
	AP	163(3,12),171(1,12)	FA20C0A3C0AB

Chapter 9

9.52

			TEMP	ANS
	ZAP	TEMP(8),B(2)	00 00 00 00 00 00 06 7C	
	MP	TEMP(8),=P'1.0'	00 00 00 00 00 00 67 0C	
	AP	TEMP(8),A(3)	00 00 00 00 00 01 90 4C	
	DP	TEMP(8),=P'1.00'	00 00 00 00 01 9C 00 4C	
			Quotient | Remainder	
	ZAP	ANS(3),TEMP(6)		00 01 9C

9.54

			ANS
	ZAP	ANS(3),B(2)	00 06 7C
	SRP	ANS(3),1,0	00 67 0C
	AP	ANS(3),A(3)	01 90 4C
	SRP	ANS(3),62,0	00 01 9C

9.56 *Note:* The question marks denote garbage.

			ANS
	MVO	ANS(3),B(2)	00 67 C?
	MVZ	ANS+2(1),=X'00'	00 67 0?
	MVN	ANS+2(1),B+1	00 67 0C
	AP	ANS(3),A(3)	01 90 4C
	MVN	ANS+1(1),ANS+2	01 9C 4C
	ZAP	ANS(3),ANS(2)	00 01 9C

9.57

			ANS
	MVO	ANS(3),B(2)	00 67 C?
	MVI	ANS+2,X'0F'	00 67 0F
	AP	ANS(3),A(3)	01 90 4C
	MVN	ANS+1(1),ANS+2	01 9C 4C
	ZAP	ANS(3),ANS(2)	00 01 9C

9.58 (a)

	LA	9,3	COUNTER
	LA	2,1	BASE REGISTER
LOOP	SRP	VARIABLE,0(2),0	
	LA	2,1(0,2)	INCREMENT BASE
	...		
	BCT	9,LOOP	

(b) Use the same technique as in part (a), except decrement the base register each time through the loop with S 2,=F'1'. The value of 0 in register 2 will cause no shift the second time through the loop. The value of −1 held as FFFFFFFF, has 6 bits of 1 as the last 6 bits, corresponding to 63, which causes a shift of one digit to the right.

9.61

	Length	Single-Length	Two-Length
Maximum		FF (255)	FF (two 15s)
1 byte		00 (0)	00 (two 0s)
2 bytes		01 (1)	11 (two 1s)

They differ because a length must be specified for each operand in a two-length SS-type instruction.

9.64 (a) 4020202021204B2020   (b) 4020202020214B2020

9.66 Two methods which will work are shown, with a trace at the right which assumes that PAY contains 012345678C.

```
        MVC  DOLLARS(4),PAY        DOLLARS CONTAINS 01234567
        MVN  DOLLARS+3(1),=X'0F'   DOLLARS CONTAINS 0123456F
        MVC  CENTS(2),PAY+3        CENTS CONTAINS 678C
        MVZ  CENTS(1),=X'00'       CENTS CONTAINS 078C
        ...
DOLLARS DS   PL4
CENTS   DS   PL2
PAY     DS   PL5
```

or

```
                                     Dollars    Cents
        ZAP  DOLLARS(6),PAY          00012345   678C (6 consecutive bytes)
        DP   DOLLARS(6),=P'1.00'     0123456C   078C
                                     Quotient   Remainder
        ...
DOLLARS DS   PL4
CENTS   DS   PL2
PAY     DS   PL5
```

9.69 (a)

```
                                      First operand
        ZAP  TEMP,DIVIDEND         000000000002200C
        MP   TEMP,=P'1.0'          000000000022000C
        DP   TEMP,DIVISOR          000000733C00010C
        ZAP  QUOTIENT,TEMP(5)               00733C
        ...
DIVIDEND  DC   PL4'22.00'
DIVISOR   DC   PL3'3.0'
QUOTIENT  DS   PL3
TEMP      DS   PL8
```

(b) You would get 7.30 instead of 7.33. If either or both are negative, a minus sign will be located in columns 6 and/or 15.

Chapter 10

10.33 (a) Register 2 holds 0, register 3 holds 100.

(b) Register 14 holds 0, register 15 holds 100, register 0 holds 200, ..., register 12 holds 1400.

(c) Register 14 holds 300, ..., register 12 holds 1700.

(d) Register 1 holds 600, ..., register 12 holds 1700.

10.34 Register 0.

10.35 From this information we can tell which program called this subprogram, and from a program dump, we can tell the values which were in the registers.

ANSWERS TO SELECTED SUPPLEMENTARY PROBLEMS

10.36 The values will be the same; they will have been reloaded by the subprogram.

10.37 No. The * needs a base address and a displacement value already established.

10.38 ST 13,SAVESUB+4 before LA 13,SAVESUB.

10.39 SUBPRO is a subroutine. It reloads register 0. The program it calls is a function, as shown by the fact that SUBPRO uses the value in register 0 after control returns to it.

10.40 Register 15 is loaded with the Load instruction, and registers 1 and 13 are loaded with Load Address:

```
LA   1,ADLIST
LA   13,SAVE
L    15,ADSUBPM
```

(*Note:* In the *called* program, register 13 is *reloaded* if necessary with

L   13,SAVE+4

10.41 Once (from the function).

10.42 It could use one, two, or three address lists, depending on whether the parameters happened to be the same or different each time.

10.43

90ECD00C	SUB	STM
05C0		BALR
98241000		LM
58503000		L
5A504000		A
50502000		ST
98ECD00C		LM
07FE		BR

Since no reference to the base address is present and no displacement is calculated, the BALR and USING instructions are not necessary.

10.44

4110C0CA	1BC042	LA	1,ADLIST	
41D0C0D2	1BC046	LA	13,SAVE	
58F0C11A	1BC04A	L	15,ADFUNC	
50E0C11E	1BC04E	ST	14,RETADD	
05EF	1BC052	BALR	14,15	
07FE	1BC100	BR	14	
05B0	1BC18C	BALR	11,0	
98231000	1BC18E	LM	2,3,0(1)	
5070B032	1BC19A	ST	7,X	
1C67	1BC19E	MR	6,7	
5A70B032	1BC1A0	A	7,X	
5A70B032	1BC1A4	A	7,X	X*X + 2*X
1807	1BC1A8	LR	0,7	

10.45 (*a*) The base register for the instructions involving X would have been C instead of B.

(*b*) The displacements would have been calculated from 1BC042 instead of from 1BC18E. [As in part (*a*), the base register would be C.]

ANSWERS TO SELECTED SUPPLEMENTARY PROBLEMS

10.46 L 13,SAVESUB+4 after BALR 14,15 and before LM 14,15,12(13).

10.47 L 13,SAVESUB+4. Since the original contents of register 13 were not stored, this instruction erases vital information—the address of the SAVE area of the calling program.

10.48

	L	15,ADSUB	LOADS ADDRESS TO WHICH TO BRANCH
	LA	13,SAVEMAIN	LOADS ADDRESS OF 18-WORD SAVE AREA
	LA	1,ADLISTM	LOADS ADDRESS OF PARAMETER ADDRESS LIST
	ST	14,RETADD	SAVES OS RETURN ADDRESS TO END EXECUTION
	BALR	14,15	BRANCH TO SUBPROGRAM
	...		
	L	14,RETADD	RELOAD OS RETURN ADDRESS FOR ENDING EXECUTION
	BR	14	END EXECUTION
SAVEMAIN	DC	18F'0'	
RETADD	DS	F	
ADSUB	DC	A(SUBPRO)	
ADLISTM	DC	A(X,Y)	
*			
SUBPRO	STM	14,12,12(13)	STORE REGISTER CONTENTS
*			IN SAVEMAIN (ADDRESS IN 13)
	BALR	12,0	ESTABLISH ADDRESSABILITY
	USING	*,12	ESTABLISH ADDRESSABILITY
	LM	2,3,0(1)	LOAD PARAMETER ADDRESSES INTO REGS 2 AND 3
	ST	13,SAVESUB+4	STORE ADDRESS OF SAVEMAIN
	LA	13,SAVESUB	LOAD ADDRESS OF SAVESUB
	L	15,ADFUNC	LOAD ADDRESS FOR LATER BRANCH TO FUNC
	LA	1,ADLIST	LOAD ADDRESS OF PARAMETER LIST
	STM	2,3,ADLIST	SETS CONTENTS OF PARAMETER LIST
*			IT PASSES TO FUNC (WITH ADDRESSES
*			IT RECEIVES FROM ITS CALLING PROGRAM)
	...	...	INSTRUCTIONS NOT DEALING WITH LINKAGE
	BALR	14,15	BRANCH TO FUNCTION
	AR	0,7	USE THE VALUE IN REG 0 (RETURNED BY FUNC)
	L	13,SAVESUB+4	RELOAD ADDRESS OF SAVE AREA
*			FROM CALLING PROGRAM
	LM	14,15,12(13)	RELOAD ALL STORED REGISTERS EXCEPT
	LM	1,12,24(13)	FOR REGISTER 0, WHICH
*			HOLDS THE VALUE TO RETURN
	BR	14	RETURN TO MAIN
SAVESUB	DC	18F'0'	
ADLIST	DS	2A	
ADFUNC	DC	A(FUNC)	

10.49 The instructions in (a) through (d) and (g) are already in proper order. Those in (e) and (f) should be changed as follows:

(e)	STM	14,12,12(13)		(f)	BALR	14,15
	ST	13,SAVESUB+4			...	
	LA	13,SAVESUB			SR	0,7
	...				LM	14,15,12(13)
	L	13,SAVESUB+4			LM	1,12,24(13)
	LM	14,12,12(13)			BR	14

10.50

	LM	2,3,0(1)		LM	2,3,0(1)	LM	2,3,0(1)
	ST	2,ADLIST		ST	2,ADLIST	ST	2,ADLIST
	LA	6,T		...		...	
	ST	6,ADLIST+4	ADLIST	DS	A	ADLIST DC	A(T,T)
	...			DC	A(T)		
ADLIST	DS	2A					

ADLIST DC A(X,T) is not legal, since X is not declared in this program. In fact, the address of X might be different on different calls to this subprogram. However, the address of X (the first parameter) is in register 2 after LM 2,3,0(1). It may simply be stored in the proper memory location, ADLIST. The address of T, the local variable, may be loaded into a register and then stored in the proper place or stored there in a declaration. Storing the address of T twice in the final ADLIST does no harm, since the address of the parameter replaces that value at ADLIST+0 before the subprogram is called. However, it is considered poor style because storing the address of T twice might be confusing.

10.51 The contents of the current program's SAVE area are loaded instead of the contents of the calling subprogram's SAVE area into 14 of the registers, and they would be loaded into a register 1 lower in number than they should have been.

10.52
```
       FUNCT   STM   14,12,12(13)
               BALR  12,0
               USING *,12
               LM    2,4,0(1)
               L     0,0(0,2)      FIRST PARAMETER IN 0
               A     0,0(0,3)      SUM OF FIRST TWO IN 0
               A     0,0(0,4)      SUM IN 0, FOR RETURN
               LM    14,15,12(13)  RELOAD REGISTERS 14 AND 15
               LM    1,12,24(13)   RELOAD REGISTERS 1 THROUGH 12
       *                           DO NOT TOUCH REGISTER 0
               BR    14            RETURN
```

10.53 No effect. Registers 14 and 15 were not changed by the subprogram anyway.

10.56 The calling program should use the contents of register 0 after it calls a function but not after it calls a subroutine. In order to work correctly, the calling program should send the correct number of parameters to a subroutine or function. Moreover, the parameters should be of the proper type—input, output, or input/output. Taking these things into consideration, main programs 10.13(b) and 10.32(a) may use the subprograms in Problems 10.55(b) and (c). No other combination will work effectively.

10.57
```
       MAX     STM   14,12,12(13)
               BALR  12,0
               USING *,12
               L     2,0(0,1)      ADDRESS OF FIRST PARAMETER
               L     0,0(0,2)      VALUE OF FIRST PARAMETER IN 0
               LA    7,4           INDEX REGISTER, START AT SECOND
       *                             PARAMETER
       LOOP    L     10,0(7,1)     ADDRESS OF AN ELEMENT IN 10
               C     0,0(0,10)
               BNL   CONTINUE
               L     0,0(0,10)     REPLACE HIGHEST SO FAR
       CONTINUE LA   7,4(0,7)      INCREMENT INDEX
               LTR   10,10         TEST FOR 1 IN BIT 0
               BNM   LOOP          LOOP IF THE VALUE IS NOT "NEGATIVE"
               LM    14,15,12(13)
               LM    1,12,24(13)
               BR    14
```

10.58

```
      BESTSALE  START  0
                BALR   12,0
                USING  *,12
                LA     1,ADLIST
                LA     13,SAVEMAIN
                L      15,ADMOST
                ST     14,SAVE14
                BALR   14,15
                LR     7,0            INDEX IN 7 (CANNOT USE 0 FOR INDEX)
                LA     3,SALES(7)
                MVC    BIG(4),0(3)
                M      6,=F'25'       THE ELEMENT IN NAME IS AT INDEX
*                                     25*N-25; SINCE REG 7 CONTAINS 4*N-4,
*                                     WE MULTIPLY THAT VALUE BY 25/4
                D      6,=F'4'
                LA     3,NAME(7)
                MVC    TOPSELLR(25),0(3)
                L      14,SAVE14
                BR     14
      TOPSELLR  DS     CL25
      BIG       DS     F
      ADLIST    DC     A(SALES)
      SAVEMAIN  DC     18F'0'
      ADMOST    DC     A(MOST)
      SAVE14    DS     A
      SALES     DC     F'221,1500,1920,888,462,923,1776,1984,1060,1392,1400'
                DC     F'132,864,909,731,1875,436,992,1680,1199,1243'
      NAME      DC     CL25'JONES'
                DC     CL25'SMITH'
                DC     CL25'PIERCE'
                DC     CL25'BROWN'
                DC     CL25'WASHINGTON'
                ...                   (REST OF THE NAMES GO HERE)
                DC     CL25'PETERS'
*
      MOST      STM    14,12,12(13)
*               RETURNS INDEX OF BEST SALES FIGURE
                BALR   12,0
                USING  *,12
                L      2,0(0,1)       ADDRESS OF ARRAY IN 2
                SR     0,0            INITIALIZE IN CASE THERE ARE NO SALES
                SR     3,3            MOST SO FAR IN 3
                SR     7,7            INDEX
                LA     10,4           INCREMENT
                LA     11,80          LIMIT FOR 21-ELEMENT FULL WORD ARRAY
      LOOP      C      3,0(7,2)       COMPARE MOST SO FAR TO PRESENT ELEMENT
                BNL    NEXT
                L      3,0(7,2)       UPDATE MOST SO FAR
                LR     0,7            RETAIN INDEX OF LARGEST SO FAR IN 0
      NEXT      BXLE   7,10,LOOP
                LM     14,15,12(13)
                LM     1,12,24(13)
                BR     14
                END
```

ANSWERS TO SELECTED SUPPLEMENTARY PROBLEMS

10.61 After the address list has been established, perhaps by a DC statement, merely use the following instruction:

        MVI   ADLIST+12,B'10000000'   EQUIVALENT TO X'80'

Alternatively, use an ADLIST defined as follows:

        ADLIST   DC   A(A,B,C)
                     DC   X'80'
                     DC   AL3(D)

The length attribute is not usually used with addresses, but it may be, as in this case. When it is used, no boundary alignment is done.

10.36 (a) In the absence of the LTORG pseudo-instruction the literal pool will be assembled at the end of the unit.

(b) The literal =F'1' will not be addressable from WRONG1. Its displacement will be calculated during assembly from the address of the USING statement in WRONG2, but when the segment is executing in WRONG1, the base address is that of the USING statement in WRONG1.

(c) The problem would be corrected since a literal =F'1' will be defined in WRONG1 by LTORG and another in WRONG2 by the END of the unit. Another LTORG in WRONG2 is not needed (unless WRONG2 is very long).

(d) Two literal memory locations for =F'1' are created, each accessible in its own CSECT.

(e) The LA 4,X instruction will not execute because X has an address before the base address of the CSECT, and a negative displacement is not legal.

Chapter 11

11.29 EXCLUSIVE OR. Subtracting a number A from a number B is the same as adding the 2's complement of A to B. First get the 1's complement by EXCLUSIVE ORing the number to be subtracted with all 1s; then add 1 to the result to get the 2's complement. Finally, add that result to the other operand.

11.30
```
              LA      2,32                COUNTER
              L       5,NUM1
              SR      4,4
LOOP          STCM    5,B'0001',TEST
              TM      TEST,B'00000001'    TEST LAST BIT
              BNO     CONTINUE
              A       4,NUM2
CONTINUE      SRDL    4,1
              BCT     2,LOOP
              ST      5,PROD
```

11.31
```
              LA      2,32                COUNTER
              L       3,DIVISOR
              X       3,=X'FFFFFFFF'      1'S COMPLEMENT
              A       3,=F'1'             2'S COMPLEMENT
              SR      4,4                 ZERO EVEN REGISTER
              L       5,DIVIDEND
LOOP          SLDA    4,1
              AR      4,3
              BNM     NOTNEG
              A       4,DIVISOR           IF MINUS, UNDO ADDITION ABOVE
              B       CONTINUE
NOTNEG        O       5,=X'00000001'      PUT 1 IN LAST BIT
CONTINUE      BCT     2,LOOP
              ST      5,QUOT
              ST      4,REMAINDR
```

388 ANSWERS TO SELECTED SUPPLEMENTARY PROBLEMS

11.32 (*a*) All bits remain unchanged.
(*b*) All bits remain unchanged.
(*c*) All bits become zero.

Chapter 12

12.32 (*a*) None.
(*b*) The second value is greater, since the assembler ignores the decimal point in packed decimal number declarations.
(*c*) The first number is greater, since the assembler rounds the full word to the nearest integer (12).
(*d*) None.

12.34 After the instruction BZ STO, delete AE 2,=E'1' and substitute the following:

```
        L     4,A
        SRDL  4,24        FRACTION IN 5
        SRL   4,1         HALVE EXPONENT
        A     4,=F'32'    CORRECT FOR EXCESS-64 NOTATION
        SRDL  4,7         EXPONENT IN 5
        SRL   5,1         ADD A ZERO AS SIGN
        ST    5,SQRTA
        DE    2,SQRTA
        AE    2,SQRTA
```

or

```
        SR    2,2         CLEAR REGISTER 2
        STE   0,SQRTA
        IC    2,A         TAKE FIRST BYTE
        S     2,=F'64'    EXCESS-64 NOTATION
        SRL   2,1         HALVE
        A     2,=F'64'    EXCESS-64 NOTATION
        STC   2,SQRTA     REPLACE FIRST BYTE
        DE    2,SQRTA
        AE    2,SQRTA
```

The first version shifts the coefficient, the last 6 bits of the exponent, and 2 zero bits (including the sign) into register 5. The second version extracts the byte containing the exponent, halves it, and restores it. The sign bit is zero. Halving the exponent requires that we take into account that the exponent is represented in excess-64 notation. We can either subtract the 64 before halving, halve, then add the 64 back in (version 2), or halve the exponent and realize that we have halved the 64 also. Therefore, we add back 32 to the exponent (version 1).

12.35
```
FUNC    STM   14,12,12(13)
        BALR  12,0
        USING *,12
        L     2,0(0,1)       ADDRESS OF NUMBER
        LE    2,0(0,2)       NUMBER IN FPR 2
        ...                  USE INSTRUCTIONS FROM PROBLEM 12.26
        STE   0,SQRT         STORE ANSWER IN MEMORY
        LA    0,SQRT         LOAD ADDRESS OF ANSWER INTO GPR 0
        LM    14,15,12(13)
        LM    1,12,24(13)
        BR    14
SQRT    DS    E
```

The main program will find the address of the answer in GPR 0, and load the value in FPR 0:

```
         BALR  14,15           CALL FUNCTION
         LR    7,0             COPY ADDRESS INTO REGISTER 7
         LE    0,0(0,7)        LOAD VALUE INTO FPR 0
```

12.36
```
ROOTS    STM   14,12,12(13)
         BALR  12,0
         USING *,12
         LM    2,6,0(1)        ADDRESSES OF A, B, C, ROOT1 AND
*                                 ROOT2 IN REGISTERS 2 THROUGH 6
         LE    0,0(0,3)        B IN FPR 0
         LER   2,0             B IN FPR 2
         MER   0,0             B*B IN FPR 0
         LE    4,0(0,2)        A IN 4
         ME    4,0(0,4)        A*C IN 4
         ME    4,=E'4'         4*A*C IN 4
         SER   0,4             B*B - 4*A*C IN 0
         STE   0,VAL           PUT DISCRIMINANT IN MEMORY FOR
*                                 CALL TO FUNCTION
         LA    0,VAL
         ST    0,ADLIST        PREPARE LIST OF PARAMETER(S)
         ST    13,SAVE+4
         LA    1,ADLIST
         LA    13,SAVE
         L     15,ADFUNC
         BALR  14,15           BRANCH TO FUNCTION OF PRIOR
*                                 PROBLEM TO FIND THE SQUARE ROOT
         LR    7,0             PUT ADDRESS OF ANSWER INTO REG 7
         LE    4,0(0,7)        SQRT OF DISCRIMINANT IN 4
         LCER  6,2             -B IN FPR 6
         AER   6,4             -B + ROOT IN 6
         HER   6,6             HALVE VALUE
         DE    6,0(0,2)        DIVIDE BY A
         STE   6,0(0,5)        STORE ONE ROOT
         LCER  6,2
         SER   6,4             -B - ROOT IN 6
         HER   6,6             HALVE
         DE    6,0(0,2)        DIVIDE BY A
         STE   6,0(0,6)        STORE SECOND ROOT IN FPR 6 AT
*                                 ADDRESS SPECIFIED IN GPR 6
         L     13,SAVE+4
         LM    14,12,12(13)
         BR    14
ADLIST   DS    F
ADFUNC   DC    A(FUNC)
SAVE     DS    18F
VAL      DS    E
```

ANSWERS TO SELECTED SUPPLEMENTARY PROBLEMS

```
12.38  SQUAREIT  STM    14,12,12(13)
                 BALR   12,0
                 USING  *,12
                 LM     2,3,0(1)          ADDRESSES OF NUM AND SQUARE
                 L      4,0(0,2)          NUM
                 LPR    4,4               ABSOLUTE VALUE OF NUM;
*                                            FLOATING POINT IS NOT IN
*                                            COMPLEMENT NOTATION
                 ST     4,UZERO+4         CONVERT N TO
                 LD     2,UZERO              FLOATING POINT
                 MDR    2,2               SQUARE IS POSITIVE NO
*                                            MATTER WHAT SIGN NUM HAS
                 STD    2,0(0,3)
                 LM     14,12,12(13)
                 BR     14
       D         DC     D'0'
       UZERO     DC     X'4E00000000000000'


12.39  MAIN      START  0
                 BALR   12,0
                 USING  *,12
                 LA     1,ADLIST
                 LA     13,SAVE
                 ST     14,SAVE14
                 SR     7,7               INDEX FOR SHORT
                 LA     10,4              INCREMENT
                 LA     11,36             LIMIT
                 SR     8,8               INDEX FOR LONG
       LOOP      L      15,ADSQ
                 LA     6,NUM(7)
                 ST     6,ADLIST
                 LA     6,SQUARE(8)
                 ST     6,ADLIST+4
                 BALR   14,15
                 LA     8,8(0,8)          INCREMENT LONG INDEX
                 BXLE   7,10,LOOP
                 L      14,SAVE14
                 BR     14
       SAVE14    DS     F
       NUM       DC     F'1,2,3,4,5,6,7,8,9,10'
       SQUARE    DS     10D
       ADLIST    DS     2F
       SAVE      DS     18F
       ADSQ      DC     A(SQUAREIT)
                 END
```

12.40 Repeat the answer to the previous problem, with the following changes:

```
                 LA     10,2    INCREMENT IS 2 FOR HALFWORDS
                 LA     11,18   LIMIT IS 18 FOR TENTH HALFWORD
```

Use the subroutine in Problem 12.38, with the following substitution:

```
                 LH     4,0(0,2)    REPLACES THE FULLWORD INSTRUCTION
```

ANSWERS TO SELECTED SUPPLEMENTARY PROBLEMS

12.41 First, squaring a halfword can be done before conversion to float, with no worry about exceeding the capacity of a single general-purpose register. In contrast, the full word should be converted to float before the number is squared, to prevent overflow. Second, before we convert a number to float, we must make it positive. Since we must convert the full word before squaring it, we must use LPR to ensure that it is positive. However, since the halfword is squared before conversion, we know that the number to be converted is positive. Thus the LPR instruction in Problem 12.38 can be omitted.

Chapter 13

13.24 (a) C: D4 BF CF
         D: B3 D8 F0 E3 A0

    (c) C: F9 D8 E1
         D: F9 B6 DE C4 E2

    (b) C: D4 BF 0E
         D: 01 D8 F0 E3 06

13.25
```
        L     2,X
        L     10,=F'-1'
        LA    11,HEX-1
        LA    7,HEX+7
LOOP    STC   2,0(0,7)
        NI    0(7),X'0F'
        SRL   2,4
        BXH   7,10,LOOP
        TR    HEX(8),TABLE
```

13.26
```
        TRT   LINE+20(9),TABLE
        BZ    PACKX
        MVI   0(1),C' '
        MVZ   LINE+28(1),=X'D0'
PACKX   PACK  X(5),LINE+20(9)
```

13.27
```
        TRT   INPUT(80),NONBLANK
        LR    4,1                    4 HOLDS ADDRESS OF 1ST DIGIT
        TRT   0(80,4),BLKORCOM       1 HOLDS ADDRESS OF NEXT BLANK
        LR    5,1                    5 HOLDS ADDRESS OF NEXT BLANK
        SR    1,4                    1 HOLDS LENGTH OF 1ST NUMBER
        BCTR  1,0                    LENGTH-1 FOR MACHINE LANGUAGE
        EX    1,PCKINSA              PACKS 1ST NUMBER AS A
        TRT   0(80,5),NONBLANK
        LR    4,1                    4 HOLDS ADDRESS OF 2ND NUMBER
        TRT   0(80,4),BLKORCOM       1 HOLDS ADDRESS OF NEXT BLANK
        SR    1,4                    1 HOLDS LENGTH OF 2ND NUMBER
        BCTR  1,0                    LENGTH-1 FOR MACHINE LANGUAGE
        EX    1,PCKINSB
        ...
PCKINSA PACK  A(6),0(0,4)            L1 FROM THIS INSTRUCTION,
PCKINSB PACK  B(6),0(0,4)              L2 FROM REGISTER 1
INPUT   DS    CL80
        DC    X'40'                  TO INSURE NO OVERSHOOTING OF 2ND NUM
NONBLANK DC   64X'01'                FINDS CHARACTERS NOT BLANK OR COMMA
        DC    X'00'                  ZERO CORRESPONDING TO BLANK
        DC    42X'01'
        DC    X'00'                  ZERO CORRESPONDING TO COMMA
        DC    148X'01'
```

```
           BLKORCOM  DC    64X'00'         FINDS BLANK OR COMMA
                     DC    X'01'           ONE CORRESPONDING TO BLANK
                     DC    42X'00'
                     DC    X'01'           ONE CORRESPONDING TO COMMA
                     DC    148X'00'
```

13.29 We wish to execute a TM instruction with various masks. In order to put this into a loop, we use the Execute (EX) instruction so that the mask may be specified in register 5. Thus, each time through the loop, we load the appropriate mask into register 5, and then we use EX to execute a TM instruction with this mask. Register 4 is the loop control, which we will also use as an index register. If the tested bit is 1, we multiply the value in register 4 by 4, use that value as an index value, and then restore the original count by dividing by 4 before continuing.

```
                     LA    4,8             INDEX REGISTER AND LOOP COUNTER
                     LA    5,1             INITIALIZE THE MASK
          * WE PUT THE MASK IN REGISTER 5, WHICH THE
          * EX INSTRUCTION WILL USE AS THE REGISTER FOR THE TM
          * INSTRUCTION.  AT THE BEGINNING, THE MASK IN TMV WILL BE
          * B'00000001'
          *
           LOOP      EX    5,TMV
                     BZ    NOTFOUND
                     MVC   LINE(121),BLANK
                     SLA   4,2             MULTIPLY BY 4
                     LA    6,CO-4(4)       FIND NAME OF PLAN
                     MVC   LINE+10(4),0(6) MOVE NAME OF PLAN TO LINE
          * PRINT OUT LINE SOME WAY
                     SRA   4,2             DIVIDE BY 4 TO RESTORE VALUE
           NOTFOUND  SLL   5,1             SHIFT MASK TO LEFT BY 1
                     BCT   4,LOOP
                     ...
           FLAG      DC    B'00101000'
           TMV       TM    FLAG,X'00'
           BLANK     DC    C' '
           LINE      DS    CL121
```

```
13.30      MAX       STM   14,12,12(13)
                     BALR  12,0
                     USING *,12
                     LM    2,4,0(1)        ADDRESSES OF ARR, N, LENGTH IN 2, 3, 4
                     L     7,0(0,4)        LENGTH IN 7
                     BCTR  7,0             LENGTH - 1
                     M     6,=F'17'        MULTIPLY BY HEXADECIMAL 11  (TO GET
          *                                   THE SAME HEX DIGIT FOR EACH LENGTH)
                     EX    7,EXZAP         FIRST ELEMENT IN LOCAL VARIABLE BIG
                     L     5,0(0,3)        N IN 5
           LOOP      EX    7,EXCP
                     BNL   ENDLOOP
                     EX    7,EXZAP         REPLACE BIG WITH CURRENT ELEMENT
```

```
        ENDLOOP  A      2,0(0,4)      INCREMENT REGISTER 2
                 BCT    5,LOOP
                 LA     0,BIG         ADDRESS OF ANSWER IN 0
                 LM     14,15,12(13)
                 LM     1,12,24(13)
                 BR     14
        BIG      DS     PL16
        EXZAP    ZAP    BIG(0),0(0,2)
        EXCP     CP     BIG(0),0(0,2)
```

The addresses of the three parameters are loaded into registers 2, 3, and 4, respectively. The length is loaded into register 7 and reduced by 1, because the machine language lengths range from 0 to F, corresponding to actual lengths of 1 to 16 bytes, respectively. Since the Execute instruction will logically OR the value in register 7 with the zero length in the ZAP and CP instructions to be executed, the machine language length must be present. These instructions require two lengths. The lengths must be placed in register 7 to be used with EX. Since the two lengths in this case happen to be the same, we can take advantage of the fact that multiplication of any hexadecimal digit by hexadecimal 11 will duplicate that digit (e.g., $2_{16} * 11_{16} = 22_{16}$). Thus we multiply the value in register 7 by $11_{16} = 17_{10}$ to get $22_{16} = 34_{10}$.

The number of elements in the array is loaded into register 5 and used to control the looping with the BCT instruction.

Because we do not know the length of the packed decimal numbers to be zapped or compared, we Execute (EX) these instructions. Both ZAP instructions of Example 10.13 can be executed with the same EXZAP instruction. The EXCP instruction is used for the Compare Packed, using the length byte in register 7. Incrementing is done by adding the length (address in register 4) to register 2. When execution returns to the calling program, the proper length of memory location BIG will be known and used. The address of BIG will be returned in register 0.

Chapter 14

14.19
```
                 MACRO
                 CVC    &BIN,&PCK,&ZON
                 LCLA   &LEN
        &LEN     SETA   L'&ZON
                 ST     6,SAVE
                 L      6,&BIN
                 CVD    6,&PCK
                 UNPK   &ZON.(&LEN),&PCK.(8)
                 MVZ    &ZON+(&LEN-1)(1),=X'F0'
                 L      6,SAVE
                 MEND
```

This is invoked by the following:

                            CVC   BIN,PCK,ZON

Note that the length attribute is used to determine the length of the zoned variable at assembly time for use in the UNPK and MVZ instructions.

14.21
```
                 MACRO
                 CPOWER &A,&B,&NUM,&REG1,&REG2
                 L      &REG2,=F'&NUM'
                 LA     &REG1+1,1
                 AIF    (&NUM EQ 0).ZERO
                 M      &REG1,&A
                 BCT    &REG2,*-4
        .ZERO    ST     &REG1+1,&B
                 MEND
```

Here are two possible invocations of the macro:

```
                CPOWER    A,B,5,8,2
                CPOWER    FW,FW2,0,4,7
```

14.23
```
        MACRO
        DIVIDHW   &FIRST,&SECOND,&REGPAIR,&REG,&HWQUOT,&HWREM
        LH        &REGPAIR,&FIRST
        SRDA      &REGPAIR,32
        LH        &REG,&SECOND
        DR        &REGPAIR,&REG
        STH       &REGPAIR+1,&HWQUOT
        STH       &REGPAIR,&HWREM
        MEND
```

Index

The letter *t* following a page number refers to a table

A (Add),26
A (address constant),233
Absolute address,70
Absolute value, of packed number,276
Accuracy,295
Add (A),26
Add Decimal (AP),173–175
Add Halfword (AH),43
Add Packed (AP),173–175
Add Register (AR),41
Addition:
  of binary numbers,8
  of floating-point numbers,302–304
  of hexadecimal numbers,8
Address,61
  absolute,70
  constant,70–71,233
  of DC and DS,65
  effective,63,66,112
  of halfword memory locations,61
  invalid,369
  of labeled instructions,65
  of labels,65
  list,235–238,244
  literal,71
  modification,111–118
  operand,61
  of save area,243
  specification (A), in DC statement,70–71
Addressability, in subprograms,231,240–241
Addressing,61–84
  in long programs,74–75
  using expressions,69–70
AGO,347
AH (Add Halfword),43
AIF,346–347
Alphabetization,142
ALU (arithmetic logical unit),91
Ampersand (&),337
AND operations,273–276
ANOP,347
AP (Add Packed),173–175
AR (Add Register),41
Arithmetic logical unit (ALU),91
Arithmetic operations,25–26,38–60
Arithmetic shifts,268,271–272
  condition code in,271
Array element number in high-level language,109–110
Arrays,106,109–135
  character strings,146–147
  declaration of,109
  floating-point,302
  fullword, using MVC,155,166

Arrays (*continued*)
  heterogeneous,147–149
    declaration of,111
  packed decimal,179–181
    declaration of,179
  replication factor in,109
  two dimensional, addresses of elements in, 110–111
Assembler,22
Assembly language format(s),22–24,359–362(*t*)
  for RR instructions,41–42
  for RX instructions,68
  for RS instructions,118
  for SI instructions,144
  for single-length SS instructions,139
  for two-length SS instructions,173
ASSIST,365
Asterisk (*):
  in instruction,66
  for check protection,204
  for comment line,24
Attribute(s):
  of symbolic parameters,348–351
    count,350–351
    length,350
    number,349–350
    type,348–349

ƀ (blank),136,206
B (binary designation in DC and DS),138
BAL (Branch and Link),232
BALR (Branch and Link Register),23,63,66–67, 71,232
  effects of,66–67
Base:
  conversion of,3–7
  designation of,3
  exponential format,295
  of number system,1
Base address,61
Base register,61–62
  explicit,116–118
  implied,112
  modification,117–118,120
    using packed instructions,180
  multiple,74
  for symbolic operands,112
  value zero,65
BC (Branch on Condition),86–88
BCR (Branch on Condition, Register),86–88
BCT (Branch on Count),106–109
BCTR (Branch on Count Register),106, 108–109
Binary digit,1

Binary format, in DC and DS,138
Binary numbers,1–21
  addition of,8
  conversion to/from other bases,3–7
  odd,18
  positional number system in,2–3
  subtraction of,9
Bit(s),1
  manipulation of,268–278
  switching,11
BL (DS designation for binary, including length), 138
Blank,22,136,206
   notation,136
  EBCDIC representation,136
  in Edit instruction,206
Blanking a string,141
Boundary requirement,67–68
  avoiding wasted bytes for,147–149,160
  double-word,67
  fullword,67–68
    basis of,19
  in heterogeneous arrays,147–149
  packed decimal,172
Branch,85
  conditional,85
  mask for,86–88,87(t)
  unconditional,85
Branch and Link (BAL),232
Branch and Link Register (BALR),23,63,66–67, 71,232
  effects of,66–67
Branch on Condition (BC),86–88
Branch on Condition Register (BCR),86–88
Branch on Count (BCT),106–109
Branch on Count Register (BCTR),106,108–109
Branch on Index High (BXH),118,120–122
Branch on Index Low or Equal (BXLE),118–122
Branching:
  in conditional assembly,346–348
  in macros,346–348
  to subprograms,232–234
  using * notation,348,349
BXH (Branch on Index High),118,120–122
BXLE (Branch on Index Low or Equal),118–122
Byte(s),22
  manipulation of,268–294

C (Compare),85,90–91
C (DC or DS designation for character),137
Carriage control (cc),364
cc (carriage control),364
cc (*see* Condition code)
CH (Compare Halfword),91
Character:
  C designation for, in DC and DS,137
  EBCDIC representation,136,136–137(t)

Character (*continued*)
  fill:
    in Edit,205
    in CLCL and MVCL,150
  message,205
Character string(s),136–170
  arrays of,146–147
  blanking of,141
  declaration of,137–138,138(t)
  literal,140,143
  looping through,149–150
Check protection, asterisk for,204
CL (Compare Logical),143
CL (DC and DS designation for character, including length),137
CLC (Compare Logical Character),139,141–143
CLCL (Compare Logical Character Long), 150–151
CLCI (Compare Logical Immediate),144–147
CLR (Compare Logical Register),143
Coefficient,295
Comment, in macro,336
Comment field,22–24
Comment line,24
Compare (C),85,90–91
Compare Decimal (CP),173,178–179
Compare Halfword (CH),91
Compare Instructions,145(t)
Compare Logical (CL),143
Compare Logical Character (CLC),139,141–143
Compare Logical Character Long (CLCL),150–151
Compare Logical Character under Mask (CLM), 278–280
Compare Logical Immediate (CLI),144–147
Compare Logical Register (CLR),143
Compare Packed (CP),173,178–179
Compare Register (CR),90–91
Comparisons:
  floating-point,301(t)
  logical,141–143
Complement notation,10–12
Concatenation, in macro,339–340
Condition code,85–90,90(t)
  set by arithmetic shifts,271
  set by binary instructions,85–86
  set by CLC,142
  set by CLI,145
  set by CLM,280
  set by Compare,90–91
  set by Compare Packed,178–179
  set by ICM,280
  set by packed decimal instructions,175
  set by SRP,192
  set by TM,277
  set by TRT,323
  settings,363(t)
Conditional assembly,346–352
  branching in,346–348

INDEX

Conditional branch,85
Constant, as parameter,256
Continuation line,23
Control sections,231
Conventions, for subprogams,230
Conversion,3–7
  binary to decimal,3
  binary to hexadecimal,7
  decimal to binary,3–7
  decimal to hexademical,3–7,298–299
    fractions,298–299
  floating-point to binary,307–308
  floating-point to/from decimal,296–299,316
  hexadecimal to binary,7
  hexadecimal to decimal,3
  of packed decimal numbers,200–210
Convert to Binary (CVB),202–203
Convert to Decimal (CVD),202–203
Core storage,22
Count, of symbolic parameter,350–351
CP (Compare Packed),173,178–179
CR (Compare Register),90–91
CR (credit balance),203–204,208–209
Credit balance,203–204,208–209
CSECT,22,231
CVB (Convert to Binary),202
CVD (Convert to Decimal),202–203

D (divide),24,39–41
D (double word),10,22,25,296
D format, double-word floating point,300
Data definition,24–25
DC (define constant),24
DC and DS format,24,138
  for addresses (A),70–71
  using B,138
  using C,138
  using D,202-203,300
  using E,300
  using F,24–25
  using P,172
  using X,138
DC statements,fractions in,25
Debugging programs,73–74
Decimal, conversion to/from other bases,3–7
Decimal, designation,3
Decimal numbers,1 (*See also* Packed decimal numbers)
Decimal places:
  amending numbers of,191–199
  rules for,189–191
Decimal point(s):
  aligning,190–191
  in packed numbers,189
Declaration(s),24–25
  of binary arrays,109
  of characters,137–138,138(*t*)

Declaration(s) (*continued*)
  dummy,148
  of floating-point numbers,300
  fractions in fullword,25
  of heterogeneous arrays,147–148
  of packed decimal arrays,179
  of packed decimal numbers,172,172(*t*)
Default length:
  in DC statements:
    for character strings,137
    for packed decimal numbers,172
  error in expressions,174
  in single-length SS instructions,139
  in two-length SS instructions,173–174
Define constant (DC),24
Define storage (DS),24
Digit, binary,1
Digit selector,205
Displacement,61–62,65–66,68
  limits of,65
Divide (D),24,39–41
Divide Decimal (DP),175,177–178
Divide Packed (DP),175,177–178
Divide Register (DR),41
Division:
  floating-point,301,303
  fullword,24,39–41
  of packed decimal numbers,174,177–178
  preparation for,39–40,283
  using shift instruction,282
  by zero,59
Dollar sign,floating,204,209–210
Double precision,296
Double word,10,22,25,296
  boundary requirements of,67,202–203
  D designation,300
Doubling,52
DP (Divide Packed),175,177–178
DR (Divide Register),41
DS (define storage),24
Dummy declaration,148

E (exponent),300
E (short floating point),300
EBCDIC,136,136–137(*t*)
  in logical comparisons,142
ED (Edit),204–210
Edit (ED),204–210
  blank in,206
  message character in,205
Edit with Mark (EDMK),204–210
EDMK (Edit with Mark),204–210
Effective address,63,66,112
END,22–25
EQ (equal),346
EQU (Equivalence),76
Equivalence pseudo-instruction (EQU),76

Even binary number,18
Even-odd register pair,38–39,46
EX (Execute),324–325
Excess-64 notation,297
EXCLUSIVE OR operations,273–276
Execute (EX),324–325
Execution,halting,26
Expansion of macro,336
Explicit address, using LA,71–72
Explicit notation,68–69,94
  base register in,116–118
  for labels,94
  for MVC,140
  for packed instructions,179–180
  for parameters,236–238
  shortened form,69
Exponent,295,300
  base of,295
  in floating-point format,297
Exponentiation,38,303–304
Expression(s):
  addressing by use of,69–70
  in operands,73
  as parameter,258
Extended mnemonics:
  after arithmetic instructions,88–89,88(t)
  after compare instruction,90(t),91–93
  after TM,278
External subprogram,231

F (full word),24–25
Factorial,45,312–313
Field:
  Comment,22–24
  Name,22–23
  Operand,22–24
  Operation,22–24
Field separator,210
Fill character:
  for CLCL and MVCL,150
  in Edit,205
Fixed-point numbers,1
Floating dollar sign,204,209–210
Floating minus sign,204
Floating-point:
  addition,302,304
  arithmetic,302–306
  arrays,302
  compare operation,301(t)
  conversion to binary,307–308
  declaration,300
  division,301,303
  E designation for,300
  exponentiation,303–304
  format,296–298
  instructions,301,306–307
  multiplication,301,303

Floating-pointing (*continued*)
  negative value in,297
  numbers,1
  operations,302–304
  registers,22,300
  sign bit,297
  subtraction,302
Format:
  assembly language,22–24,359–362(t)
    for RR instructions,41–42
    for RX instructions,68
    for SI instructions,144
    for single-length SS instructions,139
    for two-length SS instructions,173
  binary, in DC and DS,138
  errors in,44
  floating-point,296–298
  machine language,362(t)
    for RR instructions,61–62
    for RX instructions,61–63
    for SI instructions,144
    for single-length SS instructions,139
    for two-length SS instructions,173
  for packed decimal numbers,171
  for shift instructions,272
FPR (floating-point register),22,300
Fractional packed decimal numbers,189–229
Fractions:
  in DC statements,25
  in fullword declarations,25
  in hexadecimal,296(t),298–299
Full word,9–10,22,24–25
  address of,61
  boundary requirements,67–68
    basis of,19
Function byte,319
Functions,230,242–243

Garbage,10
GBL (global set symbol),343–344
GE (greater or equal),346
GEN,336
General purpose register (GPR),9,22
Generation, macro,336
Global set symbol (GBL),343–344
GPR (general purpose register),9,22
GT (greater than),346
Guard digit,305,312

H (halfword),24–25
Halfword,10,22,24–25
  address of,61
  boundary requirements,67–68
  instruction(s),43–44
    compare,91
    length of,63
Halting execution,26

INDEX

Halve (HER),315
Header, macro,335
Heterogeneous arrays,147–149
    declaration of,111
Hexadecimal digits,2
Hexadecimal format, in DC and DS,138
Hexadecimal fractions,296(*t*),298–299
Hexadecimal notation,2
Hexadecimal numbers,2–3
    addition of,8
    conversion to/from other bases,3,7,298–299
    positional number system in,2–3
    subtraction of,9
Hours-minutes-seconds,21

I2 of immediate instruction,144
I3,in SRP,192–195
IC (Insert Character),278
ICM (Insert Character under Mask),278–280
Identifiers,23
Immediate instructions,144–147
Implied base register,112
Increment, using LA,72–73
Index register,62
    modification,112–116
    value zero,65
Initial values,24
Initializing a memory location with an address,70–71
Input/output,203–204,364–368
Insert Character (IC),278
Insert Character under Mask (ICM),278–280
Instructions:
    assembly language,359–362(*t*)
    boundary requirements of,68
    floating-point,301,306–307
    length of,61
    machine language,362(*t*)
    privileged,369
Integer data type in high-level language,110
Internal subprogram,231
Interrupt codes,370
Interruptions,202,369–370
Invalid address,369
Invalid data,369
Invalid operation code,369
I/O (input/output),203–204,364–368

K' (count test in macro),350
Keyword parameters,342–343

L (Load),24–25
L' (length test in macro),350
LA (Load Address),71–73
Labeled instruction, address of,65
Labels,93–94
    address of,65

Labels (*continued*)
    explicit notation for,94
    as parameters to macro,338
LCL (local set symbol),343–344
LCR (Load Complement Register),42–43
LE (less than or equal),346
Leading zeros,10,204
    suppression of,204
Length:
    attribute of symbolic parameter,350
    specification:
        in machine language,139,173
        of single-length SS instruction,139
        of two-length SS machine format,173
LH (Load Halfword),43
Limit,for looping,114
List (*see* Array)
List, address,235–238,244
Literal,27–28
    address,71
    character string,140,143
LM (Load Multiple),234–235
LNR (Load Negative Register),42–43
Load (L),24–25
Load Address (LA),71–73
Load and Test Register (LTR),89–90
Load Complement Register (LCR),42–43
Load Halfword (LH),43
Load Multiple (LM),234–235
Load Negative Register (LNR),42–43
Load Positive Register (LPR),42–43
Load Register (LR),41
Local set symbol (LCL),343–344
Local variables, as parameters,244
Logical comparisons,141–143
Logical operations (AND, EXCLUSIVE OR, OR operations),272–276
    types of,272–273
Logical shift instructions,268–271
Long floating-point format,296–298
Long programs,addressing in,74–75
Looping,106–135
    in character string arrays,146–147
    through a character string,149–150
    in heterogeneous data,147–149
    limit for,114
LPR (Load Positive Register),42–43
LR (Load Register),41
LT (less than),346
LTORG,75,84
LTR (Load and Test Register),89–90

M (Multiply),24,38–39
Machine language format(s),362(*t*)
    for RR instructions,62
    for RX instructions,62–63
    for SI instructions,144

Machine language format(s) (*continued*)
   for single-length SS instructions,139
   for two-length SS instructions,173
Macro,334-358
   attribute tests:
      count,350
      length,350
      number,349-350
      type,348-349
   comment in,336
   concatenation in,339-340
   definition,335
   difference from subprogram,334-335
   end,335
   exit,348
   expansion,336
   generation,336
   header,335
   keyword parameter,342-343
   model statements for,335
   note,336
   prototype,335
   sublists in,340-341
   symbolic parameter,337-341
   trailer,335
Main memory,22
Mask, for BC instruction,86-88,87(*t*)
Memory,22
Memory dump,74
MEND,335
Message character, in Edit,205
MEXIT,348
MH (Multiply Halfword),43-44
Minus sign, floating,204
Mnemonic operation code,24,62
MNOTE,336
Model statements, for macro,335
Modification:
   of address,111-118
   of base register,117-118,120
   of index register,112-116
Move Character (MVC),139-141
   explicit notation for,140
   for fullword array manipulation,155,166
   for multiplication and division,196-197
   overlap in,140-141
Move Character Long (MVCL),150-151
Move Immmediate (MVI),139,144-145
Move Numeric (MVN),195-197
Move with Offset (MVO),197-199
Move Zone (MVZ),195-197
   logical alternative to,276
MP (Multiply Packed),175-177
MR (Multiply Register),41
Multiple base register,74
Multiplication:
   floating-point,301,303

Multiplication (*continued*)
   of packed numbers,175-177
   using shift instructions,282
Multiply (M),24,38-39
Multiply Decimal (MP),175-177
Multiply Halfword (MH),43-44
Multiply Packed (MP),175-177
Multiply Register (MR),41
MVC (Move Character),139-141
   explicit notation for,140
   for fullword array manipulation,155,166
   for multiplication and division,196-197
   overlap in,140-141
MVCL (Move Character Long),150-151
MVI (Move Immediate),139,144-145
MVN (Move Numeric),195-197
MVO (Move with Offset),197-199
MVZ (Move Zone),195-197
   logical alternative to,276

N' (number test in macro),349
Name field,22-23
Names,23
   absolute,70
   relocatable,70
National characters,23
NE (not equal),346
Negative numbers:
   binary,10-12
   floating-point,297
   hexadecimal,12
NOGEN,336
Normalization,299,304-305
Normalized form,297
Number (attribute of symbolic parameter),349-350
Number conversion (*See* Conversion)
Number system(s),1-21
   base of,1
   positional,2-3
Numbers:
   binary,1-21
      addition of,8
      conversion to/from other bases,3-7
      subtraction of,9
   fixed-point,1
   floating-point,1
   packed decimal,171-188 (*See also* Packed decimal numbers)
Numeric,200

Odd binary number,18
Odometer,10-11
One's complement,12
Op code,62
   invalid,369
   machine language,62
   mnemonic,24,62

INDEX

Operand, expressions in, 73
Operand address, 61
Operand field, 22–24
Operating system, 369
Operation code, 62
  invalid, 369
  machine language, 62
  mnemonic, 24, 62
Operation field, 22–24
OR operations, 273–276
Overflow, 86, 369
Overlap, in MVC, 140–141

P (packed decimal), 172
PACK, 200–201
Packed decimal instructions,
  explicit notation for, 179–180
  format, 173
Packed decimal numbers, 171–188
  absolute value of, 276
  addition of, 173–175
  advantages and disadvantages, 171–172
  arrays of, 179–180
  base register modification in, 117–118, 120
  boundary alignment, 172
  changing sign of, 185
  comparison of, 178–179
  declaration of, 172, 172(t)
  division of, 175, 177–178
  format, 171
  fractional, 189–229
  multiplication of, 175–177
  sign of, 171
  subtraction of, 175
Parameter(s) for macros:
  keyword, 342–343
  to macro, 337–338
  omission of, 339
  positional, 342
  symbolic, 337–341
    attributes, 348–351
      count, 350–351
      length, 350
      number, 349–350
      type, 348–349
  transmission by name, 337
Parameter(s) for subprograms, 230, 235–238, 246
  constant as, 256
  explicit notation for, 236–238
  expression as, 258
  local variable as, 244
Parentheses:
  with packed name, 179–180
  in RX instructions, 179–180
  in SS instructions, 179–180
Pattern, for Edit, 205
  reestablishing, 207–208

Period, in concatenation in macro, 340
Plus signs, indicating macro generation, 336
Positional number system, 2–3
Positional parameters, 342
Postnormalization, 305
Precision, double, 296
Preparation for division:
  using the multiply instruction, 39
  using a shift instruction, 283
PRINT GEN, 336
PRINT NOGEN, 336
PRINTLIN, 365
PRINTOUT, 364
Privileged instructions, 369
Problem state, 369
Program status word, 73, 370
Prototype, macro, 335
Pseudo-instructions, 22
PSW (program status word), 73, 370

Quotient, 39
  packed decimal, 177–178

READCARD, 365
Record (Pascal or COBOL), 111, 147
Register pair, 38–39, 46
Register 1, special features of:
  with EDMK, 209–210
  with TRT, 323
Register 2, special features of, with TRT, 323
Registers, 22
  floating-point, 22, 300
  general purpose, 9, 22
Relocatable names, 70
Remainder, 39
  packed decimal, 177–178
  sign of, 39
Replication factor:
  in full-word arrays, 109
  in packed decimal declarations, 179
  in strings, 138
Representation, decimal, 171
Return address, storing of, 233–234
RETURN macro, 341
Returning value from function, 242–243
Rounding, 25
  errors in, 295
RR instructions, 38, 41–42
RS instructions, 118, 234, 272
RX instructions, 41
  assembly language format for, 68
  machine language format for, 62–63

S (Subtract), 26
Save area, 239
  address of, 243
SAVE macro, 341

Saving register contents, 239–240
Scientific notation, in DC statements, 25, 295
Set Program Mask (SPM), 369
Set statements, 344
  SETA, 344
  SETB, 344
  SETC, 344
Set symbol, 343–346
  global, 343–344
  local, 343–344
  type A, 344–345
  type B, 345–346
  type C, 345–346
SH (Subtract Halfword), 43–44
Shift and Round Packed (SRP), 192–195
Shift instructions, 268–272
  arithmetic, 268, 271–272
  division using, 282
  double, 268, 270–271
  format of, 272
  logical, 268–271
  multiplication using, 282
  preparation for division using, 283
  single, 268–272
Short floating-point format, 296–298
SI instruction, 144
Sign, of remainder, 39
Sign bit, 10
  in arithmetic shifts, 268, 271
  floating-point, 297
Sign representation, packed decimal numbers, 171
Significance indicator, 207
  effect of sign on, 208
Significance starter, 205, 207
Significant digit, 207
Sine X, 313
Single-length SS instructions, 139
Single precision, 296
SNAP, 368
Social security number, 225
SP (Subtract Packed), 173–175
SPASM, 364
SPM (Set Program Mask), 369
Square root, 315
Squaring, 52
SR (Subtract Register), 41
SRP (Shift and Round Packed), 192–195, 197
SS instructions:
  lack of index register in, 179
  single-length, 139
    length in, 139
  two-length, 173
    length in, 173
ST (Store), 26
START, 22–25, 63
Statements, types of, 22
STC (Store Character), 278
STCM (Store Character under Mask), 278–280
STH (Store Halfword), 43
STM (Store Multiple), 234–235
Store (ST), 26
Store Character (STC), 278
Store Character under Mask (STCM), 278–280
Store Halfword (STH), 43
Store Multiple (STM), 234–235
Storing return address, 233–234
String(s), 136–170
  arrays of, 146–147
  blanking of, 141
  length, 137
  looping through, 149–150
  replication factor in, 138
String literal, 140, 143
Structure (PL/1), 111, 147
Sublists, in macros, 340–341
Subprograms, 230–267
  addressability in, 231, 240–241
  branching to, 232–234
  calling another, 243–244
  conventions for, 230
  difference from macro, 334–335
  external, 231
  internal, 231
Subroutines (See Subprograms)
Substrings, 346
Subtract (S), 26
Subtract Decimal (SP), 173–175
Subtract Halfword (SH), 43–44
Subtract Packed (SP), 173–175
Subtract Register (SR), 41
Subtraction:
  of binary numbers, 9
  of floating-point, 302
  of hexadecimal numbers, 9
Supervisor Call (SVC), 369
Supervisor state, 369
SVC (Supervisor Call), 369
Switching bits, 11
Symbolic parameters, 337–341
  attributes of, 348–350
    count, 350–351
    length, 350
    number, 349–350
    type, 348–349
  substring of, 346
System macros, 341
System variables, 341–342
  &SYSDATE, 341–342
  &SYSNDX, 341–342
    use in branching around DS, 350
  &SYSTIME, 341–342

T' (type test in macro), 348
Ten's complement, 11

INDEX

Test under Mask (TM),276–278
TM (Test under Mask),276–278
TR (Translate),319–322
Trailer, macro,335
Translate (TR),319–322
Translate and Test (TRT),322–324
TRT (Translate and Test),322–324
Two-dimensional arrays,110-111
Two's complement notation,10–12
Type, of symbolic parameter,348–349
Type A set symbol,344–345
Type B set symbol,345–346
Type C set symbol,345–346

Unconditional branch,85
Unnormalized instructions,306–307
Unnormalized zero,307
Unpack (UNPK),201–202
UNPK (Unpack),201–202
Unsigned data,141–142
USING,22–23,25,61,63
   effects of,66–67
   with multiple base registers,74

V (address constant),233

Word (full word),10
Word, double,10,22,25,296
   boundary requirement for,67,202–203

X (hexadecimal designation in DC and DS),138
XDECI,366–367
XDECO,366–367
XL (DS designation for hexadecimal, including length),138
XPRNT,366
XREAD,366

ZAP (Zero and Add Packed),175
Zero(s):
   leading,10,204
   unnormalized,307
Zero and Add Decimal (ZAD),175
Zero and Add Packed (ZAP),175
Zero divisor,369
ZIP code (postal),224
Zone,195,200
Zoned decimal format,200
Zoned number,200

Instructions and Pseudo-Instructions Index

A (Add),26
AD (Add Long),300–302
ADR (Add Long, Register),300–302
AE (Add Short),300–302
AER (Add Short, Register),300–302
AH (Add Halfword),43
AP (Add Packed),173–175
AR (Add Register),41
AU (Add Short, Unnormalized),306–307
AUR (Add Short Unnormalized, Register),306–307
AW (Add Long, Unnormalized),306–307
AWR (Add Long Unnormalized, Register),306–307
BAL (Branch and Link),232
BALR (Branch and Link Register),23,63,66–67,71,232
BC (Branch on Condition),86–88
BCR (Branch on Condition, Register),86–88
BCT (Branch on Count),106–109
BCTR (Branch on Count Register),106,108–109
BXH (Branch on Index High),118,120–122
BXLE (Branch on Index Low or Equal),118–122
C (Compare),85,90–91
CD (Compare Long),300–302
CDR (Compare Long, Register),300–302
CE (Compare Short),300–302
CER (Compare Short, Register),300–302
CH (Compare Halfword),91
CL (Compare Logical),143
CLC (Compare Logical Character),139,141–143
CLCL (Compare Logical Character Long),150–151
CLI (Compare Logical Immediate),144–147
CLR (Compare Logical Register),143
CP (Compare Packed),173,178–179
CR (Compare Register),90–91
CSECT,22,231
CVB (Convert to Binary),202
CVD (Convert to Decimal),202–203
D (Divide),24,39–41
DC (define constant),24
DD (Divide Long),300–302
DDR (Divide Long, Register),300–302
DE (Divide Short),300–302
DER (Divide Short, Register),300–302
DP (Divide Packed),175,177–178
DR (Divide Register),41
DS (define storage),24
ED (Edit),204–210
EDMK (Edit with Mark),204–210
END,22–25
EQU (Equivalence),76
EX (Execute),324–325
HDR (Halve Long),315
HER (Halve Short),315

IC (Insert Character),278
ICM (Insert Character under Mask),278–280
L (Load),24–25
LA (Load Address),71–73
LCDR (Load Complement, Long),300–302
LCER (Load Complement, Short),300–302
LCR (Load Complement Register),42–43
LD (Load, Long),300–302
LDR (Load Register, Long),300–302
LE (Load, Short),300–302
LER (Load Register, Short),300–302
LH (Load Halfword),43
LM (Load Multiple),234–235
LNDR (Load Negative, Long),300–302
LNER (Load Negative, Short),300–302
LNR (Load Negative Register),42–43
LPDR (Load Positive, Long),300–302
LPER (Load Positive, Short),300–302
LPR (Load Positive Register),42–43
LR (Load Register),41
LTDR (Load and Test, Long),300–302
LTER (Load and Test, Short),300–302
LTORG,75,84
LTR (Load and Test Register),89–90
M (Multiply),24,38–39
MD (Multiply Long),300–302
MDR (Multiply Long, Register),300–302
ME (Multiply Short),300–302
MER (Multiply Short, Register),300–302
MH (Multiply Halfword),43–44
MP (Multiply Packed),175–177
MR (Multiply Register),41
MVC (Move Character),139–141
MVI (Move Immediate),139,144–145
MVN (Move Numeric),195–197
MVO (Move with Offset),197–199
MVZ (Move Zone),195–197
N (And),273–276
NC (And Character),273–276
NI (And Immediate),273–276
NR (And Register),273–276
O (Or),273–276
OC (Or Character),273–276
OI (Or Immediate),273–276
OR (Or Register),273–276
PACK,200–201
S (Subtract),26
SD (Subtract Long),300–302
SDR (Subtract Long, Register),300–302
SE (Subtract Short),300–302
SER (Subtract Short, Register),300–302
SH (Subtract Halfword),43–44
SLA (Shift Left Arithmetic),268,271–272
SLDA (Shift Left Double Arithmetic),268,271–272

INSTRUCTIONS AND PSEUDO-INSTRUCTIONS INDEX

SLDL (Shift Left Double Logical),268–271
SLL (Shift Left Logical),268–271
SP (Subtract Packed),173–175
SPM (Set Program Mask),369
SR (Subtract Register),41
SRA (Shift Right Arithmetic),268,271–272
SRDA (Shift Right Double Arithmetic),268,271–272
SRDL (Shift Right Double Logical),268–271
SRL (Shift Right Logical),268–271
SRP (Shift and Round Packed),192–195,197
ST (Store),26
START,22–25,63
STC (Store Character),278
STCM (Store Character under Mask),278–280
STD (Store, Long),300–302
STE (Store, Short),300–302
STH (Store Halfword),43

STM (Store Multiple),234–235
SU (Subtract Short, Unnormalized),306–307
SUR (Subtract Short Unnormalized, Register), 306–307
SVC (Supervisor Call),369
SW (Subtract Long, Unnormalized),306–307
SWR (Subtract Long Unnormalized, Register), 306–307
TM (Test under Mask),276–278
TR (Translate),319–322
TRT (Translate and Test),322–324
UNPK (Unpack),201–202
USING,22–23,25,61,63
X (Exclusive Or),273–276
XC (Exclusive Or Character),273–276
XI (Exclusive Or Immediate),273–276
XR (Exclusive Or Register),273–276
ZAP (Zero and Add Packed),175

Catalog

If you are interested in a list of SCHAUM'S
OUTLINE SERIES send your name
and address, requesting your free catalog, to:

SCHAUM'S OUTLINE SERIES, Dept. C
McGRAW-HILL BOOK COMPANY
1221 Avenue of Americas
New York, N.Y. 10020